Oxford Primary Thesaurus

Oxford Primary Thesaurus

Editor: Alan Spooner

OXFORD
UNIVERSITY PRESS

OXFORD
UNIVERSITY PRESS

Great Clarendon Street, Oxford OX2 6DP

Oxford University Press is a department of the University of Oxford. It furthers the University's objective of excellence in research, scholarship, and education by publishing worldwide in

Oxford New York
Auckland Cape Town Dar es Salaam Hong Kong Karachi
Kuala Lumpur Madrid Melbourne Mexico City Nairobi New Delhi
Shanghai Taipei Toronto

with offices in

Argentina Austria Brazil Chile Czech Republic France Greece
Guatemala Hungary Italy Japan South Korea Poland Portugal
Switzerland Thailand Turkey Ukraine Vietnam

First published 1993
Second edition 1998
Revised second edition 2002
This edition 2005

British Library cataloguing in Publication Data available

ISBN 13: 978-0-19-911309-5

ISBN 10: 0-19-911309-2

10 9 8 7 6 5 4 3 2 1

Typeset in OUP Argo and OUP Swift

Printed in Italy by G. Canale & C S.p.A

Contents

Preface for teachers and parents

The function of a thesaurus

The function of a thesaurus is to jog the memory about words we know but which don't spring to mind, and to introduce new words to us. In these ways it can help us avoid overuse of a narrow repertory of words, and to express ourselves with greater sophistication and precision. However, young thesaurus users should not be led to assume that unearthing unfamiliar words will necessarily make their writing 'better' than using familiar ones. It would be unfortunate if 'looking it up in the thesaurus' were regarded as a kind of verbal lucky-dip. If children are to develop a proper awareness of subtle distinctions of meaning and usage, their use of a thesaurus must be complementary to - not a substitute for - their sharing of language experience with mature users of English in real situations.

The features of this thesaurus

In this thesaurus headwords are arranged in a single alphabetical sequence. Each headword is followed by an example sentence illustrating how the headword might be used. When a headword has more than one meaning, the entry is divided into numbered senses with an example sentence for each sense (see **accident**). The example sentence is then followed by a list of synonyms arranged alphabetically (for example, at **allegation** we have given the synonyms 'accusation', 'charge', and 'claim').

Where it seems useful to do so, we give a usage warning, either in the form of a brief note (e.g. under **mad**), or as a single word (e.g. *informal*) in italics and within brackets immediately before the word.

Where appropriate, an antonym - a word which is opposite in meaning to the headword - is given. If the antonym is relevant to a particular sense it is placed at the end of that numbered sense (e.g. at broad we have given the antonym narrow for sense 1 and the antonym specific for sense 2). If the antonym is relevant to all senses it is placed at the end of the entry (e.g. at **brave** we give the antonym 'cowardly').

Some entries include a boxed section of related words. These are words that belong to the same 'word family' as the headword. For example, at the entry cup we have given a list of related words that includes 'beaker', 'glass', 'mug', and 'tumbler'. These are not synonyms of the headword, but they all have a common relationship to the word 'cup'. These should provide useful material for word study and wider discussion about language.

Alan Spooner

Using this thesaurus

A thesaurus can help you to use language more interestingly and more clearly by reminding you of a variety of words you might use. In this thesaurus, you will find synonyms (words which are similar in meaning to the word you thought of); antonyms (words which mean the opposite); useful lists of words that are related in other ways, and panels focusing on words that are often overused such as 'nice' and 'good'.

A thesaurus does not give you definitions of words. If you want a definition of a word, you will need to track it down in a dictionary such as the *Oxford Primary Dictionary*.

Remember that although synonyms are similar to each other in meaning, it is very rare that two words are used in exactly the same way. For example, beautiful, pretty, and good-looking are similar in meaning, and we might talk about beautiful weather, or pretty flowers, or good-looking men; but we don't talk about pretty weather or good-looking flowers. So, when we come across a new word, we need to find out how people use it.

In this thesaurus you will find

Headwords: These are the words you look up. They are printed in colour type so that you can find them easily.

Numbers: When a headword can be used in more than one way, we number the different uses.

Example sentences: Sentences showing how you might use a word are printed in italics.

Synonyms: These are words which are similar in meaning to the headword.

Warnings: When you need to be specially careful how you use a word (for example, because it is informal) we put a warning in brackets just before the word or sentence concerned.

Cross-references: Sometimes we suggest that you look up another entry to find more useful words. This is called a cross-reference.

Opposites: If the word you look up has a useful opposite (or antonym), it appears after the synonyms.

Phrases: If a headword is often used in a phrase, the phrase appears at then end of the entry, with an example sentence and a list of synonyms, just as for the headword itself.

Related words: Words that are not necessarily synonyms, but are related to the headword in other ways are enclosed in a box.

Overused words: Words that are often overused are enclosed in a tinted panel. They provide a wide range of synonyms for these key words.

Thesaurus Features

Headwords
These are in colour to help you find words more easily

small *ADJECTIVE* This word is often overused. Here are some alternatives:
1 *The model village showed everything on a small scale.*
▸ compact, little, microscopic, miniature, minute, tiny
AN OPPOSITE IS big
2 *He complained that his helping of stew was rather small.*
▸ inadequate, insufficient, meagre, (*informal*) measly, scanty, stingy
AN OPPOSITE IS generous
3 *She had a small problem.*
▸ insignificant, minor, negligible, trifling, trivial, unimportant
AN OPPOSITE IS important

Overused words panels
Panels highlight words that are often overused and provide a range of alternatives

Opposites
If the word you look up has a useful opposite (or antonym), it appears after the synonyms

smart *ADJECTIVE*
1 *Everyone looked smart at the wedding.*
▸ chic, elegant, fashionable, neat, (*informal*) posh, spruce, stylish, tidy, trim, well-dressed
AN OPPOSITE IS scruffy
2 *It was smart of him to think of that.*
▸ acute, artful, bright, clever, crafty, ingenious, intelligent, shrewd
AN OPPOSITE IS stupid
3 *They set off at a smart pace.*
▸ brisk, fast, quick, rapid, speedy, swift
AN OPPOSITE IS slow

Word classes (parts of speech)
After the headword is the word class which shows the job that the word does when used in a sentence

Numbers
When a headword can be used in more than one way, numbers are given fot the different uses

Synonyms
These are words which are similar in meaning to the headword

Example sentences
Sentences showing how you might use a word are printed in italics

smell *NOUN*
PLEASANT SMELLS
aroma, fragrance, perfume, scent
▹ The smell of wine is its bouquet.
ADJECTIVES USED TO DESCRIBE THINGS WITH A PLEASANT SMELL
aromatic, fragrant, perfumed, savoury, scented, spicy, sweet, sweet-smelling
UNPLEASANT SMELLS
odour, (*informal*) pong, reek, stench, stink, whiff
ADJECTIVES USED TO DESCRIBE THINGS WITH AN UNPLEASANT SMELL
foul, musty, odorous, reeking, rotten, sharp, smelly, sour, stinking, (*informal*) whiffy

Topic panels and related words
Words that are not necessarily synonyms but are related to the headword in other ways are enclosed in a box

Warnings
When you need to be specially careful how you use a word (for example, because it is informal) warnings are put in brackets just before the word or sentence concerned

Topic panels

A

accommodation
adhesive
advertisement
aircraft
alarm
alcohol
ammunition
animal
anniversary
announcer
appliance
arena
armed services
armour
art
artist
astronomy
athletics
attach
audio-visual
award
axe

B

badge
bag
bandage
bank
bar
barracks
barrel
basement
basket
bathroom
bay
beam
bean
bear
bed
beetle
bell
berth
bicycle
bird
biscuit
black
blade
blemish
blind
blue
board
body
boil
book
bottle
bread
brick
bridge
broadcaster
brown
brush
builder
building
bulb
bus

C

cafe
cake
camera
captive
car
card
cash
castle
cat
cattle
cave
celebration
cereal
ceremony
cellar
certificate
channel
chasm
chess
chicken
chief
child
church
circle
circus
citrus fruit
class
clean
clergyman,
clergywoman
clerical
clinic
clock
cloth
clothes
coat
coil
comedy
committee
communication
competition
complexion
computer
container
cook
corn
correspondence
cosmetics
create
creator
cricket
crime
crockery
cross
cultivate
cup
curve
cut
cutlery

D

damage
dance

day
decorate
deer
dentist
desert
diagram
disaster
disc
dock
document
dog
door
drawing
dream
drink
drum

E

edit
education
electricity
engine
entertainer
entertainment
exercise
explosive
expression
eye

F

factory
fair
family
farm
fasten
fat
fence
fertilize
fighter
figure of speech
fire
firework
fish
floor
flower
food
forest
fort
fruit
fuel
funeral
fur
furniture

G

game
garden
gas
glass
glue
government
grass
grave
green
greeting
grey
group

H

hair
harbour
harness
hat
heat
herb
hole
holiday
horse
hospital
house
hunting

I

ice
illness
information
insect

J

jar
jewel
job
joint

K

keyboard
kill
kitchen
knife
knot

L

language
law
leg
legendary
letter
light
line
luggage

M

market
mathematics
meal
measurement
meat
medal
medicine
medium
message
metal
milk
money
monkey
monument
music

N

navy
net

news
nut

O

ocean
office
official
optical
organization

P

paint
paper
park
party
pasta
path
patrol
pave
payment
pet
photograph
picture
piece
pig
planet
plant
poem
poison
police officer
politics
pot
pottery
poultry
prayer
prehistoric
preserve
prison
prophet
protection
punctuation
punishment

R

race
railway
rain
rank
record
red
religion
renew
reptile
restaurant
restrain
road
roof
room
royalty
ruler

S

sailor
salad
sale
satirical
sauce
saw
school
science
sea
seaside
seat
sell
servant
shape
shellfish
shine
shoe
shop
shrub
signal
sing
size
sleep
smell
snake
soldier
song
sore
sound
soup
space
spice
spirit
sport
stationery
stealing
stick
stone
store
storm
story
subject
sugar
sweet
swim

T

table
talk
taste
tax
teacher
television
tent
theatre
therapy
thread
timber
time
title
tomb
tool
tooth
tower
town
toy
transport
travel
treasure
tree

trousers
twist

U

umpire
un-
underclothes
undo

V

valley
vegetables
vehicles
vessel

W

wall
war
watch
water
weapon
weather
wedding
well
whip
white
wild
window
wood
wooded
word
worker
worship
wound *noun*
wound *verb*
write
writing

Y

yard
yellow
young

Z

zodiac

Overused words

awful
bad
big
bit
clear *adjective*
clear *verb*
cry
do
eat
end
fall
fat
get
go
good
great
happy
hard
have
hit
laugh
little
like
look
lovely
make
more
new
nice
old
pleasant
put
raise
run
sad
say
see
set
short
small
strong
take
tell
thin
thing
unpleasant
use
very
walk

Aa

abandon *VERB*
1 *He abandoned his family and went off to Australia.*
▸ desert, forsake, leave
2 *The sailors abandoned the damaged ship.*
▸ evacuate, quit, withdraw from
3 *The weather was so bad that we abandoned our plan.*
▸ abort, cancel, discard, drop, give up, scrap

abbreviate *VERB*
The word 'Doctor' can be abbreviated to 'Dr'.
▸ cut, reduce, shorten

abide *VERB*
I can't abide cigarette smoke.
▸ bear, endure, put up with, stand, tolerate
to abide by *You must abide by the rules.*
▸ accept, carry out, follow, keep to, obey, stick to, submit to

ability *NOUN*
She has the ability to do well.
▸ aptitude, brains, competence, expertise, gift, intelligence, potential, power, skill, talent

ablaze *ADJECTIVE*
The whole house was ablaze before the firemen arrived.
▸ alight, blazing, burning, on fire

able *ADJECTIVE*
1 *She's an able tennis player.*
▸ accomplished, capable, clever, competent, effective, expert, gifted, skilful, skilled, talented, useful
AN OPPOSITE IS incompetent
2 *I'm able to stay until teatime.*
▸ allowed, free, permitted, ready, willing
AN OPPOSITE IS unable

abnormal *ADJECTIVE*
We had abnormal weather last winter.
▸ exceptional, extraordinary, freak, funny, odd, peculiar, queer, strange, uncharacteristic, unexpected, unnatural, unusual, weird
AN OPPOSITE IS normal

abolish *VERB*
Some people would like to abolish homework.
▸ (*informal*) do away with, eliminate, end, get rid of, put an end to
AN OPPOSITE IS create

abominable *ADJECTIVE*
Everyone was shocked by the abominable crime.
▸ appalling, awful, beastly, brutal, contemptible, cruel, despicable, detestable, disgusting, dreadful, foul, hateful, horrible, horrifying, loathsome, repulsive, revolting, terrible, vile

aboriginal *ADJECTIVE*
The aboriginal inhabitants were badly treated by the settlers.
▸ earliest, first, native, original

abort *VERB*
The control tower told the pilot to abort take-off.
▸ abandon, call off, cancel, halt, stop, terminate

abound *VERB*
Fish abound in this river.
▸ be plentiful, teem

about *PREPOSITION*
1 *We heard a story about space travellers.*
▸ concerning, connected with, involving
2 *There are about two hundred children in the school.*
▸ approximately, around, close to, roughly

abrasive *ADJECTIVE*
Don't use anything abrasive when you clean the bath.
▸ gritty, harsh, rough, scratchy, sharp

abroad *ADVERB*
I enjoy travelling abroad.
▸ in foreign countries, overseas

abrupt *ADJECTIVE*
1 *I was surprised when the film came to an abrupt end.*
▸ hasty, hurried, quick, sudden, unexpected
AN OPPOSITE IS gradual
2 *We didn't like his abrupt manner.*
▸ blunt, gruff, impolite, rude, tactless, unfriendly
AN OPPOSITE IS polite

A B C D E F G H I J K L M N O P Q R S T U V W X Y Z

absent *ADJECTIVE*
Why were you absent from school?
▸ away, missing
▹ Being absent from school without a good reason is playing truant.
AN OPPOSITE IS present

absent-minded *ADJECTIVE*
He's so absent-minded that he forgot his bus money twice last week.
▸ careless, forgetful, inattentive, vague
AN OPPOSITE IS alert

absolute *ADJECTIVE*
1 *The teacher asked for absolute silence.*
▸ complete, perfect, total, utter
2 *The king had absolute power.*
▸ dictatorial, tyrannical, unrestricted

absorb *VERB*
A sponge absorbs water.
▸ fill up with, hold, retain, soak up, suck up, take in

absorbed *ADJECTIVE*
to be absorbed in something *I was absorbed in my book.*
▸ be engrossed in, be interested in, be preoccupied with, concentrate on, think about

absorbent *ADJECTIVE*
Absorbent substances soak up liquids.
▸ porous, spongy

abstract *ADJECTIVE*
I prefer dealing with practical things rather than abstract ideas.
▸ academic, intellectual, philosophical, theoretical
AN OPPOSITE IS concrete

absurd *ADJECTIVE*
1 *I can't believe his absurd explanation.*
▸ illogical, irrational, nonsensical, senseless, silly, stupid, unreasonable
AN OPPOSITE IS sensible
2 *That dress makes her look absurd.*
▸ laughable, ludicrous, ridiculous, silly
AN OPPOSITE IS serious

abundant *ADJECTIVE*
The birds have an abundant supply of food in the summer.
▸ ample, generous, lavish, liberal, plentiful, profuse
AN OPPOSITE IS meagre

abuse *VERB*
1 *If you don't abuse your possessions, they will last a lot longer.*
▸ damage, harm, misuse, spoil, treat roughly
2 *The referee was abused by players from both teams.*
▸ be rude to, (*informal*) call someone names, insult, swear at
3 *People who abuse animals should be prosecuted.*
▸ hurt, ill-treat, injure, torment

abuse *NOUN*
They yelled abuse at us.
▸ curses, insults, obscenities, swear words

abusive *ADJECTIVE*
We were upset by their abusive language.
▸ cruel, hostile, hurtful, impolite, insulting, obscene, offensive, rude, unpleasant
AN OPPOSITE IS polite

abysmal *ADJECTIVE*
(*informal*) *The film was so abysmal that I fell asleep.*
▸ appalling, awful, bad, dreadful, terrible, worthless

abyss *NOUN*
The explorers stared down into the dark abyss.
▸ chasm, crater, gap, hole, opening, pit, rift

academic *ADJECTIVE*
1 *She's a very academic student.*
▸ (*informal*) brainy, clever, intelligent, scholarly, studious
2 *Philosophy is a very academic subject.*
▸ abstract, intellectual, theoretical
AN OPPOSITE IS practical

accelerate *VERB*
The bus accelerated.
▸ go faster, increase speed, pick up speed, speed up

accent *NOUN*
1 *She speaks English with a Welsh accent.*
▸ intonation, pronunciation, tone
2 *She told me to play the first note of each bar with a strong accent.*
▸ beat, emphasis, pulse, rhythm, stress

accept *VERB*
1 *I accepted her gift.*
▸ receive, take, welcome
AN OPPOSITE IS reject
2 *The club accepted my application for membership.*
▸ agree to, approve, consent to
AN OPPOSITE IS reject
3 *She accepts that she is guilty.*
▸ acknowledge, admit, agree, confess, recognize
AN OPPOSITE IS deny
4 *You have to accept the referee's decision.*
▸ put up with, resign yourself to, tolerate

acceptable *ADJECTIVE*
1 *I think money is always an acceptable birthday present.*
▸ appreciated, pleasant, pleasing, useful, welcome, worthwhile
2 *Our teacher complained that our behaviour was not acceptable.*
▸ adequate, appropriate, passable, permissible, satisfactory, suitable, tolerable
AN OPPOSITE IS unacceptable

accepted *ADJECTIVE*
It's accepted that she is our best player.
▸ acknowledged, agreed, recognized, undeniable, unquestioned

access *NOUN*
The access to the playing field is through the iron gates.
▸ approach, entrance, way in

access *VERB*
She showed us how to access the data we stored in the computer.
▸ get at, make use of, obtain, reach

accessible *ADJECTIVE*
Make sure the first aid box is accessible.
▸ at hand, available, convenient, handy, within reach
AN OPPOSITE IS inaccessible

accident *NOUN*
1 *Several people were injured in the accident.*
▸ calamity, catastrophe, collision, crash, disaster, misfortune, mishap
▹ An accident involving a lot of vehicles is a pile-up. A railway accident may involve a derailment.
2 *I met her in town by accident.*
▸ chance, coincidence, fluke, luck

accidental *ADJECTIVE*
1 *The damage may have been accidental.*
▸ unfortunate, unintentional, unlucky
2 *He made an accidental discovery.*
▸ casual, fortunate, lucky, unexpected, unforeseen, unplanned
AN OPPOSITE IS deliberate

acclaim *VERB*
The crowd acclaimed the arrival of the famous actor.
▸ celebrate, honour, praise

accommodate *VERB*
1 *The hostel can accommodate thirty guests.*
▸ cater for, hold, house, provide for, put up, take in
2 *If you need anything, we'll try to accommodate you.*
▸ aid, assist, help, oblige, please, serve, supply

accommodation *NOUN*
After the fire, the family was given temporary accommodation.
▸ housing, lodgings, shelter
KINDS OF HOLIDAY ACCOMMODATION
apartment, bed and breakfast, boarding house, guest house, hotel, motel, self-catering, timeshare, youth hostel
ACCOMMODATION FOR STUDENTS
(*informal*) digs, hall of residence
ACCOMMODATION FOR THE ARMED SERVICES
barracks, billet, married quarters
PLACES WHERE PEOPLE NORMALLY LIVE
bedsitter, flat, house
SEE ALSO **house**

accompany *VERB*
A friend accompanied me.
▸ escort, go with, tag along with, travel with

accomplish *VERB*
We accomplished the task she gave us.
▸ achieve, carry out, complete, do successfully, execute, finish, perform, succeed in

accomplished *ADJECTIVE*
My sister is an accomplished pianist.
▸ expert, gifted, skilful, skilled, talented

accomplishment *NOUN*
Playing the piano is one of her many accomplishments.
▸ ability, gift, skill, talent

A B C D E F G H I J K L M N O P Q R S T U V W X Y Z

accord *NOUN*
of your own accord *Mum was amazed when I washed up of my own accord.*
▸ spontaneously, unasked, voluntarily, willingly

accordingly *ADVERB*
1 *It rained, and accordingly sports day was postponed.*
▸ consequently, so, therefore
2 *You're the leader of the group, and you must behave accordingly.*
▸ appropriately, suitably

account *NOUN*
1 *I wrote an account of my trip.*
▸ chronicle, description, diary, history, log, narrative, record, report, story
2 *Money is of little account compared with your health.*
▸ concern, consideration, importance, interest, significance, use, value

account *VERB*
to account for *Can you account for your odd behaviour?*
▸ explain, give reasons for, justify, make excuses for

accumulate *VERB*
1 *Why do I accumulate so much rubbish?*
▸ collect, gather, heap up, hoard, pile up, store up
AN OPPOSITE IS scatter
2 *Your savings accumulate if you put a regular amount in the bank.*
▸ build up, grow, increase, multiply
AN OPPOSITE IS decrease

accumulation *NOUN*
There's an accumulation of odds and ends in my cupboard.
▸ collection, heap, hoard, mass, pile

accurate *ADJECTIVE*
1 *We took accurate measurements of the room.*
▸ careful, correct, exact, meticulous, minute, precise
2 *I don't think that's an accurate description of him.*
▸ factual, faithful, perfect, reliable, true, truthful
AN OPPOSITE IS inaccurate

accusation *NOUN*
She denied the accusation completely.
▸ allegation, charge, complaint

accuse *VERB*
I think it was unfair to accuse her.
▸ charge, inform against, make allegations against
AN OPPOSITE IS defend

accustomed *ADJECTIVE*
accustomed to *We are not accustomed to this hot weather.*
▸ acclimatized to, familiar with, used to

ache *NOUN*
The ache in my tooth got worse.
▸ discomfort, pain, soreness, throbbing
SEE ALSO **pain**

ache *VERB*
My legs ached from the previous day's exercise.
▸ be painful, hurt, throb

achieve *VERB*
1 *Will she ever achieve her ambition to play at Wimbledon?*
▸ accomplish, attain, carry out, fulfil, succeed in
2 *The new group achieved success with their first CD.*
▸ acquire, earn, get, score, win

achievement *NOUN*
I congratulate you on your achievement.
▸ accomplishment, attainment, success, triumph

aching *ADJECTIVE*
I slipped off my shoes to ease my aching feet.
▸ hurting, inflamed, painful, sore, tender, throbbing

acid *ADJECTIVE*
Lemons have an acid taste.
▸ bitter, sharp, sour, tart

acknowledge *VERB*
1 *I acknowledge that you are right.*
▸ accept, admit, agree, confess, grant
AN OPPOSITE IS deny
2 *Please acknowledge my letter.*
▸ answer, reply to, respond to

acquaint *VERB*
to acquaint someone with *Please acquaint me with the facts.*
▶ advise of, inform of, reveal, tell about
to be acquainted with *Are you acquainted with the area?*
▶ be familiar with, know

acquire *VERB*
Where can I acquire a copy of this book?
▶ get, get hold of, obtain
▷ To acquire something by paying for it is to **buy** or **purchase** it.

acquisition *NOUN*
His latest acquisition is a motorbike.
▶ possession, property, purchase

acquit *VERB*
Both defendants were acquitted by the magistrate.
▶ clear, declare innocent, discharge, dismiss, free, let off, release, set free
AN OPPOSITE IS convict *VERB*

across *PREPOSITION*
My friend lives across the river.
▶ beyond, on the other side of, over

act *NOUN*
1 *Rescuing the baby from the burning house was a brave act.*
▶ action, deed, exploit, feat, operation
2 *The best act at the circus involved three clowns.*
▶ item, performance, sketch, turn
to put on an act *Don't take any notice of him: he's only putting on an act.*
▶ fool about, pose, pretend, show off

act *VERB*
1 *We must act straight away.*
▶ do something, take action
2 *Give the medicine time to act.*
▶ function, have an effect, take effect, work
3 *He acted like a baby.*
▶ behave, carry on
4 *I acted the part of a shepherd in our play.*
▶ appear as, perform, play, portray, represent

action *NOUN*
1 *The driver's prompt action prevented an accident.*
▶ act, deed, effort, feat, measure
2 *The film was packed with action.*
▶ activity, drama, energy, excitement, liveliness, movement, vigour, vitality
3 *His father was killed in action in the Second World War.*
▶ battle, fighting
4 *The action of our clock needs repairing.*
▶ mechanism, works

activate *VERB*
Who activated the fire alarm?
▶ set off, start, switch on, trigger off

active *ADJECTIVE*
1 *Although he's quite old, he's still very active.*
▶ busy, dynamic, energetic, enterprising, enthusiastic, lively, vigorous
2 *I'm an active supporter of our club.*
▶ committed, dedicated, devoted, enthusiastic, hard-working, industrious, involved, zealous
AN OPPOSITE IS inactive

activity *NOUN*
1 *The market place was full of activity.*
▶ action, animation, excitement, life, liveliness, movement
2 *Gardening is Dad's favourite spare-time activity.*
▶ hobby, interest, job, occupation, pastime, pursuit, task

actor, actress *NOUNS*
A company of actors performed a play in the school hall.
▶ performer, player
▷ The most important actor in a play is the **lead** or the **star**. The other actors are the **supporting actors**. All the actors in a play are the **cast** or the **company**.
FOR OTHER PERFORMERS SEE **entertainer**

actual *ADJECTIVE*
Those were the Prime Minister's actual words.
▶ authentic, factual, genuine, real, true
AN OPPOSITE IS imaginary

actually *ADVERB*
Is this where it actually happened?
▶ certainly, definitely, genuinely, in fact, really, truly

acute *ADJECTIVE*
1 *I had an acute pain.*
▶ intense, piercing, severe, sharp, sudden, violent
AN OPPOSITE IS slight
2 *The explorers suffered from an acute shortage of food.*
▶ crucial, important, serious, urgent, vital
AN OPPOSITE IS unimportant
3 *She's too acute to be deceived by that trick.*

▸ alert, clever, intelligent, keen, observant, perceptive, quick, sharp, shrewd, smart
AN OPPOSITE IS stupid

adapt *VERB*
1 *Dad adapted the car so that we can safely put the dogs in the back.*
▸ alter, change, convert, modify, reorganize, transform
2 *They adapted to life in the country very quickly.*
▸ acclimatize, become accustomed, adjust

adaptable *ADJECTIVE*
He's an adaptable player who plays well in any position.
▸ cooperative, flexible, versatile

add *VERB*
to add to 1 *I have some things to add to what you've already got.*
▸ attach to, combine with, integrate with, join on to, put together with, tack on to, unite with
2 *I think mint sauce adds to the flavour of lamb.*
▸ enhance, improve, increase
to add up 1 *He added up the figures.*
▸ calculate, count up, find the sum of, find the total of, reckon up, work out
2 (*informal*) *Her story doesn't add up.*
▸ be convincing, make sense
to add up to *What do the figures add up to?*
▸ amount to, come to, make, total

added *ADJECTIVE*
The heavy rain was an added nuisance on our long journey.
▸ additional, extra, further

addiction *NOUN*
It is dangerous when smoking becomes an addiction.
▸ compulsion, craving, habit, obsession
▹ An addiction to alcohol is alcoholism.

additional *ADJECTIVE*
They have opened additional facilities at the leisure centre.
▸ added, extra, further, increased, more, new, supplementary

address *NOUN*
1 *I wrote the address on the envelope.*
▸ directions
2 *The Queen gave a televised address to the nation.*
▸ speech, talk
▹ An address in church is a sermon.

address *VERB*
The head addressed us in assembly.
▸ lecture to, make a speech to, speak to, talk to

adequate *ADJECTIVE*
1 *A sandwich will be adequate, thank you.*
▸ ample, enough, sufficient
2 *Your work is adequate, but I'm sure you can do better.*
▸ acceptable, competent, passable, respectable, satisfactory, tolerable
AN OPPOSITE IS inadequate

adhere *VERB*
I tried to make the stamp adhere to the envelope.
▸ cling, stick

adhesive *NOUN*
SUBSTANCES USED TO STICK THINGS
adhesive tape, cement, glue, gum, paste, (*trademark*) Sellotape, wallpaper paste

adjacent *ADJECTIVE*
adjacent to *They have a house adjacent to the park.*
▸ beside, neighbouring, next to

adjourn *VERB*
We adjourned the meeting for a cup of tea.
▸ break off, interrupt, stop, suspend

adjust *VERB*
1 *I tried to adjust the TV picture.*
▸ correct, improve, modify, put right, tune
2 *I adjusted the central heating thermostat.*
▸ alter, change, regulate, set, vary
to adjust to *At first it was hard to adjust to my new school.*
▸ adapt to, become acclimatized to, get accustomed to, get used to, settle in to

ad lib *ADJECTIVE*
Instead of making a proper speech, he made a lot of ad lib remarks.
▸ impromptu, improvised, made-up, spontaneous, unprepared, unrehearsed

ad lib *VERB*
I had to ad lib when I lost my notes.
▸ improvise, make it up

administer *VERB*
1 *The head administers the school.*
▸ administrate, control, direct, govern, lead, look after, manage, organize, preside over, run, supervise
2 *A nurse administered vitamin pills to all the children.*
▸ deal out, dispense, distribute, give out, hand out

admirable *ADJECTIVE*
She has many admirable qualities.
▸ commendable, excellent, fine, good, likeable, lovable, praiseworthy, worthy
AN OPPOSITE IS contemptible

admire *VERB*
1 *I admire her skill.*
▸ applaud, approve of, esteem, have a high opinion of, look up to, respect, think highly of, value
AN OPPOSITE IS despise
2 *We stopped to admire the view.*
▸ appreciate, be delighted by, enjoy

admission *NOUN*
1 *We were surprised by his admission that he was guilty.*
▸ acceptance, acknowledgement, confession, declaration
AN OPPOSITE IS denial
2 *Admission to the castle is by ticket only.*
▸ access, admittance, entrance, entry

admit *VERB*
1 *The hospital admitted all the victims of the accident.*
▸ accept, allow in, let in, receive, take in
AN OPPOSITE IS exclude
2 *He admits that he is guilty.*
▸ accept, acknowledge, agree, confess, grant, own up
AN OPPOSITE IS deny

adolescence *NOUN*
She spent her childhood and adolescence in France.
▸ puberty, your teens, your youth

adopt *VERB*
1 *We adopted a stray cat.*
▸ befriend, foster, take in, (*informal*) take under your wing
2 *I adopted her suggestion.*
▸ accept, choose, embrace, follow, take up

adorable *ADJECTIVE*
I have four adorable Siamese cats.
▸ attractive, charming, darling, dear, delightful, lovable, lovely, sweet

adore *VERB*
1 *She adores her grandad.*
▸ idolize, love, worship
2 (*informal*) *I adore toffee!*
▸ enjoy, like, love
AN OPPOSITE IS hate

adorn *VERB*
Before the party we adorned the room with streamers and balloons.
▸ decorate, festoon

adult *ADJECTIVE*
An adult tiger needs a large territory.
▸ full-size, fully grown, grown-up, mature
AN OPPOSITE IS immature

advance *NOUN*
1 *You can't stop the advance of science.*
▸ development, evolution, growth, progress
2 *Our new computer is a great advance on the old one.*
▸ improvement

advance *VERB*
1 *As the army advanced, the enemy fled.*
▸ approach, come near, forge ahead, gain ground, go forward, make headway, make progress, move forward, press on, proceed, progress
AN OPPOSITE IS retreat
2 *Computer technology has advanced in our lifetime.*
▸ develop, evolve, grow, improve

advanced *ADJECTIVE*
1 *The new car has advanced safety features.*
▸ the latest, modern, sophisticated, up to date
AN OPPOSITE IS obsolete
2 *Some people are shocked by his advanced ideas.*
▸ forward-looking, innovative, new, novel, progressive, revolutionary, (*informal*) trendy, unconventional
AN OPPOSITE IS old-fashioned
3 *She is advanced for her age.*
▸ grown-up, mature, well-developed
AN OPPOSITE IS backward
4 *This maths is too advanced for me.*
▸ complex, complicated, difficult, hard
AN OPPOSITE IS elementary

advantage *NOUN*
We had the advantage of the wind behind us.
▸ aid, assistance, benefit, help, use
to take advantage of *It was unfair to take advantage of him while he was ill.*
▸ exploit, impose on, make use of, use

adventure *NOUN*
1 *They set out on a dangerous adventure.*
▸ enterprise, exploit, venture
2 *She travelled the world in search of adventure.*
▸ danger, excitement, risk, thrills

adventurous *ADJECTIVE*
1 *The adventurous explorers took many risks.*
▸ bold, daring, enterprising, heroic, intrepid
2 *She gets a great thrill out of her adventurous voyages.*
▸ challenging, dangerous, eventful, exciting, perilous, risky
AN OPPOSITE IS unadventurous

adverse *ADJECTIVE*
Unfortunately, the medicine had an adverse effect on me.
▸ contrary, harmful, negative, unfavourable
AN OPPOSITE IS favourable

advertise *VERB*
We made posters to advertise our concert.
▸ announce, make known, (*informal*) plug, promote, publicize

advertisement *NOUN*
ADVERTISEMENTS IN GENERAL
advertising, promotion, publicity
AN ADVERTISEMENT ON TELEVISION
(*informal*) advert, (*informal*) break, commercial
AN ADVERTISEMENT ON A HOARDING OR NOTICEBOARD
bill, notice, placard, poster
AN ADVERTISEMENT IN A NEWSPAPER
classified advertisement, (*informal*) small ad
AN ADVERTISEMENT THROUGH THE POST OR GIVEN OUT IN THE STREET
circular, handout, leaflet

advice *NOUN*
I was glad to have his advice.
▸ counsel, guidance, help, opinion, recommendation, suggestion, tip

advisable *ADJECTIVE*
The doctor said it would be advisable to stay in bed.
▸ desirable, prudent, sensible, wise
AN OPPOSITE IS unwise

advise *VERB*
1 *What did the doctor advise?*
▸ advocate, prescribe, recommend, suggest
2 *He advised me to rest.*
▸ counsel, encourage, urge

aeroplane *NOUN*
SEE **aircraft**

affair *NOUN*
1 *The crash was a mysterious affair.*
▸ event, happening, incident, occasion, occurrence, thing
2 *She's been having an affair with an older man.*
▸ love affair, relationship, romance
affairs *Dad won't discuss his business affairs with strangers.*
▸ business, concerns, matters, questions, subjects, topics

affect *VERB*
1 *Acid rain affects trees.*
▸ act on, attack, harm, have an effect or impact on
2 *The bad news affected us deeply.*
▸ concern, disturb, grieve, trouble, upset, worry

affected *ADJECTIVE*
He gave an affected smile.
▸ assumed, false, insincere, pretended, unnatural
AN OPPOSITE IS genuine

affection *NOUN*
He felt great affection for his sister.
▸ attachment, devotion, fondness, friendliness, love, tenderness
AN OPPOSITE IS hatred

affectionate *ADJECTIVE*
She gave him an affectionate kiss.
▸ caring, devoted, fond, loving, tender
AN OPPOSITE IS unfriendly

afflict *VERB*
He was afflicted with a skin disease.
▸ bother, distress, harass, plague, torment, trouble

affluent *ADJECTIVE*
The owners of the big house must be very affluent.
▸ prosperous, rich, successful, wealthy, well off
AN OPPOSITE IS poor

afford *VERB*
Can you afford £10 for the school trip?
▸ manage, pay, spare

afloat *ADJECTIVE*
I don't enjoy life afloat because I get seasick.
▸ aboard ship, at sea, on board ship

afraid *ADJECTIVE*
He didn't let them see that he was afraid.
▸ alarmed, anxious, apprehensive, cowardly, fearful, frightened, intimidated, nervous, scared, terrified, timid
AN OPPOSITE IS brave
to be afraid *I'm afraid of huge spiders.*
▸ dread, fear, worry about

age *NOUN*
We are studying what life was like in the Victorian age.
▸ days, epoch, era, period, time

age *VERB*
1 *He's aged since we last saw him.*
▸ become older, look older
2 *Wine needs to age.*
▸ develop, mature

agenda *NOUN*
What is on your agenda for today?
▸ list, plan, programme, schedule, timetable

aggravate *VERB*
Some people think that the informal use of *aggravate* to mean *annoy* is incorrect
1 *The medicine only aggravated the pain.*
▸ add to, increase, intensify, make more serious, make worse, worsen
AN OPPOSITE IS lessen
2 (*informal*) *Their continual teasing aggravated us.*
▸ annoy, bother, irritate, provoke, trouble, vex

aggravating *ADJECTIVE*
(*informal*) *I wish they'd stop making that aggravating noise.*
▸ annoying, irritating, maddening, tiresome, trying, vexing

aggression *NOUN*
The aggression shown by our opponents was completely unjustified.
▸ aggressiveness, bullying, hostility, provocation, violence

aggressive *ADJECTIVE*
We weren't frightened by their aggressive behaviour.
▸ attacking, bullying, hostile, provocative, quarrelsome, violent, warlike
AN OPPOSITE IS friendly

agile *ADJECTIVE*
Mountain goats are extremely agile.
▸ acrobatic, lively, mobile, nimble, quick-moving, sprightly, supple, swift
AN OPPOSITE IS clumsy or slow

agitate *VERB*
1 *The thunderstorm agitated the animals.*
▸ alarm, disturb, trouble, unsettle, upset, worry
AN OPPOSITE IS calm
2 *We agitated for a proper road crossing outside the school.*
▸ campaign, make a fuss, press, push
3 *The wind agitated the surface of the water.*
▸ beat, churn, ruffle, stir

agitated *ADJECTIVE*
He was very agitated before the exam started.
▸ anxious, disturbed, edgy, excited, fidgety, flustered, nervous, restless, ruffled, unsettled, upset
AN OPPOSITE IS calm

agitator *NOUN*
▹ A person who makes a fuss to get good things done is a **campaigner**. A person who makes a fuss to cause trouble is a **troublemaker**.

agonizing *ADJECTIVE*
I had agonizing toothache.
▸ painful, severe

agony *NOUN*
I could hardly bear the agony.
▸ anguish, distress, pain, suffering, torment, torture

agree *VERB*
1 *I'm glad that we agree.*
▸ be united, think the same
AN OPPOSITE IS disagree

2 *I agree that you are right.*
▸ accept, acknowledge, admit, allow, grant
AN OPPOSITE IS disagree
3 *I agree to pay my share.*
▸ be willing, consent, promise
AN OPPOSITE IS refuse
to agree on *We agreed on a price.*
▸ choose, decide, establish, fix, settle
to agree with **1** *I don't agree with capital punishment.*
▸ advocate, argue for, defend, support
2 *Onions don't agree with me.*
▸ suit

agreement *NOUN*
1 *There's a large measure of agreement between us.*
▸ conformity, consensus, consent, harmony, sympathy, unanimity, unity
AN OPPOSITE IS disagreement
2 *The two sides signed an agreement.*
▸ alliance, treaty
▹ An agreement to end fighting is an armistice or truce. A business agreement is a bargain, contract, or deal.

aground *ADJECTIVE*
The ship was aground.
▸ beached, marooned, stranded, stuck

ahead *ADVERB*
1 *Dad went on ahead to get things ready.*
▸ before, in advance, in front
2 *I stared ahead, trying to see through the mist.*
▸ forwards, to the front

aid *NOUN*
1 *With your aid, I can do it.*
▸ assistance, backing, cooperation, help, support
2 *I think we could send more aid to the poorer countries.*
▸ contributions, donations, subsidies

aid *VERB*
The local people aided the police in their investigation.
▸ assist, back, collaborate with, cooperate with, contribute to, encourage, further, help, lend a hand to, promote, subsidize, support

ailment *NOUN*
She's suffering from some ailment.
▸ complaint, disease, illness, sickness
SEE ALSO **illness**

aim *NOUN*
What's your main aim in life?
▸ ambition, desire, dream, goal, hope, intention, objective, purpose, target, wish

aim *VERB*
1 *I aim to be a musician.*
▸ intend, mean, plan, propose, want, wish
2 *She aimed the gun at the target.*
▸ line up, point, take aim with, train
3 *She aimed the ball at the stumps.*
▸ direct, send

aimless *ADJECTIVE*
He leads an aimless life.
▸ meaningless, pointless, purposeless

air *NOUN*
1 *We shouldn't pollute the air we breathe.*
▸ atmosphere
2 *This room needs some air.*
▸ fresh air, ventilation
3 *She was singing a traditional air.*
▸ melody, song, tune
4 *There was an air of mystery about the place.*
▸ appearance, feeling, look, mood, sense

air *VERB*
1 *He opened the window to air the room.*
▸ freshen, refresh, ventilate
2 *I have a right to air my opinions.*
▸ express, make known, make public, reveal, show off, voice

aircraft *NOUN*
AIRCRAFT WHICH ARE HEAVIER THAN AIR
aeroplane, airliner, biplane, bomber, delta wing, fighter, gunship, helicopter, jet, jumbo jet, jump jet
SMALL AIRCRAFT USUALLY FLOWN AS A SPORT
glider, hang-glider, microlight
AIRCRAFT WHICH CAN LAND ON WATER
flying boat, seaplane
AIRCRAFT WHICH ARE LIGHTER THAN AIR
airship, balloon, hot-air balloon
PARTS OF AIRCRAFT
aileron, cabin, cargo hold, cockpit, elevator, engine, fin, flap, fuselage, joystick, passenger cabin, propeller, rotor, rudder, tail, tailplane, undercarriage, wing
PEOPLE WHO FLY AIRCRAFT
airman, aviator, flier, pilot
PLACES WHERE AIRCRAFT TAKE OFF AND LAND
aerodrome, airfield, airport, airstrip, heliport, landing strip, runway
TRAVELLING IN AIRCRAFT
aviation, flying

airy *ADJECTIVE*
1 *We sat and talked in a pleasant airy room.*
▶ fresh, open, ventilated
AN OPPOSITE IS stuffy
2 *He made some rather airy promises.*
▶ imprecise, indefinite, vague

ajar *ADJECTIVE*
I left the door ajar and my hamster escaped.
▶ open, unlatched

alarm *VERB*
The barking dog alarmed the sheep.
▶ agitate, distress, frighten, panic, scare, shock, startle, surprise, upset, worry
AN OPPOSITE IS reassure

alarm *NOUN*
1 *Did you hear the alarm?*
▶ alarm signal, alert, warning
THINGS THAT ACT AS AN ALARM
alarm clock, bell, fire alarm, hooter, gong, siren, whistle
2 *The sudden noise filled me with alarm.*
▶ anxiety, apprehension, distress, fear, fright, nervousness, panic, terror, uneasiness

alcohol *NOUN*
SOME ALCOHOLIC DRINKS
ale, beer, lager, spirits, wine
SOME SPIRITS
brandy, gin, rum, vodka, whisky

alert *ADJECTIVE*
A sentry must be alert at all times.
▶ attentive, awake, careful, observant, on the alert, on the lookout, ready, sharp-eyed, vigilant, wary, watchful, wide awake
AN OPPOSITE IS inattentive

alert *VERB*
We alerted them to the danger.
▶ inform, make aware, notify, signal, tip off, warn

alien *NOUN*
She felt like an alien in her new school.
▶ foreigner, immigrant, newcomer, stranger

alien *ADJECTIVE*
1 *When I was abroad, everything was so alien.*
▶ different, exotic, foreign, strange, unfamiliar
AN OPPOSITE IS familiar
2 *I read a story about alien beings and their spaceship.*
▶ extraterrestrial

alienate *VERB*
I think I alienated him when I said I didn't like his cat.
▶ antagonize, make an enemy of, offend, provoke, upset

alight *ADJECTIVE*
1 *Is the fire alight yet?*
▶ burning, ignited, on fire
2 *The sky was alight with fireworks.*
▶ ablaze, bright, illuminated, lit up, shining

alike *ADJECTIVE*
1 *The twins are alike.*
▶ identical, indistinguishable
2 *The people's reactions to our exhibition were alike.*
▶ comparable, the same, similar, uniform

alive *ADJECTIVE*
Is your goldfish still alive?
▶ breathing, existing, flourishing, in existence, live, living, surviving
▷ Living creatures in general are **animate** things.
AN OPPOSITE IS dead

allegation *NOUN*
The allegation against him was never proved.
▶ accusation, charge, claim

allege *VERB*
She alleged that he was a thief.
▶ assert, claim, contend, declare, maintain, make an accusation

allegiance *NOUN*
The king did not doubt the allegiance of his knights.
▶ devotion, duty, faithfulness, fidelity, loyalty, obedience

alliance *NOUN*
The two sides formed an alliance.
▶ association, federation, league, partnership, union
▷ An alliance between political parties is a **coalition**.

allot *VERB*
We allotted a fair share to every member of the group.
▶ assign, deal out, dispense, distribute, divide out, give out, grant, ration out, share out

allow *VERB*
1 *Dad won't allow smoking in the house.*
▸ agree to, approve of, authorize, consent to, give permission for, license, permit, put up with, stand, support, tolerate
AN OPPOSITE IS forbid
2 *We allowed £5 each for food.*
▸ budget, earmark, give, grant, set aside

allowance *NOUN*
1 *Our cats have a daily allowance of food.*
▸ amount, measure, portion, quota, ration, share
2 *Mum gives me my allowance on Saturdays.*
▸ pocket money
3 *They offered us an allowance for our old cooker.*
▸ deduction, discount, reduction

ally *NOUN*
The two countries work together as allies.
▸ friend, partner
AN OPPOSITE IS enemy

almost *ADVERB*
1 *I have almost finished.*
▸ all but, as good as, just about, nearly, not quite, practically, virtually
2 *Almost a hundred people came to our concert.*
▸ about, approximately, around

alone *ADJECTIVE, ADVERB*
1 *Did you go to the party alone?*
▸ on your own, separately, unaccompanied
2 *It's sad to be alone when everyone else is enjoying themselves.*
▸ desolate, friendless, isolated, lonely, solitary

also *ADVERB*
We also need some bread.
▸ additionally, besides, furthermore, in addition, moreover, too

alter *VERB*
I got confused because they altered their plans.
▸ adjust, amend, change, make different, modify, revise, transform, vary

alteration *NOUN*
She advised me to make some alterations to my work.
▸ adjustment, amendment, change, improvement, modification

alternate *VERB*
My brother and I alternate on washing up.
▸ rotate, take turns

alternative *NOUN*
1 *I lost my bus money, so I had no alternative but to walk home.*
▸ choice, option
2 *I don't like this book, so can I have an alternative?*
▸ replacement, substitute

altogether *ADVERB*
1 *I'm not altogether satisfied.*
▸ absolutely, completely, entirely, fully, perfectly, thoroughly, totally, utterly, wholly
2 *Altogether, it wasn't a bad holiday.*
▸ generally, in general, on the whole

always *ADVERB*
1 *The sea is always in motion.*
▸ constantly, continuously, endlessly, eternally, for ever, perpetually, unceasingly
2 *This bus is always late.*
▸ consistently, continually, invariably, persistently, regularly, repeatedly

amalgamate *VERB*
1 *The two teams amalgamated.*
▸ combine, come together, join forces, link up, merge, unite
2 *We amalgamated the two teams.*
▸ combine, fuse, integrate, join, merge, mix together, put together
AN OPPOSITE IS separate

amateur *NOUN*
All the players in this team are unpaid amateurs.
AN OPPOSITE IS professional

amateurish *ADJECTIVE*
She complained that it was amateurish work.
▸ clumsy, crude, incompetent, poor, rough, shoddy, unprofessional, unskilful
AN OPPOSITE IS skilled

amaze *VERB*
He amazed me when he said I had won first prize.
▸ astonish, astound, shock, stagger, startle, stun, surprise

amazed *ADJECTIVE*
I was amazed by the unexpected news.
▶ astonished, astounded, dumbfounded, (*informal*) flabbergasted, speechless, staggered, stunned, surprised

amazing *ADJECTIVE*
Flying over the North Pole was an amazing experience.
▶ astonishing, breathtaking, extraordinary, incredible, phenomenal, remarkable, sensational, staggering, stupendous, tremendous, wonderful

ambiguous *ADJECTIVE*
I'm still not sure what he believes because his reply was ambiguous.
▶ confusing, puzzling, uncertain, unclear, vague, woolly
AN OPPOSITE IS definite

ambition *NOUN*
1 *She has talent and ambition.*
▶ drive, enterprise, enthusiasm, zeal
2 *Her ambition is to run in the Olympics.*
▶ aim, desire, dream, goal, hope, intention, objective, target, wish

ambitious *ADJECTIVE*
If you are ambitious, you will probably succeed.
▶ committed, enterprising, enthusiastic, go-ahead, keen
AN OPPOSITE IS apathetic

ambush *NOUN*
The soldiers set up an ambush for the enemy patrol.
▶ attack, surprise attack, trap

ambush *VERB*
They ambushed the enemy patrol.
▶ attack, intercept, pounce on, surprise, swoop on, trap

amend *VERB*
I amended the poster to make its message clearer.
▶ alter, change, modify, revise

amiable *ADJECTIVE*
I don't know him well, but he seems quite amiable.
▶ agreeable, amicable, approachable, friendly, genial, good-natured, good-tempered, kind-hearted, likeable, pleasant, well-disposed

ammunition *NOUN*
KINDS OF AMMUNITION
bullet, cartridge, grenade, missile, round, shell, shrapnel

amnesty *NOUN*
The government granted an amnesty to political prisoners.
▶ pardon, reprieve

among *PREPOSITION*
I hid among the bushes.
▶ amid, between, in, in the middle of, surrounded by

amount *NOUN*
1 *Dad wrote a cheque for the correct amount.*
▶ sum, total, whole
2 *There's a large amount of food in the cupboard.*
▶ bulk, mass, measure, quantity, supply, volume

amount *VERB*
to amount to *What does the bill amount to?*
▶ add up to, come to, equal, make, total

ample *ADJECTIVE*
1 *The car has an ample boot.*
▶ big, large, roomy, spacious
AN OPPOSITE IS small
2 *We had an ample supply of food.*
▶ abundant, considerable, generous, lavish, liberal, plentiful, profuse, substantial
AN OPPOSITE IS meagre
3 *No more, thanks—that's ample.*
▶ (*informal*) heaps, lots, (*informal*) masses, more than enough, plenty, (*informal*) stacks, sufficient
AN OPPOSITE IS insufficient

amplify *VERB*
1 *She used a megaphone to amplify her voice.*
▶ boost, increase, make louder
AN OPPOSITE IS muffle
2 *Could you amplify your earlier statement?*
▶ add to, develop, elaborate, expand, fill out, lengthen, make fuller
AN OPPOSITE IS reduce

amputate *VERB*
After the accident, they thought they might have to amputate the victim's leg.
▶ cut off, remove, sever

amuse *VERB*
I think this joke will amuse you.
▸ cheer up, divert, entertain, make you laugh, (*informal*) tickle
to amuse yourself *How do you like to amuse yourself?*
▸ be entertained, occupy your time, pass the time

amusement *NOUN*
1 *What's your favourite amusement?*
▸ diversion, enjoyment, entertainment, fun, game, hobby, interest, leisure activity, pastime, pleasure, recreation, sport
2 *We tried not to show our amusement.*
▸ hilarity, laughter, merriment, mirth

amusing *ADJECTIVE*
I didn't find his jokes very amusing.
▸ comic, diverting, entertaining, funny, hilarious, humorous, witty
AN OPPOSITE IS boring or serious

analogy *NOUN*
To explain the circulation of the blood she used the analogy of a central heating system.
▸ comparison, metaphor, parallel, simile

analyse *VERB*
We analysed the results of our experiment.
▸ examine, investigate, scrutinize, study

analysis *NOUN*
What did your analysis of the data show?
▸ breakdown, examination, investigation, scrutiny, study

analytical *ADJECTIVE*
We took an analytical look at the information we collected.
▸ methodical, scientific, systematic
AN OPPOSITE IS superficial

anarchy *NOUN*
There would be anarchy if we had no police.
▸ chaos, confusion, disorder, lawlessness, mutiny, pandemonium, riot

ancestor *NOUN*
Our family's ancestors came from France.
▸ forefather, predecessor
AN OPPOSITE IS descendant

ancestry *NOUN*
She was proud of her Scottish ancestry.
▸ blood, descent, extraction, heredity, origins, pedigree, stock

ancient *ADJECTIVE*
1 *Does that ancient car still go?*
▸ antiquated, obsolete, old, old-fashioned, out of date
2 *In ancient times, our ancestors were hunters.*
▸ early, past, primitive, remote
▹ Valuable ancient furniture is **antique**. Remains of ancient animals and plants are **fossilized** remains. The times before written records were kept are **prehistoric** times. The ancient Greeks and Romans lived in **classical** times.
AN OPPOSITE IS modern

angelic *ADJECTIVE*
1 *After his naughtiness yesterday, she was amazed by his angelic behaviour today.*
▸ good, innocent, saintly, virtuous
2 *We listened to the angelic singing of the choir.*
▸ beautiful, heavenly, serene
AN OPPOSITE IS devilish

anger *NOUN*
I was filled with anger when I heard how cruel they had been.
▸ bitterness, fury, indignation, rage, (*old use*) wrath
▹ An outburst of anger is a **tantrum** or a **temper**.

anger *VERB*
His abrupt manner angered her.
▸ (*informal*) aggravate, annoy, antagonize, enrage, exasperate, incense, infuriate, irritate, madden, provoke
AN OPPOSITE IS pacify

angle *NOUN*
1 *We planted the tree in the angle between two walls.*
▸ corner, space
2 *The lecturer took an interesting angle on the topic.*
▸ approach, outlook, point of view, slant, view

angry *ADJECTIVE*
You'd better stay away from her if she's angry!
▸ annoyed, bad-tempered, bitter, cross, enraged, exasperated, fuming, furious, hostile, ill-tempered, incensed, indignant, infuriated, livid, (*informal*) mad, raging, seething, (*old use*) wrathful
AN OPPOSITE IS calm

anguish *NOUN*
He groaned in anguish.
▸ agony, anxiety, distress, grief, heartache, misery, pain, sorrow, suffering, torment, torture, woe

animal *NOUN*
We saw some strange animals in the zoo.
▸ beast, brute, creature
▹ A large or frightening animal in stories is a **monster**. A word for wild animals in general is **wildlife**. A scientific word for animals is **fauna**.
DIFFERENT KINDS OF ANIMAL
amphibian, arachnid, bird, fish, insect, invertebrate, mammal, marsupial, mollusc, reptile, rodent, vertebrate
▹ An animal that eats meat is a **carnivore**. An animal that eats plants is a **herbivore**. An animal that eats many things is an **omnivore**. Animals that sleep most of the winter are **hibernating animals**. Animals that are active at night are **nocturnal animals**.
SOME EXTINCT ANIMALS
brontosaurus, dinosaur, dodo, mastodon, pterodactyl, pterosaur, quagga
SOME MAMMALS FOUND WILD IN BRITAIN
badger, bat, coypu, deer, dormouse, fox, hare, hedgehog, mink, mouse, otter, pine marten, polecat, rabbit, rat, shrew, squirrel, stoat, vole, weasel
MAMMALS THAT LIVE IN THE SEA
dolphin, porpoise, seal, sea lion, walrus, whale
MAMMALS YOU MIGHT SEE IN A ZOO
aardvark, antelope, ape, armadillo, baboon, bear, beaver, bison, buffalo, camel, cheetah, chimpanzee, chipmunk, dromedary, elephant, elk, gazelle, gibbon, giraffe, gnu, gorilla, grizzly bear, hippopotamus, hyena, jackal, jaguar, kangaroo, koala, lemming, lemur, leopard, lion, llama, lynx, marmoset, marmot, mongoose, monkey, moose, musquash, ocelot, opossum, orang-utan, panda, panther, platypus, polar bear, porcupine, reindeer, rhinoceros, skunk, tapir, tiger, wallaby, wildebeest, wolf, wolverine, wombat, yak, zebra
MAMMALS SOMETIMES KEPT AS PETS
cat, dog, donkey, ferret, gerbil, goat, guinea pig, hamster, horse, mouse, rabbit, rat
MAMMALS SOMETIMES KEPT BY FARMERS
(*plural*) cattle, cow, goat, horse, pig, sheep
SEE ALSO **bird**, **fish**, **insect**, **reptile**

animal *NOUN*
FEMALE ANIMALS
▹ Female dog or wolf: **bitch**. Female cattle, elephant, or whale: **cow**. Female deer, hare, or rabbit: **doe**. Female sheep: **ewe**. Female deer: **hind**. Female lion: **lioness**. Female horse: **mare**. Female goat: **nanny goat**. Female pig: **sow**. Female tiger: **tigress**. Female fox: **vixen**.
MALE ANIMALS
▹ Male goat: **billy goat**. Male hare or rabbit: **buck**. Male deer: **buck**, **hart**, or **stag**. Male elephant or whale: **bull**. Male cattle: **bull** or **steer**. Male fox or wolf: **dog**. Male sheep: **ram**. Male horse: **stallion**. Male cat: **tom**.
YOUNG ANIMALS
▹ Young cattle: **calf**. Young male horse: **colt**. Young fox or lion: **cub**. Young deer: **fawn**. Young female horse: **filly**. Young horse: **foal**. Young cow: **heifer**. Young goat: **kid**. Young cat: **kitten**. Young sheep: **lamb**. Young hare: **leveret**. Young pig: **piglet**. Young dog: **pup**, **puppy**, or **whelp**. Young seal: **pup**.
GROUPS OF ANIMALS
▹ A **flock** of sheep. A **herd** of cattle or elephants. A **leap** of leopards. A **litter** of puppies or kittens. A **pack** of wolves. A **pride** of lions. A **school** of porpoises or whales.

animated *ADJECTIVE*
I could hear animated chatter from the next room.
▸ bright, brisk, bubbling, busy, cheerful, eager, enthusiastic, excited, exuberant, lively, spirited, sprightly, vivacious
AN OPPOSITE IS lethargic

animosity *NOUN*
It's obvious that there's a lot of animosity between them.
▸ antagonism, dislike, enmity, hate, hatred, hostility, ill will, malice, resentment, spite, unfriendliness
AN OPPOSITE IS friendliness

annexe *NOUN*
We slept in the annexe to the hotel.
▸ extension, wing

annihilate *VERB*
Nuclear weapons could annihilate the human race.
▸ destroy, exterminate, (*informal*) finish off, kill off, wipe out

anniversary *NOUN*
▷ The anniversary of the day you were born is your birthday. The anniversary of the day someone was married is their wedding anniversary.
SOME SPECIAL ANNIVERSARIES
bicentenary, centenary, coming-of-age, jubilee, silver wedding, golden wedding, diamond wedding, ruby wedding

announce *VERB*
1 *The head announced that sports day was cancelled.*
▸ declare, proclaim, report, reveal, state
2 *The DJ announced the next record.*
▸ introduce, lead into, present

announcement *NOUN*
1 *The head reads the announcements in assembly.*
▸ notice
2 *An official issued an announcement.*
▸ declaration, proclamation, pronouncement, statement
3 *I heard the announcement on TV.*
▸ bulletin, news flash, report

announcer *NOUN*
VARIOUS PEOPLE WHO ANNOUNCE THINGS
broadcaster, commentator, compère, herald, master of ceremonies, messenger, newscaster, newsreader, presenter, reporter, town crier

annoy *VERB*
1 *Did my sudden change of plans annoy you.*
▸ (*informal*) aggravate, anger, displease, exasperate, irritate, make you cross, upset, vex, worry
AN OPPOSITE IS please
2 *Please don't annoy me while I'm working.*
▸ badger, bother, harass, nag, pester, plague, provoke, trouble, try, worry

annoyance *NOUN*
1 *Her annoyance was obvious.*
▸ anger, exasperation, irritation, vexation
2 *Is the dog an annoyance to you?*
▸ bother, nuisance, trouble, worry

annoyed *ADJECTIVE*
Annoyed customers queued up to get their money back.
▸ angry, cross, displeased, exasperated, irritated, offended, sore, upset, vexed
AN OPPOSITE IS pleased

annoying *ADJECTIVE*
He's got a lot of very annoying habits.
▸ (*informal*) aggravating, exasperating, irritating, maddening, provoking, tiresome, troublesome, trying, vexing, worrying

anonymous *ADJECTIVE*
1 *An anonymous benefactor paid for our trip.*
▸ nameless, unidentified, unknown, unnamed
2 *I received an anonymous letter.*
▸ unsigned

answer *NOUN*
1 *Did you get an answer to your letter?*
▸ acknowledgement, reaction, reply, response
▷ A quick or angry answer is a retort.
2 *This could be the answer to all our problems.*
▸ explanation, solution

answer *VERB*
1 *I answered her question.*
▸ acknowledge, give an answer to, react to, reply to, respond to
2 *'I'm quite well,' I answered.*
▸ reply, respond, retort, return
▷ To answer quickly or angrily is to retort.
to answer back *She doesn't like it when I answer back.*
▸ argue, object, protest

antagonize *VERB*
Don't antagonize the neighbours by making a noise.
▸ alienate, anger, annoy, make an enemy of, offend, provoke, upset
AN OPPOSITE IS please

anthology *NOUN*
We put together an anthology of our favourite poems.
▸ collection, compilation, miscellany, selection

anticipate *VERB*
I anticipate that the result will be a draw.
▸ expect, forecast, foretell, hope, predict

anticlimax *NOUN*
It was an anticlimax when they abandoned the game.
▸ disappointment

antiquated *ADJECTIVE*
I was surprised that he used such an antiquated computer.
▸ aged, ancient, obsolete, old-fashioned, out of date, primitive
AN OPPOSITE IS new

antique *ADJECTIVE*
The palace was full of antique furniture.
▸ old, old-fashioned
▹ Antique cars are **veteran** or **vintage** cars.

antiseptic *ADJECTIVE*
The nurse put an antiseptic dressing on the wound.
▸ disinfected, germ-free, hygienic, sterile, sterilized

anxiety *NOUN*
1 *We waited for news with a growing sense of anxiety.*
▸ apprehension, concern, doubt, dread, fear, nervousness, strain, stress, tension, uncertainty, worry
AN OPPOSITE IS calmness
2 *In his anxiety to win, he started before the gun went off.*
▸ desire, eagerness, enthusiasm, impatience, keenness

anxious *ADJECTIVE*
1 *Are you anxious about your exams?*
▸ apprehensive, concerned, edgy, fearful, fraught, nervous, tense, troubled, uneasy, worried
AN OPPOSITE IS calm
2 *I'm anxious to do my best.*
▸ eager, enthusiastic, impatient, keen, willing

apathetic *ADJECTIVE*
You won't succeed if you are so apathetic.
▸ indifferent, listless, passive, unambitious, uncommitted, unemotional, unenthusiastic, uninterested, unmotivated
AN OPPOSITE IS enthusiastic

apologetic *ADJECTIVE*
He was apologetic about his mistake.
▸ penitent, remorseful, repentant, sorry
AN OPPOSITE IS unrepentant

apologize *VERB*
He apologized for being rude.
▸ be penitent, express regret, make an apology, repent, say sorry

appal *VERB*
The violence of the film appalled us.
▸ disgust, distress, horrify, revolt, shock, sicken

appalling *ADJECTIVE*
1 *He suffered appalling injuries in the accident.*
▸ distressing, dreadful, frightful, gruesome, horrible, horrific, horrifying, shocking, sickening
2 *My work was so appalling that I had to do it again.*
▸ (*informal*) abysmal, atrocious, awful, bad, disgraceful, terrible, unsatisfactory, worthless

apparatus *NOUN*
The firemen were wearing breathing apparatus.
▸ appliances, devices, equipment, gear, instruments, machines, mechanisms, set-up, systems, tools

apparent *ADJECTIVE*
There was no apparent reason for the crash.
▸ clear, conspicuous, detectable, evident, noticeable, obvious, perceptible, recognizable, visible
AN OPPOSITE IS concealed

appeal *VERB*
to appeal for *They appealed for our help.*
▸ ask earnestly for, beg for, cry out for, entreat, plead for, pray for, request
to appeal to *That kind of music doesn't appeal to me.*
▸ attract, fascinate, interest, tempt

appeal *NOUN*
1 *Did you hear their appeal for help?*
▸ call, cry, entreaty, request
▹ An appeal signed by a lot of people is a **petition**.
2 *Baby animals always have great appeal.*
▸ attractiveness, charm, fascination, interest

appear *VERB*
1 *Snowdrops appear in the spring.*
▸ become visible, come into view, come out, crop up, develop, emerge, occur, show, spring up, surface
2 *Our visitors didn't appear until midnight.*

▶ arrive, come, (*informal*) show up, turn up
3 *It appears that he's asleep.*
▶ look, seem
4 *I once appeared in a play.*
▶ act, feature, perform, take part

appearance NOUN
1 *I was startled by her sudden appearance.*
▶ approach, arrival, entrance, entry
2 *He had a military appearance.*
▶ air, aspect, bearing, look

appease VERB
They offered a sacrifice to appease the gods.
▶ calm, humour, pacify, satisfy, soothe, win over
AN OPPOSITE IS anger

appetite NOUN
1 *When I was ill, I completely lost my appetite.*
▶ hunger
2 *Round-the-world sailors have a great appetite for adventure.*
▶ craving, desire, eagerness, enthusiasm, keenness, longing, lust, passion, taste, thirst, urge, wish, yearning, zest

appetizing ADJECTIVE
The appetizing smell of sizzling bacon filled the room.
▶ delicious, tasty, tempting

applaud VERB
The audience laughed and applauded.
▶ cheer, clap
AN OPPOSITE IS boo

applause NOUN
At the end, the applause lasted for several minutes.
▶ cheering, clapping, congratulations

appliance NOUN
These days they make appliances to do most jobs.
▶ apparatus, device, equipment, gadget, instrument, tool
VARIOUS DOMESTIC APPLIANCES
carpet sweeper, cooker, dishwasher, freezer, fridge, microwave, vacuum cleaner, washing machine

application NOUN
1 *We sent an application for a refund.*
▶ claim, request
2 *The job needs a lot of patience and application.*
▶ commitment, dedication, devotion, effort, perseverance, persistence

apply VERB
1 *The nurse told me to apply the ointment generously.*
▶ administer, lay on, put on, spread
2 *My brother applied for a new job.*
▶ ask for, make an application for
3 *The rules apply to everyone.*
▶ be relevant, refer, relate
4 *I applied all my skill.*
▶ bring into use, employ, exercise, use, utilize

appoint VERB
1 *The school governors appointed a new teacher.*
▶ choose, elect, select, settle on, vote for
2 *We appointed a time for our meeting.*
▶ arrange, decide on, determine, fix, settle

appointment NOUN
1 *I had an appointment to meet him in town.*
▶ arrangement, date, engagement
2 *We had to be tactful about the appointment of a new captain.*
▶ choice, choosing, election, naming, selection
3 *My brother got a new appointment.*
▶ job, position, post, situation

appreciate VERB
1 *He appreciates good music.*
▶ enjoy, like, love
2 *I appreciate her good qualities.*
▶ admire, approve of, esteem, regard highly, respect, value
AN OPPOSITE IS despise
3 *I appreciate that you can't afford much.*
▶ comprehend, know, realize, recognize, see, understand
4 *Dad hopes that the value of our house will appreciate.*
▶ go up, grow, increase, mount, rise

appreciative ADJECTIVE
I enjoy playing to an appreciative audience.
▶ admiring, enthusiastic, grateful

apprehensive ADJECTIVE
Are you apprehensive about your exams?
▶ anxious, edgy, fearful, frightened, nervous, tense, troubled, uneasy, worried

a b c d e f g h i j k l m n o p q r s t u v w x y z

approach *VERB*
1 *The lion approached its prey.*
▸ advance on, come near to, draw near to, move towards
2 *I approached the head to ask if we could have a party.*
▸ contact, go to, speak to
3 *We approached the job cheerfully.*
▸ begin, embark on, set about, undertake

approach *NOUN*
1 *Footsteps signalled their approach.*
▸ advance, arrival, coming
2 *Dad made an approach to the bank manager for a loan.*
▸ appeal, application, proposal
3 *I like her positive approach.*
▸ attitude, manner, style, way
4 *The easiest approach to the castle is from the west.*
▸ access, entrance, entry, way in

approachable *ADJECTIVE*
We found him very approachable and easy to talk to.
▸ amiable, friendly, informal, kind, sympathetic, well-disposed
AN OPPOSITE IS unsympathetic

appropriate *ADJECTIVE*
It's not appropriate to wear jeans to a wedding.
▸ apt, fitting, proper, right, suitable, tactful, tasteful, well-judged
AN OPPOSITE IS inappropriate

approval *NOUN*
1 *We cheered to show our approval.*
▸ acclaim, admiration, appreciation, high regard, praise, respect, support
AN OPPOSITE IS disapproval
2 *The head gave her approval to our plan.*
▸ agreement, assent, authorization, (*informal*) blessing, consent, go-ahead, permission, support
AN OPPOSITE IS refusal

approve *VERB*
The head approved my request for a day off school.
▸ accept, agree to, allow, authorize, back, consent to, pass, permit, support
AN OPPOSITE IS refuse
to approve of *She approved of what I did.*
▸ admire, applaud, appreciate, commend, esteem, favour, like, praise, respect, value, welcome
AN OPPOSITE IS condemn

approximate *ADJECTIVE*
I gave Mum an approximate number of people coming to my party.
▸ estimated, inexact, near, rough
AN OPPOSITE IS exact

approximately *ADVERB*
Approximately twelve people are coming to my party.
▸ about, around, close to, more or less, nearly, roughly, round about

apt *ADJECTIVE*
1 *He's apt to be careless.*
▸ inclined, liable, likely, prone
2 *I need an apt quotation to put on the cover of my project.*
▸ appropriate, fitting, proper, right, suitable, well-judged
3 *She turned out to be a very apt pupil.*
▸ clever, quick, sharp

aptitude *NOUN*
He has a remarkable aptitude for music.
▸ ability, bent, expertise, gift, potential, skill, talent

arbitrary *ADJECTIVE*
He made an arbitrary decision to drop three of the best players.
▸ illogical, irrational, random, subjective
AN OPPOSITE IS rational

arbitrate *VERB*
We couldn't settle our argument, so we asked Mum to arbitrate.
▸ act as referee, adjudicate, decide the outcome, make peace, pass judgement

arch *VERB*
The cat arched its back.
▸ bend, bow, curve

area *NOUN*
1 *From the plane we saw a big area of desert.*
▸ expanse, stretch, tract
▹ A small area is a **patch**. An area of water or ice is a **sheet**.
2 *I live in an urban area.*
▸ district, locality, neighbourhood, part, region, vicinity, zone

arena NOUN
PLACES WHERE SPORT TAKES PLACE
amphitheatre, field, ground, park, pitch, ring, rink, stadium

argue VERB
1 *Whenever you two meet, you argue!*
▸ differ, disagree, fall out, fight, have an argument, quarrel, squabble
AN OPPOSITE IS agree
2 *He argued over the price.*
▸ bargain, haggle
3 *The lawyer argued that the accused was innocent.*
▸ assert, claim, maintain, reason, suggest, try to prove
to argue about something *We argue about politics.*
▸ debate, discuss

argument NOUN
1 *They was an argument about how much they should pay.*
▸ clash, controversy, debate, difference, discussion, disagreement, dispute, fight, quarrel, row, squabble
2 *Did you follow her argument?*
▸ line of reasoning, outline, theme

arid ADJECTIVE
No flowers were growing in the arid soil.
▸ barren, dry, infertile, lifeless, parched, sterile, unproductive, waterless
AN OPPOSITE IS fruitful

arise VERB
Perhaps the problem won't arise.
▸ appear, come into existence, come up, crop up, emerge, happen, occur

aristocrat NOUN
▸ noble, nobleman or noblewoman, peer

aristocratic ADJECTIVE
The castle belonged to an old aristocratic family.
▸ lordly, noble, titled, upper-class

arm VERB
They armed themselves with sticks.
▸ equip, provide, supply

armed services PLURAL NOUN
THE PRINCIPAL ARMED SERVICES
air force, army, navy
▹ Men and women in the services are troops. People who fight on horses are cavalry. People who fight on foot are infantry.
VARIOUS GROUPS IN THE ARMED SERVICES
battalion, brigade, company, corps, fleet, garrison, legion, patrol, platoon, regiment, reinforcements, squad, squadron, task force, vanguard
SERVICEMEN AND SERVICEWOMEN INCLUDE
aircraftman, aircraftwoman, cavalryman, commando, infantryman, marine, paratrooper, recruit, sailor, soldier
▹ A soldier paid to fight for a foreign country is a mercenary.
SEE ALSO **fighter**, **officer**, **rank**

armistice NOUN
An armistice ended the fighting.
▸ ceasefire, peace, truce

armour NOUN
PARTS OF A MEDIEVAL KNIGHT'S ARMOUR
breastplate, gauntlet, greave, habergeon, helmet, visor
▹ Armour made of linked rings was chain armour or chain mail.

army NOUN
SEE **armed services**

arouse VERB
The plan to build a bypass aroused strong feelings.
▸ cause, generate, lead to, produce, provoke, set off, stimulate, stir up, whip up
AN OPPOSITE IS calm

arrange VERB
1 *I tried to arrange everything logically.*
▸ categorize, classify, collate, display, lay out, line up, organize, set out, sort, sort out, tidy up
2 *Who will help me to arrange the party?*
▸ organize, plan, prepare, see to, set up

arrangement NOUN
1 *We improved the arrangement of the library.*
▸ design, layout, organization, planning, setting out
2 *I changed the arrangement of the books.*
▸ display, distribution, grouping, order, spacing

3 *We have an arrangement to pay for our TV by instalments.*
▸ agreement, bargain, contract, deal, scheme

array *NOUN*
We looked round the gleaming array of vintage cars.
▸ collection, display, exhibition, show

arrest *VERB*
1 *The police arrested the suspect.*
▸ capture, catch, detain, (*informal*) nick, seize, take into custody, take prisoner
2 *The doctors tried to arrest the spread of the disease.*
▸ check, delay, halt, hinder, prevent, stop

arrive *VERB*
When is the train due to arrive?
▸ appear, approach, come, get in, show up, turn up
▹ When a plane arrives it **lands** or **touches down**.
to arrive at *We arrived at the station.*
▸ get to, reach

arrogant *ADJECTIVE*
His arrogant manner annoys me.
▸ boastful, (*informal*) cocky, conceited, haughty, insolent, pompous, presumptuous, proud, scornful, snobbish, (*informal*) stuck-up, superior, vain
AN OPPOSITE IS modest

art *NOUN*
The art of writing letters is disappearing fast.
▸ craft, knack, skill, talent, technique, trick
VARIOUS ARTS AND CRAFTS INCLUDE
carpentry, carving, collage, crochet, drawing, embroidery, enamelling, engraving, etching, graphics, handicraft, illustration, jewellery, knitting, metalwork, modelling, needlework, origami, painting, patchwork, photography, pottery, printing, sculpture, sewing, sketching, spinning, stencilling, weaving, wickerwork, woodwork
FOR VARIOUS ARTISTS AND CRAFTSMEN SEE **artist**

artful *ADJECTIVE*
(*usually uncomplimentary*) *That was an artful trick!*
▸ clever, crafty, cunning, deceitful, devious, scheming, skilful, sly, smart, tricky, wily
AN OPPOSITE IS straightforward

article *NOUN*
1 *Have you any articles for the jumble sale?*
▸ item, object, thing
2 *Did you read my article in the magazine?*
▸ essay, piece of writing, report

articulate *ADJECTIVE*
She's a very articulate speaker.
▸ clear, eloquent, fluent, lucid
AN OPPOSITE IS inarticulate

artificial *ADJECTIVE*
1 *Organic gardeners don't use artificial fertilizers.*
▸ man-made, manufactured, synthetic, unnatural
2 *She had an artificial flower in her buttonhole.*
▸ bogus, counterfeit, fake, false, imitation
AN OPPOSITE IS genuine
3 *He gave an artificial smile.*
▸ affected, (*informal*) put on, pretended, sham, simulated
AN OPPOSITE IS genuine or natural

artist *NOUN*
ARTISTS AND CRAFTSMEN INCLUDE
blacksmith, carpenter, cartoonist, draughtsman, draughtswoman, engraver, goldsmith, graphic designer, illustrator, mason, painter, photographer, potter, printer, sculptor, silversmith, smith, weaver
FOR VARIOUS ARTS AND CRAFTS SEE **art**
FOR PERFORMING ARTISTS SEE **entertainer, performer**

artistic *ADJECTIVE*
Mum's flower arrangements are very artistic.
▸ aesthetic, attractive, beautiful, creative, imaginative, tasteful
AN OPPOSITE IS ugly

ascend *VERB*
1 *It took the rescuers a long time to ascend the mountain.*
▸ climb, go up, mount, move up, scale
2 *The plane began to ascend.*
▸ lift off, take off
3 *The eagle ascended into the air.*
▸ fly up, rise, soar
AN OPPOSITE IS descend

ascent *NOUN*
The ancient car only just managed the steep ascent.
▸ climb, gradient, hill, incline, ramp, rise, slope
AN OPPOSITE IS descent

ashamed *ADJECTIVE*
He was ashamed because of what he had done.
▸ apologetic, penitent, (*informal*) red-faced, remorseful, repentant, sorry
AN OPPOSITE IS unrepentant

ashes *PLURAL NOUN*
Next morning, the ashes of the bonfire were still glowing.
▸ cinders, embers

ask *VERB*
1 *I asked him to help me.*
▸ appeal to, beg, entreat, implore, plead with
2 *'Are you ready?' I asked.*
▸ demand, enquire, inquire
3 *I'm going to ask you to my party.*
▸ invite, (*formal*) request the pleasure of your company
to ask for 1 *He asked for silence.*
▸ appeal for, call for, demand, request, seek
2 *He was asking for trouble!*
▸ attract, cause, encourage, provoke, stir up

asleep *ADJECTIVE*
I didn't hear the phone because I was asleep.
▸ dozing, having a nap, (*informal*) nodding off, sleeping, unconscious
▹ A patient asleep for an operation is **anaesthetized** or **under sedation**. An animal asleep for the winter is **hibernating**.
AN OPPOSITE IS awake

aspect *NOUN*
1 *There's an aspect of this affair I don't understand.*
▸ angle, detail, feature, side
2 *He had an unfriendly aspect.*
▸ air, appearance, countenance, expression, face, look, manner
3 *The front room has a southern aspect.*
▸ outlook, prospect, view

assassinate *VERB*
The rebels assassinated the President.
▸ kill, murder

assault *NOUN*
The old lady was the victim of a serious assault.
▸ attack, beating, mugging

assault *VERB*
It's a serious crime to assault a policeman.
▸ attack, beat up, hit, mug, punch, strike

assemble *VERB*
1 *We assembled our luggage so that we were ready to leave.*
▸ bring together, collect, gather, pile up, put together
2 *The general assembled his troops.*
▸ muster, rally, round up
3 *A crowd assembled to watch the rescue.*
▸ accumulate, come together, converge, crowd together, flock together, gather, meet
AN OPPOSITE IS disperse

assembly *NOUN*
There was a large assembly of people in the market square.
▸ crowd, gathering, meeting, throng
▹ An assembly for worship is a **service**. A large assembly to show support for something, often out of doors, is a **rally**. An assembly to discuss political matters is a **council** or **parliament**. An assembly to discuss and learn about a particular topic is a **conference** or **congress**.

assent *NOUN*
She gave her assent to the plan.
▸ agreement, approval, consent, go-ahead, permission
AN OPPOSITE IS refusal

assert *VERB*
The accused man asserted that he was innocent.
▸ argue, claim, declare, insist, maintain, proclaim, protest, state, swear, testify

assertive *ADJECTIVE*
We need a leader who is assertive.
▸ bold, confident, decided, decisive, firm, forceful, insistent, positive, self-confident
AN OPPOSITE IS submissive

assess *VERB*
We have tests to assess our progress.
▸ appraise, determine, estimate, evaluate, gauge, judge, measure, value, weigh up

asset *NOUN*
Good health is a great asset.
▸ advantage, benefit, blessing, help
assets *It's a big company with enormous assets.*
▸ capital, funds, possessions, property, savings, wealth

assign *VERB*
He assigned the difficult jobs to the older children.
► allot, consign, distribute, give, hand over, share out

assignment *NOUN*
He gave me a hard assignment.
► duty, job, mission, piece of work, project, responsibility, task

assist *VERB*
She asked us to assist the caretaker by tidying the room.
► aid, collaborate with, cooperate with, help
AN OPPOSITE IS hinder

assistance *NOUN*
1 *That little boy needs some assistance with his shoelaces.*
► aid, encouragement, help
2 *We bought new sports equipment with the assistance of a local firm.*
► backing, collaboration, cooperation, sponsorship, subsidy, support

assistant *NOUN*
Can you manage on your own, or do you need an assistant?
► associate, colleague, helper, partner, supporter

associate *VERB*
to associate one thing with another *I associate Christmas with ice and snow.*
► connect with, link with, relate to
to associate with someone *I don't think you should associate with those people!*
► be friends with, go about with, mix with

association *NOUN*
1 *The people interested in chess formed an association.*
► alliance, club, fellowship, group, league, partnership, society, union
▷ A political association is a **party**. A business association is a **company** or **organization**.
2 *The association between us has lasted many years.*
► closeness, friendship, link, partnership, relationship

assorted *ADJECTIVE*
I bought a bag of sweets with assorted flavours.
► different, miscellaneous, mixed, several, various

assortment *NOUN*
There was an assortment of sandwiches to choose from.
► array, choice, diversity, mixture, selection, variety

assume *VERB*
1 *I assume you'd like some tea.*
► expect, guess, have a hunch, imagine, presume, suppose, suspect, think
2 *She assumed a disguise.*
► adopt, dress up in, put on, wear

assumed *ADJECTIVE*
She spoke with an assumed accent.
► bogus, counterfeit, faked, false, pretended
AN OPPOSITE IS genuine
an assumed name ► alias, pseudonym

assumption *NOUN*
My assumption is that we can average 40 miles an hour.
► belief, expectation, guess, hypothesis, supposition, theory

assure *VERB*
I assure you that I will help.
► promise

astonish *VERB*
My discovery will astonish you.
► amaze, astound, leave speechless, shock, stagger, startle, stun, surprise, take aback, take by surprise, (*informal*) take your breath away
▷ To be astonished is also to be **dumbfounded** or **flabbergasted**.

astronomy *NOUN*
SOME ASTRONOMICAL TERMS
asteroid, black hole, comet, constellation, cosmos, eclipse, galaxy, meteor, meteorite, moon, nebula, nova, planet, pulsar, quasar, satellite, shooting star, space, sun, supernova, universe, world

athlete *NOUN*
FOR VARIOUS EVENTS ATHLETES TAKE PART IN SEE **athletics**

athletic *ADJECTIVE*
He looks an athletic sort of person.
► active, energetic, fit, muscular, powerful, robust, sporting, strong, sturdy, vigorous, well-built
AN OPPOSITE IS feeble

athletics *NOUN*
VARIOUS ATHLETICS EVENTS
cross-country, decathlon, discus, high jump, hurdles, javelin, long jump, marathon, pentathlon, pole vault, relay race, running, shot, sprinting, triple jump
FOR OTHER SPORTS SEE **sport**

atmosphere *NOUN*
1 *We shouldn't pollute the atmosphere we breathe.*
▸ air
2 *There was a happy atmosphere at the party.*
▸ feeling, mood, spirit

atrocious *ADJECTIVE*
We were shocked by the atrocious crime.
▸ abominable, barbaric, bloodthirsty, brutal, callous, cruel, diabolical, dreadful, evil, fiendish, horrifying, merciless, outrageous, sadistic, savage, terrible, vicious, villainous, wicked

atrocity *NOUN*
The TV report of the atrocity shocked us.
▸ crime, horror, outrage

attach *VERB*
Attach the trailer to the back of the car.
▸ connect, couple, fasten, fix, join, link, secure
DIFFERENT WAYS TO ATTACH THINGS TO EACH OTHER
bind, bolt, chain, clamp, clip, glue, hook, nail, peg, pin, screw, solder, staple, stick, tack, tie, weld, zip
AN OPPOSITE IS detach

attached *ADJECTIVE*
The twins are very attached to each other.
▸ affectionate, close, dear, devoted, fond (of), friendly, loving, loyal
AN OPPOSITE IS hostile

attack *NOUN*
1 *The enemy's attack took them by surprise.*
▸ aggression, ambush, assault, charge, invasion, raid, strike
▹ An attack with big guns or bombs is a **blitz** or **bombardment**. An attack by planes is an **air raid**.
2 *She was upset by his attack on her character.*
▸ abuse, criticism, outburst
3 *It was embarrassing when I had a coughing attack in assembly.*
▸ bout, fit, (*informal*) turn

attack *VERB*
1 *The criminals attacked him in the street.*
▸ assail, assault, beat up, mug, (*informal*) set about, set on
▹ To attack someone else's territory is to **invade** or **raid** it. To attack someone from a hidden place is to **ambush** them. To attack the enemy with bombs or heavy guns is to **bombard** them. To attack by rushing at the enemy is to **charge**. To attack a place suddenly is to **storm** it. If an animal attacks you, it might **savage** you.
2 *He attacked her reputation.*
▸ abuse, criticize, denounce
AN OPPOSITE IS defend

attain *VERB*
I attained Grade 3 on the violin.
▸ accomplish, achieve, arrive at, complete, gain, get, obtain, reach

attempt *VERB*
We attempted to beat the record.
▸ aim, endeavour, exert yourself, make an effort, strive, try

attempt *NOUN*
I did it at the first attempt.
▸ effort, try

attend *VERB*
Are you going to attend the end-of-term concert?
▸ appear at, be present at, go to
to attend to 1 *Please attend to what I say.*
▸ concentrate on, follow carefully, heed, listen to, mark, mind, note, notice, observe, pay attention to, think about
2 *Are you going to attend to the washing up?*
▸ deal with, see to
3 *The nurses attended to the wounded.*
▸ care for, help, look after, mind, take care of, tend

attention *NOUN*
1 *It looks as if you did this without giving it proper attention.*
▸ care, concentration, consideration, thought
2 *Thank you for your attention.*
▸ courtesy, good manners, kindness, politeness, thoughtfulness

attentive *ADJECTIVE*
Drivers must be attentive at all times.
► alert, careful, listening, observant, on the alert, on the lookout, paying attention, sharp-eyed, vigilant, wary, watchful, wide awake

attitude *NOUN*
1 *Our teacher says we need a more serious attitude in class.*
► approach, behaviour, disposition, frame of mind, manner, mood
2 *I think smoking is wrong, but what's your attitude?*
► belief, feeling, opinion, outlook, position, thought, view

attract *VERB*
1 *Do you think our exhibition will attract people?*
► appeal to, fascinate, interest, tempt
2 *Baby animals attract big crowds at the zoo.*
► draw, pull in
AN OPPOSITE IS repel

attractive *ADJECTIVE*
Things can be attractive in many different ways. We give just some examples of ways we use the word here
1 *Aren't those puppies attractive?*
► adorable, appealing, captivating, charming, (*informal*) cute, delightful, enchanting, fascinating, lovable
2 *The bride and groom were an attractive couple.*
► beautiful, good-looking, handsome, pretty, striking
3 *There was an attractive picture over the fireplace.*
► artistic, beautiful, colourful
4 *Last holiday we stayed in an attractive country cottage.*
► picturesque, pretty, quaint
5 *The shop has some attractive special offers at present.*
► desirable, interesting, irresistible, tempting
AN OPPOSITE IS repulsive or unattractive

audible *ADJECTIVE*
She didn't think her rude comments were audible.
► clear, distinct
AN OPPOSITE IS inaudible

audience *NOUN*
▷ The audience for a TV programme is the **viewers**. The audience for a radio programme is the **listeners**. The audience for a sporting event is the **spectators**.

audio-visual *ADJECTIVE*
KINDS OF AUDIO-VISUAL EQUIPMENT USED IN SCHOOLS
cassette player, DVD, film-projector, interactive video, language laboratory, microfilm reader, overhead projector or OHP, slide projector, tape-slide equipment, television, video cassette recorder or VCR, whiteboard
VARIOUS KINDS OF EQUIPMENT YOU MIGHT HAVE AT HOME
amplifier, camcorder, CD, (*trademark*) Discman, DVD, earphones, headphones, hi-fi, loudspeaker, music centre, personal stereo, radio, record player, stereo, tape recorder, television, tuner, turntable, video cassette recorder or VCR, (*trademark*) Walkman

austere *ADJECTIVE*
1 *The monks led an austere kind of life.*
► comfortless, frugal, plain, puritanical, simple, sober, thrifty
AN OPPOSITE IS lavish
2 *She seemed rather an unfriendly and austere person.*
► cold, formal, hard, harsh, serious, severe, stern, strict
AN OPPOSITE IS genial

authentic *ADJECTIVE*
1 *If it's an authentic antique, it could be valuable.*
► actual, genuine, real
AN OPPOSITE IS counterfeit
2 *He gave an authentic account of his adventure.*
► accurate, dependable, factual, honest, reliable, true, truthful
AN OPPOSITE IS false

author *NOUN*
▷ An author who writes novels is a **novelist**. The author of a play is a **dramatist** or **playwright**. An author who writes for films or TV is a **scriptwriter**. An author who writes poetry is a **poet**. A person who writes music is a **composer**.
FOR OTHER WRITERS SEE **writer**

authority *NOUN*
1 *I have the head's authority to go home early.*
▸ approval, consent, permission
2 *Our teacher has the authority to tell us what to do.*
▸ influence, power, right
3 *He's an authority on steam trains.*
▸ expert, specialist

authorize *VERB*
The head authorized the purchase of a computer.
▸ agree to, approve, consent to, give permission for, permit, sign the order for

automatic *ADJECTIVE*
1 *We took our car through the automatic car wash.*
▸ automated, computerized, programmed
2 *When the lights come on, blinking is an automatic reaction.*
▸ impulsive, instinctive, involuntary, natural, reflex, spontaneous, unconscious, unthinking

auxiliary *ADJECTIVE*
The boat had an auxiliary engine.
▸ additional, emergency, extra, reserve, supplementary, supporting

available *ADJECTIVE*
Make sure the extinguisher is always available, in case there is a fire.
▸ accessible, at hand, convenient, handy, ready, usable, within reach

average *ADJECTIVE*
1 *She said that our work was above the average standard.*
▸ normal, ordinary, regular, usual
2 *It was an average kind of day at school.*
▸ commonplace, everyday, familiar, typical
AN OPPOSITE IS extraordinary

avert *VERB*
1 *I saw he was going to hit me, and I tried to avert the blow.*
▸ deflect, fend off, turn aside, ward off
2 *The firemen did all they could to avert disaster.*
▸ avoid, prevent, stave off

avid *ADJECTIVE*
She's an avid reader.
▸ eager, enthusiastic, fervent, keen
AN OPPOSITE IS apathetic

avoid *VERB*
1 *I tried hard to avoid the collision.*
▸ avert, dodge, fend off, get out of the way of, keep clear of, steer clear of
2 *The criminal avoided capture for months.*
▸ elude, escape from, evade, run away from
3 *Why does he always avoid the washing up?*
▸ get out of, shirk

await *VERB*
I await your reply.
▸ be ready for, expect, hope for, look out for, wait for

awake *ADJECTIVE*
I was awake all night.
▸ conscious, restless, sleepless, wide awake
▹ Not being able to sleep is to be suffering from **insomnia**.
AN OPPOSITE IS asleep

awaken *VERB*
1 *I awakened at dawn.*
▸ become conscious, stir, wake up
2 *Mum awakened us at seven.*
▸ alert, arouse, call, rouse, wake, waken

award *NOUN*
THINGS GIVEN TO PEOPLE WHO HAVE DONE SOMETHING SUCCESSFUL
badge, cap, cup, decoration, medal, prize, reward, scholarship, trophy

award *VERB*
They awarded first prize to my friend.
▸ confer (on), give, grant, present

aware *ADJECTIVE*
aware of *Are you aware of the rules?*
▸ acquainted with, conscious of, familiar with, informed about
AN OPPOSITE IS ignorant of

awe *NOUN*
We watched in awe as the volcano erupted.
▸ admiration, amazement, dread, fear, respect, reverence, terror, wonder

awful *ADJECTIVE* This word is often overused. It is usually vague in meaning. We give here just some of the other words you could use:
1 *The teacher complained about my awful handwriting.*
▸ (*informal*) abysmal, appalling, bad, dreadful, terrible

2 *She also complained about our awful behaviour.*
▸ disgraceful, disobedient, naughty, shameful
3 *I think he's an awful man.*
▸ detestable, disagreeable, horrid, nasty, unfriendly, unkind, unpleasant
4 *We need an awful lot of rain after this drought.*
▸ big, enormous, great, huge, large, massive
5 *We were shocked by the awful crime.*
▸ abominable, atrocious, callous, cruel, evil, horrifying, outrageous, shocking, villainous, wicked
6 *The erupting volcano was an awful sight.*
▸ awe-inspiring, dramatic, fearful

awfully *ADVERB*
It's been awfully hot today.
▸ dreadfully, exceptionally, extraordinarily, extremely, terribly, very

awkward *ADJECTIVE*
1 *The box was an awkward shape.*
▸ bulky, inconvenient, unmanageable
AN OPPOSITE IS convenient
2 *He was awkward with his hands.*
▸ clumsy, unskilful
AN OPPOSITE IS skilful
3 *I didn't know how to deal with such an awkward problem.*
▸ difficult, perplexing, thorny, (*informal*) ticklish, troublesome, trying
AN OPPOSITE IS straightforward
4 *I think the donkey was trying to be awkward.*
▸ exasperating, obstinate, stubborn, uncooperative, unhelpful
AN OPPOSITE IS cooperative
5 *He felt awkward in the smart hotel.*
▸ edgy, embarrassed, out of place, uncomfortable, uneasy
AN OPPOSITE IS comfortable

axe *NOUN*
VARIOUS TOOLS OR WEAPONS USED FOR CHOPPING
battleaxe, chopper, cleaver, hatchet, tomahawk

axe *VERB*
(*informal*) *They axed our bus service.*
▸ abolish, cancel, cut, end, get rid of, terminate, withdraw

Bb

baby *NOUN*
▸ infant
▹ A baby just learning to walk is a **toddler**.
FOR BABY ANIMALS SEE **young** *ADJECTIVE*

babyish *ADJECTIVE*
Mum got annoyed and said I was being babyish.
▸ childish, immature, infantile
AN OPPOSITE IS grown-up

back *NOUN*
The people at the front of the queue told us to go to the back.
▸ end, rear
▹ The back of a ship is the **stern**. The back end of an animal is the **hindquarters**, **rear**, or **rump**. The back of a piece of paper is the **reverse**.
AN OPPOSITE IS front

back *ADJECTIVE*
We sat on the back seat.
▸ end, rear
▹ The back legs of an animal are its **hind** legs.
AN OPPOSITE IS front

back *VERB*
1 *I watched Mum back into the drive.*
▸ drive backwards, reverse
2 *Who do you back to win?*
▸ bet on, gamble on
3 *A local business agreed to back our team.*
▸ sponsor, subsidize, support
to back away *When the dog growled, we backed away.*
▸ back off, give way, recoil, retire, retreat
AN OPPOSITE IS approach
to back out of something *I hurt my foot, so I had to back out of Saturday's game.*
▸ drop out of, withdraw from
to back someone up *Will you back me up if I need help?*
▸ help, support

background *NOUN*
1 *I drew a picture of Mum with our house in the background.*
AN OPPOSITE IS foreground
2 *We had a lesson about the background to the Gunpowder Plot.*

▷ The background to an event is the circumstances surrounding it or the history of it.
3 *My uncle's family has a military background.*
▸ tradition, upbringing

backing *NOUN*
1 *We can have a swimming competition if we get the head's backing.*
▸ approval, encouragement, help, support
2 *We got financial backing from a local firm.*
▸ aid, assistance, sponsorship, a subsidy

backwards *ADVERB*
1 *He drove backwards into the gatepost.*
▸ in reverse
AN OPPOSITE IS forwards
2 *You've got your pullover on backwards.*
▸ back to front

bad *ADJECTIVE* This word is often overused. We use the word *bad* to describe almost anything we don't like. Here are some common ways we use *bad* and some of the synonyms we might use:
1 *He was a bad man.*
▸ beastly, corrupt, criminal, cruel, dangerous, deplorable, detestable, evil, immoral, infamous, malevolent, malicious, mean, nasty, shameful, sinful, vicious, villainous, wicked
2 *I saw a bad accident on the motorway.*
▸ appalling, awful, calamitous, disastrous, dreadful, frightful, ghastly, hair-raising, hideous, horrible, shocking, terrible
3 *She went to hospital with a bad illness.*
▸ distressing, grave, painful, serious, severe, unpleasant
4 *He was punished for his bad behaviour.*
▸ abominable, (*informal*) diabolical, disgraceful, dreadful, mischievous, naughty, wrong
5 *I had to do the work again because it was so bad.*
▸ (*informal*) abysmal, awful, (*informal*) hopeless, inadequate, incompetent, inefficient, inferior, poor, shoddy, unsatisfactory, useless, weak, worthless
6 *We abandoned the journey because of the bad weather.*
▸ adverse, discouraging, harsh, hostile, unfavourable, unhelpful
7 *When the fridge went wrong we threw away a lot of bad food.*
▸ decayed, decomposing, foul, mouldy, rotten, smelly, sour, spoiled

bad
8 *The bad smell comes from the drains.*
▸ disgusting, foul, loathsome, objectionable, offensive, repulsive, revolting, sickening, vile
9 *Smoking is bad for your health.*
▸ damaging, dangerous, harmful, injurious
10 *I felt too bad to go to school today.*
▸ ill, poorly, sick, unwell
11 *I feel bad that I haven't written to Granny.*
▸ ashamed, guilty, remorseful, sorry
AN OPPOSITE IS good

badge *NOUN*
THINGS YOU WEAR OR DISPLAY TO SHOW WHO YOU ARE, WHICH ORGANIZATION YOU BELONG TO, ETC.
crest, emblem, flag, logo, medal, rosette, sign, symbol, trademark

badger *VERB*
Don't badger me while I'm busy.
▸ annoy, bother, harass, nag, pester, trouble, worry

bad-tempered *ADJECTIVE*
What made you so bad-tempered today?
▸ angry, annoyed, cross, grumpy, ill-tempered, irritable, moody, quarrelsome, rude, short-tempered, sullen
AN OPPOSITE IS good-tempered

baffle *VERB*
The problem baffled us.
▸ bewilder, confuse, defeat, foil, fox, frustrate, mystify, outwit, perplex, puzzle, stump

baffling *ADJECTIVE*
No one could explain the baffling mystery.
▸ bewildering, confusing, frustrating, inexplicable, insoluble, mysterious, mystifying, perplexing, puzzling
AN OPPOSITE IS straightforward

bag *NOUN*
VARIOUS CONTAINERS USED TO CARRY THINGS IN ARE
basket, briefcase, carrier bag, case, handbag, holdall, sack, satchel, shopping bag, shoulder bag, suitcase

baggage *NOUN*
We loaded our baggage onto a trolley.
▸ bags, belongings, cases, gear, luggage, paraphernalia, suitcases, trunks

bake *VERB*
FOR VARIOUS WAYS TO COOK THINGS SEE **cook** *VERB*

balance *NOUN*
to lose your balance *I lost my balance and fell off the branch.*
▸ totter, wobble

bald *ADJECTIVE*
He has a bald patch on the back of his head.
▸ bare, hairless

bale *VERB*
to bale out *The aircraft crashed, but the pilot had managed to bale out.*
▸ eject, escape, jump out, parachute down

ball *NOUN*
The Earth is the shape of a ball.
▸ globe, globule, orb, sphere

ban *VERB*
1 *They banned smoking on the buses.*
▸ forbid, make illegal, outlaw, prohibit, stop
2 *They banned him from swimming because he annoyed the younger children.*
▸ bar, exclude
AN OPPOSITE IS allow

band *NOUN*
1 *A band of devoted followers sat round him.*
▸ company, gang, group
2 *I play the recorder in the school band.*
▸ ensemble, group, orchestra
3 *The team's new strip has a band of red round the white shirt.*
▸ belt, hoop, line, ring, stripe

bandage *NOUN*
THINGS USED TO DRESS A WOUND ARE
dressing, gauze, lint, plaster

bandit *NOUN*
Buses travelling through the mountains have been attacked by bandits.
▸ brigand, gangster, gunman, outlaw, robber, thief

bang *NOUN*
1 *I heard a loud bang just before the crash.*
▸ blast, boom, crash, explosion, pop, report, thud, thump
FOR VARIOUS WAYS TO MAKE SOUNDS SEE **sound** *VERB*
2 *I've got a bruise where I had that bang on the head.*
▸ blow, bump, hit, knock, punch, smack, thump, (*slang*) wallop, whack

bang *VERB*
1 *You could tell she was angry by the way she banged the saucepan on the table.*
▸ hit, slam, thump
2 *The cat hates it when the fireworks bang.*
▸ crack, explode, go off

banish *VERB*
He was banished from his native land for ever.
▸ deport, eject, exile, expel, send away

bank *NOUN*
1 *I put half my pocket money in the bank.*
OTHER PLACES WHERE YOUR MONEY CAN BE LOOKED AFTER
building society, post office, savings bank
2 *There were fishermen all along the river bank.*
▸ brink, edge, margin, shore, side
3 *I sat and rested on a grassy bank.*
▸ embankment, mound, ridge, slope
4 *The pilot had to keep his eye on the bank of instruments.*
▸ array, collection, rank, row, series

bank *VERB*
1 *I banked half of my pocket money.*
▸ deposit, pay in, save
2 *The plane banked as it came in to land.*
▸ lean over, tilt, tip

banner *NOUN*
Colourful banners fluttered in the wind.
▸ flag, pennant, standard, streamer

banquet *NOUN*
They held a banquet in honour of the visiting President.
▸ dinner, feast

bar *NOUN*
LONG PIECES OF METAL OR WOOD USED FOR VARIOUS PURPOSES ARE
beam, girder, joist, pole, rail, railing, rod, shaft, stake, stick, strut
▹ A bar of chocolate can be called a **block** or **slab**. A bar of soap can be called a **cake**.

bar *VERB*
1 *The club barred her because she didn't pay her subscription.*

▸ ban, exclude, keep out, prohibit
2 *A fallen tree barred our way.*
▸ block, check, hinder, impede, obstruct, stop

barbaric ADJECTIVE
Many were killed in the barbaric attack.
▸ barbarous, brutal, cold-blooded, cruel, inhuman, ruthless, savage
AN OPPOSITE IS humane

bare ADJECTIVE
1 *He was bare from the waist up.*
▸ exposed, naked, nude, unclothed, undressed
2 *Dad's got a bare patch on top of his head.*
▸ bald, hairless
3 *There was no shelter on the bare hill.*
▸ barren, bleak, treeless
4 *The bare room looked cold and cheerless.*
▸ empty, unfurnished
5 *Shall we put some pictures on that bare wall?*
▸ blank, plain
6 *They didn't even have enough money for the bare necessities.*
▸ basic, essential, minimum

bargain NOUN
1 *I'll make a bargain with you.*
▸ agreement, deal, pact
2 *The coat I bought was a bargain.*
▸ good buy, special offer

bargain VERB
Mum bargained with the salesman about the price.
▸ argue, do a deal, haggle, negotiate

bark VERB
The dog barked fiercely.
▸ growl, yap

barracks NOUN
OTHER KINDS OF ACCOMMODATION FOR SOLDIERS
billet, camp, garrison, quarters

barrage NOUN
1 *The soldiers were attacked with a barrage of gunfire.*
▸ bombardment, volley
2 *They built a barrage to control the flow of the river.*
▸ barrier, dam, weir

barrel NOUN
VARIOUS KINDS OF BARREL ARE
butt, cask, drum, keg, oil drum, tub, water-butt
FOR OTHER THINGS TO KEEP LIQUIDS IN SEE **container**

barren ADJECTIVE
The camel train had to cross miles of barren desert.
▸ arid, bare, dried-up, infertile, lifeless, sterile, uncultivated
AN OPPOSITE IS fertile

barricade NOUN
The protesters built a barricade across the road.
▸ barrier, obstacle, obstruction
SEE ALSO **fence** NOUN

barrier NOUN
1 *They asked the spectators to stay behind the barrier.*
▸ barricade, fence, railing, wall
SEE ALSO **fence** NOUN
2 *I'd like to be friends with the French visitors, but my ignorance of their language is a barrier.*
▸ drawback, handicap, hindrance, obstacle

barter VERB
I bartered my comic for his sweets.
▸ exchange, swap, trade

base NOUN
1 *Little flowers were growing near the base of the wall.*
▸ bottom, foot
▹ The base of a statue is a **pedestal**.
2 *Dad laid some paving slabs to make a base for his new shed.*
▸ basis, foundation, support
3 *The explorers returned to their base.*
▸ camp, depot, headquarters

basement NOUN
OTHER PARTS OF A BUILDING BELOW GROUND ARE
cellar, crypt, dungeon, undercroft, vault

bashful ADJECTIVE
Don't be bashful—speak up for yourself.
▸ coy, embarrassed, modest, nervous, reserved, retiring, sheepish, shy, timid
AN OPPOSITE IS assertive

basic *ADJECTIVE*
1 *I learned the basic moves in chess.*
▸ chief, crucial, essential, fundamental, important, key, main, principal, vital
2 *My knowledge of French is very basic.*
▸ elementary, simple
AN OPPOSITE IS advanced

basin *NOUN*
I filled the basin with hot water.
▸ bowl, dish, sink
FOR OTHER THINGS TO PUT LIQUIDS IN SEE **container**

basis *NOUN*
1 *Our experienced players formed the basis of the team.*
▸ base, core, foundation
2 *On what basis did you decide to be a vegetarian?*
▸ principle

bask *VERB*
Are you going to stay basking in the sun all afternoon?
▸ enjoy yourself, lie, lounge, relax

basket *NOUN*
VARIOUS KINDS OF BASKET ARE
hamper, laundry basket, pannier, punnet, shopping-basket, trug
FOR OTHER CONTAINERS SEE **container**

bat *NOUN*
▹ In golf, you hit the ball with a club. In tennis, you hit it with a racket. In snooker, you hit it with a cue.

bath *NOUN*
▹ To wash all over you can also have a shower. Special kinds of bath are jacuzzi, sauna, and Turkish bath.

bathe *VERB*
1 *On hot days we often bathe in the river.*
▸ go swimming, splash about, swim, take a dip
▹ To walk about in shallow water is to paddle. To walk through deep water is to wade.
2 *The nurse gently bathed the wound.*
▸ clean, cleanse, rinse, wash

bathroom *NOUN*
FITTINGS YOU MAY FIND IN A BATHROOM
bath, bidet, extractor fan, jacuzzi, lavatory, medicine cabinet, mirror, shaver point, shower, shower curtain, taps, tiles, toilet, towel rail, ventilator, washbasin
THINGS PEOPLE USE IN A BATHROOM
bath mat, bath salts, comb, cosmetics, curlers, flannel, foam bath, gel, hairbrush, loofah, make-up, nail brush, nail scissors, pumice stone, razor, scales, shampoo, shaver, soap, sponge, toiletries, toilet roll, toothbrush, towel, tweezers

batter *VERB*
We battered on the door for ages, but no one came.
▸ beat, keep hitting, pound
FOR OTHER WAYS OF HITTING SEE **hit** *VERB*

battle *NOUN*
Both armies lost many soldiers in the battle.
▸ action, clash, conflict, engagement, hostilities, struggle
▹ A series of battles is a campaign or war.
SEE ALSO **fight** *NOUN*

bay *NOUN*
VARIOUS PLACES WHERE THE SEA SHORE CURVES INWARD
cove, creek, estuary, fjord, gulf, harbour, inlet, sound

be *VERB*
1 *I'll be here until lunchtime.*
▸ continue, remain, stay, survive
2 *The concert will be in November.*
▸ come about, happen, occur, take place
3 *She wants to be a writer.*
▸ become, develop into

beach *NOUN*
We played all day on the beach.
▸ sands, seashore, shore

bead *NOUN*
1 *She wore a string of pretty beads.*
FOR OTHER WORDS SEE **jewellery**
2 *Beads of sweat stood out on his forehead.*
▸ blob, drip, drop, droplet, pearl

A B C D E F G H I J K L M N O P Q R S T U V W X Y Z

beam *NOUN*
1 *The old house was full of wooden beams.*
OTHER LONG PIECES OF WOOD USED FOR VARIOUS PURPOSES
bar, boom, joist, mast, plank, pole, post, rafter, rail, railing, rod, shaft, spar, stake, stick, strut, support, timber
2 *The lighthouse sent out a strong beam of light.*
▸ gleam, ray, shaft, stream

beam *VERB*
1 *Everyone in the photo was beaming happily.*
▸ grin, laugh, smile
AN OPPOSITE IS frown
2 *The radio waves were beamed towards a satellite.*
▸ aim, broadcast, direct, radiate, send out, transmit

bean *NOUN*
SOME KINDS OF BEAN ARE
broad bean, butter-bean, French bean, haricot bean, kidney bean, runner bean, soya bean
▹ Beans, peas, lentils, etc., are **legumes** or **pulses**.

bear *VERB*
1 *The rope won't bear my weight.*
▸ carry, hold, support, take
2 *They bore the injured player off the field on a stretcher.*
▸ bring, carry, fetch, take, transfer
3 *The gravestone bears an inscription.*
▸ display, have, show
4 *I can't bear this toothache.*
▸ abide, endure, put up with, stand, suffer, tolerate
5 *She has borne three children.*
▸ give birth to

bear *NOUN*
VARIOUS KINDS OF BEAR ARE
black bear, brown bear, grizzly bear, polar bear
▹ Popular animals rather like bears are the **koala** and **giant panda**. A toy bear is a **teddy bear**.
FOR OTHER ANIMALS SEE **animal**

bearable *ADJECTIVE*
The pain is bad, but it is bearable.
▸ acceptable, endurable, tolerable
AN OPPOSITE IS unbearable

bearing *NOUN*
He was an elderly man with a military bearing.
▸ appearance, look, manner, posture
bearings *I lost my bearings in the fog.*
▸ direction, position, sense of direction

beast *NOUN*
At one time many wild beasts lived in the jungle.
▸ animal, creature
▹ You might call a large or frightening beast a **brute** or **monster**.
FOR OTHER WORDS SEE **animal**

beastly *ADJECTIVE*
I hated him for playing that beastly trick.
▸ cruel, horrid, nasty, spiteful, unkind, unpleasant
AN OPPOSITE IS kind

beat *VERB*
1 *He beat the dog with a stick.*
▸ batter, cane, flog, hit, lash, strike, thrash, whack, whip
FOR OTHER WAYS TO HIT SEE **hit** *VERB*
2 *I'm sorry to say that our opponents beat us.*
▸ conquer, defeat, get the better of, overcome, overwhelm, rout, thrash, vanquish, win against
3 *I beat some eggs to make an omelette.*
▸ mix up, stir briskly, whip, whisk
4 *My heart beat faster.*
▸ pound, thump
to beat someone up *The bully threatened to beat me up.*
▸ assault, attack, (*informal*) knock about, (*informal*) set about

beat *NOUN*
1 *After you've been running, you feel the beat of your heart.*
▸ pulse, throb
2 *I like music with a strong beat.*
▸ accent, rhythm

beautiful *ADJECTIVE*
1 *The bride looked very beautiful.*
▸ attractive, charming, (*informal*) cute, good-looking, glamorous, gorgeous, lovely, pretty, radiant
▹ A man who is pleasing to look at is **good-looking** or **handsome**.
2 *I enjoyed the beautiful views as we drove through the mountains.*
▸ delightful, glorious, magnificent, picturesque, scenic, spectacular, splendid

3 *We had beautiful weather on our holiday.*
▶ brilliant, excellent, fine, glorious, marvellous, sunny, superb, wonderful
AN OPPOSITE IS nasty or ugly

beauty *NOUN*
1 *The film star was famous for her beauty.*
▶ attractiveness, glamour, grace, loveliness
2 *We admired the beauty of the surrounding countryside.*
▶ appeal, glory, magnificence, radiance, splendour
AN OPPOSITE IS ugliness

beckon *VERB*
When he beckoned to me, I ran to see what he wanted.
▶ gesticulate, make a sign, signal

become *VERB*
1 *I hope you won't become angry if I tell the truth.*
▶ begin to be, turn
2 *If you buy a pet, remember that little puppies become big dogs!*
▶ change into, develop into, grow into, turn into
3 *That colour becomes you.*
▶ look good on, suit

bed *NOUN*
1 *This bed isn't very comfortable.*
VARIOUS KINDS OF BED
air-bed, divan, double bed, four-poster, single bed, water-bed
▷ A bed for a baby is a **cot**, **cradle**, or **crib**. Two single beds one above the other are **bunk beds**. A bed on a ship or train is a **berth**. A bed made of net or cloth hung up above the ground is a **hammock**.
PARTS OF A BED
base, bedpost, bedstead, headboard, mattress
THINGS YOU USE TO MAKE A BED WARM AND COMFORTABLE
bed linen, bedspread, blanket, bolster, continental quilt, counterpane, coverlet, duvet, eiderdown, electric blanket, mattress, pillow, pillowcase, pillowslip, quilt, sheet, sleeping bag
2 *Mum filled the flower bed with geraniums.*
▶ border, patch, plot
3 *The wreck settled on the bed of the sea.*
▶ bottom
4 *Dad erected his shed on a bed of concrete.*
▶ base, foundation, layer

bedclothes *PLURAL NOUN*
▶ bedding, sheets and blankets

bedraggled *ADJECTIVE*
The dog came in out of the rain looking very bedraggled.
▶ dirty, dishevelled, messy, scruffy, untidy, wet
AN OPPOSITE IS smart

beer *NOUN*
FOR VARIOUS DRINKS SEE **drink** *NOUN*

beetle *NOUN*
SOME OF THE MANY KINDS OF BEETLE ARE
cockchafer, cockroach, Colorado beetle, deathwatch beetle, dung-beetle, furniture beetle, ladybird, stag beetle
FOR OTHER INSECTS AND CRAWLING CREATURES SEE **insect**

before *ADVERB*
1 *Have you been here before?*
▶ already, in the past
2 *If you want to come with me, you should have told me before.*
▶ earlier, in advance, previously, sooner

beg *VERB*
1 *The next-door cat comes round to beg for food.*
▶ cadge, (*informal*) scrounge
2 *He begged me not to tell the teacher.*
▶ ask, entreat, implore, plead with

begin *VERB*
1 *We began the journey at breakfast time.*
▶ commence, embark on, set out on, start
2 *We plan to begin a chess club next term.*
▶ found, initiate, introduce, launch, set up
3 *When did the trouble begin?*
▶ arise, break out, come into existence, crop up, emerge, happen, originate, spring up
AN OPPOSITE IS end or stop

beginner *NOUN*
I'm only a beginner.
▶ learner, novice, starter
▷ A beginner in a trade or a job is an **apprentice** or **trainee**. A beginner in the police or armed services is a **cadet** or **recruit**.

a b c d e f g h i j k l m n o p q r s t u v w x y z

A B C D E F G H I J K L M N O P Q R S T U V W X Y Z

beginning *NOUN*
The beginning of the new rail service should mean fewer traffic jams.
▸ commencement, establishment, foundation, initiation, introduction, launch, opening, start
▹ The beginning of life on earth was **creation** or **genesis**. The beginning of your life was your **birth**. The beginning of the day is **dawn** or **daybreak**. The beginning of a journey is the **starting point**. The beginning of a stream or river is the **origin** or **source**. A piece of writing at the beginning of a book is an **introduction**, **preface**, or **prologue**. A piece of music at the beginning of a musical or opera is a **prelude** or **overture**.
AN OPPOSITE IS end

behave *VERB*
1 *The car behaves better since it was serviced.*
▸ act, perform, run, work
2 *I wish you would behave!*
▸ be good, be on your best behaviour

behaviour *NOUN*
She congratulated us on our good behaviour.
▸ actions, attitude, conduct, manners

being *NOUN*
They looked like beings from another planet.
▸ animal, creature, individual, person

belch *VERB*
1 *The chimney belched smoke.*
▸ discharge, emit, send out
2 *Smoke belched out of the chimney.*
▸ erupt, gush

belief *NOUN*
1 *Some people are persecuted because of their religious belief.*
▸ creed, doctrine, faith, religion
2 *My belief is that he stole the money.*
▸ conviction, feeling, notion, opinion, theory, view
3 *His belief in fairies made everyone laugh at him.*
▸ believing, confidence, faith, trust

believe *VERB*
1 *I believe what he says.*
▸ accept, have faith in, rely on, trust
AN OPPOSITE IS disbelieve
2 *I believe that she cheated.*
▸ assume, feel, know, presume, reckon, suppose, think

bell *NOUN*
VARIOUS KINDS OF BELL
alarm bell, carillon, chimes, church bells, doorbell, knell, peal of bells, tubular bells, warning bell
VERBS EXPRESSING DIFFERENT WAYS BELLS SOUND
chime, clang, clink, jangle, jingle, peal, ping, resonate, reverberate, ring, sound the knell, strike, tinkle, toll

belong *VERB*
1 *This book belongs to me.*
▸ be owned by
2 *Would you like to belong to the squash club?*
▸ be a member of, be connected with
3 *I belong here with my friends.*
▸ be at home, be welcome, have a place

belongings *PLURAL NOUN*
Make sure you take your belongings with you when you get off the train.
▸ goods, possessions, property, things

below *PREPOSITION*
1 *We saw goldfish swimming below the surface.*
▸ beneath, under, underneath
2 *The temperature never fell below 20 degrees.*
▸ less than, lower than

belt *NOUN*
We walked through a belt of woodland.
▸ band, line, stretch, strip

bench *NOUN*
1 *We sat down on a bench in the park.*
▸ form, seat
▹ A long seat in a church is a **pew**.
2 *The carpenter laid his tools out on the bench.*
▸ table, workbench, work table

bend *VERB*
The metal was bent into strange shapes.
▸ arch, buckle, coil, curl, curve, distort, flex, fold, loop, turn, twist, warp, wind
▹ A word for things which bend easily is **flexible**.
AN OPPOSITE IS straighten
to bend down *I bent down behind the wall so that they couldn't see me.*
▸ bow, crouch, duck, kneel, stoop

bend *NOUN*
Watch out for the dangerous bend in the road.
▸ angle, corner, curve, turn, twist, zigzag

benefactor *NOUN*
An anonymous benefactor paid for our trip.
▸ backer, donor, patron, promoter, sponsor, supporter, well-wisher

benefit *NOUN*
1 *One benefit of living in the country is that the air is cleaner.*
▸ advantage, convenience, gain, good thing
AN OPPOSITE IS handicap
2 *Since he lost his job he's been living on benefit.*
▸ (*informal*) dole
▹ Other terms for benefit people get from the government include income support, social security, and welfare.

benevolent *ADJECTIVE*
A benevolent sponsor gave us money for sports equipment.
▸ charitable, friendly, generous, helpful, kind, liberal, sympathetic, warm-hearted
AN OPPOSITE IS malevolent

bent *ADJECTIVE*
1 *After the accident, the car was a mass of bent metal.*
▸ arched, buckled, coiled, contorted, crooked, curved, distorted, folded, twisted, warped
AN OPPOSITE IS straight
2 (*slang*) *The bent politician was dismissed from the government.*
▸ corrupt, dishonest, untrustworthy
AN OPPOSITE IS honest

bequeath *VERB*
In her will, she bequeathed her money to her grandchildren.
▸ hand down, leave, pass on

bereaved *ADJECTIVE*
▹ Someone whose husband or wife dies is widowed. A child whose parents die is orphaned.

bereavement *NOUN*
They wore black because there was a bereavement in the family.
▸ death, loss

berserk *ADJECTIVE*
to go berserk *The dog went berserk when a wasp stung him.*
▸ (*informal*) be beside yourself, become frantic, become frenzied, go crazy, lose control of yourself, go mad, rampage, riot

berth *NOUN*
PLACES WHERE SHIPS TIE UP
anchorage, dock, harbour, haven, landing stage, moorings, pier, port, quay, slipway, wharf

beside *PREPOSITION*
They parked their car beside ours.
▸ alongside, by, close to, near, next to
beside the point *The fact that it is raining is beside the point.*
▸ irrelevant, neither here nor there, unimportant
to be beside yourself *He was beside himself when he found out they had cheated him.*
▸ become frantic, be upset, go berserk, lose control of yourself

besides *ADVERB*
I don't really want to go, and besides, I haven't got any money.
▸ additionally, also, furthermore, in addition, moreover

besiege *VERB*
1 *The Greeks besieged Troy for 10 long years.*
▸ blockade, cut off, isolate
2 *The superstar was besieged by reporters.*
▸ encircle, surround

best *ADJECTIVE*
1 *She is our best player.*
▸ finest, leading, outstanding, supreme, unequalled, unrivalled
2 *Our shop only sells vegetables of the best quality.*
▸ excellent, first-class, top
AN OPPOSITE IS worst

bet *NOUN*
I had a bet that she would win.
▸ gamble, wager

bet *VERB*
He bet everything he had on a horse race.
▸ gamble, risk

betray *VERB*
1 *He betrayed us by revealing our plans to our opponents.*
▸ be a traitor to, cheat, conspire against, double-cross
2 *He betrayed his friend to the police.*
▸ inform against, (*informal*) tell tales about

A
B
C
D
E
F
G
H
I
J
K
L
M
N
O
P
Q
R
S
T
U
V
W
X
Y
Z

3 *I thought I could trust her, but she betrayed my secret.*
▸ disclose, give away, let out, reveal, tell

better *ADJECTIVE*
1 *Which of these dresses do you think is better?*
▸ preferable, superior
2 *I had flu, but I'm better now.*
▸ cured, healed, healthier, improved, recovering, well

beware *VERB*
Beware! There are thieves about.
▸ be careful! be on your guard! look out! take care! watch out!
beware of *Beware of the bull.*
▸ avoid, guard against, heed, keep clear of, look out for, mind, watch out for

bewilder *VERB*
I was bewildered by the misleading instructions on the packet.
▸ baffle, confuse, fox, mystify, perplex, puzzle

beyond *PREPOSITION*
You'll find the post office just beyond the butchers.
▸ after, past, the other side of

bias *NOUN*
1 *She has a bias towards science.*
▸ bent, inclination, leaning, liking, preference, tendency
2 *The referee was guilty of bias.*
▸ favouritism, one-sidedness, prejudice, unfairness
▹ A bias against people of one particular race is racism. A bias against one sex is sexism.

biased *ADJECTIVE*
The crowd thought that the referee's decision was biased.
▸ one-sided, prejudiced, unfair
AN OPPOSITE IS impartial

bicycle *NOUN*
DIFFERENT KINDS OF CYCLE
bicycle or (*informal*) bike, moped, motor bike or motor cycle, mountain bike, (*old use*) penny-farthing, racer or racing bike, scooter, tandem, tricycle

bid *NOUN*
1 *I made a bid at the auction for a rare stamp.*
▸ offer
2 *His bid to beat the world record failed.*
▸ attempt, effort, go, try

big *ADJECTIVE* This word is often overused. The adjective *big* can refer to anything that is more than the normal size or importance. Here are some common ways we use *big* and some of the synonyms we might use:
1 *I need a big box to put my things in.*
▸ large, roomy, sizeable, spacious
2 *She gave us big helpings of food.*
▸ ample, considerable, enormous, great, huge, substantial, (*informal*) tremendous
3 *The weightlifter was a big man.*
▸ burly, colossal, enormous, gigantic, huge, hulking, mighty
4 *He eats so much that he's getting big.*
▸ fat, overweight, plump, stout
5 *Space exploration involves travelling big distances.*
▸ immense, infinite, vast
6 *During the storm, we were terrified by the big waves.*
▸ high, mountainous, tall, towering
7 *It's awkward carrying big parcels on the bus.*
▸ bulky, heavy, hefty, weighty
8 *We gave the winners a big round of applause.*
▸ deafening, enthusiastic, loud, thunderous
9 *I have some big decisions to make.*
▸ grave, important, serious, significant
10 *She's a big name in the music business.*
▸ famous, influential, leading, notable, powerful, prominent
AN OPPOSITE IS small or unimportant

bill *NOUN*
Dad went pale when he saw the bill for repairs to the car.
▸ account, invoice, statement

bin *NOUN*
FOR VARIOUS CONTAINERS SEE **container**

bind *VERB*
1 *I bound two sticks together with some string.*
▸ attach, connect, fasten, join, lash, rope, secure, tie
2 *The nurse started to bind the wound with a bandage.*
▸ cover, dress, wrap

bird *NOUN*
▷ The study of birds is **ornithology**.
A female bird is a **hen**. A male bird is a **cock**. A group of birds is a **flock**. A young bird is a **chick** or **fledgling**. A young bird in a nest is a **nestling**. A family of chicks is a **brood**.
FOR SPECIAL NAMES FOR YOUNG BIRDS SEE **young** *ADJECTIVE*
SOME DIFFERENT KINDS OF BIRDS ARE
birds of prey, game birds, sea birds, songbirds, waders, waterfowl, wildfowl
BIRDS SOMETIMES KEPT AS PETS ARE
budgerigar, canary, cockatoo, macaw, mynah bird, parakeet, parrot, peacock
BIRDS WHICH FARMERS KEEP FOR THEIR EGGS OR MEAT ARE
chicken, duck, goose, ostrich, turkey
▷ Birds kept by farmers are **poultry**.
BIRDS YOU MAY SEE IN BRITISH GARDENS OR COUNTRYSIDE
blackbird, blackcap, bullfinch, bunting, chaffinch, chiffchaff, corncrake, crow, cuckoo, curlew, dove, dunnock, fieldfare, finch, flycatcher, goldcrest, goldfinch, greenfinch, hedge sparrow, jackdaw, jay, lapwing, lark, linnet, magpie, martin, nightingale, nightjar, nuthatch, ousel, peewit, pigeon, pipit, plover, raven, redbreast, redstart, robin, rook, shrike, skylark, sparrow, sparrowhawk, starling, stonechat, swallow, swift, thrush, tit, treecreeper, warbler, waxwing, wheatear, whitethroat, woodpecker, wren, yellowhammer
GAME BIRDS WHICH PEOPLE HUNT, OR USED TO HUNT
grouse, partridge, pheasant, ptarmigan, quail, woodcock
BIRDS WHICH LIVE ON OR NEAR LAKES, STREAMS, OR MARSHES
avocet, bittern, coot, dabchick, dipper, diver, duck, egret, goose, grebe, heron, kingfisher, mallard, moorhen, sandpiper, snipe, spoonbill, swan, teal, wagtail, wigeon
BIRDS WHICH LIVE ON OR NEAR THE SEA
albatross, auk, chough, cormorant, dunlin, fulmar, gannet, guillemot, gull, kittiwake, oystercatcher, petrel, puffin, razorbill, redshank, seagull, shag, shearwater, shelduck, skua, tern, turnstone
SOME BIRDS OF PREY
buzzard, eagle, falcon, hawk, hen harrier, kestrel, kite, merlin, osprey, owl, peregrine, sparrowhawk

bird *NOUN*
SOME BIRDS YOU MIGHT SEE IN OTHER COUNTRIES OR IN A ZOO
cassowary, crane, emu, flamingo, humming bird, ibis, kiwi, kookaburra, ostrich, pelican, penguin, stork, toucan, vulture
PARTS OF A BIRD ARE
beak, bill, claw, crest, down, feathers, plumage, tail, talon, wing
PLACES WHERE BIRDS LIVE OR BRING UP THEIR YOUNG
aviary, cage, nest, nesting box

birth *NOUN*
▷ The movements of a woman's womb when a baby is born is **labour**. A medical specialist in childbirth is an **obstetrician**. The birth of Jesus is called the **Nativity**.

biscuit *NOUN*
SOME DIFFERENT KINDS OF BISCUIT ARE
chocolate biscuit, cracker, crispbread, digestive biscuit, ginger-nut, macaroon, oatcake, pretzel, rusk, shortbread, wafer

bisect *VERB*
The lines bisect each other.
▸ cross, divide, intersect

bit *NOUN* This word is often overused.
1 *We divided the chocolate so that we each had a bit.*
▸ chunk, fraction, hunk, lump, piece, portion, section, segment, share
2 *I swept up the bits off the floor.*
▸ chip, fragment, scrap
▷ A small bit of food is a **morsel**. A bit broken off a cake or loaf is a **crumb**. A bit of dust is a **particle** or **speck**.

bite *VERB*
▷ To bite at something hard is to **gnaw** it. To bite and crush something hard is to **crunch** it. To bite off very small bits at a time is to **nibble**. When a fierce animal bites you it **savages** you. When a dog tries to bite you it **snaps** at you. When an insect bites you it **stings** you.
FOR OTHER WORDS SEE **eat**

bitter *ADJECTIVE*
1 *The unripe plums had a bitter taste.*
▸ acid, harsh, sharp, sour, unpleasant
AN OPPOSITE IS **sweet**
2 *He was very bitter when I got the prize instead of him.*

▸ envious, jealous, malicious, resentful, sore, spiteful, unkind, unpleasant, vicious
AN OPPOSITE IS pleased
3 *I wore my anorak to keep out the bitter wind.*
▸ biting, cold, freezing, icy, (*informal*) perishing, piercing, raw, wintry
AN OPPOSITE IS mild

black *ADJECTIVE & NOUN*
WORDS TO DESCRIBE THINGS THAT ARE BLACK OR NEARLY BLACK
blackish, coal-black, dark, dirty, dusky, ebony, gloomy, inky, jet-black, murky, pitch-black, pitch-dark, raven, sooty

blade *NOUN*
VARIOUS WEAPONS AND IMPLEMENTS THAT HAVE A BLADE
axe, chopper, cutlass, dagger, knife, razor, sabre, scalpel, scissors, sword

blame *VERB*
It was unfair to blame the driver for the accident.
▸ accuse, condemn, criticize, reproach, scold

blank *ADJECTIVE*
1 *We need something to fill in that blank space.*
▸ bare, clean, empty, plain, unmarked, unused
2 *He gave me a blank look.*
▸ absent-minded, baffled, expressionless, mindless, vacant

blank *NOUN*
Fill in the blanks.
▸ break, gap, space

blasphemous *ADJECTIVE*
I was shocked to hear such blasphemous language in church.
▸ irreverent, wicked
AN OPPOSITE IS reverent

blast *NOUN*
1 *When he opened the door, I felt a blast of air.*
▸ burst, gale, gust, rush
2 *We heard the blast of a trumpet.*
▸ blare, noise, roar
3 *Windows were broken by the blast.*
▸ explosion

blaze *NOUN*
Firemen fought the blaze for hours.
▸ fire, flames, inferno

blaze *VERB*
Within a few minutes the dry timber was blazing.
▸ burn brightly, flare up

bleak *ADJECTIVE*
1 *They got lost and had to spend the night on a bleak hillside.*
▸ bare, barren, cheerless, cold, comfortless, exposed, wintry
AN OPPOSITE IS comfortable
2 *After losing so many matches, our team's future looks bleak.*
▸ depressing, dismal, gloomy, grim, hopeless, miserable
AN OPPOSITE IS promising

blemish *NOUN*
Dad noticed a blemish on the paintwork of our car.
▸ defect, fault, flaw, imperfection, mark, stain
VARIOUS KINDS OF BLEMISH YOU CAN HAVE ON YOUR SKIN ARE
birthmark, blackhead, blister, corn, freckle, mole, pimple, scar, spot, verruca, wart, whitlow, (*slang*) zit

blend *VERB*
Blend the flour with a tablespoon of water.
▸ beat together, mix, stir together, whip, whisk
to blend with *Many birds are camouflaged so that they blend with the background.*
▸ become part of, disappear into, match, merge with, tone in with

blessing *NOUN*
1 *The priest pronounced a blessing.*
▸ grace, prayer
AN OPPOSITE IS curse
2 *He gave the plan his blessing.*
▸ approval, backing, consent, permission, support
AN OPPOSITE IS disapproval
3 *Central heating is a blessing in the winter.*
▸ advantage, asset, benefit, comfort
AN OPPOSITE IS evil *NOUN*

blight *NOUN*
The problem of drugs is a blight on society.
▸ affliction, curse, evil, plague

> **blind** *ADJECTIVE*
> WORDS TO DESCRIBE PEOPLE WITH IMPAIRED VISION
> astigmatic, colour-blind, long-sighted, near-sighted or short-sighted, visually handicapped
> DISEASES CAUSING IMPAIRED VISION INCLUDE
> cataract, glaucoma
> blind to She's blind to his faults.
> c ignorant of, unaware of
> an opposite is aware of

bliss *NOUN*
She gave a sigh of bliss.
▸ delight, ecstasy, happiness, joy, pleasure
AN OPPOSITE IS misery

blissful *ADJECTIVE*
We spent a blissful week together.
▸ delightful, ecstatic, happy, heavenly, joyful
AN OPPOSITE IS miserable

blob *NOUN*
You've got a blob of ice cream on your chin.
▸ drop, lump, spot

block *NOUN*
1 *A block of stone fell from the lorry.*
▸ chunk, hunk, lump, piece
▹ We also talk about a **bar** of chocolate. a **brick** of ice cream. a **cake** of soap. an **ingot** of metal. a **slab** of concrete.
2 *The basin overflowed because there's a block in the drainpipe.*
▸ blockage, jam, obstacle, obstruction

block *VERB*
1 *A tall building blocked our view.*
▸ hamper, hinder, interfere with, obstruct
2 *A mass of leaves had blocked the drain.*
▸ (*slang*) bung up, clog, fill, stop up
▹ To block a hole is to **plug** it. To block the street with traffic is to **jam** it.
3 *The demonstrators blocked the street.*
▸ barricade, close, shut off

blockage *NOUN*
Dad spent ages clearing the blockage in the drain.
▸ block, obstacle, obstruction
▹ A blockage caused by traffic is **congestion** or a **traffic jam**. A place where a blockage is likely to happen is a **bottleneck**.

bloodshed *NOUN*
The battlefield was a scene of appalling bloodshed.
▸ butchery, killing, massacre, murder, slaughter, slaying

bloodthirsty *ADJECTIVE*
The bloodthirsty soldiers committed many atrocities.
▸ barbaric, brutal, cruel, ferocious, fierce, inhuman, murderous, pitiless, ruthless, sadistic, savage, vicious, violent, warlike

bloody *ADJECTIVE*
1 *Why is your handkerchief all bloody?*
▸ blood-soaked, blood-stained
2 *Many soldiers died in the bloody battle.*
▸ gory, gruesome, horrific

bloom *NOUN*
The branches were covered in white blooms.
▸ flower

bloom *VERB*
The daffodils bloomed early this year.
▸ blossom, flourish, flower, open
AN OPPOSITE IS fade

blossom *NOUN*
Blossom usually refers to a mass of flowers rather than a single flower
I love to see the cherry blossom in spring.
▸ blooms, buds, flowers

blot *NOUN*
The paper was covered with ink blots.
▸ blob, blotch, mark, smear, smudge, spot, stain

blot *VERB*
I accidentally blotted the page with ink.
▸ mark, smudge, spoil, spot, stain
to blot something out *Fog blotted out the view.*
▸ conceal, cover, hide, mask

blow *NOUN*
1 *The batsman gave the ball a hefty blow.*
▸ bang, (*informal*) bash, hit, knock, stroke, swipe, thump, (*informal*) wallop, whack
▹ A blow with your fist is a **punch**. A blow with the palm of your hand is a **slap** or **smack**. An accidental blow is a **bump**.
2 *The loss of her purse was a terrible blow.*
▸ calamity, disaster, misfortune, shock, surprise, upset

blow *VERB*
The heater blows out hot air.
▸ blast, puff
▹ To make a shrill sound by blowing is to whistle.
to blow up 1 *I need to blow up the tyres on my bike.*
▸ fill, inflate, pump up
2 *We heard the bomb blow up.*
▸ detonate, explode, go off
3 *The soldiers tried to blow up the enemy hideout.*
▸ blast, bomb, destroy
4 *Do you think they could blow up this photograph?*
▸ enlarge

blue *ADJECTIVE & NOUN*
VARIOUS SHADES OF BLUE ARE
azure, cobalt, indigo, navy blue, sapphire, sky-blue, turquoise

blueprint *NOUN*
The blueprint for the new car was kept very secret.
▸ design, pattern, plan, proposal
▹ The first example of an invention is a prototype.

bluff *VERB*
You'll never bluff them into letting you go.
▸ (*slang*) con, deceive, fool, trick

blunder *NOUN*
I made a terrible blunder.
▸ error, fault, (*informal*) howler, mistake, slip, slip-up

blunt *ADJECTIVE*
1 *This blunt knife is useless.*
AN OPPOSITE IS sharp
2 *I was upset by his blunt remarks about my work.*
▸ abrupt, direct, frank, honest, outspoken, plain, rude, straightforward, tactless
AN OPPOSITE IS tactful

blur *VERB*
1 *The steamy windows blurred the view.*
▸ cloud, darken, obscure, smear
2 *The accident blurred her memory.*
▸ confuse, muddle

blurred *ADJECTIVE*
1 *I couldn't make out the faces in the blurred photo.*
▸ foggy, fuzzy, hazy, out of focus, unclear, unfocused
2 *She had only a blurred memory of how the accident happened.*
▸ confused, dim, faint, indistinct, vague
AN OPPOSITE IS clear

blush *VERB*
He blushed when they accused him of lying.
▸ colour, flush, go red

blustery *ADJECTIVE*
I don't like this blustery weather.
▸ gusty, squally, windy
AN OPPOSITE IS calm

board *NOUN*
VARIOUS KINDS OF WOODEN BOARD ARE
blockboard, chipboard, panels, planks, plywood, timber, weatherboards

board *VERB*
1 *We boarded the plane for Paris.*
▸ enter, get on, go on board
▹ To board a ship is to **embark**.
2 *The victims of the fire were boarded in a hotel.*
▸ accommodate, house, lodge, put up

boast *VERB*
I hate the way he boasts about the pocket money he gets.
▸ bluster, brag, crow, gloat, show off, (*informal*) swank

boastful *ADJECTIVE*
There's no reason to be boastful because you have rich parents.
▸ arrogant, (*informal*) big-headed, (*informal*) cocky, conceited, vain
AN OPPOSITE IS modest

boat *NOUN*
FOR VARIOUS KINDS OF BOAT SEE **vessel**

bob *VERB*
Something bobbed up and down in the water.
▸ bounce, dance, move, toss

body *NOUN*
▷ The study of the human body is anatomy. The main part of your body except your head, arms, and legs is your trunk or torso. The shape of your body is your build or figure or physique. A person's dead body is a corpse. The dead body of an animal is a carcass.
VISIBLE PARTS OF THE HUMAN BODY ARE
abdomen, ankle, arm, armpit, breast, buttocks, calf, cheek, chest, chin, ear, elbow, eye, finger, foot, forehead, genitals, groin, hand, head, heel, hip, instep, jaw, knee, kneecap, knuckle, leg, lip, mouth, navel, neck, nipple, nose, pores, shin, shoulder, skin, stomach, temple, thigh, throat, waist, wrist
INNER PARTS OF THE BODY ARE
arteries, bladder, bowels, brain, eardrum, glands, gullet, gums, guts, heart, intestines, kidneys, larynx, liver, lung, muscles, nerves, ovaries, pancreas, prostate, sinews, stomach, tendons, tongue, tonsil, tooth, uterus, veins, windpipe, womb
PARTS OF YOUR SKELETON ARE
backbone or spine, collar bone, cranium or skull, pelvis, ribs, shoulder blade, vertebrae
SOME FLUIDS IN YOUR BODY ARE
bile, blood, hormones, saliva

bog *NOUN*
Take care not to sink into the bog!
▸ fen, mud, peat bog, quagmire, quicksands, swamp

bogus *ADJECTIVE*
Dad's sick of getting bogus phone calls.
▸ counterfeit, fake, false
AN OPPOSITE IS genuine

boil *VERB*
1 *I boiled the potatoes.*
FOR OTHER WAYS TO COOK THINGS SEE **cook** *VERB*
2 *Is the water boiling yet?*
▸ bubble, seethe, steam

boil *NOUN*
VARIOUS KINDS OF INFLAMED PLACE ON THE SKIN ARE
abscess, blister, carbuncle, chilblain, gumboil, inflammation, pimple, sore, spot, ulcer, (*slang*) zit

boisterous *ADJECTIVE*
We are always rather boisterous on the last day of term.
▸ disorderly, lively, noisy, rowdy, unruly, wild
AN OPPOSITE IS well-behaved

bold *ADJECTIVE*
1 *Be bold and take a risk!*
▸ adventurous, assertive, brave, confident, courageous, daring, enterprising, fearless, heroic, intrepid, valiant
AN OPPOSITE IS cowardly
2 *I put a bold heading at the top of the poster.*
▸ big, bright, clear, conspicuous, large, noticeable, obvious, prominent, striking
AN OPPOSITE IS inconspicuous

bolt *VERB*
1 *Did you remember to bolt the door?*
▸ bar, fasten, lock, secure
2 *The animals bolted when they heard the clap of thunder.*
▸ dash away, escape, flee, panic, run away, rush off, stampede
3 *Don't bolt your food.*
▸ eat hastily, gobble, gulp, guzzle

bomb *NOUN*
FOR OTHER WEAPONS SEE **weapon**

bombard *VERB*
The city was bombarded by enemy forces.
▸ assail, assault, attack, blast, bomb, fire at, pound, shell, shoot at

bombardment *NOUN*
The city was in ruins after the enemy bombardment.
▸ attack, barrage, blitz

bond *NOUN*
1 *The prisoner tried to escape from his bonds.*
▸ chains, fetters, handcuffs, ropes
2 *Their interest in music makes a bond between them.*
▸ attachment, connection, link, relationship, tie

bone *NOUN*
▷ The bones of your body are your skeleton.
SEE ALSO **body**

bonus *NOUN*
When we went on holiday, Mum gave me a bonus on top of my normal pocket money.
▸ extra, supplement

A
B
C
D
E
F
G
H
I
J
K
L
M
N
O
P
Q
R
S
T
U
V
W
X
Y
Z

book *NOUN*
How many books are there in the library?
▶ volume
▷ The particular volume which you own is your copy of the book. A book issued by a particular publisher at a particular time is an edition of the book. A book with hard covers is a hardback edition. A book with soft covers is a paperback edition. A book which is typed or handwritten but not printed is a manuscript.
THIN BOOKS IN PAPER COVERS
booklet, brochure, leaflet, pamphlet
VARIOUS KINDS OF PRINTED BOOK
album, annual, anthology, atlas, dictionary, directory, encyclopedia, guidebook, hymnal or hymn book, manual, missal, picture book, prayer book, reading book, reference book, story book, textbook, thesaurus
THINGS A BOOK MAY CONTAIN
appendix, bibliography, chapters, contents page, foreword, illustrations, index, introduction, preface, prologue, title page
BOOKS YOU CAN WRITE OR DRAW IN ARE
account book, diary, exercise book, jotter, notebook, scrapbook, sketchbook
FOR VARIOUS KINDS OF WRITING SEE **writing**

book *VERB*
1 *We booked tickets for the play.*
▶ order, reserve
2 *I've booked the disco for the party.*
▶ arrange, engage, organize

boom *VERB*
1 *The guns boomed.*
FOR VARIOUS WAYS TO MAKE SOUNDS SEE **sound** *VERB*
2 *Business is booming, I'm happy to say.*
▶ be successful, do well, expand, flourish, grow, prosper, thrive

boost *VERB*
The aim of advertising is to boost sales.
▶ aid, assist, bolster, build up, encourage, expand, help, improve, increase, promote
AN OPPOSITE IS deter

border *NOUN*
1 *The runaways were safe once they had crossed the border.*
▶ boundary, frontier
2 *We did a pretty design round the border of our poster.*
▶ edge, margin
▷ A border round the top of a wall is a frieze. A border round the bottom of a dress is a hem. A decorative border at the bottom of a curtain is a frill or fringe.
3 *Mum filled the border with geraniums.*
▶ flower bed

bore *VERB*
1 *We bored holes for the screws.*
▶ drill, pierce
2 *You can see little holes where woodworm have bored into the antique chair.*
▶ burrow, penetrate, tunnel

boring *ADJECTIVE*
1 *The film was so boring I fell asleep.*
▶ dry, dull, repetitive, tedious, tiresome, unexciting, uninteresting
2 *She's got a very boring voice.*
▶ dreary, flat, monotonous, uninspiring
AN OPPOSITE IS interesting

borrow *VERB*
1 *I borrowed her pen and forgot to give it back.*
▶ cadge, (*informal*) scrounge
AN OPPOSITE IS lend
2 *We asked if we were allowed to borrow someone else's ideas.*
▶ copy, crib, make use of, take, use

boss *NOUN*
FOR WORDS FOR PEOPLE IN CHARGE OF SOMETHING SEE **chief** *NOUN*

bossy *ADJECTIVE*
We resented her bossy manner.
▶ assertive, bullying, dictatorial, officious, tyrannical

bother *VERB*
1 *Does the noise bother you?*
▶ annoy, exasperate, irritate, upset, vex, worry
2 *Please don't bother me while I'm busy.*
▶ disturb, harass, nag, pester, plague, trouble
3 *Don't bother to wash up.*
▶ make an effort, take trouble

bother *NOUN*
1 *There was some bother in the youth club last night.*
▶ difficulty, disturbance, fuss, (*informal*) misbehaviour, problem, trouble
2 *Is the dog being a bother to you?*
▶ annoyance, inconvenience, irritation, nuisance, pest, worry

bottle *NOUN*
DIFFERENT KINDS OF BOTTLE
carafe, decanter, flagon, flask, jar, pitcher, wine bottle
FOR OTHER THINGS YOU CAN PUT LIQUIDS IN SEE **container**

bottle *VERB*
to bottle something up *She was disappointed, but she bottled up her feelings and carried on.*
▸ conceal, cover up, repress, suppress

bottom *NOUN*
1 *The mountaineers set up camp at the bottom of the mountain.*
▸ base, foot
AN OPPOSITE IS top
2 *The wreck sank to the bottom of the sea.*
▸ bed, depths, floor
AN OPPOSITE IS surface
3 *A wasp stung me on the bottom.*
▸ (*informal*) backside, behind, buttocks, rear, rump, seat

bottom *ADJECTIVE*
Who got bottom marks?
▸ least, lowest
AN OPPOSITE IS top

bough *NOUN*
The robin perched on a bough of the tree.
▸ branch, limb

bounce *VERB*
I missed the ball because it bounced at an awkward angle.
▸ rebound, ricochet

bound *ADJECTIVE*
1 *Our friends are bound to arrive by teatime.*
▸ certain, sure
2 *She felt bound to warn him of the risk.*
▸ committed, compelled, forced, obliged, pledged, required
3 *The accident was bound to happen.*
▸ destined, doomed, fated
to be bound for *The rocket was bound for the moon.*
▸ be aimed at, be directed towards, go towards, head for, make for, travel towards

bound *VERB*
1 *He bounded over the fence.*
▸ jump, leap, spring, vault
2 *Two puppies bounded across the lawn.*
▸ bounce, caper, frisk, frolic, skip

boundary *NOUN*
The fence marks the boundary of the school property.
▸ border, edge, end, frontier, limit, perimeter

bouquet *NOUN*
The bride carried a lovely bouquet of flowers.
▸ arrangement, bunch
▹ A small arrangement of flowers is a posy or spray. Flowers bound together to make a circle are a garland or wreath. A flower you wear on your lapel is a buttonhole.

bout *NOUN*
1 *I had an embarrassing bout of coughing during the concert.*
▸ attack, fit, period, (*informal*) turn
2 *The referee ended the bout after twenty minutes.*
▸ combat, contest, fight, match

bow *NOUN*
As we entered the harbour, we watched from the bow of the ship.
▸ front, prow

bow *VERB*
The men bowed respectfully in front of the queen.
▹ The corresponding movement of a woman is to curtsy.

bowl *NOUN*
Don't spill the soup when you put the bowl on the table!
▸ basin, dish

bowl *VERB*
He bowled a faster ball at the nervous batsman.
▸ fling, hurl, pitch, throw

box *NOUN*
I put my toys away in a box.
▸ carton, case, chest, crate, tea chest, trunk
▹ A small box to keep jewellery in is a casket. A box a dead person is buried in is a coffin.
FOR OTHER CONTAINERS SEE **container**

boy *NOUN*
▸ lad, schoolboy, youngster, youth

a b c d e f g h i j k l m n o p q r s t u v w x y z

A B C D E F G H I J K L M N O P Q R S T U V W X Y Z

boycott *VERB*
We boycotted the local farm shop when we heard how badly they treated their animals.
▶ avoid, stay away from

brag *VERB*
I don't think you should brag about winning.
▶ boast, crow, gloat, show off, (*informal*) swank

brain *NOUN*
Use your brain!
▶ intellect, intelligence, mind, reason, sense

brainy *ADJECTIVE*
(*informal*) *I'm good at games, but my brother is the brainy one.*
▶ bright, clever, intellectual, intelligent, wise
AN OPPOSITE IS stupid

branch *NOUN*
1 *A robin perched on a branch of the tree.*
▶ bough, limb
2 *He works in a branch of the armed services.*
▶ department, division, part, section

branch *VERB*
Follow the track until it branches into two.
▶ divide, fork
to branch out *I decided to branch out and take up water-skiing.*
▶ diversify, do something new

brand *NOUN*
Which brand of baked beans do you prefer?
▶ kind, make, sort, type, variety
▷ The sign of a particular brand of goods is a trademark.

brandish *VERB*
He brandished his gleaming sword.
▶ flourish, shake, wave

brass *NOUN*
FOR OTHER METALS SEE **metal**
MUSICAL INSTRUMENTS OFTEN MADE OF BRASS ARE
bugle, cornet, euphonium, flugelhorn, horn, trombone, trumpet, tuba

brave *ADJECTIVE*
1 *It was very brave of you to go on your own.*
▶ bold, courageous, daring, fearless, gallant, heroic, intrepid, plucky, valiant
2 *The defenders put up a brave resistance.*
▶ determined, resolute, stout
AN OPPOSITE IS cowardly

bravery *NOUN*
Everyone praised the firemen's bravery.
▶ boldness, courage, determination, fearlessness, gallantry, grit, (*informal*) guts, heroism, pluck, valour
AN OPPOSITE IS cowardice

brawl *NOUN*
After the match, there was a brawl between opposing supporters.
▶ fight, quarrel, (*informal*) scrap, scuffle, tussle

brazen *ADJECTIVE*
I don't know how he expected us to believe such a brazen lie.
▶ cheeky, impertinent, impudent, insolent, obvious, shameless, undisguised

breach *NOUN*
1 *He was disqualified because he was guilty of a breach of the rules.*
▶ breaking, violation
▷ You can also talk about an **offence** against the rules.
2 *Engineers worked all night to repair a breach in the sea wall.*
▶ crack, gap, hole, opening, split

bread *NOUN*
FORMS IN WHICH YOU BUY BREAD
bagel, baguette, bap, chappati, cob, French stick, loaf, nan, roll, sliced loaf, stick
KINDS OF BREAD ARE
brown bread, fruit loaf, granary bread, matzo, rye bread, unleavened bread, white bread, wholemeal bread

break *VERB*
1 *Don't lend him anything, because he's bound to break it.*
▶ burst, chip, crack, crumple, crush, damage, demolish, destroy, fracture, ruin, shatter, smash, snap, splinter, split, squash, wreck
2 *If you break the law, you can expect to be punished.*
▶ disobey, disregard, violate
3 *Our relay team broke the school record.*
▶ beat, better, do better than, exceed, go beyond, surpass
to break down *The car broke down on the motorway.*
▶ fail, go wrong, stop working
to break off *We'll break off for lunch at one o'clock.*

▸ finish, have a rest, pause, stop
to break out *A flu epidemic broke out just after Christmas.*
▸ begin, spread, start
to break out of *The prisoner tried to break out of gaol.*
▸ escape from, get away from
to break up *After six months, the group broke up.*
▸ disintegrate, fall apart, separate, split up

break *NOUN*
1 *They repaired a break in the pipe.*
▸ breach, crack, hole, leak, opening, puncture, rift, split, tear
2 *We'll have a break now if you are tired.*
▸ (*informal*) breather, interval, lull, pause, rest

breakable *ADJECTIVE*
Be careful with that box—there are breakable things in it.
▸ brittle, delicate, fragile, frail

breakdown *NOUN*
1 *We had a breakdown on the motorway.*
▸ engine failure, stoppage
2 *I saw a breakdown of the season's football results in the newspaper.*
▸ analysis

breakthrough *NOUN*
Doctors believe there has been a breakthrough in cancer research.
▸ development, discovery, leap forward, progress, revolution

breath *NOUN*
There wasn't a breath of wind.
▸ breeze, pant, puff, sigh, waft, whisper

breathe *VERB*
▹ To breathe in is to **inhale**. To breathe out is to **exhale**. To breathe heavily when you have been running, etc., is to **pant** or **puff**. The formal word for breathing is **respiration**.

breathless *ADJECTIVE*
I was breathless after running home from school.
▸ exhausted, gasping, out of breath, panting, puffing, tired out, wheezing

breed *VERB*
1 *Frogs usually breed in any convenient pond.*
▸ have young ones, increase, multiply, produce young, reproduce
2 *Bad hygiene breeds disease.*
▸ cause, cultivate, encourage, generate, promote

breed *NOUN*
What breed of dog is that?
▸ kind, sort, type, variety
▹ The evidence of how a dog has been bred is its **pedigree**.

breezy *ADJECTIVE*
It was a bright, breezy day.
▸ fresh, windy
FOR VARIOUS KINDS OF WIND SEE **wind** *NOUN*

brevity *NOUN*
Owing to the brevity of the speeches, we finished early.
▸ briefness, conciseness, shortness

brew *VERB*
1 *I'm just going to brew some tea.*
▸ make
▹ When you brew beer it **ferments**.
2 *I think a storm is brewing.*
▸ develop, form, loom, on the way, threatening

bribe *VERB*
They tried to bribe the referee with a large sum of money.
▸ influence, pervert, tempt

brick *NOUN*
VARIOUS KINDS OF BRICK OR BLOCK USED IN BUILDING
block, breeze-block, building block, flagstone, paving block, paving stone, set or sett, stone

bridge *NOUN*
VARIOUS KINDS OF BRIDGE
aqueduct, cantilever bridge, drawbridge, flyover, footbridge, overpass, pontoon bridge, suspension bridge, swing bridge, viaduct
▹ A structure like a bridge is an **arch** or **archway**.

brief *ADJECTIVE*
1 *We paid a brief visit to Granny.*
▸ hasty, fleeting, quick, short, temporary
2 *Give me a brief account of what happened.*
▸ abbreviated, concise, condensed, shortened
AN OPPOSITE IS long

A B C D E F G H I J K L M N O P Q R S T U V W X Y Z

brief *NOUN*
Our teacher gave us the brief for our project.
▸ directions, guidelines, information, instructions, outline, plan

brief *VERB*
Please sit down while I brief you on our plan for the match.
▸ advise, give instructions, inform, instruct, prepare, put you in the picture

bright *ADJECTIVE*
1 *I blinked in the bright sunshine.*
▸ blazing, brilliant, dazzling, glaring, intense
2 *The brass rail was bright and shiny.*
▸ gleaming, glittering, lustrous, polished
3 *We used bright colours to make an attractive poster.*
▸ glowing, showy, strong, vivid
▹ Colours that shine in the dark are luminous colours.
4 *He's a bright lad!*
▸ alert, clever, intelligent, sharp, wise
5 *She gave me a bright smile.*
▸ cheerful, good-humoured, happy, radiant, sunny
AN OPPOSITE IS dull or gloomy

brighten *VERB*
1 *Getting a letter from you brightened my day.*
▸ cheer, gladden, light up
2 *It was a cloudy morning, but it brightened after lunch.*
▸ become sunny, clear up, lighten

brilliant *ADJECTIVE*
1 *The fireworks gave off a brilliant light.*
▸ blazing, bright, dazzling, glaring, gleaming, glittering, glorious, shining, splendid, vivid
AN OPPOSITE IS dim
2 *Brunel was a brilliant engineer.*
▸ clever, exceptional, intelligent, talented
AN OPPOSITE IS incompetent or stupid
3 (*informal*) *I saw a brilliant film last week.*
▸ enjoyable, excellent, (*informal*) fabulous, (*informal*) fantastic, marvellous, outstanding, wonderful

brim *NOUN*
I filled my glass to the brim.
▸ brink, edge, rim, top

bring *VERB*
1 *Did you bring the shopping home?*
▸ carry, deliver, fetch, transport
2 *Bring your friends in.*
▸ conduct, escort, guide, invite, lead
3 *Their performance brought great applause.*
▸ attract, draw, earn, generate, lead to, result in
to bring something about *The new head brought about many changes.*
▸ arrange, be responsible for, cause, create, introduce, organize
to bring something off *Our team brought off a convincing win.*
▸ accomplish, achieve, succeed in
to bring someone up *She was brought up by her grandparents.*
▸ care for, educate, foster, look after, raise, rear, teach, train

brink *NOUN*
I stood on the brink of a deep crater.
▸ edge, lip, rim

brisk *ADJECTIVE*
1 *The doctor says I should take a brisk walk every day.*
▸ energetic, fast, invigorating, quick, rapid, vigorous
2 *He has a very brisk manner.*
▸ animated, bright, businesslike, lively, snappy, sprightly
AN OPPOSITE IS slow

brittle *ADJECTIVE*
These wafer biscuits are very brittle.
▸ breakable, crisp, delicate, easily broken, fragile, frail
AN OPPOSITE IS flexible

broad *ADJECTIVE*
1 *There was a broad square in front of the palace.*
▸ extensive, great, large, open, roomy, spacious, vast, wide
AN OPPOSITE IS narrow
2 *He just gave me a broad outline of what happened.*
▸ general, imprecise, indefinite, vague
AN OPPOSITE IS specific

broadcast *NOUN*
There is going to be a TV broadcast from our local church.
▸ programme, relay, transmission

broadcast *VERB*
They will broadcast the concert on TV.
▸ relay, send out, televise, transmit

broadcaster *NOUN*
SOME PEOPLE WHO BROADCAST ON RADIO OR TV
actor, announcer, comedian, commentator, compère, disc jockey or DJ, musician, newsreader, presenter, singer
FOR OTHER WORDS SEE **entertainer**

broaden *VERB*
Try to broaden your interests instead of watching TV all day.
▸ develop, diversify, enlarge, expand, extend, increase, widen

broad-minded *ADJECTIVE*
She likes both pop and classical music, and has a broad-minded outlook on most things.
▸ liberal, tolerant, unbiased, unprejudiced
AN OPPOSITE IS narrow-minded

brochure *NOUN*
We got some holiday brochures from the travel agent's.
▸ booklet, catalogue, leaflet, pamphlet

brood *VERB*
1 *The hen was brooding her clutch of eggs.*
▸ incubate, sit on
2 *Don't brood about mistakes you made in the past.*
▸ fret, mope, worry

brown *ADJECTIVE NOUN*
VARIOUS SHADES OF BROWN ARE
beige, bronze, buff, chestnut, chocolate, dun, fawn, khaki, russet, sepia, tan, tawny

browse *VERB*
1 *I wasn't reading carefully—I was just browsing.*
▸ dip in, look through, scan, skim
2 *The cattle were browsing in the meadow.*
▸ feed, graze

bruise *VERB*
I fell and bruised my leg.
▸ hurt, injure, mark
FOR OTHERS KINDS OF WOUND SEE **wound** *VERB*

brush *NOUN*
VARIOUS KINDS OF BRUSH
broom, hairbrush, paintbrush, scrubbing brush, toothbrush

brush *VERB*
He spent ages brushing his hair.
▸ groom, tidy
to brush up *Are you going to brush up your French before we go abroad?*
▸ improve, refresh your memory of, revise, (*informal*) swot up

brutal *ADJECTIVE*
The brutal murder was reported in all the newspapers.
▸ atrocious, barbarous, beastly, bestial, bloodthirsty, callous, cold-blooded, cruel, ferocious, heartless, inhuman, merciless, pitiless, ruthless, sadistic, savage, vicious, violent, wild
AN OPPOSITE IS gentle or humane

brute *NOUN*
1 *He was a cold-blooded brute.*
▸ barbarian, monster, sadist, savage
2 *During the storm, we were sorry for the poor brutes out in the fields.*
▸ animal, beast, creature
FOR OTHER WORDS SEE **animal**

bubble *NOUN*
▹ A word for bubbles in fizzy lemonade is effervescence. The bubbles made by soap or detergent are lather or suds. Bubbles on top of a liquid are foam or froth. The bubbles on top of beer are the head.

bubble *VERB*
A pot of coffee bubbled on the stove.
▸ fizz, foam, froth, seethe

bubbly *ADJECTIVE*
1 *I don't like bubbly drinks because they get up my nose.*
▸ effervescent, fizzy, sparkling
2 *She had a bright and bubbly personality.*
▸ animated, cheerful, lively

buck *VERB*
to buck up (*informal*) *Buck up—we're late!*
▸ be quick, hurry, make haste

bucket *NOUN*
He filled a bucket with water to wash the car.
▸ can, pail

buckle *NOUN*
She wore a belt with a large silver buckle.
▸ clasp, fastener, fastening

A B C D E F G H I J K L M N O P Q R S T U V W X Y Z

buckle *VERB*

1 *Buckle your safety belts.*
▸ clasp, clip, do up, fasten, hook up, secure
2 *The framework buckled under our weight.*
▸ bend, cave in, collapse, crumple, fold up, twist, warp

budding *ADJECTIVE*

My sister is a budding actor.
▸ potential, promising
AN OPPOSITE IS experienced

budge *VERB*

1 *The stubborn donkey wouldn't budge.*
▸ change position, give way, move, shift
2 *We kept pushing, but we couldn't budge him.*
▸ dislodge, move, shift

budget *VERB*

to budget for *Have you budgeted for a holiday this year?*
▸ allow for, plan your spending for, provide for

buffet *NOUN*

1 *We went to the buffet for a snack.*
▸ bar, café, cafeteria, snack bar
2 *Mum prepared a buffet for our party.*
FOR VARIOUS KINDS OF MEAL SEE **meal**

bug *NOUN*

1 *Birds help to control bugs in the garden.*
▸ insect, pest
2 (*informal*) *I had a stomach bug.*
▸ germ, infection, virus
3 *A bug in the computer program meant that we couldn't run it.*
▸ error, fault, mistake, virus

bug *VERB*

Spies bugged their telephone conversations.
▸ intercept, listen in to, tap

build *VERB*

Dad is going to build a shed in the garden.
▸ assemble, construct, erect, make, put together, put up, raise, set up
to build up **1** *I'm beginning to build up a collection of CDs.*
▸ accumulate, assemble, collect, put together
2 *Gloomily, we watched the opposition's excitement build up.*
▸ escalate, grow, increase, intensify, rise

builder *NOUN*

VARIOUS PEOPLE WHO WORK ON BUILDINGS
bricklayer, construction worker, contractor, joiner, labourer, mason, plasterer, plumber, surveyor
▹ A person who designs buildings is an **architect**. A person who works on very high buildings is a **steeplejack**.

building *NOUN*

▸ construction, structure
VARIOUS BUILDINGS
arcade, barn, barracks, bungalow, castle, cathedral, chapel, church, cinema, college, cottage, factory, farmhouse, filling station, flats, fortress, garage, grandstand, gurdwara, gymnasium, hall, hangar, hotel, house, inn, library, lighthouse, mansion, mill, monastery, mosque, museum, pagoda, palace, pavilion, police station, post office, power station, prison, pub or public house, restaurant, school, shed, shop, skyscraper, stable, synagogue, temple, theatre, tower, warehouse, windmill
VARIOUS PARTS OF A BUILDING
balcony, basement, cellar, corridor, courtyard, crypt, dungeon, foyer, gallery, lobby, porch, quadrangle, room, staircase, veranda
SEE ALSO **room**
VARIOUS ARCHITECTURAL FEATURES OF BUILDINGS
arch, balustrade, banister, bay window, bow window, brickwork, buttress, capital, ceiling, chimney, colonnade, column, dome, door, dormer window, eaves, floor, foundations, gable, gutter, joist, masonry, parapet, pediment, pillar, pinnacle, portal, rafter, roof, tower, turret, vault, wall, window, windowsill
SEE ALSO **castle**, **church**
SOME BUILDING MATERIALS
asphalt, bricks, cement, concrete, fibreglass, glass, hardboard, metal, mortar, paint, perspex, pipes, plaster, plasterboard, plastic, plywood, putty, rubber, slates, stone, tar, tiles, timber, wood

bulb *NOUN*

We planted some daffodil bulbs last autumn.
SOME FLOWERS THAT GROW FROM BULBS
amaryllis, bluebell, crocus, daffodil, freesia, hyacinth, lily, snowdrop, tulip
▹ Things rather like bulbs are **corms** and **tubers**.

bulge *NOUN*
What's that bulge in your shopping bag?
▸ bump, hump, knob, lump, swelling

bulge *VERB*
His pockets bulged with all sorts of odds and ends.
▸ stick out, swell

bulk *NOUN*
1 *The great bulk of the jumbo jet amazed us.*
▸ dimensions, magnitude, size
2 *We spent the bulk of our time practising for the big match.*
▸ best part, greater part, majority

bulletin *NOUN*
We waited for an official bulletin about the President's health.
▸ announcement, communication, message, newsflash, report, statement

bully *VERB*
The head said that if he continued to bully younger children he would be severely punished.
▸ frighten, intimidate, persecute, terrorize, threaten, torment

bump *VERB*
1 *He bumped us deliberately.*
▸ bang into, collide with, crash into, knock, ram, slam into, smash into, strike, thump, wallop
2 *We bumped up and down on the rough road.*
▸ bounce, jerk, jolt, shake
to bump into someone *I didn't expect to bump into you today!*
▸ come across, meet
to bump someone off (*slang*) *He tried to bump off the rest of the gang when they double-crossed him.*
▸ (*informal*) do away with, (*informal*) finish off, kill, murder

bump *NOUN*
1 *We heard a slight bump as the ship hit the quay.*
▸ bang, blow, knock, thud, thump
2 *Dad had a bump in the car.*
▸ collision, crash, smash
3 *How did you get that bump on your head?*
▸ bulge, hump, lump, swelling

bumpy *ADJECTIVE*
1 *My bottom was sore after the bumpy ride.*
▸ bouncy, jerky, jolting, rough
2 *The car jolted up and down on the bumpy road.*
▸ irregular, knobbly, lumpy, uneven

bunch *NOUN*
1 *A bunch of keys was dangling from the hook.*
▸ cluster, collection, set
FOR OTHER WORDS FOR THINGS YOU KEEP TOGETHER SEE **collection**
2 *a bunch of flowers.*
▸ bouquet, spray
3 (*informal*) *I got a bunch of friends to help me tidy the garden.*
▸ band, crowd, gang, group, mob, party, team

bunch *VERB*
Our opponents' supporters bunched together on the other side of the field.
▸ assemble, cluster, collect, crowd, gather, group, herd, huddle
AN OPPOSITE IS scatter

bundle *NOUN*
I carried a bundle of jumble down to the church hall.
▸ bale, collection, pack, package, parcel
SEE ALSO **collection**

bundle *VERB*
1 *I bundled together some old clothes for the jumble sale.*
▸ bind, fasten, pack, tie
2 *They bundled him into the car.*
▸ move hurriedly, push, remove

bungle *VERB*
If you bungle a job, you must do it again!
▸ make a mess of, mess up, ruin, spoil

buoyant *ADJECTIVE*
1 *Lifebelts are made of buoyant material.*
▸ floating, light
2 *We were in a buoyant mood after winning our match.*
▸ cheerful, happy, lively, optimistic

burden *NOUN*
1 *They moved slowly, as if carrying a heavy burden.*
▸ cargo, load, weight
2 *The captain has the burden of organizing the players.*
▸ anxiety, duty, obligation, responsibility, trouble, worry

burglar *NOUN*
The burglars made a terrible mess of the house.
▸ intruder, robber, thief

burglary *NOUN*
FOR OTHER WORDS SEE **stealing**

burly *ADJECTIVE*
The weightlifter had a burly figure.
▸ (*informal*) beefy, brawny, hefty, husky, muscular, powerful, stocky, stout, strong, sturdy, tough, well-built
AN OPPOSITE IS thin

burn *VERB*
1 *The bonfire burned all day.*
▸ be ablaze, be alight, be on fire, blaze, flame, flare, flicker
▹ To burn without flames is to **glow** or **smoulder**.
2 *The furnace will burn anything you put in it.*
▸ consume, incinerate, reduce to ashes
▹ To start something burning is to **ignite**, **kindle**, or **light** it. To burn something slightly is to **char**, **scorch**, or **singe** it. To hurt someone with boiling liquid or steam is to **scald** them. To burn a dead body is to **cremate** it. To burn a mark on an animal is to **brand** it.

burning *ADJECTIVE*
I had a burning desire to tell them my secret.
▸ acute, eager, fervent, intense, passionate, strong

burrow *NOUN*
The bank was full of rabbit burrows.
▸ hole, tunnel
▹ A piece of ground with many burrows is a **warren**. A fox's hole is an **earth**. A badger's hole is an **earth** or **set**.

burrow *VERB*
The rabbits burrow under our fence.
▸ dig, excavate, tunnel

burst *VERB*
We had so much shopping that I expected the bag to burst.
▸ break, give way, split, tear
to burst out laughing *I burst out laughing when I saw her surprise.*
▸ laugh loudly, roar with laughter, start laughing

bury *VERB*
The dog buried his bone in the garden.
▸ conceal, cover, hide, secrete

bus *NOUN*
VARIOUS KINDS OF BUS
coach, double-decker, minibus
▹ Old-fashioned words for bus are **charabanc** and **omnibus**. A bus which gets its power from overhead electric wires is a **trolleybus**. A **tram** is like a bus that runs on rails set in the road.

bush *NOUN*
Dad planted some bushes to hide the compost heap.
▸ shrub

bushy *ADJECTIVE*
He had big bushy eyebrows.
▸ hairy, shaggy, thick, untidy

business *NOUN*
1 *She runs a catering business.*
▸ company, firm, organization
2 *The new shop does a lot of business.*
▸ buying and selling, commerce, deals, trade, trading
3 *What sort of business do you want to go into?*
▸ career, employment, industry, job, occupation, profession, trade, work
4 *I have urgent business to see to.*
▸ affairs, duties, matters, problems, responsibilities, tasks, work

businesslike *ADJECTIVE*
If you are businesslike, the job won't take long.
▸ efficient, methodical, orderly, practical, systematic, well-organized

bustle *VERB*
He bustled about the kitchen preparing dinner.
▸ dash, hurry, move busily, rush, scurry, scuttle

busy *ADJECTIVE*
1 *Everyone was busy getting ready for the parents' evening.*
▸ active, bustling about, employed, (*informal*) hard at it, industrious, involved, occupied, slaving, working hard
AN OPPOSITE IS idle
2 *It's busy in town on Saturdays.*
▸ bustling, frantic, hectic, lively
AN OPPOSITE IS peaceful

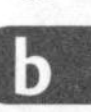

butt *VERB*
The goat butted him in the stomach.
▸ hit, knock, push, ram, shove
to butt in *Please don't butt in when I'm talking.*
▸ interrupt

buttocks *PLURAL NOUN*
▸ (*informal*) backside, behind, bottom, (*slang*) bum, rear, rump, seat

buy *VERB*
Dad is saving up until he can buy a new TV set.
▸ acquire, get, pay for, purchase
AN OPPOSITE IS sell

bystander *NOUN*
The police asked bystanders to describe the accident.
▸ eyewitness, observer, onlooker, passer-by, spectator, witness

Cc

cabin *NOUN*
1 *The climbers took refuge in a cabin in the hills.*
▸ hut, shack, shanty, shed, shelter
2 *We slept in a cabin on the cross-Channel ferry.*
▹ A sleeping place on a ship is also called a berth.

cable *NOUN*
1 *The ship was moored to the quay by strong cables.*
▸ chain, cord, line, rope
2 *Don't trip over the electric cable.*
▸ flex, lead, wire
3 *They sent a message by cable.*
▸ telegram

cadet *NOUN*
My cousin is a cadet in the police force.
▸ beginner, learner, recruit, trainee

cadge *VERB*
The cat from next door comes round to cadge food.
▸ ask for, beg for, (*informal*) scrounge

cafe *NOUN*
VARIOUS PLACES WHERE YOU CAN HAVE FOOD AND DRINK
bar, bistro, buffet, cafeteria, canteen, coffee bar, restaurant, snack bar, takeaway, tearoom

cage *NOUN*
▹ A large cage or enclosure for birds is an **aviary**. A cage or enclosure for poultry is a **coop**. A cage or enclosure for animals is a **pen**. A cage or box for a pet rabbit is a **hutch**.

cake *NOUN*
SOME KINDS OF CAKE
angel cake, birthday cake, bun, Christmas cake, doughnut, éclair, flan, fruit cake, gateau, gingerbread, macaroon, Madeira cake, meringue, muffin, parkin, sandwich cake, scone, shortbread, simnel cake, sponge, Swiss roll, teacake, wedding cake

caked *ADJECTIVE*
Our shoes were caked with mud.
▸ clogged, coated, covered, dirty

calamity *NOUN*
The earthquake was the worst calamity in the country's history.
▸ accident, catastrophe, disaster, misfortune, mishap, tragedy

calculate *VERB*
I calculated how long it would take us to drive from London to Oxford.
▸ add up, compute, count, determine, figure out, reckon, total, work out
▹ To calculate something roughly is to estimate.

call *NOUN*
1 *I thought I heard a call for help.*
▸ cry, exclamation, scream, shout, yell
2 *Grandad made an unexpected call.*
▸ stay, stop, visit
3 *There's not much call for suntan oil in winter.*
▸ demand, need

call *VERB*
1 *He called in a loud voice.*
▸ cry out, exclaim, shout, yell
2 *I wanted to call you, but the line was out of order.*
▸ phone, ring, telephone
3 *The head called me to his office.*

A B C D E F G H I J K L M N O P Q R S T U V W X Y Z

▶ invite, summon
4 *In case I overslept, I asked Mum to call me at eight.*
▶ arouse, awaken, rouse, wake, waken
5 *Grandad called on his way home from the shops.*
▶ drop in, pay a visit
6 *What did they call the baby?*
▶ baptize, christen, name
to call something off *The weather was so bad that we called the game off.*
▶ abandon, cancel, postpone
to call someone names *She thinks it's funny to call people names.*
▶ insult, make fun of, mock

calling NOUN
He is a gifted surgeon, totally dedicated to his calling.
▶ business, career, employment, job, occupation, profession, trade, work

callous ADJECTIVE
The mugging of the elderly couple was a callous crime.
▶ cold, cold-blooded, cruel, hard-hearted, heartless, inhuman, merciless, pitiless, ruthless, uncaring, unfeeling, unsympathetic
AN OPPOSITE IS kind

calm ADJECTIVE
1 *It's a lot easier to put up a tent in calm weather.*
▶ peaceful, quiet, serene, still, tranquil, windless
AN OPPOSITE IS stormy or windy
2 *The sea was calm, and we had a pleasant voyage.*
▶ flat, motionless, placid, smooth
AN OPPOSITE IS stormy
3 *He remained calm while everyone else panicked.*
▶ cool, level-headed, patient, relaxed, sedate, unemotional, unexcitable, untroubled
AN OPPOSITE IS anxious or excitable

camera NOUN
SOME TYPES OF CAMERA
(*old use*) box camera, camcorder, cine-camera, digital camera, Polaroid camera, SLR or single lens reflex camera, video camera

camouflage NOUN
We used leafy branches as camouflage for our hideout.
▶ cover, disguise, mask, screen

camp NOUN
From the hill we saw a camp in the field below us.
▶ camping ground, campsite
▷ A military camp is an encampment.

campaign NOUN
1 *Will you join our campaign to save the whale?*
▶ action, crusade, movement, struggle
2 *The army launched a campaign to recapture the city.*
▶ operation, war

cancel VERB
We had to cancel the game because of the weather.
▶ abandon, give up, scrap, (*slang*) scrub
▷ To cancel something after it has already begun is to abort it. To put something off until later is to postpone it. To cancel items on a list is to cross out or delete or erase them.
to cancel something out *The points we won today cancel out the points they won last week.*
▶ compensate for, make up for, neutralize, wipe out

candidate NOUN
▷ A candidate for a job is an applicant. A candidate in an examination is an entrant. A person competing with others in a contest is a competitor, contender, or contestant.

canopy NOUN
We sheltered from the rain under a canopy.
▶ awning, cover, shade

cap NOUN
1 *When he plays cricket, he wears his team cap.*
FOR DIFFERENT KINDS OF HAT SEE **hat**
2 *Who left the cap off the ketchup bottle?*
▶ cover, lid, top

cap VERB
The highest mountains are always capped by snow.
▶ cover, top

capable ADJECTIVE
She's a capable tennis player.
▶ able, accomplished, clever, competent,

efficient, expert, gifted, proficient, skilful, skilled, talented
AN OPPOSITE IS incompetent
to be capable of *She's capable of doing something silly.*
▷ You could also say that she is liable or likely or prone to do it.
AN OPPOSITE IS incapable of

capacity *NOUN*
1 *He has a great capacity for hard work.*
▶ ability, capability, competence, potential, power, talent
2 *What's the capacity of this oil tank?*
▶ size, volume
3 *In his capacity as captain, he has a right to tell us what to do.*
▶ function, job, position, post

cape *NOUN*
1 *We could see the island from the cape.*
▶ headland, peninsula, promontory
2 *The soldier wrapped his cape around him and tried to keep dry.*
▶ cloak, (*old use*) mantle

caper *VERB*
I watched the lambs caper about in the sunshine.
▶ bound, dance, frisk, frolic, hop, jump, leap, play, prance, romp, skip, spring

capital *NOUN*
1 *Paris is the capital of France.*
▶ chief city, centre of government
2 *Dad has enough capital to start a new business.*
▶ assets, cash, finance, funds, money, property, resources, riches, savings, wealth
capital letter *Start a new sentence with a capital letter.*
▶ block capital, block letter, initial letter

capsize *VERB*
The boat capsized in the storm.
▶ keel over, overturn, tip over, turn over, turn turtle, turn upside down

capsule *NOUN*
1 *The doctor gave her some capsules.*
▶ lozenge, pill, tablet
2 *The world's most powerful rocket launched the space capsule.*
FOR WORDS TO DO WITH TRAVEL IN SPACE SEE **space**

captain *NOUN*
The captain brought his ship safely into harbour.
▶ commander, master, skipper
FOR PEOPLE IN CHARGE OF VARIOUS THINGS SEE **chief** *NOUN*

captivating *ADJECTIVE*
She was a lively and captivating girl.
▶ appealing, attractive, charming, (*informal*) cute, delightful, enchanting, fascinating, lovable
AN OPPOSITE IS repulsive

captive *NOUN*
The captives were chained to their beds.
▶ convict, prisoner
▷ A person who is held captive until some demand is met is a hostage.

captive *ADJECTIVE*
The captive rebels were put in prison.
▶ arrested, captured, detained
PEOPLE AND ANIMALS CAN BE HELD CAPTIVE IN DIFFERENT WAYS
caged, chained, enslaved, gaoled or jailed, imprisoned, in custody, in detention, in fetters, (*old use*) in the stocks, interned, on remand, trapped
AN OPPOSITE IS free

captivity *NOUN*
No one enjoys captivity.
▶ confinement, detention, gaol, imprisonment, prison, slavery
AN OPPOSITE IS freedom

capture *VERB*
1 *After a chase, the police captured the suspect.*
▶ arrest, catch, corner, (*informal*) nab, overpower, secure, seize, take prisoner, trap
2 *In spite of the long siege, the enemy were not able to capture the castle.*
▶ conquer, occupy, take, take over, win

car *NOUN*
There are too many cars on the city streets.
▶ (*American*) automobile, motor, motor car
KINDS OF CAR
convertible, coupé, (*trademark*) Dormobile, estate, fastback, four-wheel drive, hatchback, (*trademark*) Jeep, (*trademark*) Land Rover, limousine, (*trademark*) Mini, patrol car or police car, saloon, (*old use*) shooting brake, sports car, tourer

car *NOUN*
▷ Very early cars are **veteran** or **vintage** cars.
SOME PRINCIPAL PARTS OF A CAR
battery, body, bonnet, boot, brakes, chassis, clutch, engine, exhaust pipe, fuel tank, gearbox, lights, radiator, silencer, starter, steering, suspension, transmission, wheels, windscreen
PRINCIPAL CONTROLS IN A CAR
accelerator, brake, choke, clutch, gear lever, handbrake, ignition key, indicators, steering wheel, windscreen wipers
FOR OTHER VEHICLES SEE **vehicle**

carcass *NOUN*
The carcass of the animal was hidden by the bushes.
► body, corpse, remains

card *NOUN*
CARDS WE SEND ON VARIOUS SPECIAL OCCASIONS
birthday card, Christmas card, Easter card, get well card, greetings card, invitation, notelet, picture postcard, sympathy card, Valentine
CARDS WE PLAY GAMES WITH
playing cards
▷ A complete set of playing cards is a **pack**. All the cards with the same sign on them are a **suit**.
THE SUITS IN A PACK OF CARDS
clubs, diamonds, hearts, spades
CARDS OF DIFFERENT VALUE
king, queen, jack or knave, numbers from 10 down to 2, ace, joker
▷ The king, queen, and jack are the **court cards**.
SOME CARD GAMES
beggar-my-neighbour, brag, bridge, canasta, cribbage, old maid, patience, poker, pontoon, rummy, snap, solo, whist

care *NOUN*
1 *He doesn't have a care in the world!*
► anxiety, burden, difficulty, problem, responsibility, sorrow, stress, trouble, worry
2 *He did the job with great care.*
► attention, caution, concentration, thoroughness, thought, vigilance, watchfulness
AN OPPOSITE IS carelessness
3 *She left the baby in my care.*
► charge, control, keeping, protection, safe keeping

to take care *Please take care not to spill paint on the carpet.*
► be careful, be on your guard, look out, watch out
to take care of someone or something
She had to take care of her sick mother last week.
► attend to, care for, look after, mind, nurse, tend, watch over

care *VERB*
She doesn't seem to care what happens.
► be interested, be troubled, bother, mind, worry
to care for someone or something 1 *She had to care for her sick mother last week.*
► attend to, look after, mind, nurse, take care of, tend, watch over
2 *Do you care for me?*
► be fond of, love

career *NOUN*
What sort of career do you want when you grow up?
► business, calling, employment, job, occupation, profession, trade, work
FOR VARIOUS CAREERS SEE **job**

career *VERB*
She careered down the hill into the village.
► dash, hurtle, race, rush, shoot, speed, zoom

carefree *ADJECTIVE*
The carefree days of the summer holidays were over.
► casual, cheerful, easygoing, happy, happy-go-lucky, light-hearted, peaceful, relaxed, restful, untroubled
AN OPPOSITE IS anxious or tense

careful *ADJECTIVE*
1 *She congratulated us on our careful work.*
► accurate, conscientious, methodical, meticulous, neat, orderly, organized, painstaking, precise, systematic, thorough, thoughtful
2 *Dad kept a careful watch on the bonfire.*
► alert, attentive, cautious, responsible, vigilant, wary, watchful
AN OPPOSITE IS careless
to be careful *Please be careful when you cross the road.*
► be on your guard, look out, take care, watch out

careless *ADJECTIVE*
1 *This is a very careless piece of work.*
► inaccurate, messy, shoddy, slipshod, sloppy,

slovenly, thoughtless, untidy
2 *I was careless and cut my finger.*
▸ absent-minded, inattentive, incautious, irresponsible, negligent, rash, reckless, thoughtless
AN OPPOSITE IS careful

caress *NOUN*
He gave her a loving caress.
▸ embrace, hug, kiss, pat, stroke, touch

caress *VERB*
He caressed her hair gently.
▸ smooth, stroke, touch

cargo *NOUN*
Some planes carry cargo instead of passengers.
▸ freight, goods, merchandise

carnival *NOUN*
The whole village comes out for the annual carnival.
▸ celebration, fair, festival, fête, gala, pageant, parade, procession, show

carpentry *NOUN*
You need saws and other tools for carpentry.
▸ joinery, woodwork

carriage *NOUN*
FOR VARIOUS MEANS OF TRANSPORT SEE **vehicle**

carry *VERB*
1 *I helped Mum to carry the shopping to the car.*
▸ bring, fetch, lift, lug, take, transfer
2 *Aircraft carry passengers and goods.*
▸ convey, transport
3 *The rear axle carries the greatest weight.*
▸ bear, hold up, support
to carry on *We carried on in spite of the rain.*
▸ continue, go on, keep on, persevere, persist, remain, stay, survive
to carry something out *We carried out her orders.*
▸ accomplish, achieve, complete, do, execute, finish, perform

cart *NOUN*
FOR VARIOUS MEANS OF TRANSPORT SEE **vehicle**

carton *NOUN*
He opened a new carton of cereal.
▸ box, pack, package, packet

cartoon *NOUN*
1 *There's always a political cartoon on the front page of our newspaper.*
▸ caricature, drawing, sketch
2 *My baby brother likes cartoons on TV.*
▸ animated film

carve *VERB*
1 *The statue was carved out of stone.*
▸ chisel
2 *Mum carved the chicken for Sunday dinner.*
▸ cut, slice

cascade *NOUN*
The stream poured over the rock in a cascade.
▸ torrent, waterfall

case *NOUN*
1 *What's in those cases in the attic?*
▸ box, cabinet, carton, casket, chest, crate
FOR OTHER CONTAINERS SEE **container**
2 *I loaded my case into the boot of the car.*
▸ suitcase, trunk
▹ A collection of cases that you take when you travel is your **baggage** or **luggage**.
3 *It was an obvious case of favouritism.*
▸ example, illustration, instance, occurrence
4 *The judge said he'd never known a case like this one.*
▸ inquiry, investigation, lawsuit
5 *She presented a good case for abolishing hunting.*
▸ argument, line of reasoning

cash *NOUN*
VARIOUS WORDS FOR MONEY IN THE FORM OF CASH
bank notes, change, coins, coppers, currency, loose change, notes, ready money, silver

cast *VERB*
1 *He cast a penny into the wishing-well.*
▸ drop, fling, lob, sling, throw, toss
2 *The statue was cast in bronze.*
▸ form, mould, shape

castle *NOUN*
VARIOUS KINDS OF FORTIFIED BUILDING
château, citadel, fort, fortress, motte and bailey, palace, stronghold, tower
PARTS OF A CASTLE
bailey, barbican, battlement, buttress, courtyard, donjon, drawbridge, dungeon, gate, gateway, keep, magazine, moat, motte, parapet, portcullis, postern, rampart, tower, turret, wall, watchtower

a b c d e f g h i j k l m n o p q r s t u v w x y z

A B C D E F G H I J K L M N O P Q R S T U V W X Y Z

casual *ADJECTIVE*
1 *It was just a casual remark, so don't take it too seriously.*
▸ accidental, chance, unexpected, unintentional, unplanned
AN OPPOSITE IS deliberate
2 *The restaurant had a casual atmosphere.*
▸ easy-going, informal, relaxed
AN OPPOSITE IS formal
3 *The teacher complained about our casual attitude.*
▸ apathetic, careless, slack, unenthusiastic
AN OPPOSITE IS enthusiastic

casualty *NOUN*
It was a nasty accident, but there was only one casualty.
▸ death, fatality, injury, loss, victim

> **cat** *NOUN*
> ▹ An informal word for a cat is moggy or pussy. A baby's word for a cat is pussy. A young cat is a kitten. A male cat is a tom. A cat with streaks in its fur is a tabby.
> VARIOUS WILD ANIMALS OF THE CAT FAMILY
> jaguar, leopard, lion, lynx, puma, tiger, wild cat

catalogue *NOUN*
Mum chose some curtains from a shopping catalogue.
▸ brochure

catastrophe *NOUN*
The drought is a catastrophe for the farmers.
▸ calamity, disaster, misfortune, mishap, tragedy

catch *VERB*
1 *They yelled at me to catch the ball.*
▸ clutch, grab, grasp, grip, hang on to, hold, seize, snatch, take
2 *One of the anglers caught a fish.*
▸ hook, net, trap
3 *The police hoped to catch the thief red-handed.*
▸ arrest, capture, corner, (*informal*) nab
4 *I hope you don't catch my cold.*
▸ become infected by, contract, get, (*informal*) go down with
5 *You must hurry if you want to catch the bus.*
▸ be in time for, get on
to catch on *Their latest record didn't catch on.*
▸ become popular, do well, (*informal*) make it, succeed
to catch up with someone *If we run we'll catch up with them.*
▸ gain on, overtake

catch *NOUN*
1 *They got a large catch of fish.*
▸ haul
2 *The car is so cheap that there must be a catch.*
▸ difficulty, disadvantage, drawback, obstacle, problem, snag, trap, trick
3 *The window was fitted with a safety catch.*
▸ bolt, fastening, hook, latch, lock

catching *ADJECTIVE*
Chickenpox is catching.
▸ contagious, infectious

category *NOUN*
I entered the competition in the under-twelves category.
▸ class, division, group, section, set

cater *VERB*
to cater for *The hotel catered for fifty people at my cousin's wedding.*
▸ cook for, provide food for, serve, supply

> **cattle** *PLURAL NOUN*
> VARIOUS KINDS OF CATTLE
> bulls, bullocks, calves, cows, heifers, oxen, steers
> ▹ Farm animals in general are livestock.

cause *NOUN*
1 *What was the cause of the trouble?*
▸ origin, source
▹ You can also talk about the reasons for the trouble.
2 *You've got no cause to complain.*
▸ basis, grounds, motive
3 *Who was the cause of the trouble?*
▸ creator, originator
4 *We are collecting for a good cause.*
▸ object, purpose

cause *VERB*
It'll cause trouble if you don't share things.
▸ arouse, bring about, create, generate, give rise to, lead to, provoke, result in

caution *NOUN*
1 *Proceed with caution.*
▸ attention, care, vigilance, wariness, watchfulness

2 *They let me off with a caution.*
▸ reprimand, telling-off, (*informal*) ticking-off, warning

cautious *ADJECTIVE*
Dad is a cautious driver.
▸ attentive, careful, hesitant, vigilant, wary, watchful
AN OPPOSITE IS reckless

cave *NOUN*
VARIOUS KINDS OF HOLE UNDER THE GROUND
cavern, grotto, mine, pothole, underground chamber
▹ People who lived in caves were **cavemen** or **troglodytes**.

cave *VERB*
to cave in *The miners had a lucky escape when the roof caved in.*
▸ collapse, fall in

cavity *NOUN*
The dentist filled a cavity in my tooth.
▸ hole, hollow

cease *VERB*
The fighting ceased at midnight.
▸ come to an end, end, finish, halt, stop
AN OPPOSITE IS begin

ceaseless *ADJECTIVE*
Our ceaseless noise annoyed the neighbours.
▸ constant, continual, continuous, endless, everlasting, incessant, interminable, never-ending, non-stop, perpetual, persistent, relentless, unending
AN OPPOSITE IS brief

celebrate *VERB*
1 *Let's celebrate!*
▸ be happy, have a good time, rejoice
2 *What shall we do to celebrate Granny's birthday?*
▸ commemorate, keep, observe

celebrated *ADJECTIVE*
She's one of the most celebrated poets in the country.
▸ distinguished, eminent, famous, notable, outstanding, popular, prominent, renowned, respected, well-known
AN OPPOSITE IS unknown

celebration *NOUN*
DIFFERENT KINDS OF CELEBRATION
anniversary, banquet, birthday, carnival, commemoration, feast, festival, festivity, fête, gala, jamboree, jubilee, party, reunion, wedding

celebrity *NOUN*
The head asked a TV celebrity to open our new sports centre.
▸ famous person, idol, personality, public figure, star, VIP

cellar *NOUN*
VARIOUS UNDERGROUND ROOMS
basement, crypt, dungeon, undercroft, vault, wine cellar

cemetery *NOUN*
Several famous people are buried in the local cemetery.
▸ burial ground, churchyard, graveyard
▹ A place where dead people are cremated is a **crematorium**.
SEE ALSO **tomb**

censor *VERB*
Dad says they were right to censor the violence in that film.
▸ cut out, delete, edit, remove

censure *NOUN*
He deserved the referee's censure for that foul.
▸ condemnation, criticism, disapproval, reprimand, reproach, telling-off

census *NOUN*
They did a traffic census to find out exactly how busy the road is.
▸ count, survey

central *ADJECTIVE*
1 *The traffic is very heavy in the central part of town.*
▸ inner, interior, middle
AN OPPOSITE IS outer
2 *He gave us the central facts.*
▸ chief, crucial, essential, fundamental, important, main, major, principal, vital
AN OPPOSITE IS unimportant

centre *NOUN*
We got to the centre of the maze easily, but getting outside again was more difficult.
▸ heart, inside, interior, middle

A B C D E F G H I J K L M N O P Q R S T U V W X Y Z

▷ The centre of the earth or of an apple is the core. The centre of an atom or a living cell is the nucleus. The centre of a wheel is the hub. The point at the centre of a see-saw is the pivot. The eatable part in the centre of a nut is the kernel.
AN OPPOSITE IS edge, outside, or surface

cereal *NOUN*
Many farmers grow cereals.
▸ corn, grain
DIFFERENT CEREALS
barley, corn on the cob or maize or sweetcorn, millet, oats, rice, rye, wheat

ceremonial *ADJECTIVE*
The opening of parliament is a ceremonial occasion.
▸ dignified, formal, majestic, official, solemn, stately
AN OPPOSITE IS informal

ceremony *NOUN*
1 *We watched the ceremony of the opening of parliament.*
▸ rite, ritual
▷ A plural word is formalities.
▷ A ceremony where someone is given a prize is a presentation. A ceremony where someone is given a special honour is an investiture. A ceremony to celebrate something new is an inauguration or opening. A ceremony where someone becomes a member of a society is an initiation. A ceremony to make a church or other building sacred is a dedication. A ceremony to remember a dead person or a past event is a commemoration. A ceremony held in church is a service.
VARIOUS CHURCH CEREMONIES
baptism, confirmation, funeral, wedding
2 *My sister had a quiet wedding without a lot of ceremony.*
▸ formality, pageantry, pomp, spectacle

certain *ADJECTIVE*
1 *I was certain I would win.*
▸ confident, convinced, determined, positive, sure
AN OPPOSITE IS uncertain
2 *We have certain proof that she is guilty.*
▸ absolute, clear, convincing, definite, genuine, infallible, reliable, trustworthy, undeniable, unquestionable, valid
AN OPPOSITE IS unreliable
3 *The damaged plane faced certain disaster.*
▸ inevitable, unavoidable
AN OPPOSITE IS possible
4 *If your new watch doesn't go, the shop is certain to give your money back.*
▸ bound
for certain *I'll give you the money tomorrow for certain.*
▸ certainly, definitely, for sure, without doubt
to make certain *Please make certain that you lock the doors before you go out.*
▸ ensure, make sure

certainty *NOUN*
1 *It was a certainty that we'd quarrel sooner or later.*
▸ foregone conclusion, (*informal*) sure thing
AN OPPOSITE IS impossibility
2 *I saw it happen, so I can speak with certainty.*
▸ assurance, confidence, conviction, knowledge

certificate *NOUN*
VARIOUS KINDS OF CERTIFICATE
birth certificate, death certificate, degree certificate, diploma, driver's licence, guarantee, insurance certificate, licence, marriage certificate, pass, permit, warrant

certify *VERB*
The doctor certified that I was fit to go back to school.
▸ confirm, declare, guarantee, testify, verify

chain *NOUN*
1 *The prisoners were kept in chains.*
CHAINS, ETC., USED TO SECURE PRISONERS
fetters, handcuffs, irons, manacles, shackles
▷ One ring in a chain is a link. A chain used to link railway wagons together is a coupling.
2 *The police formed a chain to keep the crowd back.*
▸ cordon, line, row
3 *The police described the chain of events that led to the murder.*
▸ sequence, series, string, succession

chair *NOUN*
FOR FURNITURE YOU SIT IN SEE **seat**

challenge *VERB*
I challenged my friend to beat me in the 100 metres race.
▸ dare, defy

champion *NOUN*
1 *The final game decides who is the champion.*
▸ conqueror, hero, medallist, prizewinner, victor, winner
2 *Martin Luther King was a great champion of civil rights.*
▸ backer, defender, supporter, upholder

championship *NOUN*
Teams from the local schools took part in a chess championship.
▸ competition, contest, tournament

chance *NOUN*
1 *They say there's a chance of rain tomorrow.*
▸ danger, possibility, probability, prospect, risk
2 *Tomorrow is our only chance for a picnic.*
▸ occasion, opportunity, time
3 *We took a chance and hoped it wouldn't rain.*
▸ gamble, risk
4 *I met him quite by chance.*
▸ accident, coincidence
▹ An unfortunate chance is bad luck or a misfortune. A fortunate chance is good luck or a fluke.

change *VERB*
1 *They changed the batting order for today's game.*
▸ adapt, adjust, alter, rearrange, reorganize, switch, vary
2 *Granny said I had changed since she last saw me.*
▸ alter, become different, develop, grow
3 *If I take these jeans back to the shop, will they change them?*
▸ exchange, replace, substitute, (*informal*) swap
to change into *Tadpoles change into frogs.*
▸ become, be transformed into, turn into

change *NOUN*
There has been no change in the weather.
▸ alteration, break, difference, variation
▹ A change to something worse is a deterioration. A change to something better is an improvement or a reform. A very big change is a revolution or transformation or U-turn. A change which involves replacing one person or thing by another is a substitution.

changeable *ADJECTIVE*
The weather has been changeable.
▸ erratic, inconsistent, unpredictable, unreliable, unstable, variable
▹ If your loyalty is changeable you are fickle.
AN OPPOSITE IS steady

channel *NOUN*
KINDS OF CHANNEL FOR WATER TO FLOW ALONG
culvert, dike, ditch, duct, gully, gutter, overflow, pipe, stream, trough, watercourse
KINDS OF CHANNEL WHICH SHIPS CAN SAIL ALONG
canal, sound, strait, waterway

chaos *NOUN*
1 *Mum said I had better tidy up the chaos in my room.*
▸ confusion, disorder, muddle, shambles
2 *There was chaos in the next class when their teacher was away.*
▸ anarchy, bedlam, pandemonium, tumult, uproar
AN OPPOSITE IS order

chaotic *ADJECTIVE*
1 *I have to admit that my room is in a chaotic state.*
▸ confused, messy, muddled, topsy-turvy, untidy, upside-down
AN OPPOSITE IS neat
2 *During the famine, the country was in a chaotic state.*
▸ anarchic, lawless, rebellious, riotous, unruly
AN OPPOSITE IS organized

chapter *NOUN*
I read one chapter of my book each evening.
▸ part, section
▹ One section of a play is an act or scene. One part of a serial is an episode or instalment.

char *VERB*
The fire charred the woodwork.
▸ blacken, scorch, singe
SEE ALSO **burn**

character *NOUN*
1 *His character is quite different from his brother's.*
▸ attitude, disposition, make-up, manner, nature, personality
2 *Our neighbour is a well-known character in our street.*

A B C D E F G H I J K L M N O P Q R S T U V W X Y Z

▸ figure, individual, person, personality
3 *Which character do you want to be in the play?*
▸ part, role

characteristic NOUN
He has some strange physical characteristics.
▸ distinguishing feature, feature, peculiarity, point

characteristic ADJECTIVE
Windmills are a characteristic feature of this area.
▸ distinctive, individual, recognizable, special, unique

characterize VERB
1 *His paintings are characterized by bright, primary colours.*
▸ distinguish
2 *The play characterizes Richard III as a villain.*
▸ depict, describe, portray, present

charge NOUN
1 *The admission charge is £2.50.*
▸ price, rate
▹ The charge made for a ride on public transport is the **fare**. The charge made to post a letter or parcel is the **postage**. A charge made to join a club is a **fee** or **subscription**. A charge made for certain things by the government is a **duty** or a **tax**. A charge made to use a private road, bridge, or tunnel is a **toll**.
2 *A policeman read out the charge against the suspect.*
▸ accusation, allegation
3 *Many soldiers were killed in the charge.*
▸ assault, attack, raid
4 *They left the dog in my charge.*
▸ care, control, keeping, protection
to be in charge of something *An experienced mountaineer was in charge of the expedition.*
▸ command, direct, lead, look after, manage, supervise

charge VERB
1 *What do they charge for a coffee?*
▸ ask for, make you pay
2 *The cavalry charged the enemy line.*
▸ assault, attack, storm

charitable ADJECTIVE
You should try to be more charitable to people.
▸ benevolent, compassionate, generous, helpful, kind, unselfish
AN OPPOSITE IS selfish

charity NOUN
1 *The whole world was impressed by the charity she showed towards the poor.*
▸ benevolence, compassion, generosity, helpfulness, humanity, kindness, love, mercy, sympathy, unselfishness
AN OPPOSITE IS selfishness
2 *The animals' hospital depends on our charity.*
▸ donations, financial support, gifts, offerings

charm NOUN
1 *He was captivated by her youthful charm.*
▸ appeal, attractiveness
2 *The sorcerer recited a magic charm.*
▸ spell

charm VERB
The books have charmed children all over the world.
▸ bewitch, captivate, delight, enchant, entrance, fascinate, please

charming ADJECTIVE
1 *We drove through some charming scenery.*
▸ attractive, beautiful, delightful, enchanting, fascinating, lovely
2 *Our neighbour's dog gave birth to four charming puppies.*
▸ adorable, appealing, captivating, (*informal*) cute, irresistible, lovable

chart NOUN
1 *The ship's captain consulted his chart.*
▸ map
2 *We made a chart to show differences in temperature for each month of the year.*
▸ diagram, graph, table

charter VERB
We chartered a coach to take us on our trip.
▸ engage, hire

chase VERB
The dog chased a rabbit.
▸ follow, hound, hunt, pursue, track, trail

chasm NOUN
VARIOUS KINDS OF DEEP HOLE
abyss, canyon, crater, crevasse, gorge, gulf, opening, pit, ravine, rift

chat, chatter *VERBS*
FOR DIFFERENT WAYS WE TALK SEE **talk** *VERB*

chatty *ADJECTIVE*
Usually he doesn't say much, but today he's quite chatty.
▶ communicative, talkative
AN OPPOSITE IS silent

cheap *ADJECTIVE*
1 *I got my anorak at a cheap price in the market.*
▶ bargain, cut-price, discount, reasonable, reduced
2 *Beans on toast is a cheap meal.*
▶ economical, inexpensive
AN OPPOSITE IS expensive
3 *That cheap watch of mine didn't last long.*
▶ inferior, shoddy, (*informal*) tacky, trashy, worthless
AN OPPOSITE IS superior

cheat *VERB*
1 *He cheated me by selling me a watch that doesn't go.*
▶ (*slang*) con, deceive, (*informal*) diddle, double-cross, (*informal*) fleece, (*slang*) fool, hoax, (*slang*) rip off, swindle, trick
2 *Anyone who cheats in a test is severely punished.*
▶ copy, crib

cheat *NOUN*
Don't trust him—he's a cheat.
▶ cheater, fraud, hoaxer, impostor, swindler

check *VERB*
1 *You must check your work carefully.*
▶ examine, inspect, scrutinize
2 *The heavy traffic checked our progress.*
▶ block, delay, halt, hamper, hinder, hold back, obstruct, slow, slow down, stop

check *NOUN*
Dad took the car to the garage for a check.
▶ check-up, examination, inspection, test

cheeky *ADJECTIVE*
Don't be so cheeky!
▶ disrespectful, facetious, flippant, impertinent, impolite, impudent, insolent, insulting, irreverent, mocking, rude, saucy, shameless
AN OPPOSITE IS respectful

cheer *VERB*
1 *We cheered when our side won.*
▶ applaud, clap, shout, yell
AN OPPOSITE IS jeer
2 *The good news cheered us.*
▶ comfort, console, delight, encourage, gladden, please
AN OPPOSITE IS sadden
to cheer up *The weather cheered up.*
▶ become more cheerful, brighten

cheerful *ADJECTIVE*
The sun was shining, and we set out in a cheerful mood.
▶ animated, bright, buoyant, delighted, elated, festive, glad, gleeful, good-humoured, happy, jolly, jovial, joyful, light-hearted, lively, merry, optimistic, pleased, radiant
AN OPPOSITE IS sad

chemist *NOUN*
▷ An old-fashioned word is **apothecary**. A chemist's shop is a **dispensary** or **pharmacy**.

chequered *ADJECTIVE*
The tablecloth had a chequered pattern.
▶ check, criss-cross
▷ Scottish cloth with a chequered pattern is **tartan**.

cherish *VERB*
I cherish the gifts she gave me.
▶ adore, be fond of, keep safe, look after, love, prize, treasure, value

chess *NOUN*
THE PIECES USED IN PLAYING CHESS
bishop, castle or rook, king, knight, pawn, queen
SOME TERMS USED IN PLAYING CHESS
castle, check, checkmate, mate, move, stalemate, take

chest *NOUN*
I found some old books in a chest in the attic.
▶ box, case, crate, trunk

chew *VERB*
The dog was still chewing his bone.
▶ crunch up, gnaw, grind up, munch

chicken *NOUN*
KINDS OF CHICKEN
bantam, broiler, chick, cockerel, fowl, hen, pullet, rooster

A B C D E F G H I J K L M N O P Q R S T U V W X Y Z

chief *NOUN*
BBC chiefs announced that the programme would be axed.
▸ boss, leader
PEOPLE IN CHARGE OF VARIOUS EVENTS, ORGANIZATIONS, OR GROUPS
administrator, captain, chairperson, chieftain, commander, commanding officer, controller, director, employer, executive, foreman, governor, head, manager, master, mistress, officer, overseer, owner, president, principal, proprietor, (*uncomplimentary*) ringleader, superintendent, supervisor
SEE ALSO **ruler**

chief *ADJECTIVE*
1 *Leave out the details, and just give me the chief facts.*
▸ basic, central, crucial, dominant, essential, foremost, fundamental, important, indispensable, key, main, major, necessary, predominant, primary, principal, prominent, significant, vital
AN OPPOSITE IS unimportant
2 *He's the Queen's chief minister.*
▸ head, senior

chiefly *ADVERB*
The snow falls chiefly in the north.
▸ especially, generally, mainly, mostly, predominantly, primarily, principally

child *NOUN*
VARIOUS WORDS FOR PEOPLE WHO ARE NOT YET GROWN UP
adolescent, baby, boy, girl, infant, juvenile, (*informal*) kid, lad, lass, toddler, youngster, youth
VARIOUS WORDS FOR SOMEONE'S CHILD
daughter, descendant, offspring, son
▹ A child who expects to inherit a title or fortune from parents is an **heir** or **heiress**. A child whose parents are dead is an **orphan**. A child looked after by a guardian is a **ward**.
WORDS FOR VARIOUS TIMES OF YOUR LIFE BEFORE YOU ARE GROWN UP
adolescence, babyhood, boyhood, childhood, girlhood, infancy, schooldays, your teens, youth

childish *ADJECTIVE*
It's childish to make rude noises.
▸ babyish, immature, infantile, juvenile
AN OPPOSITE IS mature

chill *VERB*
1 *The wind chilled us to the bone.*
▸ cool, freeze, make cold
AN OPPOSITE IS warm
2 *Chill the soup before serving it.*
▸ keep cold, refrigerate

chilly *ADJECTIVE*
1 *It's a chilly evening, so wrap up warm.*
▸ cold, cool, crisp, fresh, frosty, icy, (*informal*) nippy, raw, wintry
AN OPPOSITE IS warm *ADJECTIVE*
2 *She gave me a very chilly look.*
▸ distant, hostile, unfriendly, unsympathetic
AN OPPOSITE IS friendly

chime *NOUN*
The church clock chimed at midnight.
▸ ring, strike
FOR VARIOUS WAYS BELLS SOUND SEE **bell**

chimney *NOUN*
▹ A chimney on a ship or steam engine is a **funnel**. A pipe to take away smoke and fumes is a **flue**.

china *NOUN*
You can wash up while I put the china away.
▸ crockery, cups and saucers, porcelain
SEE ALSO **pottery**

chink *NOUN*
1 *He peeped through a chink in the fence.*
▸ crack, crevice, cut, gap, opening, rift, slit, slot, split
2 *I heard the chink of coins.*
▸ clink, ping, ring
FOR VARIOUS WAYS TO MAKE SOUNDS SEE **sound** *VERB*

chip *NOUN*
1 *I swept up the chips of wood.*
▸ bit, flake, fragment, piece, sliver, splinter, wedge
2 *This mug's got a chip in it.*
▸ crack, flaw, nick, notch

chip *VERB*
I chipped a cup while I was washing up.
▸ crack, damage, nick, notch, scratch, splinter

chivalrous *ADJECTIVE*
He's a very chivalrous man.
▸ bold, brave, courageous, heroic, valiant, worthy
AN OPPOSITE IS cowardly

choice *NOUN*
1 *We ran out of petrol, so we had no choice but to walk.*
▸ alternative, option
2 *She wouldn't be my choice as team captain.*
▸ pick, preference, vote
3 *The greengrocer has a good choice of vegetables.*
▸ array, assortment, diversity, mixture, range, selection, variety

choke *VERB*
1 *My collar is choking me.*
▸ stifle, strangle, suffocate, throttle
2 *Thick fumes made the fireman choke.*
▸ cough, gasp
choked *The main roads are choked in the rush hour.*
▸ blocked, (*informal*) bunged up, clogged, congested, impassable, jammed, obstructed

choose *VERB*
1 *We had a show of hands to choose a new captain.*
▸ appoint, elect, select, vote for
2 *I chose the green anorak.*
▸ decide on, opt for, pick out, plump for, select, settle on, single out
3 *I chose to buy the green anorak.*
▸ decide, make a decision, prefer, resolve

choosy *ADJECTIVE* (*informal*)
My baby brother is very choosy about his food.
▸ finicky, fussy, hard to please

chop *VERB*
1 *He chopped the log into thin pieces.*
▸ cut, split
2 *We chopped down the undergrowth to make a path.*
▸ hack, slash
▹ To chop down a tree is to **fell** it. To chop off an arm or leg is to **amputate** it. To chop a branch off a tree is to **lop** it. To chop food into small pieces is to **dice** or **mince** it.

chorus *NOUN*
1 *Mum sings in the chorus of the local operatic society.*
▸ choir
2 *Our teacher sang the verses, and we joined in the chorus.*
▸ refrain
in chorus *It was such an easy question that we answered in chorus.*
▸ all at once, simultaneously, together

chronic *ADJECTIVE*
1 *She has chronic pain from her rheumatism.*
▸ constant, continual, continuous, incessant, incurable, permanent, persistent
AN OPPOSITE IS acute or temporary
2 (*informal*) *He's a chronic driver!*
▸ awful, bad, dire, dreadful, terrible

chronicle *NOUN*
He wrote a chronicle of his life during the war years.
▸ account, diary, history, journal, narrative, record, story

chunk *NOUN*
I cut myself a chunk of cheese.
▸ block, hunk, lump, piece, portion, slab, wedge

church *NOUN*
THE MAIN TRADITIONS OF THE CHRISTIAN CHURCH
Orthodox, Protestant, Roman Catholic
VARIOUS PLACES WHERE CHRISTIANS WORSHIP
abbey, basilica, cathedral, chapel, convent, minster, monastery, nunnery, parish church, priory, tabernacle
FOR PLACES WHERE PEOPLE OF OTHER RELIGIONS WORSHIP SEE **worship**
PARTS OF A CHURCH
aisle, belfry, chancel, chapel, cloister, crypt, dome, nave, porch, sanctuary, spire, steeple, tower, transept, vestry
THINGS YOU MAY FIND IN A CHURCH
altar, Bible, candles, communion table, crucifix, font, hymn books, lectern, memorials, pews, prayer books, pulpit
SOME FESTIVALS AND EVENTS CELEBRATED IN CHURCH
Advent, Ascension Day, Ash Wednesday, baptism or christening, Christmas, communion, confirmation, Easter, Good Friday, Lent, mass, the Nativity, Palm Sunday, Pentecost, Whitsun
THINGS THAT MAY BE PART OF WORSHIP IN CHURCH
benediction or blessing, communion, hymn, prayer, psalm, readings from the Bible or scripture, sermon
PEOPLE CONNECTED WITH A CHURCH
archbishop, bishop, cardinal, chaplain, choirboy, choirgirl, churchwarden, clergyman or clergywoman, the congregation, curate, deacon, deaconess, elder, lay reader, minister, parson, pastor, the Pope, preacher, priest, rector, sexton, sidesman, verger, vicar

churchyard *NOUN*
▸ burial ground, cemetery, graveyard

A B C D E F G H I J K L M N O P Q R S T U V W X Y Z

cinders *PLURAL NOUN*
The cinders from the fire were still glowing.
▸ ashes, embers

circle *NOUN*
THINGS WITH A CIRCULAR SHAPE
disc, hoop, ring, wheel
THREE-DIMENSIONAL ROUND SHAPES
ball, globe, orb, sphere
▷ The distance round a circle is the circumference. The distance across a circle is the diameter. The distance from the centre to the circumference is the radius.
THINGS WITH A CURVED OR NEARLY CIRCULAR SHAPE
band, belt, coil, cordon, curl, ellipse, loop, oval, spiral
VARIOUS CIRCULAR MOVEMENTS
circulation, cycle, revolution, rotation, turn, whirl
▷ A circular race track is a circuit. Once round a circuit is a lap. A circular trip which ends where you began is a tour. A circular trip round the world is a circumnavigation. A circular trip of a satellite round a planet is an orbit.

circle *VERB*
The vultures circled overhead.
▸ turn, twist, wheel

circular *ADJECTIVE*
The pond was circular in shape.
▸ round

circular *NOUN*
I wonder if people read these circulars the postman brings?
▸ advertisement, leaflet, notice, pamphlet

circulate *VERB*
1 *Blood circulates in the body.*
▸ go round, move round
2 *I asked friends to circulate notices about our sale.*
▸ distribute, issue, send round

circulation *NOUN*
1 *We had a lesson explaining the circulation of blood round the body.*
▸ flow, movement, transmission
2 *The local newspaper has a big circulation.*
▸ distribution, sales figures

circumference *NOUN*
We raced round the circumference of the playing field.
▸ border, boundary, edge, fringe, perimeter

circumstances *PLURAL NOUN*
On the news they explained the circumstances which led to the tragedy.
▸ background, causes, conditions, context, details, facts, particulars, situation

circus *NOUN*
SOME PEOPLE WHO PERFORM IN A CIRCUS
acrobat, animal trainer, clown, conjuror, contortionist, equestrian artist or horse rider, juggler, lion-tamer, ringmaster, tightrope walker, trapeze-artist, trick cyclist

citizen *NOUN*
All adult citizens can vote in a general election.
▸ inhabitant, native, resident, subject, taxpayer, voter

citrus fruit *NOUN*
VARIOUS CITRUS FRUITS
clementine, grapefruit, lemon, lime, mandarin, orange, satsuma, tangerine

city *NOUN*
SEE **town**

civil *ADJECTIVE*
I know you're angry, but please try to be civil.
▸ civilized, considerate, courteous, obliging, polite, respectful
AN OPPOSITE IS rude

civilization *NOUN*
We have been studying the civilization of ancient Egypt.
▸ achievements, attainments, culture, society

civilized *ADJECTIVE*
Civilized people shouldn't need to use violence.
▸ cultivated, cultured, democratic, educated, polite, sophisticated, well-behaved, well-mannered
AN OPPOSITE IS uncivilized

claim *VERB*
1 *When you hand in the purse you found, are you going to claim a reward?*
▸ ask for, collect, demand, insist on, request
2 *He claims that he's an expert.*
▸ allege, argue, assert, declare, insist, maintain

clamber *VERB*
We clambered over the rocks.
▸ climb, crawl, move awkwardly, scramble

clammy *ADJECTIVE*
The walls of the cellar were unpleasantly clammy.
▸ damp, moist, slimy, sticky

clamp *VERB*
FOR VARIOUS WAYS TO FASTEN THINGS SEE **fasten**

clang, clank *VERBS*
FOR VARIOUS WAYS TO MAKE SOUNDS SEE **sound** *VERB*

clap *VERB*
1 *We clapped her performance.*
▸ applaud
2 *He clapped me on the shoulder.*
▸ hit, pat, slap, smack

clarify *VERB*
We asked the teacher to clarify what he wanted us to do.
▸ explain, make clear, simplify, throw light on
AN OPPOSITE IS confuse

clash *NOUN*
1 *The clash of cymbals made me jump.*
▸ crash
2 *There was a clash between rival supporters at the match.*
▸ argument, conflict, confrontation, fight, (*informal*) scrap, scuffle

clash *VERB*
1 *The cymbals clashed.*
▸ crash
FOR OTHER WAYS TO MAKE SOUNDS SEE **sound** *VERB*
2 *My favourite TV programmes clash at 8 o'clock tonight.*
▸ coincide, happen at the same time
3 *Demonstrators clashed with the police.*
▸ argue, fight, get into conflict, quarrel, squabble

clasp *VERB*
1 *I clasped her hand.*
▸ cling to, grasp, grip, hold, squeeze
2 *She clasped him in her arms.*
▸ embrace, hug

clasp *NOUN*
The cloak was held in place by a gold clasp.
▸ brooch, buckle, clip, fastener, fastening, hook, pin

class *NOUN*
1 *There are 32 children in our class.*
▸ form, set, stream
2 *There are many different classes of plants.*
▸ category, classification, division, group, kind, set, sort, species, type
3 *He came from a different social class.*
▸ level, rank, status
TERMS SOMETIMES USED TO LABEL SOCIAL CLASSES
aristocracy or nobility, commoners, middle class, ruling class, upper class, working class

classic *NOUN*
This book is a classic!
▸ masterpiece, model

classic *ADJECTIVE*
Notice that *classic* means *excellent of its kind*, while *classical* means either *to do with the ancient Greeks and Romans*, or *to do with serious music written in the past*
Did you see him score that classic goal on Saturday?
▸ admirable, excellent, exceptional, fine, first-class, first-rate, great, masterly, model, perfect
AN OPPOSITE IS ordinary

classified *ADJECTIVE*
The spy gave classified information to the enemy.
▸ confidential, private, secret, top secret

classify *VERB*
We classified the plants according to the shape of their leaves.
▸ class, grade, group, organize, put into sets, sort

claw *VERB*
The cat clawed his leg.
▸ savage, scratch, tear

clean *ADJECTIVE*
1 *We took care to leave the place clean after our party.*
▸ spotless, tidy
▹ Clean clothes are laundered or washed clothes. A clean piece of paper is blank or unused paper. A clean car is a polished or shiny car. A clean lavatory is hygienic or sanitary. A clean bandage is a sterile bandage. Clean water is clear, fresh, pure, or unpolluted water.
AN OPPOSITE IS dirty *ADJECTIVE*
2 *He's always led a good clean life.*

▸ decent, respectable
AN OPPOSITE IS indecent
3 *The referee said he wanted the boxers to have a clean fight.*
▸ fair, honest, honourable, sporting, sportsmanlike
AN OPPOSITE IS dishonourable

clean *VERB*
WAYS TO CLEAN THE HOUSE
dust, hoover, mop, polish, scrub, spring-clean, sweep, vacuum
WAYS TO CLEAN YOURSELF
bath, shampoo your hair, shower, soap yourself, sponge yourself, spruce yourself up, wash
WAYS TO CLEAN CLOTHES
dry-clean, launder, rinse, wash, wring out
WAYS TO CLEAN A CAR
buff up, polish, shampoo, sponge down, wax
WAYS TO CLEAN THE PANS AND DISHES
rinse, scour, scrape, sponge, swill, wipe
WAYS TO CLEAN WATER
distil, filter, purify, sterilize
WAYS TO CLEAN THE LAVATORY
cleanse, disinfect, flush, sanitize, scrub out
AN OPPOSITE IS contaminate or dirty

clear *ADJECTIVE* This word is often overused. We illustrate some common ways here, and some of the synonyms you could use:
1 *I saw fish swimming in the clear water.*
▸ clean, colourless, pure, transparent
AN OPPOSITE IS opaque
2 *It was a beautiful clear day.*
▸ bright, cloudless, sunny, unclouded
▹ A clear night is a **moonlit** or **starlit** night.
AN OPPOSITE IS cloudy
3 *She gave a clear signal.*
▸ bold, plain, unambiguous, unmistakable, visible
AN OPPOSITE IS ambiguous
4 *Her voice was clear, although she was phoning from America.*
▸ audible, distinct
AN OPPOSITE IS muffled
5 *The signature on this letter is not clear.*
▸ legible, recognizable
AN OPPOSITE IS illegible
6 *My camera takes nice clear pictures.*
▸ focused, sharp, well defined
AN OPPOSITE IS unfocused
7 *Are you sure that your conscience is clear?*
▸ blameless, innocent, untroubled
AN OPPOSITE IS guilty
8 *After hearing her clear explanation, I knew what to do.*
▸ intelligible, lucid, understandable
AN OPPOSITE IS confusing
9 *There's a clear difference between a male blackbird and a female.*
▸ conspicuous, definite, noticeable, obvious, perceptible, pronounced
AN OPPOSITE IS imperceptible
10 *The police made sure the road was clear for the ambulance.*
▸ empty, free, open, passable, uncrowded, unobstructed
AN OPPOSITE IS congested

clear *VERB* This word is often overused. We illustrate some common ways here, and some of the synonyms you could use:
1 *I cleared the weeds from the flower bed.*
▸ eliminate, get rid of, remove, strip
2 *She cleared the blocked drainpipe.*
▸ clean out, open up, unblock, unclog
▹ To clear a channel is to **dredge** it.
3 *I cleared the misty windows.*
▸ clean, polish, wipe
4 *If the fire alarm goes, clear the building.*
▸ empty, evacuate
5 *The fog cleared.*
▸ disappear, evaporate, melt away, vanish
6 *The forecast said that the weather will clear.*
▸ become clear, brighten, lighten
7 *The court cleared him of all blame.*
▸ acquit, free, release
8 *The horse cleared the fence.*
▸ bound over, get over, jump, leap over, pass over, spring over, vault
to clear off (*informal*) *Clear off and leave me alone!*
▸ get out, go away, leave
to clear up *Please clear up this mess before you go.*
▸ clean up, remove, put right, put straight, tidy up

clench *VERB*
1 *He clenched his teeth.*
▸ close tightly, grit, squeeze together
2 *She clenched the coin tightly in her hand.*
▸ clasp, grasp, grip, hold

clergyman, **clergywoman** *NOUNS*
VARIOUS MEMBERS OF THE CLERGY
archbishop, bishop, canon, cardinal, chaplain, curate, deacon, deaconess, dean, minister, parson, pastor, preacher, priest, rector, vicar

clerical *ADJECTIVE*
My job involves a lot of clerical work.
▸ office, secretarial
VARIOUS PEOPLE DOING CLERICAL WORK IN AN OFFICE
bookkeeper, clerk, computer operator, filing clerk, office boy, office girl, receptionist, secretary, shorthand typist, typist, word processor operator

clever *ADJECTIVE*
1 *My brother is very clever and always passes his exams.*
▸ able, academic, (*informal*) brainy, bright, intelligent, knowledgeable
AN OPPOSITE IS unintelligent
2 *She's very clever with her fingers.*
▸ accomplished, capable, gifted, skilful, talented
▷ If you are clever at a lot of things, you are **versatile**.
AN OPPOSITE IS unskilful
3 *They are clever enough to get away with it.*
▸ quick, sharp, shrewd, smart
▷ Uncomplimentary synonyms are **artful**, **crafty**, **cunning**, **wily**.
AN OPPOSITE IS stupid

cliff *NOUN*
The car rolled over the edge of a cliff.
▸ crag, precipice, rock face

climate *NOUN*
FOR WORDS TO DO WITH CLIMATE SEE **weather**

climax *NOUN*
The excitement built up to a climax.
▸ crisis, high point, peak
AN OPPOSITE IS anticlimax

climb *VERB*
1 *It took us several hours to climb the mountain.*
▸ ascend, clamber up, go up, scale
▷ To reach the top of a mountain is to **conquer** it.
2 *The plane climbed into the clouds.*
▸ lift off, soar, take off
3 *The road climbs steeply up to the castle.*
▸ rise, slope
to climb down 1 *It's harder to climb down the rock than to get up it.*
▸ descend, get down from
2 *We all told him he was wrong, so he had to climb down.*
▸ admit defeat, give in, surrender

climb *NOUN*
It's a steep climb up to the castle.
▸ ascent, gradient, hill, incline, rise, slope

climber *NOUN*
The climbers were all roped together.
▸ mountaineer, rock-climber

cling *VERB*
to cling to someone or **something 1** *The child clung to her mother.*
▸ clasp, clutch, embrace, grasp, hug
2 *Ivy clings to the wall.*
▸ adhere to, fasten on to, stick to

clinic *NOUN*
PLACES WHERE YOU CAN GO TO CONSULT DOCTORS OR NURSES
health centre, hospital, infirmary, medical centre, sanatorium, sickbay, surgery

clip *VERB*
1 *I clipped my papers together.*
▸ pin, staple
FOR VARIOUS WAYS TO FASTEN THINGS TOGETHER SEE **fasten**
2 *Dad was clipping the hedges in the back garden.*
▸ cut, trim
▷ To cut unwanted twigs off a tree or bush is to **prune** it.

cloak *NOUN*
She wrapped a cloak around her.
▸ cape, coat, (*old use*) mantle, wrap

clock *NOUN*
INSTRUMENTS USED TO MEASURE TIME
alarm clock, chronometer, digital clock, grandfather clock, hourglass, pendulum clock, stopwatch, sundial, timer, watch, wristwatch

clog *VERB*
In the autumn, dead leaves clog the drain.
▸ block, bung up, choke, congest, fill, jam, obstruct, stop up

close *ADJECTIVE*
1 *Our house is close to the shops.*
▸ adjacent, handy (for), near
▹ To be actually by the side of something is to be adjacent or neighbouring. To fire a gun at close range is to fire at point-blank range.
AN OPPOSITE IS distant
2 *The twins are very close.*
▸ affectionate, attached, devoted, fond of each other, friendly, intimate, loving
AN OPPOSITE IS unfriendly
3 *The police made a close examination of the stolen car.*
▸ careful, detailed, minute, painstaking, searching, thorough
AN OPPOSITE IS casual
4 *It was an exciting race because it was so close.*
▸ equal, even, level, well-matched
AN OPPOSITE IS one-sided
5 *Open the window—it's very close in here.*
▸ airless, (*informal*) fuggy, humid, muggy, stifling, stuffy, suffocating
AN OPPOSITE IS airy

close *VERB*
1 *Don't forget to close the lid.*
▸ fasten, seal, secure, shut
2 *The rioters tried to close the road.*
▸ barricade, block, obstruct, stop up
3 *He closed the meeting by thanking the chairman.*
▸ complete, conclude, end, finish, stop, terminate, (*informal*) wind up

closely *ADVERB*
Please listen closely.
▸ attentively, carefully, conscientiously

clot *VERB*
If you cut yourself, the blood will clot and form a scab.
▸ solidify, thicken

cloth *NOUN*
The curtains were made of striped cotton cloth.
▸ fabric, material, stuff
▹ A word for cloth in general is textiles.
SOME KINDS OF CLOTH
calico, canvas, cashmere, chiffon, chintz, corduroy, cotton, denim, felt, flannel, flannelette, gabardine, gauze, hessian, lace, linen, lint, mohair, muslin, nylon, oilcloth, plaid, polyester, poplin, rayon, sacking, satin, silk, taffeta, tartan, tweed, velvet, wool, worsted

clothe *VERB*
to be clothed in *They were clothed in white.*
▸ be dressed in, be wearing

clothes *PLURAL NOUN*
What clothes are you taking away on holiday?
▸ clothing, garments
▹ A set of clothes to wear is a costume, outfit, or suit. A soldier wears a uniform. A uniform worn by servants is a livery. A priest may wear a cassock, a surplice, or vestments. A nun or monk wears a habit.
VARIOUS GARMENTS
blazer, blouse, caftan, cardigan, chador or chuddar, coat, dhoti, dress, dungarees, frock, gown, gymslip, jacket, jeans, jerkin, jersey, jumper, kilt, kimono, lounge suit, miniskirt, parka, pullover, robe, sari, sarong, shirt, shorts, singlet, skirt, slacks, smock, sweater, sweatshirt, trousers, trunks, T-shirt, tunic, waistcoat
THINGS YOU WEAR ON TOP OF OTHER CLOTHES
anorak, apron, cagoule, cape, cloak, duffel coat, greatcoat, mackintosh, oilskins, overalls, overcoat, pinafore, poncho, raincoat, shawl, stole, track suit, windcheater
VARIOUS UNDERCLOTHES
bra, briefs, drawers, girdle, knickers, (*informal*) panties, pants, petticoat, slip, underpants, vest
THINGS YOU WEAR AT NIGHT OR WHEN GETTING DRESSED
dressing gown, housecoat, négligée, nightclothes, nightdress, (*informal*) nightie, pyjamas
THINGS YOU WEAR ON YOUR HANDS
gauntlets, gloves, mittens
THINGS YOU WEAR ON YOUR LEGS
garters, leggings, leg warmers, socks, stockings, tights
THINGS YOU WEAR ROUND YOUR NECK
collar, cravat, muffler, necktie, scarf, tie
FOR THINGS YOU WEAR ON YOUR HEAD AND FEET SEE **hat, shoe**
PARTS OF A GARMENT
belt, bodice, button, buttonhole, collar, cuff, hem, lapel, pocket, seam, sleeve, waistband, zip

cloud *NOUN*
A cloud of steam rose from the kettle.
▸ billow, haze, mist, puff

cloud *VERB*
to cloud over *The sky clouded over.*
► become cloudy, become dull, darken

cloudless *ADJECTIVE*
The forecast promised that it would be a cloudless day.
► bright, clear, sunny, unclouded
▷ A cloudless night is a **moonlit** or **starry** night.
AN OPPOSITE IS cloudy

cloudy *ADJECTIVE*
1 *The day was cold and cloudy.*
► dark, dismal, dull, gloomy, grey, overcast, sunless
AN OPPOSITE IS cloudless
2 *We couldn't see any fish in the cloudy water.*
► hazy, milky, muddy, murky
AN OPPOSITE IS clear or transparent

clown *NOUN*
My friend likes being a clown and making us laugh.
► comedian, comic, fool, jester, joker

club *NOUN*
1 *The intruder threatened him with a club.*
► baton, stick, truncheon
2 *Would you like to join our club?*
► association, circle, group, organization, society, union

club *VERB*
The intruder clubbed him on the head.
► (*informal*) bash, batter, hit, strike, thump, whack
FOR OTHER WAYS OF HITTING SEE **hit** *VERB*
to club together *My sister and I clubbed together and bought a new CD.*
► combine, join up, share the cost

clue *NOUN*
I don't know the answer—give me a clue.
► hint, idea, indication, lead, pointer, suggestion, tip

clump *NOUN*
We walked towards a clump of trees on the hill.
► cluster, collection, group, thicket
▷ A clump of grass, hair, etc., is a **tuft**.

clumsy *ADJECTIVE*
He's so clumsy—he's always breaking things.
► awkward, careless, inept, ungainly
AN OPPOSITE IS graceful
▷ An informal word for a clumsy person is a **butterfingers**.

cluster *NOUN*
A cluster of people waited outside the theatre.
► assembly, bunch, collection, crowd, gathering, knot
SEE ALSO **group** *NOUN*

clutch *VERB*
He clutched the rope.
► catch, clasp, cling to, grab, grasp, grip, hang on to, hold on to, seize, snatch

clutches *PLURAL NOUN*
He had her in his clutches.
► control, grasp, power

clutter *VERB*
to clutter up *My brother's belongings are cluttering up my bedroom!*
► lie about, litter, make untidy, mess up

clutter *NOUN*
We'll have to clear up all this clutter.
► junk, litter, mess, muddle, odds and ends, rubbish

coach *NOUN*
1 *We went to London by coach.*
► bus
FOR OTHER VEHICLES SEE **vehicle**
2 *Their football team has a new coach.*
► instructor, trainer

coach *VERB*
He was coached by a former champion.
► instruct, teach, train

coarse *ADJECTIVE*
1 *The blanket was made of coarse woollen material.*
► bristly, hairy, harsh, rough, scratchy
AN OPPOSITE IS soft
2 *He objected to her coarse remarks.*
► crude, impolite, improper, indecent, offensive, rude, smutty, vulgar
AN OPPOSITE IS polite

coast *NOUN*
After the disaster, oil was washed up along the coast.
► coastline, shore
SEE ALSO **seaside**

A B C D E F G H I J K L M N O P Q R S T U V W X Y Z

coast *VERB*
I coasted down the hill on my bike.
▸ cruise, freewheel, glide

coat *NOUN*
1 *Put on your coat if you are going out.*
KINDS OF COAT YOU CAN WEAR
anorak, blazer, cagoule, cardigan, dinner jacket, (*old use*) doublet, duffel coat, greatcoat, jacket, (*old use*) jerkin, mackintosh, overcoat, raincoat, waistcoat, windcheater
WORDS FOR AN ANIMAL'S COAT
fleece, fur, hair, hide, pelt, skin
FOR OTHER GARMENTS SEE **clothes**
2 *The cupboard door needs a coat of paint.*
▸ coating, covering, layer

coax *VERB*
We coaxed the animal back into its cage.
▸ persuade, tempt

cocky *ADJECTIVE* (*informal*)
I didn't like him because he was so cocky.
▸ arrogant, boastful, cheeky, conceited, pleased with yourself, vain
AN OPPOSITE IS modest

code *NOUN*
Everyone in the club must behave according to our code of conduct.
▸ laws, regulations, rules

coil *NOUN*
VARIOUS COILED SHAPES OR MOVEMENTS
corkscrew, curl, screw, spiral, twirl, twist, whirl, whorl

coil *VERB*
The snake coiled itself round a branch.
▸ curl, loop, roll, spiral, turn, twist, wind, writhe

coin *NOUN*
Have you got a 10p coin for the slot machine?
▸ bit, piece
coins *I keep come coins handy to pay my bus fare.*
▸ change, coppers, loose change, silver, small change

coin *VERB*
We coined a new name for our group.
▸ create, devise, invent, make up, produce, think up

coincide *VERB*
My birthday coincides with a bank holiday.
▸ clash, fall together, happen together

coincidence *NOUN*
We met by coincidence.
▸ accident, chance, fluke, luck

cold *ADJECTIVE*
1 *Wrap up warm in this cold weather.*
▸ arctic, bitter, chilly, cool, crisp, freezing, frosty, icy, raw, snowy, wintry
2 *I tried to shelter from the cold wind.*
▸ biting, fresh, keen, penetrating, piercing
3 *I was cold in spite of my thick anorak.*
▸ frozen, numb, (*informal*) perished, shivering, shivery
4 *The room was cold and dark.*
▸ bleak, draughty, unheated
AN OPPOSITE IS hot
to be cold *You'll be cold without a coat on.*
▸ freeze, shiver, tremble
▹ To be ill with a low temperature because of the cold is to suffer from **hypothermia**.
5 *He gave me a cold stare.*
▸ cool, distant, heartless, indifferent, reserved, stony, uncaring, unemotional, unfeeling, unfriendly, unkind, unsympathetic
AN OPPOSITE IS kind

cold-blooded *ADJECTIVE*
Cold-blooded properly refers to animals with blood that changes temperature according to the surroundings, but it is often used to describe cruel behaviour or a cruel person
We were horrified to read about the cold-blooded murder.
▸ barbaric, brutal, callous, cold, cruel, hard-hearted, heartless, inhuman, merciless, pitiless, ruthless, savage
AN OPPOSITE IS humane

collaborate *VERB*
She and her sister collaborated on the project.
▸ cooperate, work together

collaboration *NOUN*
The book is the result of several years of collaboration between the two men.
▸ association, cooperation, partnership, teamwork

collapse *VERB*
1 *Many buildings collapsed in the earthquake.*
▸ buckle, cave in, crumple, disintegrate, fall in,

fold up, tumble down
2 *Some people collapsed in the heat.*
► faint, fall down

colleague *NOUN*
He discussed the project with his colleagues.
► associate, partner

collect *VERB*
1 *Squirrels collect nuts.*
► accumulate, gather, hoard, pile up, save, store up
2 *A crowd collected to watch the fire.*
► assemble, come together, converge
AN OPPOSITE IS scatter
3 *We collected a large sum for charity.*
► raise, take
4 *I collected the bread from the baker's.*
► bring, fetch, get, obtain

collection *NOUN*
Dad has an interesting collection of old records.
► accumulation, array, assortment, hoard, pile, set
▷ A collection of books is a library. A collection of various items in a book is a compendium or omnibus. A collection of poems is an anthology. A collection of weapons is an arsenal or stockpile.

collective *ADJECTIVE*
If it affects us all, it ought to be a collective decision.
► combined, democratic, joint, shared, united
AN OPPOSITE IS individual

college *NOUN*
FOR PLACES WHERE PEOPLE STUDY SEE **education**

collide *VERB*
to collide with *The car collided with a man on a bike.*
► bump into, hit, run into, smash into, strike

collision *NOUN*
The collision dented the front wing of the car.
► accident, bump, crash, impact, knock, smash
▷ A collision involving a lot of vehicles is a pile-up.

colloquial *ADJECTIVE*
We taught our French visitor some colloquial English phrases.
► conversational, everyday, informal, slangy
AN OPPOSITE IS formal

colony *NOUN*
1 *At one time Britain had colonies all over the world.*
► possession, settlement, territory
2 *I found a colony of ants in the garden.*
FOR WORDS FOR VARIOUS GROUPS SEE **group** *NOUN*

colossal *ADJECTIVE*
A colossal statue towered above us.
► enormous, gigantic, huge, immense, massive, monstrous, monumental, towering, (*informal*) tremendous, vast
AN OPPOSITE IS small

colour *NOUN*
What do you call that colour?
► hue, shade, tinge, tint, tone
NAMES OF VARIOUS COLOURS
amber, auburn, azure, beige, black, blue, bronze, brown, buff, chestnut, chocolate, cobalt, cream, crimson, emerald, fawn, gilt, ginger, gold, golden, green, grey, indigo, ivory, jet-black, khaki, lavender, maroon, mauve, navy blue, olive, orange, pink, puce, purple, red, rosy, russet, salmon pink, sandy, scarlet, silver, tan, tawny, turquoise, vermilion, violet, white, yellow
SUBSTANCES WHICH GIVE THINGS THEIR COLOUR
colouring, cosmetics, dye, make-up, paint, pigment or pigmentation, stain
colours *The colours of the regiment fluttered in the breeze.*
► banner, flag, standard

colour *VERB*
1 *The teacher said we could colour the models we made.*
► dye, paint, tint
2 *His fair skin colours easily.*
► blush, burn, flush, redden

colourful *ADJECTIVE*
1 *The garden was ablaze with colourful flowers.*
► bright, brilliant, gaudy, showy
AN OPPOSITE IS colourless
2 *The book gave a colourful description of life in the Middle Ages.*
► exciting, lively, picturesque, striking, vivid
AN OPPOSITE IS dull

colourless *ADJECTIVE*
Everything looked colourless until the sun came out.
► drab, dull, grey, neutral, pale

A B C D E F G H I J K L M N O P Q R S T U V W X Y Z

▷ Something which has lost its colour is bleached or faded.
AN OPPOSITE IS colourful

column *NOUN*
1 *A lot of classical buildings have columns supporting the roof.*
▸ pillar, post, shaft, support
2 *A column of soldiers wound its way across the desert.*
▸ file, line, procession, row, string
3 *She writes a column in the local newspaper.*
▸ article, feature, leader, piece

comb *VERB*
1 *I had a wash and combed my hair before going out.*
▸ arrange, groom, tidy, untangle
2 *I combed the house in search of my pen.*
▸ hunt through, ransack, rummage through, scour, search thoroughly

combat *NOUN*
FOR VARIOUS KINDS OF FIGHTING SEE **fight** *NOUN*

combat *VERB*
There's a campaign to combat vandalism in our district.
▸ battle against, fight, grapple with, oppose, reduce, resist, stand up to, tackle

combination *NOUN*
▷ A combination of parts or things into one whole thing is a synthesis or unification. A combination of two businesses is an amalgamation or a merger. A combination of substances is a compound or fusion. A combination of metals is an alloy. A combination of ingredients for a cake is a blend or a mixture. When two people combine together, it is a marriage or partnership. When friends combine to help each other, it is an alliance or association. When criminals combine to do something bad, it is a conspiracy.

combine *VERB*
1 *Let's all combine our resources.*
▸ add together, amalgamate, integrate, join, put together
2 *I combined the cake ingredients in a bowl.*
▸ blend, mingle, mix, stir together
3 *The local schools combined to organize a charity concert.*
▸ band together, cooperate, get together, unite

come *VERB*
1 *We expect our guests to come at dinner time.*
▸ appear, arrive, visit
AN OPPOSITE IS go
2 *When you hear a cuckoo, you know that summer is coming.*
▸ advance, draw near
to come about *Can you tell me how the accident came about?*
▸ happen, occur, result, take place
to come across *I came across the pen you lost.*
▸ discover, find
to come round, to come to *How long did it take me to come round after the operation?*
▸ become conscious, revive
to come to **1** *Tell me when we come to my station.*
▸ approach, arrive at, get close to, near, reach
2 *What did the bill for repairs to the car come to?*
▸ add up to, amount to, total

comedy *NOUN*
VARIOUS KINDS OF COMEDY
clowning, farce, humour, jokes, satire, situation comedy or (*informal*) sitcom, slapstick, wit
PEOPLE WHO TRY TO MAKE OTHER PEOPLE LAUGH
clown, comic, entertainer, humorist, (*old use*) jester, joker, satirist

comfort *NOUN*
1 *The news brought comfort to us all.*
▸ consolation, encouragement, reassurance, relief
2 *If I had a million pounds, I could live in comfort.*
▸ affluence, contentment, ease, luxury

comfort *VERB*
He was upset, so we tried to comfort him.
▸ calm, cheer up, console, encourage, reassure, soothe, sympathize with

comfortable *ADJECTIVE*
1 *I sat in a comfortable chair and fell asleep.*
▸ cosy, easy, padded, relaxing, snug, soft, upholstered, warm
2 *On holiday you need comfortable clothes.*
▸ casual, informal, loose-fitting
3 *Our cat leads a comfortable life.*
▸ agreeable, contented, happy, luxurious, pleasant, relaxed, restful, serene
AN OPPOSITE IS uncomfortable

comic, comical *ADJECTIVES*
We laughed at his comic remarks.
▸ amusing, diverting, funny, hilarious, humorous, witty
▹ To be comical in a cheeky way is to be **facetious**. To be comical in a silly way is to be **absurd**, **farcical**, **ludicrous**, or **ridiculous**. To be comical in a hurtful way is to be **sarcastic** or **satirical**.

command *NOUN*
1 *You can start when I give the command.*
▸ instruction, order
▹ A sacred command is a **commandment**.
2 *She has command of the whole expedition.*
▸ authority (over), charge, control, management, power (over), supervision
3 *She has a good command of Spanish.*
▸ ability (in), knowledge, mastery, skill (in)

command *VERB*
1 *The officer commanded his troops to fire.*
▸ bid, direct, instruct, order, tell
2 *The captain commands the ship.*
▸ administer, be in charge of, control, direct, govern, head, lead, manage, supervise

commander *NOUN*
The commander of the expedition decided that it was too dangerous to continue.
▸ head, leader, officer-in-charge
SEE ALSO **chief** *NOUN*

commemorate *VERB*
They held a ceremony to commemorate those who died in war.
▸ be a memorial to, be a reminder of, celebrate, honour, pay tribute to, remember

commence *VERB*
You may commence work when I give the order.
▸ begin, embark on, start

commend *VERB*
The head commended us on our work.
▸ applaud, compliment, congratulate, praise
AN OPPOSITE IS **criticize**

commendable *ADJECTIVE*
She said that my effort was very commendable.
▸ admirable, good, praiseworthy, useful, worthwhile
AN OPPOSITE IS **worthless**

comment *NOUN*
Was there any comment in the newspaper about the way we played?
▸ mention, observation, opinion, reference, remark, statement
▹ A hostile comment is a **criticism**.

commentary *NOUN*
I couldn't go to the match, but I heard the commentary on the radio.
▸ account, analysis, broadcast, description, report, review

commerce *NOUN*
A lot of people in the city work in commerce.
▸ business, buying and selling, trade, trading

commercial *ADJECTIVE*
1 *Do you think the new sports centre will be a commercial success?*
▸ economic, financial
2 *Her novels are both well written and commercial.*
▸ money-making, profitable, profit-making

commercial *NOUN*
We watched the new commercial for the breakfast cereal.
▸ (*informal*) advert, advertisement, (*informal*) plug

commit *VERB*
The police intercepted the burglar before he could commit another crime.
▸ carry out, do, execute, perform
to commit yourself to something *I committed myself to help with the jumble sale.*
▸ be determined, promise, resolve, undertake, vow

commitment *NOUN*
1 *Every player has the commitment to win.*
▸ dedication, determination, enthusiasm, keenness, passion, resolution
2 *Dad has a commitment from the builder that he'll finish the job this week.*
▸ guarantee, pledge, promise, undertaking, vow

committee *NOUN*
VARIOUS GROUPS OF PEOPLE WHICH DISCUSS AND ORGANIZE THINGS
▹ A group appointed to discuss or decide something is a **panel**. A group which runs a business organization is a **board**. A group which decides whether someone is guilty or not is a **jury**. A group elected to run a town is a **council**. A group elected to govern a country is an **assembly** or **parliament**. The group of ministers who control the government is the **cabinet**.

A B C D E F G H I J K L M N O P Q R S T U V W X Y Z

common *ADJECTIVE*
1 *Colds are a common complaint in winter.*
▸ commonplace, daily, everyday, familiar, frequent, normal, ordinary, prevalent, unsurprising, well known, widespread
AN OPPOSITE IS rare
2 *'Good morning' is a common way to greet people.*
▸ conventional, customary, habitual, regular, routine, standard, traditional, typical, usual
AN OPPOSITE IS uncommon
3 *After it appeared in the paper, the story was common knowledge.*
▸ communal, general, public, universal
AN OPPOSITE IS private
4 *Mum says it's common to pick your nose.*
▸ coarse, crude, rude, vulgar
AN OPPOSITE IS refined

commonplace *ADJECTIVE*
1 *The lecturer made a lot of commonplace remarks.*
▸ boring, obvious, ordinary, predictable, routine, trivial, unexciting
SEE ALSO **common**
AN OPPOSITE IS memorable
2 *Foreign travel is commonplace these days.*
▸ common, frequent, normal, ordinary, routine, usual

commotion *NOUN*
Police had to stop the commotion when gangs of rival supporters met each other.
▸ bedlam, chaos, confusion, disorder, disturbance, excitement, fuss, hullabaloo, pandemonium, (*informal*) racket, riot, row, trouble, turbulence, turmoil, unrest, upheaval, uproar

communal *ADJECTIVE*
I didn't like the communal washing facilities at the campsite.
▸ common, public, shared
AN OPPOSITE IS private

communicate *VERB*
The head communicated her decision in a letter to our parents.
▸ announce, convey, disclose, express, indicate, make known, pass on, proclaim, publish, report
▷ To communicate in writing is to **correspond**. To communicate face to face is to **confer**, **converse**, or **discuss things**.
to communicate with *The police communicated with each other by radio.*
▸ get in touch with, make contact with, speak to, talk to

communication *NOUN*
Human beings have various methods of communication.
▸ communicating, contacting one another, understanding one another
VARIOUS KINDS OF SPOKEN COMMUNICATION
chatting, conversation, dialogue, gossip, message, rumour, telephone conversation
VARIOUS KINDS OF WRITTEN COMMUNICATION
cable, correspondence, greetings card, letter, note, postcard, telegram, text
VARIOUS OFFICIAL COMMUNICATIONS
announcement, bulletin, communiqué, dispatch, memo or memorandum, news flash, notice, proclamation, statement
VARIOUS ELECTRONIC COMMUNICATIONS
computer network, email, fax, Internet, satellite, telecommunications, text
THE MEDIA OR MASS MEDIA
advertising, broadcasting, cable television, newspapers, the press, radio, television

communicative *ADJECTIVE*
He's not very communicative, so it's hard to know what he's thinking.
▸ chatty, frank, open, talkative
AN OPPOSITE IS secretive

community *NOUN*
▷ A community sharing a home and way of life is a **commune**. A community sharing a home in Israel is a **kibbutz**.

compact *ADJECTIVE*
The computer is light and compact.
▸ portable, small
AN OPPOSITE IS large

companion *NOUN*
I'm glad I had a companion on the long journey to London.
▸ comrade, friend, (*informal*) mate, partner

company *NOUN*
1 *We enjoy other people's company.*
▸ companionship, fellowship, friendship, society
2 *My cousin works for a clothing company.*
▸ business, concern, establishment, firm, organization

comparable *ADJECTIVE*
I think your work is comparable to hers.
▸ equivalent, similar
AN OPPOSITE IS different (from)

compare *VERB*
Compare these sets of figures.
▸ match up, relate, set side by side
▹ When you compare things which are obviously different, you **contrast** them.
to compare with *We can't expect our young team to compare with theirs.*
▸ compete with, equal, match, resemble, rival

comparison *NOUN*
1 *That's an unfair comparison—we are amateurs and they are professionals.*
▸ analogy, parallel
2 *There's no comparison between their team and ours.*
▸ likeness, match, resemblance, similarity

compartment *NOUN*
Dad's toolbox has compartments for different tools.
▸ division, section, space

compassion *NOUN*
He was filled with compassion when he saw the famine victims.
▸ feeling, love, pity, sympathy, tenderness

compatible *ADJECTIVE*
1 *They discovered they weren't really compatible.*
▸ well suited
2 *We bought a new computer and a compatible printer.*
▸ matching
AN OPPOSITE IS incompatible

compel *VERB*
You can't compel me to come with you.
▸ force, make

compensate *VERB*
When I broke our neighbours' window, I had to compensate them for the damage.
▸ pay back, pay compensation to, repay

compensation *NOUN*
How much compensation did she get for the accident?
▸ damages, payment, repayment

compère *NOUN*
The compère introduced the next act.
▸ announcer, presenter
▹ A compère on a pop music programme is a **disc jockey** or **DJ**.

compete *VERB*
I'm competing in the next event.
▸ be a contestant, enter, participate, perform, take part
to compete against *We have to compete against a strong team this week.*
▸ contend with, oppose, play against

competent *ADJECTIVE*
1 *Dad wants a competent builder to build our extension.*
▸ able, accomplished, capable, efficient, experienced, expert, proficient, qualified, skilful, skilled, trained
2 *She said that my work was competent, but not brilliant.*
▸ acceptable, adequate, satisfactory
AN OPPOSITE IS incompetent

competition *NOUN*
VARIOUS KINDS OF COMPETITION
championship, contest, game, knock-out competition, match, quiz, race, rally, series, tournament, trial
SEE ALSO **sport**

competitive *ADJECTIVE*
We played in a competitive spirit.
▸ keen, lively, sporting
AN OPPOSITE IS cooperative

competitor *NOUN*
All the competitors paraded round the stadium.
▸ challenger, contender, contestant, opponent, participant, rival
▹ People who take part in an exam are **candidates** or **entrants**.

compile *VERB*
I compiled an anthology of poems about animals.
▸ assemble, collect, edit, gather together, put together

complacent *ADJECTIVE*
You can't be complacent until the job is finished.
▸ contented, pleased with yourself, self-satisfied, smug
AN OPPOSITE IS anxious

A B C D E F G H I J K L M N O P Q R S T U V W X Y Z

complain *VERB*
Don't take any notice of her—she always complains.
▸ find fault, fuss, grouse, grumble, moan, protest
to complain about *In the café, she started to complain about the food.*
▸ criticize, find fault with, object to
AN OPPOSITE IS praise

complaint *NOUN*
1 *If you have a complaint about the food, tell the manager.*
▸ criticism, grievance, objection
2 *Sore throats are a common complaint in winter.*
▸ ailment, disease, illness, infection, sickness, (*informal*) upset

complete *ADJECTIVE*
1 *Is this the complete set?*
▸ comprehensive, entire, full, intact, whole
AN OPPOSITE IS incomplete
2 *I can sit down now that my jobs are complete.*
▸ accomplished, completed, concluded, ended, finished
AN OPPOSITE IS unfinished
3 *My attempt to bake a cake was complete disaster.*
▸ absolute, downright, perfect, (*informal*) proper, pure, sheer, thorough, total, utter

complete *VERB*
She's just completed her first novel.
▸ carry out, conclude, end, finish

complex *ADJECTIVE*
Servicing an aircraft is a complex task.
▸ complicated, detailed, difficult, elaborate, (*informal*) fiddly, intricate, involved
AN OPPOSITE IS simple

complexion *NOUN*
A healthy diet is the secret of a good complexion.
▸ skin
WORDS TO DESCRIBE DIFFERENT KINDS OF COMPLEXION
clear, dark, fair, freckled, pale, pasty, ruddy, sickly, spotty, swarthy, tanned, weather-beaten

complicated *ADJECTIVE*
His ideas were too complicated for me to understand.
▸ complex, detailed, difficult, elaborate, intricate, involved, sophisticated
AN OPPOSITE IS simple

complication *NOUN*
I thought the job would be easy, but there was a complication.
▸ difficulty, problem, snag

complimentary *ADJECTIVE*
It's nice to get complimentary remarks.
▸ admiring, appreciative, approving, favourable
▹ If complimentary remarks are not deserved, they are **flattering**.
AN OPPOSITE IS critical or insulting

compliments *PLURAL NOUN*
It was nice to get compliments about my cooking.
▸ appreciation, approval, congratulations, praise, tribute
▹ Compliments which you don't deserve are **flattery**.
AN OPPOSITE IS insults

component *NOUN*
The factory made components for cars.
▸ bit, part, piece, spare, spare part

compose *VERB*
Beethoven composed nine symphonies.
▸ create, devise, make up, produce, think up, write
to be composed of *Mosaic is composed of small bits of stone and glass.*
▸ be made of, comprise, consist of

composition *NOUN*
We played a composition written by our teacher.
▸ piece, work
FOR VARIOUS KINDS OF COMPOSITION SEE **music**

compound *NOUN*
▹ A compound of substances is a **blend**, **fusion**, or **synthesis**. A compound of metals is an **alloy**.

comprehend *VERB*
She just couldn't comprehend what had happened.
▸ appreciate, figure out, follow, grasp, perceive, realize, understand

comprehensive *ADJECTIVE*
She gave us a comprehensive account of her travels.
▸ complete, detailed, encyclopedic, extensive, full, inclusive, thorough
AN OPPOSITE IS selective

compress *VERB*
I tried to compress all my clothes into one bag.
▸ cram, crush, flatten, jam, press, squash, squeeze, stuff

comprise *VERB*
The class comprised children from many different backgrounds.
▸ be composed of, consist of, contain, include

compromise *VERB*
The two sides agreed to compromise.
▸ make concessions, meet halfway, strike a balance

compulsory *ADJECTIVE*
The wearing of seat belts is compulsory.
▸ necessary, obligatory, required
AN OPPOSITE IS optional

compute *VERB*
I computed how much the project would cost.
▸ calculate, estimate, figure out, reckon, work out

computer *NOUN*
SOME KINDS OF COMPUTER
laptop, mainframe, micro or microcomputer, minicomputer, palmtop, PC or personal computer, word processor
THINGS YOU CAN DO ON A COMPUTER
calculating, data processing, desktop publishing, formatting, information retrieval, playing games, printing, producing spreadsheets, programming, storing information, word processing
SOME PARTS OF A COMPUTER SYSTEM
CD ROM drive, chip, disk drive, hard disk, interface, joystick, keyboard, microchip, microprocessor, modem, monitor, mouse, printer, processor, silicon chip, terminal, VDU
OTHER TERMS USED IN COMPUTING
bit, bug, byte, cursor, data, database, digital, diskette, floppy disk, hard copy, hardware, memory, menu, network, peripheral, printout, program, software, virus, window

comrade *NOUN*
The soldiers carried their injured comrades to safety.
▸ companion, friend, mate, partner

concave *ADJECTIVE*
AN OPPOSITE IS convex

conceal *VERB*
1 *The dog tried to conceal its bone.*
▸ bury, cover up, hide
2 *We tried to conceal our hiding place.*
▸ camouflage, disguise, make invisible, mask, screen
3 *Don't conceal the truth.*
▸ hush up, keep quiet about, keep secret, suppress

conceit *NOUN*
The conceit of that woman is ridiculous.
▸ arrogance, pride, vanity

conceited *ADJECTIVE*
He was so conceited when he won first prize!
▸ arrogant, (*informal*) big-headed, boastful, (*informal*) cocky, proud, self-satisfied, vain
AN OPPOSITE IS modest

conceive *VERB*
1 *Who conceived this silly plan?*
▸ devise, (*informal*) dream up, invent, make up, originate, plan, produce, think up, work out
2 *I could not conceive how the plan would work.*
▸ imagine, see

concentrate *VERB*
1 *Please try to concentrate and avoid mistakes.*
▸ apply yourself, be attentive, think hard, work hard
2 *The crowds concentrated in the middle of town.*
▸ collect, converge, gather

concentrated *ADJECTIVE*
This bottle contains concentrated fruit juice.
▸ condensed, strong, undiluted
AN OPPOSITE IS diluted

concept *NOUN*
I find the concept of aliens invading Earth hard to believe.
▸ idea, notion, thought

A B C D E F G H I J K L M N O P Q R S T U V W X Y Z

conception *NOUN*
1 *She has no conception of how difficult it is.*
▸ comprehension, concept, idea, inkling, notion, understanding
2 *It takes nine months from the conception of a baby to its birth.*
▸ conceiving

concern *VERB*
1 *Road safety concerns us all.*
▸ affect, be important to, be relevant to, involve, matter to, relate to
2 *It concerns me that we are destroying the rain forests.*
▸ bother, distress, trouble, upset, worry

concern *NOUN*
1 *My private life is no concern of theirs.*
▸ affair, business
2 *Global warming is a great concern to us all.*
▸ anxiety, fear, worry
3 *She's the head of a business concern.*
▸ company, enterprise, establishment, firm

concerning *PREPOSITION*
The head spoke to me concerning my future.
▸ about, regarding, relating to, relevant to, with reference to

concert *NOUN*
FOR VARIOUS ENTERTAINMENTS SEE **entertainment**

concession *NOUN*
If you are under 16, you get a concession on bus fares.
▸ allowance, reduction

concise *ADJECTIVE*
I gave the police a concise account of what happened.
▸ brief, condensed, short
▹ A concise account of something is a **précis** or **summary**.
AN OPPOSITE IS long

conclude *VERB*
1 *We concluded the Christmas concert with carols.*
▸ complete, end, finish, round off, wind up
2 *Our concert concluded with some carols.*
▸ close, culminate, terminate
3 *They concluded that he was guilty.*
▸ assume, decide, deduce, gather, infer, suppose

conclusion *NOUN*
1 *At the conclusion of the concert, everyone joined in the carols.*
▸ close, completion, culmination, end, finale, finish
2 *Now that you've heard the evidence, what is your conclusion?*
▸ decision, deduction, judgement, opinion, verdict

concrete *ADJECTIVE*
We need some concrete evidence.
▸ actual, definite, factual, firm, objective, physical, real, solid, substantial
AN OPPOSITE IS abstract

condemn *VERB*
1 *We condemn people who behave violently.*
▸ criticize, denounce, deplore, disapprove of, reproach
AN OPPOSITE IS praise
2 *The judge condemned him to death.*
▸ sentence
AN OPPOSITE IS acquit

condensation *NOUN*
I wiped the condensation off the windows.
▸ mist, steam

condense *VERB*
1 *Can you condense your story so that it fits on one page?*
▸ compress, reduce, shorten, summarize
AN OPPOSITE IS expand
2 *Steam condenses on a cold window.*
▸ become liquid, form condensation
AN OPPOSITE IS evaporate

condition *NOUN*
1 *Is your bike in good condition?*
▸ order, state
2 *A dog needs exercise to stay in good condition.*
▸ fitness, health, shape
3 *It's a condition of membership that you pay a subscription.*
▸ obligation, requirement, term
on condition that *You can come on condition that you pay your own fare.*
▸ only if, provided or providing that

conduct *VERB*
1 *A guide conducted us round the museum.*
▸ accompany, escort, guide, lead, take
2 *We asked the head to conduct our meeting.*
▸ administer, control, handle, lead, manage, organize, preside over, run, supervise
▹ To conduct an orchestra is to **direct** it.
to conduct yourself *Didn't we conduct ourselves well!*
▸ act, behave, carry on

conduct *NOUN*
Our teacher congratulated us on our good conduct.
▸ attitude, behaviour, manners

confer *VERB*
1 *The mayor conferred the freedom of the city on the victorious team.*
▸ award (to), give (to), grant (to), present (to)
2 *He conferred with his advisors before making a decision.*
▸ compare notes, consult, converse, discuss things, exchange ideas, have a discussion, talk things over

conference *NOUN*
The firm's managers had to go to a conference.
▸ consultation, discussion, meeting
SEE ALSO **meeting**

confess *VERB*
She confessed her guilt to the police.
▸ acknowledge, admit, own up to, reveal

confession *NOUN*
I was surprised by his confession that he was guilty.
▸ acknowledgement, admission, disclosure

confide *VERB*
to confide in *If you confide in me, I won't tell anyone.*
▸ open your heart to, tell secrets to

confidence *NOUN*
1 *We can face the future with confidence.*
▸ faith, hope, optimism
AN OPPOSITE IS doubt
2 *I wish I had her confidence.*
▸ assurance, boldness, conviction, firmness, self-confidence
confidence trick *He got the money with a confidence trick.*
▸ deception, fraud, hoax, swindle, trick
to have confidence in *I have confidence in her ability to succeed.*
▸ believe in, rely on, trust

confident *ADJECTIVE*
1 *I am confident that we will win.*
▸ certain, optimistic, positive, sure
AN OPPOSITE IS doubtful
2 *She is a confident sort of person.*
▸ assertive, bold, fearless, self-confident, unafraid

confidential *ADJECTIVE*
The details of the plan are confidential.
▸ private, secret
AN OPPOSITE IS public

confine *VERB*
1 *They confined their discussion to official matters.*
▸ limit, restrict
2 *The police confined our supporters at one end of the ground.*
▸ coop up, enclose, fence in, hem in, isolate, shut in, surround

confirm *VERB*
1 *The strange events confirmed his belief in ghosts.*
▸ back up, justify, prove, reinforce, support
AN OPPOSITE IS disprove
2 *I wrote to confirm my order.*
▸ make official, verify
AN OPPOSITE IS cancel

confiscate *VERB*
The police confiscated his air gun.
▸ seize, take away, take possession of

conflict *NOUN*
There's a lot of conflict in their family.
▸ antagonism, disagreement, fighting, friction, hostility, opposition, quarrelling, strife, unrest
SEE ALSO **fight** *NOUN*

conflict *VERB*
to conflict with *Her account of what happened conflicts with mine.*
▸ clash with, contradict, contrast with, differ from, disagree with
conflicting *You and I hold conflicting opinions on the subject.*
▸ contradictory, contrasting, different, incompatible, opposite

conform *VERB*
to conform to or **with** *The club expels anyone who doesn't conform with the rules.*
▸ abide by, agree with, fit in with, follow, keep to, obey, submit to
AN OPPOSITE IS disobey

confront *VERB*
I decided to confront her and ask her why she insulted me.
▸ challenge, face up to, stand up to
AN OPPOSITE IS avoid

A B C D E F G H I J K L M N O P Q R S T U V W X Y Z

confuse *VERB*
1 *Complicated rules confuse people.*
▸ baffle, bewilder, mystify, perplex, puzzle
2 *You must be confusing me with someone else.*
▸ mix up, muddle

confusion *NOUN*
1 *There was great confusion when the lights went out.*
▸ bedlam, chaos, commotion, fuss, hullabaloo, pandemonium, turmoil, uproar
2 *I saw the confusion on their faces.*
▸ bewilderment, perplexity, puzzlement

congested *ADJECTIVE*
The roads are congested during the rush hour.
▸ blocked, clogged, crowded, full, jammed, obstructed, (*informal*) snarled up
AN OPPOSITE IS clear

congratulate *VERB*
We congratulated the winners.
▸ applaud, compliment, praise
AN OPPOSITE IS criticize

connect *VERB*
1 *What's the best way to connect these wires?*
▸ attach, couple, fasten, fix together, join, link, tie together
AN OPPOSITE IS separate
2 *There was evidence connecting him with the crime.*
▸ associate, make a connection between, relate

connection *NOUN*
There is definitely a connection between smoking and cancer.
▸ association, link, relationship

conquer *VERB*
1 *They thought they could conquer their enemies if they fought one more battle.*
▸ beat, crush, defeat, get the better of, overcome, overwhelm, rout, thrash, vanquish
2 *Gaul was conquered by Julius Caesar.*
▸ capture, occupy, possess, seize, take, win
3 *Hillary conquered Everest in 1953.*
▸ climb, reach the top of

conqueror *NOUN*
Cheering crowds greeted the conquerors.
▸ victor

conquest *NOUN*
The book gave an account of the Norman conquest of Britain.
▸ invasion, occupation

conscience *NOUN*
Would your conscience allow you to kill?
▸ morals, principles, sense of right and wrong

conscientious *ADJECTIVE*
He's a conscientious worker.
▸ attentive, careful, dependable, dutiful, hard working, meticulous, painstaking, reliable, responsible, thorough
AN OPPOSITE IS careless

conscious *ADJECTIVE*
1 *In spite of the knock on his head, he remained conscious.*
▸ alert, awake, aware
AN OPPOSITE IS unconscious
2 *She made a conscious effort to improve her work.*
▸ deliberate, intentional, planned
AN OPPOSITE IS accidental

consecutive *ADJECTIVE*
She was away for three consecutive days.
▸ continuous, running (say *three days running*), successive

consent *VERB*
to consent to *She consented to my request.*
▸ agree to, approve of, authorize, grant
AN OPPOSITE IS refuse

consequence *NOUN*
1 *She did it without thinking of the consequences.*
▸ effect, outcome, result, sequel, upshot
2 *The loss of one penny is of no consequence.*
▸ importance, significance

conservation *NOUN*
The conservation of the environment is important to us all.
▸ maintenance, preservation, protection
AN OPPOSITE IS destruction

conservative *ADJECTIVE*
1 *He's conservative about what he eats.*
▸ conventional, narrow-minded, old-fashioned, reactionary, traditional, unadventurous
AN OPPOSITE IS progressive
2 *At a conservative estimate, the repairs will cost £100.*
▸ cautious, moderate, reasonable
AN OPPOSITE IS extreme

conserve *VERB*
We should conserve natural resources.
▸ be economical with, look after, preserve, protect, save, use wisely
AN OPPOSITE IS waste

consider *VERB*
1 *I considered the problem carefully.*
▸ contemplate, examine, meditate about, ponder on, reflect on, study, think about, weigh up
2 *I consider this to be very important.*
▸ believe, judge, reckon

considerable *ADJECTIVE*
We need a considerable amount of rain to fill the reservoirs.
▸ big, large, respectable, significant, sizeable, substantial
AN OPPOSITE IS negligible

considerate *ADJECTIVE*
It was considerate of you to lend her your umbrella.
▸ caring, charitable, helpful, kind, kind-hearted, neighbourly, obliging, sympathetic, thoughtful, unselfish
AN OPPOSITE IS selfish

consideration *NOUN*
1 *Thank you for your consideration.*
▸ help, kindness, sympathy, thoughtfulness, unselfishness
2 *After careful consideration, I decided not to go on the trip.*
▸ reflection, thought

consist *VERB*
to consist of 1 *The country consists largely of mountains.*
▸ be composed of, be made of, comprise, contain, include, incorporate
2 *Her job consists mostly of meeting people.*
▸ involve

consistent *ADJECTIVE*
1 *These plants need to be kept at a consistent temperature.*
▸ constant, regular, stable, steady, unchanging
2 *Fortunately, our goalkeeper is a consistent player.*
▸ dependable, predictable, reliable
AN OPPOSITE IS inconsistent

consolation *NOUN*
When you're depressed, you need some consolation.
▸ comfort, relief, support, sympathy

console *VERB*
He did his best to console me when my dog died.
▸ comfort, soothe, support, sympathize with

conspicuous *ADJECTIVE*
1 *The church spire is a conspicuous landmark.*
▸ eye-catching, notable, obvious, prominent, unmistakable, visible
2 *I had made some conspicuous mistakes.*
▸ clear, evident, glaring, noticeable, obvious
AN OPPOSITE IS inconspicuous

conspiracy *NOUN*
Guy Fawkes was involved in a conspiracy to blow up Parliament.
▸ plot, scheme

conspire *VERB*
The men conspired to cheat their employer.
▸ intrigue, plot, scheme

constant *ADJECTIVE*
1 *There is a constant noise of traffic on the motorway.*
▸ ceaseless, continual, continuous, endless, incessant, never-ending, non-stop, permanent, perpetual, persistent, relentless, steady, unending, uninterrupted
AN OPPOSITE IS changeable
2 *He has been my constant friend for many years.*
▸ dependable, devoted, faithful, firm, loyal, reliable, true, trustworthy
AN OPPOSITE IS unreliable

constitute *VERB*
In soccer, eleven players constitute a team.
▸ compose, comprise, form, make up

construct *VERB*
We constructed a shelter in the back garden.
▸ assemble, build, erect, fit together, make, put together, put up, set up
AN OPPOSITE IS demolish

A B C D E F G H I J K L M N O P Q R S T U V W X Y Z

construction *NOUN*
1 *The construction of the shelter took an hour.*
▸ assembly, building, erecting, erection, setting-up
2 *The shelter was a flimsy construction.*
▸ building, structure

constructive *ADJECTIVE*
Does anyone have any constructive suggestions?
▸ creative, helpful, positive, practical, useful, valuable, worthwhile
AN OPPOSITE IS useless

consult *VERB*
1 *If you are ill, consult the doctor.*
▸ ask, confer with, discuss things with, get advice from, speak to
2 *If you don't know how to spell a word, consult your dictionary.*
▸ refer to

consume *VERB*
1 *Our guests consumed all the food in ten minutes!*
▸ devour, gobble up, guzzle
SEE ALSO **drink, eat**
2 *The ship consumed a great deal of fuel.*
▸ use up
3 *The building was consumed by fire.*
▸ destroy

consumer *NOUN*
Shops try to give consumers what they want.
▸ buyer, customer, shopper

contact *VERB*
I'll contact you when I have some news.
▸ call, call on, communicate with, correspond with, get in touch with, notify, phone, ring, speak to, talk to, write to

contagious *ADJECTIVE*
Mumps is a very contagious disease.
▸ catching, infectious

contain *VERB*
1 *This box contains various odds and ends.*
▸ hold
2 *A dictionary contains words and definitions.*
▸ comprise, consist of, include, incorporate

container *NOUN*
SOME CONTAINERS FOR DRINKS
beaker, bottle, can, cup, decanter, flask, glass, goblet, mug, tankard, teapot, thermos, tumbler, urn, vacuum flask, wineglass
SOME CONTAINERS USED IN COOKING
billycan, bowl, casserole, cauldron, dish, jug, kettle, pan, pot, saucepan, teapot
OTHER CONTAINERS FOR LIQUIDS
barrel, basin, bath, bucket, butt, cask, churn, cistern, decanter, dish, drum, jar, keg, pail, pitcher, tank, test tube, tin, trough, tub, vase, vat, vessel, water-butt, watering can
CONTAINERS FOR NON-LIQUIDS
bag, basket, bin, box, briefcase, caddy, canister, carton, cartridge, case, casket, chest, coffer, coffin, crate, drum, dustbin, envelope, hamper, handbag, haversack, hod, holdall, knapsack, money box, pannier, pocket, pouch, punnet, purse, receptacle, rucksack, sachet, sack, satchel, scuttle, skip, suitcase, tea chest, tin, trunk, wallet

contaminate *VERB*
Chemicals contaminated the water.
▸ infect, poison, pollute
AN OPPOSITE IS purify

contemplate *VERB*
1 *She sat on the bed, contemplating herself in the mirror.*
▸ gaze at, look at, observe, stare at, survey, view, watch
2 *We contemplated what to do next.*
▸ consider, meditate about, ponder, reflect on, study, think about, weigh up
3 *I contemplate taking a holiday soon.*
▸ intend, plan, propose

contemporary *ADJECTIVE*
The two senses of *contemporary* are very different. Sense 1 describes things that belong to the same time as each other, whereas sense 2 describes things belonging to our own time
1 *The coronation of Elizabeth II and the first conquest of Mount Everest were contemporary events.*
▸ simultaneous
2 *Do you like contemporary music?*
▸ current, fashionable, the latest, modern, the newest, (*informal*) trendy, up-to-date

contempt *NOUN*
His contempt for her was quite obvious.
▸ disgust, dislike (of), hatred (of), loathing, low opinion (of), scorn
AN OPPOSITE IS admiration

contemptible *ADJECTIVE*
Mugging is a contemptible crime.
▸ despicable, detestable, disgraceful, hateful, loathsome, mean, shameful, wretched
AN OPPOSITE IS admirable

contemptuous *ADJECTIVE*
He gave a contemptuous sneer.
▸ arrogant, disrespectful, haughty, insolent, insulting, jeering, scornful, sneering
AN OPPOSITE IS admiring

contend *VERB*
I contend that I was right.
▸ argue, assert, claim, declare, maintain
to contend with **1** *They had to contend with strong opposition.*
▸ compete with, fight against, grapple with, oppose, strive against, struggle against
2 *Among other things, we had bad weather to contend with.*
▸ cope with, deal with, face, put up with

content *NOUN*
Skimmed milk has a low fat content.
▸ element, ingredient, part

content *ADJECTIVE*
Are you content to let me do it?
▸ happy, willing
AN OPPOSITE IS unwilling
SEE ALSO **contented**

contented *ADJECTIVE*
After a big dinner, he looked very contented.
▸ comfortable, (*uncomplimentary*) complacent, content, fulfilled, happy, peaceful, pleased, relaxed, satisfied, serene, tranquil, untroubled, well fed
AN OPPOSITE IS discontented

contentment *NOUN*
There was a smile of contentment on his face.
▸ comfort, contentedness, happiness, relaxation, satisfaction, serenity, tranquillity, well-being
AN OPPOSITE IS discontent

contest *NOUN*
It was an exciting contest between two excellent players.
▸ bout, challenge, competition, encounter, fight, game, match, struggle, tournament

contest *VERB*
Several players contested the referee's decision.
▸ argue against, challenge, disagree with, oppose, quarrel with, question

contestant *NOUN*
The contestants in the competition were evenly matched.
▸ competitor, contender, participant, player

continual *ADJECTIVE*
I get sick of their continual arguing.
▸ constant, eternal, frequent, perpetual, persistent, recurrent, repeated, unending
AN OPPOSITE IS occasional
SEE ALSO **continuous**

continue *VERB*
1 *They continued the search until it got dark.*
▸ keep up, persevere with, prolong, pursue, (*informal*) stick at, sustain
2 *This rain can't continue for long.*
▸ carry on, go on, keep on, last, linger, persist
3 *We'll continue our work after lunch.*
▸ proceed with, resume

continuous *ADJECTIVE*
We had continuous rain all through our holiday.
▸ ceaseless, everlasting, incessant, never-ending, non-stop, unbroken, unceasing, uninterrupted
SEE ALSO **continual**
▹ An illness which continues for a long time is a chronic illness.
AN OPPOSITE IS intermittent or occasional

contract *NOUN*
The builder's contract says that they will finish the work this month.
▸ agreement, deal, undertaking
▹ A contract to rent a house is a lease. A contract between two countries is an alliance or treaty. A contract to end a dispute about money is a settlement.

contract *VERB*
1 *Most substances contract when they get colder.*
▸ become smaller, reduce, shrink

a b c d e f g h i j k l m n o p q r s t u v w x y z

A B C D E F G H I J K L M N O P Q R S T U V W X Y Z

AN OPPOSITE IS expand
2 *A local firm contracted to build our extension.*
▸ agree, arrange, sign an agreement, undertake
3 *She contracted a mysterious illness.*
▸ become infected by, catch, develop, get

contradict *VERB*
I didn't dare to contradict her.
▸ challenge, disagree with, speak against

contradictory *ADJECTIVE*
My brother and I have contradictory opinions about eating meat.
▸ conflicting, contrary, converse, different, incompatible, opposite
AN OPPOSITE IS similar

contraption *NOUN*
Dad's got a weird contraption for sweeping up dead leaves.
▸ apparatus, contrivance, device, gadget, invention, machine, mechanism

contrary *ADJECTIVE*
1 *During the discussion, two contrary views were expressed.*
▸ contradictory, conflicting, converse, different, opposite
AN OPPOSITE IS similar
2 *She's a sulky, contrary child.*
▸ awkward, defiant, difficult, disobedient, obstinate, perverse, rebellious, stubborn, uncooperative, unhelpful, wilful
AN OPPOSITE IS cooperative

contrast *VERB*
1 *The teacher contrasted the work of the two students.*
▸ compare, emphasize differences between, make a distinction between
2 *His painting contrasts with mine.*
▸ clash, differ (from)

contrast *NOUN*
She pointed out the contrast between my work and his.
▸ difference, distinction, opposition
AN OPPOSITE IS similarity

contribute *VERB*
Will you contribute something to our charity collection?
▸ donate, give, provide
▹ If you contribute regularly to something, you **subscribe** to it.

to contribute to *Good weather contributed to our enjoyment.*
▸ add to, encourage, help

contribution *NOUN*
I gave a contribution to the local animal shelter.
▸ donation, gift
▹ A regular contribution to something is a **subscription**. An official contribution to the work of a charity is a **grant**. A contribution to a collection in church is an **offering**.

contributor *NOUN*
1 *We have some generous contributors in our fund.*
▸ benefactor, donor, patron, supporter
▹ A business which contributes to a charity is a **sponsor**. A person who contributes regularly is a **subscriber**.
2 *She is a regular contributor to the local paper.*
▸ correspondent, journalist, reporter, writer

contrive *VERB*
He contrived a way to do it.
▸ create, invent, make up, plan, think up

control *NOUN*
1 *A teacher needs to have control in the classroom.*
▸ authority, discipline, power
2 *Control of what happens in school is the job of the head teacher.*
▸ administration, command, direction, government, management, organization, supervision
to be in control of SEE **control** *VERB*

control *VERB*
1 *The government controls the country's affairs.*
▸ administer, be in charge of, be in control of, command, conduct, deal with, direct, govern, guide, look after, regulate, rule, run, superintend, supervise
2 *Can't you control that dog?*
▸ handle, manage, restrain
3 *They built a dam to control the floods.*
▸ check, contain, curb, hold back

controversial *ADJECTIVE*
The referee's decision to award a penalty was controversial.
▸ debatable, questionable

controversy *NOUN*
There is much controversy about the building of a bypass.
▸ argument, debate, disagreement, dispute, quarrelling

convalescent *ADJECTIVE*
My aunt is convalescent after an operation.
▸ getting better, improving, making progress, (*informal*) on the mend, recovering

convenient *ADJECTIVE*
1 *Is there a convenient place to put my umbrella?*
▸ accessible, appropriate, available, nearby, suitable
AN OPPOSITE IS inconvenient
2 *Dad has a convenient tool for tightening screws.*
▸ handy, helpful, labour-saving, neat, useful

convention *NOUN*
Shaking hands is a social convention.
▸ custom, tradition

conventional *ADJECTIVE*
He taught me the conventional way to say hullo in French.
▸ accepted, common, customary, everyday, habitual, normal, ordinary, orthodox, regular, routine, standard, traditional, usual
AN OPPOSITE IS unconventional

converge *VERB*
Motorways converge in one mile.
▸ coincide, combine, come together, join, meet, merge
AN OPPOSITE IS divide

conversation *NOUN*
▹ An informal conversation is a chat or gossip. A more formal conversation is a discussion. A very formal conversation is a conference. Conversation in a play or novel is dialogue.

converse *VERB*
We conversed happily for several minutes.
▸ chat, engage in conversation, have a conversation, talk
FOR DIFFERENT WAYS TO TALK SEE **talk** *VERB*

converse *NOUN*
I thought she hated me, but apparently the converse is true.
▸ opposite, reverse

conversion *NOUN*
The conversion of the house into flats has created extra accommodation for students.
▸ adaptation, alteration, changing, converting, transformation

convert *VERB*
1 *We are going to convert our attic into a games room.*
▸ adapt, alter, change, transform
2 *I never used to like football, but my cousin converted me.*
▸ change someone's mind, convince, persuade, reform, win over

convex *ADJECTIVE*
AN OPPOSITE IS concave

convey *VERB*
1 *The breakdown truck conveyed our car to a garage.*
▸ bear, bring, carry, deliver, move, take, transfer, transport
▹ To convey something by sea is to ferry or ship it.
2 *What does his message convey to you?*
▸ communicate, indicate, mean, reveal, signify, tell

convict *NOUN*
Two escaped convicts kidnapped them at gunpoint.
▸ criminal, prisoner

convict *VERB*
The burglar was convicted and sent to prison.
▸ condemn, declare guilty, prove guilty, sentence
AN OPPOSITE IS acquit

conviction *NOUN*
1 *He spoke with conviction.*
▸ assurance, certainty, confidence, firmness
2 *She has strong religious convictions.*
▸ belief, faith, opinion, principle, view

convince *VERB*
He convinced them that he was innocent.
▸ persuade, prove to someone, satisfy

convoy *NOUN*
A convoy of ships passed along the horizon.
▸ armada, fleet, group

cook *VERB*
▷ To cook food for guests or customers is to **cater** for them. Cooking as a business is **catering**. The art or skill of cooking is **cookery**.
VARIOUS WAYS TO COOK FOOD
bake, barbecue, boil, braise, brew, broil, casserole, fry, grill, poach, roast, sauté, simmer, steam, stew, toast
OTHER THINGS YOU DO WHEN YOU ARE COOKING
baste, blend, chop, grate, freeze, infuse, knead, liquidize, marinade, mix, peel, sieve, sift, stir, whisk
THINGS YOU MIGHT USE WHEN YOU ARE COOKING
baking tin, barbecue, basin, blender, bowl, breadboard, breadknife, carving knife, casserole, cauldron, chip pan, chopping board, colander, deep fat fryer, dish, food processor, frying pan, grill, hotplate, jug, kettle, ladle, liquidizer, microwave, mincer, mixer, oven, pan, pepper mill, plate, pot, pressure cooker, rolling pin, rôtisserie, salt cellar, saucepan, scales, skewer, spatula, spit, strainer, timer, tin opener, toaster, whisk, wok, wooden spoon
SEE ALSO **crockery**, **cutlery**, **kitchen**

cook *NOUN*
▷ The chief cook in a restaurant or hotel is the **chef**. A person who cooks food as a business is a **caterer**.

cool *ADJECTIVE*
1 *The weather is cool for the time of year.*
▸ chilly, coldish
AN OPPOSITE IS hot
2 *Would you like a cool drink?*
▸ chilled, iced, refreshing
AN OPPOSITE IS hot
3 *She remained cool when everyone else panicked.*
▸ calm, level-headed, patient, relaxed, sensible, unexcitable, unflustered
AN OPPOSITE IS frantic
4 *I was rather cool when she asked me to go out with her.*
▸ cold, distant, half-hearted, indifferent, lukewarm, unenthusiastic
AN OPPOSITE IS enthusiastic
5 (*informal*) *He thinks it's cool to wear sunglasses.*
▸ chic, fashionable, smart, (*informal*) trendy

cooperate *VERB*
We need everyone to cooperate on this job.
▸ assist each other, collaborate, combine, get together, help each other, join forces, support each other, work as a team, work together

cooperation *NOUN*
1 *The teacher was impressed by our cooperation.*
▸ collaboration, teamwork
2 *I could do this job quicker if I had your cooperation.*
▸ assistance, help, support

cooperative *ADJECTIVE*
As everyone was cooperative, we finished early.
▸ constructive, friendly, helpful, obliging, supportive, united, working as a team
AN OPPOSITE IS uncooperative

cope *VERB*
Shall I help you, or can you cope on your own?
▸ carry on, get by, make do, manage, survive
to cope with *She coped with her problems cheerfully.*
▸ deal with, handle, manage

copy *NOUN*
1 *She asked me to make a copy of the article.*
▸ carbon copy, duplicate, photocopy
2 *That isn't the original painting — it's a copy.*
▸ replica, reproduction
▷ A copy made to deceive someone is a **fake** or a **forgery**. A person who looks almost the same as a brother or sister born at the same time is a **twin**. A living organism which is identical to another is a **clone**.

copy *VERB*
1 *I copied the article for you.*
▸ duplicate, photocopy, reproduce, write out
2 *It's illegal to copy banknotes.*
▸ fake, forge
3 *She copied my ideas!*
▸ crib, make use of
4 *My parrot can copy my voice.*
▸ imitate, impersonate, mimic

core *NOUN*
It's very hot in the core of the earth.
▸ centre, heart, inside, middle

corn *NOUN*
Corn is one of the most important crops farmers grow.
▸ grain
VARIOUS KINDS OF CORN
barley, corn on the cob or maize or sweetcorn, oats, rye, wheat

corner *NOUN*
1 *I'll meet you at the corner of the road.*
▸ crossroads, intersection, junction, turn, turning
▹ The place where two lines meet is an **angle**.
2 *I sat in a quiet corner and read her letter.*
▸ alcove, hiding place, recess

corner *VERB*
After a chase, the police cornered him.
▸ capture, catch, trap

corpse *NOUN*
The corpse of the badger was hidden by the bushes.
▸ body, carcass, remains

correct *ADJECTIVE*
1 *Your answers are all correct.*
▸ accurate, exact, faultless, right
2 *I hope he has given us correct information.*
▸ authentic, factual, genuine, precise, reliable, true
3 *What's the correct procedure?*
▸ acceptable, appropriate, proper, regular, suitable
AN OPPOSITE IS wrong

correct *VERB*
1 *Shall I correct my mistakes?*
▸ alter, put right
2 *The optician says glasses will correct my eyesight.*
▸ cure, improve, make better
3 *He spent the day correcting exam papers.*
▸ mark

correspond *VERB*
to correspond with **1** *I didn't expect her version of the story to correspond with mine.*
▸ agree with, be consistent with, be similar to, coincide with, match, tally with
2 *I correspond with a girl in Paris.*
▸ communicate with, send letters to, write to

correspondence *NOUN*
VARIOUS KINDS OF CORRESPONDENCE
e-mail, fax, letter, memorandum or memo, message, note, postcard

corrode *VERB*
Some acids may corrode metal.
▸ eat away, rot, rust

corrupt *ADJECTIVE*
1 *His corrupt behaviour disgusted everyone.*
▸ evil, immoral, improper, perverted, sinful, wicked
2 *Corrupt officials had accepted millions of pounds in bribes.*
▸ criminal, crooked, dishonest, untrustworthy
AN OPPOSITE IS honest

cosmetics *PLURAL NOUN*
▸ make-up
SOME COSMETICS
blusher, body lotion, cleanser, deodorant, eyeliner, eyeshadow, face cream, lipstick, mascara, moisturizer, nail varnish, perfume, powder, scent, talc or talcum powder, toner

cost *VERB*
How much would this watch cost?
▸ be worth, go for, sell for

cost *NOUN*
The bill shows the total cost.
▸ amount, charge, expenditure, expense, payment, price
▹ The cost of travelling on public transport is the **fare**.

costly *ADJECTIVE*
It would be too costly to repair the car.
▸ dear, expensive
AN OPPOSITE IS cheap

costume *NOUN*
The Chinese women were wearing national costumes.
▸ outfit, set of clothes, set of garments, suit
▹ A costume you dress up in for a party is **fancy dress**. A set of clothes worn by soldiers, members of an organization, etc., is a **uniform**.
SEE ALSO **clothes**

cosy *ADJECTIVE*
It's nice to feel cosy in bed when it's cold and wet outside.
▸ comfortable, relaxed, secure, snug, soft, warm
AN OPPOSITE IS uncomfortable

couch *NOUN*
He lay on the couch watching TV all afternoon.
▸ settee, sofa
SEE ALSO **bed**, **seat**

counsel *VERB*
He was in so much trouble that they asked a social worker to counsel him.
▸ advise, give help to, guide

count *VERB*
1 *I began to count the cost of our holiday.*
▸ add up, calculate, compute, estimate, figure out, reckon, total, work out
2 *It's playing well that counts, not winning.*
▸ be important, matter
to count on *You can count on me to support you.*
▸ bank on, believe in, depend on, have faith in, rely on, trust

countenance *NOUN*
The clown had a sad countenance.
▸ appearance, expression, face, features, look

counterfeit *ADJECTIVE*
The police are on the lookout for counterfeit works of art.
▸ bogus, copied, fake, false, forged, imitation, sham
AN OPPOSITE IS genuine

countless *ADJECTIVE*
There's a countless number of stars in the sky.
▸ endless, infinite, innumerable, numerous, untold
AN OPPOSITE IS finite

country *NOUN*
1 *Delegates from all the European countries came to the conference.*
▸ land, nation, people, state, territory
▹ A country ruled by a king or queen is a kingdom, monarchy, or realm. A country governed by leaders elected by the people is a democracy. A democratic country with a President is a republic. A country governed by one person with unlimited power is a dictatorship. A group of countries ruled by one person is an empire. A group of countries cooperating together is a commonwealth.
2 *There is some very mountainous country in Norway.*
▸ countryside, landscape, scenery

couple *VERB*
The two train carriages were coupled together.
▸ connect, fasten, hitch, join, link

coupling *NOUN*
We made sure that the coupling was secure.
▸ connection, fastening, link

coupon *NOUN*
If you save ten coupons you get a free mug.
▸ ticket, token, voucher

courage *NOUN*
You need courage to be a firefighter.
▸ boldness, bravery, determination, fearlessness, grit, (*informal*) guts, heroism, nerve, pluck, valour
AN OPPOSITE IS cowardice

courageous *ADJECTIVE*
Although it was a frightening experience they were very courageous.
▸ bold, brave, daring, determined, fearless, gallant, heroic, intrepid, plucky, resolute, unafraid, valiant
AN OPPOSITE IS cowardly

courier *NOUN*
1 *A courier delivered the package.*
▸ carrier, messenger
2 *The courier showed us to our hotel.*
▸ guide

course *NOUN*
1 *The ship's course was to the west.*
▸ direction, passage, path, progress, route, way
2 *In the normal course of events we have lunch at one o'clock.*
▸ development, programme, progression, sequence, succession
of course *Of course you can come with us.*
▸ certainly, definitely, naturally, undoubtedly

court *NOUN*
If you commit a crime, you are taken to court.
▹ A court which deals with minor cases is a magistrate's court. A court which deals with important cases is the High Court. A court

which tries members of the armed services is a court martial. An inquiry into the cause of someone's death is an inquest. An inquest is held at a coroner's court.

courteous *ADJECTIVE*
I received a courteous reply to my letter.
▸ civil, considerate, friendly, helpful, polite, respectful, well-mannered
AN OPPOSITE IS rude

cover *VERB*
1 *A coat of paint will cover the graffiti.*
▸ blot out, camouflage, conceal, disguise, hide, mask, obscure
2 *She covered her face with her hands.*
▸ protect, screen, shade, shield, veil
3 *The hikers are hoping to cover twenty-five miles a day.*
▸ progress, travel
4 *An encyclopedia covers many subjects.*
▸ contain, deal with, include, incorporate
5 *Will £10 cover your expenses?*
▸ be enough for, pay for

cover *NOUN*
1 *The cover of the book was torn.*
▸ wrapper
▹ A cover for a letter is an envelope. A cover to keep papers in is a file or folder.
2 *On the bare hillside, there was no cover from the storm.*
▸ hiding place, refuge, sanctuary, shelter
3 *A helicopter gave them cover from the air.*
▸ protection, support

covering *NOUN*
There was a light covering of snow on the hills.
▸ blanket, cap, carpet, coating, film, layer, sheet, skin, veil

cowardly *ADJECTIVE*
It was cowardly to run away.
▸ faint-hearted, timid, unheroic, (*informal*) yellow
SEE ALSO **afraid**
AN OPPOSITE IS brave

coy *ADJECTIVE*
She gave him a coy smile.
▸ bashful, modest, reserved, self-conscious, shy, timid
AN OPPOSITE IS bold

crack *NOUN*
1 *There's a crack in this cup.*
▸ break, chink, chip, flaw, fracture, split
2 *He climbed into a crack between two rocks.*
▸ cranny, crevice, gap, opening, rift
3 *They heard the crack of a pistol shot.*
FOR VARIOUS WAYS TO MAKE SOUNDS SEE **sound** *VERB*
4 *She gave him a crack on the head.*
▸ blow, knock, whack
FOR OTHER WAYS OF HITTING SEE **hit** *VERB*

crack *VERB*
He cracked a bone in his foot.
▸ chip, fracture
FOR OTHER WAYS TO DAMAGE THINGS SEE **damage**

craft *NOUN*
1 *I admire the carpenter's craft.*
▸ art, expertise, handicraft, skill, technique
FOR VARIOUS ARTS AND CRAFTS SEE **art**
2 *All sorts of craft were in the harbour.*
▸ boats, ships, vessels
FOR VARIOUS BOATS AND SAILING CRAFT SEE **vessel**
3 *He got his own way by craft rather than by honest means.*
▸ cunning, deceit, deviousness, trickery

crafty *ADJECTIVE*
A crafty look came into his eyes.
▸ artful, cunning, deceitful, devious, scheming, sly, sneaky, tricky, wily
AN OPPOSITE IS straightforward

cram *VERB*
1 *We can't cram any more people in—the car is full.*
▸ compress, crush, force, jam, pack, squeeze
2 *She's cramming for a biology exam.*
▸ revise, study, (*informal*) swot

cramped *ADJECTIVE*
The classroom is very cramped.
▸ crowded, restricted, tight, uncomfortable
AN OPPOSITE IS roomy

cranky *ADJECTIVE*
I thought he was a bit cranky until I got to know him.
▸ abnormal, crazy, eccentric, odd, peculiar, strange, weird
AN OPPOSITE IS normal

cranny *NOUN*
The spider crawled into a cranny in the wall.
▸ crack, crevice, gap, hole, opening, rift, split

crash *NOUN*
1 *I heard a loud crash from the kitchen.*
▸ bang, smash

FOR OTHER WAYS TO MAKE SOUNDS SEE **sound** *VERB*
2 *We saw a nasty crash on the motorway.*
▶ accident, bump, collision, smash
▷ A crash involving a lot of vehicles is a **pile-up**. A train crash may involve a **derailment**.

crash *VERB*
1 *The car crashed into the barrier.*
▶ bump, collide, knock, smash
2 *The dishes crashed to the floor.*
▶ fall, plunge, topple

crate *NOUN*
We packed our belongings in crates.
▶ box, case, chest, packing case

crater *NOUN*
The explosion left a crater in the ground.
▶ abyss, cavity, chasm, hole, opening, pit

crawl *VERB*
I had to crawl along a narrow ledge.
▶ creep, edge, move slowly

craze *NOUN*
It's the latest teenage dance craze.
▶ cult, enthusiasm, fad, fashion, obsession, passion, trend

crazy *ADJECTIVE*
1 *The dog went crazy when it was stung by a wasp.*
▶ berserk, delirious, frantic, frenzied, hysterical, insane, mad, wild
2 *That was a crazy idea!*
▶ absurd, daft, eccentric, farcical, idiotic, ludicrous, ridiculous, senseless, silly, stupid
AN OPPOSITE IS sensible

creamy *ADJECTIVE*
Mix the ingredients together until they form a creamy liquid.
▶ rich, smooth, thick, velvety

crease *NOUN*
I need to iron the creases out of this shirt.
▶ fold, furrow, groove, line, wrinkle
▷ A crease made deliberately in a skirt, etc., is a **pleat**.

crease *VERB*
Pack the clothes carefully, so you don't crease them.
▶ crinkle, crumple, crush, wrinkle

create *VERB*
1 *We were creating a dreadful noise.*
▶ cause, make, produce
2 *The government plans to create more jobs for young people.*
▶ bring about, bring into existence, make, originate, set up, start up
YOU CREATE THINGS IN VARIOUS WAYS
▷ You **write** a poem or story. You **compose** music. You **draw** or **paint** a picture. You **carve** a statue. You **invent** or **think up** a new idea. You **design** a new product. You **devise** a plan. You **found** a new club or organization. You **manufacture** goods. You **generate** electricity. You **build** or **construct** a model or a building.
AN OPPOSITE IS destroy

creation *NOUN*
1 *We don't know much about the creation of life on earth.*
▶ beginning, birth, generation, initiation, origin
2 *Our class helped with the creation of a nature reserve.*
▶ building, construction, establishing, foundation
3 *This recipe for ice cream is my own creation.*
▶ concept, invention

creative *ADJECTIVE*
She's a very creative person.
▶ artistic, imaginative, inspired, inventive, original
AN OPPOSITE IS unimaginative

creator *NOUN*
Disney was the creator of the Mickey Mouse films.
▶ deviser, inventor, maker, originator, producer
▷ The creator of a design is an **architect** or **designer**. The creator of a novel or story is an **author** or **writer**. The creator of a piece of music is a **composer**. The creator of a work of art is an **artist**. The creator of a picture is a **painter** or **photographer**. The creator of a statue is a **sculptor**. The creator of beautiful furniture, etc., is a **craftsman** or **craftswoman**. The creator of goods for sale, etc., is a **manufacturer**.

creature *NOUN*
We should treat all living creatures with respect.
▶ animal, beast, being
SEE ALSO **animal**, **bird**, **fish**, **insect**, **reptile**

credible *ADJECTIVE*
I didn't find his story credible.
▶ believable, convincing, likely, persuasive, possible, reasonable, trustworthy
AN OPPOSITE IS incredible

credit *NOUN*
Her success brought credit to the school.
▶ approval, distinction, fame, glory, good reputation, honour, praise
AN OPPOSITE IS dishonour

credit *VERB*
1 *You won't credit her far-fetched story.*
▶ accept, believe, have faith in, trust
AN OPPOSITE IS doubt
2 *The bank credited £10 to my account.*
▶ add

creditable *ADJECTIVE*
The head said that we gave a creditable performance.
▶ admirable, commendable, excellent, good, praiseworthy, respectable, worthy
AN OPPOSITE IS worthless

creed *NOUN*
Students of all races and creeds attend the college.
▶ doctrine, faith, religion, set of beliefs

creep *VERB*
1 *I watched the lizard creep back into its hiding place.*
▶ crawl, edge, move slowly, slither, wriggle
2 *I had to creep out without waking the others.*
▶ move quietly, slink, slip, sneak, steal, tiptoe

creepy *ADJECTIVE*
The creepy noises made me a bit nervous.
▶ eerie, ghostly, (*informal*) scary, sinister, (*informal*) spooky, uncanny, unearthly, weird

crest *NOUN*
1 *The bird had a large red crest on its head.*
▶ comb, plume, tuft
2 *When we got to the crest of the hill, there was a wonderful view.*
▶ brow, crown, head, peak, summit, top

crevice *NOUN*
Plants grew in the crevices in the rock.
▶ crack, cranny, gap, opening, rift, split
▷ A deep crack in a glacier is a **crevasse**.

crew *NOUN*
FOR WORDS FOR GROUPS OF PEOPLE SEE **group** *NOUN*

crib *VERB*
He was caught cribbing in a test.
▶ cheat, copy

cricket *NOUN*
WORDS FOR PEOPLE PLAYING CRICKET
batsman, bowler, cricketer, fielder or fieldsman, wicketkeeper
▷ A person who makes sure players keep to the rules in cricket is an **umpire**.
SOME POSITIONS OF FIELDERS IN CRICKET
cover, fine leg, gulley, long-off, long-on, mid-off, mid-on, mid-wicket, point, slip, square leg, third man
SOME OTHER TERMS USED IN CRICKET
bail, boundary, crease, innings, maiden over, over, pad, run, stump, wicket

crime *NOUN*
1 *Crime is a big problem in modern society.*
▶ delinquency, dishonesty, lawbreaking, wrongdoing
2 *The law punishes anyone who commits a crime.*
▶ offence
VARIOUS CRIMES
abduction, arson, blackmail, burglary, extortion, hijacking, kidnapping, manslaughter, mugging, murder, pilfering, poaching, rape, robbery, shoplifting, smuggling, stealing, theft, vandalism
PEOPLE WHO COMMIT VARIOUS CRIMES
assassin, bandit, blackmailer, brigand, burglar, gangster, gunman, highwayman, hijacker, hooligan, kidnapper, mugger, murderer, outlaw, pickpocket, pirate, poacher, rapist, robber, shoplifter, smuggler, swindler, terrorist, thief, thug, vandal

criminal *NOUN*
These men are dangerous criminals.
▶ (*informal*) crook, delinquent, lawbreaker, offender, wrongdoer
▷ A criminal who has been sent to prison is a **convict**.
SEE ALSO **crime**

A B C D E F G H I J K L M N O P Q R S T U V W X Y Z

criminal *ADJECTIVE*
He was involved in criminal activities for years before he was caught.
▸ (*informal*) bent, corrupt, (*informal*) crooked, dishonest, illegal, unlawful, wrong
AN OPPOSITE IS honest

cripple *VERB*
1 *Will the accident cripple him permanently?*
▸ disable, handicap, maim
▹ If you are crippled, you may be lame or handicapped.
2 *The ship was crippled in the storm.*
▸ damage, immobilize, put out of action
▹ To cripple a machine or vehicle deliberately is to sabotage it.

crisis *NOUN*
We had a crisis when we found a gas leak.
▸ dangerous situation, emergency, problem

crisp *ADJECTIVE*
1 *Fry the bacon until it's crisp.*
▸ brittle, crunchy
AN OPPOSITE IS soft
2 *It was a crisp winter morning.*
▸ cold, fresh, frosty

critical *ADJECTIVE*
1 *The head made some critical comments about our behaviour.*
▸ negative, uncomplimentary, unfavourable
AN OPPOSITE IS complimentary
2 *Tomorrow's game will be critical in deciding whether the team stays in the league.*
▸ crucial, decisive, important, serious, vital
AN OPPOSITE IS unimportant

criticism *NOUN*
1 *I think his criticism was unfair.*
▸ attack, disapproval, reprimand, reproach
2 *We had to write a criticism of a favourite TV programme.*
▸ analysis, assessment, review

criticize *VERB*
She criticized us for being so careless.
▸ blame, condemn, disapprove of, find fault with, reprimand, reproach, scold
AN OPPOSITE IS praise

crockery *NOUN*
Please put the crockery away.
▸ china, dishes
VARIOUS ITEMS OF CROCKERY
basin, bowl, coffee cup, coffee pot, cup, dinner plate, dish, jug, milk jug, mug, plate, pot, sauceboat, saucer, serving dish, side plate, soup bowl, sugar bowl, teacup, teapot, tureen

crook *NOUN* (*informal*)
The crooks got away with the money.
▸ criminal, delinquent, lawbreaker, offender, wrongdoer

crooked *ADJECTIVE*
1 *I wonder why this tree grew into that crooked shape?*
▸ bent, deformed, twisted, zigzag
AN OPPOSITE IS straight
2 (*informal*) *He ran a crooked business, but the police caught him.*
▸ (*informal*) bent, corrupt, criminal, dishonest, illegal, unlawful
AN OPPOSITE IS honest

crop *NOUN*
We had a good crop of apples this year.
▸ harvest, yield

crop *VERB*
1 *The sheep were cropping the grass.*
▸ bite off, browse on, eat, graze on, nibble at
2 *I asked the hairdresser to crop my hair short.*
▸ clip, cut, snip, trim
to crop up *Several problems have cropped up.*
▸ appear, arise, come up, emerge, happen, occur, turn up

cross *VERB*
1 *Can you see the place on the map where two roads cross?*
▸ criss-cross, intersect
2 *Look out for the place where the road crosses the river.*
▸ go across, pass over, span
VARIOUS PLACES WHERE YOU CAN CROSS
bridge, causeway, flyover, ford, level crossing, overpass, pedestrian crossing, pelican crossing, subway, stepping stones, underpass, viaduct, zebra crossing
to cross something out I crossed out my name because I can't play this week.
c cancel, delete

cross *ADJECTIVE*
She's often cross when she comes in from work.
► angry, annoyed, bad-tempered, grumpy, ill-tempered, irritable, short-tempered, vexed
AN OPPOSITE IS even-tempered

cross-examine *VERB*
The lawyer began to cross-examine the witness.
► examine, interrogate, question

crossroads *NOUN*
Take great care at the crossroads.
► intersection, junction
▷ A junction of two motorways is an **interchange**.

crouch *VERB*
We crouched in the bushes.
► bend down, duck, squat, stoop

crowd *NOUN*
1 *A crowd of people waited outside the theatre.*
► assembly, bunch, cluster, company, crush, gathering, group, horde, mob, multitude, swarm, throng
SEE ALSO **group** *NOUN*
2 *The crowd at Saturday's game beat all attendance records.*
► audience, gate, spectators

crowd *VERB*
1 *People crowded on the pavement to watch the procession go past.*
► assemble, flock, gather, muster
2 *They crowded us into a small room.*
► bundle, cram, crush, herd, jam, pack, pile, push, squeeze

crowded *ADJECTIVE*
The shops are crowded at Christmas time.
► congested, full, jammed, overflowing, packed, swarming, teeming
AN OPPOSITE IS empty

crucial *ADJECTIVE*
The negotiations were at a crucial stage.
► critical, decisive, important, momentous, serious
AN OPPOSITE IS unimportant

crude *ADJECTIVE*
1 *Crude oil is taken to a refinery for processing.*
► natural, raw, unprocessed, unrefined
AN OPPOSITE IS refined
2 *I nailed together some planks to make a crude table.*
► clumsy, makeshift, primitive, rough
AN OPPOSITE IS skilful
3 *The teacher told them to stop using crude language.*
► coarse, dirty, foul, impolite, indecent, obscene, rude, smutty, vulgar
AN OPPOSITE IS polite

cruel *ADJECTIVE*
1 *I think hunting is a cruel way to kill animals.*
► atrocious, barbaric, barbarous, beastly, bloodthirsty, brutal, callous, heartless, inhuman, sadistic, savage, uncivilized
2 *He's a very cruel man.*
► diabolical, fiendish, fierce, hard, harsh, malevolent, merciless, pitiless, remorseless, ruthless, sadistic, stern, tyrannical, unjust, unkind, vicious, violent
AN OPPOSITE IS kind

crumb *NOUN*
I put out some crumbs of bread for the birds.
► bit, fragment, morsel, scrap

crumble *VERB*
1 *He crumbled the cake onto his plate.*
► break up, crush
2 *The rotten wood began crumble.*
► decay, decompose, disintegrate
▷ When rubber decays, it **perishes**.

crumpled *ADJECTIVE*
Your shirt is crumpled.
► creased, crinkled, crushed, wrinkled

crunch *VERB*
The dog crunched up a bone.
► chew, crush, grind, munch, smash

crusade *NOUN*
The local health centre started a crusade against drugs.
► campaign, movement, war

crush *VERB*
1 *I crushed my finger in the door.*
► bruise, crunch, damage, injure, mangle, squeeze
▷ To crush something into a soft mess is to

mash, pulp, or squash it. To crush something into a powder is to grind or pulverize it. To crush something out of shape is to crumple or smash it.
2 *We crushed our opponents.*
▸ conquer, defeat, humiliate, overcome, overwhelm, rout, (*informal*) thrash, vanquish

crush *NOUN*
I couldn't fight my way through the crush.
▸ congestion, crowd, jam, throng

cry *VERB* This word is often overused.
1 *She cried out for help.*
▸ bawl, bellow, call, exclaim, roar, scream, screech, shout, shriek, yell, yelp
2 *It was so sad I began to cry.*
▸ shed tears, snivel, sob, weep

cry *NOUN*
I heard a cry of pain.
▸ bellow, call, exclamation, howl, roar, scream, screech, shout, shriek, yell, yelp

cuddle *VERB*
She cuddled the baby.
▸ caress, clasp, embrace, hold closely, hug, nestle against, snuggle against

cue *NOUN*
Don't miss your cue to speak.
▸ reminder, sign, signal

culminate *VERB*
The gala culminated in a firework display.
▸ build up (to), finish, reach a climax, terminate

culprit *NOUN*
Police are searching for the culprits.
▸ criminal, delinquent, offender, troublemaker, wrongdoer

cult *NOUN*
1 *They were members of a religious cult.*
▸ group, sect
2 *The series has become a bit of a cult in Britain.*
▸ craze, fad, fashion, obsession

cultivate *VERB*
1 *They cleared more forests so they could cultivate the land.*
VARIOUS THINGS YOU DO TO CULTIVATE LAND
dig, fertilize, hoe, irrigate, manure, mulch, plough, prepare, rake, till, turn, work
THINGS YOU DO TO CULTIVATE PLANTS
feed, plant out, sow, take cuttings, tend, water
VARIOUS ASPECTS OF WORKING ON THE LAND
agriculture, farming, forestry, gardening, horticulture
2 *We want to cultivate good relations with our neighbours.*
▸ develop, encourage, further, improve, promote, try to achieve

cultivated *ADJECTIVE*
She has a cultivated way of speaking.
▸ civilized, cultured, educated, polite, (*informal*) posh, well educated
AN OPPOSITE IS vulgar

cultural *ADJECTIVE*
The festival included sporting and cultural events.
▸ artistic, educational, intellectual

culture *NOUN*
I watched a programme about the culture of ancient Greece.
▸ art, civilization, customs, learning, traditions

cultured *ADJECTIVE*
He's a cultured man with many interests.
▸ artistic, civilized, cultivated, knowledgeable, scholarly, sophisticated, well educated, well read
AN OPPOSITE IS ignorant

cunning *ADJECTIVE*
She worked out a cunning plan to get her own way.
▸ artful, clever, crafty, deceitful, devious, (*informal*) dodgy, ingenious, scheming, sly, (*informal*) sneaky, tricky, wily

cup *NOUN*
VARIOUS THINGS TO DRINK FROM
beaker, bowl, chalice, glass, goblet, mug, tankard, teacup, tumbler, wineglass
▹ A cup awarded as a prize is a trophy.

cupboard *NOUN*
Put the crockery in the cupboard.
▸ cabinet, dresser, sideboard
▹ A cupboard for food is a larder.
SEE ALSO **furniture**

curb *VERB*
You must try to curb your anger.
▸ check, control, hold back, limit, moderate, repress, restrain, restrict, suppress
AN OPPOSITE IS encourage

cure *VERB*
1 *These pills will cure your headache.*
▸ ease, heal, help, improve, make better, relieve
AN OPPOSITE IS aggravate
2 *The mechanics cured the problem with the car's steering.*
▸ correct, (*informal*) fix, mend, put an end to, put right, repair, stop

cure *NOUN*
I wish they could find a cure for colds.
▸ antidote, medicine, remedy, therapy, treatment

curiosity *NOUN*
I couldn't restrain my curiosity.
▸ inquisitiveness, interest, (*informal*) nosiness, prying

curious *ADJECTIVE*
1 *He's always curious about other people's private affairs.*
▸ inquiring, inquisitive, interested (in), (*informal*) nosy
2 *What is that curious smell?*
▸ abnormal, extraordinary, funny, mysterious, odd, peculiar, puzzling, queer, strange, unusual, weird

curl *VERB*
The snake curled itself round a branch.
▸ coil, loop, turn, twist, wind
FOR VARIOUS CURLED SHAPES SEE **curve**

curly *ADJECTIVE*
My hair's straight, but Mum's is curly.
▸ curled, curling, frizzy, kinky, permed, wavy
AN OPPOSITE IS straight

current *NOUN*
The boat drifted along with the current.
▸ flow, stream, tide
▷ A current of air is a draught or wind.

current *ADJECTIVE*
1 *My brother knows all about the current fashions in music.*
▸ contemporary, modern, prevailing, prevalent, (*informal*) trendy, up-to-date
AN OPPOSITE IS old-fashioned
2 *Have you got a current passport?*
▸ usable, valid
AN OPPOSITE IS out-of-date
3 *Who is the current prime minister?*
▸ existing, present

curriculum *NOUN*
Our teacher explained the curriculum which we have to study.
▸ course, programme of study, syllabus

curse *NOUN*
When he hit his finger, he let out a curse.
▸ oath, swearword
▷ Curses which use sacred words are blasphemy. A curse which uses rude words is an obscenity.

curse *VERB*
He cursed when he hit his finger.
▸ blaspheme, swear, utter curses

curve *NOUN*
VARIOUS CURVED SHAPES
arc, arch, bend, bow, bulge, camber, circle, coil, corkscrew, crescent, curl, loop, meander, scroll, spiral, swirl, turn, twist, wave
ADJECTIVES TO DESCRIBE VARIOUS CURVED SHAPES
arched, bent, bowed, bulging, cambered, coiled, concave, convex, crescent, crooked, curled, curving, curvy, looped, meandering, rounded, serpentine, snaking, spiral, twisted, undulating, winding

cushion *VERB*
They put mattresses on the ground to cushion his fall.
▸ protect you from, reduce the effect of, soften

custom *NOUN*
1 *It's our custom to give presents at Christmas.*
▸ convention, fashion, habit, routine, tradition, way
2 *The shop offers a discount to attract custom.*
▸ business, buyers, customers, trade

customary *ADJECTIVE*
It's the customary thing to shake hands when you meet someone.
▸ common, conventional, everyday, expected, habitual, normal, ordinary, prevailing, prevalent, regular, routine, traditional, usual
AN OPPOSITE IS unusual

customer *NOUN*
There was a queue of customers at the checkout.
▸ buyer, shopper

cut *VERB*
1 *She cut the apple in half.*
VARIOUS WAYS TO CUT THINGS
axe, carve, chip, chisel, chop, cleave, clip, gash, hack, hew, nick, notch, saw, slash, slice, slit, snick, snip, split, stab
▷ To cut off a limb is to **amputate** or **sever** it. To cut down a tree is to **fell** it. To cut branches off a tree is to **lop** them. To cut twigs off a growing plant is to **prune** it. To cut hair off your face or head is to **shave** it. To cut wool off a sheep is to **shear** it. To cut grass is to **mow** it. To cut corn is to **harvest** or **reap** it. To cut unwanted bits off something is to **trim** it. If you trim paper with a special machine you **guillotine** it. To cut food into small pieces is to **grate**, **mince**, or **shred** it. To cut something up to examine it is to **dissect** it. To cut stone, etc., to make a statue is to **carve** it. To cut an inscription in stone, etc., is to **engrave** it.
TOOLS YOU CAN USE TO CUT THINGS
axe, carving knife, chisel, chopper, cleaver, clippers, grater, guillotine, knife, mincer, mower, razor, saw, scalpel, scissors, scythe, secateurs, shears
2 *You need to cut your essay — it's too long.*
▸ condense, edit, shorten
▷ To cut parts out of a story or film because they offend people is to **censor** it.
3 *His salary was cut by 10%.*
▸ decrease, lower, reduce
▷ If you cut something by half, you **halve** it.

cut *NOUN*
1 *The nurse tried to stop the cut from bleeding.*
▸ gash, graze, injury, nick, slash, wound
2 *There's often a cut in the price of fruit in summer.*
▸ decrease, fall, reduction

cutlery *NOUN*
VARIOUS ITEMS OF CUTLERY
breadknife, butter knife, carving knife, cheese knife, dessert spoon, fish fork, fish knife, fork, knife, ladle, salad server, spoon, steak knife, tablespoon, teaspoon

cycle *NOUN*
SEE **bicycle**

cynical *ADJECTIVE*
She's cynical about whether the volunteers really intend to help.
▸ doubtful, negative, pessimistic, sceptical
AN OPPOSITE IS optimistic

Dd

daily *ADJECTIVE*
Sadly, road accidents are a daily occurrence.
▸ everyday, regular
AN OPPOSITE IS infrequent or irregular

dainty *ADJECTIVE*
The baby was wearing dainty little shoes.
▸ charming, delicate, exquisite, fine
AN OPPOSITE IS clumsy

dam *NOUN*
The dam across the river controls the flow of water.
▸ barrage, barrier, dike, weir

dam *VERB*
They plan to dam the river and create a new reservoir.
▸ block, check, hold back

damage *VERB*
I trust you not to damage the things you borrowed.
▸ harm, spoil
VARIOUS WAYS TO DAMAGE THINGS
break, buckle, burst, chip, crack, crumple, deface, fracture, mark, scar, scratch, smash, strain, weaken
▷ To damage something beyond repair is to **destroy**, **ruin**, or **wreck** it. To damage something deliberately is to **sabotage** or **vandalize** it.

damp *ADJECTIVE*
1 *Don't wear those clothes if they are damp.*
▸ clammy, moist
2 *I don't like this damp weather.*
▸ drizzly, foggy, misty, rainy, wet
▷ Weather which is both damp and warm is **humid** or **muggy** weather.
AN OPPOSITE IS dry

dampen *VERB*
1 *Just dampen the flap of the envelope and seal it.*
▸ moisten, wet
2 *Nothing could dampen her enthusiasm.*
▸ make less, reduce

dance *VERB*
I could have danced for joy.
▸ caper, cavort, frisk, frolic, gambol, hop about, jig about, jump about, leap, prance, skip, whirl
DIFFERENT KINDS OF DANCING
ballet, ballroom dancing, barn dancing, break-dancing, country dancing, disco dancing, folk dancing, Latin American dancing, line dancing, old-time dancing, tap-dancing
SOME BALLROOM DANCES
foxtrot, minuet, polka, quickstep, tango, waltz
SOME TRADITIONAL DANCES
hornpipe, Highland fling, jig, morris dancing, quadrille, reel, square dancing
SOME DANCES ASSOCIATED WITH PARTICULAR NATIONS
bolero, cancan, flamenco, limbo dancing, mazurka, polonaise, rumba, tarantella
GATHERINGS WHERE PEOPLE DANCE
ball, (*Scottish & Irish*) ceilidh, disco, party

danger *NOUN*
1 *Who knows what dangers lie ahead?*
▸ crisis, hazard, menace, peril, pitfall, threat, trap
AN OPPOSITE IS safety
2 *The forecast says there's a danger of frost.*
▸ chance, possibility, risk

dangerous *ADJECTIVE*
1 *We were in a dangerous situation.*
▸ alarming, hazardous, menacing, perilous, precarious, risky, unsafe
2 *The police arrested him for dangerous driving.*
▸ careless, reckless
3 *A dangerous criminal had escaped from prison.*
▸ desperate, ruthless, treacherous, violent
4 *Lions are dangerous animals.*
▸ unpredictable, wild
5 *It's wicked to empty dangerous chemicals into the river.*
▸ deadly, harmful, poisonous, toxic
AN OPPOSITE IS harmless or safe

dangle *VERB*
There was a bunch of keys dangling from the chain.
▸ droop, flap, hang, sway, swing, trail, wave about

dappled *ADJECTIVE*
The ground under the trees is dappled with patches of sunlight.
▸ dotted, flecked, mottled, speckled, spotted, streaked

dare *VERB*
1 *I wouldn't dare to make a parachute jump.*
▸ have the courage, take the risk
2 *He dared me to jump.*
▸ challenge, defy

daring *ADJECTIVE*
It was a very daring plan.
▸ bold, brave, courageous, fearless, intrepid, plucky, valiant
AN OPPOSITE IS timid
▹ A daring person is a daredevil.

dark *ADJECTIVE*
1 *It was a very dark night.*
▸ black, gloomy, murky, pitch black, pitch dark
AN OPPOSITE IS bright
2 *She wore a dark green coat.*
AN OPPOSITE IS pale

darken *VERB*
The sky darkened.
▸ become overcast, blacken, cloud over
AN OPPOSITE IS brighten

darling *NOUN*
I love you, darling.
▸ dear, dearest, honey, love, sweetheart

dash *NOUN*
1 *When the storm broke, we made a dash for shelter.*
▸ race, run, rush, sprint
2 *I like just a dash of milk in my tea.*
▸ drop, small amount, splash, spot

dash *VERB*
1 *We dashed home because it was raining.*
▸ hasten, hurry, race, run, rush, speed, sprint, tear, zoom
2 *She dashed her cup against the wall.*
▸ hurl, knock, smash, throw

data *PLURAL NOUN*
I entered all the data into the computer.
▸ details, facts, information
▹ Data can be in the form of figures, numbers, or statistics.

date *NOUN*
I've made a date with a friend this evening.
▸ appointment, engagement, meeting

A B C D E F G H I J K L M N O P Q R S T U V W X Y Z

dawdle *VERB*
Don't dawdle — we haven't got all day!
▸ be slow, delay, hang about, lag behind, linger, loiter, straggle
AN OPPOSITE IS hurry

dawn *NOUN*
SEE **day**

day *NOUN*
1 *There are seven days in a week.*
VARIOUS TIMES OF THE DAY
dawn or daybreak or sunrise, morning, noon or midday, afternoon, evening, nightfall or sunset, dusk or twilight, night, midnight
2 *Most people are awake during the day.*
▸ daytime
AN OPPOSITE IS night
3 *Things were different in his day.*
▸ age, epoch, era, period, time

dazed *ADJECTIVE*
He had a dazed expression on his face.
▸ bewildered, confused, muddled, perplexed

dead *ADJECTIVE*
1 *A dead fish floated by the side of the river.*
▸ deceased, lifeless
▹ Instead of 'the king who has just died', we can say 'the **late** king'. Words for a dead body are **carcass** or **corpse**.
AN OPPOSITE IS alive
2 *Latin is a dead language.*
▸ extinct, obsolete
AN OPPOSITE IS living
3 *The battery was dead.*
▸ flat, not working, useless, worn out
4 *The party was dead until the conjuror arrived.*
▸ boring, dull, slow, uninteresting
AN OPPOSITE IS lively

deaden *VERB*
1 *The dentist gave me an injection to deaden the pain.*
▸ anaesthetize, lessen, reduce, suppress
AN OPPOSITE IS increase
2 *Double glazing deadens the noise of the traffic.*
▸ dampen, muffle, quieten
AN OPPOSITE IS amplify

deadly *ADJECTIVE*
He gave her a deadly dose of poison.
▸ dangerous, destructive, fatal, harmful, lethal
AN OPPOSITE IS harmless

deafening *ADJECTIVE*
We complained about the deafening noise.
▸ blaring, booming, loud, penetrating, thunderous

deal *VERB*
1 *Who is going to deal the cards?*
▸ distribute, give out, share out
2 *My uncle used to deal in second-hand cars.*
▸ do business, trade
to deal with something **1** *I can deal with this problem.*
▸ attend to, control, cope with, grapple with, handle, look after, manage, see to, solve, sort out
2 *The book deals with the history of Rome.*
▸ be concerned with, cover, explain about

deal *NOUN*
She made a deal with the garage for her new car.
▸ agreement, arrangement, bargain, contract
a good deal, a great deal *We went to a great deal of trouble to do things properly.*
▸ a large amount, a lot

dealer *NOUN*
If the goods are faulty, return them to the dealer.
▸ merchant, shopkeeper, supplier, trader, tradesman

dear *ADJECTIVE*
1 *She is a very dear friend.*
▸ beloved, close, loved, valued
AN OPPOSITE IS distant
2 *I didn't buy it because it was too dear.*
▸ costly, expensive
AN OPPOSITE IS cheap

death *NOUN*
1 *We mourned the death of our friend.*
▸ dying, end, passing
2 *The accident resulted in several deaths.*
▸ fatality

debatable *ADJECTIVE*
It's debatable who was responsible for the accident.
▸ controversial, doubtful, questionable, uncertain
AN OPPOSITE IS certain

debate *NOUN*
We had a debate about animal rights.
▸ argument, discussion, dispute
▹ Something which people argue about a lot is a **controversy**.

debate *VERB*
1 *We debated whether it is right to kill animals for food.*
▸ argue, discuss
2 *I debated what to do next.*
▸ consider, deliberate, reflect on, weigh up

debris *NOUN*
Debris from the crashed aircraft was scattered over a large area.
▸ fragments, pieces, remains, wreckage

decay *VERB*
Dead leaves fall to the ground and decay.
▸ break down, decompose, disintegrate, rot

deceit *NOUN*
I saw through his deceit.
▸ bluff, cheating, deceitfulness, deception, dishonesty, fraud, lying, pretence, trickery
AN OPPOSITE IS honesty

deceitful *ADJECTIVE*
Don't trust him — he's a deceitful person.
▸ cheating, dishonest, hypocritical, insincere, lying, (*informal*) sneaky, treacherous, two-faced, underhand
AN OPPOSITE IS honest

deceive *VERB*
He intended to deceive you from the very beginning.
▸ cheat, (*slang*) con, (*informal*) diddle, double-cross, fool, mislead, swindle, take in, trick

decent *ADJECTIVE*
1 *I did the decent thing and owned up.*
▸ honest, honourable
2 *My friend's jokes were not decent.*
▸ acceptable, appropriate, fitting, polite, proper, respectable, suitable
AN OPPOSITE IS indecent
3 *I haven't had a decent meal for ages!*
▸ agreeable, good, nice, satisfactory
AN OPPOSITE IS bad

deception *NOUN*
SEE **deceit**

deceptive *ADJECTIVE*
Appearances can be deceptive.
▸ misleading, unreliable

decide *VERB*
1 *We decided to finish our work instead of going out to play.*
▸ choose, elect, make a decision, make up your mind, opt, resolve
2 *The referee decided that the player was offside.*
▸ conclude, judge, rule
3 *The last lap decided the result of the race.*
▸ determine, settle

decision *NOUN*
1 *Can you tell me what your decision is?*
▸ choice, preference
2 *The judge announced his decision.*
▸ conclusion, findings, judgement, verdict

decisive *ADJECTIVE*
1 *A decisive piece of evidence proved that he was innocent.*
▸ convincing, crucial, definite
AN OPPOSITE IS uncertain
2 *A referee needs to be decisive.*
▸ firm, forceful, quick-thinking, resolute, strong-minded
AN OPPOSITE IS hesitant

declaration *NOUN*
The Prime Minister issued a formal declaration.
▸ announcement, proclamation, pronouncement, statement

declare *VERB*
He declared that he was innocent.
▸ announce, assert, make known, proclaim, pronounce, state, swear

decline *VERB*
1 *Our enthusiasm declined as the day went on.*
▸ decrease, diminish, dwindle, flag, lessen, tail off, wane, weaken
AN OPPOSITE IS increase
2 *Why did you decline my invitation to the party?*
▸ refuse, reject, turn down
AN OPPOSITE IS accept

decode *VERB*
The spy tried to decode the secret message.
▸ figure out, interpret, make out, solve, understand, work out

decompose *VERB*
Dead leaves fall to the ground and decompose.
▸ break down, decay, disintegrate, rot

decorate *VERB*
1 *We decorated the church with flowers.*
▸ adorn, array, beautify, festoon
▹ To decorate a dish of food is to garnish it. To decorate clothes with lace, etc., is to trim them.
2 *Dad is going to decorate my bedroom next weekend.*
▸ (*informal*) do up, paint, paper or wallpaper
3 *They decorated her for bravery.*
▸ award or give a medal to, honour, reward
THINGS USED TO DECORATE VARIOUS THINGS INCLUDE bunting, decorations, embroidery, flags, flowers, frills, lights, ornaments, pictures, plants, streamers, tinsel, trimming

decorative *ADJECTIVE*
The book had decorative designs in the margins.
▸ attractive, beautiful, colourful, elaborate, fancy, ornamental, pretty
AN OPPOSITE IS plain

decrease *VERB*
1 *We decreased speed.*
▸ cut, lower, reduce, slacken
2 *Our enthusiasm decreased as the day went on.*
▸ become less, decline, diminish, dwindle, flag, lessen, shrink, subside, tail off, wane, weaken
AN OPPOSITE IS increase

decrease *NOUN*
There has been a decrease in the bird population.
▸ cut, decline, drop, fall, reduction
AN OPPOSITE IS increase *NOUN*

decree *NOUN*
The king issued a decree that the day should be a holiday.
▸ command, declaration, order, proclamation

decree *VERB*
The government decrees what we must pay in taxes.
▸ declare, dictate, order, prescribe, proclaim, pronounce

decrepit *ADJECTIVE*
1 *Granny says she's not a decrepit old woman yet!*
▸ feeble, frail, infirm, weak, worn out
2 *His hobby is restoring decrepit old cars.*
▸ battered, broken down, derelict

dedicate *VERB*
He dedicates himself entirely to his work.
▸ commit, devote

dedicated *ADJECTIVE*
Some dedicated fans waited all day to see the pop star.
▸ committed, devoted, enthusiastic, faithful, keen, zealous

dedication *NOUN*
I admire her dedication to her work.
▸ commitment, devotion, enthusiasm (for)

deduce *VERB*
The police managed to deduce who had committed the crime.
▸ conclude, decide, draw the conclusion, guess, reason, work out

deduct *VERB*
Tax is deducted from your salary.
▸ knock off, subtract, take away
AN OPPOSITE IS add (to)

deduction *NOUN*
1 *My deduction was correct.*
▸ conclusion
In this sense, *deduction* is related to the verb *deduce*
2 *He allowed me a deduction off the full price.*
▸ discount, reduction
In this sense, *deduction* is related to the verb *deduct*

deed *NOUN*
She was given a medal for her heroic deed.
▸ achievement, act, action, effort, exploit, feat

deep *ADJECTIVE*
1 *The well was very deep.*
AN OPPOSITE IS shallow
2 *Her letter expressed her deep sympathy.*
▸ earnest, genuine, intense, sincere
AN OPPOSITE IS insincere
3 *He fell into a deep sleep.*
▸ heavy, sound
AN OPPOSITE IS light
4 *He spoke with a deep voice.*
▸ bass, low
AN OPPOSITE IS high

deer *NOUN*
DEER AND SIMILAR ANIMALS
antelope, caribou, chamois, elk, gazelle, gnu, impala, moose, red deer, reindeer, wildebeest
▷ A male deer is a buck, hart, roebuck, or stag. A female deer is a doe or hind. Deer's flesh used as food is venison.

deface *VERB*
Vandals defaced the statue.
▶ damage, mutilate, spoil, vandalize

defeat *VERB*
1 *We defeated our opponents soundly.*
▶ beat, get the better of, overcome, thrash, vanquish
▷ To defeat someone in chess is to checkmate them. To be defeated is to lose.
2 *They defeated their enemy in a bloody battle.*
▶ conquer, crush, overwhelm, rout, triumph over, win a victory over
3 *They defeated moves to build a new road.*
▶ foil, frustrate

defeat *NOUN*
They suffered a humiliating defeat.
▶ failure, humiliation, rout, (*informal*) thrashing
AN OPPOSITE IS victory

defect *NOUN*
The cars are tested for defects before they leave the factory.
▶ failure, fault, flaw, imperfection, shortcoming, weakness
▷ A defect in a computer program is a bug.

defect *VERB*
He defected to the enemy.
▶ desert, go over
▷ A person who defects to the other side is a traitor or turncoat.

defective *ADJECTIVE*
If the goods are defective, take them back to the shop.
▶ damaged, faulty, imperfect
AN OPPOSITE IS perfect

defence *NOUN*
1 *What was the accused woman's defence?*
▶ case, excuse, explanation, justification
2 *We have no defence against this illness.*
▶ guard, protection, safeguard
3 *The enemy soon broke through their defences.*
▶ barricade, fortification, rampart, shield

defend *VERB*
1 *We defended ourselves against the rival gang.*
▶ guard, keep safe, protect
AN OPPOSITE IS attack
2 *His lawyer defended him in court.*
▶ plead for, speak up for, stand up for, support
AN OPPOSITE IS accuse

defer *VERB*
She decided to defer her departure until Saturday.
▶ delay, postpone, put off

defiant *ADJECTIVE*
He didn't like her defiant attitude.
▶ aggressive, disobedient, insolent, mutinous, obstinate, quarrelsome, rebellious, stubborn, uncooperative
AN OPPOSITE IS cooperative

deficient *ADJECTIVE*
Their diet is deficient in vitamins.
▶ inadequate, insufficient, lacking, unsatisfactory, wanting
AN OPPOSITE IS adequate

defile *VERB*
He felt that the filth he lived in defiled him.
▶ contaminate, degrade, dirty, infect, make dirty, pollute, soil, tarnish

define *VERB*
A thesaurus simply lists words, while a dictionary defines them.
▶ clarify, explain, give the meaning of, interpret

definite *ADJECTIVE*
1 *Is it definite that we're going to move?*
▶ certain, fixed, settled, sure
2 *He's very definite in his opinions.*
▶ confident, decided, determined, emphatic, exact, precise, specific, unambiguous
3 *She said there were definite signs of improvement in my work.*
▶ clear, distinct, marked, noticeable, obvious, positive, pronounced, unmistakable
AN OPPOSITE IS indefinite

definitely *ADVERB*
I'll definitely come tomorrow.
▸ beyond doubt, certainly, doubtless, for certain, positively, surely, unquestionably, without doubt, without fail
AN OPPOSITE IS perhaps

definition *NOUN*
The dictionary gives definitions for most words.
▸ explanation, interpretation

deflate *VERB*
1 *Vandals deflated the tyres of her car.*
▸ let down
AN OPPOSITE IS inflate
2 *She was deflated when she came last.*
▸ depress, humble, humiliate

deflect *VERB*
I was able to deflect the blow.
▸ avert, fend off, intercept, turn aside, ward off

deformed *ADJECTIVE*
He has a deformed foot.
▸ bent, buckled, crooked, distorted, gnarled, twisted, warped

deft *ADJECTIVE*
She folded the paper with deft movements of her fingers.
▸ agile, clever, expert, nimble, proficient, quick, skilful
AN OPPOSITE IS clumsy

defy *VERB*
1 *It's not a good idea to defy the teacher.*
▸ confront, disobey, refuse to obey, resist, stand up to
AN OPPOSITE IS obey
2 *I defy you to produce evidence.*
▸ challenge, dare
3 *The jammed door defied my attempts to open it.*
▸ beat, defeat, frustrate, resist, withstand

degenerate *VERB*
The game degenerated into a series of fouls.
▸ become worse, decline, deteriorate, sink, worsen
AN OPPOSITE IS improve

degrading *ADJECTIVE*
It was a degrading experience.
▸ humiliating, shameful, undignified

degree *NOUN*
She showed a high degree of skill in shaping the clay.
▸ extent, grade, level, measure, standard

dejected *ADJECTIVE*
I felt dejected when I failed the test.
▸ depressed, desolate, discouraged, (*informal*) down, downcast, forlorn, gloomy, glum, (*informal*) low, melancholy, miserable, sad, unhappy, woeful, wretched
AN OPPOSITE IS happy

delay *VERB*
1 *Please don't let me delay you.*
▸ detain, hinder, hold up, keep waiting, make late, slow down
2 *They delayed the start of the race because of the weather.*
▸ defer, postpone, put off
3 *You'll miss the bus if you delay.*
▸ dawdle, (*informal*) hang about or around, hesitate, linger, loiter, pause, wait

delay *NOUN*
What caused the delay?
▸ hold-up, pause, wait

delete *VERB*
I deleted his name from the list.
▸ cancel, cross out, erase, remove

deliberate *ADJECTIVE*
1 *It was a deliberate insult.*
▸ calculated, conscious, intentional, planned, premeditated
AN OPPOSITE IS accidental or unintentional
2 *I walked with deliberate steps across the icy pavement.*
▸ careful, cautious, slow, unhurried
AN OPPOSITE IS hasty or careless

deliberate *VERB*
We deliberated where to go for the summer holiday.
▸ confer about, consider, debate, discuss, think carefully about, weigh up

delicacy *NOUN*
1 *We admired the delicacy of the embroidery.*
▸ daintiness, exquisiteness, fineness, precision
2 *She described the unpleasant details with great delicacy.*
▸ sensitivity, tact
3 *The table was loaded with delicacies.*
▸ speciality, treat

delicate *ADJECTIVE*
1 *Her blouse had delicate embroidery on the collar.*
▸ dainty, exquisite, intricate
2 *Take care not to damage the delicate material.*
▸ fine, flimsy, fragile, soft, thin
3 *Protect delicate plants if there's a chance of frost.*
▸ sensitive, tender
4 *He's often away from school — he has a delicate constitution.*
▸ feeble, sickly, unhealthy, weak
5 *The nurse's fingers had a delicate touch.*
▸ gentle, light, soft
6 *He discussed the matter in a delicate way.*
▸ careful, considerate, diplomatic, discreet, prudent, sensitive, tactful
7 *Can you help me with a delicate problem?*
▸ awkward, embarrassing, ticklish

delicious *ADJECTIVE*
The food was delicious.
▸ appetizing, enjoyable, (*informal*) mouth-watering, tasty
SEE ALSO **taste** *VERB*
AN OPPOSITE IS horrible

delight *NOUN*
Imagine my delight when I saw my friend again!
▸ bliss, ecstasy, enjoyment, happiness, joy, pleasure

delight *VERB*
The film's special effects delighted us.
▸ amuse, charm, divert, enchant, entertain, entrance, fascinate, please, thrill
AN OPPOSITE IS dismay

delighted *ADJECTIVE*
The delighted spectators cheered the victorious team.
▸ ecstatic, elated, exultant, joyful, happy, pleased, thrilled

delightful *ADJECTIVE*
The flower arrangements were delightful.
▸ attractive, beautiful, charming, lovely, pleasant, pleasing

delinquent *NOUN*
The police know most of the delinquents in our area.
▸ criminal, hooligan, vandal, young offender

delirious *ADJECTIVE*
The supporters were delirious with joy when we scored the winning goal.
▸ beside yourself, crazy, ecstatic, excited, frantic, frenzied, hysterical, mad, wild
AN OPPOSITE IS calm

delirium *NOUN*
In his delirium he didn't know what he was saying.
▸ excitement, fever, frenzy, hysteria, madness

deliver *VERB*
1 *How many letters does our postman deliver each day?*
▸ bring, convey, distribute, hand over, present, supply, take round
2 *The head delivered a lecture on good behaviour.*
▸ give, make, read out

delude *VERB*
He deluded us into thinking he could do real magic.
▸ bluff, (*slang*) con, deceive, fool, hoax, mislead, trick

deluge *NOUN*
The crops were ruined in the deluge.
▸ downpour, flood, inundation, rainstorm

deluge *VERB*
They deluged me with questions.
▸ overwhelm, swamp

delusion *NOUN*
His belief that he ruled the world was a delusion.
▸ dream, fantasy, self-deception

demand *VERB*
1 *I demand a refund!*
▸ call for, claim, insist on, require, want
2 *'What do you want?' she demanded.*
▸ ask, enquire, inquire

demand *NOUN*
The manager agreed to the workers' demands.
▸ claim, request, requirement

demanding *ADJECTIVE*
1 *My baby sister is very demanding.*
▸ difficult, impatient, insistent, selfish
AN OPPOSITE IS patient
2 *He has a very demanding job.*
▸ challenging, difficult, exhausting
AN OPPOSITE IS easy

A B C D E F G H I J K L M N O P Q R S T U V W X Y Z

democratic *ADJECTIVE*
Britain has a democratic government.
▸ elected

demolish *VERB*
They will have to demolish several buildings to make way for the new road.
▸ bulldoze, destroy, dismantle, flatten, knock down, level, pull down, tear down
AN OPPOSITE IS build

demonstrate *VERB*
1 *The teacher demonstrated how warm air rises.*
▸ explain, illustrate, show
2 *People were so angry about the heavy lorries that they decided to demonstrate in the street.*
▸ march, parade, protest

demonstration *NOUN*
1 *She gave a demonstration of what the new computer could do.*
▸ display, presentation, show
2 *Everyone joined the demonstration against the heavy lorries.*
▸ (*informal*) demo, march, parade, protest, rally

demote *VERB*
At the end of the season, the team was demoted to a lower division.
▸ put down, relegate
AN OPPOSITE IS promote

den *NOUN*
We built a den in the garden.
▸ hideout, hiding place, secret place, shelter
▹ The den of a wild animal is its lair.

denote *VERB*
What does this symbol denote?
▸ be a sign for, express, indicate, mean, signify, stand for

denounce *VERB*
1 *She denounced cruelty to animals.*
▸ complain about, condemn, deplore, speak against
2 *Even his friends denounced him as a traitor.*
▸ accuse, blame, complain about, condemn, inform against, report, reveal
AN OPPOSITE IS praise

dense *ADJECTIVE*
1 *The accident happened in dense fog.*
▸ heavy, thick
2 *A dense crowd waited in the square.*
▸ compact, packed, solid
3 (*insulting*) *You are dense today!*
▸ SEE **stupid**

dent *NOUN*
There was a large dent in the car door.
▸ depression, hollow, indentation

dent *VERB*
He dented the car door.
▸ knock in, push in

dentist *NOUN*
▹ A dentist who specializes in straightening teeth is an orthodontist.
OTHER PEOPLE WHO WORK AT THE DENTIST'S
dental nurse, hygienist, receptionist
THINGS THAT CAN BE DONE AT THE DENTIST'S
extractions, fillings, fitting a brace or a bridge, fitting a crown, fitting dentures, injections, scaling teeth, X-rays
FOR OTHER PEOPLE WHO LOOK AFTER OUR HEALTH SEE **medicine**

deny *VERB*
1 *In spite of the evidence, he continued to deny the accusation.*
▸ dispute, oppose, reject
AN OPPOSITE IS accept
2 *Her parents don't deny her anything.*
▸ deprive of, refuse
AN OPPOSITE IS give

depart *VERB*
1 *What time is the train due to depart?*
▸ begin a journey, get going, leave, set off, set out, start
2 *It looks as if the criminals departed in a hurry.*
▸ (*informal*) clear off, exit, go away, make off, retreat, withdraw
AN OPPOSITE IS arrive

department *NOUN*
I spent ages looking for the right department to pay my bill.
▸ branch, division, office, section

depend *VERB*
to depend on someone *I depend on you to help me.*
▸ bank on, count on, rely on, trust
to depend on something *My success will depend on good luck.*
▸ be decided by, hinge on, rest on

dependable *ADJECTIVE*
We need dependable people who will finish the work on time.
▸ conscientious, honest, loyal, reliable, responsible, sound, steady, trustworthy
AN OPPOSITE IS unreliable

dependent *ADJECTIVE*
dependent on 1 *Everything is dependent on the weather.*
▸ controlled by, determined by, subject to
2 *Don't ever become dependent on drugs.*
▸ addicted to, (*informal*) hooked on, reliant on

depict *VERB*
1 *The artist depicted the scene brilliantly.*
▸ draw, paint, sketch
2 *The film depicted what life was like in medieval times.*
▸ describe, illustrate, outline, portray, represent, show

deplorable *ADJECTIVE*
Their rudeness was deplorable.
▸ disgraceful, lamentable, scandalous, shameful, shocking, unforgivable
AN OPPOSITE IS praiseworthy

deplore *VERB*
We all deplore cruelty to animals.
▸ condemn, disapprove of, hate

deport *VERB*
He was deported from Australia.
▸ banish, exile, expel, send abroad

deposit *NOUN*
1 *Dad paid the deposit on a new car.*
▸ down-payment, first instalment, initial payment
2 *There was a deposit of mud at the bottom of the river.*
▸ layer, sediment

depot *NOUN*
The explorers set up a depot at the base of the mountain.
▸ base, store
▹ A depot where you store weapons is an arsenal.

depress *VERB*
The weather depressed us.
▸ discourage, sadden
AN OPPOSITE IS cheer

depressed *ADJECTIVE*
He was depressed by the news.
▸ dejected, desolate, discouraged, (*informal*) down, downcast, gloomy, glum, in despair, (*informal*) low, melancholy, miserable, sad, unhappy, wretched
AN OPPOSITE IS cheerful

depressing *ADJECTIVE*
It was a depressing situation to be in.
▸ discouraging, distressing, gloomy, sad, unhappy, unwelcome
AN OPPOSITE IS cheerful

depression *NOUN*
1 *She sank into a state of depression.*
▸ dejection, desolation, despair, gloom, glumness, hopelessness, low spirits, melancholy, misery, pessimism, sadness, unhappiness
AN OPPOSITE IS cheerfulness
2 *Most businesses do badly during a depression.*
▸ recession, slump
AN OPPOSITE IS boom
3 *The rain had collected in several depressions in the ground.*
▸ dip, hole, hollow, indentation, pit, rut, sunken area
AN OPPOSITE IS bump

deprived *ADJECTIVE*
The charity tries to help deprived families.
▸ needy, poor, underprivileged
AN OPPOSITE IS privileged or wealthy

deputize *VERB*
to deputize for *Will you deputize for the captain while she is ill?*
▸ do the job of, replace, represent, stand in for, substitute for, take over from

deputy *NOUN*
The deputy has been running the company for the last six months.
▸ assistant, second-in-command, stand-in, substitute
There are several words with the prefix *vice*, which mean 'the deputy for a particular person': e.g. *vice-captain*, *vice-president*, etc

derelict *ADJECTIVE*
It's about time they pulled down those derelict buildings.
▸ abandoned, broken down, crumbling, decrepit, deserted, neglected, ruined

derision *NOUN*
Her idea was greeted with shouts of derision.
▸ mockery, ridicule, satire, scorn

derivation *NOUN*
It's interesting to learn about the derivation of words.
▸ origin, source

derive *VERB*
1 *She derived a lot of pleasure from her garden.*
▸ gain, get, obtain, receive
2 *He derived a lot of his ideas from a text book.*
▸ borrow, collect, crib, draw, (*informal*) lift, pick up, take

descend *VERB*
1 *After admiring the view, we began to descend the mountain.*
▸ climb down, come down, go down, move down
▹ To descend through the air is to **drop** or **fall**. To descend through water is to **sink**.
2 *The road descends gradually into the valley.*
▸ dip, drop, fall, incline, slope
AN OPPOSITE IS ascend
to be descended from someone *She's descended from a French family.*
▸ come from, originate from
to descend from something *I helped my little sister to descend from the pony.*
▸ dismount from, get down from, get off

descendant *NOUN*
▹ A person's descendants are their **heirs** or **successors**.
AN OPPOSITE IS ancestor

descent *NOUN*
The path makes a steep descent into the valley.
▸ dip, drop, fall, incline
AN OPPOSITE IS ascent

describe *VERB*
1 *An eyewitness described how the accident happened.*
▸ depict, explain, outline, report, tell about
2 *She described him as a quiet, shy man.*
▸ characterize, portray, present, represent

description *NOUN*
1 *I wrote a description of our day at the seaside.*
▸ account, report, story
2 *We had to write a description of our favourite character in the novel.*
▸ portrait, representation, sketch

descriptive *ADJECTIVE*
She said my writing was very descriptive.
▸ colourful, detailed, expressive, graphic, vivid

desert *NOUN*
FEATURES OF A DESERT MIGHT BE
cactus, mirage, oasis, palm tree, sandhill, sandstorm
ADJECTIVES WHICH MIGHT DESCRIBE A DESERT
arid, barren, dry, dusty, infertile, inhospitable, sandy, sterile, uncultivated, waterless
▹ A group of people travelling together across a desert is a **caravan**. A desert island is an **uninhabited** island. People who live in the desert are often **nomads**.

desert *VERB*
He deserted his friends when they needed him most.
▸ abandon, betray, forsake, leave, (*informal*) walk out on
▹ To desert someone in a place they can't get away from is to **maroon** or **strand** them.

deserter *NOUN*
Deserters from the army are severely punished.
▸ absentee, runaway

deserve *VERB*
Her brave action deserves a reward.
▸ be worthy of, justify, merit, warrant

design *NOUN*
1 *We produced a design for a car of the future.*
▸ blueprint, drawing
▹ A first example of something, used as a model for making others, is a **prototype**.
2 *The head showed us some school uniforms and asked which design we liked best.*
▸ style, type, version
3 *The wallpaper had a flowery design.*
▸ arrangement, composition, pattern

design *VERB*
She designs all her own clothes.
▸ conceive, create, devise, sketch, think of

desirable *ADJECTIVE*
1 *The house has many desirable features.*
▸ appealing, attractive, interesting, irresistible, tempting
AN OPPOSITE IS worthless
2 *It is desirable for you to come with us.*
▸ advisable, prudent, sensible, wise
AN OPPOSITE IS unwise

desire *VERB*
What do you most desire?
► crave, fancy, hanker after, long for, need, set your heart on, want, wish for, yearn for, yen

desire *NOUN*
What is your greatest desire?
► ambition, craving, fancy, hankering, longing, urge, want, wish, yearning
▷ A desire for food is appetite or hunger. A desire for drink is thirst. Excessive desire for money or other things is greed.

desolate *ADJECTIVE*
1 *He felt desolate when she died.*
► dejected, depressed, forlorn, hopeless, lonely, melancholy, miserable, sad, wretched
AN OPPOSITE IS cheerful
2 *No one wants to live in that desolate place.*
► abandoned, bare, barren, bleak, cheerless, depressing, deserted, dismal, dreary, forsaken, gloomy, inhospitable, isolated, lonely, remote, uninhabited, wild
AN OPPOSITE IS pleasant

despair *NOUN*
She was overcome by feelings of despair.
► anguish, dejection, depression, desperation, gloom, hopelessness, melancholy, misery, pessimism, wretchedness
AN OPPOSITE IS hope

despatch *NOUN, VERB*
SEE **dispatch** *NOUN, VERB*

desperate *ADJECTIVE*
1 *The refugees were in a desperate situation.*
► critical, drastic, grave, hopeless, serious, severe
2 *The police warned people not to approach the desperate criminals.*
► dangerous, reckless, violent

despicable *ADJECTIVE*
We were horrified by the despicable way he treated his dog.
► contemptible, disgraceful, hateful, shameful

despise *VERB*
He despises people who aren't good at sport.
► be contemptuous of, deride, feel contempt for, have a low opinion of, look down on, scorn, sneer at
AN OPPOSITE IS admire

dessert *NOUN*
For dessert there's ice cream or fruit salad.
► (*informal*) afters, pudding, sweet

destination *NOUN*
The train arrived at its destination five minutes early.
► terminus

destined *ADJECTIVE*
1 *My plans were destined to fail.*
► bound, certain, doomed, fated
2 *We felt that the disaster was destined.*
► inevitable, intended, unavoidable

destiny *NOUN*
Was it destiny that brought us together?
► fate, fortune

destroy *VERB*
1 *An avalanche destroyed the village.*
► break down, crush, demolish, devastate, flatten, knock down, level, pull down, shatter, smash, sweep away
2 *He tried to destroy the good work we had done.*
► ruin, sabotage, undo, wreck

destruction *NOUN*
The war caused terrible destruction of life and property.
► annihilation, demolition, devastation, elimination, extermination, extinction, killing, ruin, wrecking
AN OPPOSITE IS conservation or creation

destructive *ADJECTIVE*
The storm had a destructive effect on the crops.
► catastrophic, damaging, devastating, disastrous, harmful, injurious, ruinous, violent

detach *VERB*
He detached the wires to make sure he didn't get an electric shock.
► disconnect, part, release, remove, separate, take off, undo, unfasten
▷ To detach a caravan from a car, etc., is to unhitch it. To detach railway wagons from a locomotive is to uncouple them. To detach something by cutting it off is to sever it.
AN OPPOSITE IS attach

detached *ADJECTIVE*
I don't support either team, so I can watch from a detached point of view.
► disinterested, impartial, independent,

A B C D E F G H I J K L M N O P Q R S T U V W X Y Z

neutral, objective, unbiased, uncommitted, uninvolved, unprejudiced
AN OPPOSITE IS biased

detail *NOUN*
Her account was accurate in every detail.
▸ aspect, fact, feature, item, particular, point, respect

detain *VERB*
1 *The police detained the suspect.*
▸ arrest, capture, imprison, restrain
AN OPPOSITE IS release
2 *I'll try not to detain you for long.*
▸ delay, hinder, hold up, keep waiting

detect *VERB*
The mechanic detected a fault in the car.
▸ diagnose, discover, find, identify, recognize, reveal, spot, track down

deter *VERB*
How can we deter the blackbirds from eating the strawberries?
▸ discourage, dissuade, prevent, put off, stop
AN OPPOSITE IS encourage

deteriorate *VERB*
1 *His health began to deteriorate.*
▸ decline, degenerate, get worse, go downhill, worsen
2 *The buildings will deteriorate if we don't maintain them.*
▸ crumble, decay, disintegrate
AN OPPOSITE IS improve

determination *NOUN*
Marathon runners show great determination.
▸ commitment, courage, dedication, drive, grit, (*informal*) guts, perseverance, persistence, resolve, spirit, will-power

determine *VERB*
Our task was to determine the height of the tower.
▸ calculate, compute, decide, figure out, reckon, work out

determined *ADJECTIVE*
1 *She's a determined woman!*
▸ assertive, decisive, persistent, resolute, strong-minded, tough
AN OPPOSITE IS weak-minded
2 *I'm determined to win!*
▸ committed, resolved

detest *VERB*
I detest the smell of cigarette smoke.
▸ dislike, hate, loathe
▹ Informal expressions are **can't bear** and **can't stand**.
AN OPPOSITE IS love

detestable *ADJECTIVE*
I found the film's violence detestable.
▸ (*informal*) awful, contemptible, disgusting, hateful, horrible, horrid, repulsive, revolting
AN OPPOSITE IS adorable

detonate *VERB*
1 *They set a timer to detonate the bomb.*
▸ explode, set off
2 *Fortunately the bomb didn't detonate.*
▸ blow up, go off

detour *NOUN*
I wasted time by taking a detour.
▸ diversion, indirect route, roundabout route

devastate *VERB*
A hurricane devastated the town.
▸ demolish, destroy, flatten, level, ruin, wreck

develop *VERB*
1 *The manager wants to develop the business.*
▸ build up, diversify, enlarge, expand, extend
2 *The teacher said I should develop my ideas.*
▸ amplify, elaborate
3 *This group's music has developed in their recent albums.*
▸ advance, evolve, get better, improve, progress
4 *The plants develop quickly in the spring.*
▸ grow, flourish
5 *How did he develop that posh accent?*
▸ acquire, cultivate, get, pick up

development *NOUN*
1 *Were there any developments while I was away?*
▸ change, happening, incident, occurrence
2 *He is pleased with the development of his business.*
▸ expansion, growth, improvement, progress, spread
3 *The land is set aside for industrial development.*
▸ building, exploitation, use

device *NOUN*
It's a device for opening tins more easily.
▸ apparatus, appliance, contraption, contrivance, gadget, implement, instrument, tool

devilish *ADJECTIVE*
He showed devilish cunning.
▸ cruel, diabolical, evil, fiendish, hellish, infernal, savage, wicked
AN OPPOSITE IS angelic

devilment *NOUN*
(*usually joking*) *What devilment have you children been up to?*
▸ mischief, naughtiness, pranks, trouble

devious *ADJECTIVE*
1 *I don't trust his devious explanations.*
▸ cunning, deceitful, dishonest, evasive, furtive, insincere, misleading, sly, (*informal*) sneaky, treacherous, wily
2 *Because of the roadworks, we took a devious route home.*
▸ indirect, meandering, roundabout, winding
AN OPPOSITE IS direct or straightforward

devise *VERB*
We need to devise a strategy for Saturday's game.
▸ conceive, contrive, form, formulate, invent, make up, map out, organize, plan, prepare, think out, think up

devote *VERB*
They devote all their free time to sport.
▸ assign, commit, set aside

devoted *ADJECTIVE*
She's a devoted supporter of our team.
▸ committed, enthusiastic, faithful, loyal
AN OPPOSITE IS apathetic

devotion *NOUN*
She has always shown a great devotion to her children.
▸ adoration (of), commitment, love (of), loyalty

devour *VERB*
They devoured a whole plateful of sandwiches.
▸ consume, eat, gobble up, gulp down, swallow

diabolical *ADJECTIVE*
It was a diabolical plan.
▸ devilish, evil, fiendish, hellish, infernal, wicked

diagnose *VERB*
The doctor diagnosed the cause of my illness.
▸ detect, determine, identify, name, recognize

diagnosis *NOUN*
What is the doctor's diagnosis?
▸ conclusion, explanation, interpretation, opinion, verdict

diagram *NOUN*
VARIOUS KINDS OF DIAGRAM
block diagram, chart, cutaway diagram, figure, flow chart, graph, outline, pie chart, plan, sketch

dial *VERB*
I picked up the phone and dialled his number.
▸ call, phone, ring, telephone

dialogue *NOUN*
The book consisted of a series of dialogues.
▸ chat, conversation, debate, discussion, exchange, talk

dictate *VERB*
to dictate to someone *You've got no right to dictate to me!*
▸ (*informal*) boss about, command, give orders to, impose on, (*informal*) lay down the law to, order about

dictatorial *ADJECTIVE*
I didn't like her dictatorial manner.
▸ (*informal*) bossy, tyrannical

die *VERB*
1 *Her dog died last week.*
▸ expire, pass away, perish
▹ To die of hunger is to starve.
2 *The flowers will die if they don't have water.*
▸ droop, fade, wilt, wither
to die down *The flames died down.*
▸ become less, decline, decrease, dwindle, fizzle out, go out, subside, wane, weaken
to die out *When did the dinosaurs die out?*
▸ become extinct, cease to exist, come to an end, disappear, vanish

A B C D E F G H I J K L M N O P Q R S T U V W X Y Z

diet *NOUN*
The doctor asked me about my normal diet.
▸ food, nourishment, nutrition
▹ If you choose what to eat in order to lose weight, you are on a **slimming** diet. If you don't eat meat, you are on a **vegetarian** diet. If you don't eat any animal products at all, you are on a **vegan** diet.
SEE ALSO **food**

differ *VERB*
We differed about what to do.
▸ argue, clash, conflict, contradict each other, disagree, fall out, oppose each other, quarrel
AN OPPOSITE IS agree
to differ from
My opinions differ from yours.
▸ be different from, contrast with

difference *NOUN*
1 *The salesman explained the difference between the computers we were looking at.*
▸ contrast, distinction
AN OPPOSITE IS similarity
2 *This will make a difference to our plans.*
▸ alteration, change, modification, variation

different *ADJECTIVE*
1 *We have different opinions on this issue.*
▸ clashing, conflicting, contradictory, opposite
2 *It's important that the teams wear different colours.*
▸ contrasting, dissimilar, distinguishable
3 *The packet contains sweets of different flavours.*
▸ assorted, diverse, miscellaneous, mixed, numerous, several, various
4 *We always go to the park — haven't you got any different ideas?*
▸ fresh, new, original
5 *Everyone's handwriting is different.*
▸ distinct, distinctive, individual, special, unique
AN OPPOSITE IS identical or similar

difficult *ADJECTIVE*
1 *The questions were very difficult.*
▸ baffling, complex, complicated, hard, involved, perplexing, tricky
AN OPPOSITE IS simple
2 *We were worn out by the difficult climb to the top of the hill.*
▸ challenging, demanding, exhausting, formidable, gruelling, laborious, strenuous, tough
AN OPPOSITE IS easy
3 *Mum says I was a difficult child when I was small.*
▸ annoying, awkward, disruptive, obstinate, stubborn, tiresome, troublesome, trying, uncooperative, unhelpful
AN OPPOSITE IS cooperative

difficulty *NOUN*
1 *The explorers were used to facing difficulty.*
▸ adversity, challenges, hardship, trouble
2 *There were many difficulties to be overcome.*
▸ complication, dilemma, hitch, obstacle, problem, snag

dig *VERB*
1 *He spent the afternoon digging the garden.*
▸ cultivate, fork over, turn over
2 *Rabbits dig holes in the ground.*
▸ burrow, excavate, gouge out, hollow out, scoop out, tunnel
3 *Did you dig me in the back?*
▸ jab, poke, prod, punch, shove

dignified *ADJECTIVE*
She was a very dignified old lady.
▸ calm, formal, grave, proper, refined, sedate, serious
AN OPPOSITE IS undignified

dignity *NOUN*
1 *Please don't do anything to spoil the dignity of the occasion.*
▸ formality, importance, seriousness, solemnity
2 *She handled the problem with dignity.*
▸ calmness, poise, self-control

dilemma *NOUN*
I can wait for my friend and miss the bus, or catch the bus and leave her behind — it's a real dilemma!
▸ difficulty, problem

dilute *VERB*
You should dilute orange squash with water.
▸ thin, water down, weaken
AN OPPOSITE IS concentrate

dim *ADJECTIVE*
1 *I could just see a dim outline in the mist.*
▸ blurred, cloudy, faint, fuzzy, hazy, indistinct, misty, pale, shadowy, vague
AN OPPOSITE IS clear
2 *The light is rather dim.*
▸ dark, dingy, dull, gloomy, murky
AN OPPOSITE IS bright

dimensions *PLURAL NOUN*
We measured the dimensions of the room.
▸ capacity, extent, measurements, size
FOR WORDS USED IN MEASURING SEE **measurement**

diminish *VERB*
1 *Don't diminish his confidence by making fun of him.*
▸ lessen, make smaller, minimize, reduce
2 *Our enthusiasm diminished as time went on.*
▸ become less, decline, decrease, dwindle, subside, wane
AN OPPOSITE IS increase

din *NOUN*
I can't hear you because of that awful din!
▸ clatter, hullabaloo, noise, racket, row

dingy *ADJECTIVE*
How can we brighten up this dingy room?
▸ colourless, dark, depressing, dim, dirty, dismal, drab, dreary, dull, faded, gloomy, grimy, murky, shabby
AN OPPOSITE IS bright

dip *VERB*
1 *I dipped my hand in the water.*
▸ immerse, lower, plunge, submerge
2 *The road dips down into the valley.*
▸ descend, go down, slope down

dip *NOUN*
1 *There was a dip in the ground.*
▸ depression, hole, hollow, slope
2 *It was so hot we decided to have a dip in the sea.*
▸ bathe, swim

diplomacy *NOUN*
She showed great diplomacy in ending the dispute.
▸ delicacy, tact, tactfulness

diplomatic *ADJECTIVE*
Her questions were very diplomatic.
▸ careful, considerate, delicate, discreet, polite, sensitive, tactful
AN OPPOSITE IS tactless

dire *ADJECTIVE*
It was a dire emergency when the bridge collapsed.
▸ acute, dangerous, dreadful, frightful, horrible, nasty, serious, terrible

direct *ADJECTIVE*
1 *Let's take the most direct route.*
▸ shortest, straight
AN OPPOSITE IS indirect
2 *Please give me a direct answer.*
▸ blunt, frank, honest, outspoken, plain, sincere, straightforward, unambiguous
AN OPPOSITE IS evasive

direct *VERB*
1 *Can you direct me to the station?*
▸ guide, indicate the way, point, show the way, tell the way
2 *They appointed someone to direct the company's affairs while the boss was ill.*
▸ administer, be in charge of, command, control, handle, lead, manage, run, superintend, supervise, take charge of
▹ To direct an orchestra is to **conduct** it.
3 *He directed us to begin.*
▸ command, instruct, order, tell

direction *NOUN*
Which direction did they go in?
▸ course, path, route, way
directions *The kit comes with directions for assembling it.*
▸ guidance, guidelines, instructions, plans

director *NOUN*
FOR PEOPLE IN CHARGE OF THINGS SEE **chief** *NOUN*

dirt *NOUN*
1 *The floor was covered in dirt.*
▸ dust, filth, grime, mess, muck, mud
2 *Chickens scratched about in the dirt.*
▸ clay, earth, loam, mud, soil

dirty *ADJECTIVE*
1 *Those dirty clothes need washing.*
▸ dusty, filthy, foul, grimy, grubby, messy, mucky, muddy, soiled, sooty, stained
AN OPPOSITE IS clean
2 *We refused to drink the dirty water.*
▸ cloudy, impure, polluted
AN OPPOSITE IS pure
3 *The other team used dirty tactics.*
▸ dishonest, illegal, mean, unfair, unsporting
AN OPPOSITE IS honest
4 *He used a lot of dirty words.*
▸ coarse, crude, improper, indecent, obscene, offensive, rude, smutty, vulgar
AN OPPOSITE IS decent

A B C D E F G H I J K L M N O P Q R S T U V W X Y Z

disability *NOUN*
She leads a normal life in spite of her disabilities.
▸ affliction, complaint, handicap, impairment, infirmity

disabled *ADJECTIVE*
He has been disabled since the accident.
▸ handicapped
▹ A person who has difficulty in walking is **lame**. A person who has to spend all the time in bed is **bedridden**. A person who cannot move on their own is **immobile**. A person who cannot move part of their body is **paralysed**. A person who is paralysed in the legs is **paraplegic**.

disadvantage *NOUN*
It's a disadvantage to be small if you play basketball.
▸ drawback, handicap, hindrance, inconvenience, snag

disagree *VERB*
Unfortunately, my brother and I often disagree.
▸ argue, clash, differ, fall out, quarrel, squabble
AN OPPOSITE IS agree
to disagree with **1** *He disagrees with everything I say.*
▸ argue with, contradict, object to, oppose
2 *Onions disagree with me.*
▸ have a bad effect on, upset

disagreement *NOUN*
We had a disagreement about who should use the computer first.
▸ argument, clash, conflict, debate, difference of opinion, dispute, quarrel, row, squabble
AN OPPOSITE IS agreement

disagreeable *ADJECTIVE*
There's no need to be so disagreeable.
▸ annoying, horrible, nasty, offensive, spiteful, tiresome, uncooperative, unfriendly, unkind, unpleasant
AN OPPOSITE IS pleasant

disappear *VERB*
1 *The fog disappeared.*
▸ clear, disperse, dissolve, evaporate, fade away, melt away
2 *The rabbits disappeared in the long grass.*
▸ become invisible, vanish
3 *He disappeared round the corner.*
▸ depart, escape, flee, go away, run away, withdraw
AN OPPOSITE IS appear

disappoint *VERB*
I was disappointed by her behaviour.
▸ dismay, displease, upset
AN OPPOSITE IS delight or satisfy

disapproval *NOUN*
Her frown showed her disapproval.
▸ condemnation, criticism, dislike, dissatisfaction
AN OPPOSITE IS approval

disapprove *VERB*
to disapprove of *They all disapprove of smoking.*
▸ condemn, criticize, denounce, deplore, dislike, frown on, object to, take exception to, (*informal*) take a dim view of
AN OPPOSITE IS approve of

disapproving *ADJECTIVE*
She made some disapproving comments about my work.
▸ critical, reproachful, uncomplimentary, unfavourable
AN OPPOSITE IS favourable

disaster *NOUN*
The pilot managed to land the damaged plane and avoided a disaster.
▸ calamity, catastrophe, tragedy
SOME DIFFERENT KINDS OF DISASTER
air crash, avalanche, collision, crash, derailment, earthquake, epidemic, fire, flood, hurricane, landslide, plague, road accident, shipwreck, tidal wave, tornado, volcanic eruption

disastrous *ADJECTIVE*
The disastrous fire cost millions of pounds.
▸ calamitous, catastrophic, destructive, devastating, dire, dreadful, fatal, ruinous, terrible

disc *NOUN*
THINGS SHAPED LIKE A DISC
circle, counter, plate, record, wheel
VARIOUS KINDS OF RECORDED DISC
album, CD or compact disc, LP, recording, single
VARIOUS KINDS OF COMPUTER DISK
CD ROM, diskette, floppy disk, hard disk
Note that in computing, the word is usually spelt *disk*

discard *VERB*
I discarded some old clothes and sent them to the jumble sale.
▸ cast off, dispose of, dump, get rid of, reject, scrap, throw away

discharge *VERB*
1 *The accused man was found not guilty and discharged.*
▸ acquit, allow to leave, clear, free, let off, liberate, release
2 *The chimney discharged thick smoke.*
▸ belch, eject, emit, expel, give off, give out, pour out, produce

disciple *NOUN*
The religious leader had many disciples.
▸ admirer, devotee, follower, supporter
▹ The disciples of Jesus were the **apostles**.

discipline *NOUN*
Discipline is important in the army.
▸ control, order

disclose *VERB*
He never disclosed the truth.
▸ confess, make known, make public, reveal, tell
AN OPPOSITE IS conceal

discolour *VERB*
The smoke discoloured the paint.
▸ mark, spoil the colour of, stain

discomfort *NOUN*
He still experiences a lot of discomfort from his injury.
▸ pain, soreness

disconnect *VERB*
Disconnect the electricity supply before you start to mend the fuse.
▸ cut off, detach

discontented *ADJECTIVE*
She felt very discontented with her job.
▸ dejected, dissatisfied, miserable, unhappy, upset
AN OPPOSITE IS happy

discount *NOUN*
I got a discount on the full price.
▸ allowance, concession, cut, deduction, reduction

discourage *VERB*
1 *Did her criticism discourage you?*
▸ demoralize, depress, (*informal*) put you off
2 *How can we discourage the blackbirds from eating the strawberries?*
▸ deter, dissuade, prevent, restrain, stop
AN OPPOSITE IS encourage

discover *VERB*
I discovered some old toys in the attic.
▸ come across, find, spot, stumble across, uncover
▹ To discover something that has been buried is to **unearth** it. To discover something that has been under water is to **dredge it up**. To discover something you have been pursuing is to **track it down**.
AN OPPOSITE IS hide

discovery *NOUN*
Scientists have made an exciting new discovery.
▸ breakthrough, find

discreet *ADJECTIVE*
I asked a few discreet questions about her illness.
▸ careful, cautious, delicate, diplomatic, polite, prudent, sensitive, tactful
AN OPPOSITE IS tactless

discriminate *VERB*
It's sometimes hard to discriminate between poisonous mushrooms and edible ones.
▸ distinguish, judge the difference, tell the difference
to discriminate against *It's wrong to discriminate against people because of their race, religion, or sex.*
▸ be biased against, be intolerant of, be prejudiced against, persecute

discrimination *NOUN*
1 *She shows discrimination in her choice of music.*
▸ good judgement, good taste
2 *Discrimination against people because of their race, religion, or sex is wrong.*
▸ bias, intolerance, prejudice, unfairness
▹ Discrimination against people because of their sex is **sexism**. Discrimination against people because of their race is **racism**. Discrimination against people of a different nation is **chauvinism**.

discuss *VERB*
He discussed the situation with his wife.
▸ confer about, debate, talk about

a b c **d** e f g h i j k l m n o p q r s t u v w x y z

A B C D E F G H I J K L M N O P Q R S T U V W X Y Z

discussion *NOUN*
We had a lively discussion.
▸ argument, conversation, exchange of views
▹ A formal discussion is a **conference** or **debate**.

disease *NOUN*
He was suffering from a serious disease.
▸ affliction, ailment, (*informal*) bug, complaint, illness, sickness
SEE ALSO **illness**

diseased *ADJECTIVE*
Gardeners throw away diseased plants.
▸ infected, sickly, unhealthy
AN OPPOSITE IS healthy
SEE ALSO **ill**

disembark *VERB*
The passengers disembarked from the ferry.
▸ go ashore
AN OPPOSITE IS embark

disgrace *NOUN*
1 *He never got over the disgrace of being caught cheating.*
▸ dishonour, embarrassment, humiliation, shame
2 *The way he treats them is a disgrace!*
▸ outrage, scandal

disgraceful *ADJECTIVE*
We were horrified by their disgraceful behaviour.
▸ appalling, outrageous, scandalous, shameful, shocking
AN OPPOSITE IS honourable

disguise *VERB*
I tried to disguise my feelings.
▸ camouflage, conceal, cover up, hide, mask
to disguise yourself as *The spy disguised himself as a member of the ship's crew.*
▸ dress up as, pretend to be

disguise *NOUN*
I didn't recognize him in that disguise.
▸ camouflage, costume, make-up, mask

disgust *NOUN*
I couldn't hide my disgust at his behaviour.
▸ detestation, dislike, hatred, horror, loathing, repulsion
AN OPPOSITE IS liking

disgust *VERB*
Didn't those horrible pictures disgust you?
▸ appal, distress, horrify, offend, (*informal*) put you off, repel, revolt, shock, sicken, (*informal*) turn your stomach
AN OPPOSITE IS please

disgusting *ADJECTIVE*
Cruelty to animals is disgusting.
▸ appalling, horrible, loathsome, nasty, offensive, repulsive, revolting, sickening
AN OPPOSITE IS delightful

dish *NOUN*
1 *She cooked the casserole in an earthenware dish.*
▸ basin, bowl
▹ A dish to serve soup from is a **tureen**.
SEE ALSO **container**
2 *What's your favourite dish?*
▸ food, item on the menu

dishevelled *ADJECTIVE*
He looked tired and dishevelled.
▸ messy, ruffled, scruffy, untidy
AN OPPOSITE IS neat

dishonest *ADJECTIVE*
1 *There are too many dishonest traders about.*
▸ (*informal*) bent, cheating, corrupt, criminal, (*informal*) crooked, deceitful, disreputable, (*informal*) dodgy, immoral, lying, (*informal*) shady, swindling, thieving, untrustworthy
2 *The judge reprimanded him for making dishonest statements.*
▸ devious, false, fraudulent, misleading, untruthful
AN OPPOSITE IS honest

dishonesty *NOUN*
He was accused of dishonesty.
▸ cheating, corruption, (*informal*) crookedness, deceit, deviousness, insincerity, lying
AN OPPOSITE IS honesty

disinfect *VERB*
The nurse disinfected my wound.
▸ cleanse, sterilize
▹ To disinfect an infected area is to **decontaminate** it. To disinfect a room with fumes is to **fumigate** it.
AN OPPOSITE IS infect

disinfectant *NOUN*
Mum poured disinfectant into the drain.
▸ antiseptic

disintegrate *VERB*
1 *Pounded by the waves, the wreck disintegrated.*
▸ break into pieces, break up, crack up, fall apart
2 *Dead leaves fall to the ground and gradually disintegrate.*
▸ crumble, decay, decompose, rot

disinterested *ADJECTIVE*
A referee must be disinterested.
▸ detached, fair, impartial, neutral, unbiased, unprejudiced
AN OPPOSITE IS biased

disk *NOUN*
SEE **disc**

dislike *NOUN*
His colleagues regarded him with intense dislike.
▸ detestation, disapproval, disgust, hatred, loathing, revulsion
AN OPPOSITE IS liking

dislike *VERB*
I dislike people who hunt wild animals.
▸ detest, disapprove of, hate, loathe
AN OPPOSITE IS like

dislocate *VERB*
1 *He dislocated his shoulder playing rugby.*
▸ (*informal*) put out, put out of joint
2 *Floods dislocated the train service.*
▸ disrupt, interfere with, interrupt, throw into confusion or disorder, upset

dislodge *VERB*
The wind dislodged some tiles on the roof.
▸ displace, disturb, move, shift

disloyal *ADJECTIVE*
He was disloyal to his friends.
▸ faithless, false, treacherous, unfaithful, unreliable, untrustworthy
AN OPPOSITE IS loyal

dismal *ADJECTIVE*
How can we brighten up this dismal room?
▸ cheerless, dark, depressing, dingy, drab, dreary, dull, gloomy, murky
AN OPPOSITE IS bright or cheerful

dismantle *VERB*
After the school fair, we had to dismantle all the stalls.
▸ take apart, take down
▹ To dismantle a tent is to strike it.
AN OPPOSITE IS assemble

dismay *NOUN*
We listened with dismay to the bad news.
▸ alarm, anxiety, disappointment, distress, gloom, shock

dismayed *ADJECTIVE*
I was dismayed by the failure of our plan.
▸ appalled, depressed, devastated, disappointed, discouraged, distressed, shocked, surprised
AN OPPOSITE IS encouraged

dismiss *VERB*
1 *The teacher dismissed the class.*
▸ free, let go, release, send away
2 *The firm dismissed ten workers.*
▸ (*informal*) fire, give notice to, make redundant, sack
3 *The weather was so bad that we dismissed the idea of having a picnic.*
▸ discard, drop, reject

dismount *VERB*
I dismounted from my bike to open the gate.
▸ descend, get off

disobedient *ADJECTIVE*
She said she had never known such a disobedient child.
▸ badly behaved, contrary, defiant, disorderly, disruptive, mutinous, naughty, rebellious, uncontrollable, undisciplined, ungovernable, unmanageable, unruly
AN OPPOSITE IS obedient

disobey *VERB*
1 *You will be penalized if you disobey the rules.*
▸ break, defy, disregard, ignore, violate
2 *Soldiers are trained never to disobey.*
▸ be disobedient, mutiny, rebel, revolt
AN OPPOSITE IS obey

disorder *NOUN*
1 *Police were called in to deal with the disorder.*
▸ anarchy, brawling, commotion, disturbance, fighting, lawlessness, quarrelling, rioting, uproar

2 *It's time I tidied up the disorder in my room.*
▸ chaos, confusion, mess, muddle, untidiness
AN OPPOSITE IS order

disorderly *ADJECTIVE*
The head came in to reprimand the disorderly class.
▸ badly behaved, disobedient, uncontrollable, undisciplined, ungovernable, unmanageable, unruly
AN OPPOSITE IS orderly

dispatch *NOUN*
The messenger brought a dispatch from headquarters.
▸ bulletin, communication, letter, message, report

dispatch *VERB*
1 *They dispatched a letter to him.*
▸ post, send
2 *They decided it was kindest to dispatch the wounded animal.*
▸ dispose of, (*informal*) finish off, kill

dispense *VERB*
1 *Villagers dispensed tea to the people who had been involved in the accident.*
▸ deal out, distribute, give out, provide, share out
2 *The pharmacist dispenses medicine prescribed by the doctor.*
▸ make up, prepare, supply
to dispense with *His leg had healed and he was able to dispense with his crutches.*
▸ dispose of, do without, get rid of, remove

disperse *VERB*
1 *The police dispersed the crowd.*
▸ break up, drive away, send away, send in different directions, separate
2 *The crowd dispersed quickly after the match.*
▸ disappear, dissolve, melt away, scatter, spread out, vanish
AN OPPOSITE IS gather

displace *VERB*
1 *The vibration displaced part of the mechanism.*
▸ dislodge, disturb, put out of place, shift
2 *A brilliant new player displaced me in the team.*
▸ replace, succeed, take the place of

display *VERB*
We planned the best way to display our work.
▸ demonstrate, exhibit, present, put on show, set out, show, show off
▹ To display something boastfully is to flaunt it.

display *NOUN*
We set out a display of our work.
▸ demonstration, exhibition, presentation, show

displease *VERB*
I didn't do anything to displease her.
▸ annoy, anger, exasperate, irritate, upset, vex

dispose *VERB*
to dispose of something *Let's dispose of this old carpet.*
▸ discard, (*informal*) dump, get rid of, give away, scrap, throw away
to be disposed to do something *He didn't seem disposed to do anything about the problem.*
▸ be inclined to, be likely to, be ready to, be willing to

disposition *NOUN*
He has a friendly disposition.
▸ character, nature, personality

dispute *NOUN*
They settled the dispute about who should use the computer first.
▸ argument, controversy, debate, difference of opinion, disagreement, quarrel

disqualify *VERB*
She was disqualified from the competition.
▸ bar, prohibit

disregard *VERB*
I disregarded her advice.
▸ ignore, pay no attention to, reject, take no notice of
AN OPPOSITE IS heed

disrespect *NOUN*
She didn't intend any disrespect by the remark.
▸ insolence, rudeness

disrespectful *ADJECTIVE*
Don't be disrespectful towards her.
▸ bad-mannered, impolite, insolent, insulting, rude
AN OPPOSITE IS respectful

disrupt *VERB*
Floods disrupted the train service.
► dislocate, interfere with, interrupt, throw into confusion or disorder, upset

dissatisfied *ADJECTIVE*
Dissatisfied customers may return the goods and get a refund.
► annoyed, disappointed, discontented, displeased, frustrated
AN OPPOSITE IS satisfied

dissolve *VERB*
Stir your tea until the sugar dissolves.
► disintegrate, disperse, melt

dissuade *VERB*
to dissuade someone from doing something *We tried to dissuade him from going out in the storm.*
► argue someone out of, deter someone from, discourage someone from, persuade someone not to, warn someone against
AN OPPOSITE IS persuade

distance *NOUN*
What is the distance from here to London?
► measurement, mileage
▷ The distance across something is the **breadth** or **width**. The distance along something is the **length**. The distance between two points is a **gap** or **interval**.
FOR UNITS FOR MEASURING DISTANCE SEE **measurement**

distant *ADJECTIVE*
1 *I'd love to travel to distant countries.*
► faraway, inaccessible, out-of-the-way, remote
AN OPPOSITE IS close
2 *His distant manner puts me off.*
► cool, formal, haughty, reserved, unapproachable, unfriendly, withdrawn
AN OPPOSITE IS friendly

distinct *ADJECTIVE*
1 *You have made a distinct improvement.*
► definite, evident, noticeable, obvious, perceptible
AN OPPOSITE IS imperceptible
2 *It was a small photo, but the details were quite distinct.*
► clear, distinguishable, plain, recognizable, sharp, unmistakable, visible, well defined
AN OPPOSITE IS indistinct
3 *Organize your essay into distinct sections.*
► individual, separate

distinction *NOUN*
1 *I can't see the distinction between the expensive coat and the cheap one.*
► contrast, difference, distinctiveness
2 *My cousin had the distinction of getting the highest mark.*
► credit, glory, honour, merit, prestige

distinctive *ADJECTIVE*
We have a distinctive blue football strip.
► characteristic, different, recognizable, special, unique, unmistakable

distinguish *VERB*
1 *Can you distinguish between butter and margarine?*
► choose, decide, discriminate, make a distinction, tell apart
2 *In the dark we couldn't distinguish who she was.*
► determine, identify, make out, perceive, recognize, single out, tell

distinguished *ADJECTIVE*
1 *The school has a distinguished academic reputation.*
► excellent, exceptional, first-rate, outstanding
AN OPPOSITE IS ordinary
2 *She's a very distinguished writer.*
► celebrated, eminent, famous, notable, prominent, renowned, well known
AN OPPOSITE IS unknown

distort *VERB*
1 *When my bike hit the kerb, it distorted the wheel.*
► bend, buckle, contort, twist, warp
2 *The newspaper distorted the facts.*
► slant, twist

distract *VERB*
Don't distract the driver.
► divert the attention of

distress *NOUN*
1 *We tried to comfort her in her distress.*
► anguish, anxiety, dismay, grief, misery, pain, sadness, sorrow, suffering, torment, worry, wretchedness
2 *We saw that the man in the boat was in distress.*
► danger, difficulty, trouble

A B C D E F G H I J K L M N O P Q R S T U V W X Y Z

distress *VERB*
We could see that the bad news distressed her.
▸ alarm, dismay, disturb, torment, trouble, upset, worry
AN OPPOSITE IS comfort

distribute *VERB*
1 *They distributed free samples.*
▸ circulate, (*informal*) dish out, dispense, give out, hand round, issue, share out, take round
2 *Distribute the seeds evenly.*
▸ disperse, scatter, spread

district *NOUN*
Granny lives in a quiet district.
▸ area, locality, neighbourhood, region, vicinity

distrust *VERB*
I distrust her motives for being so nice to me.
▸ be sceptical about, be suspicious or wary of, doubt, feel uncertain or uneasy or unsure about, mistrust, question, suspect
AN OPPOSITE IS trust

disturb *VERB*
1 *Don't disturb her if she's asleep.*
▸ annoy, bother, interrupt, pester
2 *The bad new disturbed us.*
▸ alarm, distress, frighten, trouble, upset, worry
3 *Don't disturb the papers on my desk.*
▸ mess about with, move, muddle

disused *ADJECTIVE*
They made the disused railway line into a cycle track.
▸ abandoned, closed down, unused

ditch *NOUN*
They dug a ditch to help drain the marshy land.
▸ dike, drain, gully, trench

dither *VERB*
Don't dither — get on with it!
▸ delay, falter, hang about, hesitate, waver

dive *VERB*
1 *She dived into the water.*
▸ jump, leap, plunge
2 *The eagle dived towards its prey.*
▸ pounce, swoop

diver *NOUN*
▹ A diver who wears a rubber suit and flippers and breathes air from tanks carried on their back is a scuba diver or frogman.

diverse *ADJECTIVE*
People from many diverse cultures live in the area.
▸ contrasting, different, differing, varied, various

diversify *VERB*
His business has diversified into a wider range of goods.
▸ branch out

diversion *NOUN*
1 *Because of an accident, we had to follow a diversion.*
▸ detour, indirect route, roundabout route
2 *His chief diversion is reading.*
▸ amusement, entertainment, recreation

divert *VERB*
1 *They diverted the plane to another airport.*
▸ direct, switch
2 *She diverted herself by playing the piano.*
▸ amuse, cheer up, delight, entertain, keep happy

divide *VERB*
1 *We divided into two groups.*
▸ break up, move apart, part, separate, split
AN OPPOSITE IS combine
2 *He divided the food between us.*
▸ allot, deal out, dispense, distribute, give out, share out
3 *Which way do we go? The path divides here.*
▸ branch, fork
AN OPPOSITE IS converge

divine *ADJECTIVE*
1 *The holy book deals with divine things.*
▸ heavenly, holy, religious, sacred, spiritual
2 *Ancient Greeks believed divine beings lived on Mount Olympus.*
▸ godlike, immortal

division *NOUN*
1 *The government discussed the division of the country into smaller areas.*
▸ dividing, partition, splitting
2 *There was a division in the government.*
▸ disagreement, split
3 *There is a movable division between the two classrooms.*
▸ divider, dividing wall, partition, screen
4 *Dad now works in a different division of his company.*
▸ branch, department, section, unit

dizzy *ADJECTIVE*
I feel dizzy when I look down from a height.
▶ dazed, faint, giddy, reeling, unsteady

do *VERB* This word is often overused. It can mean many things. We give here only a few of the ways we use the word, and some of the many synonyms:
1 *Can you do a job for me?*
▶ attend to, cope with, deal with, handle, look after, perform, undertake
2 *I managed to do the job in two hours.*
▶ accomplish, achieve, carry out, complete, execute, finish
3 *Can you do these sums?*
▶ answer, puzzle out, solve, work out
4 *I tried to help, but it didn't do any good.*
▶ bring about, cause, produce, result in
5 *You can do as you like.*
▶ act, behave, conduct yourself
6 *He asked for £10, but he said £8 would do.*
▶ be acceptable, be enough, be satisfactory, be sufficient, serve
to do away with *I would like to do away with homework.*
▶ abolish, eliminate, end, get rid of, put an end to
to do up *Do up your coat before you go out.*
▶ button up, fasten
SEE ALSO **fasten**

docile *ADJECTIVE*
Don't be afraid of the dog — he's quite docile.
▶ gentle, manageable, meek, obedient, safe, submissive, tame
AN OPPOSITE IS fierce

dock *NOUN*
PLACES WHERE SHIPS TIE UP, UNLOAD, ETC.
berth, boatyard, dockyard, dry dock, harbour, jetty, landing stage, marina, pier, port, quay, wharf

dock *VERB*
We can't disembark until the ship docks.
▶ moor, tie up

doctor *NOUN*
FOR PEOPLE WHO LOOK AFTER OUR HEALTH SEE **medicine**

doctrine *NOUN*
He explained the main doctrine of his religion.
▶ principle, teaching
▷ A set of doctrines of a particular religion is a **creed**.

document *NOUN*
VARIOUS KINDS OF DOCUMENTS
birth certificate, death certificate, diploma, driver's licence, insurance certificate, insurance policy, marriage certificate, marriage licence, passport, television licence, visa
▷ Legal documents concerning a house you own are the **deeds**. A legal document concerning a business agreement is a **contract**. A document stating what is to happen to your property when you die is a **will**. An official document giving people certain rights is a **charter**. A document giving police a right to search a property is a **warrant**. Historical documents are **records**. A collection of documents relating to a particular thing or issue is the **documentation**.

dodge *VERB*
I dodged the snowball she threw at me.
▶ avoid, evade

dodge *NOUN*
He used various dodges to avoid paying tax.
▶ knack, manoeuvre, technique, trick

dodgy *ADJECTIVE*
Don't buy anything from him — he's a dodgy character.
▶ cunning, deceitful, dishonest, disreputable, shady, unreliable, wily

dog *NOUN*
▷ A female dog is a **bitch**. A young dog is a **puppy** or **whelp**. An uncomplimentary word for a dog is **cur**. A dog of pure breed with known ancestors has a **pedigree**. A dog of mixed breeds is a **mongrel**. A dog used for hunting is a **hound**.
SOME BREEDS OF DOG
Alsatian, basset-hound, beagle, bloodhound, boxer, bulldog, bull-terrier, cairn terrier, chihuahua, chow, cocker spaniel, collie, corgi, dachshund, Dalmatian, foxhound, fox terrier, Great Dane, greyhound, husky, Labrador, mastiff, Pekingese or Pekinese, Pomeranian, poodle, pug, retriever, Rottweiler, setter, spaniel, terrier, whippet

A B C D E F G H I J K L M N O P Q R S T U V W X Y Z

dogged *ADJECTIVE*
I admire the dogged way she kept going.
▸ determined, persistent, resolute, stubborn
▹ If you are dogged in an annoying or unhelpful way you are **obstinate** or stubborn.

domestic *ADJECTIVE*
1 *At weekends I do various domestic chores.*
▸ family, household
2 *Cats and dogs are popular domestic animals.*
▸ domesticated, tame

domesticated *ADJECTIVE*
Is your puppy domesticated yet?
▸ house-trained, trained

dominant *ADJECTIVE*
1 *Russia and the USA are two dominant world powers.*
▸ chief, dominating, leading, main, major, powerful, principal, supreme
AN OPPOSITE IS unimportant
2 *The castle is a dominant feature in the landscape.*
▸ big, conspicuous, eye-catching, imposing, large, obvious, outstanding
AN OPPOSITE IS insignificant

dominate *VERB*
The visiting team dominated the game.
▸ control, govern, monopolize, take control of, take over

donate *VERB*
Will you donate something to our collection?
▸ contribute, give

donor *NOUN*
A generous donor gave us money for new sports equipment.
▸ benefactor, contributor, sponsor

doom *NOUN*
She went to her doom bravely.
▸ end, fate, ruin

door *NOUN*
VARIOUS KINDS OF DOOR OR BARRIER
doorway, emergency exit, entrance, exit, French window, gate, gateway, patio door, portal, postern, revolving door, swing door, turnstile, way out
▹ A door in a floor or ceiling is a **hatch** or **trapdoor**. The plank or stone underneath a door is the **threshold**. The beam or stone above a door is the **lintel**. The device on which most doors swing is the **hinge**.

dose *NOUN*
The nurse gave me a dose of the medicine.
▸ correct amount or quantity, measure

dossier *NOUN*
The spy stole a dossier containing secret plans.
▸ file, folder, set of documents

dot *NOUN*
She was furious when she saw dots of paint on the carpet.
▸ fleck, point, speck, spot
▹ The dot you always put at the end of a sentence is a **full stop**.

double *ADJECTIVE*
There are several words which we use differently to mean 'consisting of two' or 'having two parts':
binary, dual, duplicate, paired, twin

double *NOUN*
She's so like you — she's almost your double.
▸ (*informal*) lookalike, (*informal*) spitting image, twin
▹ A living organism created as an exact copy of another living organism is a **clone**.

double-cross *VERB*
The gangsters hunted down the man who double-crossed them.
▸ betray, cheat

doubt *NOUN*
1 *Have you any doubt about his honesty?*
▸ distrust, hesitation, mistrust, reservation, scepticism, suspicion
AN OPPOSITE IS confidence
2 *There's some doubt about what we're going to do.*
▸ ambiguity, confusion, question, uncertainty
AN OPPOSITE IS certainty

doubt *VERB*
There is no reason to doubt her story.
▸ be sceptical about, be suspicious or wary of, distrust, feel uncertain or uneasy or unsure about, mistrust, question, suspect
AN OPPOSITE IS trust

doubtful *ADJECTIVE*
1 *He looked doubtful, but agreed to let us go.*
▸ distrustful, hesitant, sceptical, suspicious, uncertain, unconvinced, unsure
AN OPPOSITE IS certain
2 *The referee made a doubtful decision there.*
▸ arguable, debatable, questionable

downcast *ADJECTIVE*
What's the matter? You seem downcast today.
▸ dejected, depressed, gloomy, glum, (*informal*) low, melancholy, miserable, sad, unhappy
AN OPPOSITE IS cheerful

downfall *NOUN*
After the government's downfall, we had a general election.
▸ collapse, fall, ruin

downward *ADJECTIVE*
We took the downward path into the valley.
▸ descending, downhill
AN OPPOSITE IS upward

doze *VERB*
Dad often dozes in the evening.
▸ (*informal*) drop off, nod off, rest, sleep

drab *ADJECTIVE*
We brightened up the drab room with some new wallpaper.
▸ cheerless, colourless, dingy, dismal, dreary, dull, gloomy, grey
AN OPPOSITE IS bright

draft *NOUN*
I jotted down a draft of my story.
▸ outline, plan, rough version, sketch

draft *VERB*
I began to draft my story.
▸ plan, prepare, sketch, work out

drag *VERB*
The tractor dragged the car out of the ditch.
▸ draw, haul, lug, pull, tow, tug
AN OPPOSITE IS push
to drag something up *They dragged up a lot of rubbish from the bottom of the canal.*
▸ dredge, lift, raise

drain *NOUN*
Surplus water runs away along a drain.
▸ channel, ditch, drainpipe, gutter, pipe, sewer

drain *VERB*
1 *If they drain the marsh, lots of waterbirds will die.*
▸ dry out, remove water from
2 *She drained the oil from the engine.*
▸ draw off, empty
3 *The water slowly drained away.*
▸ ooze, seep, trickle
4 *The tough climb drained my energy.*
▸ consume, exhaust, use up

drama *NOUN*
1 *Drama is one of my favourite subjects.*
▸ acting
SEE ALSO **theatre**
2 *I witnessed the drama of a real robbery.*
▸ action, excitement, suspense, turmoil

dramatic *ADJECTIVE*
We watched the dramatic rescue on TV.
▸ eventful, exciting, gripping, sensational, tense, thrilling

dramatize *VERB*
1 *They dramatized the story for TV.*
▸ adapt, make into a play
2 *The policeman thought I was dramatizing what had happened.*
▸ exaggerate, make too much of

drastic *ADJECTIVE*
After being without food for three days, the explorers needed to take drastic action.
▸ desperate, extreme, harsh, severe

draught *NOUN*
I felt a draught of air from the open window.
▸ breeze, current, movement, puff

draw *VERB*
1 *I drew pictures while she was talking.*
▸ doodle, sketch, trace
2 *She told us to draw the castle.*
▸ depict, portray, represent
3 *The horse was drawing a cart.*
▸ drag, haul, lug, pull, tow, tug
4 *We expect tomorrow's match to draw a big crowd.*
▸ attract, bring in, pull in
5 *The two teams drew 1–1.*
▸ finish equal, tie
to draw near *As the ship drew near, I got more excited.*
▸ advance, approach, come near

draw *NOUN*
▹ Kinds of prize draw are a lottery and a raffle.

A B C D E F G H I J K L M N O P Q R S T U V W X Y Z

drawback *NOUN*
It's a drawback to be small if you play basketball.
▸ disadvantage, handicap, hindrance, inconvenience

drawing *NOUN*
VARIOUS KINDS OF DRAWING
caricature, cartoon, design, doodle, illustration, outline, sketch
▹ Drawing done on a computer is **computer graphics**.
SEE ALSO **picture** *NOUN*

dread *NOUN*
He has a dread of spiders.
▸ anxiety (about), fear, horror, phobia (about), terror

dreadful *ADJECTIVE*
1 *We saw a dreadful accident on the motorway.*
▸ alarming, appalling, distressing, fearful, frightful, ghastly, grisly, gruesome, horrible, horrifying, shocking, terrible, tragic, upsetting
2 *We had dreadful weather on holiday.*
▸ abominable, awful, bad, dire, (*informal*) filthy, foul, horrid, nasty
AN OPPOSITE IS pleasant

dream *NOUN*
▹ A bad dream is a **nightmare**. A dreamlike experience you have while awake is a **daydream**, **fantasy**, or **reverie**. Something you see in dreams or daydreams is a **vision**. The dreamlike state when you are hypnotized is a **trance**. Something you think you see that is not real is a **hallucination** or **illusion**. Something you dream of achieving in the future is an **ambition**. An ambition you dream of which is not likely to happen is a **pipedream**.

dream *VERB*
I dreamed that I could fly.
▸ daydream, fancy, have a vision, imagine
▹ To have a fantasy is to **fantasize**.

dreary *ADJECTIVE*
1 *Unfortunately, the lecturer had a dreary voice.*
▸ boring, dull, flat, tedious, unexciting, uninteresting
AN OPPOSITE IS lively
2 *When will this dreary weather end?*
▸ cheerless, depressing, dismal, dull, gloomy, murky, overcast
AN OPPOSITE IS bright or sunny

drench *VERB*
The rain drenched me to the skin.
▸ soak, wet thoroughly

dress *NOUN*
1 *She bought a dress to wear to the party.*
▸ frock, gown
2 *She told us to wear appropriate dress for a picnic.*
▸ clothes, clothing, costume, garments, outfit
SEE ALSO **clothes**

dress *VERB*
1 *I helped to dress my little brother.*
▸ clothe, put clothes on
AN OPPOSITE IS undress
2 *A nurse dressed my wound.*
▸ bandage, bind up, put a dressing on

dressing *NOUN*
1 *Do you want dressing on your salad?*
▸ French dressing, mayonnaise
2 *The nurse put a dressing on the wound.*
▸ bandage, compress, plaster, poultice

dribble *VERB*
1 *Careful, the baby's dribbling on your jumper.*
▸ drool
2 *Water dribbled out of the hole in the tank.*
▸ drip, leak, ooze, seep, trickle

drift *VERB*
1 *The boat drifted downstream.*
▸ be carried, float, move slowly
2 *The crowd lost interest and drifted away.*
▸ meander, ramble, stray, walk aimlessly, wander
3 *The snow will drift in this wind.*
▸ accumulate, make drifts, pile up

drift *NOUN*
1 *The car was stuck in a snow drift.*
▸ accumulation, bank, heap, mound, pile, ridge
2 *Did you understand the drift of the speech?*
▸ gist, main idea, point

drill *NOUN*
1 *Drill is an important part of a soldier's life.*
▸ practice, training
2 *You know the drill, so make a start on erecting the tent.*
▸ procedure, routine, system

drill *VERB*
It took a long time to drill through the concrete.
▸ bore, penetrate, pierce

drink *NOUN*
SOME HOT DRINKS
chocolate, cocoa, coffee, tea
SOME NON-ALCOHOLIC COLD DRINKS
barley water, cola, cordial, fruit juice, ginger beer, lemonade, lime juice, milk, milkshake, mineral water, orangeade, pop, sodawater, squash, tonic water, water
SOME ALCOHOLIC DRINKS
ale, beer, champagne, cider, lager, mead, port, punch, red wine, shandy, sherry, white wine
▹ Very strong alcoholic drinks are **spirits**. Specially flavoured spirits are **liqueurs**.
SOME SPIRITS
brandy, gin, rum, vodka, whisky
THINGS YOU DRINK FROM
beaker, cup, glass, goblet, mug, tankard, tumbler, wineglass

drink *VERB*
▹ To drink greedily is to **gulp**, **guzzle**, or **swig**. To drink a small amount at a time is to **sip**. To drink with the tongue as a cat does is to **lap**.

drip *NOUN*
Dad was worried by the drips of oil underneath the car.
▸ dribble, splash, spot, trickle

drip *VERB*
The oil dripped onto the garage floor.
▸ dribble, drop, leak, splash, trickle

drive *VERB*
1 *The dog drove the sheep through the gate.*
▸ direct, guide, herd
2 *I couldn't drive the spade into the hard ground.*
▸ hammer, plunge, push, ram, thrust
3 *When can I learn to drive a car?*
▸ control, handle, manage
4 *Lack of money drove him to steal.*
▸ compel, force, oblige
to drive someone out *The invading soldiers drove the people out.*
▸ eject, expel, throw out
▹ To drive people out of their homes is to **evict** them. To drive people out of their country is to **banish** or **exile** them.

drive *NOUN*
1 *We went for a drive in the country.*
▸ excursion, jaunt, journey, outing, ride, trip
2 *Have you got the drive to succeed?*
▸ ambition, determination, energy, enterprise, enthusiasm, initiative, keenness, motivation, persistence, zeal

driver *NOUN*
Many drivers go too fast.
▸ motorist
▹ A person who drives someone's car as a job is a **chauffeur**.

droop *VERB*
Plants tend to droop in dry weather.
▸ be limp, bend, flop, sag, wilt

drop *NOUN*
1 *Large drops of rain began to fall.*
▸ bead, blob, drip, droplet, spot
2 *Could I have another drop of milk in my tea?*
▸ dash, small quantity
3 *We expect a drop in the price of fruit in the summer.*
▸ cut, decrease, reduction
4 *There's a drop of two metres on the other side of the wall.*
▸ descent, fall, plunge

drop *VERB*
1 *The hawk dropped onto its prey.*
▸ descend, dive, plunge, swoop
2 *I dropped to the ground exhausted.*
▸ collapse, fall, sink, slump, subside, tumble
3 *Why did you drop me from the team?*
▸ eliminate, exclude, leave out, omit
4 *They dropped the plan for a new bypass.*
▸ abandon, discard, give up, reject, scrap
to drop in *Drop in on your way home.*
▸ call, pay a call, visit
to drop out *Why did you drop out at the last minute?*
▸ back out, pull out, (*informal*) quit, withdraw

drown *VERB*
The music drowned our conversation.
▸ overwhelm

drowsy *ADJECTIVE*
If you feel drowsy, why not go to bed?
▸ sleepy, tired, weary

A B C D E F G H I J K L M N O P Q R S T U V W X Y Z

drug *NOUN*
The doctor knows which drugs will make you better.
▸ medicine, remedy, treatment
▹ A drug which relieves pain is an **analgesic** or **painkiller**. A drug which calms you down is a **sedative** or **tranquillizer**. Drugs which make you sleepy are **narcotics**. Drugs which make you more active are **stimulants**. An informal word for addictive or narcotic drugs is **dope**.

drum *NOUN*
We heard the warlike sound of drums and trumpets.
VARIOUS DRUMS
bass drum, bongo drum, kettledrum or timpani, side drum, snare drum, tabor, tambour, timpani, tom-tom
FOR OTHER PERCUSSION INSTRUMENTS SEE **music**

drunk *ADJECTIVE*
He got drunk and had to be taken home.
▸ intoxicated, (*informal*) tight
AN OPPOSITE IS sober

drunkard *NOUN*
He lost his job because he was a drunkard.
▸ alcoholic, drunk
AN OPPOSITE IS teetotaller

dry *ADJECTIVE*
1 *Nothing will grow in this dry soil.*
▸ arid, barren, dehydrated, moistureless, parched, waterless
AN OPPOSITE IS wet
2 *He gave rather a dry speech.*
▸ boring, dreary, dull, tedious, uninteresting
AN OPPOSITE IS interesting
3 *He has a dry sense of humour — you can't tell whether he is joking or not.*
▸ ironic, quiet, subtle

dry *VERB*
1 *She took the clothes out of the washing machine and hung them up to dry.*
▸ dry out, get dry
2 *Will you please dry the dishes?*
▸ wipe dry
to dry out, to dry up *The young plants all dried up in the drought.*
▸ become dry, shrivel, wilt, wither
▹ When you dry food to preserve it, you **dehydrate** it. When your throat feels very dry, you are **parched**.
3 (*informal*) *Why don't you just dry up!*
▸ become silent, stop talking

dual *ADJECTIVE*
There are several words which we use differently to mean *consisting of two* or *having two parts*:
binary, double, duplicate, paired, twin

duck *NOUN*
▹ A male duck is a **drake**. A young duck is a **duckling**.

duck *VERB*
1 *I ducked when he threw a stone at me.*
▸ bend down, bob down, crouch, stoop
2 *They ducked me in the pool.*
▸ immerse, plunge, push under, submerge

due *ADJECTIVE*
1 *The train is due in five minutes.*
▸ anticipated, expected
2 *Subscriptions are now due.*
▸ owed, owing, payable
3 *I give her due credit for what she did.*
▸ appropriate, deserved, fitting, proper, suitable, well-earned

dull *ADJECTIVE*
1 *I don't like the dull colours in this room.*
▸ dim, dingy, dismal, drab, dreary, faded, gloomy, sombre, subdued
AN OPPOSITE IS bright
2 *The sky was dull that day.*
▸ cloudy, grey, heavy, murky, overcast, sunless
AN OPPOSITE IS clear
3 *I heard a dull thud from upstairs.*
▸ indistinct, muffled, muted
AN OPPOSITE IS distinct
4 *He's rather a dull student.*
▸ (*informal*) dense, dim, obtuse, slow, stupid, (*informal*) thick, unimaginative, unintelligent
AN OPPOSITE IS clever
5 *The lecture was so dull that I fell asleep.*
▸ boring, dry, monotonous, tedious, unexciting, uninteresting
AN OPPOSITE IS interesting

dumb *ADJECTIVE*
1 *I was struck dumb with amazement.*
▷ If you do not speak, you are **mute** or **silent**. If you cannot speak because you are surprised, confused, or embarrassed, you are **speechless** or **tongue-tied**. If you find it hard to express yourself, you are **inarticulate**.
2 (*informal*) *He's too dumb to understand.*
▸ (*informal*) dense, dim, obtuse, slow, stupid, (*informal*) thick, unintelligent

dumbfounded *ADJECTIVE*
I was dumbfounded when I heard the news.
▸ amazed, astonished, astounded, (*informal*) flabbergasted, speechless, struck dumb, stunned

dummy *NOUN*
The revolver used in the robbery was a dummy.
▸ copy, imitation, toy

dump *VERB*
1 *I decided to dump the old toys I never use.*
▸ discard, dispose of, get rid of, scrap, throw away
2 *Dump your things on the table.*
▸ drop, place, put down, throw down, tip

duplicate *NOUN*
We made a duplicate of the original document.
▸ carbon copy, copy, photocopy, reproduction
▷ An exact copy of a historic document or manuscript is a **facsimile**. An exact copy of a thing is a **replica**. A person who looks like you is your **double** or **twin**. A living organism which is a duplicate of another living organism is a **clone**.

duplicate *VERB*
She used the photocopier to duplicate some papers.
▸ copy, photocopy

durable *ADJECTIVE*
These expensive trainers ought to be more durable than the cheap ones.
▸ hard-wearing, lasting, robust, strong, tough
AN OPPOSITE IS flimsy

duration *NOUN*
They stayed there for the duration of the holiday.
▸ length, period

dusk *NOUN*
I'll meet you at dusk.
▸ nightfall, sundown, sunset, twilight
AN OPPOSITE IS dawn

dust *NOUN*
There was a lot of dust on the furniture.
▸ dirt, particles, powder

dust *VERB*
1 *I dusted the bookshelves.*
▸ clean, polish, wipe over
2 *Mum dusted the top of the cake with icing sugar.*
▸ powder, sprinkle

dusty *ADJECTIVE*
The things we found in the attic were very dusty.
▸ dirty, grimy
AN OPPOSITE IS clean

dutiful *ADJECTIVE*
She is a kind and dutiful daughter.
▸ conscientious, devoted, faithful, loyal, obedient, reliable, responsible, thorough, trustworthy
AN OPPOSITE IS irresponsible or lazy

duty *NOUN*
1 *I have a duty to help my parents.*
▸ obligation, responsibility
2 *I carried out my duties conscientiously.*
▸ assignment, job, task
3 *You may have to pay a duty if you bring things into the country from abroad.*
▸ charge, tax

dwarf *VERB*
He was so tall that he dwarfed the others.
▸ look much bigger than, tower over

dwell *VERB*
to dwell in *Groups of gypsies still dwell in these caves.*
▸ inhabit, live in, occupy, reside in
to dwell on *Try not to dwell on things that happened in the past.*
▸ brood over, keep thinking about, worry about

dwelling *NOUN*
SEE **house** *NOUN*

A B C D E F G H I J K L M N O P Q R S T U V W X Y Z

dwindle *VERB*
Our enthusiasm dwindled as the day went on.
▶ become less, decline, decrease, diminish, lessen, subside, wane, weaken
AN OPPOSITE IS increase

dying *ADJECTIVE*
1 *The vet put the dying animal out of its misery.*
▶ expiring
2 *I pulled up the dying plants.*
▶ drooping, fading, wilting, withering
AN OPPOSITE IS lively or thriving

dynamic *ADJECTIVE*
The new captain gave the team the dynamic leadership it needed.
▶ active, energetic, enterprising, enthusiastic, forceful, lively, powerful, vigorous
AN OPPOSITE IS apathetic

Ee

eager *ADJECTIVE*
We were eager to help.
▶ anxious, enthusiastic, keen
AN OPPOSITE IS apathetic

eagerness *NOUN*
The teacher was impressed by our eagerness to begin work.
▶ desire, enthusiasm, keenness

early *ADJECTIVE*
1 *The bus was early today.*
▶ ahead of schedule, ahead of time
AN OPPOSITE IS late
2 *The early computers were huge machines.*
▶ first, old
AN OPPOSITE IS advanced or recent

earmark *VERB*
I decided to earmark £10 of my birthday money to buy a CD.
▶ reserve, set aside

earn *VERB*
1 *My cousin earns extra pocket money washing cars.*
▶ bring in, get, make, obtain, receive, work for
2 *You trained hard and earned your success.*
▶ deserve, merit

earnest *ADJECTIVE*
He's a terribly earnest young man.
▶ grave, serious, sincere, solemn, thoughtful
AN OPPOSITE IS casual or flippant

earnings *PLURAL NOUN*
My brother's earnings are not enough for him to live on.
▶ income, pay
▷ Earnings that you are paid week by week are your **wages**. Regular yearly earnings, usually paid in monthly instalments, are your **salary**. A payment someone receives for doing a single job is a **fee**.

earth *NOUN*
The earth was so dry that many plants died.
▶ ground, land, soil
▷ Rich, fertile earth is **loam**. The top layer of fertile earth is **topsoil**. Rich earth consisting of decayed plants is **humus**. A heavy, sticky kind of earth is **clay**.

earthquake *NOUN*
▷ When there is an earthquake, you feel a **shock** or **tremor**. An instrument which detects and measures earthquakes is a **seismograph**.

ease *NOUN*
1 *He did the job with ease.*
▶ facility, skill, speed
AN OPPOSITE IS difficulty
2 *She leads a life of ease.*
▶ comfort, contentment, leisure, peace, quiet, relaxation, rest, tranquillity
AN OPPOSITE IS stress

ease *VERB*
1 *The doctor gave her some pills to ease her pain.*
▶ lessen, moderate, relieve, soothe
AN OPPOSITE IS aggravate
2 *After taking the pills, the pain began to ease.*
▶ decrease, reduce, slacken
AN OPPOSITE IS increase
3 *We eased the piano into position.*
▶ edge, guide, manoeuvre, move gradually, slide, slip

east *NOUN, ADJECTIVE, ADVERB*
▷ The parts of a country or continent in the east are the **eastern** parts. The countries of east Asia, east of the Mediterranean, are called **oriental** countries. To travel towards the east is to travel **eastward** or **eastwards** or **in an easterly direction**. A wind from the east is an **easterly** wind.

easy *ADJECTIVE*
1 *The work was easy.*
▶ effortless, light, undemanding
2 *The instructions were easy to understand.*
▶ clear, elementary, plain, simple, straightforward
3 *She is an easy person to get on with.*
▶ amiable, friendly, good-natured, informal, pleasant, tolerant
4 *Our cat has an easy life.*
▶ carefree, comfortable, leisurely, peaceful, relaxed, relaxing, restful, tranquil, untroubled
AN OPPOSITE IS difficult

eat *VERB* This word is often overused.
He was eating a hot dog.
▶ consume, devour
▷ When cattle eat grass they are **grazing**.
VARIOUS WAYS TO EAT
bite, chew, crunch, gnaw, munch
▷ To eat very quickly is to **bolt** or **gobble** your food. To eat a lot of food is to **gorge yourself** or **overeat**. To eat in large mouthfuls is to **gulp** your food. To eat in small mouthfuls is to **nibble** or **peck** at your food. If you eat a little food to see what it is like, you **taste** it. To eat a large, formal meal is to **banquet** or **dine** or **feast**.
FOR THINGS TO EAT SEE **food**
to eat something away *The flood began to eat away the river bank.*
▶ erode, wear away

eatable *ADJECTIVE*
Is the food eatable?
▶ edible, fit to eat, good, safe to eat
AN OPPOSITE IS inedible or uneatable

ebb *VERB*
1 *The fishermen waited for the tide to ebb.*
▶ fall, flow back, go down, recede, retreat
2 *She fell ill and her strength began to ebb.*
▶ decline, fade, lessen, wane, weaken

eccentric *ADJECTIVE*
What is the reason for his eccentric behaviour?
▶ abnormal, curious, odd, peculiar, strange, unconventional, unusual, weird, zany
AN OPPOSITE IS conventional

echo *VERB*
1 *The sound echoed across the valley.*
▶ resound
2 *'He's gone home.' 'Gone home?' she echoed.*
▶ repeat

economic *ADJECTIVE*
1 *The Chancellor of the Exchequer looks after the country's economic affairs.*
▶ business, financial
2 *It's not economic to open the shop on Sundays.*
▶ profitable, worthwhile

economical *ADJECTIVE*
1 *My uncle is very economical with his money.*
▶ careful, frugal, prudent, thrifty
▷ If you are economical with money in a selfish way, you are **mean** or **miserly**.
AN OPPOSITE IS wasteful
2 *It's an economical car to run.*
▶ cheap, inexpensive, reasonable
AN OPPOSITE IS expensive

economize *VERB*
If you're poor you have to economize.
▶ be economical, cut back, spend less

economy *NOUN*
1 *The Chancellor of the Exchequer looks after the national economy.*
▶ budget, economic affairs, wealth
2 *They turned off the light for reasons of economy.*
▶ frugality, prudence, saving, thrift

ecstasy *NOUN*
You should see my dog's ecstasy when I come home!
▶ bliss, delight, elation

ecstatic *ADJECTIVE*
They gave me an ecstatic welcome.
▶ blissful, delighted, delirious, elated, enthusiastic, exultant, fervent, frenzied, gleeful, joyful, passionate

A B C D E F G H I J K L M N O P Q R S T U V W X Y Z

edge *NOUN*
▹ The edge of a cliff or other steep place is the **brink**. The edge of a cup or other container is the **brim** or **rim**. The line round the edge of a circle is the **circumference**. The line round the edge of any other shape is its **outline**. The distance round the edge of an area is the **perimeter**. The stones along the edge of a road are the **kerb**. Grass along the edge of a road is the **verge**. The space down the edge of a page is the **margin**. The space round the edge of a picture is a **border**. Something that fits round the edge of a picture is a **frame**. The edge of a skirt, etc., is the **hem**. An edge with threads or hair hanging loosely down is a **fringe**. The edge of a crowd also is the **fringe** of the crowd. The area round the edge of a city is the **outskirts** or **suburbs**. The edge of a cricket field is the **boundary**. The edge of a football pitch is the **touchline**.

edge *VERB*
1 *I edged away from the lion.*
▸ creep, move stealthily, slink, steal
2 *Mum edged the curtains with a fringe.*
▸ trim

edgy *ADJECTIVE*
The horses became edgy during the thunderstorm.
▸ agitated, anxious, excitable, fidgety, fraught, irritable, jumpy, nervous, restless, tense, (*informal*) uptight
AN OPPOSITE IS calm

edible *ADJECTIVE*
Are these toadstools edible?
▸ eatable, fit to eat, good to eat, safe to eat
AN OPPOSITE IS poisonous or uneatable

edit *VERB*
Her job was to edit the magazine.
▸ compile, get ready, organize, prepare, put together
WAYS YOU MIGHT EDIT CONTRIBUTIONS TO A MAGAZINE, ETC.
abridge or shorten, adapt or alter, censor, condense or cut or shorten, correct, format, proof-read, revise or rewrite

edition *NOUN*
1 *We prepared a Christmas edition of our magazine.*
▸ copy, issue, number
2 *Our teacher bought the latest edition of the Junior Dictionary.*
▸ version

educate *VERB*
The job of a school is to educate young people.
▸ inform, instruct, teach, train

educated *ADJECTIVE*
She is an educated woman.
▸ cultivated, cultured, knowledgeable, learned, literate, well informed, well read

education *NOUN*
Education is important if you want to get on in life.
▸ instruction, schooling, teaching, training
▹ A programme of education is the **curriculum** or **syllabus**.
PEOPLE WHO MAY HELP TO EDUCATE US
coach, counsellor, governess, headteacher, instructor, lecturer, professor, teacher, trainer, tutor
PLACES WHERE WE RECEIVE EDUCATION
academy, college, kindergarten, playgroup, primary school, secondary school, sixth-form college, university

eerie *ADJECTIVE*
I heard some eerie sounds in the night.
▸ creepy, frightening, ghostly, mysterious, (*informal*) scary, sinister, (*informal*) spooky, strange, uncanny, unearthly, unnatural, weird

effect *NOUN*
1 *The effect of eating too much was that I became fat!*
▸ consequence, outcome, result, sequel, upshot
2 *Does this music have any effect on you?*
▸ impact, influence
3 *The lighting gives an effect of warmth.*
▸ feeling, illusion, impression, sense

effective *ADJECTIVE*
1 *I wish they could find an effective cure for colds.*
▸ successful
2 *Our team needs an effective goalkeeper.*
▸ able, capable, competent, proficient, skilled
3 *He presented an effective argument against hunting.*
▸ compelling, convincing, impressive, persuasive, telling
AN OPPOSITE IS useless

effervescent *ADJECTIVE*
He preferred effervescent drinks to the still kind.
▸ bubbly, fizzy, sparkling
AN OPPOSITE IS still

efficient *ADJECTIVE*
1 *An efficient worker can do the job in an hour.*
▸ able, capable, competent, effective, proficient
2 *Dad tried to work out an efficient way of heating our house.*
▸ economic, productive
AN OPPOSITE IS inefficient

effort *NOUN*
1 *A lot of effort went into making that piece of work.*
▸ exertion, hard work, industry, labour, toil, work
2 *She congratulated us on a good effort.*
▸ attempt, endeavour, go, performance, try

effortless *ADJECTIVE*
She's so good at it that she makes it look effortless.
▸ easy, painless, undemanding
AN OPPOSITE IS hard

egg *VERB*
to egg someone on *We egged him on, even though we knew it was dangerous to climb the tree.*
▸ encourage, spur on

eject *VERB*
1 *Lava was ejected from the volcano when it erupted.*
▸ discharge, emit
2 *The caretaker ejected an intruder from the building.*
▸ banish, evict, expel, kick out, remove, throw out, turn out

elaborate *ADJECTIVE*
The plan was so elaborate that it was hard to remember all the details.
▸ complex, complicated, detailed, intricate, involved
AN OPPOSITE IS simple

elaborate *VERB*
He refused to elaborate his plan.
▸ add to, amplify, develop, expand, fill out, improve on
AN OPPOSITE IS simplify

elated *ADJECTIVE*
We were elated when we beat our rivals.
▸ delighted, delirious, ecstatic, exultant, gleeful, joyful, (*slang*) over the moon, pleased, thrilled

elder *ADJECTIVE*
My elder brother is in the football team.
▸ older

elderly *ADJECTIVE*
I helped the elderly couple to get on the bus.
▸ aged, rather old
AN OPPOSITE IS young

eldest *ADJECTIVE*
Jane is my eldest sister.
▸ oldest

elect *VERB*
We elected a new captain.
▸ appoint, vote for

election *NOUN*
We had an election to choose a new captain.
▸ ballot, poll, vote

electricity *NOUN*
Is the electricity on?
▸ current, power, power supply
▹ Someone whose job is to fit and repair electrical equipment is an **electrician**.
SOME THINGS AN ELECTRICIAN MIGHT FIT OR REPAIR
adaptor, battery, cable, charger, circuit, dynamo, flex, fuse, generator, heating, insulation, lead, lighting, meter, plug, power point, socket, switch, terminal, transformer, wiring

elegant *ADJECTIVE*
She always wears elegant clothes.
▸ chic, fashionable, graceful, smart, sophisticated, stylish, tasteful
AN OPPOSITE IS inelegant

element *NOUN*
They discussed various elements of the book.
▸ component, constituent, feature, part
to be in your element *A duck would be in its element in this wet weather.*
▸ be at home, be comfortable, be happy, enjoy yourself
the elements 1 *The mountaineers battled against the elements.*
▸ the forces of nature, the weather
SEE ALSO **weather**

2 *We were taught the elements of algebra.*
▸ the basic facts, the fundamental facts, the principles

elementary *ADJECTIVE*
Anyone can solve such an elementary problem.
▸ basic, easy, fundamental, simple, straightforward, uncomplicated
AN OPPOSITE IS advanced or complex

eligible *ADJECTIVE*
Children over twelve are not eligible to enter this race.
▸ allowed, authorized, qualified, suitable
AN OPPOSITE IS ineligible

eliminate *VERB*
The government wants to eliminate crime.
▸ get rid of, put an end to
▹ To be eliminated from a competition is to be knocked out.

eloquent *ADJECTIVE*
The lawyer's eloquent speech convinced the jury.
▸ articulate, expressive, fluent, persuasive

elude *VERB*
The police chased him, but he managed to elude them.
▸ avoid, escape from, evade, get away from

elusive *ADJECTIVE*
Deer are elusive animals.
▸ evasive, hard to find

emancipate *VERB*
Wilberforce worked for years to emancipate the slaves.
▸ free, liberate, release, set free

embark *VERB*
The passengers embarked in time for the ship to sail at high tide.
▸ board, go aboard
AN OPPOSITE IS disembark
to embark on something *Today we embarked on a big project.*
▸ begin, commence, start, undertake

embarrass *VERB*
Will it embarrass you if I tell people our secret?
▸ distress, humiliate, make you blush

embarrassed *ADJECTIVE*
Don't feel embarrassed — it happens to everyone!
▸ ashamed, awkward, bashful, distressed, flustered, humiliated, self-conscious, uncomfortable

embers *PLURAL NOUN*
The embers of the fire were still glowing next morning.
▸ ashes, cinders

emblem *NOUN*
The dove is an emblem of peace.
▸ sign, symbol

embrace *VERB*
1 *She embraced him lovingly.*
▸ clasp, cuddle, hold, hug
2 *She's always ready to embrace new ideas.*
▸ accept, adopt, take on, welcome
3 *The syllabus embraces all aspects of the subject.*
▸ include, incorporate, take in

embryo *NOUN*
A human embryo is in the mother's womb for nine months.
▸ foetus

emerge *VERB*
He didn't emerge from his bedroom until ten o'clock.
▸ appear, come out

emergency *NOUN*
Try to keep calm in an emergency.
▸ crisis, danger, difficulty, serious situation

emigrant *NOUN*
AN OPPOSITE IS immigrant

emigrate *VERB*
During the famine, many Irish people were forced to emigrate to America.
▸ leave the country, move abroad
AN OPPOSITE IS immigrate

eminent *ADJECTIVE*
An eminent author came to give us a talk.
▸ celebrated, distinguished, famous, great, notable, prominent, renowned, respected, well known
AN OPPOSITE IS unknown

emit *VERB*
1 *The exhaust pipe emitted clouds of smoke.*
▸ belch, blow out, discharge, expel, give off
2 *The satellite was emitting radio signals.*
▸ give out, send out, transmit
AN OPPOSITE IS receive

emotion *NOUN*
His voice was full of emotion.
▸ feeling, fervour, passion, sentiment

emotional *ADJECTIVE*
1 *He made an emotional farewell speech.*
▸ moving, touching
2 *The music for the love scenes was very emotional.*
▸ romantic, sentimental
3 *She's a very emotional woman.*
▸ intense, passionate
AN OPPOSITE IS unemotional

emphasis *NOUN*
In the word 'dictionary' the emphasis is on the first syllable.
▸ accent, stress, weight

emphasize *VERB*
She emphasized the important points.
▸ dwell on, focus on, give emphasis to, highlight, stress, underline

employ *VERB*
1 *The new factory plans to employ 100 workers.*
▸ engage, give work to, hire, take on
2 *The factory will employ the latest methods.*
▸ use, utilize

employee *NOUN*
100 employees will work at the new factory.
▸ worker
▹ A word for all the employees of an organization is **staff** or **workforce**.

employer *NOUN*
He asked his employer for a pay rise.
▸ (*informal*) boss, chief, head, manager, owner

employment *NOUN*
There are a lot of people in our area looking for employment.
▸ a job, an occupation, a profession, a trade, work
FOR PARTICULAR KINDS OF EMPLOYMENT SEE **job**

empty *ADJECTIVE*
1 *Please put the empty milk bottles outside the door.*
AN OPPOSITE IS full
2 *The house next to ours has been empty for weeks.*
▸ deserted, uninhabited, unoccupied, vacant
AN OPPOSITE IS occupied
3 *After we put up our display, there was still some empty space on the wall.*
▸ bare, blank, clear, unused

empty *VERB*
1 *Empty the dirty water into the sink.*
▸ drain, pour out
AN OPPOSITE IS fill
2 *The building emptied when the fire alarm went off.*
▸ clear, evacuate
3 *Did you empty all the shopping out of the trolley?*
▸ remove, unload

enable *VERB*
1 *The fine weather enabled us to do the job quickly.*
▸ aid, assist, help, make it possible for
2 *A passport enables you to travel abroad.*
▸ allow, authorize, entitle, permit
AN OPPOSITE IS prevent

enchant *VERB*
The ballet enchanted us.
▸ bewitch, charm, delight, entrance, fascinate

enchantment *NOUN*
The forest had an air of enchantment.
▸ delight, magic, pleasure, wonder

encircle *VERB*
The pond was encircled by trees.
▸ ring, surround

enclose *VERB*
1 *The documents were enclosed in a brown paper envelope.*
▸ contain, insert, sheathe, wrap
2 *The animals were enclosed within a wire fence.*
▸ confine, fence in, imprison, restrict, shut in

enclosure *NOUN*
▹ An animal's enclosure with bars is a **cage**. An enclosure for chickens is a **coop** or **run**. An enclosure for cattle and other animals is a **pen** or **corral**. An enclosure for horses is a **paddock**. An enclosure for sheep is a **fold**. An enclosure for lost animals or towed-away vehicles is a **pound**. An enclosure with buildings in it is a **compound**. An enclosure for sporting events is an **arena** or **stadium**.

A B C D E F G H I J K L M N O P Q R S T U V W X Y Z

encounter *VERB*
1 *He encountered her outside the station.*
▸ come face to face with, meet, run into
2 *We encountered some problems.*
▸ come upon, confront, experience, be faced with

encourage *VERB*
1 *We went to the match to encourage our team.*
▸ applaud, cheer, egg on, inspire, motivate, spur on, support
2 *Our doctor encourages people to stop smoking.*
▸ persuade, urge
3 *Is advertising likely to encourage sales?*
▸ aid, boost, further, help, increase, promote, stimulate
AN OPPOSITE IS discourage

encouragement *NOUN*
Our team needs some encouragement.
▸ applause, incentive, inspiration, reassurance, stimulation, stimulus, support

encouraging *ADJECTIVE*
The results of the tests were encouraging.
▸ cheering, favourable, hopeful, optimistic, positive, promising, reassuring

end *NOUN*
1 *The fence marks the end of the garden.*
▸ boundary, limit
2 *The end of the film was the most exciting part.*
▸ close, conclusion, culmination, ending, finish
▹ The last part of a show or piece of music is the **finale**. A section added at the end of a letter is a **postscript**. A section added at the end of a story is an **epilogue**.
3 *I was tired by the time we got to the end of the journey.*
▸ destination, termination
4 *We arrived late and found ourselves at the end of the queue.*
▸ back, rear, tail
5 *What end did you have in view when you started?*
▸ aim, intention, objective, outcome, plan, purpose, result

end *VERB* This word is often overused.
1 *We ended our work just in time for dinner.*
▸ break off, complete, conclude, finish, halt, (*informal*) round off
2 *When did they end public executions?*
▸ abolish, do away with, eliminate, get rid of, put an end to
3 *The concert ended with the National Anthem.*
▸ cease, close, come to an end, culminate, stop, terminate, wind up

endanger *VERB*
Bad driving endangers other people.
▸ put at risk, threaten
AN OPPOSITE IS protect

endeavour *VERB*
Please endeavour to behave well.
▸ aim, attempt, make an effort, strive, try

ending *NOUN*
The ending of the film was the most exciting part.
▸ close, conclusion, culmination, end, finish, last part
▹ The ending of a show or piece of music is the **finale**.

endless *ADJECTIVE*
1 *Teachers need endless patience.*
▸ inexhaustible, infinite, limitless, unending, unlimited
2 *There's an endless procession of cars along the main road.*
▸ ceaseless, constant, continual, continuous, everlasting, incessant, interminable, perpetual, unbroken, uninterrupted

endurance *NOUN*
The climb was a test of their endurance.
▸ determination, perseverance, persistence, resolution, stamina

endure *VERB*
1 *She had to endure a lot of pain.*
▸ bear, cope with, experience, go through, put up with, stand, suffer, tolerate, undergo
2 *These traditions have endured for centuries.*
▸ carry on, continue, keep going, last, persist, survive

enemy *NOUN*
They used to be friends but now they are bitter enemies.
▸ adversary, foe, opponent, rival
AN OPPOSITE IS ally or friend

energetic *ADJECTIVE*
1 *She's a very energetic person.*
▸ active, dynamic, enthusiastic, hard-working, tireless
2 *It was a very energetic exercise routine.*
▸ brisk, fast, lively, quick moving, strenuous, vigorous
AN OPPOSITE IS lethargic

energy *NOUN*
1 *The dancers had tremendous energy.*
▸ drive, enthusiasm, liveliness, spirit, stamina, strength, vigour, vitality, zest
2 *Industry needs a reliable supply of energy.*
▸ fuel, power

enforce *VERB*
The umpire's job is to enforce the rules.
▸ administer, apply, carry out, implement, impose, insist on, put into effect

engage *VERB*
1 *The builder engaged extra workers in order to complete the job on time.*
▸ employ, hire, take on
2 *The general decided to engage the enemy at dawn.*
▸ attack, start fighting
to engage someone in conversation *She engaged me in conversation and I couldn't get away.*
▸ converse with, talk to

engaged *ADJECTIVE*
1 *He was engaged in his work.*
▸ absorbed, busy, engrossed, immersed, occupied, tied up
AN OPPOSITE IS idle
2 *I tried to phone but the line was engaged.*
▸ being used, busy, unavailable
AN OPPOSITE IS available

engagement *NOUN*
1 *Dad has a business engagement this afternoon.*
▸ appointment, commitment, date, meeting
2 *The engagement between the two armies was brief and bloody.*
▸ action, battle, clash, conflict, (*plural*) hostilities

engine *NOUN*
VARIOUS KINDS OF ENGINE
diesel engine, electric motor, internal-combustion engine, jet engine, outboard motor, petrol engine, steam engine, turbine, turbojet, turboprop
▷ A railway engine is a **locomotive**.
PARTS OF A PETROL ENGINE
alternator, carburettor, cooling system, crankshaft, cylinder block, cylinders, distributor, fuel injection, oil filter, pistons, starter motor, throttle, valves

engrave *VERB*
An inscription was engraved on the stone.
▸ carve, cut, etch

engrossed *ADJECTIVE*
She was engrossed in her work.
▸ absorbed, busy, engaged, immersed, occupied

engulf *VERB*
The tidal wave engulfed several villages near the coast.
▸ drown, flood, immerse, inundate, overwhelm, submerge, swallow up, swamp

enhance *VERB*
The team's victory enhanced their reputation.
▸ improve, strengthen

enjoy *VERB*
I really enjoyed the film.
▸ admire, appreciate, be pleased by, get pleasure from, like, love

enjoyable *ADJECTIVE*
It was an enjoyable party.
▸ agreeable, amusing, delightful, entertaining, pleasant
AN OPPOSITE IS unpleasant

enlarge *VERB*
Business is so good that they plan to enlarge the shop.
▸ build on to, develop, expand, extend, increase the size of, make bigger
▷ To make something wider is to **broaden** or **widen** it. To make something longer is to **extend**, **lengthen**, or **stretch** it. To make something seem larger is to **magnify** it.
AN OPPOSITE IS reduce

enlist *VERB*
Many men decided to enlist in the army.
▸ enrol, join up, sign on, volunteer

enormity *NOUN*
The enormity of the crime shocked the whole country.
▸ dreadfulness, evil, villainy, wickedness

enormous *ADJECTIVE*
Enormous waves battered the ship.
▸ colossal, gigantic, huge, immense, massive, monstrous, monumental, mountainous, towering, tremendous, vast
AN OPPOSITE IS small

A B C D E F G H I J K L M N O P Q R S T U V W X Y Z

enough ADJECTIVE
Is there enough food for ten people?
▸ adequate, ample, sufficient

enquire VERB
He enquired if I was well.
▸ ask, inquire
to enquire about *I enquired about train times to London.*
▸ ask for, get information about, investigate, request

enquiry NOUN
The librarian help me with my enquiry.
▸ investigation, question, request, research

enrage VERB
I was enraged by their stupidity.
▸ anger, exasperate, incense, infuriate, madden, provoke
AN OPPOSITE IS pacify

enrol VERB
I enrolled as a member of the drama club.
▸ join, put your name down, sign up, volunteer

ensure VERB
Please ensure that you lock the door before you go out.
▸ confirm, make certain, make sure, see

enter VERB
1 *Silence fell as I entered the room.*
▸ come in, walk in
▹ To enter a place without permission is to invade it.
AN OPPOSITE IS leave
2 *The bullet entered his leg.*
▸ go into, penetrate, pierce
3 *Can I enter my name on the list?*
▸ inscribe, insert, put down, record, register, set down, sign, write
AN OPPOSITE IS cancel
4 *We all decided to enter the competition.*
▸ enrol in, go in for, join in, participate in, sign up for, take part in, volunteer for
AN OPPOSITE IS withdraw from

enterprise NOUN
1 *She showed enterprise in starting her own business.*
▸ drive, initiative
2 *The expedition was a very rash enterprise.*
▸ adventure, effort, mission, operation, project, undertaking, venture

enterprising ADJECTIVE
Some enterprising girls organized a sponsored walk.
▸ adventurous, ambitious, bold, courageous, daring, eager, energetic, enthusiastic, hard-working, imaginative, industrious, intrepid, keen
AN OPPOSITE IS unadventurous

entertain VERB
1 *He entertained us for hours with his stories and jokes.*
▸ amuse, cheer up, divert, keep amused, make you laugh, please
AN OPPOSITE IS bore
2 *Members can entertain friends in the club's private dining room.*
▸ cater for, give hospitality to, receive, welcome

entertainer NOUN
VARIOUS ENTERTAINERS
acrobat, actor, actress, ballerina, broadcaster, busker, clown, comedian or comic, conjuror, dancer, disc jockey or DJ, juggler, lion-tamer, magician, musician, singer, street entertainer, stunt man, trapeze artist, ventriloquist
▹ A famous entertainer is a **star** or **superstar**. In past times, an entertainer in an important household was a **fool**, **jester**, or **minstrel**.

entertainment NOUN
We like to have our holiday in a place with plenty of entertainment.
▸ amusements, diversions, enjoyment, fun, nightlife, pastimes, pleasure, recreation, sport
VARIOUS KINDS OF ENTERTAINMENT
air show, ballet, cabaret, ceilidh, cinema, circus, comedy, concert, dance, disco, fair, firework display, flower show, gymkhana, motor show, musical, nightclub, opera, pageant, pantomime, play, radio, recitation, revue, rodeo, show, son et lumière, tattoo, television, theatre, variety show, waxworks, zoo
SEE **music, sport**

enthusiasm NOUN
1 *To be successful you need enthusiasm.*
▸ ambition, commitment, drive, eagerness, keenness, zeal, zest
AN OPPOSITE IS apathy
2 *Gardening is one of her many enthusiasms.*
▸ craze, diversion, fad, hobby, interest, passion, pastime

enthusiast *NOUN*
Her brother is a football enthusiast.
▶ addict, devotee, fan, fanatic, (*informal*) freak, lover, supporter

enthusiastic *ADJECTIVE*
1 *He's an enthusiastic supporter of our local team.*
▶ avid, devoted, energetic, fervent, keen, passionate, zealous
2 *The audience burst into enthusiastic applause.*
▶ eager, excited, exuberant, hearty, lively, vigorous
AN OPPOSITE IS apathetic

entire *ADJECTIVE*
She spent the entire evening watching television.
▶ complete, full, total, whole

entitle *VERB*
The voucher entitles you to claim a discount.
▶ allow, authorize, enable, permit

entrance *NOUN*
1 *Please pay at the entrance.*
▶ access, door, entry, gate, turnstile, way in
▷ When you go through the entrance to a building, you cross the **threshold**.
2 *I'll meet you in the entrance.*
▶ entrance hall, foyer, lobby, porch
3 *Her sudden entrance took everyone by surprise.*
▶ appearance, arrival, entry
AN OPPOSITE IS exit

entrance *VERB*
The music entranced us.
▶ charm, delight, enchant, please

entrant *NOUN*
A prize of £50 will be awarded to the winning entrant.
▶ candidate, competitor, contender, contestant, participant

entreat *VERB*
We entreated him to drive slowly.
▶ ask earnestly, beg, implore, plead with, request

entrust *VERB*
to entrust someone with something
Can I entrust you with the money?
▶ let you look after, put you in charge of, trust you with

entry *NOUN*
1 *Please don't block the entry.*
▶ access, door, entrance, gate, way in
2 *Every evening I write an entry in my diary.*
▶ item, note

envelop *VERB*
Mist enveloped the top of the mountain.
▶ conceal, cover, hide, mask

envious *ADJECTIVE*
He was envious of his brother's success.
▶ jealous, resentful

environment *NOUN*
Animals should live in their natural environment, not in cages.
▶ conditions, habitat, setting, situation, surroundings
the environment *We must do all we can to protect the environment.*
▶ nature, the earth, the natural world, the world

envy *NOUN*
I didn't feel any envy, even when I saw how rich she was.
▶ bitterness, jealousy, resentment

envy *VERB*
He envies her success.
▶ begrudge, grudge, resent

episode *NOUN*
1 *I paid for the broken window, and I want to forget the whole episode.*
▶ event, experience, incident
2 *I missed last night's episode of my favourite programme.*
▶ instalment, part

equal *ADJECTIVE*
1 *Give everyone an equal amount.*
▶ corresponding, equivalent, fair, identical, matching, similar
2 *The scores were equal at half-time.*
▶ even, level, the same, square

A B C D E F G H I J K L M N O P Q R S T U V W X Y Z

equalize *VERB*
Our opponents equalized just before half-time.
▸ level the scores, make the scores equal or even

equip *VERB*
All the bedrooms are equipped with a colour television.
▸ provide, supply
▹ To equip soldiers with weapons is to **arm** them. To equip a room with furniture is to **furnish** it.

equipment *NOUN*
Dad has got all the equipment you need to repair the car.
▸ apparatus, gear, implements, instruments, kit, machinery, materials, paraphernalia, tackle, things, tools
▹ Computing equipment is **hardware**.

equivalent *ADJECTIVE*
You need 250 grams or an equivalent amount in ounces.
▸ corresponding, identical, matching, similar

era *NOUN*
Shakespeare lived in the Elizabethan era.
▸ age, epoch, period, time

erase *VERB*
I erased the writing on the board.
▸ delete, get rid of, remove, rub out, wipe out

erect *ADJECTIVE*
The dog stood with its ears erect.
▸ perpendicular, upright, vertical

erect *VERB*
The town hall was erected in 1892.
▸ build, construct, put up, raise, set up
▹ To erect a tent is to **pitch** it.

erode *VERB*
The flood water eroded the river bank.
▸ destroy, eat away, wear away

errand *NOUN*
I went on an errand to the shop.
▸ assignment, job, journey, task, trip

erratic *ADJECTIVE*
Our goalkeeper's performance has been erratic this season.
▸ changeable, fluctuating, inconsistent, irregular, uneven, unpredictable, variable
AN OPPOSITE IS **consistent**

error *NOUN*
1 *The accident was the result of an error by the driver.*
▸ blunder, fault, lapse, mistake
2 *I think there is an error in your argument.*
▸ fallacy, flaw, inaccuracy, inconsistency, misunderstanding
▹ The error of leaving something out is an **omission** or **oversight**.

erupt *VERB*
Smoke began to erupt from the volcano.
▸ be discharged, be emitted, belch, burst out, gush, issue, pour out, shoot out, spout, spurt

escalate *VERB*
The police were afraid that the rioting would escalate.
▸ become worse, build up, develop, grow, increase, intensify

escape *VERB*
1 *Why did you let him escape?*
▸ break free, break out, get away, get out, (*informal*) give you the slip, run away
2 *She always escapes the nasty jobs.*
▸ avoid, dodge, evade, get out of, shirk

escape *NOUN*
1 *The prisoner's escape was filmed by security cameras.*
▸ breakout, flight, getaway
2 *The explosion was caused by an escape of gas.*
▸ leak, leakage, seepage

escort *NOUN*
1 *The president always has an escort to protect him.*
▸ bodyguard, guard
2 *The actress arrived with her escort.*
▸ companion, partner

escort *VERB*
The queen was escorted by a number of attendants.
▸ accompany, guard, look after, protect

especially *ADVERB*
I like biscuits, especially chocolate biscuits.
▸ above all, chiefly, most of all

espionage *NOUN*
In a time of war, many people are involved in espionage.
▸ intelligence, spying

essence *NOUN*
Don't give me all the details, but what is the essence of your problem?
▸ centre, core, gist, heart, substance

essential *ADJECTIVE*
Fresh fruit and vegetables are an essential part of our diet.
▸ basic, chief, crucial, fundamental, important, indispensable, necessary, principal, vital

establish *VERB*
1 *He plans to establish a new business.*
▸ begin, create, found, initiate, institute, introduce, launch, originate, set up, start
2 *The police have not managed to establish his guilt.*
▸ confirm, prove, show to be true, verify

establishment *NOUN*
1 *Since its establishment last year, many people have joined the drama club.*
▸ creation, formation, foundation, introduction
2 *The restaurant is a very well run establishment.*
▸ business, concern, organization

estate *NOUN*
1 *There's a new housing estate near our school.*
▸ area, development
2 *The Duke does not allow hunting on his estate.*
▸ grounds, land
3 *When he died, the millionaire left his estate to his partner.*
▸ fortune, possessions, property, wealth

esteem *VERB*
He was highly esteemed by all his colleagues.
▸ admire, appreciate, honour, look up to, respect, think highly of, value

estimate *NOUN*
What is your estimate of how much it will cost?
▸ assessment, calculation, evaluation, guess, judgement, opinion
▹ An official estimate of the value of something is a valuation. An official estimate of what a job is going to cost is a quotation or tender.

estimate *VERB*
Dad asked the builder to estimate how much the job will cost.
▸ assess, calculate, compute, count up, evaluate, judge, reckon, think out, work out

eternal *ADJECTIVE*
1 *He seemed to have the secret of eternal youth.*
▸ everlasting, infinite, lasting, timeless, unending
▹ Beings with eternal life are said to be immortal.
2 *I'm sick of your eternal quarrelling!*
▸ ceaseless, constant, continual, incessant, never-ending, non-stop, perpetual, persistent, recurrent, repeated, unceasing

evacuate *VERB*
1 *The firemen had to evacuate us from the smoke-filled building.*
▸ clear, move out, remove, send away
2 *You must evacuate the building when the fire alarm goes.*
▸ abandon, empty, leave, quit, withdraw from

evade *VERB*
Don't try to evade your responsibilities.
▸ avoid, dodge, escape from, fend off, shirk, steer clear of
AN OPPOSITE IS confront

evaluate *VERB*
The government is evaluating the success of the training scheme.
▸ assess, calculate, estimate, judge, reckon, work out

evaporate *VERB*
Dew evaporates in the morning.
▸ disappear, disperse, dry up, melt away, vanish
AN OPPOSITE IS condense

evasive *ADJECTIVE*
I still don't know the truth because his answers were so evasive.
▸ ambiguous, devious, indirect, oblique, roundabout, unhelpful
AN OPPOSITE IS straightforward

A B C D E F G H I J K L M N O P Q R S T U V W X Y Z

even *ADJECTIVE*
1 *You need an even surface for cricket.*
▸ flat, level, smooth, straight
AN OPPOSITE IS uneven
2 *They travelled at an even pace.*
▸ monotonous, regular, rhythmical, steady, unvarying
AN OPPOSITE IS irregular
3 *He has an even temper.*
▸ calm, cool, placid, predictable, unexcitable
AN OPPOSITE IS excitable
4 *The scores were even at half time.*
▸ equal, identical, level, matching, the same, square
AN OPPOSITE IS different
5 *2, 4, and 6 are even numbers.*
AN OPPOSITE IS odd

even *VERB*
to even something up *If I go over to their team, that will even up the numbers.*
▸ balance, equalize, level, match, square

evening *NOUN*
Towards evening it clouded over and began to rain.
▸ dusk, nightfall, sundown, sunset, twilight

event *NOUN*
1 *There were no unexpected events while you were away.*
▸ happening, incident, occurrence
2 *They held a special event to celebrate the opening of the sports club.*
▸ ceremony, entertainment, function, occasion, party, reception
3 *For some people, the Cup Final is the most important sporting event of the year.*
▸ competition, contest, engagement, fixture, game, match, meeting, tournament

eventful *ADJECTIVE*
We had an eventful journey.
▸ active, busy, exciting, interesting, lively
AN OPPOSITE IS boring or restful

eventual *ADJECTIVE*
We worked hard, but we were delighted with the eventual outcome.
▸ ensuing, final, overall, resulting, ultimate

eventually *ADVERB*
The journey took ages, but eventually we arrived safely.
▸ at last, finally, in the end, ultimately

evergreen *ADJECTIVE*
Most pine trees are evergreen.
AN OPPOSITE IS deciduous

everlasting *ADJECTIVE*
I'm sick of your everlasting chatter!
▸ ceaseless, constant, continual, eternal, incessant, never-ending, non-stop, perpetual, persistent, recurrent, repeated, unceasing, unending
AN OPPOSITE IS occasional
▹ Everlasting life is **immortality**.

everyday *ADJECTIVE*
Don't bother to dress up — come in your everyday clothes.
▸ customary, normal, ordinary, regular, usual

evict *VERB*
The landlord threatened to evict the tenants.
▸ eject, expel, put out, remove, throw out, turn out

evidence *NOUN*
I have evidence that what I say is true.
▸ confirmation, proof
▹ Evidence that someone accused of a crime was not there when the crime was committed is an **alibi**. Evidence given in a lawcourt is a **testimony**. To give evidence in court is to **testify**.

evident *ADJECTIVE*
It's evident that someone has made a mistake.
▸ apparent, certain, clear, noticeable, obvious, perceptible, plain, undeniable, unmistakable, visible

evil *ADJECTIVE*
1 *Whoever committed this murder is an evil person.*
▸ corrupt, immoral, perverted, sinful, treacherous, vicious, villainous, wicked
2 *Who would do such an evil deed?*
▸ atrocious, cruel, diabolical, dreadful, fiendish, foul, hateful, malevolent, malicious, vile, wrong
AN OPPOSITE IS good

evil *NOUN*
1 *You cannot pretend there is no evil in the world.*
▸ corruption, crime, cruelty, dishonesty, immorality, malevolence, malice, mischief, sin, treachery, vice, villainy, wickedness, wrongdoing

2 *Throughout history, people have endured many evils.*
▸ affliction, calamity, catastrophe, curse, disaster, misfortune, pain, suffering, wrong

evolution *NOUN*
The evolution of life on earth has taken millions of years.
▸ development, emergence, growth, progress

evolve *VERB*
Over millions of years, simple forms of life evolved into complex organisms.
▸ develop, emerge, grow, mature, modify, progress

exact *ADJECTIVE*
1 *I gave the police an exact account of what happened.*
▸ accurate, correct, detailed, faithful, meticulous, precise, strict, true
2 *Is this an exact copy of the original document?*
▸ identical, indistinguishable, perfect
AN OPPOSITE IS inaccurate

exaggerate *VERB*
He tends to exaggerate his problems.
▸ inflate, magnify, make too much of, overdo
AN OPPOSITE IS minimize

examination *NOUN*
1 *The results of the examinations will be announced next month.*
▸ assessment, (*informal*) exam, test
▹ A sheet of questions to which you must write answers is an exam paper. An examination in which you speak the answers is an oral exam.
2 *The judge made a thorough examination of the facts.*
▸ analysis, appraisal, inspection, investigation, review, study, survey
3 *He was subjected to a long examination by the police.*
▸ cross-examination, interrogation, questioning
4 *He was sent to hospital for an examination.*
▸ check-up
▹ A medical examination of a dead person is a post-mortem.

examine *VERB*
1 *The judge examined the evidence.*
▸ analyse, appraise, explore, inquire into, inspect, investigate, look closely at, pore over, probe, scrutinize, sift, sort out, study, test, weigh up
2 *The prosecution examined the witness.*
▸ cross-examine, grill, interrogate, question

example *NOUN*
1 *Give me an example of what you mean.*
▸ case, illustration, instance, sample, specimen
2 *She's an example to us all.*
▸ ideal, model

exasperate *VERB*
Dad was exasperated because the phone was continually engaged.
▸ (*informal*) aggravate, anger, annoy, irritate, provoke, upset, vex

excavate *VERB*
The builder excavated a trench for the foundations.
▸ dig, hollow out, scoop out

exceed *VERB*
She exceeded the previous long jump record by six centimetres.
▸ beat, better, excel, go over, outdo, pass, surpass

exceedingly *ADVERB*
The team played exceedingly well.
▸ amazingly, especially, exceptionally, extraordinarily, extremely, outstandingly, specially, unusually, very

excel *VERB*
She's a good all-round player, but she excels at tennis.
▸ do best, shine, stand out

excellent *ADJECTIVE*
She's fairly good at most games, but she's excellent at tennis.
▸ (*informal*) brilliant, exceptional, extraordinary, (*informal*) fabulous, (*informal*) fantastic, first-class, first-rate, (*informal*) great, impressive, (*informal*) incredible, magnificent, marvellous, outstanding, (*informal*) phenomenal, remarkable, (*informal*) sensational, (*informal*) superb, superlative, (*informal*) supreme, (*informal*) terrific, tremendous, unequalled, wonderful
AN OPPOSITE IS bad

except *PREPOSITION*
Everyone got a prize except me.
▸ apart from, but, excluding, with the exception of

exception *NOUN*
to take exception to something *She took exception to what he said about her clothes.*
▸ be upset by, complain about, disapprove of, dislike, object to

exceptional *ADJECTIVE*
It is exceptional to have such cold weather in June.
▸ abnormal, amazing, extraordinary, odd, peculiar, phenomenal, rare, special, strange, surprising, uncommon, unexpected, unheard-of, unusual
AN OPPOSITE IS normal

excerpt *NOUN*
She recited an excerpt from the poem.
▸ extract, part, passage, section
▹ A short excerpt is a **quotation**. The most interesting excerpts from something are the **highlights**. Excerpts from a film are **clips**.

excess *NOUN*
▹ If there is an excess of something so that it is hard to sell it, there is a **glut**. When a business has an excess of income over its expenses, it has a **profit** or a **surplus**.

excessive *ADJECTIVE*
1 *I think his enthusiasm for football is excessive.*
▸ exaggerated, extreme, fanatical
2 *Mum prepared excessive amounts of food for the party.*
▸ extravagant, needless, superfluous, unnecessary, unreasonable, wasteful

exchange *VERB*
The shop will exchange faulty goods.
▸ change, replace
▹ To exchange goods for other goods without using money is to **barter**. To exchange an old thing for part of the cost of a new one is to **trade it in**. To exchange things with your friends is to **swap** or **swop** them. To exchange players for other players in football, etc., is to **substitute** them.

excitable *ADJECTIVE*
Horses can be very excitable before a race.
▸ agitated, edgy, jumpy, nervous, restless
AN OPPOSITE IS calm

excite *VERB*
The prospect of going to America really excited her.
▸ arouse, electrify, rouse, stimulate, stir up, thrill
AN OPPOSITE IS calm

excited *ADJECTIVE*
On Christmas Eve he was too excited to sleep.
▸ animated, eager, elated, enthusiastic, exuberant, lively, thrilled
AN OPPOSITE IS calm

excitement *NOUN*
1 *The crowd's excitement increased as the final whistle drew near.*
▸ agitation, delirium, eagerness, elation, enthusiasm, exuberance, passion
2 *I could hardly bear the excitement!*
▸ drama, stimulation, suspense, tension, thrill

exciting *ADJECTIVE*
The last minutes of the match were the most exciting of all!
▸ dramatic, electrifying, eventful, gripping, rousing, sensational, stimulating, stirring, thrilling
AN OPPOSITE IS boring

exclaim *VERB*
'Get out of my house!' she exclaimed.
▸ call, cry out, shout, yell

exclamation *NOUN*
He gave an exclamation of surprise.
▸ cry, shout, yell
▹ When we discuss language, the formal word for an exclamation is **interjection**. An impolite exclamation is an **oath** or **swear word**.

exclude *VERB*
1 *Anyone who doesn't pay the subscription is excluded from the club.*
▸ ban, banish, bar, keep out, prohibit, reject, remove, shut out
2 *She's excluded dairy products from her diet.*
▸ leave out, omit
AN OPPOSITE IS include

exclusive *ADJECTIVE*
It's a very exclusive hotel.
▸ (*informal*) posh, private, select, snobbish

excursion *NOUN*
We went on an excursion to the seaside.
▸ expedition, jaunt, journey, outing, trip

excuse *NOUN*
He had no excuse for his behaviour.
▸ defence, explanation, justification, reason

excuse *VERB*
I am prepared to excuse your bad behaviour on this occasion.
▸ forgive, overlook, pardon
AN OPPOSITE IS punish
to be excused something *May I be excused swimming?*
▸ be exempt from, be let off, be released from

execute *VERB*
1 *In some countries, criminals may still be executed.*
▸ put to death
▹ To execute someone unofficially without a proper trial is to lynch them.
2 *She executed a perfect somersault.*
▸ accomplish, carry out, complete, perform, produce

exempt *ADJECTIVE*
Old age pensioners are exempt from paying for their prescriptions.
▸ excused, let off, spared

exercise *NOUN*
Exercise helps to keep you fit.
▸ activity, effort, exertion
SOME FORMS OF EXERCISE
aerobics, circuit training, dancing, games, gymnastics, jogging, keep fit, PE, running, sport, step aerobics, swimming, walking, workout
SEE ALSO **sport**
exercise book *I wrote a few notes in my exercise book.*
▸ jotter, notebook, writing pad
exercises *Piano exercises are important if you want to improve your playing.*
▸ practice, training

exercise *VERB*
1 *If you exercise regularly, it helps you to keep fit.*
▸ exert yourself, keep fit, train
2 *I sometimes exercise our neighbour's dog.*
▸ take for a walk, take out, walk
3 *You must exercise patience.*
▸ apply, display, employ, show, use

exert *VERB*
He exerted all his strength to lift the box.
▸ apply, employ, use

exertion *NOUN*
The exertion made him red in the face.
▸ effort, hard work, labour, toil

exhaust *NOUN*
The exhaust from cars damages the environment.
▸ emissions, fumes, gases, smoke

exhaust *VERB*
1 *The steep climb up the hill exhausted me.*
▸ tire, wear out
2 *We exhausted our supply of food before we'd gone half way!*
▸ consume, finish, go through, (*informal*) polish off, use up

exhausted *ADJECTIVE*
After a hard race, we lay exhausted on the grass.
▸ (*informal*) all in, breathless, fatigued, gasping, panting, (*informal*) puffed out, tired, weary, worn out

exhausting *ADJECTIVE*
Digging the garden is exhausting work.
▸ demanding, difficult, gruelling, hard, laborious, strenuous, tiring
AN OPPOSITE IS easy

exhaustion *NOUN*
He was overcome by sheer exhaustion.
▸ fatigue, tiredness, weakness, weariness

exhibit *VERB*
1 *Her paintings were exhibited in galleries all over Europe and America.*
▸ arrange, display, present, put up, set up, show
2 *He was exhibiting signs of anxiety.*
▸ demonstrate, reveal, show off
AN OPPOSITE IS hide

exhibition *NOUN*
We went to see an exhibition of paintings by Picasso.
▸ display, show

A B C D E F G H I J K L M N O P Q R S T U V W X Y Z

exile *VERB*
As a result of the war, many people were exiled from their own country.
▸ banish, deport, drive out, eject, expel, send away

exile *NOUN*
He returned to his country after 24 years of exile.
▸ banishment, deportation, expulsion
▹ A person who has been exiled is a **refugee**.

exist *VERB*
1 *Some people claim that ghosts actually exist.*
▸ be real, occur
2 *We can't exist without food.*
▸ continue, endure, keep going, last, live, remain alive, survive

existence *NOUN*
1 *I don't believe in the existence of ghosts.*
▸ reality
2 *Our existence depends on preserving our environment.*
▸ life, survival

existing *ADJECTIVE*
1 *Many animals have become extinct, so we must protect existing species.*
▸ living, remaining, surviving
2 *Next season, the existing rules will be replaced by new ones.*
▸ current, present

exit *NOUN*
1 *I'll wait for you by the exit.*
▸ barrier, door, doorway, gate, way out
2 *We made a hurried exit.*
▸ departure

exit *VERB*
The actors exited from the left of the stage.
▸ depart, go out, leave, withdraw

exotic *ADJECTIVE*
She's travelled to many exotic places.
▸ alien, different, exciting, foreign, remote, romantic, strange, unfamiliar, wonderful
AN OPPOSITE IS familiar

expand *VERB*
Business is good, and they hope to expand it.
▸ build up, develop, enlarge, extend, increase, make bigger
▹ To become larger is to **grow** or **swell**. To become wider is to **broaden**, **thicken**, or **widen**. To become longer is to **extend**, **lengthen**, or **stretch**.
AN OPPOSITE IS contract or reduce

expanse *NOUN*
The explorers crossed a large expanse of desert.
▸ area, stretch, tract
▹ An expanse of water or ice is a **sheet**.

expect *VERB*
1 *I expect that it will rain.*
▸ anticipate, forecast, foresee, imagine, predict, prophesy
2 *He expects complete obedience from his troops.*
▸ ask for, count on, demand, insist on, require, want
3 *I expect he missed the bus.*
▸ assume, believe, guess, imagine, presume, suppose, think

expedition *NOUN*
▹ An expedition into unknown territory is an **exploration**. An expedition to see or hunt wild animals is a **safari**. An expedition to find something is a **quest**. An expedition to carry out a special task is a **mission**. An expedition to worship at a holy place is a **pilgrimage**.
SEE ALSO **journey**, **travel**

expel *VERB*
1 *A fan expels the stale air and fumes.*
▸ force out, send out
2 *He was expelled from school.*
▸ ban, dismiss, remove, send away, throw out
▹ To expel someone from their home is to **eject** or **evict** them. To expel someone from their country is to **banish** or **exile** them. To expel evil spirits is to **exorcise** them.

expense *NOUN*
He was worried about the expense involved in running a car.
▸ charges, cost, expenditure, overheads

expensive *ADJECTIVE*
Houses are very expensive in this area.
▸ costly, dear
AN OPPOSITE IS cheap

experience *NOUN*
1 *She's had a lot of experience in the catering business.*
▸ involvement, participation, practice
2 *I had an unusual experience today.*
▸ event, happening, incident, occurrence
▹ An exciting experience is an **adventure**. A frightening or difficult experience is an **ordeal**.

experienced *ADJECTIVE*
She's an experienced nurse and is used to dealing with emergencies.
▸ expert, knowledgeable, professional, qualified, skilled, specialized, trained
AN OPPOSITE IS inexperienced

experiment *NOUN*
We carried out a scientific experiment.
▸ test, trial
▹ A series of experiments is **research** or an **investigation**.

experiment *VERB*
We experimented to see if our invention would work.
▸ do tests
▹ To experiment on or with something is to **test** it or **try it out**.

expert *NOUN*
He's an expert at chess.
▸ authority, genius, specialist, wizard

expert *ADJECTIVE*
You need an expert craftsman to mend these antiques.
▸ brilliant, capable, clever, competent, experienced, knowledgeable, professional, proficient, qualified, skilful, skilled, specialized, trained
AN OPPOSITE IS amateur or unskilful

expertise *NOUN*
I haven't got the expertise you need to mend a computer.
▸ ability, competence, know-how, knowledge, skill, training

expire *VERB*
1 *The television licence expires next month.*
▸ become invalid, come to an end, finish, run out
2 *The animal expired before the vet arrived.*
▸ die, pass away

explain *VERB*
1 *The solicitor explained the procedure carefully.*
▸ clarify, describe, give an explanation of, make clear
2 *I can explain my behaviour.*
▸ account for, excuse, give reasons for, justify, make excuses for

explanation *NOUN*
1 *He'd better have a good explanation for his behaviour.*
▸ excuse, justification, reason
2 *He gave us a brief explanation of how the device worked.*
▸ account, demonstration, description

explode *VERB*
1 *The firework exploded with a bang.*
▸ blow up, burst, go off, make an explosion, shatter
2 *The slightest movement might explode the bomb.*
▸ detonate, set off

exploit *NOUN*
The book describes his exploits as a fighter pilot in the war.
▸ adventure, deed, escapade, feat, venture

exploit *VERB*
1 *My music teacher says I should exploit my talent.*
▸ build on, (*informal*) cash in on, develop, make use of, profit by, take advantage of, use, utilize
2 *Some workers are exploited by their employers.*
▸ impose on, misuse, oppress, (*slang*) rip off, take unfair advantage of, treat unfairly

explore *VERB*
1 *The spacecraft will explore the solar system.*
▸ probe, search, survey, travel through
2 *We must explore all the possibilities.*
▸ analyse, examine, inspect, investigate, look into, research, scrutinize

explosion *NOUN*
The explosion rattled the windows.
▸ bang, blast, detonation
▹ An explosion from a volcano is an **eruption**. An explosion of laughter is an **outburst**. The sound of a gun going off is a **report**. The sudden loud noise of thunder is a **clap** of thunder.

explosive *NOUN*
SOME EXPLOSIVES
cordite, dynamite, gelignite, gunpowder, (*trademark*) Semtex, TNT

A B C D E F G H I J K L M N O P Q R S T U V W X Y Z

export *VERB*
The factory exports a lot of the cars it makes.
▸ sell abroad, send abroad, ship overseas
AN OPPOSITE IS import

expose *VERB*
1 *He yawned, exposing a set of white teeth.*
▸ uncover
2 *He kept his secret for years, until a newspaper exposed the truth.*
▸ betray, disclose, make known, publish, reveal

express *VERB*
He's always quick to express his opinions.
▸ communicate, convey, phrase, put into words, voice
▹ To express yourself by word of mouth is to **speak**. To express yourself on paper is to **write**. To express your feelings is to **give vent** to them.
SEE ALSO **talk** *VERB*

expression *NOUN*
1 *The English language contains many colloquial expressions.*
▸ phrase, saying, term, wording
▹ An expression that people use too much is a **cliché**.
2 *Did you see her expression when I told her the news?*
▸ appearance, countenance, face, look
SOME EXPRESSIONS YOU SEE ON PEOPLE'S FACES
beam, frown, glare, glower, grimace, grin, laugh, leer, long face, poker-face, pout, scowl, smile, smirk, sneer, wince, yawn
3 *My sister plays the piano with great expression.*
▸ emotion, feeling, sympathy, understanding

expressive *ADJECTIVE*
1 *She gave me an expressive look.*
▸ meaningful, revealing, significant, telling
2 *An actor needs to have an expressive voice.*
▸ eloquent, lively, varied
AN OPPOSITE IS expressionless

exquisite *ADJECTIVE*
There was some exquisite embroidery on the wedding dress.
▸ beautiful, dainty, delicate, intricate

extend *VERB*
1 *Delays on the motorway extended our journey by an hour.*
▸ delay, draw out, lengthen, make longer, prolong
AN OPPOSITE IS shorten
2 *He plans to extend his business.*
▸ add to, build up, develop, enlarge, expand, increase, widen the scope of
AN OPPOSITE IS reduce
3 *He sat back and extended his legs.*
▸ hold out, put out, reach out, stick out, stretch out
4 *We extended a warm welcome to the visitors.*
▸ give, offer

extension *NOUN*
They are building an extension to the runway.
▸ addition, continuation

extensive *ADJECTIVE*
The palace gardens cover an extensive area.
▸ big, broad, large, spread out, wide
AN OPPOSITE IS small

extent *NOUN*
1 *The map shows the extent of the estate.*
▸ area, breadth, dimensions, expanse, length, limits, measurement, spread
2 *After the storm we went out to see the extent of the damage.*
▸ amount, degree, level, magnitude, range, scope, size

exterior *NOUN*
He painted the exterior of his house.
▸ outside
AN OPPOSITE IS interior

exterminate *VERB*
They used poison to exterminate the rats.
▸ annihilate, destroy, get rid of, kill, wipe out

external *ADJECTIVE*
We liked the external appearance of the house, but inside it was rather gloomy.
▸ exterior, outer, outside
AN OPPOSITE IS internal

extinct *ADJECTIVE*
▹ An extinct species is one that has **died out** or **vanished**. An extinct volcano is an **inactive** volcano.

extinguish *VERB*
We managed to extinguish the fire before the fire engine arrived.
▸ put out, quench, smother
AN OPPOSITE IS ignite

extra *ADJECTIVE*
1 *There is an extra charge for taking your bike on the train.*
▶ added, additional, excess, further, increased, supplementary
2 *There is extra food in the kitchen if we need it.*
▶ more, reserve, spare, surplus

extract *NOUN*
I read an extract from the book in a magazine.
▶ excerpt, part, passage, section
▷ A short extract is a quotation. Specially interesting extracts from something are the highlights. An extract from a newspaper is a cutting. An extract from a film is a clip.

extract *VERB*
1 *The dentist decided to extract my tooth.*
▶ draw out, pull out, remove, take out, (*informal*) whip out, withdraw
2 *She extracted passages from the book for the students to translate.*
▶ derive, gather, get, obtain, quote, select

extraordinary *ADJECTIVE*
I can't explain the extraordinary things that happened.
▶ abnormal, amazing, astonishing, curious, exceptional, (*informal*) fantastic, incredible, marvellous, miraculous, mysterious, odd, outstanding, peculiar, phenomenal, queer, rare, remarkable, special, strange, surprising, unbelievable, unheard of, unique, unusual, weird, wonderful
AN OPPOSITE IS ordinary

extravagant *ADJECTIVE*
He held a large, extravagant party for all his friends.
▶ expensive, lavish, uneconomical, wasteful
AN OPPOSITE IS economical

extreme *ADJECTIVE*
1 *They suffered dreadfully in the extreme cold.*
▶ acute, excessive, great, intense, severe
2 *She lives on the extreme edge of the town.*
▶ farthest, furthest

exuberant *ADJECTIVE*
After our team's victory, we were in an exuberant mood.
▶ animated, boisterous, bubbly, cheerful, eager, elated, energetic, enthusiastic, excited, exultant, high-spirited, lively, sprightly, vivacious
AN OPPOSITE IS apathetic

exultant *ADJECTIVE*
The fans were exultant after their team's victory.
▶ delighted, (*slang*) over the moon, pleased, thrilled
SEE ALSO **exuberant**

eye *NOUN*
PARTS OF YOUR EYE
cornea, eyeball, eyebrow, eyelash, eyelid, iris, lens, pupil, retina
SOME PROBLEMS WITH EYESIGHT
astigmatism, long-sightedness, myopia or short-sightedness
SOME DISEASES OF THE EYE
cataract, glaucoma
▷ A person who tests your eyesight is an optician. A specialist in eye diseases is an oculist. An adjective describing things connected with the eyes is optical. Instruments you look through are optical instruments.

eye *VERB*
The dog eyed the sausages hungrily.
▶ contemplate, gaze at, look at, regard, stare at, watch

eyewitness *NOUN*
An eyewitness described the accident.
▶ bystander, observer, onlooker, spectator, witness

fabric *NOUN*
Mum bought some fabric to make curtains.
▶ cloth, material, stuff
▷ A plural word is textiles.
FOR VARIOUS KINDS OF FABRIC SEE **cloth**

fabulous *ADJECTIVE*
1 (*informal*) *We had a fabulous time at the party.*
▶ (*informal*) brilliant, excellent, (*informal*)

A B C D E F G H I J K L M N O P Q R S T U V W X Y Z

fantastic, first-class, marvellous, outstanding, (*informal*) smashing, superb, tremendous, wonderful
2 *Dragons are fabulous creatures.*
▶ fictitious, imaginary, legendary, mythical

face *NOUN*

1 *You could tell by her face that she had bad news.*
▶ countenance, expression, features, look
SEE ALSO **expression**
2 *Put the cards face down.*
▶ front
3 *A cube has six faces.*
▶ side, surface

face *VERB*

1 *Stand and face your partner.*
▶ be opposite to, look towards
2 *I had to face all my problems on my own.*
▶ confront, cope with, encounter, face up to, meet, stand up to, tackle
AN OPPOSITE IS avoid

facetious *ADJECTIVE*

Don't make facetious remarks.
▶ cheeky, flippant

facility *NOUN*

1 *The crèche is a useful facility for busy parents.*
▶ amenity, convenience, resource, service
2 *The facility with which he did the job surprised me.*
▶ ease, skill

fact *NOUN*

It's a fact that cuckoos lay their eggs in other birds' nests.
▶ certainty, reality, truth
AN OPPOSITE IS fiction
the facts *The police want to know all the facts.*
▶ circumstances, details, information, particulars
▷ Facts which are useful in trying to prove something are **evidence**. Facts expressed as numbers are **statistics**. Facts which you put into a computer are **data**.

factor *NOUN*

Hard work was an important factor in her success.
▶ aspect, component, element, influence, ingredient

factory *NOUN*

PLACES WHERE THINGS ARE MANUFACTURED
assembly line, forge, foundry, manufacturing plant, mill, production line, refinery, workshop

factual *ADJECTIVE*

1 *The documentary provides a factual account of what actually happened.*
▶ accurate, authentic, correct, exact, genuine, objective, precise, reliable, true
AN OPPOSITE IS false
2 *The film is based on factual occurrences.*
▶ real, real life, true
▷ A film or story based on a person's life is **biographical**. A film or story based on history is **historical**. A film telling you about real events is a **documentary**.
AN OPPOSITE IS fictional

fade *VERB*

1 *Sunlight has faded the curtains.*
▶ bleach, make paler, whiten
AN OPPOSITE IS brighten
2 *After a couple of days, the flowers faded.*
▶ droop, flag, shrivel, wilt, wither
AN OPPOSITE IS flourish
3 *Gradually, the light began to fade.*
▶ decline, diminish, disappear, dwindle, fail, melt away, vanish, wane, weaken
AN OPPOSITE IS increase

fail *VERB*

1 *Peace talks between the two sides have failed.*
▶ be unsuccessful, come to an end, fall through, (*informal*) flop, founder, meet with disaster
AN OPPOSITE IS succeed
2 *The plane's engines failed just after it had taken off.*
▶ break down, cut out, give up, stop working
3 *The light began to fail.*
▶ decline, diminish, disappear, dwindle, fade, get worse, vanish, wane, weaken
AN OPPOSITE IS improve
4 *She failed to keep her appointment.*
▶ forget, neglect, omit
AN OPPOSITE IS remember

failing *NOUN*

She loved him, despite his failings.
▶ bad habit, defect, fault, imperfection, shortcoming, weakness

failure *NOUN*
1 *There was a failure in the computer system.*
▸ breakdown, collapse, crash, stoppage
2 *Our attempt to beat the record ended in failure.*
▸ defeat, disappointment, disaster, (*informal*) a flop, (*slang*) a wash-out
AN OPPOSITE IS success

faint *ADJECTIVE*
1 *The picture was faint and I couldn't make out the details.*
▸ blurred, dim, faded, hazy, indistinct, misty, pale, shadowy, unclear, vague
AN OPPOSITE IS clear
2 *I noticed a faint smell of roses.*
▸ delicate, slight
AN OPPOSITE IS strong
3 *I heard a faint cry for help.*
▸ distant, hushed, low, muffled, muted, soft, thin, weak
AN OPPOSITE IS loud
4 *He was so hungry that he felt faint.*
▸ dizzy, exhausted, feeble, giddy, light-headed, unsteady, weak

faint *VERB*
He thought he was going to faint.
▸ become unconscious, collapse, (*informal*) flake out, pass out, (*old use*) swoon

faint-hearted *ADJECTIVE*
This is not time to be faint-hearted.
▸ apprehensive, fearful, nervous, timid, unadventurous
AN OPPOSITE IS bold

fair *ADJECTIVE*
1 *I think the referee made a fair decision.*
▸ disinterested, fair-minded, honest, honourable, impartial, just, proper, right, unbiased, unprejudiced
AN OPPOSITE IS unfair
2 *The twins both have fair hair.*
▸ blond or blonde, golden, light, yellow
AN OPPOSITE IS dark
3 *Her work is fair, but not outstanding.*
▸ acceptable, adequate, average, moderate, passable, reasonable, respectable, satisfactory, tolerable
4 *The forecast says the weather will be fair today.*
▸ bright, clear, cloudless, dry, favourable, fine, pleasant, sunny

fair *NOUN*
PLACES AND EVENTS WITH OUTDOOR AMUSEMENTS
amusement park, carnival, fairground or funfair, gala, theme park
SOME AMUSEMENTS YOU FIND IN FAIRS
big dipper, big wheel, bouncy castle, bumper cars or dodgems, coconut shy, fortune-teller, ghost train, helter-skelter, merry-go-round, roller coaster, roundabout, shooting gallery, sideshow, slot-machine, stalls, swingboat, switchback
OTHER KINDS OF FAIR WHERE THINGS ARE ON EXHIBITION OR FOR SALE
antiques fair, bazaar, Christmas fair, craft fair, market

fairly *ADVERB*
1 *We were not treated fairly.*
▸ honestly, impartially, justly, properly
2 *I saw a fairly good film on TV last night.*
▸ moderately, (*informal*) pretty, quite, rather, reasonably, somewhat, tolerably, up to a point

fairy *NOUN*
FOR OTHER LEGENDARY CREATURES SEE **legendary**

faith *NOUN*
1 *I have the utmost faith in you.*
▸ belief, confidence, trust
AN OPPOSITE IS doubt
2 *The school is attended by pupils of many different faiths.*
▸ creed, doctrine, religion

faithful *ADJECTIVE*
1 *His dog is his faithful friend.*
▸ close, constant, dependable, devoted, firm, loyal, reliable, trustworthy
AN OPPOSITE IS unfaithful
2 *It's a faithful reproduction of the original painting.*
▸ accurate, exact, precise, true

fake *NOUN*
I thought the painting might be valuable, but it was a fake.
▸ copy, forgery, imitation, replica, reproduction
▹ An event which fakes a real event is a **hoax**, or **sham**, or **simulation**. A person who pretends to be another person is an **impostor**.

A B C D E F G H I J K L M N O P Q R S T U V W X Y Z

fake *VERB*
He tried to fake a posh accent.
▸ copy, imitate, pretend, put on, reproduce, simulate
▹ To fake someone's signature is to **forge** it.

fall *VERB* This word is often overused. These are some of the ways we use it, and some of the synonyms we could use:
1 *He fell off the wall.*
▸ crash down, pitch, topple, tumble
2 *I fell into the water.*
▸ drop, plunge, sink
3 *The tide began to fall.*
▸ ebb, go down, subside
4 *The water-level in the reservoir fell during the summer.*
▸ become lower, decline, decrease, diminish, dwindle, lessen
5 *Prices are likely to fall after Christmas.*
▸ be reduced, come down, slump
6 *After a long siege, the town fell to the enemy.*
▸ give in, surrender
7 *Millions of soldiers fell in the war.*
▸ die
8 *We arrived at the hotel as night was falling.*
▸ come, happen, occur
9 *His eyes fell on an advertisement in the paper.*
▸ be directed at, come to rest on
to fall in *We were afraid the roof would fall in.*
▸ cave in, collapse
to fall out *Those two fall out over the slightest little thing!*
▸ argue, differ, disagree, quarrel, squabble
to fall through *Our plans for a picnic fell through because of the rain.*
▸ be unsuccessful, come to nothing, fail, founder

fall *NOUN*
1 *He had a fall and cut his knee.*
▸ tumble
2 *I noticed a fall in the water-level.*
▸ drop, lowering
3 *There has been a fall in the price of vegetables.*
▸ decline, decrease, reduction
4 *The fall of the town led to the signing of a peace treaty.*
▸ defeat, surrender

fallacy *NOUN*
It is a fallacy to think that money always makes people happy.
▸ error, falsehood, mistake

false *ADJECTIVE*
1 *The police charged him with giving false information.*
▸ deceptive, fallacious, fictitious, inaccurate, incorrect, invented, misleading, mistaken, untrue, wrong
AN OPPOSITE IS correct
2 *He was arrested for travelling with a false passport.*
▸ bogus, counterfeit, fake
AN OPPOSITE IS authentic
3 *She's wearing false eyelashes.*
▸ artificial, imitation
AN OPPOSITE IS real
4 *He turned out to be a false friend.*
▸ deceitful, dishonest, disloyal, treacherous, unfaithful, unreliable, untrustworthy
AN OPPOSITE IS trustworthy

falsehood *NOUN*
1 *She accused me of falsehood.*
▸ deceit, dishonesty
2 *He accused them of spreading falsehoods about him.*
▸ fib, lie

falter *VERB*
1 *She didn't falter as she walked up to the lion's cage.*
▸ flinch, hesitate, hold back, lose confidence, pause, stumble, waver
▹ To falter in your speech is to **stammer** or **stutter**.
2 *My courage began to falter.*
▸ become weaker, flag, wane, weaken

fame *NOUN*
The film brought him international fame.
▸ distinction, eminence, glory, honour, importance, prestige, prominence, renown

familiar *ADJECTIVE*
1 *Starlings are a familiar sight in our garden.*
▸ accustomed, common, customary, everyday, frequent, mundane, normal, ordinary, regular, routine, usual, well known
AN OPPOSITE IS rare
2 *I thought he was a bit too familiar with me.*
▸ chatty, close, confidential, friendly, informal, intimate, relaxed
AN OPPOSITE IS formal or unfriendly
to be familiar with something *Are you familiar with this music?*
▸ be acquainted with, be aware of, be an expert in, know

family *NOUN*
My family lives in Scotland.
▸ relations, relatives
▹ Your family is your **relations** or **relatives**. An old-fashioned term for your family is your **kin**.
MEMBERS OF A FAMILY MAY INCLUDE
adopted child, aunt, brother, child, cousin, daughter, father, foster-child, foster-parent, grandchild, grandparent, guardian, husband, mother, nephew, niece, parent, sister, son, step-child, step-parent, uncle, ward, wife
▹ The official term for your closest relative is **next of kin**. A single stage in a family is a **generation**. The line of ancestors from which a family is descended is its **ancestry** or **pedigree**. A diagram showing how people in your family are related is a **family tree** or **genealogy**. A powerful family which goes on from generation to generation is a **dynasty**. A number of families with the same ancestor, especially in Scotland, is a **clan**. In certain societies, a group of families living together is a **tribe**. The children in a family are the **offspring**. A family of young birds is a **brood**. A family of puppies, etc., is a **litter**.

famine *NOUN*
The drought caused widespread famine.
▸ hunger, malnutrition, scarcity, shortage, starvation, want
AN OPPOSITE IS plenty

famished *ADJECTIVE*
What's for dinner? I'm famished!
▸ hungry, ravenous, (*informal*) starving
▹ If you are rather hungry, you are **peckish**.

famous *ADJECTIVE*
He's one of the world's most famous actors.
▸ celebrated, distinguished, eminent, notable, outstanding, prominent, renowned, well known
AN OPPOSITE IS unknown

fan *NOUN*
1 *I switched on the fan in the kitchen.*
▸ blower, extractor fan, ventilator
2 *I used to be a Manchester United fan.*
▸ admirer, devotee, enthusiast, follower, supporter

fanatic *NOUN*
My brother is a football fanatic.
▸ addict, devotee, enthusiast, (*informal*) freak

fanatical *ADJECTIVE*
He is a fanatical supporter of our local team.
▸ enthusiastic, extreme, fervent, over-enthusiastic, passionate, rabid, zealous
AN OPPOSITE IS moderate

fanciful *ADJECTIVE*
His story included some fanciful ideas about fairies and goblins.
▸ fantastic, fictitious, imaginary, unrealistic
AN OPPOSITE IS realistic

fancy *ADJECTIVE*
The furniture was very fancy.
▸ decorative, elaborate, ornamental, pretty
AN OPPOSITE IS plain

fancy *VERB*
1 *What do you fancy to eat?*
▸ feel like, long for, prefer, want, wish for
2 *I fancied I heard a noise downstairs.*
▸ imagine, think

fantastic *ADJECTIVE*
1 *He told some fantastic story about little green men.*
▸ amazing, extraordinary, fanciful, far-fetched, incredible, strange, unbelievable, unlikely, unrealistic, weird
AN OPPOSITE IS realistic
2 (*informal*) *We had a fantastic time.*
▸ (*informal*) brilliant, excellent, (*informal*) fabulous, first-class, marvellous, outstanding, (*informal*) smashing, superb, tremendous, wonderful

fantasy *NOUN*
Those ideas about becoming rich and famous are all his fantasy.
▸ daydream, delusion, dream, fancy, hallucination, vision

far *ADJECTIVE*
1 *She lives in the far north.*
▸ distant, faraway, remote
2 *The ferry took us to the far side of the river.*
▸ opposite, other
AN OPPOSITE IS near

farcical *ADJECTIVE*
The whole idea is farcical.
▸ absurd, laughable, ludicrous, ridiculous

fare *NOUN*
How much is the fare on the train to London?
▸ charge, cost, payment, price

far-fetched *ADJECTIVE*
His explanations sounded a bit far-fetched to me.

A B C D E F G H I J K L M N O P Q R S T U V W X Y Z

▶ amazing, extraordinary, fanciful, fantastic, incredible, strange, unbelievable, unlikely, unrealistic
AN OPPOSITE IS likely

farm *NOUN*
KINDS OF FARM
arable farm, cattle farm, dairy farm, fish farm, fruit farm, hill farm, mixed farm, pig farm, poultry farm, stud farm
▷ The formal word for farming is **agriculture**. A farm which uses no artificial fertilizers or chemicals is an **organic farm**. A very small farm is a **smallholding**. A small farm growing fruit and vegetables is a **market garden**. A small farm in Scotland is a **croft**. A large cattle farm in America is a **ranch**.
FARM BUILDINGS
barn, battery unit, byre or cowshed, dairy, Dutch barn, farmhouse, granary, milking parlour, outhouse, pigsty, stable
OTHER PARTS OF A FARM
barnyard or farmyard, cattle pen, fallow or set-aside land, fields, haystack, meadow, paddock, pasture, rick, sheep fold, silo
ITEMS OF FARM EQUIPMENT
baler, combine harvester, cultivator, drill, harrow, harvester, irrigation system, manure spreader, mower, planter, plough, tedder, tractor, trailer
PEOPLE WHO WORK ON A FARM
agriculturalist, agricultural worker, (*old use*) dairymaid, farm labourer, farm manager, ploughman, shepherd, stockbreeder, tractor driver
ACTIVITIES THAT TAKE PLACE ON A FARM
breeding animals, cultivating or tilling the land, fertilizing the land, growing crops, harvesting, irrigation, ploughing, reaping, rearing livestock, sowing
CROPS GROWN ON FARMS
barley, cereals or corn, fodder, fruit, maize, oats, potatoes, rape, rye, sugar beet, sweet corn, vegetables, wheat
SOME FARM ANIMALS
bull, bullock, chicken or hen, cow, duck, goat, goose, horse, pig, sheep, turkey
▷ Birds kept on a farm are **poultry**. Animals kept for milk or beef are **cattle**. Farm animals in general are **livestock**.

fascinate *VERB*
I was fascinated by his stories.
▶ attract, bewitch, captivate, charm, delight, enchant, entrance, interest, please
AN OPPOSITE IS bore

fashion *NOUN*
1 *He behaved in a strange fashion.*
▶ manner, way
2 *She always dresses according to the latest fashion.*
▶ craze, fad, look, style, taste, trend

fashion *VERB*
We fashioned the clay into animal figures.
▶ form, make, mould, shape

fashionable *ADJECTIVE*
She always wears fashionable clothes.
▶ chic, contemporary, current, elegant, the latest, modern, smart, sophisticated, stylish, tasteful, (*informal*) trendy, up-to-date
AN OPPOSITE IS unfashionable

fast *ADJECTIVE*
1 *He made a fast exit when he saw me coming.*
▶ brisk, hasty, headlong, high-speed, hurried, lively, quick, rapid, smart, speedy, swift, unhesitating
▷ Something which goes faster than sound is **supersonic**.
AN OPPOSITE IS slow
2 *Make the rope fast.*
▶ firm, secure, tight
AN OPPOSITE IS loose
3 *Before you put clothes in the washing machine, make sure the colours are fast.*
▶ indelible, permanent

fast *ADVERB*
1 *He was driving too fast.*
▶ briskly, quickly, rapidly, swiftly
2 *The boat was stuck fast on the rocks.*
▶ firmly, tightly

fast *VERB*
The monks used to fast on holy days.
▶ go hungry, go without food

fasten *VERB*
He fastened the strap to the camera.
▶ attach, connect, fix, join, link, secure
▷ To fasten something with rope, etc., is to **bind**, **hitch**, **knot**, **lash**, or **tie** it. To fasten something with adhesive is to **glue**, **paste**, or **stick** it. To fasten a door, you **bolt**, **lock**, or **padlock** it. To fasten a caravan or railway wagon to something, you **couple** them, or **hitch** them up. To fasten the front of your coat, etc., you **button** it, **zip** it, or **do it up**. To fasten an envelope, you **seal** it or **stick it down**. To fasten pieces of paper together,

you clip, pin, or staple them. To fasten pieces of wood together, you nail or screw them. To fasten pieces of metal together, you rivet, solder, or weld them. To secure a boat is to anchor or moor it. To secure an animal is to tether it.

THINGS YOU CAN USE FOR FASTENING VARIOUS THINGS
adhesive, anchor, bolt, buckle, button, catch, chain, clamp, clasp, clip, drawing pin, glue, gum, hook, knot, lace, latch, lock, nail, padlock, painter, paste, peg, pin, rivet, rope, safety pin, screw, seal, (*trademark*) Sellotape, solder, staple, strap, string, tack, tape, tether, tie, (*trademark*) Velcro, wedge, zip

fastener, **fastening** *NOUNS*
FOR THINGS YOU CAN USE AS FASTENINGS SEE **fasten**

fat *ADJECTIVE* This word is often overused.
1 *You'll get fat if you eat so much chocolate!*
▸ chubby, dumpy, flabby, gross, heavy, overweight, plump, podgy, portly, round, stout
Note that synonyms for *fat* are often insulting.
2 *She was reading a fat book.*
▸ bulky, thick, weighty
AN OPPOSITE IS thin

fat *NOUN*
KINDS OF FAT USED IN COOKING
butter, dripping, ghee, lard, margarine, olive oil, suet, various vegetable oils
▹ Different kinds of fat are saturated fats and polyunsaturated fats.

fatal *ADJECTIVE*
1 *If it had been an inch lower, the wound would have been fatal.*
▸ deadly, lethal, mortal
▹ A fatal illness is an incurable or terminal illness.
2 *He made a fatal mistake half way through the match.*
▸ calamitous, disastrous, dreadful

fatality *NOUN*
Did the accident result in fatalities?
▸ casualty, death, loss

fate *NOUN*
1 *Fate was kind to her.*
▸ chance, destiny, fortune, luck
2 *He met a terrible fate.*
▸ death, end

fatigue *NOUN*
By the end of the journey, I was overcome with fatigue.
▸ exhaustion, tiredness, weakness, weariness

fatigued *ADJECTIVE*
We were all fatigued by the time we got home.
▸ (*informal*) all in, exhausted, tired, weary, worn out

fatty *ADJECTIVE*
I don't like fatty food.
▸ fat, greasy, oily

fault *NOUN*
1 *There's a fault in the loudspeakers.*
▸ defect, flaw, weakness
2 *I'm really sorry about the confusion — it's all my fault.*
▸ responsibility

faultless *ADJECTIVE*
It was a faultless piece of work.
▸ flawless, ideal, perfect
AN OPPOSITE IS imperfect

faulty *ADJECTIVE*
1 *The stereo was faulty, so Dad took it back to the shop.*
▸ broken, damaged, defective, out of order, unusable
2 *She said that my argument was faulty.*
▸ flawed, illogical, inaccurate, incorrect, invalid
AN OPPOSITE IS perfect

favour *NOUN*
1 *He did me a favour.*
▸ courtesy, good deed, good turn, kindness, service
2 *They looked on him with favour.*
▸ approval, friendliness, goodwill
3 *We complained that the referee showed favour towards the other side.*
▸ bias, favouritism, preference, prejudice
to be in favour of something *I didn't expect you to be in favour of fox hunting.*
▸ approve of, like, support

A B C D E F G H I J K L M N O P Q R S T U V W X Y Z

favour *VERB*
1 *I favour our original plan.*
▸ advocate, approve of, back, be in sympathy with, choose, (*informal*) fancy, (*informal*) go for, like, opt for, prefer
AN OPPOSITE IS oppose
2 *In the second half, the strong wind favoured our team.*
▸ aid, be advantageous to, help
AN OPPOSITE IS hinder

favourable *ADJECTIVE*
1 *The weather conditions were very favourable.*
▸ advantageous, helpful
AN OPPOSITE IS unfavourable
2 *The film received favourable reviews.*
▸ agreeable, approving, complimentary, encouraging, friendly, generous, kind, positive, reassuring
AN OPPOSITE IS critical or hostile

favourite *ADJECTIVE*
What is your favourite book?
▸ best-loved, dearest, preferred, top

favouritism *NOUN*
A referee must not show favouritism.
▸ bias, one-sidedness, prejudice

fear *NOUN*
She huddled in the corner, trembling with fear.
▸ alarm, anxiety, apprehension, dread, fright, horror, panic, terror, timidity, uneasiness, worry
▹ A formal word for a special type of fear is **phobia**. A fear of open spaces is **agoraphobia**. A fear of spiders is **arachnophobia**. A fear of enclosed spaces is **claustrophobia**. A fear or dislike of foreigners is **xenophobia**.
AN OPPOSITE IS courage

fear *VERB*
What do you fear most?
▸ be afraid or frightened of, dread, worry about

fearful *ADJECTIVE*
1 *There was a fearful look on his face.*
▸ afraid, anxious, apprehensive, frightened, nervous, scared, terrified, timid
AN OPPOSITE IS brave
2 *The erupting volcano was a fearful sight.*
▸ dreadful, fearsome, frightening, horrifying, intimidating, (*informal*) scary, terrifying
3 (*informal*) *Your friends made a fearful mess in the kitchen.*
▸ awful, frightful, horrid, nasty, unpleasant, upsetting

fearless *ADJECTIVE*
The fearless explorers pressed on into the unknown.
▸ brave, courageous, daring, heroic, intrepid, plucky, valiant
AN OPPOSITE IS cowardly

fearsome *ADJECTIVE*
The tiger yawned, revealing a fearsome set of teeth.
▸ dreadful, fearful, frightening, horrifying, intimidating, (*informal*) scary, terrifying

feasible *ADJECTIVE*
1 *Is it feasible to get to London and back before teatime?*
▸ possible, practicable, practical, realistic, workable
AN OPPOSITE IS impractical
2 *He gave a feasible excuse, but I don't know whether to believe it.*
▸ credible, likely, reasonable
AN OPPOSITE IS incredible

feast *NOUN*
The king held a great feast to celebrate his coronation.
▸ banquet, dinner
SEE ALSO **meal**

feat *NOUN*
The trapeze artists performed many daring feats.
▸ achievement, act, action, deed, exploit, performance

feather *NOUN*
▹ A large feather is a **plume**. All the feathers on a bird are its **plumage**. Soft, fluffy feathers are **down**. A feather used as a pen is a **quill**.

feathery *ADJECTIVE*
The duvet is full of feathery stuff.
▸ fluffy, light, soft

feature *NOUN*
1 *The crime had several unusual features.*
▸ aspect, characteristic, detail, peculiarity, point
▹ A person's features are their face.
2 *There was a feature about our school in the local paper last week.*
▸ article, item, piece, report, story

feature *VERB*
1 *The film features a brilliant new actor.*
▸ give prominence to, highlight, star
2 *A brilliant new actor features in this film.*
▸ appear, figure, star, take part

fee *NOUN*
If you want to join, there's an annual membership fee of £10.
▸ charge, cost, payment, price
▹ A fee to use a private road or bridge is a toll.

feeble *ADJECTIVE*
1 *I still feel feeble after my illness.*
▸ delicate, exhausted, faint, frail, listless, poorly, puny, sickly, useless, weak, weary, weedy
AN OPPOSITE IS strong
2 *I made a feeble attempt to stop the ball.*
▸ hesitant, indecisive, ineffectual
AN OPPOSITE IS decisive
3 *Do you expect me to believe that feeble excuse?*
▸ flimsy, lame, poor, tame, unconvincing, weak
AN OPPOSITE IS convincing

feed *VERB*
It costs a lot to feed a family.
▸ cater for, give food to, nourish, provide for
to feed on *Sheep feed on grass.*
▸ consume, eat

feel *VERB*
1 *I let the baby feel the cat's warm fur.*
▸ caress, stroke, touch
2 *When the light went out, I had to feel my way to the door.*
▸ fumble, grope
3 *It feels cold today.*
▸ appear, seem
4 *Old people tend to feel the cold.*
▸ be aware of, be conscious of, experience, notice, suffer from
5 *I feel that it's time to go home.*
▸ believe, consider, think

feeling *NOUN*
1 *She lost the feeling in her right hand.*
▸ sensation, sense of touch, sensitivity
2 *Cruelty to animals arouses strong feelings.*
▸ emotion, passion, sentiment
3 *My sister has a feeling for this kind of music.*
▸ fondness, sympathy, understanding (of)
4 *I have a feeling that something is wrong.*
▸ belief, hunch, idea, impression, instinct, intuition, notion, thought
5 *There was a good feeling at the party.*
▸ atmosphere, mood

female *ADJECTIVE*
FOR FEMALE HUMAN BEINGS SEE **woman**
FOR FEMALE ANIMALS SEE **animal**
AN OPPOSITE IS male

feminine *ADJECTIVE*
Her style of dress is very feminine.
AN OPPOSITE IS masculine

fence *NOUN*
THINGS USED TO SURROUND A PIECE OF LAND
electric fence, fencing, hedge, paling, palisade, railing, stockade, wall, wire fence
THINGS SET UP TO BLOCK THE WAY
barricade, barrier, hurdle, obstacle

fence *VERB*
The farmyard was fenced with a thorn hedge.
▸ encircle, enclose, surround
to fence something in *The animals are fenced in at night.*
▸ confine, coop up, wall in

fend *VERB*
to fend for yourself *It's time you learned to fend for yourself!*
▸ care for, look after, take care of
to fend someone or **something off** *He raised his arm to fend off the blow.*
▸ drive away, fight off, hold off, push away, repel, ward off

ferment *VERB*
Dad left his home-made wine to ferment in a glass jar.
▸ bubble, fizz, foam, seethe

ferment *NOUN*
The country was in a state of ferment.
▸ agitation, commotion, confusion, excitement, tumult, turbulence, turmoil, unrest, upheaval

A B C D E F G H I J K L M N O P Q R S T U V W X Y Z

ferocious *ADJECTIVE*
The ferocious dog made me very nervous.
▸ dangerous, fearsome, fierce, savage, vicious, violent, wild
AN OPPOSITE IS tame

ferry *VERB*
The lifeboat ferried passengers to safety.
▸ carry, convey, ship, take, transfer, transport

fertile *ADJECTIVE*
The surrounding countryside was green and fertile.
▸ flourishing, fruitful, productive
AN OPPOSITE IS barren or sterile

fertilize *VERB*
If you want good crops, you must fertilize the soil.
▸ cultivate, enrich, feed, manure
THINGS USED TO FERTILIZE THE SOIL
chemical fertilizer, compost, dung or manure, mulch, organic fertilizer

fervent *ADJECTIVE*
She's a fervent supporter of the local team.
▸ avid, committed, enthusiastic, fanatical, keen, passionate, vigorous, zealous
AN OPPOSITE IS apathetic

festival *NOUN*
The town holds a festival every summer.
▸ carnival, celebration, fair, feast, fête, gala, jamboree
▹ A celebration of a special anniversary is a **jubilee**.

festive *ADJECTIVE*
The opening of the new community centre was a festive occasion.
▸ cheerful, happy, jolly, jovial, joyful, joyous, light-hearted, merry
AN OPPOSITE IS gloomy

fetch *VERB*
1 *I fetched the shopping from the car.*
▸ bring, carry, collect, convey, get, obtain, pick up, retrieve, transfer, transport
2 *If we sell our car, how much will it fetch?*
▸ be sold for, bring in, earn, go for, make, raise, sell for

feud *NOUN*
The feud between the gangs resulted in violence.
▸ antagonism, conflict, dispute, enmity, fighting, hostility, quarrel, rivalry, strife

feverish *ADJECTIVE*
1 *I had a feverish cold.*
▹ When you are feverish you are **hot** and **shivery**. With a bad fever you may become **delirious**.
2 *There was feverish activity to get the hall ready before everyone arrived.*
▸ agitated, busy, excited, frantic, frenzied, hectic, hurried, impatient, restless

few *ADJECTIVE*
Yesterday was one of the few times I have been absent from school.
▸ infrequent, rare, uncommon
AN OPPOSITE IS many

fibre *NOUN*
Cloth consists of many fibres woven together.
▸ filament, hair, strand, thread

fickle *ADJECTIVE*
His supporters turned out to be very fickle.
▸ changeable, disloyal, erratic, inconsistent, unfaithful, unpredictable, unreliable
AN OPPOSITE IS loyal

fiction *NOUN*
1 *I enjoy reading fiction.*
FOR VARIOUS KINDS OF LITERATURE SEE **writing**
2 *Her account of what happened was a fiction from start to finish.*
▸ fantasy, invention, lie
AN OPPOSITE IS fact

fictional *ADJECTIVE*
I enjoy fictional writing best.
▸ creative, imaginative
AN OPPOSITE IS factual

fictitious *ADJECTIVE*
1 *Peter Pan is a fictitious character.*
▸ imaginary, invented, made-up, non-existent, unreal
AN OPPOSITE IS real
2 *He gave the police a fictitious name.*
▸ assumed, bogus, fake, false, fraudulent
AN OPPOSITE IS genuine

fiddle *VERB*
1 *Don't fiddle with the knobs on the TV.*
▸ fidget, meddle, mess about, play about, tamper, twiddle
2 (*informal*) *He tried to fiddle his expenses.*
▹ To fiddle something is to **be dishonest** about it, or to **cheat** or **swindle** someone.

fiddling *ADJECTIVE*
I don't want to go into a lot of fiddling details.
▸ insignificant, minor, petty, small, tedious, trivial, unimportant
AN OPPOSITE IS important

fiddly *ADJECTIVE*
Mending this torch is a fiddly job.
▸ awkward, complicated, intricate, involved
AN OPPOSITE IS straightforward

fidelity *NOUN*
The dog displayed amazing fidelity to its owner.
▸ devotion, faithfulness, loyalty

fidget *VERB*
I begin to fidget when I'm bored.
▸ be restless, fiddle about, mess about, move restlessly, play about

fidgety *ADJECTIVE*
After waiting an hour, we began to get fidgety.
▸ agitated, impatient, restless
AN OPPOSITE IS calm

field *NOUN*
1 *Cattle were grazing in the field.*
▸ meadow, pasture
▹ A small field for horses is a **paddock**. An area of grass in a village is a **green**.
2 *The field is too wet for games today.*
▸ ground, pitch, playing field, recreation ground
3 *Electronics is not my field.*
▸ area of study, special interest, speciality, special subject

fiendish *ADJECTIVE*
The tyrant used fiendish methods to gain power.
▸ cruel, devilish, diabolical, evil, hellish, infernal, savage, wicked
AN OPPOSITE IS angelic

fierce *ADJECTIVE*
1 *The travellers were killed in a fierce attack by armed bandits.*
▸ brutal, cruel, ferocious, fiendish, merciless, murderous, pitiless, ruthless, sadistic, savage, vicious, violent, wild
2 *We played against fierce opposition last Saturday.*
▸ aggressive, competitive, eager, keen, passionate, relentless, strong
3 *We walked out into the fierce heat of the sun.*
▸ blazing, intense, raging

fiery *ADJECTIVE*
1 *We could feel the fiery heat of the furnace.*
▸ blazing, burning, fierce, flaming, glowing, hot, intense, raging, red, red-hot
2 *Take care — he has a fiery temper.*
▸ angry, excitable, furious, irritable, passionate, violent

fight *NOUN*
1 *He's always getting into fights with other boys.*
▹ Fighting is **combat** or **hostilities**. A fight between armies is an **action** or a **battle**. A minor unplanned battle is a **skirmish**. A series of actions or battles is a **campaign** or a **war**. A confused fight in a public place is a **brawl**, **punch-up**, or **scuffle**. A minor fight over something unimportant is a **scrap**, **squabble**, or **tussle**. A long-lasting series of fights or squabbles is a **feud**. A fight arranged between two people is a **duel**. A fight in a boxing or wrestling ring is a **bout** or **match**. Fighting sports such as karate and judo are **martial arts**. A fight between knights on horseback in the Middle Ages was a **joust** or **tilting match**.
2 *We must continue the fight against poverty.*
▸ crusade, struggle

fight *VERB*
1 *Two men were fighting in the street.*
▸ exchange blows, have a fight, scrap, scuffle
2 *The two countries fought each other in the war.*
▸ attack, do battle with, wage war with
▹ Fighting with foils or swords is **fencing**. Fighting with fists is **boxing**. A fight in which you try to throw your opponent to the ground is **wrestling**.
3 *Local people decided to fight the decision to build a bypass.*
▸ campaign against, make a stand against, oppose, protest against, resist

fighter *NOUN*
PEOPLE WHO FIGHT IN A WAR OR CONFLICT
freedom fighter, gladiator, guerrilla, gunman, knight, sniper, soldier, swordsman, terrorist, warrior
PEOPLE WHO FIGHT AS A SPORT
boxer, contender, contestant, wrestler
FOR PEOPLE WHO FIGHT IN THE ARMY, ETC. SEE **armed services**

A B C D E F G H I J K L M N O P Q R S T U V W X Y Z

figure *NOUN*
1 *Write the figure '8' on the blackboard.*
▸ digit, integer, number, numeral
2 *Bargaining over the price of the new car, the salesman asked Dad what figure he had in mind.*
▸ amount, price, sum, value
3 *She's always had a very good figure.*
▸ body, build, form, shape
4 *She was looking at a small bronze figure of a horse.*
▸ carving, sculpture, statue
5 *The figure on page 22 shows the average rainfall for the area.*
▸ diagram, drawing, graph, illustration
figures *You must be good with figures to work in the bank.*
▸ accounts, mathematics, statistics, sums

figure *VERB*
The same character figures in many of her novels.
▸ appear, feature, take part
to figure out 1 *Have you figured out how much this holiday will cost?*
▸ add up, calculate, compute, count, reckon, work out
2 *I can't figure out what this means.*
▸ comprehend, follow, make out, puzzle out, see, understand

figure of speech *NOUN*
SOME COMMON FIGURES OF SPEECH
alliteration, assonance, hyperbole, irony, metaphor, onomatopoeia, personification, simile

file *NOUN*
1 *I keep my papers in a file.*
▸ binder, cover, folder
▹ A file containing information, especially secret information, is a **dossier**.
2 *Please walk in a single file.*
▸ column, line, procession, queue, rank, row

file *VERB*
1 *I file all my letters in a pink folder.*
▸ organize, put away, store
2 *We filed into the hall for assembly.*
▸ march, parade, troop, walk in a line

fill *VERB*
1 *We filled the trolley with shopping.*
▸ cram, load, pack, stuff, top up
▹ To fill a tyre with air is to **inflate** it.
AN OPPOSITE IS **empty**
2 *What can I use to fill this hole?*
▸ block up, close up, plug, seal, stop up
3 *Sightseers filled the streets.*
▸ block, (*informal*) bung up, crowd, jam, obstruct

filling *NOUN*
The chair has a padded seat with a foam filling.
▸ padding, stuffing

film *NOUN*
1 *I watched a good film last night.*
▸ (*American*) motion picture, movie, video
▹ To go to a cinema to see a film is to **go to the pictures**. A long film is a **feature film**. A short excerpt from a film is a **clip**. A script for a film is a **screenplay**.
KINDS OF FILM
biopic, cartoon, comedy, documentary, horror film, love story or romance, space or science fiction film, war film, western
2 *There was a film of oil on the water.*
▸ coat, coating, covering, layer, sheet, skin
▹ A large patch of oil floating on water is a **slick**.

filter *NOUN*
▹ A filter used to separate tea leaves from tea, etc., is a **strainer**. A device used in the kitchen to separate lumps from liquid or from flour, etc., is a **sieve**. A coarse sieve used in the garden is a **riddle**.

filter *VERB*
Dad filters his home-made wine to get rid of the cloudiness.
▸ clarify, purify, strain

filth *NOUN*
The floor was covered with a layer of filth.
▸ dirt, grime, mess, muck, mud, scum, slime, sludge

filthy *ADJECTIVE*
1 *Your shoes are filthy!*
▸ dirty, grimy, grubby, messy, mucky, muddy, soiled, stained
AN OPPOSITE IS **clean**
2 *You mustn't drink that filthy water!*
▸ cloudy, contaminated, foul, impure, polluted, slimy, smelly, stinking
AN OPPOSITE IS **pure**
3 *We were offended by their filthy language.*
▸ coarse, crude, dirty, improper, indecent, obscene, offensive, rude, vulgar
AN OPPOSITE IS **decent**

final *ADJECTIVE*
1 *The final moments of the game were very tense.*
▸ closing, concluding, last
AN OPPOSITE IS opening
2 *What was the final result?*
▸ eventual, ultimate

finale *NOUN*
The fireworks were the finale to the whole festival.
▸ conclusion, culmination, end

finance *NOUN*
I'm not very interested in finance.
▸ commerce, economics, investments, money
finances *What's the state of your finances?*
▸ bank account, funds, money, resources, wealth

finance *VERB*
The bank helped them finance the business.
▸ back, invest in, pay for, provide money for, subsidize, support

find *VERB*
1 *Did you find the money you lost?*
▸ get back, recover, retrieve, trace, track down
AN OPPOSITE IS lose
2 *Did you find what you wanted?*
▸ come across, discover, encounter, locate, see, spot, stumble across, unearth
3 *Did the doctor find what was wrong?*
▸ detect, diagnose, identify
4 *I think you will find that digging is hard work.*
▸ become aware, learn, notice, realize, recognize

findings *PLURAL NOUN*
The judge announced his findings.
▸ conclusion, decision, judgement, verdict

fine *ADJECTIVE*
1 *We applauded his fine performance.*
▸ admirable, commendable, excellent, first-class, good
AN OPPOSITE IS bad
2 *As the weather was fine, we took a picnic.*
▸ bright, clear, cloudless, fair, pleasant, sunny
AN OPPOSITE IS dull
3 *The spider spins a very fine thread.*
▸ delicate, flimsy, fragile, slender, slim, thin
AN OPPOSITE IS thick
4 *The dunes were made of fine sand.*
▸ dusty, powdery
AN OPPOSITE IS coarse

fine *NOUN*
She had to pay a fine for speeding.
▸ penalty

finger *NOUN*
▹ Your short fat finger is your **thumb**. The finger next to your thumb is your **index finger**, because it is the finger you point with or indicate things with. The next finger is your **middle finger**. The next finger is your **ring finger**, because you can wear a wedding or engagement ring on that finger of your left hand. Your small thin finger is your **little finger**. The joints in your fingers are your **knuckles**.

finger *VERB*
Please don't finger the food on the table.
▸ feel, touch

finicky *ADJECTIVE*
Our cat is finicky about her food.
▸ (*informal*) choosy, fussy, hard to please, particular

finish *VERB*
1 *When are you likely to finish your work?*
▸ cease, complete, reach the end of, round off, stop
2 *The concert is likely to finish at about nine o'clock.*
▸ conclude, end, reach the end, terminate, (*informal*) wind up
3 *I've finished my chocolates.*
▸ consume, exhaust, get through, (*informal*) polish off, use up
AN OPPOSITE IS start

finish *NOUN*
The finish of the race was very exciting.
▸ close, completion, conclusion, end, result, termination
AN OPPOSITE IS start

fire *NOUN*
1 *A crowd gathered to watch the fire.*
▸ blaze, flames
2 *The heat of the fire melted the steel frame.*
▸ burning, combustion

▷ A very big hot fire is an inferno. An open fire out of doors is a bonfire. A metal container for an outdoor fire is a brazier. A metal container for burning rubbish is an incinerator. An enclosed fire which produces great heat is a furnace. An enclosed fire for cooking food is an oven. An enclosed fire for making pottery, etc., is a kiln.
VARIOUS KINDS OF HEATING APPARATUS AT HOME, IN SCHOOL, ETC.
boiler, central heating, convector, electric fire, fan heater, fireplace, gas fire, immersion heater, radiator, stove, underfloor heating

fire *VERB*
1 *Vandals fired the barn.*
► burn, ignite, kindle, light, put a light to, set alight, set fire to
2 *You fire pottery in a kiln.*
► bake, harden, heat
3 *He claimed that he fired the gun by mistake.*
► discharge, let off, set off, shoot
▷ To fire a missile is to launch it.
4 (*informal*) *The boss fired him because he was continually late for work.*
► dismiss, sack
to fire at something *I fired at the target.*
► aim at, shoot at

firework *NOUN*
VARIOUS FIREWORKS
banger, cascade, Catherine wheel, cracker or firecracker, fountain, rocket, Roman candle, sparkler, squib

firm *NOUN*
Mum works for a firm that sells computers.
► business, company, concern, organization

firm *ADJECTIVE*
1 *Make sure the ladder rests on firm ground.*
► hard, solid
AN OPPOSITE IS soft
2 *Is the ladder firm?*
► fixed, secure, stable, steady
AN OPPOSITE IS unsteady
3 *She has a firm belief in fate.*
► decided, definite, determined, obstinate, persistent, resolute, sure
AN OPPOSITE IS unsure
4 *I trust him — he's a firm friend.*
► close, constant, dependable, devoted, faithful, loyal, reliable, trustworthy
AN OPPOSITE IS unreliable

first *ADJECTIVE*
1 *The first cars were slow and unreliable.*
► earliest, original
2 *The first thing to do in an emergency is to keep calm.*
► basic, chief, fundamental, key, main, principal
at first *At first, I thought the lesson was going to be boring, but then I got interested.*
► at the beginning, initially, originally, to start with

first-class, **first-rate** *ADJECTIVES*
The team's performance was first-class.
► excellent, outstanding, supreme, unequalled
INFORMAL SYNONYMS
brilliant, fabulous, fantastic, great, tremendous

first-hand *ADJECTIVE*
Do you have first-hand knowledge of this firm?
► direct, personal

fish *NOUN*
VARIOUS FISH
brill, carp, catfish, chub, cod, conger, cuttlefish, dace, eel, flounder, goldfish, grayling, gudgeon, haddock, hake, halibut, herring, jellyfish, lamprey, ling, mackerel, minnow, mullet, perch, pike, pilchard, piranha, plaice, roach, salmon, sardine, sawfish, shark, skate, sole, sprat, squid, starfish, stickleback, sturgeon, swordfish, trout, tuna, turbot, whitebait, whiting
▷ Bloater and kipper are kinds of smoked herring. Young fish are fry. An informal word for a very small fish is a tiddler. A large number of fish swimming together is a shoal.
▷ A fisherman who uses a rod and line is an angler. A man whose job is to catch fish at sea is a trawlerman.
▷ The sport or job of catching fish is fishing. Fishing with a rod and line is angling. Fishing with nets from a boat is trawling. Fishing equipment is tackle.
SOME EQUIPMENT USED IN FISHING
bait, creel, float, fly, gaff, hook, keepnet, line, lure, net, reel, rod, trawl line, trawl net

fishy *ADJECTIVE*
(*informal*) *Tell the police if you see anything fishy going on.*
► shady, suspicious

fit *ADJECTIVE*
1 *They gave us a dinner fit for a king!*
▸ appropriate, fitting, good enough, proper, right, suitable
AN OPPOSITE IS unsuitable
2 *You should try to keep fit.*
▸ healthy, in good form, robust, strong, well
AN OPPOSITE IS unhealthy
3 *We worked till we were fit to collapse.*
▸ liable, likely, ready

fit *VERB*
1 *My new jeans don't seem to fit.*
▸ be the right size
2 *We need to fit a new lock on the door.*
▸ install, put in place
3 *The pieces of this jigsaw don't fit.*
▸ go together, join up, match
4 *Wear clothes to fit the occasion.*
▸ be suitable for, go with, suit

fit *NOUN*
I had a fit of coughing.
▸ attack, bout, outburst

fitting *ADJECTIVE*
Scoring the winning goal was a fitting end to his great career.
▸ appropriate, apt, proper, suitable
AN OPPOSITE IS inappropriate

fix *VERB*
1 *He fixed a bayonet to the end of his rifle.*
▸ attach, connect, fasten, join, link
SEE ALSO **fasten**
2 *We set the post in concrete to fix it in its proper position.*
▸ make firm, secure, stabilize
3 *Let's fix a time for the party.*
▸ agree on, arrange, decide, establish, settle, specify
4 (*informal*) *Dad says he can fix my bike.*
▸ mend, put right, repair

fix *NOUN*
(*informal*) *Can you help me? I'm in a fix.*
▸ difficulty, dilemma, (*informal*) jam, mess, plight

fixture *NOUN*
Our team has three fixtures next week.
▸ date, engagement, game, match

fizz *VERB*
The lemonade fizzed when I opened the bottle.
▸ bubble, foam, froth, hiss

fizzy *ADJECTIVE*
The baby hates fizzy drinks.
▸ bubbly, effervescent, foaming, sparkling
AN OPPOSITE IS still

flabbergasted *ADJECTIVE* (*informal*)
I was flabbergasted when they said I had won first prize.
▸ amazed, astonished, astounded, dumbfounded, speechless, stunned, surprised, taken aback

flabby *ADJECTIVE*
This exercise is good for flabby thighs.
▸ fat, fleshy, out of condition, slack
AN OPPOSITE IS firm

flag *NOUN*
The street was decorated with flags for the carnival.
▸ banner, pennant, streamer
▹ The flag of a regiment is its colours or standard. A flag flown on a ship is an ensign.

flag *VERB*
Our enthusiasm flagged as the day went on.
▸ decline, decrease, diminish, dwindle, lessen, tail off, wane, weaken

flames *PLURAL NOUN*
Don't put your hand near the flames.
▸ blaze, fire

flap *VERB*
The sail flapped in the wind.
▸ flutter, sway, thrash about, wave about

flare *VERB*
to flare up **1** *The bonfire flared up when he threw dry grass on it.*
▸ blaze, burn brightly, flame
2 *She flares up at the slightest provocation.*
▸ become angry, lose your temper

flash *NOUN VERB*
FOR VARIOUS EFFECTS OF LIGHTS SEE **light** *NOUN*

flat *ADJECTIVE*
1 *You need a flat surface to write on.*
▸ even, level, smooth
AN OPPOSITE IS uneven
2 *I lay flat on the ground.*
▸ horizontal, outstretched, spread out

AN OPPOSITE IS upright
▷ To be lying face downwards is to be **prone**. To be lying face upwards is to be **supine**.
3 *He spoke in a flat, quiet voice.*
▸ boring, dull, lifeless, monotonous, tedious, uninteresting
AN OPPOSITE IS lively
4 *The front tyre of my bike was flat.*
▸ deflated, punctured
AN OPPOSITE IS inflated

flat *NOUN*
FOR PLACES WHERE PEOPLE LIVE SEE **house**

flatten *VERB*
1 *She flattened the crumpled paper.*
▸ smooth
▷ To flatten clothes that have been washed is to **iron** or **press** them.
2 *They flattened the old buildings and built a new road.*
▸ demolish, destroy, knock down, level, pull down
3 *The wheat had been flattened by the rain.*
▸ crush, squash

flaunt *VERB*
He likes to flaunt his expensive clothes.
▸ display, exhibit, show off

flavour *NOUN*
1 *I don't like the flavour of raw onions.*
▸ taste
FOR WORDS TO DESCRIBE HOW THINGS TASTE SEE **taste** *VERB*
2 *Which flavour of ice cream do you like best?*
▸ kind, sort, variety

flavour *VERB*
▷ To flavour food with salt, pepper, etc., is to **season** it.

flaw *NOUN*
1 *Pride was the greatest flaw in his character.*
▸ imperfection, weakness
2 *There's a flaw in your argument.*
▸ error, fallacy, inaccuracy, mistake, slip
3 *There's a small flaw in the glass.*
▸ blemish, break, chip, crack

fleck *NOUN*
He brushed a few flecks of dust from his jacket.
▸ dot, mark, speck, spot

flee *VERB*
When they saw the police arrive, the attackers fled.
▸ escape, get away, retreat, run away

fleet *NOUN*
▷ A group of ships or vehicles travelling together is a **convoy**. A fleet of warships is an **armada**. A number of ships belonging to a particular country is its **navy**.

fleeting *ADJECTIVE*
I only caught a fleeting glimpse of him.
▸ brief, momentary, quick, short
AN OPPOSITE IS lengthy or permanent

flesh *NOUN*
▷ Your flesh is **muscle** and **fat**. An animal's flesh used for food is **meat**.

flex *NOUN*
Don't trip over the flex of the iron!
▸ cable, lead, wire

flexible *ADJECTIVE*
1 *The wire was flexible enough to wind round the post.*
▸ pliable, soft, springy, supple
AN OPPOSITE IS rigid
2 *My plans are flexible, so I can come at any time.*
▸ adjustable, alterable, variable
AN OPPOSITE IS fixed
3 *He's quite flexible — he'll play in any position.*
▸ adaptable, versatile
AN OPPOSITE IS inflexible

flicker *VERB*
The candlelight flickered in the draught.
▸ glimmer, quiver, tremble, twinkle, waver

flight *NOUN*
1 *The Wright brothers played an important part in the history of flight.*
▸ aviation, flying
2 *The refugees began their flight from danger under cover of darkness.*
▸ escape

flimsy *ADJECTIVE*
1 *A butterfly's wings are so flimsy that the slightest touch damages them.*
▸ brittle, delicate, fine, fragile, frail, light, thin
2 *The gale blew down our flimsy shelter.*
▸ rickety, shaky, weak, wobbly
AN OPPOSITE IS strong

flinch *VERB*
She didn't even flinch when he threatened her.
▸ back off, draw back, falter, recoil, shrink back, start, wince

fling *VERB*
I flung a stone into the pond.
▸ cast, (*informal*) chuck, hurl, pitch, sling, throw, toss

flippant *ADJECTIVE*
Don't make flippant remarks about people's misfortunes.
▸ facetious, frivolous, silly, stupid
AN OPPOSITE IS serious

float *VERB*
1 *The raft floated gently down the river.*
▸ drift, sail
2 *There wasn't enough water to float the ship.*
▸ launch
AN OPPOSITE IS sink

flock *NOUN*
FOR VARIOUS GROUPS SEE **group** *NOUN*

flock *VERB*
People flocked round to see what was happening.
▸ crowd, gather, herd, jostle

flog *VERB*
He flogged the poor donkey mercilessly.
▸ beat, cane, lash, thrash, (*slang*) wallop, whack, whip

flood *NOUN*
The flood of water swept away the bridge.
▸ deluge, inundation, rush, torrent

flood *VERB*
The river burst its banks and flooded the valley.
▸ cover, drown, engulf, immerse, inundate, overwhelm, submerge, swamp
to flood in *Donations to the charity flooded in.*
▸ flow in, keep coming, pour in

floor *NOUN*
1 *There weren't enough chairs, so I had to sit on the floor.*
SOME THINGS USED TO MAKE OR COVER A FLOOR
carpet, flagstones, floorboards, lino or linoleum, mat, matting, parquet, rug, tiles, vinyl
2 *Her flat is on the top floor.*
▸ level, storey
▹ A floor on a ship is a **deck**.

flop *VERB*
1 *I was so tired that I just flopped onto my bed.*
▸ collapse, drop, fall, slump
2 *The plants in the hanging basket will flop if you don't water them.*
▸ dangle, droop, hang down, sag, wilt
3 (*informal*) *Their first single flopped, but their second was a big hit.*
▸ be unsuccessful, fail, founder, meet with disaster

floppy *ADJECTIVE*
The dog had long, floppy ears.
▸ droopy, limp, soft

flounder *VERB*
1 *We floundered through the mud.*
▸ stagger, struggle, stumble, wallow
2 *The question took him by surprise and he began to flounder.*
▸ falter, get confused, make mistakes, talk aimlessly

flourish *VERB*
1 *The plants may flourish if we get some rain.*
▸ be fruitful, bloom, blossom, flower, grow, thrive
AN OPPOSITE IS die
2 *The company has continued to flourish.*
▸ be successful, boom, develop, do well, increase, prosper, succeed
AN OPPOSITE IS fail
3 *He flourished his umbrella to attract the taxi driver's attention.*
▸ brandish, shake, twirl, wave

flow *VERB*
Water flowed along the gutter.
▸ glide, run, stream
▹ To flow slowly is to **dribble**, **drip**, **ooze**, **seep**, or **trickle**. To flow fast is to **cascade** or **pour**. To flow with sudden force is to **spurt**, **squirt**, or **well up**. To flow over the edge of something is to **overflow** or **spill**. When blood flows from a wound, we say that it **bleeds**. When the tide flows out, it **ebbs**.

flow *NOUN*
1 *It's hard work rowing against the flow.*
▸ current, stream, tide
2 *There was a steady flow of water into the pond.*
▸ cascade, flood, gush, rush

A B C D E F G H I J K L M N O P Q R S T U V W X Y Z

flower *NOUN*
▷ A single flower is a **bloom**. A mass of small flowers growing together is **blossom**. Flowers in a vase are an **arrangement**. A bunch of flowers arranged for a special occasion is a **bouquet**, **posy**, or **spray**. Flowers arranged to make a circle are a **garland** or **wreath**.
SOME WILD FLOWERS
bluebell, buttercup, catkin, celandine, coltsfoot, cornflower, cowslip, daisy, dandelion, foxglove, harebell, kingcup, orchid, poppy, primrose
SOME POPULAR CULTIVATED FLOWERS
begonia, candytuft, carnation, chrysanthemum, columbine, crocus, cyclamen, daffodil, dahlia, forget-me-not, freesia, geranium, gladiolus, hollyhock, hyacinth, iris, lilac, lily, lupin, marigold, nasturtium, pansy, pelargonium, peony, petunia, phlox, pink, polyanthus, rose, snowdrop, sunflower, tulip, wallflower, water lily
PARTS OF A FLOWER
axil, bract, calyx, carpel, corolla, perianth, pistil, pollen, sepal, stamen, whorl

flower *VERB*
Most plants flower in the summer.
▸ bloom, blossom, have flowers

fluent *ADJECTIVE*
I wish I was fluent in French.
▸ articulate, eloquent
AN OPPOSITE IS hesitant

fluffy *ADJECTIVE*
Seven fluffy ducklings were swimming in the pond.
▸ downy, feathery, furry, fuzzy, hairy, soft

fluid *NOUN*
▷ Fluids are either **liquids** or **gases**.
AN OPPOSITE IS solid

fluke *NOUN*
It was just a fluke that the ball went into the net.
▸ accident, chance, stroke of good luck

flush *VERB*
He flushed with embarrassment.
▸ blush, colour, go red, redden

flustered *ADJECTIVE*
I get flustered when I have to read in assembly.
▸ confused, mixed up, nervous
AN OPPOSITE IS confident

flutter *VERB*
The moth's wings fluttered.
▸ flap, quiver, tremble, vibrate

fly *NOUN*
FOR VARIOUS INSECTS SEE **insect**

fly *VERB*
1 *The swallows were flying high in the sky.*
▸ flit, glide, hover, rise, soar, swoop
2 *The ship was flying the British flag.*
▸ display, hang up, hoist, raise, show, wave
3 *Doesn't time fly!*
▸ go quickly, pass quickly, rush by

foam *NOUN*
1 *This detergent makes a lot of foam.*
▸ bubbles, froth, lather, suds
2 *These cushions are filled with foam.*
▸ sponge, spongy rubber

foam *VERB*
The lemonade foamed as I poured it into the glass.
▸ boil, bubble, fizz, froth up

focus *NOUN*
1 *Can you adjust the focus on the projector?*
▸ clarity, sharpness
2 *The club's new player is the focus of attention in the papers.*
▸ centre, focal point
in focus *These photos are not in focus.*
▸ clear, focused, sharp, well defined
out of focus *The photos are out of focus.*
▸ blurred, foggy, fuzzy, hazy, indistinct, unclear, unfocused

focus *VERB*
Can you focus the projector?
▸ adjust the focus of, get into focus
to focus on *We ought to focus on the main problem.*
▸ concentrate on, examine, look at, think about

fog *NOUN*
There was fog on the motorway.
▸ bad visibility
▷ Thin fog is **haze** or **mist**. A thick mixture of fog and smoke is **smog**.

foggy *ADJECTIVE*
1 *Dad doesn't like driving in this foggy weather.*
▸ hazy, misty, murky

2 *The photo was foggy.*
▸ blurred, fuzzy, indistinct
AN OPPOSITE IS clear

foil *VERB*
1 *The security officer foiled the attempted robbery.*
▸ block, check, halt, prevent, stop
2 *The security officer foiled the thieves.*
▸ frustrate, outwit

fold *VERB*
Fold the paper along the dotted line.
▸ bend, crease, double over

fold *NOUN*
1 *She smoothed the soft folds of her dress.*
▹ A fold which is part of the way a garment is made is a **pleat**.
2 *The dog drove the sheep into the fold.*
▸ enclosure, pen

folder *NOUN*
I keep my project work in a folder.
▸ cover, file

follow *VERB*
1 *James I followed Elizabeth I.*
▸ come after, replace, succeed, take the place of
AN OPPOSITE IS precede
2 *Follow that car!*
▸ chase, go after, keep up with, pursue
3 *The lion followed its prey.*
▸ hunt, stalk, tail, track, trail
4 *Try to follow his example.*
▸ be guided by, imitate, model yourself on
5 *Follow the rules.*
▸ heed, keep to, obey, observe, pay attention to, take notice of
6 *Do you follow snooker?*
▸ be a fan of, know about, support, take an interest in
7 *Try to follow what I say.*
▸ comprehend, grasp, understand
8 *It's sunny now, but it doesn't follow that it'll be fine tonight.*
▸ be inevitable, come about, ensue, happen, mean, result

follower *NOUN*
▹ Someone who follows you in a job, etc., is your **successor**. Someone who follows a person or animal to try to catch them is a **hunter** or **pursuer**. Someone who continually follows a person about is a **stalker**. Someone who follows a person's teaching is a **disciple**. Someone who follows a football team, etc., is a **fan** or **supporter**.

fond *ADJECTIVE*
1 *He gave me a fond kiss.*
▸ affectionate, loving, tender
2 *Winning the lottery is just a fond dream.*
▸ fanciful, silly, unrealistic
to be fond of *I'm very fond of her.*
▸ admire, adore, like, love

food *NOUN*
All living things need food.
▸ nourishment
▹ The food that we normally eat or that we choose to eat is our **diet**. Something specially tasty to eat is a **delicacy**. Food for farm animals is **fodder**. A word used for the food which plants need is **nutrients**.
PRINCIPAL CONSTITUENTS OF OUR FOOD
carbohydrate, fat, fibre, protein, roughage, starch, vitamins
Cereal foods
VARIOUS CEREALS
barley, maize or sweetcorn, oats, rice, rye, wheat
SOME FOODS MADE FROM CEREALS
bran, cornflakes, cornflour, flour, muesli, oatmeal, porridge
FOODS MADE LARGELY FROM FLOUR
batter, biscuits, bread, cake, dumplings, noodles, pancakes, pasta, pastry, pizza, tortilla, Yorkshire pudding
VARIOUS KINDS OF BREAD
bagel, baguette, brown bread, chapatti, French bread or French stick, fruit loaf, granary bread, matzo, nan, rye bread, white bread, wholemeal bread
▹ You can use bread to make **sandwiches** or **toast**.
SOME KINDS OF CAKE
bun, doughnut or donut, fruitcake, gingerbread, meringue, muffin, scone, shortbread, sponge cake
SOME KINDS OF PASTA
lasagne, macaroni, ravioli, spaghetti, tagliatelle
SOME THINGS MADE WITH PASTRY
flan, pasty, pie, quiche, samosa, sausage roll, tart

Food from animals
DIFFERENT KINDS OF MEAT
bacon, beef, chicken, duck, game, gammon, goose, ham, lamb, mutton, pork, turkey, veal, venison
DIFFERENT WAYS A BUTCHER CUTS AND SELLS MEAT
burgers, chops, cutlets, mince, roasting joint, sausages, steak
SOME FOODS OFTEN MADE WITH MEAT
casserole, chop suey, chow mein, curry, fritters, goulash, hash, hotpot, kebab, meat pie, paté, rissoles, stew
▷ Other foods which come from animals are eggs and milk.
FOODS MADE WITH EGGS
omelette, soufflé
FOODS MADE WITH MILK
blancmange, butter, cheese, cream, custard, ice cream, milk pudding, yoghurt
▷ A diet which includes no meat is a vegetarian diet. A diet which includes no animal products is a vegan diet.
Fish used as food
SOME FISH THAT PEOPLE EAT
bream, cod, eel, haddock, halibut, herring, mackerel, pilchard, plaice, salmon, sardine, sole, sprat, trout, tuna
▷ Bloaters and kippers are kinds of smoked herring. An expensive food from a fish called sturgeon is caviare. Very small young herrings or sprats are called whitebait.
SOME SHELLFISH THAT PEOPLE EAT
crab, lobster, mussels, oysters, prawn, scampi, shrimp, whelks
▷ A mixture of fish, shellfish, etc., is seafood.
Fruits and vegetables
FOR FRUITS AND VEGETABLES SEE **fruit, vegetable**
Sweet foods s
THINGS WE USE TO MAKE FOOD TASTE SWEET INCLUDE
artificial sweeteners, honey, saccharin, sugar, syrup, treacle
SWEET FOODS USUALLY CONTAINING A LOT OF SUGAR INCLUDE
biscuit, cake, chocolate, gateau, ice cream, icing, jam, jelly, marmalade, pudding, sweet
SOME PUDDINGS OR DESSERTS
charlotte, cheesecake, crumble, fool, fruit pies, fruit salad, fruit tarts, gateau, milk pudding, mousse, sundae, trifle
Other ingredients and flavourings
KINDS OF FAT USED IN FOOD
butter, dripping, ghee, lard, margarine, olive oil, suet, vegetable oil

THINGS YOU ADD TO FOOD TO MAKE THE TASTE MORE INTERESTING
chilli, chutney, curry powder, dressing, garlic, gravy, herbs, ketchup, mayonnaise, mustard, pepper, pickle, salt, sauce, spice, sugar, vinegar
▷ Things like salt and pepper which you add to food are condiments or seasoning. Artificial chemicals added to food before you buy it are called additives. Additives may be colourings, flavourings, or preservatives.

fool *NOUN*
1 *Only a fool would have believed him.*
▸ ass, clown, dope, idiot, moron
Fool and its synonyms are used informally, and they are insulting if you use them to describe other people
2 (*old use*) *The king's fool entertained the court.*
▸ jester

fool *VERB*
He fooled you completely!
▸ bluff, (*slang*) con, deceive, (*informal*) have you on, hoax, (*informal*) kid, mislead, take you in, trick
to fool about *The teacher told us not to fool about.*
▸ be naughty, misbehave, play about

foolish *ADJECTIVE*
What a foolish thing to do!
▸ absurd, crazy, idiotic, irresponsible, pointless, ridiculous, senseless, silly, stupid, thoughtless, unintelligent, unwise
AN OPPOSITE IS sensible

foolproof *ADJECTIVE*
The plan was completely foolproof.
▸ certain, guaranteed, infallible, safe, sure, unfailing

foot *NOUN*
1 *These shoes hurt my feet.*
▷ An animal's foot is a paw. A horse's foot is a hoof. A pig's foot is a trotter. A bird's feet are its claws. The feet of a bird of prey are its talons.
2 *We set up camp at the foot of the mountain.*
▸ base, bottom

footprint *NOUN*
We followed the footprints in the snow.
▸ footmark, track

forbid *VERB*
I think they ought to forbid smoking in public places.
▸ ban, bar, make illegal, prohibit, rule out, stop
AN OPPOSITE IS allow

forbidding *ADJECTIVE*
Despite her forbidding appearance, she's actually quite a kind woman.
▸ gloomy, grim, menacing, ominous, stern, threatening, unfriendly, unwelcoming
AN OPPOSITE IS friendly

force *NOUN*
1 *I had to use all my force to open the door.*
▸ effort, energy, might, power, strength
2 *The force of the explosion broke all the windows.*
▸ effect, impact, shock, violence
3 *They sent a military force to stop the riots.*
▸ army, troops
in force *Is that rule still in force?*
▸ effective, legal, valid

force *VERB*
1 *You can't force me to do it.*
▸ compel, make, order, require
2 *They forced the change on us.*
▸ impose, inflict
3 *We had to force the door.*
▸ break open, burst open, prise open, smash, wrench, (*informal*) yank

forceful *ADJECTIVE*
I'm a bit afraid of her forceful personality.
▸ dominant, energetic, overpowering, powerful, strong
AN OPPOSITE IS weak

ford *VERB*
There's no bridge, but you can ford the stream here.
▸ drive through, ride through, wade across

forecast *NOUN*
The forecast is for more rain.
▸ outlook, prediction

forecast *VERB*
Did they forecast rain for today?
▸ foresee, foretell, predict

foreground *NOUN*
I painted my dog in the foreground of my picture.
▸ front, nearest part
AN OPPOSITE IS background

foreign *ADJECTIVE*
1 *You see a lot of foreign people in London.*
▸ overseas, visiting
AN OPPOSITE IS native
2 *I would love to travel to foreign places.*
▸ distant, exotic, far-away, remote, strange, unfamiliar
AN OPPOSITE IS familiar
3 *Lying is foreign to her nature.*
▸ uncharacteristic (of), untypical (of)
AN OPPOSITE IS natural

foreigner *NOUN*
Many foreigners visit the centre every year.
▸ alien, immigrant, outsider, overseas visitor, stranger
▹ A formal word is **alien**. A word describing people who come from abroad to live in a country is **immigrant**.

foremost *ADJECTIVE*
He is one of the foremost actors of our time.
▸ best known, chief, distinguished, eminent, leading, major, most important, outstanding, principal, prominent
AN OPPOSITE IS unimportant

foresee *VERB*
I foresaw what would happen.
▸ anticipate, forecast, foretell, predict, prophesy

forest *NOUN*
VARIOUS KINDS OF AREA WHERE TREES GROW
coppice, copse, jungle, plantation, wood, woodland

foretell *VERB*
1 *He foretold that an accident would happen.*
▸ forecast, foresee, predict, prophesy
2 *The cold wind foretold a change in the weather.*
▸ herald, signify

forfeit *NOUN*
He had to pay a forfeit.
▸ fine, penalty

forfeit *VERB*
If you broke the rules, you'll have to forfeit your prize.
▸ give up, lose, surrender

A B C D E F G H I J K L M N O P Q R S T U V W X Y Z

forge *VERB*
1 *He forged the iron into a sword.*
▸ beat into shape, cast, hammer out, shape
2 *It is a serious offence to forge someone's signature.*
▸ copy, counterfeit, fake
to forge ahead *After a slow start, the company is now forging ahead.*
▸ advance quickly, make good progress, make headway, progress quickly

forgery *NOUN*
The painting was a forgery.
▸ copy, counterfeit, fake, fraud, imitation, replica, reproduction

forget *VERB*
1 *I forgot my toothbrush when I packed my suitcase.*
▸ leave out, miss out, omit
2 *I forgot my umbrella when I got off the bus.*
▸ leave behind, overlook
AN OPPOSITE IS remember

forgetful *ADJECTIVE*
You'd better remind him — he's so forgetful!
▸ absent-minded, careless, inattentive, negligent, unreliable, vague

forgive *VERB*
Please forgive me — I won't do it again!
▸ excuse, let off, pardon

fork *VERB*
The path forks here, and I don't know which way to go.
▸ branch, divide, split

forlorn *ADJECTIVE*
I felt quite forlorn after she had left.
▸ abandoned, alone, deserted, forsaken, friendless, lonely, sad, solitary, unhappy
AN OPPOSITE IS cheerful

form *NOUN*
1 *I made out the form of a man through the mist.*
▸ figure, outline, shape, silhouette
2 *Ice is a form of water.*
▸ kind, sort, type, variety
3 *My brother moves up into a higher form next term.*
▸ class, group, level, set, stream, tutor-group
4 *If you want to join the club, sign this form.*
▸ document, paper

form *VERB*
1 *The potter formed the clay into a tall vase.*
▸ cast, mould, shape
2 *We formed a chess club.*
▸ bring into existence, create, establish, found, make, organize, set up
3 *Two friends and I form the committee.*
▸ act as, compose, constitute, make up
4 *Icicles formed under the bridge.*
▸ appear, come into existence, develop, grow, take shape

formal *ADJECTIVE*
1 *I went to the formal opening of the sports centre.*
▸ ceremonial, official
2 *We shook hands in a formal way.*
▸ conventional, correct, dignified, proper, solemn

format *NOUN*
1 *They've changed the format of the newspaper.*
▸ appearance, design, presentation, style
▹ The format of a document includes its layout, shape, and size.
2 *I'd like to change the format of our weekly meetings.*
▸ arrangements, organization, plan

former *ADJECTIVE*
In former times, the house was an inn.
▸ earlier, previous

formula *NOUN*
What is your formula for success?
▸ blueprint, method, prescription, procedure, recipe, set of rules

formulate *VERB*
We formulated a plan so that everyone knew exactly what to do.
▸ define, express clearly, set out in detail, work out

forsake *VERB*
She knew he would never forsake her.
▸ abandon, desert, leave

fort, fortification *NOUNS*
VARIOUS FORTIFIED PLACES
castle, citadel, fortress, garrison, military camp, stronghold, tower

fortify *VERB*
1 *The soldiers tried to fortify the town.*
▸ defend, protect, reinforce, secure
2 *A good breakfast will fortify you for the day ahead.*
▸ bolster, boost, cheer, encourage, strengthen, sustain
AN OPPOSITE IS weaken

fortunate *ADJECTIVE*
We were fortunate to have good weather.
▸ in luck, lucky

fortune *NOUN*
1 *Mum had the good fortune to win a prize in a raffle.*
▸ accident, chance, luck
2 *The millionaire left his fortune to a charity.*
▸ assets, estate, (*informal*) millions, possessions, property, riches, wealth

forward *ADJECTIVE*
1 *It's a good idea to do some forward planning.*
▸ advance, early
2 *Wasn't he rather forward, telling the teacher what to do?*
▸ bold, cheeky, eager, familiar, impudent

forwards *ADVERB*
1 *The queue moved forwards very slowly.*
▸ along, on, onwards
2 *Will you all face forwards, please.*
▸ ahead, to or toward the front
AN OPPOSITE IS backwards

foster *VERB*
My aunt decided to foster a child.
▸ bring up, care for, look after, take care of
▹ To **adopt** a child is to make the child legally a full member of your family.

foul *ADJECTIVE*
1 *The refugees were living in foul conditions.*
▸ dirty, disgusting, filthy, loathsome, messy, mucky, offensive, repulsive, revolting, rotten, smelly, stinking, vile
AN OPPOSITE IS clean
2 *Foul drinking water was blamed for the epidemic.*
▸ contaminated, impure, infected, polluted, slimy, unclean
AN OPPOSITE IS pure
3 *He was sent off for using foul language.*
▸ abusive, blasphemous, coarse, crude, dirty, improper, indecent, insulting, obscene, offensive, rude, vulgar
AN OPPOSITE IS decent
4 *The referee blew her whistle for a foul tackle.*
▸ illegal, prohibited, unfair
AN OPPOSITE IS fair

found *VERB*
The school was founded a hundred years ago.
▸ begin, create, establish, initiate, institute, set up, start

foundation *NOUN*
1 *Dad and I laid the foundation for a garden shed.*
▸ base
2 *There's no foundation for the rumour they are spreading.*
▸ basis, grounds
3 *It's a hundred years since the foundation of the hospital.*
▸ beginning, establishment, setting up, starting

founder *VERB*
1 *The ship struck a rock and foundered.*
▸ go under, sink
2 *The project foundered because of a lack of money.*
▸ be unsuccessful, come to an end, fail, fall through, (*informal*) flop, meet with disaster

fountain *NOUN*
A fountain of water shot into the air.
▸ jet, spout, spray, spurt

fox *NOUN*
▹ A female fox is a **vixen**. A young fox is a **cub**.

fox *VERB*
The riddle completely foxed me.
▸ baffle, bewilder, deceive, mystify, perplex, puzzle

foyer *NOUN*
We'll meet you in the cinema foyer.
▸ entrance, entrance hall, lobby, reception

fraction *NOUN*
I can afford only a fraction of what they asked for.
▸ bit, part, portion

fractionally *ADVERB*
Their house is fractionally bigger than ours.
▸ a little, marginally, slightly

fracture *VERB*
He fell off his bike and fractured a bone in his arm.
▸ break, chip, crack

A B C D E **F** G H I J K L M N O P Q R S T U V W X Y Z

fracture *NOUN*
The X-ray showed a fracture in the bone.
▸ break, breakage, chip, crack

fragile *ADJECTIVE*
Old people's bones are more fragile than ours.
▸ breakable, brittle, delicate, easily damaged, frail, weak
AN OPPOSITE IS strong

fragment *NOUN*
1 *I dug up a fragment of broken pottery.*
▸ bit, chip, piece, sliver
2 *She overheard fragments of their conversation.*
▸ part, portion, scrap

fragrant *ADJECTIVE*
The room was fragrant with the smell of roses.
▸ perfumed, scented, sweet smelling

frail *ADJECTIVE*
1 *She still feels rather frail after her illness.*
▸ feeble, unsteady, weak
2 *The balcony looks a bit frail.*
▸ delicate, easily damaged, flimsy, fragile, rickety, unsound
AN OPPOSITE IS strong

frame *NOUN*
1 *The frame of the building is made of steel girders.*
▸ framework, shell, skeleton
2 *I put the photo of my friend in a frame.*
▸ border, case, edging, mount
frame of mind *Let's wait till he's in a better frame of mind.*
▸ humour, mood, temper

frank *ADJECTIVE*
Please give me a frank reply, even if it is bad news.
▸ blunt, direct, genuine, honest, outspoken, plain, sincere, straightforward, truthful
AN OPPOSITE IS insincere or tactful

frantic *ADJECTIVE*
1 *She was frantic with worry.*
▸ berserk, beside yourself, delirious, fraught, hysterical, uncontrollable, worked up
2 *There was frantic activity to get everything ready before the visitors arrived.*
▸ desperate, excited, frenzied, furious, hectic, wild
AN OPPOSITE IS calm

fraud *NOUN*
1 *He was guilty of fraud.*
▸ (*slang*) con-trick, deceit, deception, dishonesty, forgery, swindling, trickery
2 *The 'special offer' was a fraud.*
▸ hoax, pretence, sham, swindle, trick
3 *The salesman was a fraud.*
▸ cheat, hoaxer, impostor, swindler

fraudulent *ADJECTIVE*
He was accused of fraudulent business activities.
▸ bogus, cheating, corrupt, criminal, (*informal*) crooked, deceitful, devious, dishonest, illegal, lying, swindling, underhand
AN OPPOSITE IS honest

frayed *ADJECTIVE*
I can't wear this shirt — the collar is frayed.
▸ tattered, worn

freak *NOUN*
(*informal*) *My sister is a keep-fit freak.*
▸ addict, devotee, enthusiast, fanatic

freakish *ADJECTIVE*
We've had freakish weather conditions this summer.
▸ abnormal, exceptional, extraordinary, odd, peculiar, queer, unpredictable, unusual
AN OPPOSITE IS normal

free *ADJECTIVE*
1 *We are free to do what we want.*
▸ able, allowed, at liberty, permitted
AN OPPOSITE IS restricted
2 *After ten years in prison, he was free at last.*
▸ emancipated, freed, independent, liberated, released
AN OPPOSITE IS enslaved or imprisoned
3 *I got a free drink with my burger.*
▸ complimentary, free of charge
4 *Look out — the end of that rope has worked free.*
▸ loose, untied
AN OPPOSITE IS secure
5 *Is the bathroom free?*
▸ available, unoccupied, vacant
AN OPPOSITE IS engaged
6 *He is free with his money.*
▸ generous, lavish, liberal
AN OPPOSITE IS mean

free *VERB*

1 *The soldiers freed the prisoners of war.*
▸ liberate, release, rescue, save, set free
▹ To free slaves is to **emancipate** them. To free prisoners by paying money to the captors is to **ransom** them.
AN OPPOSITE IS imprison
2 *We freed the dogs and let them run about.*
▸ loose, turn loose, untie
AN OPPOSITE IS confine
3 *The judge freed the accused man.*
▸ acquit, clear, discharge, let go, let off, pardon
AN OPPOSITE IS condemn
4 *Can you free those tangled ropes?*
▸ undo, untangle
AN OPPOSITE IS tangle

freedom *NOUN*

We all like to have the freedom to do what we want.
▸ independence, liberty

freeze *VERB*

1 *Water begins to freeze at 0°C.*
▸ become ice, harden, solidify
2 *If you freeze food, you can store it for a long time.*
▸ refrigerate
▹ To make food cold to store it for a short time is to **chill** it.
3 *They decided to freeze prices until next year.*
▸ fix, hold, keep as they are

freight *NOUN*

They unloaded the freight from the wagons.
▸ cargo, goods, load

frequent *ADJECTIVE*

1 *I've given you frequent warnings about your behaviour.*
▸ constant, continual, countless, many, numerous, recurrent, recurring, repeated
AN OPPOSITE IS infrequent
2 *Cuckoos used to be frequent visitors to this part of the country.*
▸ common, familiar, habitual, ordinary, persistent, regular
AN OPPOSITE IS rare

frequent *VERB*

The restaurant is frequented by actors from the nearby theatre.
▸ visit

fresh *ADJECTIVE*

1 *The youth club needs some fresh ideas.*
▸ additional, different, extra, up-to-date
AN OPPOSITE IS old
2 *We need some fresh bread.*
▸ freshly baked, new
AN OPPOSITE IS stale
3 *I prefer fresh fruit to tinned.*
▸ natural, raw, unprocessed
AN OPPOSITE IS preserved or tinned
4 *After being indoors all day, I felt like some fresh air.*
▸ clean, cool, invigorating
AN OPPOSITE IS stuffy
5 *Can I get a fresh duvet cover out of the cupboard?*
▸ clean, laundered, washed
AN OPPOSITE IS dirty
6 *Having a shower makes me feel nice and fresh.*
▸ energetic, healthy, invigorated, lively, revived, vigorous
AN OPPOSITE IS weary
7 *When you are camping, you need a supply of fresh water.*
▸ drinkable, pure
AN OPPOSITE IS salty

freshen *VERB*

to freshen someone up *The swim had freshened her up.*
▸ invigorate, revive

fret *VERB*

The dog frets if we leave her tied up.
▸ be anxious, be upset, become stressed, worry

friction *NOUN*

1 *Bike brakes work by friction against the wheel.*
▸ resistance, rubbing, scraping
2 *There was some friction between the two sides.*
▸ antagonism, conflict, disagreement, hostility, opposition, quarrelling

friend *NOUN*

I was playing with my friends.
▸ companion, comrade, (*informal*) mate, (*informal*) pal
▹ A friend you play games with is a **playmate**. A friend you work with or live with is your **partner**. A friend you write to but don't normally meet is a **penfriend**. A friend you know only slightly is an **acquaintance**.
AN OPPOSITE IS enemy

friendless *ADJECTIVE*
I felt quite friendless when everyone went away on holiday.
► abandoned, alone, deserted, forlorn, forsaken, lonely, solitary, unloved

friendly *ADJECTIVE*
1 *You will like her — she's a friendly person.*
► affectionate, amiable, amicable, approachable, genial, good-natured, gracious, helpful, kind, kind-hearted, likeable, sympathetic
2 *Those two have a very friendly relationship.*
► close, familiar, intimate, loving
3 *They gave me a friendly welcome.*
► civil, courteous, hospitable, neighbourly, polite, warm, welcoming
AN OPPOSITE IS unfriendly

friendship *NOUN*
Their friendship has lasted for many years.
► affection, association, attachment, closeness, comradeship, familiarity, fellowship, fondness
▷ A formal friendship between countries or parties is an **alliance**.
AN OPPOSITE IS hostility

frieze *NOUN*
We painted a decorative frieze around the wall.
► border, edging

fright *NOUN*
1 *She jumped up in fright and began to scream.*
► alarm, dismay, dread, fear, horror, panic, terror
2 *The explosion gave us a dreadful fright!*
► scare, shock, surprise

frighten *VERB*
Sorry — I didn't mean to frighten you.
► alarm, horrify, make afraid, petrify, scare, shock, startle, terrify
AN OPPOSITE IS reassure

frightened *ADJECTIVE*
If we stick together, there's no need to be frightened.
► afraid, alarmed, apprehensive, dismayed, fearful, nervous, panicky, scared, terrified

frightening *ADJECTIVE*
The film was very frightening.
► creepy, eerie, ghostly, horrifying, nightmarish, (*informal*) scary, sinister, spine-chilling, (*informal*) spooky

frightful *ADJECTIVE*
1 *There was a frightful accident on the motorway.*
► alarming, appalling, awful, dreadful, fearful, ghastly, grisly, gruesome, hideous, horrible, horrid, horrific, horrifying, shocking
2 (*informal*) *It was a frightful shame you couldn't come to my party.*
► dreadful, great, terrible

fringe *NOUN*
1 *She fiddled with the fringe of the tablecloth.*
► border, edging, frill
2 *We live on the fringe of the town.*
► border, edge, margin, outskirts

frisk *VERB*
to frisk about *Lambs were frisking about in the field.*
► bound, caper, dance, frolic, hop about, jump about, leap about, play about, prance, romp, skip

fritter *VERB*
If you fritter your money on sweets, you'll have nothing to spend on holiday.
► spend unwisely, squander, use up, waste

frivolous *ADJECTIVE*
1 *We were in a frivolous mood before we went on holiday.*
► flippant, frisky, high-spirited, jaunty, joking, jolly, light-hearted, lively, playful, sprightly
2 *Don't waste my time asking frivolous questions.*
► facetious, foolish, petty, pointless, ridiculous, silly, stupid, superficial, trivial, unimportant, worthless
AN OPPOSITE IS serious

frock *NOUN*
FOR THINGS YOU WEAR SEE **clothes**

frolic *VERB*
Lambs were frolicking in the field.
► bound, caper, dance, frisk about, have fun, hop about, jump about, leap about, play about, prance, romp, skip

front *NOUN*
1 *We stood at the front of the queue.*
► head
▷ The front of a ship is the **bow** or **prow**. The front of a picture is the **foreground**.
AN OPPOSITE IS back
2 *Troops were sent to the front.*
► battle area, danger zone, front line

front *ADJECTIVE*
The front runners came into sight round the corner.
▸ first, leading, most advanced
AN OPPOSITE IS back

frontier *NOUN*
We crossed the frontier between France and Belgium.
▸ border, boundary

frosty *ADJECTIVE*
It was a clear, frosty night.
▸ cold, crisp, freezing, icy, wintry

froth *NOUN*
I love the froth you get on hot chocolate.
▸ bubbles, foam
▹ The froth on top of soapy water is lather or suds. Dirty froth is scum.

frown *NOUN*
FOR EXPRESSIONS ON PEOPLE'S FACES SEE **expression**

frugal *ADJECTIVE*
1 *We try to be frugal with our pocket money.*
▸ careful, economical, prudent, sparing, thrifty
AN OPPOSITE IS wasteful
2 *I had very little money left, so I had a frugal meal.*
▸ cheap, inexpensive
AN OPPOSITE IS lavish

fruit *NOUN*
VARIOUS FRUITS WHICH PEOPLE USE AS FOOD
apple, apricot, avocado, banana, bilberry, blackberry, blackcurrant, cherry, coconut, crab apple, cranberry, damson, date, fig, gooseberry, grape, greengage, guava, kiwi fruit, loganberry, lychee, mango, melon, nuts, olive, pawpaw or papaya, peach, pear, pineapple, plum, pomegranate, quince, raspberry, redcurrant, rosehip, sloe, strawberry, tomato
CITRUS FRUITS
grapefruit, lemon, lime, nectarine, orange, satsuma, tangerine
DRIED FRUITS
currant, prune, raisin, sultana
▹ Rhubarb is not a fruit, but we eat it as if it was a fruit.

fruitful *ADJECTIVE*
1 *Did you have a fruitful shopping trip?*
▸ profitable, rewarding, successful, useful, worthwhile
AN OPPOSITE IS fruitless
2 *We drove through miles of fruitful farmland.*
▸ fertile, flourishing, productive
AN OPPOSITE IS unproductive

fruitless *ADJECTIVE*
I looked everywhere for my purse, but it was a fruitless search.
▸ futile, pointless, unproductive, unprofitable, unsuccessful, useless, vain
AN OPPOSITE IS successful

frustrate *VERB*
The police frustrated an attempted robbery.
▸ baffle, block, check, defeat, foil, halt, hinder, prevent, stop

fry *VERB*
FOR WAYS TO COOK THINGS SEE **cook** *VERB*

fuel *NOUN*
▹ Fuels found in the earth which are formed from decomposed living matter are fossil fuels.
KINDS OF FOSSIL FUEL
coal, crude oil or petroleum, natural gas
FUELS REFINED FROM CRUDE OIL
diesel, gasoline, paraffin, petrol
KINDS OF COAL INCLUDE
anthracite, coke, smokeless coal
OTHER KINDS OF SOLID FUEL
charcoal, logs, peat
OTHER FUELS INCLUDE
butane, (*trademark*) Calor gas, electricity, methylated spirit, nuclear fuel, propane

fugitive *NOUN*
Police searched for the fugitives.
▸ deserter, outlaw, runaway
▹ Someone who is a fugitive from war or persecution is a refugee.

fulfil *VERB*
1 *She fulfilled her ambition to play at Wimbledon.*
▸ accomplish, achieve, attain, bring about, carry out, complete, succeed in
2 *To be a member of the team, you must fulfil certain conditions.*
▸ meet, satisfy

A B C D E F G H I J K L M N O P Q R S T U V W X Y Z

full *ADJECTIVE*
1 *The basin was full, so I turned the tap off.*
▸ brimming, filled, overflowing, topped-up
AN OPPOSITE IS empty
2 *The shopping centre was full on Saturday.*
▸ busy, congested, crammed, crowded, jammed, packed
AN OPPOSITE IS uncrowded
3 *The head wanted a full explanation of what had happened.*
▸ complete, comprehensive, detailed, entire, whole
AN OPPOSITE IS incomplete
4 *We drove at full speed.*
▸ greatest, highest, maximum, top
AN OPPOSITE IS minimum
5 *She was wearing a full skirt.*
▸ broad, loose, wide
AN OPPOSITE IS tight

fumes *PLURAL NOUN*
People could hardly breathe because of the fumes.
▸ exhaust, gases, pollution, smoke

fun *NOUN*
Let's have some fun!
▸ amusement, diversion, enjoyment, entertainment, games, jokes, laughter, merriment, play, pleasure, recreation, sport
to make fun of someone *It was cruel to make fun of her when she fell over.*
▸ jeer at, laugh at, mock, ridicule, taunt, tease
▹ To make fun of someone in a story, poem, or play, etc., is to satirize them.

function *NOUN*
1 *The function of a doctor is to cure sick people.*
▸ duty, job, responsibility, task, work
2 *They held an official function to open the new sports centre.*
▸ ceremony, event, reception

function *VERB*
The computer doesn't function properly.
▸ go, operate, work

functional *ADJECTIVE*
1 *The drinks machine is functional again.*
▸ going, operating, usable, working
2 *The kitchen was small but functional.*
▸ practical, useful

fundamental *ADJECTIVE*
He taught me the fundamental rules of chess.
▸ basic, elementary, essential, important, main, necessary, principal, underlying
AN OPPOSITE IS advanced

funds *PLURAL NOUN*
He invested all his funds.
▸ capital, money, riches, savings, wealth

funeral *NOUN*
▹ A funeral at which a dead person is buried is an interment. An interment takes place in a cemetery or graveyard. A funeral at which a dead person's body is burned is a cremation. A cremation takes place in a crematorium. A vehicle which carries a dead person to a funeral is a hearse. A formal funeral procession is a cortège. People who attend a funeral are mourners. A person who organizes funerals is an undertaker.

funfair *NOUN*
SEE **fair** *NOUN*

funny *ADJECTIVE*
1 *He told us a funny joke.*
▸ amusing, comic, diverting, entertaining, hilarious, humorous, (*informal*) priceless, witty
AN OPPOSITE IS serious
2 *There's a funny smell in here.*
▸ abnormal, curious, mysterious, odd, peculiar, puzzling, queer, strange, unusual, weird

fur *NOUN*
VARIOUS COVERINGS ON ANIMALS' SKINS
bristles, coat, down, fleece, hair, hide, pelt, wool

furious *ADJECTIVE*
1 *He was furious because he didn't win.*
▸ angry, enraged, fuming, incensed, infuriated, livid, mad, raging, seething
2 *We worked at a furious rate to try to get things finished.*
▸ desperate, excited, frantic, frenzied, hectic, intense, tempestuous, tumultuous, turbulent, violent, wild
AN OPPOSITE IS calm

furniture *NOUN*

VARIOUS ITEMS OF FURNITURE FOR SITTING OR SLEEPING ON

armchair, bed, bunk, chair, cot, couch, cradle, dining chair, divan, pew, pouffe, rocking chair, seat, settee, sofa, stool

VARIOUS ITEMS OF FURNITURE TO KEEP THINGS IN OR PUT THINGS ON

bench, bookcase, bureau, cabinet, chest of drawers, coffee table, cupboard, desk, dresser, dressing table, filing cabinet, sideboard, table, trestle table, wardrobe, workbench

▷ A set of pieces of furniture that go together is a suite. The soft covering on armchairs, sofas, etc., is upholstery. Old and valuable pieces of furniture are antiques.

furrow *NOUN*

▷ A furrow to sow seeds in is a drill. A furrow made by the wheels of vehicles is a rut. A furrow in someone's skin is a wrinkle.

furry *ADJECTIVE*

A small, furry creature was curled up inside the box.

▸ downy, feathery, fleecy, fuzzy, hairy, woolly

further *ADJECTIVE*

We need further information.

▸ additional, extra, fresh, more, new, supplementary

further *VERB*

We want to further the cause of peace.

▸ advance, aid, assist, back, encourage, help along, promote, support, urge on

furthermore *ADVERB*

We started late and, furthermore, we ran out of petrol on the motorway.

▸ additionally, also, besides, moreover, too

furtive *ADJECTIVE*

She cast a furtive glance over her shoulder and then unlocked the door.

▸ cautious, concealed, crafty, disguised, secretive, sly, (*informal*) sneaky, stealthy, underhand

fury *NOUN*

1 *He didn't disguise his fury at what had happened.*

▸ anger, indignation, rage, wrath

2 *There was no shelter from the fury of the storm.*

▸ ferocity, fierceness, force, intensity, power, savagery, tempestuousness, turbulence, violence

fuse *VERB*

The metals had fused together into a solid mass.

▸ blend, combine, join, melt, merge, unite

▷ To fuse metals together when you are making or mending something is to solder or weld them.

fuss *NOUN*

There was a lot of fuss when someone was accused of cheating.

▸ bother, commotion, excitement, hullabaloo, trouble

fuss *VERB*

Please don't fuss!

▸ get excited, make a commotion, worry

fussy *ADJECTIVE*

1 *Our cat is fussy about her food.*

▸ (*informal*) choosy, finicky, hard to please, particular

2 *I don't like clothes with fussy designs.*

▸ complicated, detailed, elaborate

futile *ADJECTIVE*

I made a futile attempt to stop him going.

▸ fruitless, pointless, unproductive, unprofitable, unsuccessful, useless, vain, wasted

AN OPPOSITE IS successful

future *NOUN*

Now that we have sponsorship, the team's future looks bright.

▸ outlook, prospects

AN OPPOSITE IS past

fuzzy *ADJECTIVE*

1 *The TV picture has gone fuzzy.*

▸ blurred, cloudy, hazy, indistinct, out of focus, unclear, unfocused

AN OPPOSITE IS clear

2 *She was wearing a fuzzy sweater.*

▸ fleecy, fluffy, woolly

Gg

gadget *NOUN*
It's a handy little gadget.
▸ contraption, device, implement, instrument, tool

gain *VERB*
1 *They had nothing to gain by lying.*
▸ acquire, earn, get, obtain, win
AN OPPOSITE IS lose
2 *They finally gained the shore.*
▸ achieve, get to, reach

gains *PLURAL NOUN*
The stock market saw large gains yesterday.
▸ increases, profits

gala *NOUN*
The village annual gala is in July.
▸ carnival, fair, festival, fête

gallant *ADJECTIVE*
1 *In the old days, a gallant knight defended the weak and the poor.*
▸ brave, courageous, fearless, heroic, valiant
AN OPPOSITE IS cowardly
2 *The gallant young man did everything he could to make the ladies comfortable.*
▸ gentlemanly, polite
AN OPPOSITE IS rude

gamble *VERB*
He gambled £10 on the horse.
▸ bet, risk, wager
DIFFERENT WAYS OF GAMBLING
betting, bingo, cards, dice, lottery, the pools, raffle

game *NOUN*
1 *Their favourite game was hide-and-seek.*
▸ amusement, fun, pastime, sport
2 *I've been selected to play in the game on Saturday.*
▸ competition, contest, match, tournament
GAMES YOU USUALLY PLAY INDOORS
bagatelle, billiards, bingo, cards, charades, chess, darts, dice, dominoes, draughts, lotto, ludo, marbles, ping-pong, pool, skittles, snooker, solitaire, table tennis, tiddlywinks, tombola
CHILDREN'S GAMES OFTEN PLAYED OUT OF DOORS
conkers, hide-and-seek, hopscotch, leapfrog, roller skating, skateboarding, skating, sledging, tag
OTHER OUTDOOR GAMES SEE **sport**

gang *NOUN*
A gang of workmen dug a hole in the road.
▸ crowd, group, team

gangster *NOUN*
The film was about a group of ruthless gangsters.
▸ criminal, (*informal*) crook, gunman

gaol *VERB*
The thief was gaoled for six months.
▸ detain, imprison, lock up, (*informal*) shut away

gap *NOUN*
1 *The animals escaped through a gap in the fence.*
▸ breach, break, hole, opening
2 *She returned to work after a gap of two years.*
▸ interval, pause, rest

gaping *ADJECTIVE*
He nearly fell into a gaping hole.
▸ broad, wide, wide open, yawning

garbage *NOUN*
Put the garbage in the bin.
▸ junk, litter, refuse, rubbish, trash, waste

garden *NOUN*
VARIOUS FEATURES OF A GARDEN
border, compost heap, flower bed, greenhouse, hedge, lawn, orchard, path, patio, pond, rockery or rock garden, shed, shrubbery, terrace, trellis
SEE ALSO **flower**, **fruit**, **tree**, **vegetable**
TOOLS GARDENERS USE
cultivator, fork, hoe, lawnmower, rake, riddle, secateurs, shears, shovel, sieve, spade, trowel, watering can
SUBSTANCES USED IN THE GARDEN
compost, fertilizer, insecticide, manure, peat, pesticide, weedkiller

garment *NOUN*
SEE **clothes**

gas *NOUN*
A cloud of poisonous gas escaped from the factory.
▸ fumes, vapour
SOME KINDS OF GAS
carbon dioxide, carbon monoxide, coal gas, helium, hydrogen, methane, nitrogen, oxygen, ozone, sulphur dioxide, tear gas

gash *NOUN*
The broken glass made a nasty gash in my foot.
▸ cut, slash, slit, wound

gasp *VERB*
At the end of the race we lay down gasping for breath.
▸ gulp, pant

gate *NOUN*
We waited at the gate to be let in.
▸ barrier, entrance, gateway

gather *VERB*
1 *A crowd gathered to watch the performers.*
▸ assemble, collect, come together, swarm round
AN OPPOSITE IS disperse
2 *The captain gathered her team to give them a talk.*
▸ bring together, get together, muster, round up
3 *They were gathering mushrooms in the forest.*
▸ collect, harvest, pick
4 *I gather that you've just been on holiday.*
▸ hear, learn, understand

gathering *NOUN*
There was a big family gathering for her birthday.
▸ assembly, crowd, meeting, party

gaudy *ADJECTIVE*
He wore a rather gaudy shirt.
▸ flashy, showy, too bright, too colourful

gauge *VERB*
I tried to gauge how much further she had to go.
▸ assess, estimate, judge, measure

gaze *VERB*
The dog gazed hungrily at the food.
▸ look, stare

gear *NOUN*
We put the fishing gear in the back of the car.
▸ equipment, paraphernalia, tackle, things

gem *NOUN*
The gems glittered under the bright lights.
▸ jewel, precious stone
SEE ALSO **jewellery**

gender *NOUN*
▹ The gender of a man is male or masculine. The gender of a woman is female or feminine. The gender of a thing is neuter.

general *ADJECTIVE*
1 *There's a general feeling that our team will win.*
▸ common, popular, prevailing, prevalent, widespread
2 *I've only got a general idea of where we are.*
▸ approximate, broad, indefinite, vague

generally *ADVERB*
We generally buy our food at the shop down the road.
▸ as a rule, chiefly, commonly, mainly, mostly, normally, on the whole, principally, usually

generate *VERB*
The shop generated a lot of business when it started giving away free gifts.
▸ bring about, create, give rise to, produce

generous *ADJECTIVE*
1 *It was generous of you to give him your last sweet.*
▸ charitable, unselfish
AN OPPOSITE IS selfish
2 *We all had generous second helpings.*
▸ ample, large, liberal
AN OPPOSITE IS meagre

genial *ADJECTIVE*
His genial smile made us feel welcome.
▸ cheerful, friendly, good-natured, kind, pleasant, warm-hearted
AN OPPOSITE IS unfriendly

genius *NOUN*
She's a genius at maths.
▸ expert, mastermind, wizard

gentle *ADJECTIVE*
1 *The vet is very gentle with the sick animals.*
▸ good-tempered, humane, kind, tender
2 *She had a gentle voice.*
▸ low, mild, peaceful, pleasant, quiet, reassuring, soft
3 *The yacht hardly moved in the gentle wind.*
▸ faint, imperceptible, light, slight
AN OPPOSITE IS rough or severe

genuine *ADJECTIVE*
1 *Is that a genuine diamond?*
▸ actual, authentic, real
AN OPPOSITE IS fake
2 *He seemed like a very genuine person.*
▸ honest, sincere, true
AN OPPOSITE IS false

A B C D E F **G** H I J K L M N O P Q R S T U V W X Y Z

germs *PLURAL NOUN*
Many germs cause diseases.
▸ bacteria, (*informal*) bugs, microbes, viruses

germinate *VERB*
The seeds will germinate when the weather gets warmer.
▸ sprout, start growing

gesture *NOUN*
She made an angry gesture.
▸ action, movement, sign

get *VERB* This word is often overused.
1 *It's getting cold.*
▸ become, grow, turn
2 *I got a new bike yesterday.*
▸ acquire, buy, obtain, purchase, receive
3 *What time did you get home?*
▸ arrive, reach
4 *The dog got the ball.*
▸ bring, fetch, find, pick up, retrieve
5 *Shall I get the tea?*
▸ make ready, prepare
6 *Get him to do the washing up.*
▸ order, persuade
7 *I don't get what you mean.*
▸ comprehend, follow, grasp, understand
to get on with something *She told us to get on with our work.*
▸ continue, concentrate on, keep on with, persevere with
to get out of something *He always gets out of the hard jobs.*
▸ avoid, shirk
to get over something *Have you got over your cold?*
▸ get better from, recover from

ghastly *ADJECTIVE*
We saw a ghastly accident on the motorway.
▸ appalling, awful, dreadful, frightful, grim, grisly, horrible, horrifying, shocking, terrible

ghost *NOUN*
Do you believe in ghosts?
▸ spectre, spirit

giant *ADJECTIVE*
The giant tree towered above us.
▸ colossal, enormous, gigantic, huge, immense, mammoth, massive, monstrous
SEE ALSO **big**
AN OPPOSITE IS tiny

giddy *ADJECTIVE*
I felt giddy when I stood at the edge of the cliff.
▸ dizzy, faint, unsteady

gift *NOUN*
1 *I received some nice gifts on my birthday.*
▸ present
2 *She has a gift for music.*
▸ genius, talent

gifted *ADJECTIVE*
There are some gifted players in the team.
▸ able, accomplished, clever, skilful, talented

gigantic *ADJECTIVE*
There was a gigantic statue in the square.
▸ colossal, enormous, giant, huge, immense, mammoth, massive, monstrous
AN OPPOSITE IS tiny

girder *NOUN*
The roof was supported by a framework of iron girders.
▸ bar, beam

girl *NOUN*
▹ A synonym used in some parts of Britain is lass. Old-fashioned words are damsel, maid, and maiden.

give *VERB*
1 *He gave each person a present.*
▸ deal out, distribute, hand over, issue, pass, supply
2 *The sponsors gave a prize to the winner.*
▸ award, offer, present
3 *Will you give something to our collection for charity?*
▸ contribute, donate
4 *He gave a laugh.*
▸ let out, utter
5 *We gave a concert at the end of term.*
▸ arrange, organize, perform, present, put on
6 *Will this branch give if I sit on it?*
▸ bend, break, buckle, collapse, give way
to give in *They gave in after a long fight.*
▸ submit, surrender, yield
to give up *We gave up trying to beat the record.*
▸ abandon, end, finish, (*informal*) scrap

glad *ADJECTIVE*
I was glad to hear that she was feeling better.
▸ delighted, happy, pleased
AN OPPOSITE IS sad

glamorous *ADJECTIVE*
She looks very glamorous in that dress.
▸ attractive, beautiful, gorgeous, (*informal*) sexy
AN OPPOSITE IS unattractive

glamour *NOUN*
She was excited by the glamour of a career in television.
▸ appeal, attraction, excitement, fascination

glance *VERB*
1 *I glanced at my watch.*
▸ look quickly, peep
2 *The ball glanced off the edge of the bat.*
▸ bounce, ricochet

glare *VERB*
He glared angrily at me.
▸ frown, glower, scowl

glare *NOUN*
1 *The glare of the lights dazzled me.*
▸ brightness, brilliance
SEE ALSO **light** *NOUN*
2 *She gave me an angry glare.*
▸ frown, nasty look, scowl

glaring *ADJECTIVE*
1 *The car's glaring headlights nearly caused an accident.*
▸ blinding, bright, brilliant, dazzling
2 *The book was full of glaring mistakes.*
▸ conspicuous, gross, noticeable, obvious

glass, glasses *NOUNS*
WORDS FOR GLASS USED IN WINDOWS
double glazing, glazing, pane, plate glass
KINDS OF GLASS FOR DRINKS OR LIQUIDS
beaker, goblet, tumbler, wineglass
GLASSES YOU WEAR TO HELP YOU SEE OR TO PROTECT YOUR EYES
bifocals, contact lenses, goggles, reading glasses, spectacles, sunglasses
INSTRUMENTS WITH LENSES TO MAKE THINGS LOOK BIGGER
binoculars, field glasses, magnifying glass, microscope, opera glasses, telescope

glassy *ADJECTIVE*
1 *The road was glassy after the frost.*
▸ icy, shiny, slippery, smooth
2 *He stared at us with glassy eyes.*
▸ blank, dull, empty, expressionless, glazed, staring, vacant

gleam *NOUN*
I saw a gleam of moonlight between the clouds.
▸ glimmer, glint, ray, shaft

gleam *VERB*
The lights gleamed on the water.
▸ glimmer, glint, glisten, shimmer, shine

gleeful *ADJECTIVE*
She gave a gleeful laugh.
▸ delighted, exultant, happy, joyful, pleased
AN OPPOSITE IS gloomy

glide *VERB*
The boat glided gently across the lake.
▸ move smoothly, slide, slip

glimpse *VERB*
He glimpsed a deer running through the forest.
▸ catch sight of, make out, see, spot

glint *VERB*
The sunlight glinted on the polished brass.
▸ flash, glitter, sparkle

glisten *VERB*
The reflection of the lights glistened on the wet road.
▸ gleam, shine

glitter *VERB*
The jewels glittered under the bright lights.
▸ flash, shine, sparkle, twinkle

gloat *VERB*
There's no need to gloat, even if you did win by five goals!
▸ boast, crow, exult, show off

global *ADJECTIVE*
The global effects of pollution are alarming.
▸ international, universal, worldwide

globe *NOUN*
1 *I'd like to travel all round the globe.*
▸ earth, planet, world
2 *The light was enclosed in a glass globe.*
▸ ball, sphere

gloom *NOUN*
1 *We could hardly see in the gloom.*
▸ darkness, dimness, shade, shadow
▹ The gloomy light late in the evening is **dusk** or **twilight**.
2 *We were filled with gloom when we heard the news.*
▸ dejection, depression, misery, sadness, unhappiness

A B C D E F G H I J K L M N O P Q R S T U V W X Y Z

gloomy *ADJECTIVE*
1 *It was a gloomy day.*
▸ cloudy, dark, dim, murky, overcast, shadowy
2 *What are you looking so gloomy about?*
▸ dejected, depressed, glum, melancholy, miserable, sad, unhappy
3 *This gloomy room needs some bright curtains to cheer it up.*
▸ depressing, dingy, dismal, dreary, sombre
AN OPPOSITE IS bright or cheerful

glorify *VERB*
They didn't like the film because it glorified war.
▸ celebrate, honour, praise

glorious *ADJECTIVE*
1 *It was a glorious victory.*
▸ celebrated, famous, heroic, illustrious, noble, renowned, triumphant
AN OPPOSITE IS shameful
2 *Look at that glorious sunset!*
▸ beautiful, gorgeous, lovely, magnificent, spectacular, splendid, superb, wonderful
AN OPPOSITE IS ugly

glossy *ADJECTIVE*
The book was printed on glossy paper.
▸ gleaming, lustrous, shining, shiny
AN OPPOSITE IS dull

glow *NOUN*
1 *The fire gave out a warm glow.*
▸ brightness, heat, redness, warmth
2 *She felt a glow of pleasure when she passed the exam.*
▸ feeling, sensation

glow *VERB*
The embers of the bonfire glowed in the dark.
▸ gleam, shine
FOR VARIOUS EFFECTS OF LIGHT SEE **light** *NOUN*

glower *VERB*
He glowered at them when they interrupted him.
▸ frown, glare, scowl, stare angrily

glue *NOUN*
VARIOUS THINGS YOU USE FOR GLUING
adhesive, cement, gum, paste, sealant, (*trademark*) Sellotape, sticky tape, wallpaper paste

glum *ADJECTIVE*
What are you looking so glum about?
▸ dejected, depressed, gloomy, melancholy, miserable, sad, unhappy
AN OPPOSITE IS cheerful

gluttonous *ADJECTIVE*
She has a gluttonous appetite for ice cream!
▸ greedy, insatiable

gnarled *ADJECTIVE*
The branches of the tree were gnarled with age.
▸ bent, crooked, distorted, knobbly, knotty, lumpy, twisted

gnaw *VERB*
The dog gnawed at his bone.
▸ bite, chew

go *VERB* This word is often overused. Here are some alternatives:
1 *I'd like to go round the world one day.*
▸ journey, travel
SEE ALSO **travel**
2 *We'll go in a minute.*
▸ be off, depart, get away, leave, proceed, set out, start
3 *This road goes to Bristol.*
▸ extend, lead, reach, stretch
4 *The milk went sour.*
▸ become, turn
5 *My watch isn't going.*
▸ function, operate, work
6 *Plates go on that shelf.*
▸ belong, have a place
7 *The show went well.*
▸ happen, pass, proceed, take place
to go off *The bomb went off.*
▸ detonate, explode
to go on 1 *What went on while I was away?*
▸ happen, occur, take place
2 *Please go on with what you're saying.*
▸ carry on, continue, keep going, persevere, proceed

go *NOUN*
Whose go is it next?
▸ chance, opportunity, try, turn

goal *NOUN*
What is your goal in life?
▸ aim, ambition, intention, object, objective, purpose, target

gobble *VERB*
They gobbled up all the food.
▸ bolt, eat quickly, gulp, guzzle

good *ADJECTIVE* This word is often overused. We use the adjective *good* to describe anything we like or approve of. Here are just some of the many words you could use
1 *We had a good time at the party.*
▸ agreeable, (*informal*) brilliant, delightful, enjoyable, excellent, (*informal*) fabulous, (*informal*) fantastic, fine, (*informal*) incredible, lovely, marvellous, nice, outstanding, perfect, pleasant, pleasing, remarkable, satisfactory, (*informal*) sensational, splendid, superb, (*informal*) terrific, wonderful
2 *She's a good friend.*
▸ caring, charitable, considerate, decent, friendly, helpful, humane, loving, loyal, merciful, noble
3 *They promised they would be good in future.*
▸ honest, just, law-abiding, moral, obedient, truthful, virtuous
4 *He's a good tennis player.*
▸ able, accomplished, capable, clever, competent, efficient, gifted, proficient, skilful, skilled, talented
5 *She did a good job.*
▸ commendable, competent, correct, creditable, conscientious, neat, praiseworthy, thorough, well done
6 *After our long walk we were looking forward to a good meal.*
▸ delicious, eatable, healthy, nourishing, nutritious, tasty, well-cooked, wholesome
AN OPPOSITE IS bad

good-looking *ADJECTIVE*
He's a very good-looking man.
▸ attractive, handsome
AN OPPOSITE IS ugly

good-natured *ADJECTIVE*
He told us what we did wrong in a good-natured way, so no one got upset.
▸ considerate, friendly, helpful, kind, pleasant, sympathetic
AN OPPOSITE IS unkind

goods *PLURAL NOUN*
Lorries take the goods from the ship to the warehouse.
▸ cargo, freight, merchandise, produce, wares

goodwill *NOUN*
The meeting was a success because of the goodwill shown by both sides.
▸ friendliness, good intentions

gorgeous *ADJECTIVE*
She always wore gorgeous clothes.
▸ beautiful, colourful, lovely, magnificent, splendid, superb
AN OPPOSITE IS ugly

gossip *VERB*
Those two are always gossiping!
▸ chatter, spread rumours, tell tales

gossip *NOUN*
1 *Don't believe all the gossip you hear.*
▸ chat, chatter, rumour, scandal
2 *He's an awful gossip.*
▸ busybody, chatterbox, Nosy Parker, telltale

gouge *VERB*
He gouged a hole in the wall.
▸ cut, dig, hollow out, scoop out

govern *VERB*
They governed the country fairly.
▸ administer, be in charge of, control, direct, look after, manage, regulate, rule, run, supervise

government *NOUN*
DIFFERENT TYPES OF GOVERNMENT
democracy, dictatorship, monarchy, republic
GROUPS OF PEOPLE INVOLVED IN GOVERNMENT
the Cabinet, the civil service, government departments or ministries, local authorities, parliament
INDIVIDUAL PEOPLE INVOLVED IN GOVERNMENT
Chancellor of the Exchequer, civil servants, Members of Parliament, ministers, politicians, the premier, the President, the Prime Minister, Secretaries of State, senators
PEOPLE INVOLVED IN LOCAL GOVERNMENT
councillors, the mayor
PEOPLE WHO WORK FOR THEIR GOVERNMENT IN FOREIGN COUNTRIES
ambassadors, consuls, diplomats

grab *VERB*
I grabbed the reins of the runaway horse.
▸ catch, clutch, get hold of, grasp, seize, snatch

A B C D E F G H I J K L M N O P Q R S T U V W X Y Z

graceful *ADJECTIVE*
I admired the dancer's graceful movements.
▸ flowing, nimble, pliant, supple
AN OPPOSITE IS clumsy

gracious *ADJECTIVE*
She gave a gracious smile.
▸ agreeable, courteous, good-natured, kind, pleasant, polite
AN OPPOSITE IS rude or unkind

grade *NOUN*
The butcher sells only top grade meat.
▸ class, quality, standard

grade *VERB*
Eggs are graded according to size.
▸ classify, group, sort

gradient *NOUN*
They struggled up the steep gradient.
▸ ascent, bank, hill, incline, rise, slope

gradual *ADJECTIVE*
There has been a gradual increase in prices.
▸ even, gentle, moderate, regular, slow, steady
AN OPPOSITE IS sudden

grain *NOUN*
1 *They grow a lot of grain in this part of the country.*
▸ cereals, corn
2 *He had some grains of sand in his shoes.*
▸ bit, particle, speck

grand *ADJECTIVE*
The wedding was a grand occasion.
▸ big, great, important, imposing, impressive, magnificent, (*informal*) posh, splendid, stately
AN OPPOSITE IS insignificant

grant *VERB*
They granted his request for leave.
▸ allow, give, let you have, permit

grant *NOUN*
She got a grant to help her pay for a music course.
▸ allowance, award, scholarship, sponsorship, subsidy

graphic *ADJECTIVE*
The newspaper printed a graphic account of the battle.
▸ clear, descriptive, detailed, lifelike, lively, vivid

graphics *PLURAL NOUN*
The graphics were produced by computer.
▸ diagrams, drawings, pictures

grapple *VERB*
They grappled with the intruder, but he got away.
▸ struggle, wrestle

grasp *VERB*
1 *He grasped the end of the rope.*
▸ catch, clutch, grab, grip, hang on to, hold, seize, take hold of
2 *The ideas were quite difficult to grasp.*
▸ appreciate, comprehend, follow, understand

grasp *NOUN*
She has a good grasp of mathematics.
▸ comprehension, understanding

grasping *ADJECTIVE*
He's a grasping old miser.
▸ greedy, miserly, money-grabbing, selfish, tight
AN OPPOSITE IS generous

grass *NOUN*
VARIOUS GRASS-COVERED AREAS
field, green, lawn, meadow, pasture, playing field, prairie, recreation ground, savannah, steppe, village green

grate *VERB*
1 *I grated the cheese.*
▸ shred
2 *The chalk grated on the board.*
▸ rub, scrape, scratch
to grate on *The parrot's screeching grates on me.*
▸ annoy, irritate, upset, vex

grateful *ADJECTIVE*
I'm grateful for your help.
▸ appreciative, thankful
AN OPPOSITE IS ungrateful

grating *NOUN*
There was an iron grating over the top of the well.
▸ framework, grid, grill

gratitude *NOUN*
How can we show our gratitude for her help?
▸ appreciation, thanks

grave *NOUN*
THINGS PUT UP TO MARK A GRAVE
gravestone, headstone, memorial, monument, plaque, tombstone
PLACES WHERE DEAD PEOPLE ARE BURIED
catacomb, cemetery, crypt, graveyard, mausoleum, tomb, vault

grave *ADJECTIVE*
1 *They looked grave when they heard the news.*
▸ grim, sad, serious, thoughtful
AN OPPOSITE IS cheerful
2 *She made a grave mistake.*
▸ crucial, important, serious, vital
AN OPPOSITE IS trivial

graveyard *NOUN*
He was buried in the local graveyard.
▸ burial ground, cemetery, churchyard

graze *VERB*
I grazed my knee when I fell off my bike.
▸ scrape, scratch

greasy *ADJECTIVE*
I don't like greasy foods.
▸ fatty, oily

great *ADJECTIVE* This word is often overused. Here are some alternatives:
1 *Our voices echoed round the great cavern.*
▸ big, enormous, extensive, huge, immense, large, tremendous, vast
AN OPPOSITE IS small
2 *Crime is a great problem in this area.*
▸ considerable, crucial, major, serious, severe
AN OPPOSITE IS trivial
3 *The opening of the Olympic Games is a great event.*
▸ grand, important, large scale, magnificent, spectacular
AN OPPOSITE IS unimportant
4 *Shakespeare was a great writer.*
▸ brilliant, celebrated, classic, exceptional, famous, notable, outstanding, well-known
AN OPPOSITE IS ordinary

greed *NOUN*
Because of his greed, there was nothing left for me!
▸ gluttony, overeating, selfishness

greedy *ADJECTIVE*
1 *She was so greedy that she ate all the cakes.*
▸ gluttonous, (*informal*) piggish
2 *The greedy shopkeeper cheated his customers.*
▸ grasping, miserly, money-grabbing, selfish, tight-fisted
AN OPPOSITE IS generous or unselfish

green *ADJECTIVE, NOUN*
VARIOUS SHADES OF GREEN
emerald, grass-green, jade, khaki, lime, olive, pea-green, turquoise

greens *PLURAL NOUN*
SEE **vegetable**

greet *VERB*
She greeted me with a friendly wave.
▸ hail, receive, salute, welcome

greeting *NOUN*
GREETINGS USED WHEN WE MEET SOMEONE
good day (good morning, etc.), hallo or hello or hullo, how do you do, welcome
GREETINGS USED ON CARDS FOR SPECIAL OCCASIONS
congratulations, happy anniversary, happy birthday, many happy returns, merry Christmas, well done

grey *ADJECTIVE, NOUN*
VARIOUS SHADES OF GREY
ashen, blackish, leaden, off-white, silvery, slate grey, smoky, sooty, whitish

grid *NOUN*
There was an iron grid covering the hole.
▸ framework, grating, grill

grief *NOUN*
He could not hide his grief when his grandfather died.
▸ anguish, misery, regret, sadness, sorrow, unhappiness
AN OPPOSITE IS joy

grievance *NOUN*
If you have a grievance, speak to the manager.
▸ complaint, grumble

a b c d e f g h i j k l m n o p q r s t u v w x y z

A B C D E F G H I J K L M N O P Q R S T U V W X Y Z

grieve *VERB*
1 *They are still grieving over her death.*
▸ lament, mourn, weep
AN OPPOSITE IS rejoice
2 *Her bad behaviour grieved her parents.*
▸ distress, hurt, sadden, upset
AN OPPOSITE IS please

grievous *ADJECTIVE*
1 *Her death was a grievous loss.*
▸ distressing, sad, tragic
2 *The school suffered grievous damage in the storm.*
▸ grave, heavy, serious, severe

grim *ADJECTIVE*
1 *I could tell she was angry by the grim expression on her face.*
▸ bad-tempered, severe, stern, unfriendly
AN OPPOSITE IS friendly
2 *The monster's grim appearance made us shudder.*
▸ frightening, frightful, grisly, gruesome, hideous, horrible, menacing, terrible, threatening
AN OPPOSITE IS attractive

grime *NOUN*
The windows were covered in grime.
▸ dirt, dust, filth

grin *VERB*
FOR VARIOUS WAYS TO SHOW AMUSEMENT SEE **laugh**

grind *VERB*
1 *He ground the coffee beans.*
▸ crush, mill, powder, pulverize
2 *He ground the blades of the lawn mower.*
▸ polish, sharpen

grip *VERB*
1 *Grip the handle tightly.*
▸ clutch, grasp, hold, seize
2 *The audience was gripped by the film.*
▸ absorb, engross, fascinate

grisly *ADJECTIVE*
We found the grisly remains of a dead sheep.
▸ dreadful, gory, gruesome, hideous, horrible, nasty, revolting, sickening

grit *NOUN*
1 *I've got some grit in my shoe.*
▸ gravel, stones
2 *The runners in the marathon showed real grit.*
▸ bravery, courage, determination, endurance, (*informal*) guts, pluck, toughness

groan *VERB*
He groaned with pain.
▸ cry out, moan, sigh, wail

groom *VERB*
The stable girl was grooming the horse.
▸ brush, clean, smarten, tidy

groove *NOUN*
He cut a groove in the table.
▸ channel, cut, furrow, rut, scratch, slot

grope *VERB*
I groped in the dark for the light switch.
▸ feel about, fumble

gross *ADJECTIVE*
1 *He was so gross he could hardly fit into the chair.*
▸ fat, heavy, overweight
2 *I was disgusted by their gross behaviour.*
▸ coarse, indecent, offensive, rude, shocking, vulgar
3 *It was a gross injustice.*
▸ conspicuous, extreme, glaring, noticeable, obvious

grotesque *ADJECTIVE*
1 *He can twist himself into grotesque shapes.*
▸ deformed, distorted, fantastic, strange, unnatural, weird
2 *It was a grotesque idea.*
▸ absurd, ludicrous, ridiculous

ground *NOUN*
1 *I planted some seeds in the ground.*
▸ earth, land, soil
2 *The ground was too wet to play on.*
▸ arena, field, pitch, stadium
grounds *What were her grounds for accusing you?*
▸ argument, basis, justification, reason

group *NOUN*
1 *I like to feel I'm a member of a group.*
► community, family, society
2 *People with similar interests often form a group.*
► alliance, association, club, guild, league, society, union
3 *We formed a group to discuss sports day.*
► assembly, committee, gathering, meeting
4 *She sorted her clothes into different groups.*
► category, collection, pack, set
5 *A group of soldiers marched down the road.*
► army, company, force, platoon, squad, squadron, troop
SPECIAL WORDS FOR GROUPS OF PEOPLE
▷ a band of musicians. a class of children in school. a company of actors. a congregation of worshippers in church. a coven of witches. a crew of sailors. a gang of workers. a horde of invaders. a mob of rioters. a rabble of troublemakers. a team of players.
SPECIAL WORDS FOR GROUPS OF ANIMALS
▷ a brood of chicks. a covey of partridges. a flock of sheep or birds. a gaggle of geese. a herd of cattle or elephants. a litter of pigs or puppies. a pack of wolves. a pride of lions. a school of whales. a shoal of fish. a swarm of insects.
SPECIAL WORDS FOR GROUPS OF THINGS
▷ a battery of guns. a bunch of flowers. a clump of trees. a clutch of eggs in a nest. a constellation or galaxy of stars. a convoy or fleet of ships.

group *VERB*
I want you to group in fours for the next game.
► assemble, collect, come together, gather, get together, swarm round, team up

grouse *VERB*
He's always grousing about work.
► complain, grumble, moan, object, protest, whine

grow *VERB*
1 *The flowers I planted are growing fast.*
► become bigger, develop, get bigger, spring up, sprout, swell
2 *His business has grown this year.*
► build up, enlarge, expand, flourish, increase, prosper
3 *She likes growing roses.*
► cultivate, produce, raise
4 *You'll grow more confident with practice.*
► become, get
to grow up *She's growing up fast.*
► become adult, mature

growth *NOUN*
1 *He is pleased with the growth of his business.*
► development, enlargement, expansion, increase, spread
2 *The doctor examined the growth on my foot.*
► lump, swelling, tumour

grub *NOUN*
I found a grub in my apple.
► caterpillar, larva, maggot

grubby *ADJECTIVE*
Wash your hands if they are grubby.
► dirty, grimy, messy, mucky, soiled
AN OPPOSITE IS clean

grudge *VERB*
to grudge someone something *I don't grudge him his success.*
► be jealous or resentful about, envy, resent

gruelling *ADJECTIVE*
The marathon is a gruelling race.
► challenging, exhausting, hard, laborious, strenuous, tough
AN OPPOSITE IS easy

gruesome *ADJECTIVE*
The battlefield was a gruesome sight.
► appalling, bloody, dreadful, frightful, gory, grisly, hideous, horrible, nasty, revolting, sickening, terrible

gruff *ADJECTIVE*
He spoke in a gruff voice.
► harsh, hoarse, husky, rough

grumble *VERB*
She grumbles if I'm late.
► complain, grouse, moan, object, protest, whine

grumpy *ADJECTIVE*
He's grumpy because he's got a headache.
► bad-tempered, cross, ill-tempered, irritable, short-tempered, sour
AN OPPOSITE IS good-tempered

guarantee *VERB*
They guaranteed that they'd deliver it today.
▸ pledge, promise, undertake, vow

guard *VERB*
1 *We had injections to guard us against various diseases.*
▸ defend, protect, safeguard, shield
2 *Two policemen guarded the prisoner.*
▸ escort, keep watch on, look after, mind, stand guard over, tend, watch over

guard *NOUN*
A guard was on duty at the gate.
▸ lookout, security officer, sentinel, sentry, warder, watchman

guardian *NOUN*
The guardian of the treasure was a fierce dragon.
▸ defender, keeper, minder, protector

guess *NOUN*
My answer was just a guess.
▸ estimate, feeling, hunch

guess *VERB*
1 *I didn't know the answer, so I guessed.*
▸ estimate, have a shot, make a guess
2 *I guess you are tired after your journey.*
▸ assume, imagine, suppose, think

guest *NOUN*
We had guests on Sunday.
▸ caller, visitor

guide *NOUN*
1 *The guide showed us around.*
▸ courier, escort, leader, tour leader
2 *We bought a useful guide to the city.*
▸ guidebook, handbook

guide *VERB*
She guided me out of the maze.
▸ direct, escort, lead, show the way, steer

guidelines *PLURAL NOUN*
She gave us some guidelines to help us with our project.
▸ advice, a brief, guidance, instructions, tips

guilt *NOUN*
1 *He admitted his guilt.*
▸ guiltiness, wickedness, wrongdoing
2 *You could see the look of guilt on her face.*
▸ bad conscience, penitence, regret, remorse, shame
AN OPPOSITE IS innocence

guilty *ADJECTIVE*
1 *The jury found him guilty.*
▸ at fault, in the wrong, liable, responsible, to blame
AN OPPOSITE IS innocent
2 *She had a guilty look on her face.*
▸ ashamed, conscience-stricken, penitent, remorseful, repentant
AN OPPOSITE IS unrepentant

gulf *NOUN*
There's a great gulf between their points of view.
▸ difference, gap, opening, separation, split

gullible *ADJECTIVE*
He's so gullible he'll believe anything.
▸ innocent, naive, trusting, unsuspecting

gulp *VERB*
1 *Don't gulp your food.*
▸ bolt, gobble, guzzle
2 *She gulped in amazement.*
▸ gasp, swallow

gun *NOUN*
FOR VARIOUS TYPES OF GUN SEE **weapon**

gush *NOUN*
There was a gush of water from the pipe.
▸ cascade, flood, jet, spout, spurt, stream, torrent

gush *VERB*
Oil gushed from the well.
▸ burst, erupt, flood, flow, pour, rush, spout, spurt, squirt, stream

guts *PLURAL NOUN*
(*informal*) *The players showed real guts.*
▸ bravery, courage, determination, endurance, grit, pluck, toughness

guzzle *VERB*
They guzzled down all the cakes.
▸ bolt, gobble, gulp

Hh

habit *NOUN*
1 *It was his habit to go for a walk each morning.*
▸ convention, custom, practice, routine
2 *He has a habit of scratching his head.*
▸ mannerism, way

habitual *ADJECTIVE*
1 *She soon recovered her habitual good humour.*
▸ accustomed, customary, normal, ordinary, predictable, regular, routine, standard, traditional, usual
AN OPPOSITE IS abnormal
2 *He is a a habitual smoker.*
▸ addicted, confirmed, dependent, persistent

hack *VERB*
They hacked through the undergrowth.
▸ chop, cut, slash, slice
SEE ALSO **cut** *VERB*

haggard *ADJECTIVE*
He looked haggard after his ordeal.
▸ exhausted, gaunt, ill, thin, tired out, withered, worn out
AN OPPOSITE IS healthy

haggle *VERB*
They haggled over the price.
▸ argue, bargain, negotiate

hair *NOUN*
WORDS FOR THE HAIR ON YOUR HEAD
hank, lock, (*informal*) mop, tress
VARIOUS HAIRSTYLES
bob, braids, crew-cut, curls, dreadlocks, fringe, Mohican, perm or permanent wave, pigtail, plaits, ponytail, quiff, ringlets, short back and sides, sideboards, sideburns, topknot
PEOPLE WHO CUT AND CARE FOR YOUR HAIR
barber, coiffeur or coiffeuse, hairdresser, hairstylist
WORDS TO DESCRIBE THE COLOUR OF HAIR
auburn, (*male*) blond, (*female*) blonde, brunette, (*informal*) carroty, dark, fair, flaxen, ginger, grey, grizzled, mousy, platinum blonde, red, silver
FALSE HAIR
hairpiece, toupee, wig
HAIR ON AN ANIMAL
bristles, down, fleece, fur, mane

hair-raising *ADJECTIVE*
The drive along the mountain road was hair-raising.
▸ alarming, dangerous, frightening, scary, terrifying

hairy *ADJECTIVE*
The dog had a thick hairy coat.
▸ bristly, furry, fuzzy, hirsute, long-haired, shaggy, woolly

half-hearted *ADJECTIVE*
There's no point playing if you're going to be half-hearted about it.
▸ apathetic, indifferent, lukewarm, uncommitted, unenthusiastic
AN OPPOSITE IS enthusiastic

hall *NOUN*
1 *The hall was full for the concert.*
▸ assembly hall, auditorium, concert hall, theatre
2 *When you go through the front door, you find yourself in the hall.*
▸ entrance hall, foyer, hallway, lobby

hallucination *NOUN*
She's been having hallucinations.
▸ delusion, dream, fantasy, illusion, mirage, vision

halt *VERB*
1 *A traffic jam halted the traffic.*
▸ check, obstruct, stop
2 *The car halted at the red light.*
▸ come to a halt, draw up, pull up, stop, wait
3 *Work halted when the whistle went.*
▸ break off, cease, end, terminate
AN OPPOSITE IS go or start

halve *VERB*
1 *Halve the tomatoes and scoop out the seeds.*
▸ cut in half, divide into halves, split in two
2 *The workforce has been halved in the last five years.*
▸ cut by half, reduce by half

hammer *VERB*
I hammered on the door, but no one answered.
▸ (*informal*) bash, batter, beat, knock, strike
SEE ALSO **hit** *VERB*

hamper *VERB*
Bad weather hampered the rescuers.
▸ curb, foil, frustrate, get in the way of,

A B C D E F G H I J K L M N O P Q R S T U V W X Y Z

handicap, hinder, hold up, interfere with, obstruct, restrict, slow down
AN OPPOSITE IS help

hand *NOUN*
▷ When you clench your hand you make a fist. The flat part of the inside of your hand is the palm.

hand *VERB*
Hand your essay in at the end of the week.
▶ deliver, give, offer, pass, present, submit
to hand something down *The family home was handed down from generation to generation.*
▶ bequeath, leave as a legacy, pass down, pass on

handicap *NOUN*
1 *In this job, lack of experience can be a handicap.*
▶ difficulty, disadvantage, drawback, hindrance, inconvenience, nuisance, obstacle, problem
AN OPPOSITE IS advantage
2 *He was born with a visual handicap.*
▶ disability, impairment

handicap *VERB*
Lack of money handicapped the research project.
▶ create problems for, hamper, hinder, hold back, restrict
AN OPPOSITE IS help

handicraft *NOUN*
FOR VARIOUS ARTS AND CRAFTS SEE **art**

handiwork *NOUN*
Is this your handiwork?
▶ creation, doing, invention, work

handle *NOUN*
The handle on my bag has broken.
▶ grip, handgrip
▷ The handle of a sword is the hilt.

handle *VERB*
1 *It's important to handle the puppies very carefully.*
▶ feel, finger, grasp, hold, stroke, touch
2 *The referee handled the game well.*
▶ conduct, control, cope with, deal with, look after, manage, supervise

handsome *ADJECTIVE*
1 *He's a very handsome man.*
▶ attractive, good-looking
AN OPPOSITE IS unattractive
2 *The stately home was full of handsome furniture.*
▶ admirable, beautiful, elegant, tasteful, well-made
AN OPPOSITE IS ugly
3 *They made a handsome profit when they sold the house.*
▶ big, large, sizeable, valuable
AN OPPOSITE IS mean

handy *ADJECTIVE*
1 *It's a handy gadget for peeling potatoes.*
▶ convenient, easy to use, helpful, practical, useful, well-designed
AN OPPOSITE IS awkward
2 *Keep your tools handy.*
▶ accessible, available, close at hand, easy to reach, nearby, ready
AN OPPOSITE IS inaccessible

hang *VERB*
1 *A blue flag hung from the flagpole.*
▶ dangle, droop, swing, trail down
2 *I hung the picture on the wall.*
▶ attach, fasten, fix, peg, pin, stick, suspend
3 *Smoke hung in the air.*
▶ drift, float, hover
to hang about or **around** *Don't hang about, we'll miss the bus.*
▶ dawdle, linger, loiter
to hang on (*informal*) *Try to hang on a bit longer.*
▶ carry on, continue, hold on, keep going, persevere, persist, stick it out, wait
to hang on to something **1** *Hang on to the rope.*
▶ catch, grasp, hold, seize
2 *Hang on to your ticket in case they ask to see it.*
▶ keep, retain, save

haphazard *ADJECTIVE*
The arrangement of the exhibition was haphazard.
▶ arbitrary, chaotic, confusing, disorderly, disorganized, higgledy-piggledy, random, unplanned
AN OPPOSITE IS orderly

happen *VERB*
Did anything interesting happen?
▶ arise, come about, crop up, emerge, occur, result, take place

happening *NOUN*
There have been some strange happenings here lately.
▶ event, incident, occurrence, phenomenon

happiness *NOUN*
Her face glowed with happiness.
▶ bliss, cheerfulness, contentment, delight, ecstasy, elation, exuberance, gaiety, gladness, high spirits, joy, jubilation, light-heartedness, merriment, pleasure, well-being
AN OPPOSITE IS sorrow

happy *ADJECTIVE* This word is often overused. Here are some alternatives:
1 *She came in looking happy and excited.*
▶ cheerful, contented, delighted, ecstatic, elated, exultant, glad, gleeful, good-humoured, joyful, light-hearted, merry, overjoyed, over the moon, pleased, proud, radiant, thrilled
2 *They spent many happy days on the beach.*
▶ blissful, heavenly, idyllic, joyous
AN OPPOSITE IS unhappy

harass *VERB*
The dog had been harassing the sheep on the farm.
▶ annoy, badger, bait, bother, disturb, hound, molest, persecute, pester, plague, torment, trouble

harassed *ADJECTIVE*
She felt tired and harassed.
▶ distressed, hassled, irritated, stressed, troubled, vexed, worried
AN OPPOSITE IS carefree

harbour *NOUN*
PLACES WHERE SHIPS CAN TIE UP OR SHELTER
anchorage, dock, haven, jetty, landing stage, marina, moorings, pier, port, quay, wharf

harbour *VERB*
He was suspected of harbouring an escaped criminal.
▶ conceal, give refuge to, give sanctuary to, hide, protect, shelter, shield

hard *ADJECTIVE* This word is often overused. Here are some alternatives:
1 *The ground was hard and covered with frost.*
▶ dense, firm, flinty, rigid, rocky, solid, stony
AN OPPOSITE IS soft
2 *Shovelling the snow from the drive was very hard work.*
▶ exhausting, gruelling, heavy, laborious, strenuous, tiring, tough, wearying
AN OPPOSITE IS easy
3 *That's a hard question to answer.*
▶ baffling, complex, complicated, confusing, difficult, intricate, involved, perplexing, puzzling
AN OPPOSITE IS simple
4 *It's been a long, hard winter.*
▶ disagreeable, harsh, painful, severe, unpleasant
AN OPPOSITE IS pleasant
5 *He was a hard man.*
▶ callous, cruel, hard-hearted, heartless, intolerant, merciless, pitiless, ruthless, severe, stern, strict, unfeeling, unkind
AN OPPOSITE IS kind
6 *She gave the rope a hard pull.*
▶ energetic, forceful, heavy, powerful, strong, violent
AN OPPOSITE IS slight
hard up *They are too hard up to buy new clothes.*
▶ badly off, needy, poor

harden *VERB*
We left the cement to harden.
▶ set, solidify, stiffen
▷ If you harden clay in a kiln, you bake or fire it.
AN OPPOSITE IS soften

hardly *ADVERB*
I could hardly see in the fog.
▶ barely, only just, scarcely, with difficulty

hardship *NOUN*
They suffered years of hardship during the war.
▶ adversity, affliction, difficulty, misery, misfortune, suffering, trouble, unhappiness, want

hardware *NOUN*
The ship's cargo consisted entirely of military hardware.
▶ equipment, implements, instruments, machines, machinery, tools
FOR VARIOUS TOOLS SEE **tool**

A B C D E F G **H** I J K L M N O P Q R S T U V W X Y Z

hard-wearing *ADJECTIVE*
Denim is a hard-wearing material.
▸ durable, lasting, stout, strong, sturdy, tough, well-made
AN OPPOSITE IS flimsy

hardy *ADJECTIVE*
You must be hardy to go camping in this weather.
▸ fit, healthy, hearty, robust, strong, sturdy, tough, vigorous
AN OPPOSITE IS tender

harm *VERB*
1 *His captors didn't harm him.*
▸ hurt, ill-treat, injure, misuse, treat badly, wound
2 *Too much direct sunlight may harm this plant.*
▸ damage, ruin, spoil

harm *NOUN*
I didn't mean to cause him any harm.
▸ damage, hurt, injury, pain
AN OPPOSITE IS benefit

harmful *ADJECTIVE*
The harmful effects of smoking are now well known.
▸ bad, damaging, dangerous, deadly, injurious, poisonous, unhealthy, unwholesome
AN OPPOSITE IS beneficial or harmless

harmless *ADJECTIVE*
1 *It was just a bit of harmless fun.*
▸ acceptable, innocuous, safe
2 *The dog looks fierce, but really he's quite harmless.*
▸ innocent, inoffensive, mild
AN OPPOSITE IS dangerous or harmful

harmonize *VERB*
Choose colours which will harmonize in an attractive way.
▸ blend, coordinate, go together, match, suit each other

harmony *NOUN*
They lived together in perfect harmony.
▸ agreement, compatibility, cooperation, friendliness, goodwill, peace, sympathy, understanding
AN OPPOSITE IS disagreement

harness *NOUN*
PARTS OF A HORSE'S HARNESS
bit, blinker, bridle, collar, crupper, girth, halter, headstall, noseband, pommel, rein, saddle, spurs, stirrups, trace

harness *VERB*
Attempts have been made to harness the sun's energy.
▸ control, make use of, use, utilize

harsh *ADJECTIVE*
1 *She had a loud harsh voice.*
▸ croaking, disagreeable, grating, jarring, rasping, raucous, rough, shrill, strident, unpleasant
AN OPPOSITE IS gentle
2 *We blinked in the harsh light.*
▸ bright, brilliant, dazzling, gaudy, glaring, lurid
AN OPPOSITE IS subdued
3 *Conditions in the prison are harsh.*
▸ arduous, difficult, hard, severe, stressful, tough, uncomfortable
AN OPPOSITE IS easy
4 *The material had a harsh, unpleasant texture.*
▸ abrasive, coarse, rough
AN OPPOSITE IS smooth
5 *He has had to endure a lot of harsh criticisms.*
▸ brutal, cruel, hard-hearted, merciless, pitiless, severe, stern, strict, unforgiving, unkind, unsympathetic
AN OPPOSITE IS lenient

harvest *NOUN*
The farmers had a good harvest this year.
▸ crop, return, yield
▹ Things grown on a farm are produce.

harvest *VERB*
The weather was too wet for the wheat to be harvested.
▸ bring in, collect, gather, mow, pick, reap, take in

hassle *NOUN*
(*informal*) *They had a lot of hassle getting their money back.*
▸ argument, bother, fuss, inconvenience, trouble

haste *NOUN*
More haste, less speed.
▸ hurry, rush, speed, urgency

hasty *ADJECTIVE*
1 *They made a hasty exit.*
▸ abrupt, fast, headlong, hurried, quick, rapid, speedy, sudden, swift
2 *He soon regretted his hasty decision.*
▸ foolhardy, impulsive, rash, reckless, thoughtless
AN OPPOSITE IS careful or leisurely

hat *NOUN*
THINGS PEOPLE WEAR ON THE HEAD
balaclava, baseball cap, bearskin, beret, boater, bonnet, bowler, cap, coronet, crash helmet, crown, fez, hard hat, headband, headdress, helmet, hood, mitre, mortarboard, skullcap, sou'wester, stetson, sunhat, tiara, top hat, trilby, turban, wig, yarmulke

hatch *VERB*
Those troublemakers are hatching a plot.
▸ conceive, contrive, (*informal*) cook up, devise, (*informal*) dream up, invent, plan, plot, scheme, think up

hate *VERB*
1 *He hates spiders.*
▸ can't bear, can't stand, detest, dislike, loathe
2 *I hate her superior attitude.*
▸ deplore, despise, resent, scorn
AN OPPOSITE IS like or love

hateful *ADJECTIVE*
They were in a hateful mood.
▸ awful, contemptible, despicable, detestable, disgusting, foul, horrible, nasty, vile
AN OPPOSITE IS lovable

hatred *NOUN*
She looked at him with hatred.
▸ animosity, antagonism, contempt, detestation, dislike, enmity, hate, hostility, intolerance, loathing
AN OPPOSITE IS love

haughty *ADJECTIVE*
She had a haughty expression.
▸ arrogant, boastful, conceited, lofty, lordly, pompous, presumptuous, proud, (*informal*) stuck-up, superior
AN OPPOSITE IS modest

haul *VERB*
He hauled his bike out of the shed.
▸ drag, draw, pull, tow

haunt *VERB*
1 *He returned to one of the cafés he used to haunt when he was younger.*
▸ frequent, visit frequently
2 *The sight haunted me for years.*
▸ linger in the memory, obsess, prey on

have *VERB* This word is often overused. The verb *have* has many meanings and can be used in many ways. Here are just some of the ways you might use it:
1 *I have my own radio.*
▸ own, possess
2 *Our house has six rooms.*
▸ consist of, include, incorporate
3 *We had a good party.*
▸ enjoy
4 *She had a bad time.*
▸ endure, experience, feel, go through, live through, put up with, suffer
5 *I had some really nice presents.*
▸ be given, get, obtain, receive
6 *She had the last toffee.*
▸ consume, eat, steal, take
to have someone on (informal) Don't believe him — he's having you on.
c deceive, fool, hoax, mislead, trick
to have to do something They had to pay for the damage.
c be compelled or forced to, have an obligation to, must, need to, ought to, should

haven *NOUN*
The lake is a haven for a variety of wild birds.
▸ refuge, place of safety, sanctuary, shelter
SEE **harbour** *NOUN*

hazard *NOUN*
Beware of the hazards along the way.
▸ danger, pitfall, risk, snag, threat, trap

hazardous *ADJECTIVE*
He made the hazardous journey to the South Pole.
▸ dangerous, risky, unsafe
AN OPPOSITE IS safe

haze *NOUN*
I could hardly see through the haze.
▸ cloud, fog, mist, steam, vapour

hazy *ADJECTIVE*
1 *The things in the distance were rather hazy.*
▸ blurred, dim, faint, misty, unclear
2 *He's only got a hazy knowledge of history.*
▸ uncertain, vague
AN OPPOSITE IS clear

head *NOUN*
1 *Use your head!*
▸ ability, brains, intellect, intelligence, mind, understanding
PARTS OF YOUR HEAD
brain, brow, cheek, chin, cranium, crown, dimple, ear, eye, forehead, gums, hair, jaw, jowl, lip, mouth, nose, nostril, scalp, skull, teeth, temple, tongue
FOR OTHER PARTS OF YOUR BODY SEE **body**
2 *She's head of a large business.*
▸ (*informal*) boss, controller, director, manager
SEE ALSO **chief** *NOUN*

head *VERB*
1 *The department is headed by a government minister.*
▸ be in charge of, command, control, direct, govern, guide, lead, manage, rule, run, superintend, supervise
2 *At the end of the day we headed for home.*
▸ aim, go, make, set out, start, steer, turn
to head someone or **something off** *Police headed off the approaching cars.*
▸ deflect, divert, intercept, turn aside

headache *NOUN*
▹ Severe kinds of headache are **migraine** and **neuralgia**.

heading *NOUN*
Each chapter had a different heading.
▸ caption, headline, title

headlong *ADJECTIVE*
We made a headlong dash to get out of the rain.
▸ breakneck, hasty, hurried, impulsive, quick, reckless

headquarters *PLURAL NOUN*
They phoned headquarters for instructions.
▸ base, depot, head office, (*informal*) HQ

headteacher *NOUN*
The headteacher runs the school.
▸ headmaster or headmistress, principal

headway *NOUN*
They are making little headway with the negotiations.
▸ advance, breakthrough, progress

heal *VERB*
1 *It took two months for my leg to heal properly.*
▸ get better, knit, mend, recover
2 *Part of a doctor's job is to heal the sick.*
▸ cure, make better, restore, treat

health *NOUN*
1 *Unfortunately, his health is poor.*
▸ condition, constitution
2 *He's bursting with health and vitality.*
▸ fitness, strength, vigour, well-being
FOR VARIOUS MEDICAL TREATMENTS SEE **medicine**
FOR VARIOUS ILLNESSES SEE **illness**

healthy *ADJECTIVE*
1 *He's always been a healthy child.*
▸ fit, flourishing, (*informal*) in good shape, robust, sound, strong, sturdy, vigorous, well
AN OPPOSITE IS ill
2 *The air in the mountains is said to be very healthy.*
▸ bracing, health-giving, invigorating, wholesome
AN OPPOSITE IS unhealthy

heap *NOUN*
There was an untidy heap of books on her desk.
▸ collection, mass, mound, mountain, pile, stack
heaps of (*informal*) *We had heaps of food.*
▸ ample, lots of, plenty of

heap *VERB*
We heaped up all the rubbish.
▸ bank, collect, pile, stack

hear *VERB*
1 *Did you hear what she said?*
▸ catch, listen to, overhear, pay attention to, pick up
2 *Have you heard the news?*
▸ be told, discover, find out, gather, learn, receive

heart *NOUN*
1 *Have you no heart?*
▸ affection, compassion, feeling, humanity, kindness, love, sympathy, tenderness, understanding
2 *It's a new hotel, located right in the heart of the city.*
▸ centre, middle
3 *They tried to get to the heart of the problem.*
▸ core, essence

heartbreaking *ADJECTIVE*
The animal's condition was heartbreaking.
▸ distressing, moving, pitiful, tragic
AN OPPOSITE IS cheering

heartbroken *ADJECTIVE*
He was heartbroken when his dog died.
▸ dejected, depressed, desolate, grieving, miserable, sad, sorrowful, tearful
AN OPPOSITE IS cheerful

heartless *ADJECTIVE*
How could she be so heartless?
▸ callous, cruel, hard-hearted, inhuman, pitiless, ruthless, unfeeling, unkind
AN OPPOSITE IS kind

hearty *ADJECTIVE*
1 *He gave me a hearty slap on the back.*
▸ forceful, strong, vigorous
AN OPPOSITE IS feeble
2 *He had a hearty appetite after his walk.*
▸ big, healthy
AN OPPOSITE IS poor
3 *They gave us a hearty welcome.*
▸ enthusiastic, sincere, warm
AN OPPOSITE IS unenthusiastic

heat *NOUN*
1 *The cat basked in the heat of the fire.*
▸ glow, hotness, warmth
2 *Last summer, the heat made me feel ill.*
▸ closeness, high temperatures, hot weather
▹ A long period of hot weather is a **heatwave**.

heat *VERB*
VERBS WHICH MEAN TO BE HOT, TO BECOME HOT, OR TO MAKE SOMETHING HOT
bake, blister, boil, burn, cook, fry, grill, inflame, make hot, melt, reheat, roast, scald, scorch, simmer, sizzle, smoulder, steam, stew, swelter, toast, warm up
AN OPPOSITE IS cool

heath *NOUN*
I took the dog for a walk across the heath.
▸ common land, moor, moorland, open country, wasteland

heave *VERB*
They heaved the sacks onto a lorry.
▸ drag, draw, haul, hoist, lift, lug, pull, raise, throw, tug

heaven *NOUN*
1 *They believed that when they died they would go to heaven.*
▸ the afterlife, eternal rest, the next world, paradise
AN OPPOSITE IS hell
2 *Lying by the pool with a good book is her idea of heaven.*
▸ bliss, contentment, delight, ecstasy, happiness, joy, pleasure
the heavens *The rocket soared into the heavens.*
▸ the sky, space

heavenly *ADJECTIVE*
(*informal*) *The weather was heavenly.*
▸ beautiful, blissful, delightful, (*informal*) divine, exquisite, lovely, (*informal*) out of this world, wonderful
AN OPPOSITE IS horrible

heavy *ADJECTIVE*
1 *The box was too heavy for me to lift.*
▸ bulky, burdensome, large, massive, ponderous, weighty
2 *Digging the garden is heavy work.*
▸ back-breaking, exhausting, gruelling, hard, laborious, strenuous, tiring, tough, wearying
3 *The book made heavy reading.*
▸ deep, demanding, intellectual, serious
4 *The heavy rain caused flooding.*
▸ severe, torrential
5 *In the morning there was a heavy mist.*
▸ dense, thick
6 *The apple tree had a heavy crop of fruit.*
▸ abundant, copious, profuse
7 *She said goodbye with a heavy heart.*
▸ depressed, gloomy, miserable, sad, sorrowful, unhappy
AN OPPOSITE IS light

hectic *ADJECTIVE*
The next few days were hectic.
▸ bustling, busy, chaotic, feverish, frantic, lively
AN OPPOSITE IS leisurely

A B C D E F G **H** I J K L M N O P Q R S T U V W X Y Z

hedge *VERB*

1 *The garden was hedged with privet.*
▸ encircle, enclose, fence in, surround
2 *When she asked for an answer, he hedged.*
▸ be evasive

heed *VERB*

She didn't heed his warning.
▸ attend to, consider, listen to, mark, mind, note, notice, obey, pay attention to, regard, take notice of
AN OPPOSITE IS ignore

heedless *ADJECTIVE*

Heedless of other people, they raced through the streets.
▸ inconsiderate, neglectful, thoughtless, unconcerned (about), unsympathetic (towards)
AN OPPOSITE IS careful

hefty *ADJECTIVE*

The wrestler was a hefty man.
▸ (*informal*) beefy, big, brawny, burly, heavy, hulking, large, mighty, muscular, powerful, solid, strong, tough
AN OPPOSITE IS slight

height *NOUN*

The plane was flying at its normal height.
▸ altitude, elevation

heighten *VERB*

The crowd's excitement heightened as the kick-off approached.
▸ increase, intensify
AN OPPOSITE IS lessen

hell *NOUN*

Some people believe that sinners go to hell.
▸ eternal punishment, the lower regions, the underworld
AN OPPOSITE IS heaven

helmet *NOUN*

▹ A helmet worn by builders, etc., is a hard hat. A helmet worn by motor cyclists is a crash helmet. Part of a helmet that protects the face is a visor.

help *NOUN*

Thank you for your help.
▸ advice, aid, assistance, backing, benefit, collaboration, cooperation, friendship, guidance, support
AN OPPOSITE IS hindrance

help *VERB*

1 *She helped him when he was in trouble.*
▸ advise, aid, assist, back, befriend, be helpful to, collaborate with, cooperate with, (*informal*) give a hand to, serve, side with, stand by, support, take pity on
AN OPPOSITE IS hinder
2 *This medicine will help your cough.*
▸ cure, ease, improve, make better, relieve
AN OPPOSITE IS aggravate
3 *I can't help coughing.*
▸ avoid, prevent, stop

helpful *ADJECTIVE*

1 *The staff were friendly and helpful.*
▸ considerate, cooperative, kind, neighbourly, obliging, sympathetic, thoughtful
AN OPPOSITE IS unhelpful
2 *She gave us some helpful advice.*
▸ beneficial, profitable, useful, valuable, worthwhile
AN OPPOSITE IS worthless

helping *NOUN*

I got a huge helping of ice cream.
▸ amount, plateful, portion, ration, serving, share

helpless *ADJECTIVE*

Kittens are born blind and helpless.
▸ defenceless, dependent, feeble, powerless, weak
AN OPPOSITE IS independent

hem *VERB*

to hem someone in *They were hemmed in by the crowd.*
▸ encircle, surround

herald *NOUN*

The cuckoo is said to be the herald of spring.
▸ announcer, messenger

herald *VERB*

Thunder often heralds a change in the weather.
▸ advertise, announce, foretell, indicate, make known, predict, proclaim, promise

herb *NOUN*

VARIOUS HERBS USED FOR FLAVOURING
balm, balsam, basil, borage, camomile, caraway, chervil, chicory, chive, coriander, cumin, dill, fennel, fenugreek, hyssop, liquorice, lovage, marjoram, mint, oregano, parsley, peppermint, rosemary, rue, sage, savory, spearmint, tansy, tarragon, thyme

herd *NOUN*
FOR WORDS FOR GROUPS OF ANIMALS SEE **group** *NOUN*

hereditary *ADJECTIVE*
Cystic fibrosis is a hereditary disease.
▸ handed down, inherited, passed on

heritage *NOUN*
These ancient buildings are part of our heritage.
▸ culture, history, inheritance, legacy, tradition

hero, heroine *NOUNS*
Everyone turned out to welcome the heroes.
▸ champion, idol, victor, winner

heroic *ADJECTIVE*
He made a heroic effort to rescue her.
▸ bold, brave, courageous, daring, fearless, gallant, intrepid, noble, selfless, valiant
AN OPPOSITE IS cowardly

hesitant *ADJECTIVE*
He was hesitant about accepting their offer.
▸ cautious, dithering, faltering, hesitating, nervous, shy, timid, uncertain, undecided, unsure, wary, wavering
AN OPPOSITE IS confident

hesitate *VERB*
She hesitated, unsure of what to say.
▸ be cautious, delay, dither, falter, hang back, pause, (*informal*) think twice, wait, waver

hidden *ADJECTIVE*
1 *She kept the money hidden in a drawer.*
▸ concealed, covered, invisible, out of sight, private, shrouded, unseen
AN OPPOSITE IS visible
2 *There's a hidden meaning in the message.*
▸ coded, mysterious, obscure, secret
AN OPPOSITE IS obvious

hide *VERB*
1 *Quick! — someone's coming — we'd better hide.*
▸ go into hiding, go to ground, lie low, lurk, take cover, take refuge
AN OPPOSITE IS reveal yourself
2 *They hid the gold in a cave.*
▸ bury, conceal, put out of sight, secrete
AN OPPOSITE IS discover
3 *The clouds hid the sun.*
▸ blot out, cover, mask, screen, shroud, veil
AN OPPOSITE IS uncover
4 *I tried to hide my feelings.*
▸ camouflage, cloak, disguise, keep secret, suppress
AN OPPOSITE IS show

hideous *ADJECTIVE*
His smile made him look even more hideous than before.
▸ appalling, dreadful, frightful, ghastly, gruesome, repulsive, shocking, terrible, ugly
AN OPPOSITE IS beautiful

hideout *NOUN*
We made a hideout in the garden.
▸ den, hiding place, lair, refuge

hiding *NOUN*
His father gave him a hiding.
▸ beating, caning, thrashing

high *ADJECTIVE*
1 *The house was surrounded by a high wall.*
▸ high-rise, lofty, soaring, tall, towering
2 *The lounge was a spacious room with a high ceiling.*
▸ elevated, raised
3 *His father was a high official in the Civil Service.*
▸ chief, distinguished, eminent, important, leading, powerful, prominent, top
4 *House prices are very high at the moment.*
▸ dear, excessive, expensive, unreasonable
5 *A high wind was blowing.*
▸ exceptional, great, intense, strong
6 *She had a high squeaky voice.*
▸ high-pitched, piercing, sharp, shrill
▹ A high singing voice is **soprano** or **treble**.

highlight *NOUN*
The day in Paris was the highlight of the trip.
▸ best moment, high spot

hike *VERB*
They hiked across the moors.
▸ ramble, tramp, trek, walk

hilarious *ADJECTIVE*
They thought the film was hilarious.
▸ amusing, comic, funny, (*informal*) hysterical

hill *NOUN*
1 *From the top of this hill you can see for miles around.*
▸ mound, mountain, peak, ridge, summit
2 *She pushed her bike up the steep hill.*
▸ ascent, gradient, incline, rise, slope

A B C D E F G H I J K L M N O P Q R S T U V W X Y Z

hinder *VERB*
Snowdrifts hindered their progress.
▸ bar, check, curb, delay, deter, frustrate, get in the way of, hamper, handicap, hold up, obstruct, prevent, restrict, slow down, stand in the way of, stop
AN OPPOSITE IS help

hindrance *NOUN*
Lack of money was a hindrance to the progress of the research.
▸ difficulty, disadvantage, drawback, handicap, inconvenience, obstacle
AN OPPOSITE IS help

hinge *VERB*
to hinge on *Everything hinges on your decision.*
▸ depend on, rely on, rest on

hint *NOUN*
I've no idea what it is — give me a hint.
▸ clue, indication, inkling, sign, suggestion

hint *VERB*
She hinted that we'd get a surprise.
▸ give a hint, imply, indicate, suggest

hire *VERB*
▹ If you hire a bus or aircraft you **charter** it. If you hire someone to do a job you **engage** or **employ** them. If you hire a building for a time you **lease** or **rent** it.

historic *ADJECTIVE*
Notice that there is a difference between *historic*, which means famous or important in history, and *historical*, which simply refers to anything that happened in the past
The Battle of Hastings was a historic event.
▸ celebrated, eminent, famous, important, momentous, notable, renowned, significant, well-known
AN OPPOSITE IS unimportant

historical *ADJECTIVE*
See note under *historic*
No one is sure whether Robin Hood is a historical character.
▸ actual, authentic, past, real, real-life, true
AN OPPOSITE IS fictitious

history *NOUN*
1 *I'm interested in our country's history.*
▸ heritage, past
2 *He wrote a history of the First World War.*
▸ account, chronicle, record

hit *NOUN*
1 *He got a nasty hit on the head.*
▸ bang, blow, bump, knock, whack
▹ A hit with your fist is a **punch**. A hit with your open hand is a **clap** or **slap** or **smack**. A hit with a bat or club is a **drive** or **stroke** or **swipe**.
2 *The new record was an instant hit.*
▸ success, triumph, (*informal*) winner

hit *VERB* This word is often overused.
1 *She hit him on the head with her umbrella.*
THERE ARE VARIOUS WAYS TO HIT THINGS
▹ To hit with your fist is to **punch**. To hit with the palm of your hand is to **clap**, **slap**, **smack**, or **spank**. To punish someone by hitting them is to **beat**, **birch**, **cane**, **flog**, **lash**, **scourge**, **thrash**, or **whip** them. To hit someone with a stick or blunt instrument is to **club**, **cosh**, or **cudgel** them. To hit your toe on something is to **stub** it. To hit a ball with a bat or club is to **drive** it. To kill an insect by hitting it is to **swat** it. To hit something repeatedly is to **batter** or **pound** it. To hit another vehicle in an accident is to **collide** with it or **ram** it.
OTHER WORDS MEANING TO HIT
These words can be used as nouns as well as verbs. Many of them are used informally
bang, bash, belt, biff, bump, butt, clonk, clout, crack, cuff, jab, jog, kick, knock, nudge, prod, rap, slam, slap, slog, sock, strike, swipe, tap, thump, thwack, wallop, whack, wham
2 *The drought hit the farmers.*
▸ affect, bring disaster to, damage, do harm to, harm, hurt, ruin
to hit on something *They hit on a new way of making money.*
▸ discover, think of

hoard *NOUN*
He kept a hoard of sweets in his drawer.
▸ heap, pile, stockpile, store, supply

hoard *VERB*
Squirrels hoard nuts.
▸ collect, gather, keep, pile up, put by, save, store

hoarse *ADJECTIVE*
Her voice was hoarse after shouting so much.
▸ croaking, grating, growling, gruff, harsh, husky, rough

hoax *NOUN*
The telephone call was a hoax.
▸ fake, fraud, joke, practical joke, trick

hobby *NOUN*
What's your favourite hobby?
▸ activity, interest, pastime, pursuit, recreation, relaxation

hoist *VERB*
The crane hoisted the crates onto a ship.
▸ heave, lift, pull up, raise, winch up

hold *NOUN*
She took a firm hold on the dog's lead.
▸ clasp, clutch, grasp, grip, purchase

hold *VERB*
1 *Please hold the dog's lead.*
▸ clasp, cling to, clutch, grasp, grip, hang on to, seize
2 *Can I hold the baby?*
▸ embrace, hug
3 *They held the suspect until the police arrived.*
▸ confine, detain, keep, stop
4 *Will the shelf hold all these books?*
▸ bear, carry, support, take
5 *If our luck holds, we could reach the final.*
▸ carry on, continue, last, persist, stay
6 *She holds strong opinions.*
▸ believe in, maintain, stick to
to hold out **1** *Hold out your hand.*
▸ extend, offer, reach out, stick out, stretch out
2 *They can't hold out much longer.*
▸ carry on, continue, endure, hang on, keep going, last, persevere, persist, resist, stand fast
to hold something up **1** *Hold up your hand.*
▸ lift, put up, raise
2 *The accident held up the traffic.*
▸ delay, halt, hinder, obstruct, slow down

hold-up *NOUN*
1 *As long as there aren't any hold-ups, we should arrive before lunch.*
▸ delay, interruption
2 *There was a hold-up at the bank.*
▸ robbery

hole *NOUN*
VARIOUS KINDS OF HOLE IN THE GROUND
abyss, burrow, cave, cavern, cavity, chasm, crater, depression, excavation, hollow, mine, pit, pothole, shaft, tunnel, underground passage
VARIOUS HOLES RIGHT THROUGH THINGS
breach, break, chink, crack, cut, gap, gash, leak, opening, perforation, puncture, slit, split, tear, vent, window

holiday *NOUN*
I spent my summer holiday in France.
▸ break, day off, leave, time off, vacation
TIMES WHEN MANY PEOPLE DO NOT GO TO WORK OR SCHOOL
bank holiday, half-term, holy day, school holidays, weekend
VARIOUS KINDS OF HOLIDAY
camping, caravanning, cruise, honeymoon, pony-trekking, safari, seaside holiday, touring, travelling, walking
PLACES WHERE YOU MIGHT STAY ON HOLIDAY
apartment, bed and breakfast, boarding house, campsite, cruise ship, flat, guesthouse, hostel, hotel, motel, self-catering apartment or studio, villa

hollow *ADJECTIVE*
Tennis balls are hollow.
▸ empty, unfilled
AN OPPOSITE IS solid

hollow *VERB*
Some birds make their nests by hollowing out holes in tree trunks.
▸ dig, excavate, gouge, scoop

hollow *NOUN*
The cat tried to hide in a hollow in the ground.
▸ crater, dent, depression, dip, hole
▷ A hollow between two hills is a **valley**.

holy *ADJECTIVE*
1 *The pilgrims knelt to pray in the holy shrine.*
▸ blessed, divine, revered, sacred
2 *The pilgrims were holy people.*
▸ pious, religious, righteous, saintly

home *NOUN*
The floods forced people to flee their homes.
▸ abode, dwelling, house, lodging, residence
SEE ALSO **house**
▷ A home for the sick is a **convalescent home** or **nursing home**. A place where a bird or animal lives is its **habitat**.

A B C D E F G **H** I J K L M N O P Q R S T U V W X Y Z

homely *ADJECTIVE*
It's a traditional hotel with a homely atmosphere.
▸ comfortable, cosy, easygoing, friendly, informal, natural, ordinary, relaxed, simple
AN OPPOSITE IS sophisticated

homework *NOUN*
I have to do homework every night.
▸ assignments, (*informal*) prep, preparation, private study

honest *ADJECTIVE*
1 *He's an honest boy, so he gave the money back.*
▸ conscientious, good, honourable, law-abiding, moral, reliable, trustworthy, upright, virtuous
AN OPPOSITE IS dishonest
2 *She gave me an honest reply.*
▸ direct, frank, genuine, outspoken, plain, sincere, straight, straightforward, truthful, unbiased
AN OPPOSITE IS insincere

honesty *NOUN*
1 *I don't doubt your honesty.*
▸ goodness, honour, integrity, morality, reliability, trustworthiness, truthfulness, uprightness, virtue
AN OPPOSITE IS dishonesty
2 *I was surprised by the honesty of his comments.*
▸ directness, frankness, outspokenness, plainness, sincerity, straightforwardness
AN OPPOSITE IS insincerity

honour *NOUN*
1 *Her success brought honour to the school.*
▸ credit, fame, good reputation, renown, respect
2 *It's an honour to meet you.*
▸ distinction, privilege

honour *VERB*
The winners were honoured at a special ceremony.
▸ celebrate, give credit to, glorify, pay respect or tribute to, praise

honourable *ADJECTIVE*
1 *He's an honourable man.*
▸ decent, fair, good, honest, loyal, moral, respectable, respected, righteous, sincere, trustworthy, trusty, upright, virtuous, worthy
2 *It was an honourable thing to do.*
▸ admirable, creditable, noble, praiseworthy
AN OPPOSITE IS unworthy

hook *VERB*
1 *He hooked the trailer to the car.*
▸ connect, couple, fasten, hitch, link
2 *He hooked an enormous fish.*
▸ capture, catch, take

hooligan *NOUN*
Hooligans did a lot of damage in the park.
▸ delinquent, lout, ruffian, troublemaker, vandal

hooter *NOUN*
A hooter sounded to warn everyone of the danger.
▸ horn, siren, whistle

hop *VERB*
They were hopping about in excitement.
▸ bound, caper, dance, jump, leap, prance, skip, spring

hope *NOUN*
1 *Her dearest hope was to see her family again.*
▸ ambition, desire, dream, wish
2 *There's hope of better weather tomorrow.*
▸ expectation, likelihood, prospect

hope *VERB*
I hope that we win the championship.
▸ be hopeful or optimistic, expect, have faith, trust, wish

hopeful *ADJECTIVE*
1 *She was in a hopeful mood.*
▸ confident, expectant, optimistic, positive
AN OPPOSITE IS pessimistic
2 *The future is beginning to look more hopeful.*
▸ encouraging, favourable, promising, reassuring
AN OPPOSITE IS discouraging

hopeless *ADJECTIVE*
1 *The situation seems hopeless.*
▸ beyond hope, desperate, wretched
AN OPPOSITE IS hopeful
2 *I'm hopeless at cricket.*
▸ bad, incompetent, poor, useless, worthless
AN OPPOSITE IS competent

horde *NOUN*
Hordes of people were queuing for tickets.
▸ crowd, gang, group, mob, swarm, throng

horizontal ADJECTIVE
He lay in a horizontal position.
▸ flat, level
AN OPPOSITE IS vertical

horrible ADJECTIVE
What a horrible smell!
▸ appalling, awful, beastly, disagreeable, disgusting, dreadful, ghastly, hateful, horrid, loathsome, nasty, objectionable, offensive, repulsive, revolting, terrible, unpleasant
AN OPPOSITE IS pleasant

horrid ADJECTIVE
SEE **horrible**

horrific ADJECTIVE
The accident was horrific.
▸ appalling, atrocious, disgusting, dreadful, frightening, ghastly, grisly, gruesome, hideous, horrifying, shocking, sickening

horrify VERB
We were horrified by the news.
▸ appal, disgust, frighten, scare, shock, sicken, terrify

horror NOUN
1 *He has a horror of snakes.*
▸ detestation, disgust, dislike, dread, fear, loathing, terror
2 *Photographs showed the full horror of the tragedy.*
▸ awfulness, frightfulness, ghastliness, gruesomeness, hideousness

horse NOUN
VARIOUS KINDS OF HORSE
bronco, carthorse, (*old use*) charger, cob, colt, filly, foal, gelding, hunter, mare, (*informal*) nag, piebald, pony, race horse, Shetland pony, shire-horse, skewbald, stallion, steed, warhorse
PEOPLE WHO RIDE HORSES
cavalryman, equestrian, horseman or horsewoman, jockey, rider
SEE ALSO **harness** NOUN
▹ A cross between a donkey and a horse is a mule.

hospitable ADJECTIVE
She's a very hospitable woman.
▸ friendly, generous, sociable, warm, welcoming
AN OPPOSITE IS unfriendly

hospital NOUN
PLACES WHERE PEOPLE GO FOR MEDICAL TREATMENT
clinic, convalescent home, hospice, infirmary, nursing home, sanatorium
PARTS OF A HOSPITAL
accident and emergency, dispensary, intensive care unit, operating theatre, outpatients, pharmacy, X-ray department, ward
SEE ALSO **medicine**

hospitality NOUN
They thanked us for our hospitality.
▸ friendliness, sociability, welcome

hostage NOUN
The hijackers treated their hostages well.
▸ captive, prisoner

hostile ADJECTIVE
1 *The supporters of the other team looked hostile.*
▸ aggressive, antagonistic, inhospitable, malevolent, unfriendly, unwelcoming, warlike
AN OPPOSITE IS friendly
2 *The weather conditions were too hostile to make the journey.*
▸ adverse, bad, unfavourable, unhelpful
AN OPPOSITE IS favourable

hostility NOUN
The hostility between the opposing sides was obvious.
▸ aggression, antagonism, bad feeling, detestation, dislike, enmity, hate, hatred, ill will, malevolence, opposition, unfriendliness
AN OPPOSITE IS friendship

hot ADJECTIVE
1 *The sun was extremely hot.*
▸ blistering, burning, roasting, scorching
2 *Do you like this hot weather?*
▸ humid, oppressive, steamy, stifling, sweltering, tropical, warm
3 *Careful — the soup's really hot.*
▸ baking hot, boiling, piping hot, scalding, sizzling, steaming
4 *I like curry, but only if it's not too hot.*
▸ gingery, peppery, spicy
5 *He's got a hot temper.*
▸ angry, emotional, excited, fierce, impatient, passionate, violent
AN OPPOSITE IS cold or mild

A B C D E F G H I J K L M N O P Q R S T U V W X Y Z

house *NOUN*
WORDS FOR THE PLACE YOU LIVE IN
abode, dwelling, home, lodging, quarters, residence
BUILDINGS WHERE PEOPLE LIVE
apartment, bungalow, chalet, cottage, council house, croft, detached house, farmhouse, flat, hovel, hut, igloo, lodge, maisonette, manor, manse, mansion, rectory, semi-detached house, shack, shanty, terraced house, thatched house, vicarage, villa
FOR ROOMS IN A HOUSE SEE **room**

house *VERB*
The refugees were housed in temporary accommodation.
▸ accommodate, board, lodge, place, put up, shelter, take in

hover *VERB*
1 *Army helicopters hovered overhead.*
▸ fly
2 *He hovered in the doorway, afraid to go inside.*
▸ dally, dither, hang about, hesitate, linger, loiter, pause, wait about

howl *VERB*
FOR VARIOUS WAYS TO MAKE SOUNDS SEE **sound** *VERB*

huddle *VERB*
We huddled together to get warm.
▸ cluster, crowd, cuddle, flock, gather, nestle, snuggle, squeeze
AN OPPOSITE IS scatter

hue *NOUN*
FOR VARIOUS COLOURS SEE **colour** *NOUN*

hug *VERB*
She flung her arms round him and hugged him tight.
▸ clasp, cling to, cuddle, embrace, hold close, snuggle against, squeeze

huge *ADJECTIVE*
Elephants are huge animals.
▸ colossal, enormous, giant, gigantic, great, (*informal*) hulking, immense, imposing, impressive, massive, mighty, monstrous, monumental, stupendous, (*informal*) terrific, towering, tremendous, vast, weighty
AN OPPOSITE IS tiny

hum *NOUN*
She could hear the hum of bees.
▸ buzz, drone, murmur

human *ADJECTIVE*
She'll forgive you — she's quite human.
SEE **humane**

human beings *PLURAL NOUN*
Human beings are supposed to be more intelligent than animals.
▸ folk, humanity, humans, mankind, men and women, mortals, people

humane *ADJECTIVE*
A humane society should treat animals well.
▸ benevolent, charitable, civilized, compassionate, human, humanitarian, kind, kind-hearted, loving, merciful, sympathetic, tender, warm-hearted
AN OPPOSITE IS cruel

humble *ADJECTIVE*
1 *Her humble manner makes you forget how famous she is.*
▸ docile, meek, modest, polite, respectful, submissive, unassertive
AN OPPOSITE IS proud
2 *She comes from a humble background.*
▸ commonplace, lowly, obscure, ordinary, simple, undistinguished, unimportant
AN OPPOSITE IS important

humid *ADJECTIVE*
I don't like this humid weather.
▸ muggy, steamy, sticky, sweaty
AN OPPOSITE IS fresh

humiliate *VERB*
He humiliated her in front of all her colleagues.
▸ crush, deflate, disgrace, embarrass, humble, make ashamed, (*informal*) put you in your place, shame, (*informal*) take you down a peg

humiliating *ADJECTIVE*
They suffered a humiliating defeat.
▸ crushing, degrading, embarrassing, humbling, undignified
AN OPPOSITE IS glorious

humility *NOUN*
They were impressed by his gentleness and humility.
▸ humbleness, meekness, modesty
AN OPPOSITE IS pride

humorous *ADJECTIVE*
She made a humorous and entertaining speech.
▸ amusing, comic, funny, witty
AN OPPOSITE IS serious

humour *NOUN*
1 *His stories were full of humour.*
▸ sense of humour, wit
2 *The arguments had not improved her humour.*
▸ disposition, frame of mind, mood, spirits, temper

hump *NOUN*
Camels have humps on their backs.
▸ bulge, bump, lump, swelling

hump *VERB*
He humped the suitcases upstairs.
▸ carry, cart, fetch, haul, lift, lug, take, transfer

hunch *NOUN*
I have a hunch that she won't come.
▸ feeling, guess, idea, impression, inkling, intuition, suspicion

hunch *VERB*
He hunched his shoulders.
▸ arch, bend, curl, curve, hump, shrug

hunger *NOUN*
Many people died from cold and hunger.
▸ famine, lack of food, starvation
▹ Bad health caused by not having enough food is **malnutrition**.

hungry *ADJECTIVE*
Our dog always seems to be hungry.
▸ famished, greedy, (*informal*) peckish, ravenous, starving

hunt *NOUN*
After searching for hours, the police abandoned the hunt.
▸ chase, pursuit, quest, search

hunt *VERB*
1 *I think it's cruel to hunt animals.*
▸ chase, hound, pursue, stalk, track, trail
2 *I hunted in the attic for our old photos.*
▸ ferret, look, rummage, search, seek

hunting *NOUN*
KINDS OF HUNTING
badger-baiting, beagling, deer stalking, falconry, ferreting, fishing, fox-hunting, hare coursing, hawking, shooting, whaling

hurdle *NOUN*
1 *I jumped over the hurdle easily.*
▸ barricade, barrier, fence, hedge, obstacle
2 *There are many hurdles to overcome in life.*
▸ difficulty, handicap, hindrance, obstruction, problem, snag, stumbling block

hurl *VERB*
I hurled the ball as far as I could.
▸ cast, (*informal*) chuck, fling, launch, pitch, sling, throw, toss

hurry *VERB*
1 *If you want to catch the bus, you'd better hurry.*
▸ (*informal*) buck up, dash, fly, hasten, hurtle, rush, speed
AN OPPOSITE IS dawdle
2 *It's no good trying to hurry him.*
▸ quicken, speed up
AN OPPOSITE IS slow down

hurry *NOUN*
What's the hurry for?
▸ haste, rush, speed, urgency

hurt *VERB*
1 *Put that knife down — you might hurt someone.*
▸ damage, harm, injure, wound
▹ To hurt someone deliberately is to **torment** or **torture** them.
2 *My feet hurt.*
▸ ache, be painful, smart, sting, throb, tingle
3 *The insult hurt her.*
▸ distress, grieve, upset

hurtle *VERB*
The train hurtled along at top speed.
▸ charge, dash, fly, race, rush, shoot, speed, tear, zoom

A B C D E F G H I J K L M N O P Q R S T U V W X Y Z

hush *VERB*
He told us all to hush.
▸ be quiet, be silent, (*informal*) pipe down, shut up, stop talking
to hush something up *They tried to hush up the scandal.*
▸ conceal, cover up, hide, keep quiet, keep secret, suppress

husky *ADJECTIVE*
1 *Her voice is still a bit husky.*
▸ croaking, grating, gravelly, growling, gruff, harsh, hoarse, rough
2 *The wrestler was a big, husky fellow.*
▸ (*informal*) beefy, brawny, burly, hefty, large, mighty, muscular, powerful, solid, strong, tough

hustle *VERB*
The police hustled him into a car.
▸ bustle, force, hasten, hurry, push, rush, shove

hut *NOUN*
He keeps his fishing tackle in hut by the river.
▸ cabin, chalet, den, shack, shanty, shed

hybrid *NOUN*
▷ An animal that combines two different species is a **cross-breed**. A dog that combines two different breeds is a **mongrel**.

hygienic *ADJECTIVE*
Hygienic conditions are essential in hospital.
▸ clean, disinfected, germ free, healthy, sanitary, sterilized, unpolluted, wholesome
AN OPPOSITE IS unhygienic

hypocrisy *NOUN*
He accused the newspapers of hypocrisy.
▸ falsity, insincerity

hypocritical *ADJECTIVE*
It's hypocritical to say one thing and do another.
▸ false, insincere, two-faced

hypothesis *NOUN*
His hypothesis was proved to be correct.
▸ suggestion, supposition, theory

hypothetical *ADJECTIVE*
This is a hypothetical situation, not a real one.
▸ academic, imaginary, supposed, theoretical
AN OPPOSITE IS actual

hysteria *NOUN*
Hysteria swept the town when a tiger escaped from the zoo.
▸ frenzy, hysterics, madness

hysterical *ADJECTIVE*
1 *The fans became hysterical when the band appeared.*
▸ crazy, delirious, frenzied, mad, raving, uncontrollable, wild
2 (*informal*) *Listen to his joke — it's hysterical.*
▸ funny, hilarious, ridiculous

Ii

ice *NOUN*
KINDS OF ICE
black ice, floe, frost, glacier, iceberg, icicle

icy *ADJECTIVE*
1 *You need to dress warmly in icy weather.*
▸ arctic, bitter, cold, crisp, freezing, frosty, wintry
2 *Icy roads are dangerous.*
▸ frozen, glassy, slippery

idea *NOUN*
1 *I've got a great idea!*
▸ inspiration, plan, proposal, scheme, suggestion
2 *She has some funny ideas about life.*
▸ belief, concept, conception, hypothesis, notion, opinion, theory, view
3 *What's the main idea of this poem?*
▸ intention, meaning, point, thought
4 *Give me an idea of what you are planning.*
▸ clue, hint, impression, inkling

ideal *ADJECTIVE*
It's ideal weather for a picnic.
▸ the best, excellent, faultless, perfect, suitable

identical *ADJECTIVE*
They were wearing identical clothes.
▸ alike, indistinguishable, interchangeable, matching, similar
AN OPPOSITE IS different

identify *VERB*
1 *The police asked if I could identify the thief.*
▸ distinguish, name, pick out, recognize, single out
2 *The doctor couldn't identify what was wrong.*
▸ diagnose, discover, (*informal*) put a name to, spot
to identify with *Can you identify with the hero of the story?*
▸ feel for, (*informal*) put yourself in the shoes of, sympathize with, understand

idiom *NOUN*
It's hard for foreigners to understand English idioms.
▸ choice of words, expression, manner of speaking, phrase, phrasing, usage

idiotic *ADJECTIVE*
It was an idiotic thing to do.
▸ daft, foolish, irrational, mad, ridiculous, silly, stupid, thoughtless, unintelligent, unwise
AN OPPOSITE IS sensible

idle *ADJECTIVE*
1 *He lost his job for being so idle.*
▸ apathetic, lazy, slothful, uncommitted
AN OPPOSITE IS enthusiastic
2 *The machines lay idle during the strike.*
▸ doing nothing, inactive, inoperative, unemployed, unused
AN OPPOSITE IS busy

idol *NOUN*
1 *The people worshipped the idol.*
▸ deity, god, image, statue
2 *He was a pop idol of the fifties.*
▸ favourite, hero, star

idolize *VERB*
She idolized her mother.
▸ adore, be devoted to, love, worship

ignite *VERB*
1 *We ignited the lantern with a match.*
▸ kindle, light, set alight, set on fire
2 *The fire refused to ignite.*
▸ burn, catch fire

ignorant *ADJECTIVE*
1 *He was ignorant of the facts.*
▸ lacking knowledge, unacquainted (with), unaware, unconscious, unfamiliar (with)
AN OPPOSITE IS knowledgeable
2 *He's an ignorant young man.*
▸ illiterate, uneducated
AN OPPOSITE IS educated
3 (*informal and insulting*) *You're just ignorant!*
▸ SEE **stupid**

ignore *VERB*
1 *He ignored the warning and got into difficulties.*
▸ disobey, disregard, take no notice of, (*informal*) turn a blind eye to
2 *I ignored the difficult questions.*
▸ leave out, miss out, neglect, omit, overlook, skip

ill *ADJECTIVE*
1 *You can't work properly if you are ill.*
▸ ailing, bedridden, diseased, feeble, frail, infected, infirm, poorly, queasy, sick, sickly, suffering, under the weather, unfit, unhealthy, unwell, weak
AN OPPOSITE IS healthy or well
2 *Did the plants suffer ill effects in the frost?*
▸ adverse, bad, damaging, harmful, injurious, unfavourable
AN OPPOSITE IS good
FOR VARIOUS ILLNESSES SEE **illness**

illegal *ADJECTIVE*
Stealing is illegal.
▸ against the law, banned, criminal, forbidden, outlawed, prohibited, unlawful, wrong
AN OPPOSITE IS legal

illegible *ADJECTIVE*
His signature was illegible.
▸ unclear, unreadable
AN OPPOSITE IS legible

illiterate *ADJECTIVE*
They're illiterate because they didn't go to school.
▸ unable to read, uneducated
AN OPPOSITE IS literate

illness *NOUN*
What kind of illness is he suffering from?
▸ abnormality, affliction, ailment, attack, (*informal*) bug, complaint, condition, disability, disease, disorder, health problem, infection, infirmity, sickness, (*informal*) upset
▹ A sudden illness is an attack or fit. A period of illness is a bout. A general outbreak of illness in a particular area is an epidemic.

a b c d e f g h i j k l m n o p q r s t u v w x y z

A B C D E F G H I J K L M N O P Q R S T U V W X Y Z

VARIOUS ILLNESSES OR COMPLAINTS
acne, allergy, anaemia, appendicitis, arthritis, asthma, bronchitis, cancer, cataract, catarrh, chickenpox, chilblains, chill, cholera, cold, colic, constipation, convulsions, cough, diabetes, diarrhoea, diphtheria, dysentery, eczema, epilepsy, fever, flu, gangrene, gastric flu, glandular fever, haemorrhage, hay fever, headache, hernia, hypothermia, indigestion, influenza, jaundice, laryngitis, leprosy, leukaemia, lumbago, malaria, measles, meningitis, migraine, multiple sclerosis, mumps, neuralgia, piles, plague, pneumonia, polio or poliomyelitis, rabies, rheumatism, rickets, scarlet fever, sciatica, scurvy, shingles, smallpox, spina bifida, stomach-ache, stroke, tetanus, thrombosis, tonsillitis, tuberculosis, typhoid, typhus, ulcer, whooping cough
SEE ALSO **medicine**

illogical *ADJECTIVE*
His argument was illogical.
▸ absurd, fallacious, inconsistent, irrational, senseless, silly, unreasonable
AN OPPOSITE IS logical

illuminate *VERB*
1 *The floodlights illuminated the pitch.*
▸ decorate with lights, light up
2 *Her explanation illuminated the problem.*
▸ clarify, clear up, explain, make clear, throw light on

illusion *NOUN*
The magician fooled us with his illusions.
▸ conjuring, deception, trick

illustrate *VERB*
1 *I used some photos to illustrate my story.*
▸ depict, picture, portray
2 *The accident illustrates the importance of road safety.*
▸ demonstrate, make clear, show

illustration *NOUN*
1 *She likes books with illustrations.*
▸ decoration, diagram, drawing, photograph, picture, sketch
2 *I'll give you an illustration of what I mean.*
▸ demonstration, example, instance, specimen

image *NOUN*
1 *The film contained frightening images of war.*
▸ depiction, picture, portrayal, representation
2 *The temple contained images of the gods.*
▸ carving, figure, idol, statue
3 *You can see your image in the mirror.*
▸ likeness, reflection
4 *She's the image of her mother.*
▸ double, twin

imaginary *ADJECTIVE*
Her fears were imaginary.
▸ fanciful, fictional, fictitious, imagined, invented, made up, non-existent, unreal
AN OPPOSITE IS real

imagination *NOUN*
Use your imagination.
▸ artistry, creativity, fancy, ingenuity, inventiveness, originality, sensitivity, thought, vision

imaginative *ADJECTIVE*
His paintings were very imaginative.
▸ artistic, attractive, beautiful, clever, creative, fanciful, ingenious, inspired, inventive, original, poetic, sensitive, thoughtful, vivid
AN OPPOSITE IS boring or unimaginative

imagine *VERB*
1 *Imagine what it would be like to be rich.*
▸ conjure up, dream up, fancy, make up, picture, pretend, think up, visualize
2 *I imagine you'd like a drink.*
▸ assume, believe, guess, presume, suppose

imitate *VERB*
1 *She was very good at imitating his voice.*
▸ counterfeit, impersonate, make fun of, mimic, parody, reproduce, (*informal*) send up, simulate
2 *Try to imitate my example.*
▸ copy, follow, match

imitation *ADJECTIVE*
The coat was made from imitation leather.
▸ artificial, counterfeit, dummy, model, sham, simulated
AN OPPOSITE IS real

imitation *NOUN*
It's an imitation, not the real thing.
▸ copy, counterfeit, dummy, duplicate, fake, forgery, impersonation, impression, likeness, mock-up, model, replica, reproduction, sham, simulation
▷ An imitation which you want people to laugh at is a **caricature** or **parody**.

immature *ADJECTIVE*
She's very immature for her age.
▸ babyish, childish, infantile, juvenile
AN OPPOSITE IS mature

immediate *ADJECTIVE*
1 *Please can I have an immediate reply.*
▸ direct, instantaneous, prompt, quick, (*informal*) snappy, speedy, swift, top priority, urgent
AN OPPOSITE IS slow
2 *Fortunately we get on well with our immediate neighbours.*
▸ adjacent, closest, nearest
AN OPPOSITE IS distant

immediately *ADVERB*
I want you to do it immediately!
▸ at once, directly, instantly, now, promptly, right away, straight away

immense *ADJECTIVE*
It was an immense building.
▸ big, colossal, enormous, giant, gigantic, great, huge, imposing, impressive, large, majestic, massive, mighty, monstrous, monumental, stupendous, towering, tremendous, vast
AN OPPOSITE IS tiny

immerse *VERB*
I immersed the potatoes in cold water to cool them down.
▸ dip, lower, plunge, submerge

immersed *ADJECTIVE*
I didn't hear because I was immersed in my work.
▸ absorbed, busy, engrossed, interested, involved, occupied, preoccupied

immobile *ADJECTIVE*
He sat immobile in his chair.
▸ motionless, stationary, still, unmoving
AN OPPOSITE IS mobile

immobilize *VERB*
The car was immobilized by water in the engine.
▸ cripple, disable, paralyse, put out of action, stop

immoral *ADJECTIVE*
We were shocked by their immoral behaviour.
▸ bad, corrupt, deceitful, dishonest, evil, impure, indecent, naughty, scandalous, sinful, wicked, wrong
AN OPPOSITE IS moral

immortal *ADJECTIVE*
They believed their gods were immortal.
▸ ageless, everlasting, undying
AN OPPOSITE IS mortal

immune *ADJECTIVE*
immune from or **to** *We are immune to many diseases.*
▸ free from, immunized against, inoculated against, protected from, resistant to, safe from, unaffected by, vaccinated against

immunize *VERB*
▹ You can be immunized by inoculation or vaccination.

impact *NOUN*
1 *Was the car damaged in the impact?*
▸ bang, blow, bump, collision, crash, knock, smash
2 *Computers have a big impact on our lives.*
▸ effect, influence

impair *VERB*
Very loud noise can impair your hearing.
▸ damage, harm, weaken

impartial *ADJECTIVE*
The referee must be impartial.
▸ disinterested, fair, fair-minded, independent, just, neutral, objective, open-minded, unbiased, unprejudiced
AN OPPOSITE IS biased

impassable *ADJECTIVE*
The road was impassable because of the flood.
▸ blocked, closed, obstructed, unusable

impatient *ADJECTIVE*
1 *Don't be so impatient!*
▸ eager, in a hurry, keen
2 *We were impatient because of the delay.*
▸ agitated, anxious, edgy, fidgety, irritable
3 *He was very impatient with her.*
▸ abrupt, hasty, quick-tempered
AN OPPOSITE IS patient

imperceptible *ADJECTIVE*
He gave an almost imperceptible smile.
▸ faint, gradual, insignificant, invisible, negligible, slight, undetectable, unnoticeable
AN OPPOSITE IS noticeable

imperfect *ADJECTIVE*
The goods are rejected if they are imperfect.
▸ broken, damaged, defective, deficient, faulty, incomplete, marked, spoilt, unfinished
AN OPPOSITE IS perfect

impersonal *ADJECTIVE*
He was put off by her impersonal manner.
▸ cool, detached, distant, formal, official, remote, unapproachable, unemotional, unfriendly, uninvolved, unsympathetic
AN OPPOSITE IS friendly

impersonate *VERB*
He made us laugh by impersonating the Prime Minister.
▸ counterfeit, disguise yourself as, imitate, mimic, parody, (*informal*) send up, simulate

impertinent *ADJECTIVE*
He made some rather impertinent remarks.
▸ cheeky, disrespectful, impolite, impudent, insolent, irreverent, rude, saucy
AN OPPOSITE IS respectful

implement *NOUN*
We have a cupboard full of implements for doing jobs round the house.
▸ appliance, device, gadget, instrument, tool, utensil

implement *VERB*
The bad weather made it impossible to implement the plan.
▸ bring about, carry out, execute, fulfil, perform, put into practice, try out

implore *VERB*
We implored her to help us.
▸ beg, entreat, plead with

imply *VERB*
He implied that they were wrong.
▸ hint, indicate, suggest

impolite *ADJECTIVE*
There's no need to be impolite when someone asks a civil question.
▸ abrupt, abusive, bad-mannered, disrespectful, impertinent, insulting, rude, uncomplimentary, uncouth
AN OPPOSITE IS polite

import *VERB*
The country has to import most of the oil it uses.
▸ bring in, ship in
AN OPPOSITE IS export

important *ADJECTIVE*
1 *The World Cup is an important sporting event.*
▸ big, central, historic, major, momentous, outstanding, significant
2 *They have some important things to do.*
▸ pressing, serious, urgent, weighty
3 *The prime minister is an important person.*
▸ distinguished, eminent, famous, great, influential, leading, notable, powerful, prominent, renowned, well-known
AN OPPOSITE IS unimportant

impose *VERB*
1 *The plans for a bypass were imposed against the wishes of local people.*
▸ enforce, insist on, introduce
2 *The government imposed a tax on fuel.*
▸ fix, inflict, prescribe, set
to impose on *I don't want to impose on you.*
▸ put a burden on, take advantage of

imposing *ADJECTIVE*
The castle is an imposing building.
▸ big, dignified, grand, great, impressive, magnificent, majestic, splendid, stately, striking
AN OPPOSITE IS insignificant

impossible *ADJECTIVE*
Years ago, people said that space travel was impossible.
▸ absurd, hopeless, impracticable, impractical, insoluble, out of the question, ridiculous
AN OPPOSITE IS possible

impostor *NOUN*
The man who claimed to be a detective was an impostor.
▸ cheat, (*slang*) con man, impersonator, swindler, trickster

impracticable *ADJECTIVE*
The scheme turned out to be impracticable.
▸ absurd, hopeless, impossible, impractical, out of the question, ridiculous
AN OPPOSITE IS possible

impractical *ADJECTIVE*
1 *He's impractical when it comes to doing jobs round the house.*
▸ clumsy, incompetent, ineffective, ineffectual, useless
2 *The inventor's designs were impractical.*
▸ impossible, impracticable, inconvenient, unachievable, unrealistic
AN OPPOSITE IS practical

impress *VERB*
They were impressed by his hard work.
▸ influence, leave its mark on, make an impression on, stick in your mind
to impress something on someone *She impressed on us the need to be careful.*
▸ emphasize, stress

impression *NOUN*
1 *She had the impression something was wrong.*
▸ feeling, hunch, idea, notion, sense, suspicion
2 *The film made a big impression on them.*
▸ effect, impact, influence, mark
3 *She does a good impression of the boss.*
▸ imitation, impersonation, (*informal*) send-up

impressive *ADJECTIVE*
The cathedral is an impressive building.
▸ grand, great, important, imposing, large, magnificent, majestic, remarkable, spectacular, splendid, stately, striking
AN OPPOSITE IS insignificant

imprison *VERB*
The thief was imprisoned for two years.
▸ commit to prison, confine, detain, gaol or jail, (*informal*) keep under lock and key, lock up, (*informal*) put away
AN OPPOSITE IS liberate

imprisonment *NOUN*
He was sentenced to two years' imprisonment.
▸ confinement, detention, gaol or jail
▹ A person who is held by the police is in custody. A person who is in prison awaiting trial is on remand.

improbable *ADJECTIVE*
It seemed a rather improbable story.
▸ far-fetched, incredible, questionable, unbelievable, unconvincing, unlikely
AN OPPOSITE IS probable

impromptu *ADJECTIVE*
The musicians gave us an impromptu concert.
▸ ad lib, improvised, spontaneous, unplanned, unprepared, unrehearsed
AN OPPOSITE IS rehearsed

improper *ADJECTIVE*
1 *Improper use of the equipment may cause damage.*
▸ careless, inappropriate, incorrect, irresponsible, silly, wrong
2 *They used language that was considered improper.*
▸ coarse, crude, dirty, indecent, obscene, offensive, rude, smutty, unseemly, vulgar
AN OPPOSITE IS proper

improve *VERB*
1 *Her work improved during the term.*
▸ advance, develop, get better, move on, progress
AN OPPOSITE IS deteriorate
2 *Has he improved since his illness?*
▸ pick up, rally, recover, revive
AN OPPOSITE IS get worse
3 *How can I improve this story?*
▸ amend, correct, enhance, make better, refine, revise
4 *She got a grant to improve the house.*
▸ decorate, modernize, upgrade
▹ To improve something by making small changes is to touch it up.

improvement *NOUN*
1 *There's been an improvement in her health.*
▸ advance, gain, progress, recovery
2 *He made some improvements to the article.*
▸ amendment, correction, revision
3 *They've made a lot of improvements to the house since they moved in.*
▸ decoration, modernization, modification

improvise *VERB*
We had nothing ready, so we had to improvise.
▸ ad lib, make up, perform impromptu

impudent *ADJECTIVE*
She made some impudent remarks.
▸ bold, brazen, cheeky, disrespectful, forward, impertinent, impolite, insolent, insulting, irreverent, rude, saucy, shameless
AN OPPOSITE IS respectful

impulse *NOUN*
1 *He did it on a sudden wild impulse.*
▸ desire, instinct, urge
2 *What was the impulse behind your decision?*
▸ force, motive, pressure, stimulus

A B C D E F G H **I** J K L M N O P Q R S T U V W X Y Z

impulsive *ADJECTIVE*
I didn't think about it: it was just an impulsive action.
▶ hasty, impromptu, instinctive, intuitive, involuntary, natural, spontaneous, sudden, thoughtless, unconscious, unplanned, unrehearsed, unthinking, wild
AN OPPOSITE IS deliberate

impure *ADJECTIVE*
He became ill through drinking impure water.
▶ contaminated, defiled, dirty, infected, polluted, unclean
AN OPPOSITE IS pure

inaccessible *ADJECTIVE*
1 *The medicines were inaccessible on the top shelf.*
▶ hard to find, inconvenient, out of reach, out of the way
2 *The plane crashed in an inaccessible area.*
▶ desolate, isolated, lonely, outlying, out-of-the-way, remote, unfrequented
AN OPPOSITE IS accessible

inaccurate *ADJECTIVE*
The police said that the witness's story was inaccurate.
▶ faulty, imperfect, incorrect, inexact, misleading, mistaken, unreliable, untrue, wrong
AN OPPOSITE IS accurate

inactive *ADJECTIVE*
Hedgehogs are inactive in winter.
▶ asleep, doing nothing, hibernating, idle, immobile, passive, quiet, sleepy, slow
AN OPPOSITE IS active

inadequate *ADJECTIVE*
The inadequate rainfall means that water must be rationed.
▶ insufficient, limited, meagre, poor, scanty, scarce, unsatisfactory
AN OPPOSITE IS adequate

inanimate *ADJECTIVE*
Rocks and stones are inanimate.
▶ dead, inactive, lifeless
AN OPPOSITE IS animate

inappropriate *ADJECTIVE*
Her remarks were thought to be inappropriate.
▶ improper, out of place, tactless, unseemly, unsuitable, untimely, wrong
AN OPPOSITE IS appropriate

inattentive *ADJECTIVE*
She shouts at him if he's inattentive.
▶ absent-minded, careless, daydreaming, dreaming, heedless, lacking concentration, negligent, unobservant
AN OPPOSITE IS attentive

inaudible *ADJECTIVE*
Their cries for help were inaudible.
▶ faint, indistinct, low, muffled, muted, unclear, weak
AN OPPOSITE IS audible

incapable *ADJECTIVE*
He's incapable of doing things for himself.
▶ helpless, incompetent, ineffective, ineffectual, stupid, useless
All these synonyms are followed by *at* rather than *of*
AN OPPOSITE IS capable

incentive *NOUN*
They were offered incentives to work harder.
▶ encouragement, inducement, motivation, stimulus

incessant *ADJECTIVE*
They were tired of his incessant complaints.
▶ ceaseless, chronic, constant, continual, endless, eternal, everlasting, never-ending, non-stop, perpetual, persistent, relentless, unceasing, unending
AN OPPOSITE IS occasional

incident *NOUN*
He told us about an amusing incident that happened last week.
▶ event, happening, occasion, occurrence

incidental *ADJECTIVE*
Let's discuss the main point, not incidental details.
▶ inessential, minor, odd, secondary, subordinate, unimportant
AN OPPOSITE IS essential

inclination *NOUN*
He has an inclination to eat too much.
▶ bias, disposition, instinct, leaning, readiness, tendency, willingness

incline *VERB*
The yacht inclined to one side in the strong wind.
▶ bend, lean, slant, slope, tilt, tip
to be inclined *He's inclined to eat too much.*
▶ be disposed, have a habit (of), be liable, like, prefer, tend

incline *NOUN*
We had to push the car up the incline.
▸ gradient, hill, rise, slope

include *VERB*
This CD includes some of my favourite songs.
▸ combine, comprise, consist of, contain, incorporate, take in
AN OPPOSITE IS exclude

income *NOUN*
She gets a monthly income from her employer.
▸ pay, salary, wage
▹ Income that you get from savings is interest. Income that a retired person gets is a pension.
AN OPPOSITE IS expenditure

incompatible *ADJECTIVE*
They split up because they were incompatible.
▸ unsuited
AN OPPOSITE IS incompatible

incompetent *ADJECTIVE*
He was so incompetent that he had to do the work again.
▸ hopeless, ineffective, inefficient, unsatisfactory, unskilful, useless
AN OPPOSITE IS competent

incomplete *ADJECTIVE*
She was punished because her work was incomplete.
▸ imperfect, unfinished
AN OPPOSITE IS complete

incomprehensible *ADJECTIVE*
Can you explain this incomprehensible message?
▸ baffling, meaningless, obscure, perplexing, puzzling, unclear, unintelligible
AN OPPOSITE IS intelligible

incongruous *ADJECTIVE*
His business suit seemed incongruous at a pop concert.
▸ inappropriate, odd, out of place, unsuitable, unsuited
AN OPPOSITE IS appropriate

inconsiderate *ADJECTIVE*
It's inconsiderate to play the radio so loudly.
▸ insensitive, rude, selfish, tactless, thoughtless, uncaring, unfriendly, unhelpful, unkind, unthinking
AN OPPOSITE IS considerate

inconsistent *ADJECTIVE*
1 *His performance has been inconsistent this season.*
▸ changeable, erratic, fickle, unpredictable, unreliable, variable
2 *The stories of the two witnesses are inconsistent.*
▸ contradictory, different
AN OPPOSITE IS consistent

inconspicuous *ADJECTIVE*
The policeman thought he would be inconspicuous in plain clothes.
▸ camouflaged, hidden, insignificant, invisible, unnoticed
AN OPPOSITE IS conspicuous

inconvenience *NOUN*
She said she didn't want to cause any inconvenience.
▸ annoyance, bother, disadvantage, disruption, drawback, encumbrance, hindrance, irritation, nuisance, trouble

inconvenient *ADJECTIVE*
The visitors arrived at an inconvenient moment.
▸ annoying, awkward, difficult, embarrassing, irritating, tiresome, troublesome, unsuitable
AN OPPOSITE IS convenient

incorporate *VERB*
The CD incorporates some of his favourite songs.
▸ combine, comprise, consist of, contain, include, take in
AN OPPOSITE IS exclude

incorrect *ADJECTIVE*
Nine out of ten of his answers were incorrect.
▸ false, inaccurate, mistaken, wrong
AN OPPOSITE IS correct

increase *VERB*
1 *They plan to increase the size of the road to cope with more traffic.*
▸ add to, broaden, develop, enlarge, expand, make bigger, widen
2 *They increased the time allowed for the work.*
▸ extend, lengthen, prolong
3 *The police increased their efforts to find the murderer.*
▸ intensify, step up
4 *They've increased the bus fares.*
▸ put up, raise
5 *Can you increase the volume of the TV?*
▸ amplify, boost, turn up

A B C D E F G H I J K L M N O P Q R S T U V W X Y Z

6 *The number of cars on the roads continues to increase.*
▸ become bigger, build up, escalate, go up, grow, mount, multiply, rise, soar
FOR OPPOSITES SEE **decrease**

incredible *ADJECTIVE*
Do you expect us to believe that incredible story?
▸ amazing, extraordinary, fantastic, far-fetched, improbable, surprising, unbelievable, unconvincing, unlikely, untrustworthy
AN OPPOSITE IS credible

incredulous *ADJECTIVE*
She seemed incredulous when told she'd won.
▸ disbelieving, distrustful, sceptical, suspicious, uncertain, unconvinced

incurable *ADJECTIVE*
Sadly, he has an incurable illness.
▸ fatal, hopeless, untreatable

indecent *ADJECTIVE*
We were embarrassed by their indecent behaviour.
▸ coarse, crude, dirty, improper, obscene, offensive, rude, smutty, vulgar
AN OPPOSITE IS decent

indefinite *ADJECTIVE*
His answer was rather indefinite.
▸ ambiguous, general, uncertain, unclear, vague
AN OPPOSITE IS definite

independence *NOUN*
They value their independence.
▸ freedom, liberty

independent *ADJECTIVE*
1 *She led an independent life.*
▸ carefree, free
AN OPPOSITE IS dependent
2 *He wanted an independent opinion about the matter.*
▸ disinterested, impartial, neutral, objective, open-minded, unbiased, unprejudiced
AN OPPOSITE IS biased

indicate *VERB*
1 *She indicated where we could get a drink.*
▸ describe, make known, point out, show, specify
2 *A red light indicates danger.*
▸ communicate, convey, denote, express, mean, signal, signify, stand for, symbolize

indication *NOUN*
He gave no indication that he felt ill.
▸ clue, evidence, hint, inkling, sign, signal, symptom, token, warning

indicator *NOUN*
The indicators showed that the machine was working normally.
▸ clock, dial, display, gauge, instrument, meter, pointer, screen, sign, signal

indifferent *ADJECTIVE*
1 *They were indifferent to the result of the game.*
▸ apathetic, not bothered, unconcerned, unenthusiastic, uninterested
AN OPPOSITE IS enthusiastic
2 *The food was indifferent.*
▸ fair, mediocre, ordinary, unexciting
AN OPPOSITE IS excellent

indignant *ADJECTIVE*
We were indignant about the way they mistreated the animals.
▸ angry, annoyed, cross, exasperated, furious, infuriated, irritated, resentful, (*informal*) sore

indirect *ADJECTIVE*
1 *She was late because she came by an indirect route.*
▸ devious, meandering, rambling, roundabout, winding, zigzag
2 *He gave an indirect answer to the question.*
▸ disguised, euphemistic, implied, oblique
AN OPPOSITE IS direct

indispensable *ADJECTIVE*
He is an indispensable member of the team.
▸ crucial, essential, necessary, vital
AN OPPOSITE IS unnecessary

indistinct *ADJECTIVE*
1 *The photo was rather indistinct.*
▸ blurred, faint, fuzzy, hazy, indefinite, obscure, shadowy, unclear
AN OPPOSITE IS clear
2 *They could hear indistinct sounds of people talking.*
▸ deadened, incomprehensible, muffled, mumbled, unintelligible, vague
AN OPPOSITE IS distinct

indistinguishable *ADJECTIVE*
The two sisters look almost indistinguishable.
▸ identical, interchangeable, the same
AN OPPOSITE IS different

individual *ADJECTIVE*
Her singing has an individual style.
▸ characteristic, different, distinct, distinctive, personal, special, unique

individual *NOUN*
Who was that odd individual?
▸ character, man, person, woman

induce *VERB*
1 *She couldn't be induced to take part.*
▸ coax, encourage, persuade, prevail on, tempt
2 *Her illness was induced by stress.*
▸ bring on, cause, give rise to, lead to, produce, provoke

indulge *VERB*
They indulged their children too much.
▸ humour, pamper, spoil, treat
to indulge in *I indulged in a nice hot bath.*
▸ enjoy, wallow in

indulgent *ADJECTIVE*
They are very indulgent parents.
▸ easygoing, generous, lenient, liberal, permissive, tolerant
AN OPPOSITE IS strict

industrious *ADJECTIVE*
She's a very industrious worker.
▸ busy, conscientious, enterprising, hard-working, keen, persistent, productive, tireless, zealous
AN OPPOSITE IS lazy

industry *NOUN*
1 *Many people in the town work in industry.*
▸ business, commerce, manufacturing, trade
2 *He admired her for her industry.*
▸ application, commitment, determination, effort, energy, hard work, industriousness, keenness, perseverance, persistence, zeal

ineffective *ADJECTIVE*
1 *Sadly, the medicine was ineffective.*
▸ fruitless, futile, unproductive, unsuccessful, useless, vain, worthless
AN OPPOSITE IS effective
2 *He was an ineffective leader.*
▸ SEE **ineffectual**

ineffectual *ADJECTIVE*
He was an ineffectual captain of the team.
▸ feeble, inadequate, incompetent, ineffective, inefficient, unconvincing, unsuccessful, weak
AN OPPOSITE IS competent

inefficient *ADJECTIVE*
1 *He lost his job for being inefficient.*
▸ ineffective, slow, unproductive, useless
2 *The car was inefficient in its use of fuel.*
▸ extravagant, prodigal, uneconomical, wasteful
AN OPPOSITE IS efficient

inert *ADJECTIVE*
He lay inert on the pavement.
▸ immobile, lifeless, motionless, still

inertia *NOUN*
It was sheer inertia that stopped her from doing anything.
▸ apathy, idleness, inactivity, laziness
AN OPPOSITE IS liveliness

inevitable *ADJECTIVE*
When two men were sent off, it was inevitable that they would lose the game.
▸ certain, sure, unavoidable

inexhaustible *ADJECTIVE*
The supply of fossil fuels is not inexhaustible.
▸ endless, infinite, limitless, never-ending, unlimited

inexpensive *ADJECTIVE*
He bought some inexpensive clothes in the market.
▸ cheap, cut-price, low-priced, reasonable
AN OPPOSITE IS expensive

inexplicable *ADJECTIVE*
The origins of the universe are an inexplicable mystery.
▸ baffling, bewildering, incomprehensible, insoluble, mysterious, mystifying, puzzling, unsolvable
AN OPPOSITE IS understandable

infallible *ADJECTIVE*
She has an infallible way of making me laugh.
▸ certain, dependable, foolproof, never-failing, perfect, reliable, sound, sure, trustworthy, unbeatable
AN OPPOSITE IS unreliable

infamous *ADJECTIVE*
Dick Turpin was an infamous highwayman.
▸ notorious, villainous, wicked

infant *NOUN*
He was a very demanding infant.
▸ baby, small child, toddler

infantile *ADJECTIVE*
(*uncomplimentary*) *She said their behaviour had been infantile.*
▸ babyish, childish, immature, silly
AN OPPOSITE IS mature

infect *VERB*
They were afraid that chemicals had infected the water supply.
▸ contaminate, defile, poison, pollute, spoil

infected *ADJECTIVE*
The nurse treated the infected wound with antiseptic.
▸ inflamed, poisoned, septic

infection *NOUN*
The infection spread rapidly.
▸ blight, contagion, contamination, epidemic, virus
FOR VARIOUS ILLNESSES SEE **illness**

infectious *ADJECTIVE*
The flu is very infectious.
▸ catching, contagious, transmittable

infer *VERB*
Note: *infer* and *imply* are not synonyms
He inferred from her silence that she agreed.
▸ assume, conclude, deduce, gather, guess, work out

inferior *ADJECTIVE*
1 *The clothes were of inferior quality.*
▸ bad, cheap, indifferent, mediocre, poor, shoddy, (*informal*) tacky, trashy
2 *The officer can give orders to everyone of inferior rank.*
▸ junior, lesser, lower, subordinate
AN OPPOSITE IS superior

infested *ADJECTIVE*
The garden shed was infested with mice.
▸ alive, crawling, overrun, plagued, swarming, teeming

infiltrate *VERB*
Spies infiltrated the enemy's camp.
▸ enter secretly, penetrate

infinite *ADJECTIVE*
There's an infinite number of stars in the sky.
▸ countless, endless, inexhaustible, innumerable, limitless, never-ending, uncountable, unending, unlimited, untold
AN OPPOSITE IS finite

infirm *ADJECTIVE*
Infirm people need a lot of help.
▸ elderly, feeble, frail, ill, old, poorly, weak
▹ People who have to stay in bed are **bedridden**.
AN OPPOSITE IS healthy

inflame *VERB*
The sight of the badly treated animals inflamed our anger.
▸ arouse, kindle, provoke, rouse, stimulate
AN OPPOSITE IS soothe

inflamed *ADJECTIVE*
The nurse put antiseptic on the inflamed wound.
▸ infected, poisoned, red, septic

inflammation *NOUN*
This ointment will soothe the inflammation.
▸ infection, redness, soreness

inflate *VERB*
1 *The tyres need to be inflated.*
▸ blow up, pump up
2 *Don't inflate the importance of the experiment.*
▸ exaggerate, make too much of

inflexible *ADJECTIVE*
1 *The material becomes inflexible as it dries.*
▸ firm, hard, rigid, solid, stiff, unbending, unyielding
2 *The rules of the game are inflexible.*
▸ invariable, unalterable
3 *This referee is inflexible about applying the rules.*
▸ obstinate, resolute, strict, stubborn, uncompromising
AN OPPOSITE IS flexible

inflict *VERB*
I hate seeing someone inflict pain on an animal.
▸ administer, apply, deal out, impose

influence *NOUN*
The influence of parents is important for children.
▸ authority, control, dominance, effect, guidance, impact, power

influence *VERB*
The money he was offered influenced his decision.
▸ affect, change, control, direct, guide, have an effect on, modify, motivate

influential *ADJECTIVE*
Members of the government are influential people.
▸ important, leading, powerful, significant
AN OPPOSITE IS unimportant

inform *VERB*
I'll inform you if I can't come.
▸ advise, let you know, notify, tell
to inform against *The spy informed against his colleague.*
▸ accuse, betray, denounce, give information about, report, (*informal*) sneak on, (*slang*) split on, (*informal*) tell tales about

informal *ADJECTIVE*
1 *They were surprised how informal she was.*
▸ approachable, easygoing, familiar, free and easy, friendly, homely, natural, ordinary, relaxed
2 *I can wear informal clothes to the party.*
▸ casual, comfortable, everyday
3 *He talked to us in a quite informal way.*
▸ chatty, colloquial, personal, slangy
AN OPPOSITE IS formal

information *NOUN*
VARIOUS KINDS OF INFORMATION
data, evidence, facts, intelligence, knowledge, propaganda, public records, statistics
VARIOUS WAYS INFORMATION IS PASSED ON
advertisements, announcements, a brief, a bulletin, communications, gossip, instructions, the Internet, letters, the media, messages, the news, notices, reports, statements, teaching
VARIOUS WAYS INFORMATION CAN BE STORED
database, documents, dossier, file

informative *ADJECTIVE*
The travel agent gave us an informative booklet about holidays abroad.
▸ helpful, illuminating, instructive, revealing, useful
AN OPPOSITE IS unhelpful

informer *NOUN*
The informer gave the police some vital information.
▸ informant, spy, telltale

infrequent *ADJECTIVE*
This bird is an infrequent visitor to this area.
▸ irregular, occasional, rare, uncommon, unusual
AN OPPOSITE IS frequent

infuriate *VERB*
He was infuriated by their bad behaviour.
▸ anger, enrage, exasperate, incense, provoke

ingenious *ADJECTIVE*
It seemed like an ingenious plan.
▸ artful, brilliant, clever, crafty, cunning, imaginative, inspired, inventive, original, shrewd, skilful, subtle

inhabit *VERB*
People inhabited the caves thousands of years ago.
▸ dwell in, live in, make a home in, occupy, reside in, settle in, set up home in

inhabitant *NOUN*
The inhabitants of the remote island had few visitors.
▸ citizen, occupant, occupier, resident
▹ The inhabitants of a town, etc., are the town's population.

inhabited *ADJECTIVE*
Is the castle inhabited?
▸ lived-in, occupied
AN OPPOSITE IS uninhabited

inherent *ADJECTIVE*
The instinct to survive is inherent in all animals.
▸ fundamental, hereditary, ingrained, inherited, natural

inheritance *NOUN*
She was left a small inheritance in her uncle's will.
▸ bequest, legacy

inherited *ADJECTIVE*
Eye colour is an inherited characteristic.
▸ hereditary, passed down

A B C D E F G H I J K L M N O P Q R S T U V W X Y Z

inhibited *ADJECTIVE*
He was too inhibited to join the fun.
▸ bashful, prim and proper, reserved, self-conscious, shy, tense, (*informal*) uptight
AN OPPOSITE IS uninhibited

inhospitable *ADJECTIVE*
1 *They were so inhospitable that he didn't even get a cup of tea.*
▸ cool, hostile, unfriendly, unsociable, unwelcoming
AN OPPOSITE IS hospitable
2 *The explorers were glad to leave those inhospitable mountains.*
▸ comfortless, desolate, forbidding

inhuman *ADJECTIVE*
She thought it was inhuman to hunt animals.
▸ barbaric, barbarous, bloodthirsty, cruel, diabolical, fiendish, heartless, merciless, pitiless, ruthless, savage
AN OPPOSITE IS humane

initial *ADJECTIVE*
The initial work on the bypass starts next week.
▸ earliest, first, introductory, opening, preliminary
AN OPPOSITE IS final

initiate *VERB*
We initiated negotiations to buy a new house.
▸ begin, commence, enter into, launch, open, start
AN OPPOSITE IS finish

initiative *NOUN*
She was given the job because she showed initiative.
▸ ambition, drive, enterprise, leadership, originality

injection *NOUN*
The nurse gave me an injection.
▸ inoculation, (*informal*) jab, vaccination

injure *VERB*
Was anyone injured in the accident?
▸ harm, hurt, wound
FOR VARIOUS KINDS OF INJURY SEE **wound** *VERB*

injustice *NOUN*
The injustice of the decision made them angry.
▸ bias, dishonesty, favouritism, illegality, prejudice, unfairness, unlawfulness
AN OPPOSITE IS justice

inner *ADJECTIVE*
1 *The inner rooms of the palace are not open to visitors.*
▸ central, inside, interior, internal, middle
2 *She tried to hide her inner feelings.*
▸ concealed, hidden, innermost, intimate, inward, personal, private, secret
AN OPPOSITE IS outer

innocent *ADJECTIVE*
1 *The jury found him innocent.*
▸ blameless, free from blame, guiltless
AN OPPOSITE IS guilty
2 *Sleeping babies look so innocent.*
▸ angelic, faultless, harmless, inexperienced, naïve, pure, simple, sinless, virtuous
AN OPPOSITE IS wicked

innovation *NOUN*
The club introduced some innovations this year.
▸ change, new feature, reform

innovator *NOUN*
George Stephenson was an important innovator in the history of railways.
▸ discoverer, experimenter, inventor, pioneer, reformer

innumerable *ADJECTIVE*
There are innumerable stars in the sky.
▸ countless, numberless, uncountable, untold

inquest *NOUN*
They held an inquest to determine how she died.
▸ hearing, inquiry, investigation

inquire *VERB*
If you have any problems, please inquire at the desk.
▸ ask, enquire, seek help

inquiry *NOUN*
There will be an inquiry into how the accident happened.
▸ enquiry, inquest, investigation

inquisitive *ADJECTIVE*
Who's that inquisitive man asking all those questions?
▸ curious, inquiring, interfering, meddling, nosy, prying, snooping
▹ An inquisitive person is a busybody.

insane *ADJECTIVE*
Although they are often used as a joke, synonyms of *insane* are usually insulting, and show that the person using the word does not understand mental illnesses
▸ crazy, daft, mad, (*informal*) out of your mind, unbalanced, unhinged

inscribe *VERB*
He read the words inscribed on the tomb.
▸ engrave, set down, write

inscription *NOUN*
He read the inscription on the tomb.
▸ engraving, wording, writing

insect *NOUN*
VARIOUS INSECTS
ant, aphid, bee, beetle, blackbeetle, blackfly, bluebottle, bumble-bee, butterfly, cicada, cockroach, cricket, daddy-long-legs, damselfly, dragonfly, earwig, firefly, fly, glow-worm, gnat, grasshopper, hornet, ladybird, locust, mantis, mayfly, midge, mosquito, moth, termite, tsetse fly, wasp, weevil
OTHER FORMS OF AN INSECT
caterpillar, chrysalis, grub, larva, maggot, pupa
CRAWLING CREATURES WHICH PEOPLE OFTEN CALL INSECTS WHICH STRICTLY SPEAKING ARE NOT INSECTS
arachnid, centipede, earthworm, mite, slug, spider, woodlouse, worm

insecure *ADJECTIVE*
1 *Be careful — that scaffolding is insecure.*
▸ dangerous, loose, precarious, shaky, unsafe, unstable, unsteady, wobbly
2 *She felt insecure in her new job.*
▸ anxious, apprehensive, nervous, uncertain, unconfident, uneasy
AN OPPOSITE IS secure

insensitive *ADJECTIVE*
Her remarks were a bit insensitive.
▸ callous, cruel, tactless, thoughtless, uncaring, unfeeling, unsympathetic
AN OPPOSITE IS sensitive

insert *VERB*
He inserted the key into the lock.
▸ drive in, introduce, push in, put in, tuck in

inside *ADJECTIVE*
We painted the inside walls of the hut with emulsion.
▸ indoor, inner, interior, internal
AN OPPOSITE IS outside

inside *NOUN*
The inside of the apple was rotten.
▸ centre, core, heart, interior, middle
AN OPPOSITE IS outside

insignificant *ADJECTIVE*
There was an insignificant amount of rainfall last month.
▸ inconsiderable, negligible, small, trivial, unimportant, unimpressive, valueless, worthless
AN OPPOSITE IS significant

insincere *ADJECTIVE*
He paid her some rather insincere compliments.
▸ deceitful, deceptive, dishonest, false, flattering, hypocritical, lying, pretended, (*informal*) two-faced
AN OPPOSITE IS sincere

insist *VERB*
He insisted that he was innocent.
▸ assert, declare, emphasize, maintain, state, stress, swear, vow
to insist on *She insists on obedience.*
▸ demand, expect, require

insistent *ADJECTIVE*
In the end he gave in to their insistent requests.
▸ assertive, emphatic, forceful, persistent, relentless, repeated, unrelenting, urgent

insolence *NOUN*
He was punished for his insolence.
▸ arrogance, boldness, cheek, disrespect, forwardness, impertinence, impudence, rudeness, (*informal*) sauce
AN OPPOSITE IS politeness

insolent *ADJECTIVE*
Her insolent stare annoyed him.
▸ arrogant, bold, brazen, (*informal*) cheeky, disrespectful, forward, impertinent, impolite, impudent, insulting, rude, saucy, shameless, sneering
AN OPPOSITE IS polite

insoluble *ADJECTIVE*
The problem seemed insoluble.
▸ baffling, incomprehensible, inexplicable, mysterious, mystifying, puzzling, unanswerable, unsolvable
AN OPPOSITE IS soluble

inspect *VERB*
The builders inspected the damage done by the storm.
▸ check, examine, investigate, scrutinize, study, survey

inspection *NOUN*
They had a school inspection last term.
▸ check, check-up, examination, investigation, review, scrutiny, survey

inspector *NOUN*
The inspector checked the standard of work.
▸ examiner, investigator, official, tester

inspiration *NOUN*
1 *What was the inspiration behind your story?*
▸ impulse, motivation, stimulus
2 *I had a sudden inspiration.*
▸ idea, thought

inspire *VERB*
The crowd inspired them to play well.
▸ animate, arouse, egg on, encourage, motivate, prompt, stimulate

install *VERB*
They installed the central heating boiler in the bathroom.
▸ establish, fix, place, position, put in, set up
AN OPPOSITE IS remove

instalment *NOUN*
Did you see the first instalment of the new serial?
▸ episode, part

instance *NOUN*
Give me an instance of what you mean.
▸ case, example, illustration, sample

instant *ADJECTIVE*
Gardeners don't expect instant results.
▸ direct, fast, immediate, instantaneous, prompt, quick, rapid, snappy, speedy, swift

instant *NOUN*
The shooting star was gone in an instant.
▸ flash, moment, second, split second

instantaneous *ADJECTIVE*
SEE **instant** *ADJECTIVE*

instinct *NOUN*
1 *Animals have an instinct to look after their young.*
▸ impulse, inclination, tendency, urge
2 *Some instinct told him that they would come today.*
▸ feeling, hunch, intuition

instinctive *ADJECTIVE*
1 *It's instinctive for a mother to protect her baby.*
▸ inherent, intuitive, natural
2 *Blinking in bright light is an instinctive reaction.*
▸ automatic, impulsive, involuntary, reflex, spontaneous, unconscious, unthinking
AN OPPOSITE IS deliberate

institute *VERB*
They've instituted a one-way system in town.
▸ create, establish, initiate, introduce, launch, set up, start

institution *NOUN*
1 *It was an institution for blind people.*
▸ academy, college, foundation, home, hospital, institute, organization, school, society
2 *Sunday dinner is a regular institution in their house.*
▸ convention, custom, habit, ritual, routine, tradition

instruct *VERB*
1 *The teacher instructed them in how to use the new computer.*
▸ coach, teach, train
2 *He instructed us to wait.*
▸ command, order, tell

instructive *ADJECTIVE*
It was instructive watching the professional players training.
▸ educational, helpful, illuminating, informative, revealing
AN OPPOSITE IS unhelpful

instructor *NOUN*
The swimming instructor taught them life-saving.
▸ coach, teacher, trainer

instrument *NOUN*
The surgeon uses instruments specially designed for doing operations.
▸ appliance, contraption, device, gadget, implement, tool, utensil
FOR MUSICAL INSTRUMENTS SEE **music**

instrumental *ADJECTIVE*
She was instrumental in getting him a job.
▶ active, helpful, influential, useful

insufficient *ADJECTIVE*
Many plants died because there was insufficient rain.
▶ inadequate, meagre, poor, scanty, scarce, unsatisfactory
AN OPPOSITE IS enough or excessive

insulate *VERB*
He insulated the water pipes to prevent loss of heat.
▶ cover, enclose, lag, protect, surround, wrap up

insult *VERB*
It was wrong to insult him in public.
▶ abuse, call you names, mock, sneer at, snub, taunt
AN OPPOSITE IS compliment

insult *NOUN*
She was offended by his insults.
▶ abuse, cheek, impudence, insulting behaviour, rudeness, slur, snub, taunt
AN OPPOSITE IS compliment

insulting *ADJECTIVE*
She was infuriated by his insulting remarks.
▶ abusive, contemptuous, impolite, insolent, mocking, offensive, rude, scornful
AN OPPOSITE IS complimentary

insurance *NOUN*
Have you got insurance against loss or accident?
▶ cover, protection
▷ The insurance document is the policy.

intact *ADJECTIVE*
The vase remained intact despite being dropped.
▶ complete, (*informal*) in one piece, perfect, unbroken, undamaged, unharmed

integral *ADJECTIVE*
1 *The boiler is an integral part of the heating system.*
▶ essential, indispensable, necessary
2 *The equipment is supplied as an integral unit.*
▶ combined, complete, full, integrated, whole

integrate *VERB*
They decided to integrate the two groups.
▶ amalgamate, bring together, combine, harmonize, join, merge, put together, unify, unite
AN OPPOSITE IS separate *VERB*

integrity *NOUN*
You can trust her integrity.
▶ fidelity, goodness, honesty, honour, loyalty, reliability, sincerity, trustworthiness, virtue
AN OPPOSITE IS dishonesty

intellect *NOUN*
SEE **intelligence**

intellectual *ADJECTIVE*
1 *It was an intellectual book about philosophy.*
▶ demanding, difficult, educational, improving
2 *The professor is very intellectual.*
▶ academic, brainy, clever, cultured, intelligent, scholarly, studious, thoughtful

intelligence *NOUN*
1 *Use your intelligence!*
▶ ability, brains, cleverness, genius, insight, intellect, judgement, mind, reason, sense, understanding, wisdom, wit
2 *They received intelligence about the enemy's plans.*
▶ data, facts, information, knowledge, news, reports, warnings

intelligent *ADJECTIVE*
The professor must be a very intelligent person.
▶ able, brainy, bright, brilliant, clever, intellectual, perceptive, quick, sharp, shrewd, smart, wise
AN OPPOSITE IS stupid

intelligible *ADJECTIVE*
The message was not very intelligible.
▶ clear, comprehensible, legible, lucid, meaningful, plain, straightforward, unambiguous, understandable
AN OPPOSITE IS incomprehensible

intend *VERB*
1 *What do you intend to do?*
▶ aim, have in mind, mean, plan, plot, propose
2 *The surprise was intended to please you.*
▶ design, set up

intense *ADJECTIVE*
1 *She suffered the intense pain bravely.*
▶ acute, agonizing, extreme, great, severe, sharp, strong, violent
AN OPPOSITE IS slight
2 *The contest aroused intense feelings.*
▶ burning, deep, emotional, fanatical, passionate, powerful, profound
AN OPPOSITE IS mild

intensify *VERB*
1 *They intensified their attack in the second half of the game.*
▸ boost, make greater, reinforce, sharpen, step up, strengthen
2 *The excitement intensified.*
▸ become greater, build up, escalate, heighten, increase
AN OPPOSITE IS reduce

intensive *ADJECTIVE*
They made an intensive search.
▸ concentrated, detailed, thorough
AN OPPOSITE IS superficial

intent *ADJECTIVE*
She had an intent look on her face.
▸ absorbed, concentrating, eager, engrossed, interested, preoccupied

intention *NOUN*
It's his intention to work with computers.
▸ aim, ambition, goal, intent, objective, plan, target

intentional *ADJECTIVE*
He was penalized for an intentional foul.
▸ calculated, conscious, deliberate, intended, planned, wilful
AN OPPOSITE IS accidental

intercept *VERB*
He managed to intercept the pass.
▸ catch, check, cut off, deflect, head off, stop

interest *VERB*
Astronomy interests a lot of people.
▸ absorb, appeal to, attract, capture the imagination of, excite, fascinate, intrigue, stimulate
AN OPPOSITE IS bore

interest *NOUN*
1 *Did he show any interest?*
▸ attention, concern, curiosity, involvement
2 *The information was of no interest to anyone.*
▸ consequence, importance, significance, value
3 *He asked him about his interests.*
▸ activity, diversion, hobby, pastime, pursuit

interesting *ADJECTIVE*
They listened intently to the interesting story.
▸ absorbing, appealing, curious, engrossing, entertaining, exciting, fascinating, intriguing, riveting, stimulating
AN OPPOSITE IS boring

interfere *VERB*
Don't interfere in other people's affairs.
▸ be a busybody, butt in, interrupt, intervene, intrude, meddle, (*informal*) poke your nose in, pry, snoop
to interfere with *The bad weather interfered with the plans for sports day.*
▸ get in the way of, hamper, hinder, obstruct

interior *ADJECTIVE, NOUN*
SEE **inside** *ADJECTIVE, NOUN*

intermediate *ADJECTIVE*
She's reached an intermediate stage in her studies, but she's still got a long way to go.
▸ half-way, middle, midway, transitional

intermittent *ADJECTIVE*
The TV has an intermittent fault.
▸ irregular, occasional, recurrent
AN OPPOSITE IS continual

internal *ADJECTIVE*
She didn't know much about the internal parts of computers.
▸ inner, inside, interior
AN OPPOSITE IS external

international *ADJECTIVE*
Interpol is an international police organization.
▸ global, inter-continental, worldwide

interpret *VERB*
Can you interpret this old writing?
▸ clarify, decipher, decode, explain, make clear, make sense of, paraphrase, translate, understand

interrogate *VERB*
The police interrogated the suspect for several hours.
▸ cross-examine, examine, grill, interview, question

interrupt *VERB*
1 *Please don't interrupt while I am speaking.*
▸ barge in, break in, butt in, cut in, intervene
2 *A fire alarm interrupted work.*
▸ cut short, disrupt, halt, hold up, stop, suspend

3 *The new houses interrupt their view.*
▸ get in the way of, interfere with, obstruct, spoil

interruption *NOUN*
They worked for an hour without any interruption.
▸ break, check, disruption, gap, halt, pause, stop, suspension

intersection *NOUN*
Drivers need to take special care at the intersection.
▸ crossroads, interchange, junction

interval *NOUN*
1 *There was an interval of two hours before they came back.*
▸ break, delay, lapse, lull, pause, wait
▹ Another word for an interval in a play or film is **interlude** or **intermission**. An interval in a meeting is a **recess**. An interval when you take a rest is a **breather** or **breathing space**.
2 *There were signs at regular intervals along the road.*
▸ distance, gap, space

intervene *VERB*
1 *Many events intervened before he saw her again.*
▸ come between, happen, occur
2 *He intervened to stop the fight.*
▸ butt in, interfere, interrupt, (*informal*) step in

interview *VERB*
If you witnessed the accident, the police will want to interview you.
▸ examine, interrogate, question, sound you out

intimate *ADJECTIVE*
1 *They have been intimate friends for many years.*
▸ affectionate, close, familiar, friendly, loving
AN OPPOSITE IS impersonal
2 *He had no right to ask for intimate details of her life.*
▸ confidential, personal, private, secret

intimidate *VERB*
They attempted to intimidate witnesses in the trial.
▸ bully, frighten, menace, persecute, scare, terrify, terrorize, threaten

intolerable *ADJECTIVE*
The doctor will give you an injection if the pain becomes intolerable.
▸ impossible to bear, unacceptable, unbearable, unendurable
AN OPPOSITE IS tolerable

intolerant *ADJECTIVE*
Don't be so intolerant — try to understand their point of view.
▸ biased, chauvinistic, narrow-minded, prejudiced, racialist, racist, sexist
AN OPPOSITE IS tolerant

intoxicated *ADJECTIVE*
He couldn't drive because he was intoxicated.
▸ drunk, (*informal*) tight
AN OPPOSITE IS sober

intoxicating *ADJECTIVE*
1 *Children are not allowed to buy intoxicating drinks.*
▸ alcoholic, strong
2 *Reaching the top of the mountain was an intoxicating experience.*
▸ exciting, stimulating

intricate *ADJECTIVE*
The clock has an intricate mechanism.
▸ complex, complicated, elaborate, involved, sophisticated
AN OPPOSITE IS simple

intrigue *VERB*
1 *Science intrigues me.*
▸ appeal to, attract, fascinate, interest
2 *Guy Fawkes intrigued against Parliament.*
▸ conspire, plot, scheme

introduce *VERB*
1 *Let me introduce you to my friend.*
▸ make known, present
2 *It was his job to introduce the various acts in the concert.*
▸ announce, give an introduction to, lead into
3 *They introduced a new bus service.*
▸ begin, bring in, commence, create, establish, initiate, set up, start

introduction *NOUN*
▹ Something which happens as an introduction to a bigger event is a **prelude**. An introduction to a book is a **preface**. An introduction to a play is a **prologue**. A piece played as an introduction to a concert or opera is an **overture**.

introductory *ADJECTIVE*
The chairman made some introductory remarks.
▸ initial, opening, preliminary
AN OPPOSITE IS final

intrude *VERB*
This is a private conversation — please don't intrude!
▸ break in, butt in, interfere, intervene, push in

intruder *NOUN*
They called the police when they saw an intruder in the garden.
▸ burglar, prowler, trespasser

intuition *NOUN*
I had an intuition that you'd come today.
▸ feeling, hunch, instinct

invade *VERB*
The country has been invaded many times in its history.
▸ attack, enter, march into, occupy, raid

invalid *ADJECTIVE*
1 *The passport is invalid because the photograph has come off.*
▸ out-of-date, unacceptable, unusable, worthless
2 *The arguments that he used were invalid.*
▸ fallacious, false, illogical, irrational, unconvincing
AN OPPOSITE IS valid

invaluable *ADJECTIVE*
Your help was invaluable.
▸ precious, priceless, useful, valuable
AN OPPOSITE IS worthless

invariable *ADJECTIVE*
It's an invariable rule that we must wash our hands before meals.
▸ constant, inflexible, unalterable, unchangeable
AN OPPOSITE IS variable

invasion *NOUN*
Fortunately, the expected invasion never happened.
▸ attack, raid

invent *VERB*
Who invented computers?
▸ conceive, create, design, devise, originate, think up

invention *NOUN*
1 *This system is his own invention.*
▸ (*informal*) brainchild, creation, design, discovery
2 *She made a lot of money from her new invention.*
▸ contraption, device
3 *Her story was pure invention.*
▸ deceit, fantasy, fiction, lies

inventive *ADJECTIVE*
She's full of inventive ideas.
▸ creative, enterprising, imaginative, ingenious, inspired, original

inventor *NOUN*
The device was sold to a big company by its inventor.
▸ creator, designer, discoverer, originator

investigate *VERB*
They were investigating the possibility of establishing a new business.
▸ consider, examine, explore, follow up, gather evidence about, (*informal*) go into, inquire into, look into, research, scrutinize, study

investigation *NOUN*
An investigation showed how the accident happened.
▸ enquiry, examination, inquiry, inspection, research, study, survey

invigorating *ADJECTIVE*
He took an invigorating shower.
▸ healthy, refreshing, stimulating, reviving
AN OPPOSITE IS tiring

invisible *ADJECTIVE*
They planted trees so that the sewage works will be invisible from the road.
▸ camouflaged, concealed, covered, disguised, hidden, inconspicuous, obscured, out of sight, undetectable, unnoticeable, unnoticed, unseen
AN OPPOSITE IS visible

invite *VERB*
He invited them to join in.
▸ ask, encourage, request, urge

inviting *ADJECTIVE*
An inviting smell came from the kitchen.
▸ appealing, attractive, encouraging, irresistible, tantalizing, tempting
AN OPPOSITE IS repulsive

involuntary *ADJECTIVE*
Blinking is an involuntary movement.
▸ impulsive, instinctive, reflex, spontaneous, unconscious, unthinking
AN OPPOSITE IS deliberate

involve *VERB*
1 *What does the job involve?*
▸ comprise, contain, incorporate, take in
2 *Protecting the environment involves us all.*
▸ affect, concern, interest

involved *ADJECTIVE*
1 *The problem was too involved for him.*
▸ complex, complicated, confusing, difficult, elaborate, intricate
AN OPPOSITE IS simple
2 *Once she started the work, she got really involved.*
▸ absorbed, active, busy, committed, engrossed, enthusiastic, interested, keen, preoccupied
AN OPPOSITE IS uninterested

irrational *ADJECTIVE*
They couldn't understand his irrational behaviour.
▸ absurd, crazy, illogical, mad, nonsensical, senseless, silly, unreasonable
AN OPPOSITE IS rational

irregular *ADJECTIVE*
1 *The buses run at irregular times.*
▸ erratic, haphazard, intermittent, occasional, odd, random, unpredictable, unreliable, varying
AN OPPOSITE IS regular
2 *His behaviour is highly irregular.*
▸ abnormal, exceptional, illegal, improper, unconventional, unusual
AN OPPOSITE IS normal

irrelevant *ADJECTIVE*
She left out the irrelevant details.
▸ inappropriate, inessential, meaningless, pointless, unnecessary
AN OPPOSITE IS relevant

irresistible *ADJECTIVE*
On such a hot day, ice cream was an irresistible temptation!
▸ overpowering, overwhelming, persuasive, powerful, unavoidable

irresponsible *ADJECTIVE*
It's irresponsible to drive too fast.
▸ immoral, inconsiderate, negligent, reckless, selfish, thoughtless, uncaring, untrustworthy
AN OPPOSITE IS responsible

irreverent *ADJECTIVE*
They were reprimanded for their irreverent behaviour in church.
▸ blasphemous, disrespectful, rude
AN OPPOSITE IS reverent

irritable *ADJECTIVE*
She's in an irritable mood!
▸ angry, bad-tempered, grumpy, ill-tempered, impatient, short-tempered, touchy

irritate *VERB*
She was irritated by their attitude.
▸ anger, annoy, bother, exasperate, provoke, vex

island *NOUN*
▷ A small island is an **islet**. A coral island is an **atoll**. A group of islands is an **archipelago**.

isolate *VERB*
1 *The police isolated the troublemakers.*
▸ keep apart, segregate, separate, single out
2 *The hospital isolates infectious patients.*
▸ place in quarantine, set apart

isolated *ADJECTIVE*
1 *The isolated farm had few visitors.*
▸ desolate, inaccessible, lonely, outlying, out-of-the-way, remote, unfrequented
AN OPPOSITE IS accessible
2 *There had been a few isolated cases of cheating.*
▸ abnormal, exceptional, single, uncommon, unique, unusual
AN OPPOSITE IS common

issue *VERB*
1 *They issued blankets to the refugees.*
▸ distribute, give out, supply
2 *They have issued a new set of stamps.*
▸ bring out, circulate, print, produce, publish, put out, release
3 *Smoke issued from the chimney.*
▸ appear, come out, emerge, erupt, flow out, gush

A B C D E F G H I J K L M N O P Q R S T U V W X Y Z

issue *NOUN*
1 *Do they deal with the issue of passports here?*
▸ distribution, issuing
2 *The new issue of the magazine comes out this week.*
▸ copy, edition, number, publication
3 *They print stories about local issues in the magazine.*
▸ affair, controversy, dispute, matter, problem, question, subject, topic
4 *They were eager to know the issue of the election.*
▸ consequence, effect, outcome, result, upshot

itch *NOUN*
1 *She had an itch in her foot.*
▸ irritation, tickle, tingling
2 *He had an itch to travel.*
▸ ache, desire, impulse, longing, restlessness, urge, wish, yearning

item *NOUN*
1 *There were some interesting items in the sale.*
▸ article, bit, object, thing
2 *Did you read this item in the paper?*
▸ article, feature, piece, report

Jj

jab *VERB*
She jabbed me in the ribs.
▸ elbow, nudge, poke, prod, stab, thrust

jacket *NOUN*
1 *He took off his jacket and hung it in the wardrobe.*
▸ SEE **coat** *NOUN*
2 *The hot water tank has an insulating jacket.*
▸ cover, covering, sheath, wrapper, wrapping

jaded *ADJECTIVE*
I felt tired and jaded at the end of a long day.
▸ bored, (*informal*) fed up, listless, weary
AN OPPOSITE IS lively

jagged *ADJECTIVE*
The knife had a jagged edge.
▸ rough, uneven, zigzag
AN OPPOSITE IS smooth

jail *NOUN*
SEE **prison**

jam *NOUN*
1 *She was delayed in a jam on the motorway.*
▸ blockage, bottleneck, hold-up, tailback, traffic jam
2 (*informal*) *I'm in a bit of a jam.*
▸ difficulty, dilemma, (*informal*) tight corner

jam *VERB*
1 *The door was jammed open.*
▸ prop, stick, wedge
2 *Cars jammed the street.*
▸ block, (*informal*) bung up, fill, obstruct
3 *I jammed my kit into a holdall.*
▸ cram, crowd, crush, pack, ram, squash, squeeze, stuff

jangle *VERB*
A bell jangled loudly.
▸ clang, clink, jingle, ring, tinkle

jar *NOUN*
VARIOUS KINDS OF JAR
carafe, flagon, glass, jam jar, jug, mug, pitcher, pot, urn
FOR OTHER CONTAINERS SEE **container**

jar *VERB*
He jarred his back badly when he fell.
▸ jerk, jolt, shake, shock

jarring *ADJECTIVE*
Her voice was jarring.
▸ disagreeable, discordant, grating, grinding, harsh, unpleasant

jaunt *NOUN*
They're planning a jaunt to Paris.
▸ excursion, expedition, outing, trip

jaunty *ADJECTIVE*
He whistled a jaunty tune.
▸ bright, carefree, cheerful, lively, sprightly
AN OPPOSITE IS gloomy

jazzy *ADJECTIVE*
The band were playing some jazzy music.
▸ lively, rhythmic, spirited, syncopated

jealous *ADJECTIVE*
He's jealous because I won.
▸ bitter, envious, grudging, resentful

jeer *VERB*
to jeer at *Some of the younger men jeered at him.*
▸ barrack, boo, deride, hiss, laugh at, make fun of, mock, ridicule, scoff at, sneer at, taunt
AN OPPOSITE IS cheer

jerk *VERB*
He jerked the fishing rod out of the water.
▸ pluck, pull, tug, twitch, wrench, yank

jerky *ADJECTIVE*
The coach drew to a jerky halt.
▸ bouncy, bumpy, jolting, jumpy, shaky, uneven
AN OPPOSITE IS steady

jest *NOUN, VERB*
SEE **joke** *NOUN, VERB*

jester *NOUN*
The king's jester kept the court amused.
▸ clown, entertainer, fool, joker

jet *NOUN*
A jet of water shot high in the air.
▸ fountain, gush, rush, spout, spurt, squirt, stream

jetty *NOUN*
A boat tied up at the jetty.
▸ landing stage, pier, quay

jewel, jewellery *NOUNS*
VARIOUS ITEMS OF JEWELLERY
anklet, bangle, beads, bracelet, brooch, chain, charm, choker, clasp, cufflinks, earring, engagement ring, locket, necklace, pendant, pin, ring, signet ring, tiepin, wedding ring
VARIOUS STONES OR GEMS USED TO MAKE JEWELLERY
agate, amber, amethyst, aquamarine, beryl, carnelian or cornelian, coral, diamond, emerald, garnet, jade, jasper, jet, lapis lazuli, onyx, opal, pearl, ruby, sapphire, topaz, turquoise
METALS USED TO MAKE JEWELLERY
gold, platinum, silver

jingle *VERB*
Coins jingled as he emptied his pocket.
▸ chink, clink, ring, tinkle

job *NOUN*
1 *He's got a well-paid job.*
▸ appointment, business, career, employment, livelihood, living, occupation, position, post, profession, trade, work
▹ The job you particularly want to do is your **mission** or **vocation**.
2 *It's not my job to do the washing-up.*
▸ assignment, chore, duty, errand, task
JOBS PEOPLE DO
accountant, architect, artist, banker, barber, barmaid or barman, barrister, blacksmith, bookseller, brewer, bricklayer, broadcaster, builder, cameraman, caretaker, carpenter, cashier, caterer, chauffeur, chef, cleaner, clergyman, clerk, coastguard, composer, conductor, cook, courier, curator, decorator, dentist, designer, detective, driver, docker, doctor, dustman, electrician, engineer, entertainer, estate agent, executive, farmer, fireman, forester, gamekeeper, gardener, groundsman, hairdresser, handyman, hotelier, industrialist, interpreter, joiner, journalist, labourer, lawyer, lecturer, librarian, machinist, mason, mechanic, midwife, milkman, miller, miner, model, musician, nightwatchman, nurse, nurseryman, office worker, optician, pharmacist, photographer, physiotherapist, pilot, plumber, policeman or policewoman, politician, porter, postman, printer, probation officer, professor, programmer, projectionist, psychiatrist, publisher, receptionist, reporter, sailor, scientist, secretary, shepherd, shopkeeper, signalman, social worker, soldier, solicitor, steward or stewardess, stockbroker, surgeon, surveyor, tailor, teacher, technician, telephonist, test pilot, traffic warden, typist, undertaker, vet, waiter or waitress

jog *VERB*
1 *He jogs round the park every morning.*
▸ go jogging, run, trot
2 *She jogged my elbow.*
▸ jar, jerk, jolt, knock, nudge, push
3 *The photograph may jog her memory.*
▸ prompt, refresh, set off, stimulate, stir

join *NOUN*
They mended it so well that you can't see the join.
▸ joint, link, mend, seam

A B C D E F G H I J K L M N O P Q R S T U V W X Y Z

join *VERB*

1 *The countries joined together to abolish trade restrictions.*
▸ amalgamate, combine, come together, merge, unite
AN OPPOSITE IS separate

2 *Join one section of pipe to the other.*
▸ attach, connect, fasten, fix, link, put together, tack on
SEE ALSO **fasten**
AN OPPOSITE IS detach

3 *Two roads join here.*
▸ converge, meet, merge
AN OPPOSITE IS divide

4 *I joined the crowd going into the cinema.*
▸ follow, go with, tag along with
AN OPPOSITE IS leave

5 *He joined the navy.*
▸ become a member of, enlist in, enrol in, volunteer for
AN OPPOSITE IS resign from

joint *ADJECTIVE*

The preparation of the meal was a joint effort.
▸ combined, communal, cooperative, shared, united
AN OPPOSITE IS individual

joint *NOUN*

IMPORTANT JOINTS IN YOUR BODY
ankle, elbow, hip, knee, knuckle, shoulder, vertebra, wrist

joist *NOUN*

Long joists support the ceiling.
▸ beam, girder, rafter

joke *NOUN*

Do you know any good jokes?
▸ funny story, (*informal*) gag, jest, pun

joke *VERB*

They're always laughing and joking.
▸ be facetious, clown, jest, make jokes

jolly *ADJECTIVE*

We had a jolly time last night.
▸ cheerful, happy, joyful, merry
AN OPPOSITE IS gloomy

jolt *VERB*

The car jolted over the track.
▸ bounce, bump, jar, jerk, jog, shake

jostle *VERB*

He was jostled by the journalists and photographers.
▸ crowd in on, hustle, press, push, shove

jot *VERB*

I quickly jotted down some ideas.
▸ note, scrawl, scribble, write

jotter *NOUN*

He made some notes in his jotter.
▸ exercise book, notebook, writing pad

journal *NOUN*

1 *He subscribes to several medical journals.*
▸ magazine, newspaper, paper, periodical, publication

2 *The captain kept a journal of the voyage.*
▸ account, chronicle, diary, log, record

journalist *NOUN*

She works as a journalist on the local newspaper.
▸ contributor, correspondent, reporter, writer

journey *NOUN*

His journey took him through France, Germany, and Italy.
▸ itinerary, route, travels
SEE ALSO **travel**

jovial *ADJECTIVE*

He was in a very jovial mood.
▸ cheerful, good-humoured, happy, jolly, joyful, merry, warm-hearted
AN OPPOSITE IS sad

joy *NOUN*

Her eyes filled with tears of joy.
▸ bliss, cheerfulness, delight, ecstasy, elation, exultation, gaiety, gladness, glee, happiness, joyfulness, jubilation, mirth, rejoicing
AN OPPOSITE IS sorrow

joyful *ADJECTIVE*

They arrived home amid joyful scenes in London.
▸ cheerful, delighted, ecstatic, elated, exultant, gleeful, happy, jolly, jovial, joyous, jubilant, merry, rejoicing, triumphant
AN OPPOSITE IS sad

judge *NOUN*

▹ A judge in a local court is a **magistrate**. A judge in a dispute is an **arbitrator** or a **mediator**. A judge in a competition is an **adjudicator**. A judge in a sport is a **linesman**, **referee**, **referee's assistant**, **touch judge**, or **umpire**.

judge *VERB*
1 *He was judged and found innocent.*
▸ examine, try
2 *The umpire judged that the ball was out.*
▸ adjudicate, decide, decree, pass judgement, rule
3 *She has been asked to judge the entries in the art competition.*
▸ appraise, assess, evaluate, give your opinion of
4 *They judged him to be about 25 years old.*
▸ consider, estimate, gauge, guess, reckon, suppose

judgement *NOUN*
1 *The judgement was given by the chairman of the committee.*
▸ arbitration, award, conclusion, decision, decree, finding, outcome, result, ruling, verdict
2 *His comments show a lack of political judgement.*
▸ common sense, discrimination, expertise, good sense, intelligence, reason, wisdom
3 *They have formed an unfair judgement of his character.*
▸ belief, estimation, evaluation, impression, opinion, point of view

judicious *ADJECTIVE*
It was a judicious change of tactics.
▸ clever, prudent, sensible, shrewd, thoughtful, well-judged, wise
AN OPPOSITE IS unwise

juice *NOUN*
The juice from the vegetables was kept in the fridge.
▸ fluid, liquid, sap

jumble *NOUN*
There was a jumble of books on the floor.
▸ chaos, clutter, confusion, mess, muddle

jumble *VERB*
The drawer was full of letters jumbled together.
▸ mess up, mix up, muddle, shuffle
AN OPPOSITE IS arrange

jump *VERB*
1 *Lambs were jumping about in the field.*
▸ bound, leap, spring
2 *I bet you can't jump the fence.*
▸ clear, vault
▹ When a cat jumps it pounces.

jump *NOUN*
The horse easily cleared the last jump.
▸ ditch, fence, gate, hurdle, obstacle

junction *NOUN*
Two cars collided at the junction.
▸ crossroads, interchange, intersection, T-junction

junior *ADJECTIVE*
1 *The junior members of the club go swimming on Thursdays.*
▸ younger
2 *He's only a junior employee in the firm.*
▸ inferior, lesser, lower, minor, subordinate
AN OPPOSITE IS senior

junk *NOUN*
The garage is full of junk.
▸ clutter, garbage, jumble, lumber, oddments, odds and ends, rubbish, scrap, trash, waste

just *ADJECTIVE*
It was a just punishment, considering the crime.
▸ appropriate, deserved, fair, justified, legitimate, merited, proper, reasonable, rightful, unbiased, unprejudiced
AN OPPOSITE IS unjust

justice *NOUN*
1 *Justice demands that everyone should be treated the same.*
▸ fairness, honesty, impartiality, integrity, right
AN OPPOSITE IS injustice
2 *They were tried in a court of justice.*
▸ law

justifiable *ADJECTIVE*
He had a justifiable reason for being late.
▸ acceptable, defensible, excusable, forgivable, justified, permissible, reasonable, right
AN OPPOSITE IS unjustifiable

justify *VERB*
1 *He attempted to justify his actions.*
▸ defend, excuse, explain
2 *The dreadful crime justifies the severe punishment.*
▸ deserve, merit, warrant

jut *VERB*
The mantelpiece juts over the fireplace.
▸ extend, overhang, poke out, project, protrude, stick out

juvenile *ADJECTIVE*
The government introduced new measures to deal with juvenile offenders.
▸ adolescent, young, youthful
AN OPPOSITE IS adult or mature

A B C D E F G H I J **K** L M N O P Q R S T U V W X Y Z

Kk

keel *VERB*
to keel over *The boat keeled over in the wind.*
► capsize, lean, overturn, tilt

keen *ADJECTIVE*
1 *All the players are very keen.*
► ambitious, committed, diligent, eager, enthusiastic, fervent, industrious, interested, motivated, zealous
AN OPPOSITE IS apathetic
2 *The carving knife has a keen edge.*
► cutting, razor-sharp, sharp, sharpened
AN OPPOSITE IS blunt
3 *Owls must have keen eyesight.*
► acute, perceptive, sensitive, sharp
AN OPPOSITE IS poor
4 *A keen wind was blowing and flakes of snow began to fall.*
► bitter, cold, icy, penetrating, severe
AN OPPOSITE IS mild

keep *VERB*
1 *I'll keep these things for later.*
► conserve, guard, hang on to, hold on to, preserve, retain, safeguard, save, store up
AN OPPOSITE IS abandon or lose
2 *Please keep still.*
► remain, stay
3 *She kept laughing.*
► carry on, continue, keep on, persevere in, persist in
4 *You're late. What kept you?*
► delay, detain, hamper, hinder, hold up, obstruct, restrain
5 *Will the milk keep until tomorrow?*
► be preserved, be usable, last, stay good
6 *They kept chickens and a few pigs.*
► look after, manage, mind, own
7 *It costs a lot to keep a family.*
► feed, maintain, pay for, provide for, support
to keep something up *Keep up the good work!*
► carry on, continue, maintain

keeper *NOUN*
▷ The keeper of something precious is the **custodian**. The keeper of a museum is the **curator**. The keeper of a prison is a **jailer** or **warder**. The keeper of a hostel is the **warden**.

key *NOUN*
The key to his behaviour may lie in his unhappy past.
► answer, clue, explanation, solution

keyboard *NOUN*
VARIOUS KEYBOARD INSTRUMENTS
accordion, celesta, electronic keyboard, harmonium, harpsichord, organ, piano, spinet, synthesizer

kidnap *VERB*
She was kidnapped by terrorists.
► abduct, carry off, run away with, snatch

kill *VERB*
1 *He was killed by a gunman.*
► (*slang*) bump off, dispatch, do away with, (*informal*) finish off, (*old use*) slay
2 *Careless driving can kill.*
► take life
▷ To kill people deliberately is to **murder** them. To kill people brutally is to **butcher** them. To kill large numbers of people is to **annihilate**, **exterminate**, or **massacre** them. To kill people as a punishment is to **execute** them or **put them to death**. To kill people for political reasons is to **assassinate** them. To kill people for their beliefs is to **martyr** them. To kill an animal humanely is to **put it down** or **put it to sleep**. To kill an animal for food is to **slaughter** it. To kill animals selectively is to **cull** them.
VARIOUS WAYS TO KILL
behead, choke, crucify, decapitate, drown, electrocute, garrotte, gas, guillotine, hang, knife, lynch, poison, shoot, smother, stab, starve, stone, strangle, suffocate, throttle
PEOPLE WHO KILL FOR VARIOUS REASONS
assassin, butcher, cut-throat, executioner, gunman, hunter, murderer, slayer, trapper
VARIOUS KINDS OF KILLING
assassination, euthanasia, execution, homicide, manslaughter, martyrdom, murder, suicide
THE KILLING OF LARGE NUMBERS OF PEOPLE OR ANIMALS
annihilation, bloodshed, butchery, carnage, elimination, extermination, extinction, genocide, massacre, slaughter

kind *NOUN*
1 *I like all kinds of music.*
► category, class, sort, type
2 *What kind of animal is that?*
► breed, family, race, species
3 *What kind of baked beans do you prefer?*
► brand, make, variety

kind *ADJECTIVE*
It was very kind of you to help me.
▸ affectionate, amiable, benevolent, brotherly, caring, charitable, comforting, compassionate, considerate, courteous, fatherly, friendly, generous, genial, gentle, good-natured, good-tempered, gracious, helpful, hospitable, humane, indulgent, kind-hearted, kindly, lenient, loving, merciful, motherly, neighbourly, obliging, polite, sensitive, sisterly, soft-hearted, sweet, sympathetic, tactful, tender, thoughtful, understanding, unselfish, warm-hearted, well-meaning
AN OPPOSITE IS unkind

kindle *VERB*
1 *The sparks kindled the dry grass.*
▸ ignite, light, set fire to, set light to
2 *The damp wood refused to kindle.*
▸ burn, catch fire, start burning

kindly *ADJECTIVE*
SEE **kind** *ADJECTIVE*

king *NOUN*
SEE **ruler**

kink *NOUN*
The rope had a kink in it.
▸ bend, coil, knot, loop, tangle, twist

kiosk *NOUN*
He bought a newspaper at the kiosk.
▸ bookstall, booth, news-stand, stall

kit *NOUN*
1 *I've forgotten my games kit.*
▸ gear, outfit, paraphernalia, tackle
2 *I've bought a repair kit for my bike.*
▸ equipment, set of tools

kitchen *NOUN*
EQUIPMENT YOU MIGHT FIND IN A KITCHEN
blender, cooker, crockery, cutlery, dish rack, dishwasher, draining board, extractor fan, food processor, freezer, fridge, grill, kettle, liquidizer, microwave oven, mincer, mixer, oven, percolator, refrigerator, scales, sink, stove, thermos, toaster, tray, vacuum flask
FOR VARIOUS COOKING UTENSILS SEE **cook, crockery, cutlery**

knack *NOUN*
You need a special knack to do this.
▸ expertise, gift, skill, talent, trick

knead *VERB*
He kneaded the athlete's tired muscles.
▸ manipulate, massage, pound, press, squeeze

knickers *PLURAL NOUN*
SEE **underclothes**

knife *NOUN*
VARIOUS KINDS OF KNIFE
butter knife, carving knife, clasp-knife, cleaver, dagger, flick knife, machete, penknife, pocket knife, scalpel, sheath knife
FOR OTHER KINDS OF CUTLERY SEE **cutlery**

knob *NOUN*
The trunk of the gnarled old tree was covered with knobs.
▸ bulge, bump, lump, projection, swelling
▹ A knob on a door is a handle. A knob in the middle of a shield is a boss.

knock *VERB*
I knocked my head on a beam.
▸ (*informal*) bash, bump, smack, strike, thump
SEE ALSO **hit** *VERB*
to knock off 1 (*informal*) *They knocked off work early today.*
▸ cease, end, finish, stop
2 (*informal*) *He's planning to knock off some videos.*
▸ (*informal*) make off with, (*slang*) pinch, steal, take, walk off with

knot *VERB*
We knotted the two ropes together.
▸ bind, do up, entwine, fasten, join, lash, link, tie
AN OPPOSITE IS untie
VARIOUS KNOTS
bow, bowline, clovehitch, fisherman's knot, granny knot, hitch, noose, reef knot, sheepshank, sheetbend, slipknot

know *VERB*
1 *I don't know how to mend a puncture.*
▸ comprehend, have experience of, remember, understand
2 *The police know who committed the crime.*
▸ be certain, have confidence

A B C D E F G H I J K L M N O P Q R S T U V W X Y Z

3 *As soon as he saw her, he knew who she was.*
▸ identify, perceive, recognize, realize
4 *Do you know Martin well?*
▸ be acquainted with, be familiar with, be a friend of

knowing *ADJECTIVE*
She gave him a knowing look.
▸ expressive, meaningful

knowledge *NOUN*
1 *She has the knowledge and ability to do well in the exam.*
▸ awareness, background, education, experience, grasp, know-how, learning, skill, talent, training, understanding, wisdom
AN OPPOSITE IS ignorance
2 *An encyclopedia contains a lot of knowledge.*
▸ data, facts, information, learning, scholarship, science

knowledgeable *ADJECTIVE*
He's very knowledgeable about antiques.
▸ familiar (with), learned, well educated, well informed
SEE ALSO **clever**
AN OPPOSITE IS ignorant

Ll

label *NOUN*
The washing instructions are on the label.
▸ sticker, tag, ticket

label *VERB*
They labelled all the boxes, so they know what's in them.
▸ identify, mark, name, put a label on, tag

laborious *ADJECTIVE*
It was a laborious climb to the top of the hill.
▸ difficult, exhausting, gruelling, hard, stiff, strenuous, tiring, tough
AN OPPOSITE IS easy

labour *NOUN*
1 *They were paid for their labour.*
▸ effort, exertion, industry, pains, toil, work
2 *The firm took on extra labour.*
▸ employees, workers
3 *She began labour in the night, and the baby was born by morning.*
▸ childbirth, labour pains
▹ Labour pains are also called contractions.

labour *VERB*
They laboured to get the job finished on time.
▸ exert yourself, (*informal*) slave away, toil, work hard

labyrinth *NOUN*
He got lost in the labyrinth of corridors.
▸ maze, network, tangle

lace *NOUN*
1 *They have lace curtains in their front room.*
▸ net, netting
2 *He left the laces on his trainers undone.*
▸ cord, string

lack *NOUN*
The judge dismissed the case because of a lack of evidence.
▸ absence, scarcity, shortage, want
▹ A general lack of food is a famine. A general lack of water is a drought.
AN OPPOSITE IS abundance

lack *VERB*
The game lacked excitement.
▸ be short of, be without, miss, need, require, want

laden *ADJECTIVE*
We came home laden with shopping.
▸ burdened, loaded, weighed down

lady *NOUN*
SEE **woman**

ladylike *ADJECTIVE*
She behaved in a ladylike manner.
▸ cultured, modest, polite, (*informal*) posh, prim and proper, refined, respectable, well-bred
AN OPPOSITE IS vulgar

lag *VERB*

1 *He soon became tired and started lagging behind.*

▸ dawdle, drop behind, fall behind, linger, loiter, straggle, trail

2 *We lagged our water pipes to conserve heat.*

▸ insulate, wrap up

lair *NOUN*

They tracked the animal back to its lair.

▸ den, hideout, hiding place, refuge, shelter

lake *NOUN*

We rowed across the lake.

▸ boating lake, lagoon, (*Scottish*) loch, pond, pool, reservoir

lame *ADJECTIVE*

1 *The horse was lame and had to be withdrawn from the race.*

▸ crippled, disabled, limping, maimed

2 *He didn't believe her lame excuse.*

▸ feeble, flimsy, inadequate, poor, tame, unconvincing, weak

lament *VERB*

They lamented the death of their friend.

▸ grieve for, mourn, shed tears for, weep for

lamp *NOUN*

SEE **light** *NOUN*

land *NOUN*

1 *They returned to their native land after many years abroad.*

▸ country, nation, region, state, territory

2 *This land produces good crops.*

▸ earth, farmland, ground, soil

3 *The duke owns this land.*

▸ estate, grounds, property

land *VERB*

1 *The plane landed exactly on time.*

▸ arrive, touch down

2 *They landed at Dover.*

▸ berth, come ashore, disembark, dock

landlady, landlord *NOUNS*

▹ The landlady or landlord of a pub is the licensee. The landlady or landlord of a rented property is the owner or proprietor.

landscape *NOUN*

We sat on the hill and admired the landscape.

▸ countryside, panorama, scene, scenery, view

lane *NOUN*

SEE **road**

language *NOUN*

▹ The words we know and use are the lexical items or vocabulary of our language. The rules for using words are the grammar of the language. A computer language is a code.

WAYS WE USE LANGUAGE

listening, reading, speaking or speech, writing

VARIETIES OF LANGUAGE

colloquial language, dialect, formal language, informal language, jargon, register, slang

PARTS OF A WORD

letter, consonant, vowel; syllable, prefix, suffix

UNITS OF LANGUAGE WE USE IN WRITING

clause, paragraph, phrase, sentence, word

NAMES OF PARTS OF SPEECH

adjective, adverb, conjunction, exclamation or interjection, noun, preposition, pronoun, verb

PUNCTUATION MARKS USED IN WRITING

apostrophe, brackets, colon, comma, dash, exclamation mark, full stop, hyphen, question mark, quotation marks or speech marks, semicolon

WORDS USED TO DESCRIBE THE WAY LANGUAGE SOUNDS

accent, intonation, pronunciation

lanky *ADJECTIVE*

The lanky figure ran clumsily.

▸ awkward, bony, gaunt, lean, long, skinny, tall, thin, ungraceful, weedy

AN OPPOSITE IS graceful or sturdy

lap *NOUN*

1 *The cat sat on my lap.*

▸ knees, thighs

2 *The cars were on the last lap of the race.*

▸ circuit

lapse *NOUN*

1 *She made a mistake because of a lapse in concentration.*

▸ failure, fault, flaw, shortcoming, slip, weakness

2 *He's started playing tennis again after a lapse of six months.*

▸ break, gap, interruption, interval, lull, pause

A B C D E F G H I J K **L** M N O P Q R S T U V W X Y Z

larder *NOUN*
There's some cheese in the larder.
▸ food cupboard, pantry

large *ADJECTIVE*
1 *Elephants are large animals.*
▸ big, bulky, colossal, enormous, giant, gigantic, great, heavy, hefty, huge, immense, mighty, monstrous, weighty
2 *She gave them large helpings of food.*
▸ above average, abundant, ample, generous, substantial, tremendous
3 *The cathedral is a large building.*
▸ grand, high, imposing, lofty, massive, tall, towering, vast
4 *They need a large room if they're going to dance.*
▸ roomy, sizeable, spacious
5 *The gales caused damage over a large area.*
▸ broad, extensive, vast, wide
6 *The meeting was attended by a large number of people.*
▸ considerable, incalculable
AN OPPOSITE IS small

lash *VERB*
1 *It was terrible to see him lash the poor donkey.*
▸ beat, flog, strike, thrash, whip
2 *They lashed oil drums together with rope to make a raft.*
▸ bind, fasten, secure, tie

last *ADJECTIVE*
1 *Z is the last letter of the alphabet.*
▸ closing, concluding, final, terminating, ultimate
AN OPPOSITE IS first
2 *What was his last record called?*
▸ latest, most recent
AN OPPOSITE IS next

last *VERB*
1 *I hope the fine weather lasts.*
▸ carry on, continue, endure, hold, keep on, persist, remain, stay
2 *They don't expect the sick animal to last much longer.*
▸ hold out, keep going, linger, live, survive

latch *NOUN*
Make sure the latch is holding the door shut.
▸ bolt, catch, fastener

late *ADJECTIVE*
1 *The bus is late.*
▸ delayed, overdue
AN OPPOSITE IS early or punctual
2 *They had a great deal of respect for the late king.*
▸ dead, deceased, former

latent *ADJECTIVE*
She was encouraged to develop her latent talent.
▸ hidden, potential, undeveloped, undiscovered

laugh *VERB* This word is often overused. Here are some alternatives:
VARIOUS WAYS TO SHOW AMUSEMENT
beam, burst into laughter, chortle, chuckle, giggle, go into hysterics, grin, guffaw, roar with laughter, simper, smile, smirk, sneer, snigger, titter
to laugh at *Don't laugh at people less fortunate than you.*
▸ deride, make fun of, mock, ridicule, scoff at, tease

laughable *ADJECTIVE*
They found the idea laughable.
▸ absurd, comic, funny, hilarious, ludicrous, ridiculous, silly

laughter *NOUN*
She heard peals of laughter coming from the room.
▸ hilarity, merriment, mirth

launch *VERB*
1 *They watched the rocket being launched.*
▸ blast off, fire, send off, set off
2 *She has launched a new business.*
▸ begin, embark on, establish, found, initiate, open, set up, start

lavatory *NOUN*
They put up a notice showing where the lavatory is.
▸ cloakroom, convenience, (*informal*) loo, public convenience, toilet, WC

lavish *ADJECTIVE*
1 *She was lavish with her gifts for the children.*
▸ extravagant, free, generous
AN OPPOSITE IS mean
2 *There was a lavish supply of food.*
▸ abundant, bountiful, copious, liberal, plentiful
AN OPPOSITE IS meagre

law *NOUN*
▷ A law passed by parliament is an **act**. A proposed law to be discussed by parliament is a **bill**. The process of making laws is **legislation**. The laws of a game are **regulations** or **rules**. A regulation which must be obeyed is a **commandment**, **decree**, **edict**, or **order**. A set of laws or rules is a **code**.
EVENTS THAT TAKE PLACE IN A LAWCOURT
court martial, hearing, inquest, lawsuit, legal proceedings, trial
PEOPLE WHO MAY BE INVOLVED IN A LAWCOURT
the accused, advocate, barrister, clerk, coroner, counsel for the defence, counsel for the prosecution, defendant, judge, juror, lawyer, magistrate, plaintiff, police, prosecutor, solicitor, usher, witness
TERMS OFTEN USED IN LAWCOURTS
accusation, appeal, arrest, bail, case, charge, dock, evidence, judgement, plea, probation, punishment, remand, sentence, suing, summons, testimony, verdict

lawful *ADJECTIVE*
Stealing is not a lawful act.
▸ allowed, just, legal, legitimate, permissible, permitted, right
AN OPPOSITE IS illegal

lawless *ADJECTIVE*
A lawless mob attacked the building.
▸ anarchic, badly behaved, disobedient, disorderly, mutinous, rebellious, riotous, rowdy, turbulent, uncontrolled, undisciplined, unruly, wild
AN OPPOSITE IS well behaved

lay *VERB*
1 *She laid her books on the table.*
▸ deposit, leave, place, position, put down, set down, spread
2 *Please lay the table for dinner.*
▸ arrange, set out

layer *NOUN*
1 *The walls needed two layers of paint.*
▸ coat, coating, covering, film, sheet, skin, thickness
2 *You can see layers of white and pink rock in the cliff.*
▸ seam, stratum

laze *VERB*
I spent most of the holiday lazing in the sun.
▸ be lazy, do nothing, lie about, loaf, lounge, relax, (*informal*) unwind

laziness *NOUN*
He was annoyed by the laziness of his workers.
▸ idleness, inactivity, sloth, slowness

lazy *ADJECTIVE*
She accused him of being lazy.
▸ idle, slack, slothful, slow, unenterprising
AN OPPOSITE IS hard-working

lead *VERB*
1 *The rescuers led them to safety.*
▸ conduct, escort, guide, pilot, steer
AN OPPOSITE IS follow
2 *Scott led an expedition to the South Pole.*
▸ be in charge of, direct, head, manage, preside over, supervise
3 *She led from the start of the race.*
▸ be in front, be in the lead, head the field

lead *NOUN*
1 *We followed the captain's lead.*
▸ example, guidance, leadership
2 *He was in the lead from the start.*
▸ first place, front position
3 *He was given the lead in the play.*
▸ chief part, starring role, title role
4 *Keep the dog on a lead.*
▸ chain, leash, strap
5 *Don't trip over the electrical lead.*
▸ cable, flex, wire

leader *NOUN*
▷ The leader of a team is the **captain**. The leader of a business is the **boss**, **director**, or **head**. The leader of a group of wrongdoers is the **ringleader**. The leader of a military expedition is the **commander**. The leader of a party of tourists is a **courier** or **guide**. The leader of a tribe is the **chief** or **chieftain**. The leader of a government is the **premier** or **prime minister**. The leader of a country is the **president** or **ruler**.
SEE ALSO **ruler**

leaf *NOUN*
1 *Deciduous trees lose their leaves in autumn.*
▷ A mass of leaves is **foliage** or **greenery**.
2 *She tore a leaf out of her book.*
▸ page, sheet

leaflet *NOUN*
People keep on putting advertising leaflets through our door.
▸ brochure, circular, pamphlet

league *NOUN*
to be in league with someone *The two criminals are in league with each other.*
▸ collaborate with, conspire with, join forces with, plot with, scheme with

leak *NOUN*
The plumber mended a leak in the water tank.
▸ crack, drip, hole
▹ A leak in a tyre is a **puncture**.

leak *VERB*
1 *The oil made a mess when it leaked onto the floor.*
▸ drip, escape, ooze, seep, trickle
2 *The plan was leaked to the newspaper.*
▸ disclose, give away, let out, make known, pass on, reveal

lean *VERB*
1 *I leaned against the wall.*
▸ prop yourself, recline, rest, support yourself
2 *The yacht leaned to one side in the wind.*
▸ bank, incline, list, slant, slope, tilt, tip

lean *ADJECTIVE*
The athlete has a strong, lean figure.
▸ slender, slim, thin, wiry
SEE ALSO **thin**
AN OPPOSITE IS fat

leap *VERB*
The dog leaped in the air to catch the ball.
▸ bound, jump, spring, vault

learn *VERB*
1 *They learned a lot on the school trip.*
▸ discover, find out, gain understanding of, gather, grasp, pick up
2 *I've got to learn my words for the play.*
▸ learn by heart, memorize

learned *ADJECTIVE*
The author of this book is very learned.
▸ academic, clever, cultured, educated, intellectual, knowledgeable, scholarly
AN OPPOSITE IS ignorant or uneducated

learner *NOUN*
He's a very slow learner.
▸ beginner, novice, starter
▹ Someone learning things at school or college is a **pupil** or **student**. Someone learning a trade is an **apprentice** or **trainee**. Someone being trained for the armed services or the police is a **cadet**.

learning *NOUN*
She's a woman of great learning.
▸ culture, education, knowledge, scholarship, wisdom

least *ADJECTIVE*
1 *Whoever has the least points has to drop out of the game.*
▸ fewest, lowest
2 *The least amount of this poison is deadly.*
▸ slightest, smallest, tiniest

leave *VERB*
1 *Do you have to leave now?*
▸ depart, go away, go out, make off, say goodbye, set off, take your leave, withdraw
AN OPPOSITE IS arrive or enter
2 *Don't leave me here on my own!*
▸ abandon, desert, forsake
3 *All the passengers left the damaged ship.*
▸ evacuate, get out of
4 *He has left his job.*
▸ give up, quit, resign from, (*informal*) walk out of
5 *Leave the milk bottles by the front door.*
▸ deposit, place, position, put down, set down
6 *He left all the arrangements to her.*
▸ entrust, refer
7 *She left him some money in her will.*
▸ bequeath, hand down
to leave someone or **something out** *They left him out of the team.*
▸ exclude, miss out, omit, reject

leave *NOUN*
1 *Will you give me leave to speak?*
▸ freedom, liberty, permission
2 *She gets 30 days' leave a year.*
▸ holiday, time off, vacation

lecture *NOUN*
1 *They heard an interesting lecture on astronomy.*
▸ address, speech, talk
2 *She gave them a lecture on how to behave.*
▸ reprimand, (*informal*) telling off, warning

lecture *VERB*
He lectured on English literature.
▸ give a lecture, speak, talk

lecturer *NOUN*
SEE **teacher**

ledge *NOUN*
The climbers rested on a ledge of rock.
▸ projection, shelf
▹ A ledge under a door is a sill. A ledge under a window is a windowsill.

left *ADJECTIVE*
▹ The left side of a ship when you face the bow is the port side.
AN OPPOSITE IS right

leg *NOUN*
PARTS OF YOUR LEG
ankle, calf, foot, knee, shin, thigh
WORDS WHICH DESCRIBE PEOPLE'S LEGS
bandy, bow-legged, knock-kneed

legacy *NOUN*
He left her a legacy in his will.
▸ bequest, inheritance

legal *ADJECTIVE*
It's not legal for children to buy cigarettes.
▸ allowed, lawful, legalized, legitimate, permissible, permitted
AN OPPOSITE IS illegal

legalize *VERB*
They won't ever legalize the sale of cigarettes to children.
▸ allow, make legal, permit
AN OPPOSITE IS ban

legendary *ADJECTIVE*
Unicorns are legendary beasts.
▸ fabulous, fictional, fictitious, invented, made-up, mythical, non-existent
AN OPPOSITE IS real
CREATURES YOU READ ABOUT IN LEGENDS
brownie, centaur, dragon, dwarf, elf, fairy, giant, gnome, goblin, griffin, imp, leprechaun, leviathan, mermaid, monster, nymph, ogre, phoenix, pixie, troll, unicorn, vampire, werewolf, witch, wizard

legible *ADJECTIVE*
She has good, legible handwriting.
▸ clear, neat, readable
AN OPPOSITE IS illegible

legitimate *ADJECTIVE*
Are you the legitimate owner of this car?
▸ authorized, legal, licensed, permitted, proper, rightful

leisure *NOUN*
He has plenty of leisure since he retired.
▸ holiday time, recreation, relaxation, rest, spare time, time off

leisurely *ADJECTIVE*
She went for a leisurely walk by the river.
▸ gentle, lingering, peaceful, relaxed, relaxing, restful, slow, unhurried
AN OPPOSITE IS fast

lend *VERB*
She lent him £50.
▸ loan
AN OPPOSITE IS borrow

length *NOUN*
The passengers complained about the length of the delay.
▸ duration, time

lengthen *VERB*
1 *She had to lengthen the skirt after she bought it.*
▸ extend, make longer
2 *The days lengthen in spring.*
▸ draw out, get longer
AN OPPOSITE IS shorten

lengthy *ADJECTIVE*
She had a lengthy wait for the bus.
▸ drawn out, extended, long, longish, prolonged, time-consuming
AN OPPOSITE IS short

lenient *ADJECTIVE*
The teacher was lenient and let her off.
▸ easygoing, forgiving, indulgent, kind, merciful, soft-hearted, tolerant
AN OPPOSITE IS strict

lessen *VERB*
1 *The nurse gave him some ointment to lessen the pain.*
▸ minimize, reduce, relieve
2 *The force of the storm lessened during the night.*
▸ become less, decrease, die away, diminish, dwindle, ease off, moderate, slacken, subside, tail off, weaken
AN OPPOSITE IS increase

let *VERB*
1 *His parents wouldn't let him go out.*
▸ allow, give permission to, permit
AN OPPOSITE IS forbid
2 *They are letting the house next door.*
▸ hire, lease, rent

A B C D E F G H I J K L M N O P Q R S T U V W X Y Z

lethal *ADJECTIVE*
A tiny amount of this drug is lethal.
▸ deadly, fatal, mortal, poisonous

letter *NOUN*
LETTERS WE USE TO MAKE WORDS IN WRITING
The letters a, e, i, o, u, and sometimes y are vowels. The other letters are consonants
LETTERS WE SEND TO EACH OTHER
correspondence, mail, post
VARIOUS LETTERS AND WRITTEN MESSAGES
business letter, card, circular, communication, dispatch, email, greetings card, love letter, memorandum, note, postcard, text
▹ The letters which form part of the New Testament are **epistles**.

level *ADJECTIVE*
1 *You need a level field for playing rounders.*
▸ even, flat, horizontal, smooth
AN OPPOSITE IS uneven
2 *At half-time the scores were level.*
▸ equal, even, matching, (*informal*) neck-and-neck, the same

level *VERB*
1 *He levelled the garden to make a lawn.*
▸ even out, flatten, smooth
2 *A serious earthquake levelled the town.*
▸ demolish, destroy, devastate, knock down

level *NOUN*
1 *The water had reached a high level.*
▸ height
2 *The lift takes you up to the sixth level.*
▸ floor, storey
3 *What level have you reached in your piano exams?*
▸ grade, stage, standard
4 *She was promoted to a higher level in the firm.*
▸ degree, position, rank, standing, status

lever *VERB*
I levered the lid off the box.
▸ force, prise, wrench

liable *ADJECTIVE*
1 *He is liable to make mistakes when he's tired.*
▸ disposed, inclined, likely, prone, ready
AN OPPOSITE IS unlikely
2 *The drunken driver was liable for the accident.*
▸ responsible, to blame

liar *NOUN*
She didn't trust him — she knew he was a liar.
▸ deceiver, fibber

liberal *ADJECTIVE*
1 *He poured a liberal amount of milk into his tea.*
▸ abundant, bountiful, copious, lavish, plentiful
AN OPPOSITE IS miserly
2 *She has a liberal attitude towards most things.*
▸ broad-minded, easygoing, indulgent, lenient, permissive, tolerant, unprejudiced
AN OPPOSITE IS strict

liberate *VERB*
There was great rejoicing when they liberated the prisoners.
▸ discharge, emancipate, free, let out, release, rescue, save, set free, untie
AN OPPOSITE IS imprison

liberty *NOUN*
1 *They had the liberty to do what they wanted.*
▸ freedom, independence
2 *Eventually the slaves were given their liberty.*
▸ emancipation, liberation, release

licence *NOUN*
He has a licence to practise as a doctor.
▸ certificate, document, permit, warrant

license *VERB*
Certain shops are licensed to sell alcohol.
▸ allow, authorize, entitle, permit

lid *NOUN*
She couldn't get the lid off the jar.
▸ cap, cover, covering, top

lie *NOUN*
They weren't taken in by his lies.
▸ deceit, dishonesty, falsehood, fib
AN OPPOSITE IS truth

lie *VERB*
1 *It's twelve o'clock and he's still lying in bed!*
▸ lounge, recline, rest, sprawl, stretch out
▹ To lie face down is to be **prone**. To lie face upwards is to be **supine**.
2 *The house lies in a valley.*
▸ be located, be situated
3 *I don't trust her — I think she's lying.*
▸ bluff, deceive someone, fib
to lie low *We'll lie low until the danger passes.*
▸ go into hiding, hide, take cover, take refuge

life *NOUN*
1 *He has a very easy life.*
▸ existence, way of life
2 *His life depended on finding water.*
▸ survival
3 *You seem to be full of life today!*
▸ animation, energy, liveliness, spirit,

sprightliness, vigour, vitality
4 *She was reading a life of Elvis Presley.*
▸ autobiography, biography

lifeless *ADJECTIVE*
1 *The lifeless body lay on the bed.*
▸ dead, deceased, killed
AN OPPOSITE IS living
2 *Nothing grows in that lifeless desert.*
▸ arid, barren, sterile
AN OPPOSITE IS fertile
3 *He lay lifeless on the ground.*
▸ inanimate, inert, motionless, unconscious
AN OPPOSITE IS conscious or moving

lifelike *ADJECTIVE*
The waxworks are very lifelike.
▸ convincing, natural, realistic, true to life
AN OPPOSITE IS unrealistic

lift *VERB*
1 *The crane lifted the girder.*
▸ elevate, hoist, pick up, pull up, raise
2 *The plane lifted off the ground.*
▸ ascend, rise, soar

light *NOUN*
VARIOUS KINDS OF NATURAL LIGHT
daylight, half-light, moonlight, starlight, sunlight, twilight
SOURCES OF ARTIFICIAL LIGHT
arc light, bulb, candle, chandelier, electric light, floodlight, fluorescent lamp, headlamp or headlight, illuminations, lamp, lantern, laser, neon light, pendant light, searchlight, spotlight, standard lamp, street light, strobe, taper, torch
LIGHTS USED AS SIGNALS
beacon, flare, traffic lights, warning light
LIGHTS USED TO IGNITE THINGS
cigarette lighter, lighter, match, pilot light
DIFFERENT EFFECTS OF LIGHT WHICH YOUR EYE CAN DETECT
beam, blaze, brightness, diffused light, flame, flash, flicker, fluorescence, glare, gleam, glint, glitter, glow, halo, illumination, lustre, phosphorescence, radiance, ray, reflection, shaft
ADJECTIVES WHICH DESCRIBE DIFFERENT KINDS OF LIGHT
bright, blazing, dazzling, flashing, flickering, fluorescent, glaring, gleaming, glimmering, glinting, glistening, glittering, glowing, luminous, lustrous, phosphorescent, reflected, shimmering, shining, sparking, sparkling, twinkling

light *ADJECTIVE*
1 *They had a light and airy room to work in.*
▸ bright, illuminated, well-lit
AN OPPOSITE IS dim or gloomy
2 *She was wearing light blue jeans.*
▸ pale
AN OPPOSITE IS dark
3 *Modern laptop computers are very light.*
▸ lightweight, portable
AN OPPOSITE IS heavy
4 *A light wind rippled the surface of the water.*
▸ faint, gentle, imperceptible, slight
AN OPPOSITE IS strong
5 *Since his illness he can only do light work.*
▸ easy, undemanding
AN OPPOSITE IS strenuous
6 *She prefers light music.*
▸ cheerful, entertaining, pleasant
AN OPPOSITE IS serious

light *VERB*
1 *It was so cold that she lit the fire.*
▸ fire, ignite, kindle, set alight, set fire to, put a match to, switch on
AN OPPOSITE IS extinguish
2 *The bonfire lit the sky.*
▸ brighten, illuminate, light up, shed light on, shine on
AN OPPOSITE IS darken

like *PREPOSITION*
She bought some jeans like her sister's.
▸ indistinguishable from, resembling, similar to, the same as

like *VERB* This word is often overused. Here are some alternatives:
What sort of films do you like?
▸ admire, appreciate, approve of, be fond of, be interested in, be partial to, be pleased by, delight in, enjoy, prefer
AN OPPOSITE IS dislike

likeable *ADJECTIVE*
She's a very likeable person.
▸ attractive, charming, friendly, lovable, nice, pleasant
AN OPPOSITE IS hateful

likely *ADJECTIVE*
It's likely that we'll win on Saturday.
▸ anticipated, expected, foreseeable, predictable, probable
AN OPPOSITE IS unlikely

likeness *NOUN*
1 *There's a strong likeness between the two sisters.*
▸ resemblance, similarity
AN OPPOSITE IS difference
2 *This photo is a good likeness of him.*
▸ copy, image, picture, portrait, representation

liking *NOUN*
She has a liking for classical music.
▸ affection, fondness, love, preference, taste
AN OPPOSITE IS dislike

limb *NOUN*
▹ Your limbs are your **arms** and **legs**. Birds have **wings**. Seals, etc., have **flippers**. An octopus has **tentacles**. The limbs of a tree are its **boughs** or **branches**.

limit *NOUN*
1 *She put a limit of ten on the number he could invite to the party.*
▸ ceiling, maximum, restriction
▹ A limit on time is a **deadline** or **time limit**.
2 *The fence marks the limit of the school grounds.*
▸ border, boundary, bounds, edge, extent, perimeter

limit *VERB*
They had to limit the number of tickets they sold for the concert.
▸ control, put a limit on, ration, restrict

limited *ADJECTIVE*
1 *The supply of food was limited.*
▸ finite, fixed, inadequate, insufficient, rationed, restricted, short, unsatisfactory
2 *It was hard to move about in the limited space.*
▸ cramped, narrow, small
AN OPPOSITE IS limitless

limitless *ADJECTIVE*
What would you do if you had a limitless amount of money?
▸ endless, inexhaustible, infinite, never-ending, unending, unlimited, vast
AN OPPOSITE IS limited

limp *VERB*
She managed to limp home after she cut her foot.
▸ falter, hobble, hop

limp *ADJECTIVE*
The leaves of the plant looked limp.
▸ drooping, flabby, flexible, floppy, sagging, soft, wilting
AN OPPOSITE IS rigid

line *NOUN*
LINES MARKED ON PAPER OR OTHER SURFACES
dash, streak, stripe, stroke, underlining
LINES CUT OR FOLDED INTO THE SURFACE OF SOMETHING
crease, furrow, groove, score, scratch, slash, wrinkle
LINES OF PEOPLE
column, cordon, crocodile, file, procession, queue, rank
LINES OF THINGS
rank, row, series, stream
LINES WHICH MARK THE EDGE OF SOMETHING
border, boundary, edging, frontier
LINES USED TO FASTEN THINGS
cord, hawser, rope, string, thread, wire
LINES WHICH CARRY ELECTRICITY
cable, flex, lead, wire
VARIOUS KINDS OF RAILWAY LINE
branch line, commuter line, main line, route, track

line *VERB*
to line up *They lined up to get into the cinema.*
▸ form a line, queue

linger *VERB*
1 *The smell of burning lingered after the fire was put out.*
▸ continue, last, persist, remain, stay
AN OPPOSITE IS disappear
2 *Don't linger outside in this cold weather.*
▸ dawdle, delay, hang about, lag behind, loiter, stay behind, wait about
AN OPPOSITE IS hurry

link *NOUN*
The two countries have close links with each other.
▸ association, connection, relationship
FOR THINGS YOU CAN USE TO LINK THINGS TOGETHER SEE **fasten**

link *VERB*
They linked the trailer to the tractor.
▸ attach, connect, couple, fasten, join
to link up *The two teams linked up for training sessions.*
▸ amalgamate, merge, unite
AN OPPOSITE IS separate

liquid *ADJECTIVE*
He poured the liquid jelly into a mould.
▸ flowing, fluid, molten, runny, sloppy, thin, watery, wet
AN OPPOSITE IS solid

liquid *NOUN*
▷ Substances which flow like liquids and gases are **fluids**.

list *NOUN*
▷ A list of people's names is a **roll**. A list of people with their addresses and phone numbers is a **directory**. A list of the pupils attending school is a **register**. A list of people who have tasks to do is a **rota**. A list of books in the library or of goods for sale is a **catalogue**. A list of topics mentioned in a book is an **index**. A list of numbers or facts is a **table**. A list of things to choose from is a **menu**. A list of things to be done is a **schedule**.

list *VERB*
1 *I helped to list the books in the library.*
▸ catalogue, index, make a list of, record, register, write down
2 *The damaged ship listed to one side.*
▸ incline, lean, slope, tilt, tip

listen *VERB*
to listen to something *They listened carefully to what he said.*
▸ attend to, concentrate on, hear, heed, overhear, pay attention to, take notice of

listless *ADJECTIVE*
The audience was listless because it was so hot.
▸ apathetic, feeble, lifeless, tired, unenthusiastic, uninterested, weary
AN OPPOSITE IS lively

literal *ADJECTIVE*
She gave a literal translation of the Latin motto.
▸ exact, precise, strict, word for word

literary *ADJECTIVE*
She's a literary person — she has read a lot of books.
▸ cultured, educated, refined, well-read

literature *NOUN*
1 *He has read a lot of English literature.*
▸ books, writings
FOR KINDS OF LITERATURE SEE **writing**
2 *The travel agent gave them some literature about their holiday destination.*
▸ brochures, handouts, leaflets, pamphlets

litter *NOUN*
The street was covered with litter.
▸ clutter, garbage, junk, mess, odds and ends, refuse, rubbish, waste

litter *VERB*
Why are these bits of paper littered round the room?
▸ scatter, strew

little *ADJECTIVE* This word is often overused.
1 *He's got a little dictionary that fits in his pocket.*
▸ compact, miniature, small, tiny
2 *Did you see those little lambs?*
▸ newborn, young
AN OPPOSITE IS big

live *ADJECTIVE*
You can see live animals in the zoo.
▸ SEE **living** *ADJECTIVE*

live *VERB*
Will these plants live through the winter?
▸ continue, exist, flourish, last, remain, stay alive, survive
AN OPPOSITE IS die
to live in a place *We live in a flat.*
▸ dwell in, inhabit, occupy, reside in
to live on *What do polar bears live on?*
▸ eat, feed on

livelihood *NOUN*
SEE **living** *NOUN*

lively *ADJECTIVE*
A lively crowd enjoyed an entertaining match.
▸ animated, boisterous, bubbly, bustling, cheerful, energetic, enthusiastic, excited, exuberant, frisky, high-spirited, merry, spirited, sprightly
AN OPPOSITE IS apathetic

living *ADJECTIVE*
1 *She has no living relatives.*
▸ alive
AN OPPOSITE IS dead
2 *There are no dinosaurs still living.*
▸ existing, surviving
AN OPPOSITE IS extinct

A B C D E F G H I J K **L** M N O P Q R S T U V W X Y Z

living *NOUN*
1 *He makes a living from painting.*
▸ income, livelihood
2 *What does she do for a living?*
▸ career, job, occupation, profession, trade

load *NOUN*
1 *I could hardly carry such a big load.*
▸ burden, weight
2 *A lorry was delivering its load to the supermarket.*
▸ cargo, consignment, freight, goods

load *VERB*
1 *We loaded the luggage into the car.*
▸ heap, pack, pile, stow
2 *They loaded him with their shopping.*
▸ weigh down

loaf *VERB*
He loafed about all day without offering to help us.
▸ dawdle, loiter, mess about, (*informal*) stand around, waste time

loan *NOUN*
She needs a loan to pay for her holiday.
▸ advance
▷ A system which allows you to pay for something later is **credit**. A loan to buy a house is a **mortgage**.

loan *VERB*
Can you loan me 50p?
▸ advance, lend
AN OPPOSITE IS borrow

loathe *VERB*
He loathes football.
▸ despise, detest, dislike, hate

loathsome *ADJECTIVE*
Rats are loathsome creatures.
▸ abominable, despicable, detestable, disgusting, foul, hated, horrible, nasty, repellent, repulsive, revolting, unpleasant, vile
AN OPPOSITE IS lovable

lobby *NOUN*
They waited for him in the lobby.
▸ entrance hall, foyer, hall

local *ADJECTIVE*
He always uses the local shops.
▸ nearby, neighbourhood, neighbouring

locality *NOUN*
There are some good schools in the locality.
▸ area, community, district, neighbourhood, parish, region, residential area, town, vicinity

locate *VERB*
1 *She located the book she wanted in the library.*
▸ detect, discover, find, search out, unearth
AN OPPOSITE IS lose
2 *They located the new offices in the middle of town.*
▸ build, establish, place, position, put, set up, situate, station

location *NOUN*
The coastguard asked the yachtsman to give his location.
▸ place, position, situation, spot, whereabouts

lock *NOUN*
He fixed a lock on the shed door.
▸ bolt, catch, padlock

lock *VERB*
Make sure you lock the door when you go out.
▸ bolt, close, fasten, seal, secure, shut

lodge *VERB*
1 *Where are you lodging at present?*
▸ rest, stay
2 *The authorities lodged the homeless family in a hostel.*
▸ accommodate, board, house, put up
3 *The ball lodged in a tree.*
▸ became fixed, get caught or jammed or stuck

lodger *NOUN*
She earns some money taking in lodgers.
▸ boarder, paying guest

lodgings *NOUN*
Where can we find lodgings for a few nights?
▸ accommodation, a boarding house, (*informal*) digs, a lodging house, quarters, rooms, temporary home

lofty *ADJECTIVE*
You can see the church's lofty spire from miles away.
▸ high, soaring, tall, towering
AN OPPOSITE IS low

log *NOUN*
1 *They collected logs to burn on the fire.*
FOR VARIOUS FORMS OF TIMBER SEE **wood**
2 *The ship's captain kept a log of the voyage.*
▸ account, diary, journal, record

logic *NOUN*
He admired the logic of her argument.
▸ clarity, good sense, orderly thinking, reasoning, validity

logical *ADJECTIVE*
She presents ideas in a logical way.
▸ clear, intelligent, lucid, methodical, rational, reasonable, sensible, systematic, valid
AN OPPOSITE IS illogical

loiter *VERB*
They were late because they loitered on the way.
▸ be slow, dawdle, hang back, linger, loaf about, mess about, straggle

lone *ADJECTIVE*
A lone rider galloped past.
▸ isolated, single, solitary, unaccompanied

lonely *ADJECTIVE*
1 *He felt lonely while his friends were away.*
▸ alone, desolate, forlorn, forsaken, friendless, neglected, solitary
2 *The climbers sheltered in a lonely hut.*
▸ abandoned, distant, faraway, isolated, out-of-the-way, remote, secluded

long *ADJECTIVE*
It seemed a long time before the bus came.
▸ endless, interminable, lengthy, longish, prolonged, unending
AN OPPOSITE IS short

long *VERB*
to long for something *I'm longing for a drink.*
▸ (*informal*) be dying for, crave, desire, fancy, have an appetite for, itch for, pine for, want, wish for, yearn for
▹ If you long for food or drink you are hungry or thirsty.

look *VERB* This word is often overused. Here are some alternatives:
1 *Look carefully so that you recognize it when you see it again.*
▸ keep your eyes open, take note, watch
2 *You look pleased today.*
▸ appear, seem
to look after someone or **something** *He looked after their things while they went swimming.*
▸ care for, guard, keep an eye on, mind, protect, tend, watch over
▹ To look after sick people is to nurse them.
to look at something **1** *We stopped to look at the view.*
▸ contemplate, eye, gape at, gaze at, observe, peep at, peer at, regard, scan, see, stare at, survey, view
2 *She looked at their work.*
▸ cast an eye over, consider, examine, glance at, inspect, scrutinize, skim through, study, take a look at
to look down on someone *Don't look down on them just because they are younger than you.*
▸ despise, scorn, sneer at
to look for something *He spent ages looking for his keys.*
▸ hunt for, search for, seek
to look out *If you don't look out, you'll get wet.*
▸ beware, keep an eye open, pay attention, take care, watch out
to look up to someone *He looks up to his older sister.*
▸ admire, have a high opinion of, respect, think highly of

look *NOUN*
1 *Did you have a look at what she was wearing?*
▸ glance, glimpse, peep, sight, view
2 *She has a friendly look.*
▸ air, appearance, aspect, bearing, countenance, expression, face, manner

lookout *NOUN*
The lookout reported that a stranger was approaching.
▸ guard, sentinel, sentry, watchman

loom *VERB*
1 *A figure loomed out of the mist.*
▸ appear, arise, emerge
2 *The grim castle loomed above us.*
▸ rise, stand out, stick up, tower

A B C D E F G H I J K L M N O P Q R S T U V W X Y Z

loop *NOUN*
His foot was caught in a loop in the rope.
▸ bend, circle, coil, curl, hoop, kink, noose, ring, twist

loop *VERB*
The sailor looped the rope round a bollard.
▸ bend, coil, curl, turn, twist, wind

loose *ADJECTIVE*
1 *The fire was started by a loose wire.*
▸ detached, disconnected, unattached
AN OPPOSITE IS secure
2 *These guy ropes are too loose.*
▸ slack
AN OPPOSITE IS tight
3 *Don't stumble on these loose stones.*
▸ insecure, movable, shaky, unsteady, wobbly
AN OPPOSITE IS firm
4 *The animals wander loose in the safari park.*
▸ at large, free, roaming, uncaged, unconfined, unrestricted
AN OPPOSITE IS confined

loosen *VERB*
Can you loosen these knots?
▸ ease, free, loose, release, slacken, undo, unfasten, unloose, untie
AN OPPOSITE IS tighten

loot *NOUN*
The loot was buried near the church.
▸ haul, plunder, takings

loot *VERB*
Rioters looted the shops.
▸ pillage, plunder, raid, ransack, rob, steal from

lopsided *ADJECTIVE*
The lopsided load on the lorry looked dangerous.
▸ crooked, tilting, unbalanced, uneven

lorry *NOUN*
FOR VARIOUS VEHICLES SEE **vehicle**

lose *VERB*
1 *She's lost her purse.*
▸ be unable to find, mislay
2 *He lost his way in the forest.*
▸ miss, stray from
AN OPPOSITE IS find
3 *Unfortunately, we lost on Saturday.*
▸ be defeated or unsuccessful, get beaten, suffer a defeat
AN OPPOSITE IS win

loss *NOUN*
1 *The loss of their water supply caused a lot of problems.*
▸ deprivation, disappearance, failure
2 *He was devastated by the loss of his friend.*
▸ death

lot *NOUN*
a lot of, lots of *She gave him a lot of help. He's got lots of money.*
▸ a large amount of, ample, heaps of, much, plenty of
the lot *I don't want any, so you can give her the lot.*
▸ all, everything

lotion *NOUN*
He needed some lotion for his sunburn.
▸ cream, ointment

loud *ADJECTIVE*
1 *She couldn't sleep because of the loud noise.*
▸ audible, blaring, booming, deafening, echoing, noisy, penetrating, piercing, resounding, rowdy, shrieking, shrill, (*informal*) terrific, thunderous
▹ A noise which is loud enough to hear is **audible**.
AN OPPOSITE IS quiet
2 *They were wearing rather loud shirts.*
▸ bright, flashy, gaudy, showy
AN OPPOSITE IS soft

lounge *VERB*
They lounged in the garden all day.
▸ be lazy, hang about, idle, laze, loaf, lie around, loiter, mess about, relax, sprawl, stand about, take it easy, waste time

lovable *ADJECTIVE*
She's got a lovable little puppy.
▸ adorable, appealing, attractive, charming, cuddly, enchanting, likeable, lovely
AN OPPOSITE IS hateful

love *NOUN*
He talked about her love for him.
▸ admiration, adoration, affection, devotion, fondness, friendship, liking, passion
to be in love with *My sister is in love with a boy at her college.*
▸ be devoted to, be fond of
love affair *Do you think their love affair will lead to marriage?*
▸ affair, courtship, relationship, romance

love *VERB*
1 *They love each other and want to get married.*
▸ admire, adore, be in love with, care for, cherish, have a passion for, idolize, treasure, value, worship
2 *I love fish and chips.*
▸ appreciate, approve of, be fond of, be partial to, enjoy
AN OPPOSITE IS hate

lovely *ADJECTIVE* This word is often overused. Here are some alternatives:
The flowers look lovely.
▸ appealing, attractive, beautiful, charming, delightful, enjoyable, fine, nice, pleasant, pretty, sweet
AN OPPOSITE IS nasty

lover *NOUN*
People send cards to their lovers on Valentine's Day.
▸ boyfriend, fiancé, fiancée, girlfriend, sweetheart, valentine

loving *ADJECTIVE*
She gave him a loving kiss.
▸ affectionate, devoted, fond, friendly, kind, passionate, tender, warm
AN OPPOSITE IS unfriendly

low *ADJECTIVE*
1 *The low land is often flooded in winter.*
▸ low-lying, sunken
2 *He resented his low status in the firm.*
▸ humble, inferior, junior, lowly, modest
3 *We spoke in low whispers.*
▸ muffled, muted, quiet, soft, subdued
4 *The tuba plays low notes.*
▸ bass, deep
AN OPPOSITE IS high

lower *VERB*
1 *The supermarket has lowered its prices.*
▸ bring down, cut, decrease, lessen, reduce, (*informal*) slash
2 *Will you please lower the volume of your radio?*
▸ quieten, turn down
3 *At sunset they lower the flag.*
▸ dip, haul down, let down, take down
AN OPPOSITE IS raise

lowly *ADJECTIVE*
He has a lowly position at present, but he hopes he'll be promoted soon.
▸ humble, inferior, insignificant, junior, low, modest

loyal *ADJECTIVE*
She has always been a loyal friend.
▸ constant, dependable, devoted, faithful, reliable, sincere, true, trustworthy
AN OPPOSITE IS disloyal

lubricate *VERB*
He spent the morning lubricating his bike.
▸ grease, oil

lucid *ADJECTIVE*
She gave a lucid explanation of the process.
▸ clear, logical, rational, sensible, unambiguous, understandable
AN OPPOSITE IS confused

luck *NOUN*
1 *He found his watch by luck.*
▸ accident, chance, coincidence, destiny, fate, fluke
2 *She had a bit of luck today.*
▸ good fortune, happiness, success

lucky *ADJECTIVE*
1 *He made a lucky discovery.*
▸ accidental, chance, unintentional, unplanned
2 *Some lucky person won a million pounds.*
▸ favoured, fortunate, happy, successful
AN OPPOSITE IS unlucky

ludicrous *ADJECTIVE*
They laughed at such a ludicrous idea.
▸ absurd, daft, foolish, laughable, ridiculous, senseless, silly

luggage *NOUN*
They packed their luggage in the boot of the car.
▸ baggage, belongings, paraphernalia, things
VARIOUS ITEMS OF LUGGAGE
bag, basket, box, briefcase, case, chest, hamper, handbag, hand luggage, haversack, holdall, knapsack, pannier, purse, rucksack, satchel, suitcase, trunk, wallet

lull *VERB*
She lulled the baby by singing quietly.
▸ calm, hush, pacify, quieten, soothe, subdue

lull *NOUN*
He took advantage of a lull in the storm and ran home.
▸ break, calm, gap, interval, pause

lumber *NOUN*
They cleared the lumber out of the garage.
▸ bits and pieces, clutter, jumble, junk, odds and ends, rubbish, trash

lumber *VERB*
1 *A rhinoceros lumbered towards them.*
▸ blunder, move clumsily, shamble
2 (*informal*) *They lumbered him with the clearing up.*
▸ burden, (*informal*) saddle

luminous *ADJECTIVE*
The alarm clock has a luminous dial.
▸ glowing, phosphorescent, shining

lump *NOUN*
1 *Lumps of sticky clay stuck to his boots.*
▸ cake, chunk, mass, slab
▹ A round lump of something is a **ball**. An oblong lump of something is a **brick**. A lump of metal is an **ingot**. A lump of gold is a **nugget**. A lump of wood is a **block**. A lump of earth is a **clod**. A lump of blood is a **clot**.
2 *After the stone hit him he got a lump on his head.*
▸ bulge, bump, protrusion, swelling

lump *VERB*
to lump things together *Just lump the ingredients together and give them a stir.*
▸ blend, combine, mingle, mix

lunge *VERB*
1 *Robin lunged at the sheriff with his sword.*
▸ jab, stab, strike, thrust
2 *The policeman lunged after the escaping robber.*
▸ charge, dash, dive, pounce, rush, throw yourself

lurch *VERB*
1 *The passengers lurched forward as the bus stopped suddenly.*
▸ reel, stagger, stumble, sway, totter
2 *The ship lurched as the waves pounded it.*
▸ heave, lean, list, pitch, roll, wallow

lure *VERB*
They lured him into their trap.
▸ attract, coax, draw, invite, persuade, tempt

lurk *VERB*
The lion lurked in wait for its prey.
▸ crouch, hide, lie in wait, lie low

luscious *ADJECTIVE*
She ate a bowl of luscious strawberries.
▸ appetizing, delicious, juicy, sweet

lust *NOUN*
He had a lust for power.
▸ appetite, craving, desire, greed, hunger, itch, longing, passion

luxurious *ADJECTIVE*
They were amazed by the luxurious surroundings in the hotel.
▸ comfortable, costly, expensive, grand, lavish, lush, magnificent, rich, splendid, wealthy
AN OPPOSITE IS austere or poor

luxury *NOUN*
It must be nice to live a life of luxury.
▸ affluence, comfort, ease, extravagance, pleasure, self-indulgence, wealth
AN OPPOSITE IS poverty

lying *NOUN*
The judge accused him of lying.
▸ deceit, dishonesty, falsehood

lyrical *ADJECTIVE*
His writing had a very lyrical quality.
▸ emotional, expressive, songlike

Mm

machine *NOUN*
Do you know how this machine works?
▸ apparatus, appliance, contraption, contrivance, device, engine, gadget, instrument, robot, tool
▹ A collection of machines is **machinery**. The moving parts of a machine is the **mechanism** or **works**.

machinery *NOUN*
1 *A lot of machinery has been installed.*
▸ equipment, machines, plant
2 *They set out to reform the machinery of government.*
▸ method, organization, procedure, system

mad *ADJECTIVE*
1 *You must be mad to go swimming on a day like this.*
▸ crazy, daft, insane, irrational, manic, mental, out of your mind, out of your senses, unbalanced, unstable
Note that these words are used informally, and they are often insulting
AN OPPOSITE IS sane
2 (*informal*) *He's mad about football.*
▸ enthusiastic, fanatical, keen (on), passionate
3 *He was mad with rage.*
▸ angry, berserk, beside yourself, frenzied, hysterical

madden *VERB*
She was maddened beyond endurance by his behaviour.
▸ anger, enrage, exasperate, incense, inflame, infuriate, make mad, provoke, vex

madman *NOUN*
He must be a madman to drive like that.
▸ lunatic, maniac
It is important to avoid giving offence when using words connected with mental illness

madness *NOUN*
He was driven to the brink of madness.
▸ frenzy, hysteria, insanity, lunacy, mania, mental illness
Make sure that if you use a synonym listed here it will not be insulting

magazine *NOUN*
1 *She bought a magazine to read on the train.*
▸ comic, journal, paper, periodical, publication
2 *The ammunition was stored in a secret magazine.*
▸ ammunition dump, arsenal, storehouse

magic *ADJECTIVE*
He disappeared as if by a magic trick.
▸ conjuring, magical, miraculous, supernatural

magic *NOUN*
Do you believe in magic?
▸ charms, enchantments, sorcery, spells, witchcraft, wizardry

magician *NOUN*
1 *They hired a magician for the children's party.*
▸ conjuror
2 *According to legend, King Arthur was helped by the medieval magician Merlin.*
▸ sorcerer, witch, wizard

magnetize *VERB*
His dark brown eyes magnetized those around him.
▸ attract, captivate, charm, fascinate, hypnotize
AN OPPOSITE IS repel

magnificent *ADJECTIVE*
1 *The mountain scenery was magnificent.*
▸ beautiful, glorious, gorgeous, impressive, majestic, noble, spectacular, splendid, superb
2 *The President lived in a magnificent palace.*
▸ dignified, grand, imposing, (*informal*) posh, stately
3 *It was a magnificent meal.*
▸ excellent, (*informal*) fabulous, (*informal*) fantastic, first-class, marvellous, wonderful
AN OPPOSITE IS ordinary

magnify *VERB*
1 *The image was magnified to 100 times its actual size.*
▸ (*informal*) blow up, enlarge, make larger
AN OPPOSITE IS reduce
2 *She tended to magnify the faults of the people she disliked.*
▸ exaggerate, make too much of, maximize, overdo
AN OPPOSITE IS minimize

magnifying glass SEE **glass**

magnitude *NOUN*
He exaggerates the magnitude of his problems.
▸ dimensions, extent, importance, size

mail *NOUN*
The postman brings the mail.
▸ correspondence, letters and parcels, post

mail *VERB*
He mailed the birthday card too late to get there in time.
▸ dispatch, post, send

maim *VERB*
He was maimed for life in the car accident.
▸ cripple, disable, injure, mutilate, wound

main *ADJECTIVE*
1 *What was the main point of the story?*
▸ basic, central, chief, crucial, dominant, essential, fundamental, greatest, important, outstanding, predominant, primary, prime, supreme

a b c d e f g h i j k l **m** n o p q r s t u v w x y z

A B C D E F G H I J K L M N O P Q R S T U V W X Y Z

2 *They are the main suppliers of coal in the district.*
▸ biggest, foremost, largest, leading, major, principal
AN OPPOSITE IS minor or unimportant

mainly *ADVERB*
The chimpanzees eat mainly fruit and vegetables.
▸ chiefly, especially, generally, in the main, largely, mostly, normally, on the whole, predominantly, primarily, principally, usually

maintain *VERB*
1 *It pays to maintain your bike in good order.*
▸ keep, look after, preserve, take care of
2 *He has always maintained that he was innocent.*
▸ argue, assert, claim, contend, declare, insist, proclaim, state
3 *It costs a lot to maintain a family.*
▸ feed, keep, pay for, provide for, support

maintenance *NOUN*
The maintenance of an old car can be expensive.
▸ care, repairs, servicing, upkeep

majestic *ADJECTIVE*
The town was dominated by the majestic castle.
▸ awe-inspiring, awesome, dignified, grand, imposing, impressive, magnificent, noble, splendid, stately
AN OPPOSITE IS commonplace

major *ADJECTIVE*
1 *They decided to keep to the major roads.*
▸ bigger, chief, greater, larger, primary, principal
2 *She had a major part in the play.*
▸ big, considerable, great, important, leading, outstanding, significant
AN OPPOSITE IS minor

majority *NOUN*
The majority of the people prefer television to radio.
▸ bulk, greater number, most
AN OPPOSITE IS minority
to be in the majority *Those who agreed with the decision were in the majority.*
▸ be greater, dominate, outnumber the others, predominate

make *VERB*
The verb *make* is used in many ways. We give just a selection of the main ways you can use the word here
1 *They made a shelter out of leaves and branches.*
▸ assemble, build, construct, produce, put together
▹ To make a cake is to **bake** or **cook** it. To make clothes, etc., is to **knit**, **sew**, or **weave** them. To make a model, statue, etc., is to **carve**, **cast**, or **mould** it. To make something in a factory is to **manufacture** or **mass-produce** it.
2 *They're always making trouble.*
▸ bring about, cause, give rise to, provoke
3 *They made me captain.*
▸ appoint, elect, nominate
4 *They've made the attic into a games room.*
▸ alter, change, convert, modify, transform, turn
5 *She'll make a good actress when she's older.*
▸ become, change into, grow into, turn into
6 *The regulations were made to protect children.*
▸ agree, decide on, establish, fix
7 *You made me jump!*
▸ cause you to
8 *If I don't want to come, you can't make me.*
▸ compel, force, order
9 *He made a lot of money last year.*
▸ earn, gain, get, obtain, receive, win
10 *The swimmer just made the shore.*
▸ arrive at, get as far as, get to, reach
11 *What do you make the total?*
▸ calculate, compute, count, estimate, reckon
12 *2 and 2 make 4.*
▸ add up to, come to, total
13 *The garage made an offer for her car.*
▸ propose, suggest
14 *Have you made your bed this morning?*
▸ arrange, tidy
to make fun of *Don't make fun of her.*
▸ deride, jeer at, laugh at, mock, ridicule, scoff at, (*informal*) send up, tease
to make off *The thieves made off in a stolen car.*
▸ depart, disappear, go away, leave, set off
to make someone or **something out** *I can't make out why everything went wrong.*
▸ appreciate, comprehend, fathom, make sense of, recognize, understand, work out
to make up *She made up a lot of lies.*
▸ compose, create, invent, originate, think up
to make up your mind *Make up your mind about what you want to do.*
▸ choose, decide, make a decision, resolve

make *NOUN*
There were many different makes of computer.
▸ brand, kind, model, sort, type, variety

make-believe *NOUN*
His story was all make-believe.
▸ fantasy, imagination, pretence, pretending, sham

maker *NOUN*
The company is the country's largest car maker.
▸ manufacturer, producer

make-up *NOUN*
She hardly ever wears make-up.
▸ cosmetics
FOR VARIOUS ITEMS OF MAKE-UP SEE **cosmetics**

male *ADJECTIVE*
FOR MALE HUMAN BEINGS SEE **man**
FOR MALE CREATURES SEE **animal**
AN OPPOSITE IS female

malevolent *ADJECTIVE*
SEE **malicious**

malice *NOUN*
He gave her a look of pure malice.
▸ enmity, hatred, hostility, ill will, malevolence, nastiness, spite, spitefulness, viciousness
AN OPPOSITE IS kindness

malicious *ADJECTIVE*
They've been spreading malicious rumours.
▸ bitchy, evil-minded, hateful, ill-natured, malevolent, mischievous, nasty, revengeful, spiteful, vicious, wicked
AN OPPOSITE IS kind

mammal *NOUN*
FOR VARIOUS KINDS OF ANIMAL SEE **animal**

man *NOUN*
▷ A polite word for a man is gentleman. Informal words are bloke, chap, fellow, guy. A married man is a husband. A man who has children is a father. An unmarried man is a bachelor. A man whose wife has died is a widower. A man on his wedding day is a bridegroom. A man who is engaged to be married is a fiancé. A man who is going out with a woman is her boyfriend. Words for a young man are boy, lad, youth.

manage *VERB*
1 *How much work can you manage before dinner?*
▸ achieve, bring about, carry out, cope with, deal with, do, finish, perform
2 *You'll have to manage with what you've got.*
▸ be satisfied, cope, make do
3 *If you can't pay it all, pay what you can manage.*
▸ afford, spare
4 *His eldest son manages the business now.*
▸ administer, administrate, be in charge of, be the manager of, direct, govern, lead, look after, preside over, regulate, rule, run, superintend, supervise, take control of
5 *She has a knack for managing difficult horses.*
▸ control, dominate, handle

manager *NOUN*
If you have a problem, talk to the manager.
▸ (*informal*) boss, chief, director, proprietor
FOR PEOPLE IN CHARGE OF VARIOUS THINGS SEE **chief** *NOUN*

mangle *VERB*
His hand was mangled in the machine.
▸ crush, damage, injure, maim, mutilate, squash, tear, wound

manhandle *VERB*
1 *The journalists were manhandled by the security guards.*
▸ (*informal*) beat up, knock about, mistreat, misuse, treat roughly
2 *They had to manhandle the piano up the stairs.*
▸ carry, haul, heave, hump, lift, pull, push

mania *NOUN*
A mania for the pop group swept the country.
▸ craze, enthusiasm, fad, hysteria, obsession, passion
SEE ALSO **madness**

maniac *NOUN*
SEE **madman**

manic *ADJECTIVE*
SEE **mad**

manifesto *NOUN*
Each political party issues a manifesto before an election.
▸ declaration, policy, statement

A B C D E F G H I J K L M N O P Q R S T U V W X Y Z

manipulate *VERB*
1 *He carefully manipulated the dials of the radio set.*
► control, guide, handle, manage, steer
2 *She uses her charm to manipulate people.*
► exploit, impose on, take advantage of, use

mankind *NOUN*
Conservation of this planet is important for all mankind.
► human beings, humanity, the human race, men and women, people

manner *NOUN*
1 *She does things in a professional manner.*
► fashion, style, way
2 *He had a very cheeky manner.*
► air, attitude, bearing, behaviour, character, conduct, disposition, look
good manners, or simply **manners** *He has no manners at all.*
► courtesy, good behaviour, politeness

manoeuvre *NOUN*
1 *Their victory was the result of a very skilful manoeuvre.*
► dodge, plan, plot, scheme, strategy, tactic, trick
2 *Getting the car into the garage is a tricky manoeuvre.*
► move, operation

manoeuvre *VERB*
The captain manoeuvred the ship into the dock.
► guide, move, pilot, steer

mansion *NOUN*
We had to pay £3 each to look round the mansion.
► manor, manor house, palace, stately home
SEE ALSO **house** *NOUN*

manufacture *VERB*
The factory manufactures pine furniture.
► assemble, build, fabricate, make
▷ Manufacturing something in large quantities is **mass-production**.

many *ADJECTIVE*
I have been to London many times.
► countless, frequent, innumerable, numerous, untold, various
AN OPPOSITE IS **few**

map *NOUN*
He drew us a map to show us how to get to the party.
► chart, diagram, plan
▷ A book of maps is an **atlas** or a **roadbook**.

map *VERB*
They had to map the area around the school.
► chart, survey
to map something out *They sat down and mapped out a strategy for the next game.*
► arrange, devise, organize, plan, prepare, work out

mar *VERB*
The match was marred by bad weather.
► make a mess of, mess up, ruin, spoil

marauder *NOUN*
Marauders came down from the hills to attack the village.
► bandit, invader, plunderer, raider

march *VERB*
Soldiers marched into the town.
► file, parade, stride, troop

margin *NOUN*
Don't write in the margin of the paper.
► border, edge

marginal *ADJECTIVE*
The difference between the two estimates is marginal.
► borderline, minimal, negligible, small, unimportant
AN OPPOSITE IS **great**

mark *NOUN*
1 *There were dirty marks all over the kitchen floor.*
► blemish, blot, blotch, dot, fingermark, line, scar, scratch, scribble, smear, smudge, smut, spot, stain, streak
▷ A mark on a person's skin is a **birthmark**, **freckle**, **mole**, or **tattoo**.
2 *The flag was at half-mast as a mark of respect for the dead man.*
► emblem, indication, sign, symbol, token
3 *The manufacturer's mark is on the label.*
► badge, brand, seal, stamp

mark *VERB*
1 *He picked up the photograph gently, careful not to mark it.*
▸ damage, deface, smudge, stain
▹ To mark your skin is to **bruise**, **cut**, **graze**, **scar**, or **scratch** it.
2 *She had a pile of English essays to mark.*
▸ assess, correct, grade
3 *There will be trouble, you mark my words!*
▸ attend to, heed, listen to, mind, note, notice, observe, take note of

market *NOUN*
PLACES WHERE THINGS ARE BOUGHT AND SOLD
auction, bazaar, car boot sale, fair, sale, street market
SEE ALSO **shop**

market *VERB*
The company needs to market its goods in Europe.
▸ advertise, promote, sell, trade in

maroon *VERB*
They were marooned on a desert island.
▸ abandon, cast away, desert, forsake, leave, put ashore, strand

marriage *NOUN*
1 *My grandparents celebrated 40 years of marriage.*
▸ matrimony
2 *Today is the anniversary of their marriage.*
▸ wedding

marsh *NOUN*
The birds breed on coastal marshes.
▸ bog, fen, mud, swamp

marshy *ADJECTIVE*
His feet squelched in the marshy ground.
▸ boggy, muddy, soft, soggy, swampy, waterlogged, wet
AN OPPOSITE IS firm or dry

marvel *NOUN*
The exhibition featured all the marvels of modern science.
▸ miracle, wonder

marvel *VERB*
to marvel at *She marvelled at his courage.*
▸ admire, applaud, be amazed by, be astonished by, be surprised by, wonder at

marvellous *ADJECTIVE*
1 *Medical science can do marvellous things these days.*
▸ amazing, astonishing, extraordinary, incredible, miraculous, phenomenal, remarkable, surprising, unbelievable, wonderful
2 *She looked marvellous.*
▸ excellent, (*informal*) fabulous, (*informal*) fantastic, glorious, magnificent, sensational, (*informal*) smashing, spectacular, splendid, superb
AN OPPOSITE IS ordinary

masculine *ADJECTIVE*
He was rugged, handsome, and very masculine.
▸ male, manly
AN OPPOSITE IS feminine

mash *VERB*
Mash the fruit into a pulp.
▸ beat, crush, pound, smash, squash
▹ To make something into powder is to **grind** or **pulverize** it.

mask *VERB*
The factory was masked by a row of poplar trees.
▸ camouflage, cloak, conceal, cover, disguise, hide, obscure, screen, shield, shroud, veil

mass *NOUN*
She began sifting through the mass of papers on her desk.
▸ accumulation, heap, (*informal*) load, lot, lump, mound, pile, quantity, stack

massacre *VERB*
SEE **kill**

massage *VERB*
She massaged his aching back.
▸ knead, manipulate, rub

massive *ADJECTIVE*
SEE **huge**

mast *NOUN*
▹ A radio mast is an **aerial** or **transmitter**. A mast to fly a flag on is a **flagpole**. A mast to carry power lines is a **pylon**.

A B C D E F G H I J K L **M** N O P Q R S T U V W X Y Z

master *NOUN*
▷ A master in a school is a schoolmaster or teacher. The master of a dog is its keeper or owner. The master of a ship is the captain. A master in a particular sport or skill is an ace, expert, or genius.

master *VERB*
Some people think it is sexist to use the verb *master*
1 *I've mastered the basic moves of chess.*
► (*informal*) get the hang of, grasp, learn, understand
2 *She succeeded in mastering her fear of heights.*
► conquer, control, curb, defeat, dominate, get the better of, govern, manage, overcome, regulate, restrain, subdue, tame, triumph over

mastermind *NOUN*
1 *She's a scientific mastermind.*
► expert, genius, intellectual
2 *Who was the mastermind behind the plan?*
► brains, creator, inventor, originator, planner

masterpiece *NOUN*
This piece of music is a masterpiece.
► classic

mastery *NOUN*
1 *He struggled to gain mastery over his emotions.*
► authority, control, dominance, power, (*informal*) the upper hand
2 *His tactical mastery helped him to win the match.*
► cleverness, knowledge, skill

match *NOUN*
1 *The semi-final was a really exciting match.*
► competition, contest, game, tie, tournament
2 *The jacket and tie are a good match.*
► combination, double, pair

match *VERB*
Does this tie match my shirt?
► be compatible with, be the same colour as, be similar to, blend with, combine with, correspond with, fit with, go with, harmonize with, tone in with
AN OPPOSITE IS contrast

matching *ADJECTIVE*
He wore a blue shirt with a matching tie.
► comparable, compatible, complimentary, coordinating, corresponding, equivalent, harmonizing, similar, twin
AN OPPOSITE IS contrasting

mate *NOUN*
1 (*informal*) *He's one of my best mates.*
► (*informal*) chum, friend, (*informal*) pal
2 *He's got a job as a plumber's mate.*
► assistant, colleague, companion, helper, partner

mate *VERB*
Many birds mate in spring.
► become partners, copulate, have intercourse, have sex

material *NOUN*
1 *She's collecting material for a newspaper article.*
► data, facts, ideas, information, notes, subject matter
2 *He needed to buy some cleaning materials.*
► building materials, raw materials, stuff, substances, things
FOR VARIOUS BUILDING MATERIALS SEE **building**
3 *Her skirt was made of soft, woollen material.*
► cloth, fabric
FOR VARIOUS KINDS OF FABRIC SEE **cloth**

mathematics *NOUN*
He had to finish his mathematics homework before going out.
► (*informal*) maths, number work
VARIOUS BRANCHES OF MATHEMATICS
algebra, arithmetic, geometry, statistics
WORDS FOR THINGS YOU DO IN MATHS
addition or adding, calculation or calculating, counting, division or dividing, investigating, measuring, multiplication or multiplying, subtraction or subtracting, sums
VARIOUS MATHEMATICAL INSTRUMENTS
calculator, compasses, computer, dividers, protractor, ruler, set square
SOME WORDS YOU MIGHT USE IN MATHS
angle, answer, area, binary system, capacity, concentric, congruence, decimal fraction, decimal point, diagonal, diameter, difference, digit, equation, equilateral, factor, figure, fraction, function, graph, index, locus, logarithm, matrix, measurement, mensuration, minus, negative, number, parallel, pattern, percentage, perpendicular, plus, positive, problem, radius, ratio, right angle, shape, sine, sum, symmetry, tangent, tessellation, theorem, times, total, unit, volume
FOR OTHER WORDS YOU MIGHT USE IN MATHS SEE **measurement, shape**

matted *ADJECTIVE*
Her hair was dirty and matted.
▸ knotted, tangled, uncombed

matter *NOUN*
1 *The manager will deal with this matter.*
▸ affair, business, concern, incident, issue, situation, subject, thing, topic
2 *Peat consists mainly of vegetable matter.*
▸ material, stuff, substance
3 *What's the matter with the car?*
▸ difficulty, problem, trouble, worry

matter *VERB*
Will it matter if I'm late?
▸ be important, count, make a difference

mature *ADJECTIVE*
1 *She's mature for her age.*
▸ adult, advanced, grown-up, well developed
2 *There is a large garden, with mature chestnut and oak trees.*
▸ established, fully grown
AN OPPOSITE IS immature

maximum *ADJECTIVE*
The maximum number of people allowed in the minibus is 16.
▸ biggest, fullest, greatest, highest, largest, top
AN OPPOSITE IS minimum

maximum *NOUN*
Temperatures usually reach their maximum after noon.
▸ ceiling, highest point, peak, top, upper limit

maybe *ADVERB*
Maybe I'll come, maybe I won't!
▸ perhaps, possibly
AN OPPOSITE IS definitely

maze *NOUN*
They were lost in a confusing maze of corridors.
▸ labyrinth, network, tangle, web

meadow *NOUN*
Cows were grazing in the meadow.
▸ field, pasture

meagre *ADJECTIVE*
She was forced to supplement her meagre wages by taking another job.
▸ inadequate, insufficient, (*informal*) measly, scanty, small, stingy

meal *NOUN*
MEALS YOU HAVE AT VARIOUS TIMES OF DAY
breakfast, dinner, (*informal*) elevenses, high tea, lunch or luncheon, supper, tea
▹ A big formal meal is a **banquet** or **feast**. A quick informal meal is a **snack**. A meal you eat out of doors is a **barbecue** or **picnic**. A meal where you help yourself to food is a **buffet**. A meal you buy ready cooked is a **takeaway**.
VARIOUS COURSES OF A MEAL
(*informal*) afters, dessert, main course, pudding, starter, sweet
SEE ALSO **food**

mean *ADJECTIVE*
1 *He's too mean to give to charity.*
▸ (*informal*) mingy, miserly, selfish, stingy, tight, uncharitable
AN OPPOSITE IS generous
2 *That was a mean trick to play.*
▸ callous, contemptible, cruel, despicable, malicious, nasty, shabby, shameful, (*informal*) sneaky, spiteful, unkind, vicious
AN OPPOSITE IS kind

mean *VERB*
1 *What does that sign mean?*
▸ communicate, convey, denote, express, hint at, imply, indicate, say, signify, stand for, suggest, symbolize
2 *I mean to work harder.*
▸ aim, desire, intend, plan, propose, want, wish

meander *VERB*
We meandered round the town looking at the shops.
▸ ramble, roam, stray, wander

meaning *NOUN*
The expression has several different meanings in English.
▸ definition, explanation, interpretation, sense, significance

meaningless *ADJECTIVE*
1 *She felt that her life was meaningless.*
▸ empty, futile, pointless, worthless
2 *I can't speak Japanese, so it was meaningless to me.*
▸ incomprehensible, nonsensical, pointless, senseless

means *PLURAL NOUN*
1 *Scientists now have the means to travel to other planets.*
▸ ability, capacity, method, process, way

a b c d e f g h i j k l **m** n o p q r s t u v w x y z

2 *He hasn't got the means to buy a house.*
▸ capital, finances, funds, income, money, resources, riches, wealth

measly *ADJECTIVE*
(*informal*) *They offered him a measly £2 for all the work he did.*
▸ inadequate, insufficient, meagre, poor, scanty, small, (*informal*) stingy

measure *VERB*
Measure the length and width of the window.
▸ assess, calculate, compute, gauge, survey, take measurements of

measure *NOUN*
1 *They now know the measure of the problem.*
▸ extent, magnitude, measurement, size
2 *The government introduced new measures to curb crime.*
▸ act, action, law, procedure, step

measurement *NOUN*
What are the measurements of this room?
▸ dimensions, extent, measure, size
METRIC UNITS USED TO MEASURE DISTANCE (BREADTH OR WIDTH, GAUGE, HEIGHT, AND LENGTH)
millimetre, centimetre, metre, kilometre
OLD UNITS USED TO MEASURE DISTANCE (BREADTH OR WIDTH, GAUGE, HEIGHT, AND LENGTH)
inch, foot, yard, furlong, mile
UNIT USED TO MEASURE DISTANCE IN SPACE
light year
UNIT USED TO MEASURE DEPTH AT SEA
fathom
METRIC UNITS USED TO MEASURE AREA
square centimetre (metre, etc.), hectare
OLD UNITS USED TO MEASURE AREA
square inch (foot, etc.), acre
METRIC UNITS USED TO MEASURE CAPACITY OR VOLUME
millilitre, cubic centimetre, litre
OLD UNITS USED TO MEASURE CAPACITY OR VOLUME
cubic inch, pint, quart, gallon
METRIC UNITS USED TO MEASURE WEIGHT
milligram, gram, kilo or kilogram, tonne
OLD UNITS USED TO MEASURE WEIGHT
ounce, pound, stone, hundredweight, ton
UNITS USED TO MEASURE TIME
second, minute, hour, day, week, month, year, decade, century, millennium
UNITS USED TO MEASURE SPEED OR VELOCITY
kilometres per hour, miles per hour, (*informal*) ton
UNIT USED TO MEASURE SPEED AT SEA
knot
UNITS USED TO MEASURE TEMPERATURE
degrees Celsius, degrees centigrade, degrees Fahrenheit
INFORMAL MEASUREMENTS OF AMOUNT OR QUANTITY
cupful, handful, pinch, plateful, spoonful

meat *NOUN*
KINDS OF MEAT
bacon, beef, chicken, game, gammon, ham, lamb, mutton, pork, poultry, turkey, veal, venison
VARIOUS CUTS OR JOINTS OF MEAT
breast, brisket, chops, cutlet, fillet, leg, loin, rib, rump, scrag, shoulder, silverside, sirloin, spare-rib, steak, topside
INNER ORGANS OF ANIMALS WHICH CAN BE EATEN
liver, kidney, offal, tripe
KINDS OF PROCESSED MEAT
brawn, burger, corned beef, hamburger, mince, pasty, pàté, pie, potted meat, rissole, sausage

mechanic *NOUN*
The mechanic said it would take an hour to mend the engine.
▸ engineer, technician

medal *NOUN*
OTHER THINGS GIVEN TO PEOPLE FOR SOMETHING GOOD OR BRAVE THEY HAVE DONE
award, certificate, decoration, honour, medallion, prize, reward, ribbon, rosette, star, trophy

medallist *NOUN*
Everyone cheered when the medallists received their awards.
▸ champion, victor, winner

meddle *VERB*
1 *She's always meddling in other people's affairs.*
▸ interfere, intervene, intrude, (*informal*) poke your nose in, pry
2 *Don't meddle with my things.*
▸ fiddle about, tinker

media *PLURAL NOUN*
SEE **medium** *NOUN*

medicine *NOUN*
1 *Has he taken his medicine?*
▸ drug, medication, prescription, remedy, treatment
▹ An amount of medicine taken at one time is a **dose**.
2 *My cousin is at university studying medicine.*
▸ healing, therapy, treatment of diseases
COMMON MEDICINES AND TREATMENTS
anaesthetic, antibiotic, antidote, antiseptic, aspirin, gargle, herbs, iodine, linctus, morphia, narcotic, painkiller, penicillin, sedative, tonic, tranquillizer

FORMS IN WHICH YOU TAKE MEDICINE
capsule, inhaler, injection, lotion, lozenge, ointment, pastille, pill, tablet
THINGS USED TO DRESS WOUNDS
bandage, dressing, lint, plaster, poultice
EQUIPMENT USED IN MEDICAL TREATMENT
forceps, hypodermic syringe, scalpel, sling, splint, stethoscope, syringe, thermometer, tweezers
PLACES WHERE YOU CAN GET MEDICAL TREATMENT
clinic, doctor's surgery, health centre, hospital, infirmary, nursing home, sickbay
VARIOUS DEPARTMENTS AND AREAS IN A HOSPITAL
accident and emergency, dispensary, intensive-care unit, operating theatre, outpatients' department, ward, X-ray department
PEOPLE WHO LOOK AFTER OUR HEALTH
▷ A person trained to heal sick people is a **doctor** or **physician**. A doctor who works in a local health centre is a **general practitioner**. A person trained to look after sick people is a **nurse**. Someone who performs medical operations is a **surgeon**. A specialist in repairing people's faces or bodies after accidents is a **plastic surgeon**. A person who puts you to sleep during operations is an **anaesthetist**. A person who takes X-rays is a **radiologist**. A person who tests your hearing is an **audiometrician**. A person who tests your eyes is a **optician**. A person who looks after your feet is a **chiropodist**. People who look after your teeth are **dentists** and **hygienists**.
A specialist in skin problems is a **dermatologist**. A specialist in what you eat is a **dietician**. A specialist in women's health is a **gynaecologist**. A specialist in childbirth is an **obstetrician**. Someone who helps to deliver babies is a **midwife**. A specialist in children's health is a **paediatrician**. A specialist in mental illnesses is a **psychiatrist**. People who treat you by rubbing or twisting your body in various ways: **chiropractor**, **masseur**, **osteopath**, and **physiotherapist**.
SEE ALSO **ill**, **illness**

mediocre *ADJECTIVE*
I thought the film was rather mediocre.
▸ indifferent, inferior, ordinary, second-rate, undistinguished, unexciting

meditation *NOUN*
Monks spend a lot of their time in meditation.
▸ contemplation, prayer, reflection

meditate *VERB*
She sat in silence, meditating on the day's events.
▸ brood (over), contemplate, deliberate (on), ponder, reflect (on), think (about)

medium *ADJECTIVE*
The man was of medium height.
▸ average, middle, moderate, normal, ordinary, usual

medium *NOUN*
This artist's favourite medium is watercolour.
▸ means of expression, method, way
the media or **the mass media**
Media is plural, so we should not say *a media*, but *the media*
THE MEDIA, OR THE MASS MEDIA, INCLUDE
advertising, broadcasting, cable television, magazines, newspapers, the press, radio, satellite television, terrestrial television

meek *ADJECTIVE*
She looks meek, but she has a fierce temper.
▸ docile, gentle, humble, mild, modest, obedient, patient, quiet, resigned, tame
AN OPPOSITE IS aggressive

meet *VERB*
1 *A week later, I met him in the street.*
▸ (*informal*) bump into, come across, encounter, run into, see
2 *My parents met me at the station.*
▸ greet, pick up, welcome
3 *We were told to meet in the playground.*
▸ assemble, collect, gather, muster, rally
4 *Two roads meet here.*
▸ come together, connect, converge, cross, intersect, join, link up, merge, unite
5 *Improvements were carried out to meet the new safety requirements.*
▸ agree with, comply with, fulfil, satisfy

meeting *NOUN*
▷ A meeting of children in school is an **assembly**. A formal meeting to discuss business is a **committee** or **council**. A meeting to discuss and learn about a particular topic is a **conference** or **congress**. A meeting to receive information from someone is a **briefing**. A meeting to give information to reporters is a **press conference**. A large meeting to show support for something, often out of doors, is a **rally**. A meeting for

worship is a service. A meeting with a friend is a rendezvous or date. A formal meeting with a king or queen is an audience.

melancholy *ADJECTIVE*
She sat on her own with a melancholy look on her face.
▸ cheerless, dejected, depressed, gloomy, miserable, mournful, sad, sombre, sorrowful, unhappy, woeful
AN OPPOSITE IS cheerful

mellow *ADJECTIVE*
1 *The fruit had a ripe, mellow flavour.*
▸ pleasant, rich, smooth, sweet
AN OPPOSITE IS sharp
2 *The subdued lighting gave the room a mellow atmosphere.*
▸ agreeable, comforting, friendly, peaceful, reassuring, soft, warm
AN OPPOSITE IS harsh

melody *NOUN*
He picked up the guitar and began to play a familiar melody.
▸ air, theme, tune

melt *VERB*
The ice melted in the sun.
▸ soften, thaw, unfreeze
▹ To melt frozen food is to defrost it. To treat ore to get metal from it is to smelt it.
to melt away *The crowd melted away.*
▸ disappear, disperse, dissolve, dwindle, fade, go away, vanish

member *NOUN*
to be a member of something *She's a member of the local tennis club.*
▸ belong to, join, subscribe to

memorable *ADJECTIVE*
The atmosphere, music, and beautiful surroundings created a truly memorable occasion.
▸ impressive, notable, outstanding, remarkable, striking, unforgettable
AN OPPOSITE IS ordinary

memorial *NOUN*
SEE **monument**

memorize *VERB*
I tried to memorize my words for the play.
▸ commit to memory, learn, learn by heart, remember
AN OPPOSITE IS forget

memory *NOUN*
He has lots of happy memories of his holiday in America.
▸ impression, recollection, remembrance, reminder, reminiscence

menace *VERB*
They were menaced by a man wielding a knife.
▸ bully, intimidate, terrorize, threaten

menace *NOUN*
1 *People who drink and drive are a menace to society.*
▸ danger, threat
2 *That cat is an absolute menace!*
▸ annoyance, inconvenience, irritation, nuisance

mend *VERB*
1 *Workmen were mending holes in the roof.*
▸ fix, put right, renovate, repair, restore
2 *Those socks need mending.*
▸ darn, patch, sew up, stitch up

mental *ADJECTIVE*
1 *She is getting old, but her mental powers are as sharp as ever.*
▸ intellectual, rational
2 *After his accident, he was in a dreadful mental state.*
▸ emotional, psychological

mention *VERB*
1 *She mentioned the idea to her boss.*
▸ comment on, hint at, refer to, speak about, touch on
2 *He mentioned that his father was meeting him later.*
▸ *(informal)* let out, remark, say
3 *The speaker mentioned all the prizewinners.*
▸ acknowledge, draw attention to, name

merciful *ADJECTIVE*
Perhaps the judge will be merciful.
▸ compassionate, forgiving, generous, gracious, humane, humanitarian, kind, lenient, mild, pitying, sympathetic, tender-hearted, tolerant
AN OPPOSITE IS merciless

merciless *ADJECTIVE*
It was a merciless attack on the two people.
▸ barbaric, callous, cruel, hard, hard-hearted, harsh, heartless, intolerant, pitiless, relentless, remorseless, ruthless, savage, severe, stern, strict, unfeeling, unforgiving, unkind, unrelenting, vicious
AN OPPOSITE IS merciful

mercy *NOUN*
Their attackers showed no mercy.
▸ charity, compassion, feeling, forgiveness, goodwill, grace, humanity, kindness, lenience, love, pity, sympathy, understanding
AN OPPOSITE IS cruelty

merge *VERB*
1 *The authorities merged two schools.*
▸ amalgamate, combine, integrate, join together, link up, put together, unite
2 *Motorways merge in one mile.*
▸ come together, converge, join, meet
AN OPPOSITE IS separate

merit *NOUN*
It's a painting of considerable merit.
▸ distinction, excellence, quality, talent, value, virtue, worth

merit *VERB*
Her suggestion merits careful consideration.
▸ be entitled to, deserve, earn, justify, rate, warrant

merriment *NOUN*
Her eyes sparkled with merriment.
▸ amusement, gaiety, hilarity, joking, jollity, joviality, laughter, mirth

merry *ADJECTIVE*
He walked off, whistling a merry tune.
▸ bright, carefree, cheerful, happy, jolly, jovial, joyful, light-hearted, lively, spirited
AN OPPOSITE IS gloomy

mess *NOUN*
1 *Clear up this mess!*
▸ chaos, clutter, confusion, dirt, disorder, jumble, litter, muddle, (*informal*) shambles, untidiness
2 *I made a real mess of it.*
▸ (*informal*) hash, mix-up
3 *I got into a mess.*
▸ difficulty, dilemma, (*informal*) fix, (*informal*) jam, plight, problem

mess *VERB*
to mess about *We were just messing about.*
▸ loaf, lounge about, (*informal*) muck about, play about
to mess things up *I hope you haven't messed up my tapes.*
▸ confuse, jumble, make a mess of, mix up, muddle, tangle
to mess something up *He said he knew how to do it, but he messed it up.*
▸ bungle, (*informal*) make a hash of

message *NOUN*
Did you get my message?
▸ communication
VARIOUS KINDS OF MESSAGE
announcement, bulletin, cable, dispatch, email, letter, memo or memorandum, note, notice, phone call, report, statement, text
PEOPLE WHO DELIVER MESSAGES
bearer, carrier, courier, dispatch rider, go-between, herald, messenger, postman, runner

messy *ADJECTIVE*
Her bedroom is really messy.
▸ chaotic, dirty, disorderly, filthy, grubby, mucky, muddled, untidy
AN OPPOSITE IS neat

metal *NOUN*
SOME COMMON METALS
aluminium, chromium, copper, gold, iron, lead, magnesium, mercury, nickel, platinum, silver, tin, zinc
SOME METAL ALLOYS
brass, bronze, gunmetal, pewter, solder, steel

metallic *ADJECTIVE*
1 *The copper vase had a metallic sheen.*
▸ gleaming, lustrous, shiny
2 *A funny metallic sound came from inside the engine.*
▸ clanking, clinking, ringing

method *NOUN*
1 *She had a secret method for baking cakes.*
▸ procedure, process, technique, way
▷ A specially skilful method for doing something is a knack.
2 *There's method in everything he does.*
▸ a design, order, organization, a pattern, a plan, a routine, a system

A B C D E F G H I J K L M N O P Q R S T U V W X Y Z

methodical ADJECTIVE
She's very methodical and keeps a record of everything.
▸ businesslike, careful, deliberate, efficient, logical, meticulous, neat, orderly, organized, systematic, tidy
AN OPPOSITE IS careless

microbe NOUN
▹ Microbes are **bacteria**, **germs**, **micro-organisms**, or **viruses**.

middle ADJECTIVE
The ball knocked the middle stump out of the ground.
▸ central, inner, inside, midway

middle NOUN
There's a maggot in the middle of this apple.
▸ centre, core, heart
▹ The middle of a wheel is the **hub**. The middle part of an atom or cell is the **nucleus**.

might NOUN
I banged at the door with all my might.
▸ energy, force, power, strength, vigour

mighty ADJECTIVE
He split the log with one mighty blow.
▸ big, enormous, forceful, great, hefty, muscular, powerful, strong, vigorous
AN OPPOSITE IS weak

mild ADJECTIVE
1 *He's a mild person who never complains.*
▸ amiable, docile, easygoing, gentle, good-tempered, harmless, kind, lenient, merciful, placid, soft-hearted
2 *The weather has been mild for this time of year.*
▸ pleasant, temperate, warm
AN OPPOSITE IS severe

militant ADJECTIVE
The protesters became more militant.
▸ aggressive, assertive, attacking, fighting, hostile, warlike

milk NOUN
KINDS OF MILK
condensed, dried, evaporated, long-life, pasteurized, semi-skimmed, skimmed, UHT, whole milk
▹ Foods made from milk are **dairy products**.
SOME DAIRY PRODUCTS
butter, cheese, cream, creme fraiche, custard, fromage frais, junket, milk pudding, yoghurt

milky ADJECTIVE
The sun was hazy in the milky grey sky.
▸ cloudy, misty, opaque, whitish
AN OPPOSITE IS clear

mill VERB
Wheat is milled to make flour.
▸ grind
to mill about *Everyone was milling about wondering what to do.*
▸ move aimlessly, swarm, throng

mimic VERB
Children often mimic their teachers.
▸ copy, do impressions of, imitate, impersonate, pretend to be, (*informal*) take off
▹ If you mimic people specially to make fun of them, you **caricature** or **parody** them.

mind NOUN
1 *Her mind was as sharp as ever.*
▸ brain, head, intellect, intelligence, judgement, mental powers, reasoning, sense, understanding, wits
2 *He changed his mind.*
▸ beliefs, intentions, opinion, outlook, point of view, view, way of thinking, wishes

mind VERB
1 *Will you mind my bag for a minute?*
▸ care for, guard, (*informal*) keep an eye on, look after, watch
2 *Mind the step.*
▸ be careful about, beware of, heed, look out for, note, pay attention to, remember, take notice of, watch out for
3 *I won't mind if you're late.*
▸ be upset, bother, care, complain, disapprove, grumble, object, take offence, worry

mine NOUN
▹ A coal mine is a **colliery** or **pit**. A place where coal is removed from the surface of the ground is an **opencast mine**. A place where stone or slate is removed is a **quarry**.

mine VERB
People used to mine lead in these caves.
▸ dig for, excavate, extract, remove

mingle VERB
The detectives mingled with the crowd.
▸ blend, combine, get together, mix

miniature *ADJECTIVE*
A piccolo looks like a miniature flute.
▸ minute, tiny, toy
SEE ALSO **small**

minimum *ADJECTIVE*
This task can be done with the minimum amount of effort.
▸ least, littlest, lowest, smallest
AN OPPOSITE IS maximum

minor *ADJECTIVE*
1 *They decided to travel on the minor roads.*
▸ lesser, less important, secondary, smaller
2 *I only had a minor part in the play.*
▸ inferior, insignificant, little, small, subordinate, trivial, unimportant
3 *He was guilty of a minor crime.*
▸ petty
AN OPPOSITE IS major

minority *NOUN*
Only a minority are opposed to the scheme.
▸ lesser number, smaller number
AN OPPOSITE IS majority
to be in a minority *Some of them opposed the scheme, but they were in a minority.*
▸ be outnumbered, lose

mint *ADJECTIVE*
in mint condition *His bike was in mint condition.*
▸ brand new, fresh, new, perfect, unmarked, unused

minute *ADJECTIVE*
You can hardly see it, it's so minute.
▸ insignificant, little, microscopic, negligible, tiny
AN OPPOSITE IS large

miracle *NOUN*
It was a miracle that she recovered from her illness.
▸ marvel, mystery, wonder

miraculous *ADJECTIVE*
She made a miraculous recovery.
▸ amazing, astonishing, extraordinary, incredible, inexplicable, marvellous, mysterious, unbelievable, wonderful

mirage *NOUN*
He thought he saw a lake in the distance, but it was a mirage.
▸ illusion, vision

misbehave *VERB*
She has been misbehaving in class again.
▸ behave badly, be naughty, disobey, do wrong, fool about, make mischief, mess about, (*informal*) muck about
AN OPPOSITE IS behave

misbehaviour *NOUN*
We were punished for our misbehaviour.
▸ disobedience, mischief, naughtiness, rudeness, wrongdoing

miscellaneous *ADJECTIVE*
The box was full of miscellaneous odds and ends.
▸ assorted, different, mixed, various

mischief *NOUN*
She'll make sure he doesn't get into any mischief.
▸ misbehaviour, naughtiness, pranks, scrapes, trouble

mischievous *ADJECTIVE*
The mischievous puppy chewed up my slippers.
▸ badly behaved, boisterous, disobedient, impish, naughty, playful, roguish, wicked
AN OPPOSITE IS well behaved

miserable *ADJECTIVE*
1 *You look miserable — what's the matter?*
▸ anguished, broken-hearted, dejected, depressed, distressed, gloomy, glum, melancholy, mournful, sad, sorrowful, tearful, unhappy, woeful
AN OPPOSITE IS cheerful or happy
2 *The poor animals lived in miserable conditions.*
▸ distressing, heartbreaking, pathetic, pitiful, squalid, uncomfortable, wretched
AN OPPOSITE IS comfortable
3 *The weather was cold and miserable.*
▸ depressing, dismal, dreary, grey, unpleasant
AN OPPOSITE IS pleasant

miserly *ADJECTIVE*
He was too miserly to contribute to the collection.
▸ (*informal*) grasping, mean, mercenary, (*informal*) mingy, stingy
AN OPPOSITE IS generous

misery *NOUN*
He saw the misery in her eyes.
▸ anguish, dejection, depression, despair, distress, gloom, grief, heartache, melancholy,

sadness, sorrow, suffering, unhappiness, wretchedness
AN OPPOSITE IS happiness

misfortune *NOUN*
She seems to revel in the misfortunes of other people.
▸ adversity, affliction, bad luck, calamity, catastrophe, disaster, hardship, mishap, tragedy, trouble
AN OPPOSITE IS good luck

mishap *NOUN*
She had a slight mishap with the car.
▸ accident, calamity, catastrophe, disaster, misfortune

mislay *VERB*
I mislaid my purse.
▸ lose
AN OPPOSITE IS find

mislead *VERB*
Don't try to mislead us!
▸ bluff, confuse, deceive, fool, (*informal*) kid, trick

misleading *ADJECTIVE*
The article in the paper contained a number of misleading statements.
▸ ambiguous, confusing, deceptive, muddling, puzzling, unclear, unreliable, wrong

miss *VERB*
1 *I missed the bus.*
▸ be too late for
2 *The arrow missed the target.*
▸ fall short of, go wide of
3 *If we leave now, we should miss the traffic.*
▸ avoid
4 *I missed dad when he was in hospital.*
▸ grieve for, long for, need, pine for, want, yearn for
to miss something out *I missed out the boring parts of the story.*
▸ ignore, leave out, omit, overlook, skip

missile *NOUN*
FOR VARIOUS MISSILES SEE **weapon**

missing *ADJECTIVE*
We found the missing cat two days later.
▸ absent, lost, straying

mission *NOUN*
1 *His mission was to improve staff morale.*
▸ aim, campaign, job, objective, purpose, task
2 *The devices were tested on a recent space mission.*
▸ expedition, exploration, journey, voyage

mist *NOUN*
1 *We drove slowly through the mist.*
▸ cloud, drizzle, fog, haze
2 *I can't see out because of the mist on the windows.*
▸ condensation, steam

mistake *NOUN*
Her work is always full of mistakes.
▸ blunder, error, inaccuracy, lapse, slip, slip-up
▹ A spelling mistake is a misspelling. A mistake where something is left out is an omission. A mistake in a printed book is a misprint.

mistake *VERB*
She mistook my meaning entirely.
▸ get wrong, misunderstand, mix up

mistreat *VERB*
A dog which has been mistreated will remain wary of strangers.
▸ abuse, hurt, misuse, treat badly

mistrust *VERB*
He had no reason to mistrust her.
▸ be sceptical about, distrust, have doubts about, suspect
AN OPPOSITE IS trust

misty *ADJECTIVE*
1 *The weather forecast said that it will be misty.*
▸ foggy, hazy
2 *I can't see out because the windows are misty.*
▸ cloudy, opaque, smoky, steamy
3 *I could just make out a misty shape in the distance.*
▸ blurred, dim, faint, fuzzy, indistinct, shadowy, vague
AN OPPOSITE IS clear

misunderstand *VERB*
He misunderstood her remarks.
▸ get wrong, miss the point of, mistake
AN OPPOSITE IS understand

misunderstanding *NOUN*
The problem was due to a misunderstanding on my part.
▸ error, mistake, (*informal*) mix-up

misuse *VERB*
They felt that they had been deceived and misused.
▸ abuse, hurt, mistreat, treat badly

mix *VERB*
Mix the ingredients in a bowl.
▸ blend, combine, mingle
to mix something up *Don't mix up those papers — I've only just sorted them out.*
▸ confuse, jumble, muddle
▹ To mix up playing cards is to shuffle them.

mixed *ADJECTIVE*
Add a teaspoon of mixed herbs.
▸ assorted, different, miscellaneous, various
AN OPPOSITE IS separate

mixture *NOUN*
1 *Whisk the ingredients and put the mixture in a saucepan.*
▸ blend, combination, mix
2 *There's an odd mixture of things in this drawer.*
▸ assortment, collection, jumble, variety
▹ A mixture of metals is an alloy. A mixture of two different species of plant or animal is a hybrid. A mixture of a solid in a liquid is an emulsion.

moan *VERB*
1 *He moaned in pain.*
▸ cry, groan, sigh, wail
2 *We moaned about the food.*
▸ complain, grouse, grumble

mob *NOUN*
Troops were called in to control the mob.
▸ bunch, crowd, gang, horde, riot, throng

mob *VERB*
Autograph hunters mobbed the pop star.
▸ crowd round, hem in, jostle, surround, swarm round, throng round

mobile *ADJECTIVE*
1 *A mobile library visits once a fortnight.*
▸ movable, travelling
▹ Something that you can carry about is portable.
2 *It wasn't long after the accident before he was mobile again.*
▸ active, moving about, (*informal*) up and about
AN OPPOSITE IS immobile

mobilize *VERB*
The organizers of the demonstration mobilized a lot of supporters.
▸ enlist, gather, get together, muster, organize, rally, summon

mock *VERB*
The winner mocked the other competitors.
▸ deride, jeer at, laugh at, make fun of, ridicule, scoff at, scorn, (*informal*) send up, sneer at

mockery *NOUN*
His smile was full of mockery.
▸ derision, jeering, laughter, ridicule, scorn, sneering
▹ Mocking someone by saying the opposite of what you mean is sarcasm. A piece of writing which mocks someone or something is parody or satire.

model *ADJECTIVE*
1 *They've decided to build a model railway.*
▸ miniature, toy
2 *She's a model pupil.*
▸ ideal, perfect

model *NOUN*
1 *They bought a little model of the aeroplane.*
▸ copy, replica, toy
2 *This year's models will be on display at the motor show.*
▸ design, type, version
3 *She's a model of good behaviour.*
▸ example, ideal

model *VERB*
He models figures in clay.
▸ construct, fashion, make, mould, shape

moderate *ADJECTIVE*
The company offers good quality work at moderate prices.
▸ average, fair, medium, modest, normal, ordinary, reasonable, sensible
AN OPPOSITE IS excessive

moderate *VERB*
1 *The storm moderated.*
▸ become less severe, decrease, die down, ease off, subside, wear off
2 *They moderated their demands.*
▸ lessen, reduce

a b c d e f g h i j k l **m** n o p q r s t u v w x y z

A B C D E F G H I J K L M N O P Q R S T U V W X Y Z

moderately *ADVERB*
He answered the questions moderately well.
▸ fairly, (*informal*) pretty, quite, rather, reasonably, to some extent

modern *ADJECTIVE*
1 *All the equipment in their kitchen was modern.*
▸ advanced, the latest, up to date
AN OPPOSITE IS out of date
2 *She always dresses in modern clothes.*
▸ contemporary, fashionable, present-day, progressive, (*informal*) trendy
AN OPPOSITE IS old-fashioned

modernize *VERB*
The farmhouse had been fully modernized.
▸ improve, rebuild, update

modest *ADJECTIVE*
1 *He's modest about his success.*
▸ bashful, coy, humble, quiet, shy
AN OPPOSITE IS conceited
2 *There has been a modest increase in sales.*
▸ average, medium, moderate, reasonable

modify *VERB*
The present law needs to be modified.
▸ adapt, adjust, alter, change, refine, revise, vary

moist *ADJECTIVE*
1 *The walls of the cellar were moist.*
▸ clammy, damp, watery, wet
2 *Tropical plants grow well in this moist atmosphere.*
▸ humid, muggy, rainy, steamy
AN OPPOSITE IS dry

moisture *NOUN*
Moisture caused the model to disintegrate.
▸ condensation, damp, dampness, dew, mist, steam, vapour, water, wetness

molest *VERB*
The crowd were shouting abuse and molesting the two police officers.
▸ abuse, annoy, assault, attack, bother, harass, interfere with, irritate, pester, torment, vex, worry

molten *ADJECTIVE*
The molten metal is poured into a mould.
▸ liquid, melted

moment *NOUN*
1 *I'll be ready in a moment.*
▸ (*informal*) flash, instant, minute, second
2 *It was one of the great moments of aviation history.*
▸ occasion, time

momentary *ADJECTIVE*
His momentary lack of concentration almost caused an accident.
▸ brief, fleeting, short, temporary
AN OPPOSITE IS permanent

momentous *ADJECTIVE*
It was a momentous decision to declare war.
▸ critical, crucial, decisive, historic, important, serious, significant
AN OPPOSITE IS unimportant

monarch *NOUN*
SEE **ruler**

money *NOUN*
I haven't got any money.
▸ (*slang synonyms*) bread, dough, lolly
DIFFERENT FORMS IN WHICH YOU CAN SPEND MONEY
banknotes, cash, change, cheque, coins, credit card, currency, notes, traveller's cheques
WORDS FOR THE MONEY PEOPLE MAY OWN
finances, fortune, funds, resources, riches, wealth
DIFFERENT FORMS IN WHICH YOU CAN OWN MONEY
assets, capital, estate, investments, property, savings
MONEY YOU RECEIVE FOR DOING A JOB
earnings, income, pay, salary, wages
MONEY YOU RECEIVE FOR OTHER REASONS
dividends, grant, interest, pension, pocket money, profits, winnings
MONEY YOU OWE OR PAY TO OTHER PEOPLE
debts, duty, tax
MONEY WHICH SOMEONE LENDS YOU
advance, loan, mortgage

monkey *NOUN*
VARIOUS KINDS OF MONKEY
ape, baboon, chimpanzee, gibbon, gorilla, marmoset, orang-utan

monopolize *VERB*
He monopolized the conversation all evening.
▸ hog, keep others out of, take over
AN OPPOSITE IS share

monotonous *ADJECTIVE*
Her monotonous voice almost sent me to sleep.
▸ boring, dreary, dull, flat, tedious, unchanging, unexciting, uninteresting
AN OPPOSITE IS interesting

monster *NOUN*
The film featured several frightening monsters.
▸ beast, brute, giant, ogre

monstrous *ADJECTIVE*
1 *The monstrous tidal wave swamped the surrounding countryside.*
▸ big, colossal, enormous, gigantic, great, huge, hulking, immense, mighty, towering, vast
2 *The whole nation was shocked by the monstrous crime.*
▸ abhorrent, atrocious, cruel, dreadful, evil, gross, gruesome, hideous, horrible, horrifying, inhuman, obscene, outrageous, repulsive, shocking, terrible, villainous, wicked

monument *NOUN*
VARIOUS THINGS SET UP AS MONUMENTS
column, cross, gravestone or headstone or tombstone, mausoleum, memorial, obelisk, pillar, shrine, statue, tombstone

mood *NOUN*
What sort of mood is he in today?
▸ disposition, humour, state of mind, temper

moody *ADJECTIVE*
1 *She had been moody and withdrawn for several weeks.*
▸ bad-tempered, cross, depressed, gloomy, grumpy, melancholy, miserable, sulky, sullen
AN OPPOSITE IS cheerful
2 *He's such a moody person that I don't know whether to joke with him or not.*
▸ changeable, touchy, unpredictable, unreliable

moor *VERB*
We moored the boat in the harbour.
▸ fasten, make fast, secure, tie up

mope *VERB*
It's no use moping — things could be worse.
▸ be sad, brood, grieve, pine, sulk

moral *ADJECTIVE*
1 *We have a moral responsibility to help people in need.*
▸ ethical
2 *She's a very moral person.*
▸ honest, innocent, law-abiding, pure, righteous, trustworthy, truthful, upright, virtuous
AN OPPOSITE IS immoral

moral *NOUN*
The moral of this story is that crime does not pay.
▸ lesson, meaning, message
morals *Hasn't he got any morals?*
▸ decency, goodness, honesty, ideals, integrity, morality, principles, standards

morale *NOUN*
The team's morale is high, so we have a good chance of winning.
▸ attitude, confidence, courage, mood, spirit, state of mind

more *ADJECTIVE*
The soup needs more pepper.
▸ added, additional, extra, further
AN OPPOSITE IS less

moreover *ADVERB*
They know the painting is a forgery. Moreover, they know who painted it.
▸ also, besides, further, furthermore, in addition

morsel *NOUN*
She hadn't eaten a morsel of food all day.
▸ bite, crumb, fragment, mouthful, nibble, piece, scrap, taste

mortal *ADJECTIVE*
1 *All human beings are mortal.*
▸ bodily, earthly, human, physical
AN OPPOSITE IS immortal
2 *He received a mortal wound.*
▸ deadly, fatal, lethal

mortality *NOUN*
Sadly, there is high mortality among young birds.
▸ death rate, fatalities, loss of life
AN OPPOSITE IS survival

mostly *ADVERB*
Nowadays, houses are mostly lit by electricity.
▸ chiefly, commonly, generally, largely, mainly, normally, predominantly, primarily, principally, typically, usually

motherly *ADJECTIVE*
All her motherly instincts were aroused by the sight of the babies.
► caring, kind, loving, maternal, protective, tender

motion *NOUN*
He summoned the waiter with a motion of his hand.
► gesture, movement

motionless *ADJECTIVE*
The cat sat motionless, watching the bird.
► immobile, stationary, still, unmoving
AN OPPOSITE IS moving

motivate *VERB*
He was motivated solely by the desire for power.
► encourage, induce, persuade, prompt, provoke, spur, stimulate, urge

motive *NOUN*
The police believe jealousy was the motive for the crime.
► cause, motivation, purpose, reasoning, thinking

motor *NOUN*
The toy train had an electric motor.
► engine
motor car
SEE **car**

motorist *NOUN*
Some motorists drive too fast in bad weather.
► driver

mottled *ADJECTIVE*
The sunlight made a mottled pattern under the trees.
► dappled, patchy, speckled, spotty

motto *NOUN*
Her motto has always been, 'keep smiling'.
► catchphrase, proverb, saying, slogan

mould *VERB*
We moulded the figures from clay.
► fashion, form, model, shape

mouldy *ADJECTIVE*
There was nothing in the fridge but some mouldy cheese.
► damp, decaying, decomposing, musty, rotten, rotting

mound *NOUN*
1 *She sat at her desk, surrounded by mounds of paper.*
► heap, mass, pile, stack
2 *There used to be a castle on top of that mound.*
► hill, hump, rise
▷ An ancient mound of earth over a grave is a barrow.

mount *VERB*
1 *She mounted the pony and rode off.*
► get on, jump onto
2 *He mounted the steps.*
► ascend, climb, go up
3 *The gallery is mounting an exhibition of 16th century drawings.*
► display, put up, set up
to mount up *Her debts were beginning to mount up.*
► accumulate, get bigger, grow, increase, pile up

mountain *NOUN*
▷ The top of a mountain is the peak or summit. A line of mountains is a range. A long, narrow mountain is a ridge. A mountain with a hole at the top caused by an eruption is a volcano.

mountainous *ADJECTIVE*
1 *Travelling is difficult in mountainous country.*
► alpine, hilly, rugged
2 *The ship was battered by mountainous waves.*
► colossal, enormous, gigantic, high, huge, steep, towering

mourn *VERB*
He mourned for his dead dog.
► go into mourning, grieve, lament, pine, weep
AN OPPOSITE IS rejoice

mournful *ADJECTIVE*
1 *The farewell party was a mournful occasion.*
► dismal, distressing, gloomy, sad, sorrowful, tearful, unhappy
2 *They could hear the mournful cries of the abandoned animals.*
► desolate, distressed, forlorn, melancholy, woeful
AN OPPOSITE IS cheerful

mouth *NOUN*
1 *Don't talk with your mouth full.*
► jaws, lips
▷ A dog's nose and mouth is its muzzle.
2 *They travelled the whole length of the river, from its source to its mouth.*
► outlet
▷ A wide river mouth is an estuary. A river

mouth where the river divides into branches is a **delta**.
3 *She saw the mouth of a cave in the cliff above her.*
▸ entrance, opening

move *NOUN*
1 *Don't make a move!*
▸ movement
2 *What will his next move be?*
▸ action, deed, manoeuvre, step
3 *It's your move next.*
▸ chance, go, opportunity, turn

move *VERB* This word is often overused. People and things can move in many different ways. We give some of the commoner senses of the word, followed by synonyms you could use:
1 *To move things from one place to another.*
▸ carry, remove, shift, transfer, transport
2 *To move from a certain position.*
▸ budge, depart, go, leave, quit
3 *To move restlessly.*
▸ fidget, flap, shake, stir, toss, turn, twist, twitch
4 *To move from side to side.*
▸ swing, wag, wave, wiggle
5 *To move along.*
▸ make progress, proceed, travel, walk
6 *To move along quickly.*
▸ career, dash, fly, hasten, hurry, hurtle, race, run, rush, shoot, speed, sweep, zoom
7 *To move along slowly.*
▸ amble, crawl, dawdle, stroll
8 *To move towards something.*
▸ advance, approach, come, proceed, progress
9 *To move away from something.*
▸ back, retreat, reverse, withdraw
10 *To move downwards.*
▸ descend, drop, fall, sink, swoop
11 *To move upwards.*
▸ arise, ascend, climb, mount, rise, soar
12 *To move round and round.*
▸ revolve, roll, rotate, spin, turn, twirl, twist, wheel, whirl
13 *To move gracefully.*
▸ dance, flow, glide
14 *To move clumsily.*
▸ flounder, lumber, lurch, shuffle, stagger, stumble, totter, trip, trundle
15 *To move stealthily.*
▸ crawl, creep, edge, slink

movement *NOUN*
1 *He felt incapable of movement.*
▸ action, gesture, motion, moving
2 *Has there been any movement in their attitude?*
▸ change, development, progress, shift
3 *She's keen to join the anti-hunting movement.*
▸ campaign, crusade, group, organization, party

moving *ADJECTIVE*
His moving story nearly made her cry.
▸ emotional, inspiring, stirring, (*informal*) tear-jerking, touching

muck *NOUN*
They were clearing the muck out of the stable.
▸ dirt, dung, filth, grime, manure, mud, rubbish, sewage, slime, sludge

mucky *ADJECTIVE*
His hands are all mucky.
▸ dirty, filthy, foul, grimy, grubby, messy, muddy, soiled, squalid
AN OPPOSITE IS clean

mud *NOUN*
The tractor left a trail of mud on the road.
▸ clay, dirt, muck, slime, sludge, soil

muddle *NOUN*
1 *There was a muddle over the arrangements.*
▸ confusion, misunderstanding, (*informal*) mix-up
2 *There was a muddle of clothes on the floor.*
▸ jumble, mess, tangle

muddle *VERB*
1 *He muddled all the books on her desk.*
▸ jumble up, make a mess of, (*informal*) mess up, mix up, shuffle, tangle
AN OPPOSITE IS tidy
2 *Don't talk so fast — you'll muddle him.*
▸ bewilder, confuse, mislead, perplex, puzzle

muddy *ADJECTIVE*
1 *Take off your muddy shoes before you come in.*
▸ caked, dirty, filthy, messy, mucky, soiled
AN OPPOSITE IS clean
2 *I got filthy walking across the muddy ground.*
▸ boggy, marshy, soft, spongy, waterlogged, wet
AN OPPOSITE IS dry or firm

A B C D E F G H I J K L M N O P Q R S T U V W X Y Z

muffle *VERB*
1 *They muffled themselves up to play in the snow.*
▸ cover, wrap
2 *She tried to muffle her sneeze.*
▸ deaden, disguise, mask, silence, stifle, suppress

muffled *ADJECTIVE*
She could hear muffled voices coming from next door.
▸ indistinct, muted, unclear, woolly
AN OPPOSITE IS clear

muggy *ADJECTIVE*
The weather's been very muggy recently.
▸ close, damp, humid, moist, oppressive, steamy
AN OPPOSITE IS fresh

multiply *VERB*
Mice multiply quickly.
▸ breed, increase, reproduce, spread

multitude *NOUN*
She's got a multitude of things to do.
▸ crowd, host, large number, mass

mumble *VERB*
He was mumbling and they could hardly understand what he was saying.
▸ mutter, talk indistinctly

munch *VERB*
He sat munching crisps through the whole film.
▸ chew, crunch

murder *NOUN*
▹ A synonym commonly used in America is **homicide**. The murder of an important person is an **assassination**. The murder of a king is **regicide**. Killing someone without meaning to do so is **manslaughter**.
SEE ALSO **kill**

murderous *ADJECTIVE*
They launched a murderous attack on their enemy.
▸ bloodthirsty, brutal, cruel, deadly, ferocious, fierce, pitiless, ruthless, savage, vicious, violent

murky *ADJECTIVE*
It was so murky that they had to put the headlights on.
▸ cloudy, dark, dim, dull, foggy, gloomy, grey, misty, sombre
AN OPPOSITE IS clear

murmur *NOUN*
There was a murmur of voices from the next room.
▸ buzz, drone, hum, whispering

muscular *ADJECTIVE*
The wrestler was a muscular man.
▸ (*informal*) beefy, brawny, burly, hefty, husky, powerful, robust, strong, sturdy, tough, well built, well developed
AN OPPOSITE IS puny or weak

music *NOUN*
DIFFERENT KINDS OF MUSIC
blues, classical music, country and western, dance music, disco music, folk music, gospel, jazz, orchestral music, pop music, punk, ragtime, rap, reggae, rock, soul, swing
MUSICAL COMPOSITIONS FOR SINGING
anthem, ballad, carol, hymn, lullaby, sea shanty, song, spiritual
LONG MUSICAL COMPOSITIONS FOR SINGING OR DANCING
ballet, musical, opera, operetta, oratorio
SOME OTHER KINDS OF MUSICAL COMPOSITION
concerto, fanfare, fugue, march, nocturne, overture, prelude, rhapsody, sonata, symphony

Musical instruments
FAMILIES OF MUSICAL INSTRUMENTS
brass, keyboard, percussion, strings, woodwind
STRINGED INSTRUMENTS THAT CAN BE PLAYED WITH A BOW
cello, double bass, viola, violin or fiddle
INSTRUMENTS WITH STRINGS PLAYED BY PLUCKING OR STRUMMING
banjo, guitar, harp, lute, lyre, sitar, ukulele, zither
BRASS INSTRUMENTS
bugle, cornet, euphonium, flugelhorn, French horn, trombone, trumpet, tuba
OTHER INSTRUMENTS YOU PLAY BY BLOWING
bagpipes, bassoon, clarinet, cor anglais, flute, harmonica or mouth organ, oboe, piccolo, recorder, saxophone
KEYBOARD INSTRUMENTS
accordion, harmonium, harpsichord, keyboard, organ, piano, synthesizer
PERCUSSION INSTRUMENTS
bass drum, bongo drum, castanets, celesta, chime bars, cymbals, drum, glockenspiel, gong, kettledrum, maracas, marimba, rattle, side drum, snare drum, tabor, tambour, tambourine, timpani, tom-tom, triangle, tubular bells, vibraphone, wood block, xylophone

music *NOUN*
DIFFERENT SINGING VOICES
alto, bass, contralto, soprano, tenor, treble
PEOPLE WHO PLAY VARIOUS INSTRUMENTS
bugler, cellist, clarinettist, drummer, fiddler, flautist, guitarist, harpist, oboist, organist, percussionist, pianist, piper, timpanist, trombonist, trumpeter, violinist
VARIOUS OTHER MUSICIANS
accompanist, composer, conductor, instrumentalist, singer, vocalist
GROUPS OF MUSICIANS
band, choir or chorus, duet or duo, ensemble, group, orchestra, quartet, quintet, trio
Musical terms
TERMS USED IN MUSIC
chord, chromatic scale, counterpoint, diatonic scale, discord, harmony, melody, note, octave, pitch, rhythm, scale, semitone, tempo, theme, tone, tune
NAMES OF NOTES IN WRITTEN MUSIC
crotchet, minim, quaver, semibreve, semiquaver
OTHER SIGNS USED IN WRITTEN MUSIC
clef sign, flat, key signature, natural, sharp, stave, time signature

musical *ADJECTIVE*
She has a very musical voice.
▸ harmonious, melodious, pleasant, sweet sounding, tuneful

muster *VERB*
Can they muster a full team for Saturday?
▸ assemble, call together, collect, gather, get together, mobilize, rally, round up

musty *ADJECTIVE*
There's a musty smell in the spare room.
▸ airless, damp, mouldy, stale, stuffy
AN OPPOSITE IS fresh

mute *ADJECTIVE*
He stared in mute amazement.
▸ dumb, silent, speechless, tongue-tied

mutilate *VERB*
The soldier was horribly mutilated in the explosion.
▸ cripple, injure, lame, maim, mangle, wound

mutinous *ADJECTIVE*
The captain was unable to control his mutinous crew.
▸ defiant, disobedient, rebellious, uncontrollable

mutiny *VERB*
The sailors mutinied because of the bad conditions on their ship.
▸ disobey, rebel, revolt, rise up

mutter *VERB*
I can't understand what you're saying when you mutter.
▸ mumble, murmur, talk indistinctly

mutual *ADJECTIVE*
They had a mutual interest in doing the deal.
▸ common, joint, reciprocal, shared

mysterious *ADJECTIVE*
1 *The doctors were puzzled by her mysterious illness.*
▸ baffling, incomprehensible, inexplicable, miraculous, mystifying, perplexing, puzzling, unexplained
2 *Someone had drawn a mysterious sign on the wall.*
▸ eerie, obscure, secret, strange, uncanny, weird

mystery *NOUN*
What really happened was a mystery.
▸ miracle, mysterious happening, puzzle, riddle, secret

mystify *VERB*
He was mystified by her disappearance.
▸ baffle, bewilder, perplex, puzzle

mythical *ADJECTIVE*
The unicorn is a mythical beast.
▸ fabulous, fanciful, fictional, imaginary, invented, legendary, mythological, non-existent, unreal
AN OPPOSITE IS real

Nn

nag *VERB*
He was always nagging her to work harder.
▸ badger, pester, scold

naïve *ADJECTIVE*
He's so naïve that he believes her promises.
▸ gullible, inexperienced, innocent, simple-minded

naked *ADJECTIVE*
He walked naked into the bathroom.
▸ bare, nude, stripped, unclothed, undressed
AN OPPOSITE IS clothed

name *NOUN*
▹ The official names you have are your first names or forenames, and surname. Names a Christian is given at baptism are **Christian names**. A false name is an **alias**. A name people use instead of your real name is a **nickname**. A false name an author uses is a **pen name** or **pseudonym**. The name of a book is its **title**.

name *VERB*
His parents named him Antony.
▸ call
▹ To name someone at the ceremony of baptism is to **baptize** or **christen** them.

nap *NOUN*
to take a nap *He always takes a nap on Sunday afternoons.*
▸ doze, nod off, rest, sleep

narrate *VERB*
He narrated the story of his life.
▸ recount, relate, tell

narration *NOUN*
Who did the narration in that film?
▸ commentary, description, storytelling

narrative *NOUN*
The sailor wrote an exciting narrative of his lonely voyage.
▸ account, chronicle, history, story, tale, (*informal*) yarn

narrow *ADJECTIVE*
He squeezed through a narrow opening.
▸ slender, slim, thin
AN OPPOSITE IS wide

narrow-minded *ADJECTIVE*
She has a very narrow-minded view of life.
▸ biased, conservative, intolerant, prejudiced, prim
AN OPPOSITE IS broad-minded

nasty *ADJECTIVE*
The adjective *nasty* can refer to almost anything you don't like. We give some of the common uses of the word, followed by synonyms you could use instead
1 *A nasty person.*
▸ cruel, unfriendly, unkind, unpleasant
2 *A nasty experience.*
▸ awful, dreadful, fearful, frightening, grim, horrifying, (*informal*) scary, terrifying
3 *A nasty problem.*
▸ baffling, complicated, difficult, hard, insoluble, puzzling, ticklish, tricky
4 *A nasty mess.*
▸ dirty, disgusting, filthy, horrible, loathsome, (*informal*) mucky, revolting, squalid
5 *A nasty smell.*
▸ bad, disagreeable, foul, objectionable, repulsive, rotten, sickening, stinking
6 *A nasty crime.*
▸ barbaric, beastly, brutal, cruel, ruthless, savage, vicious
7 *A nasty film.*
▸ immoral, indecent, obscene, offensive, shocking, (*informal*) sick, violent
8 *A nasty illness.*
▸ acute, critical, dangerous, life threatening, painful, serious, severe
AN OPPOSITE IS nice

nation *NOUN*
1 *The president addressed the nation on television.*
▸ community, population, society
2 *People from many nations compete in the Olympic Games.*
▸ country, land, state

national *ADJECTIVE*
1 *She bought the national and local newspapers.*
▸ general, nationwide
AN OPPOSITE IS local
2 *It's interesting to learn about other people's national customs.*
▸ ethnic

nationalist *NOUN*
▹ People who love their country are **patriots**. People who think their country is better than any other are **chauvinists**.

natural *ADJECTIVE*
1 *It's natural for birds to defend their territory.*
▸ inherited, instinctive, intuitive
2 *It's natural for most people to write with the right hand.*
▸ normal, ordinary, spontaneous, usual
AN OPPOSITE IS unnatural

nature *NOUN*

1 *I like TV programmes about nature.*
▸ the countryside, natural history, wildlife
2 *He has a kind nature.*
▸ character, disposition, manner, personality
3 *I collect coins, medals, and things of that nature.*
▸ description, kind, sort, type, variety

naughty *ADJECTIVE*

The naughty children felt ashamed of themselves.
▸ bad, badly behaved, bad-mannered, disobedient, impolite, mischievous, rebellious, rude, stubborn, troublesome, uncontrollable, unmanageable, unruly, wicked
AN OPPOSITE IS well behaved
to be naughty ▸ behave badly, disobey, (*informal*) mess about, misbehave

navigate *VERB*

The captain navigated his ship between the dangerous rocks.
▸ direct, guide, manoeuvre, pilot, sail, steer

navy *NOUN*
WORDS FOR GROUPS OF SHIPS
armada, convoy, fleet

near *ADJECTIVE*

1 *We get on well with our near neighbours.*
▸ adjacent, close, next door
2 *My birthday is near.*
▸ approaching, coming
3 *I invited all my near relatives to the party.*
▸ close, dear, familiar, intimate
AN OPPOSITE IS distant

nearly *ADVERB*

It's nearly dinner time.
▸ almost, approaching, not quite, practically, virtually

neat *ADJECTIVE*

1 *My friend keeps her bedroom neat.*
▸ clean, orderly, tidy, uncluttered
2 *Mum always looks neat when she goes out.*
▸ elegant, smart, spruce, trim
3 *He congratulated me on doing a neat job.*
▸ accurate, deft, expert, meticulous, precise, skilful
AN OPPOSITE IS untidy

necessary *ADJECTIVE*

The policeman said that the repairs to the car were absolutely necessary.
▸ compulsory, essential, indispensable, inevitable, needed, unavoidable
AN OPPOSITE IS unnecessary

necessity *NOUN*

Is it a necessity, or can we do without it?
▸ essential, requirement

need *NOUN*

There's a need for more shops in our area.
▸ call, demand, requirement

need *VERB*

1 *I need £10.*
▸ be short of, lack, require, want
2 *The charity needs our support.*
▸ depend on, rely on

needless *ADJECTIVE*

Why are they making that needless noise?
▸ excessive, superfluous, unnecessary, unwanted

needlework *NOUN*

Gran says you need good eyesight for needlework.
▸ embroidery, sewing

needy *ADJECTIVE*

Don't you think we should help needy people?
▸ badly off, hard up, poor
AN OPPOSITE IS rich

negative *ADJECTIVE*

He has a very negative attitude to his job.
▸ contrary, grudging, obstinate, pessimistic, uncooperative, unenthusiastic, unhelpful, unwilling
AN OPPOSITE IS positive

neglect *VERB*

She's been neglecting her work.
▸ abandon, disregard, forget, ignore, leave alone, overlook, pay no attention to, shirk

negligent *ADJECTIVE*

The doctor was accused of being negligent.
▸ careless, forgetful, inattentive, inconsiderate, irresponsible, slack, sloppy, slovenly, thoughtless, uncaring, unprofessional, unthinking
AN OPPOSITE IS careful

A B C D E F G H I J K L M N O P Q R S T U V W X Y Z

negligible *ADJECTIVE*
There has been a negligible amount of rain this summer.
▸ imperceptible, insignificant, slight, small, tiny, trivial, unimportant
AN OPPOSITE IS considerable

negotiate *VERB*
1 *She negotiated with the car salesman.*
▸ bargain, confer, discuss terms, haggle
2 *The driver failed to negotiate the bend and crashed the car.*
▸ get past, manoeuvre round

negotiation *NOUN*
Instead of fighting, the two sides settled the dispute by negotiation.
▸ arbitration, bargaining, diplomacy, discussion

neighbourhood *NOUN*
They live in a very nice neighbourhood.
▸ area, community, district, locality, vicinity

neighbouring *ADJECTIVE*
She invited people from the neighbouring houses to her party.
▸ adjacent, bordering, close, near, nearby, nearest, next door

neighbourly *ADJECTIVE*
It was neighbourly to water their plants while they were away.
▸ friendly, helpful, kind
AN OPPOSITE IS unfriendly

nerve *NOUN*
1 *That steeplejack has some nerve!*
▸ bravery, courage, daring, pluck
2 *She's got a nerve, taking my pen without asking!*
▸ cheek, impertinence, impudence, rudeness

nerve-racking *ADJECTIVE*
His driving test was a nerve-racking experience.
▸ agonizing, distressing, tense, worrying
AN OPPOSITE IS relaxing

nervous *ADJECTIVE*
She always feels nervous before an exam.
▸ agitated, anxious, apprehensive, edgy, fearful, fidgety, flustered, insecure, jumpy, on edge, tense, uneasy, (*informal*) uptight, worried
AN OPPOSITE IS calm

nestle *VERB*
The puppies nestled against their mother.
▸ cuddle, curl up, lie comfortably, snuggle

net, network *NOUNS*
THINGS WITH A CRISS-CROSS ARRANGEMENT OF LINES, ETC.
grid, lace, lattice, mesh, net, netting, network, trellis, web
▷ A network of paths is a **labyrinth** or **maze**. An organization with many connected parts, like a railway network, is a **system**.

neutral *ADJECTIVE*
1 *A referee has to be neutral.*
▸ disinterested, impartial, unbiased, unprejudiced
AN OPPOSITE IS prejudiced
2 *The room was decorated in neutral colours.*
▸ drab, indefinite, pale
AN OPPOSITE IS distinctive

new *ADJECTIVE* This word is often overused. Here are some alternatives:
1 *Start on a new sheet of paper.*
▸ brand new, clean, fresh, unused
▷ A new stamp or coin is in **mint** condition.
2 *They went to the motor show to see the new models.*
▸ current, latest, modern, recent, up to date
3 *She thought she'd sorted everything out, but then a new problem arose.*
▸ additional, different, extra, unexpected, unfamiliar
4 *Haven't you got any new ideas?*
▸ innovative, radical, revolutionary
AN OPPOSITE IS old

newcomer *NOUN*
The teacher introduced the newcomer to the class.
▸ arrival, beginner, new boy, new girl
▷ A person who has just come to a new country is an **immigrant** or **settler**.

news *NOUN*
What's the latest news?
▸ information, (*old use*) tidings, word
VARIOUS FORMS IN WHICH YOU GET NEWS
announcement, bulletin, dispatch, message, newsflash, newsletter, newspaper, notice, poster, press release, proclamation, report, statement
SEE ALSO **communication**

next *ADJECTIVE*
1 *He lives in the house next to the chip shop.*
▸ adjacent, closest, nearest
AN OPPOSITE IS distant
2 *If she's not on this bus, she's bound to be on the next one.*
▸ following, subsequent
AN OPPOSITE IS previous

nice *ADJECTIVE* This word is often overused. People often use the adjective *nice* because it can refer to almost anything we like; but its meaning is vague, and there are a lot of more precise words we can use. We give here some of the uses of the word, followed by synonyms you could use instead:
1 *A nice person.*
▸ friendly, generous, helpful, kind, likeable
2 *A nice experience.*
▸ delightful, enjoyable, good
3 *Nice food.*
▸ delicious, satisfying, tasty, well cooked
4 *A nice smell.*
▸ agreeable, fragrant
5 *Nice weather.*
▸ fine, sunny, warm
6 *Nice manners.*
▸ courteous, elegant, polished, polite, refined
7 *A nice picture.*
▸ attractive, beautiful, pleasing
AN OPPOSITE IS nasty
Other senses in which you can use the word *NICE*:
1 *There is a nice distinction between borrowing and stealing.*
▸ delicate, fine
2 *A watchmaker must have a nice eye for small details.*
▸ accurate, discriminating, exact, meticulous, precise

nimble *ADJECTIVE*
She soon sewed the button on with her nimble fingers.
▸ agile, deft, quick, quick-moving, skilful
AN OPPOSITE IS clumsy

nip *VERB*
1 *She nipped her finger in the door.*
▸ pinch, snip, squeeze
2 *The dog nipped my leg.*
▸ bite
3 (*informal*) *She nipped along to the shops.*
▸ dash, go, (*informal*) pop, run, rush

noble *ADJECTIVE*
1 *She comes from an ancient noble family.*
▸ aristocratic, high-born, upper-class
AN OPPOSITE IS ordinary
2 *The rescue team were congratulated for their noble efforts.*
▸ brave, chivalrous, courageous, gallant, heroic, honourable, virtuous, worthy
AN OPPOSITE IS cowardly or unworthy
3 *The noble building could be seen from miles around.*
▸ dignified, distinguished, elegant, grand, great, imposing, impressive, magnificent, majestic, splendid, stately
AN OPPOSITE IS insignificant

nobleman, noblewoman *NOUNS*
▸ aristocrat, noble
FOR VARIOUS NOBLE TITLES SEE **title**

nod *VERB*
He nodded his head in agreement.
▸ bend, bob, bow
to nod off *He sometimes nods off in front of the television.*
▸ be drowsy, doze, fall asleep, have a nap, rest, sleep

noise *NOUN*
There's a dreadful noise coming from the house.
▸ din, hullabaloo, pandemonium, racket, row, screaming, screeching, shrieking, shouting, tumult, uproar, yelling
FOR VARIOUS WAYS TO MAKE SOUNDS SEE **sound** *VERB*

noisy *ADJECTIVE*
1 *They complained about the noisy children.*
▸ chattering, rowdy, screaming, screeching, shrieking, shrill, talkative
2 *The people next door were playing noisy music.*
▸ blaring, booming, deafening, ear-splitting, loud, thunderous
AN OPPOSITE IS quiet

nominate *VERB*
They nominated her as captain.
▸ appoint, choose, elect, name, select

non-existent *ADJECTIVE*
The danger was non-existent.
▸ fictitious, imaginary, imagined, made-up
AN OPPOSITE IS real

nonsense *NOUN*
She's talking nonsense!
▸ (These synonyms are normally used *INFORMALLY*) bilge, rot, rubbish, stuff and nonsense, tripe

nonsensical *ADJECTIVE*
His nonsensical idea just wasn't worth talking about.
▸ absurd, crazy, foolish, illogical, incomprehensible, irrational, laughable, ludicrous, meaningless, ridiculous, senseless, silly, stupid, unreasonable
AN OPPOSITE IS sensible

non-stop *ADJECTIVE*
1 *Their non-stop chattering annoyed her.*
▸ ceaseless, constant, continual, continuous, endless, incessant, never-ending, unbroken, unceasing
2 *They took a non-stop train from Leicester to London.*
▸ direct, express, fast

normal *ADJECTIVE*
1 *He had a normal kind of day at work.*
▸ average, common, customary, familiar, habitual, ordinary, predictable, regular, routine, standard, typical, unsurprising, usual
2 *No normal person would sleep on a bed of nails.*
▸ healthy, rational, reasonable, sane
AN OPPOSITE IS abnormal

north *NOUN, ADJECTIVE, & ADVERB*
▹ The parts of a continent or country in the north are the **northern** parts. To travel towards the north is to travel **northward** or **northwards** or in a **northerly** direction. A wind from the north is a **northerly** wind. A person who lives in the north of Britain is a **northerner**.

nose *NOUN*
1 *Someone punched him on the nose.*
▹ The openings in your nose are **nostrils**. Words for an animal's nose are **muzzle** or **snout**.
2 *She sat in the nose of a boat looking out for dangerous rocks.*
▸ bow, front, prow

nostalgia *NOUN*
He felt a nostalgia for the old days.
▸ longing, pining, yearning

nostalgic *ADJECTIVE*
He has nostalgic memories of his childhood.
▸ emotional, romantic, sentimental, wistful

nosy *ADJECTIVE* (*informal*)
She resented his nosy questions about her private life.
▸ inquisitive, interfering, meddlesome, prying

notable *ADJECTIVE*
1 *Many notable writers and artists were present at the ceremony.*
▸ celebrated, distinguished, eminent, famous, important, outstanding, prominent, renowned, well known
2 *The Prince's visit was a notable event.*
▸ memorable, rare, remarkable, uncommon, unusual
AN OPPOSITE IS insignificant or ordinary

note *NOUN*
1 *He sent a note thanking her for the present.*
▸ communication, letter, message
2 *There was a note of anger in her voice.*
▸ feeling, quality, sound, tone

note *VERB*
1 *He noted the car number on a piece of paper.*
▸ jot down, make a note of, record, scribble, write down
2 *Did you note what he was wearing?*
▸ heed, mark, notice, observe, pay attention to, see, take note of

notebook *NOUN*
She jotted down a few ideas in a notebook.
▸ diary, exercise book, jotter, writing book

nothing *NOUN*
Four minus four equals nothing.
▸ nought, zero
▹ In cricket a score of nothing is a **duck**, in tennis it is **love**, and in football it is **nil**.

notice *NOUN*
Someone put up a notice about the meeting.
▸ advertisement, placard, poster, sign, warning
to take notice of something *She took notice of the warning.*
▸ heed, pay attention to

notice *VERB*
1 *Did you notice what he was wearing?*
▸ heed, mark, note, observe, pay attention to, see, take note of
2 *I noticed a funny smell.*
▸ become aware of, detect

noticeable *ADJECTIVE*
1 *There has been a noticeable improvement in the weather.*
▸ definite, distinct, measurable, notable, perceptible, significant
2 *The power station is noticeable from many miles away.*
▸ conspicuous, visible
3 *He spoke with a noticeable foreign accent.*
▸ audible, obvious, pronounced, unmistakable
AN OPPOSITE IS imperceptible

notion *NOUN*
He has some strange notions about life.
▸ belief, concept, idea, opinion, theory, thought, view

notorious *ADJECTIVE*
The police finally arrested the notorious criminal.
▸ infamous, outrageous, scandalous, shocking, well known, wicked

nourish *VERB*
Plants are nourished by water drawn up through their roots.
▸ feed, strengthen, sustain

nourishing *ADJECTIVE*
The refugees were in need of nourishing food.
▸ health-giving, nutritious, sustaining, wholesome

novel *ADJECTIVE*
The designer had a novel approach to fashion.
▸ different, fresh, imaginative, innovative, new, original, uncommon, unconventional, unfamiliar, unusual
AN OPPOSITE IS familiar

novel *NOUN*
FOR VARIOUS KINDS OF WRITING SEE **writing**

now *ADVERB*
1 *She is now living in Glasgow.*
▸ at present, at the moment, currently
2 *The job must be done now.*
▸ immediately, straight away, without delay

nude *ADJECTIVE*
Several children swam nude.
▸ bare, naked, stripped, undressed
AN OPPOSITE IS clothed

nudge *VERB*
She nudged me with her elbow.
▸ bump, jog, jolt, poke, prod, shove, touch

nuisance *NOUN*
The dog's constant barking is a real nuisance.
▸ annoyance, bother, inconvenience, irritation, menace, worry

numb *ADJECTIVE*
My toes are numb with cold.
▸ dead, frozen, insensitive, paralysed
AN OPPOSITE IS sensitive

number *NOUN*
1 *He added the numbers together to get the answer.*
▸ figure, numeral
▹ Any of the numbers from 0 to 9 is a **digit**. A negative or positive whole number is an **integer**. An amount used in measuring or counting is a **unit**.
2 *A large number of people welcomed the team home.*
▸ collection, crowd, multitude
3 *He'd lost the current number of the magazine.*
▸ edition, issue
4 *The band played some well-known numbers.*
▸ piece, song

numerous *ADJECTIVE*
The car had numerous faults.
▸ abundant, countless, innumerable, many, plenty of, untold
AN OPPOSITE IS few

nurse *VERB*
1 *He nursed her while she was ill.*
▸ care for, look after, tend
2 *She nursed the baby in her arms.*
▸ cradle, cuddle, hold, hug

nursery *NOUN*
1 *Her little brother starts at a nursery next month.*
▸ crèche, kindergarten, nursery school
2 *They went to the nursery to buy plants for the garden.*
▸ garden centre

nut *NOUN*
KINDS OF NUT
almond, brazil, cashew, chestnut, cobnut, coconut, filbert or hazelnut, peanut, pecan, pistachio, walnut

A B C D E F G H I J K L M N O P Q R S T U V W X Y Z

Oo

oath *NOUN*
1 *He swore a solemn oath that he was telling the truth.*
▸ pledge, promise, vow, word of honour
2 *He let out a terrible oath when the door slammed on his finger.*
▸ blasphemy, curse, exclamation, swear word

obedient *ADJECTIVE*
The dog seemed very obedient.
▸ disciplined, docile, manageable, submissive, well behaved
AN OPPOSITE IS disobedient

obey *VERB*
1 *The soldiers refused to obey orders.*
▸ abide by, adhere to, carry out, follow, heed, implement, keep to, observe, submit to
2 *He obeyed without question.*
▸ be obedient, conform, do what you are told, take orders
AN OPPOSITE IS disobey

object *NOUN*
1 *She saw some strange objects in the museum.*
▸ article, item, thing
2 *What is the object of this exercise?*
▸ aim, goal, intention, objective, point, purpose

object *VERB*
to object to something *He objected to the plan.*
▸ argue against, be opposed to, complain about, disapprove of, grumble about, mind, protest against, raise questions about, take exception to
AN OPPOSITE IS accept or agree to

objection *NOUN*
Her objections were ignored.
▸ complaint, disapproval, opposition, outcry, protest, query, question

objectionable *ADJECTIVE*
The drains were giving off an objectionable smell.
▸ disagreeable, disgusting, foul, hateful, intolerable, loathsome, nasty, offensive, repellent, revolting, sickening, undesirable, unpleasant
AN OPPOSITE IS acceptable

objective *ADJECTIVE*
1 *There was no objective evidence of his guilt.*
▸ actual, real, scientific
2 *He gave an objective account of what happened.*
▸ disinterested, factual, impartial, rational, unbiased, unemotional, unprejudiced
AN OPPOSITE IS subjective

objective *NOUN*
Their objective was to reach the top of the hill.
▸ aim, ambition, goal, intention, object, purpose, target

obligation *NOUN*
Everyone has an obligation to pay taxes.
▸ commitment, duty, liability, requirement, responsibility
AN OPPOSITE IS option

obligatory *ADJECTIVE*
The wearing of seat belts is obligatory.
▸ compulsory, necessary, required
AN OPPOSITE IS optional

oblige *VERB*
Would you oblige me by passing the salt?
▸ help, please

obliged *ADJECTIVE*
1 *He felt obliged to help them.*
▸ bound, compelled, forced, required
2 *I'm much obliged to you for your kindness.*
▸ appreciative, grateful, indebted, thankful

oblique *ADJECTIVE*
1 *After the earthquake, the floor ended up at an oblique angle.*
▸ inclined, slanting, sloping, tilted
2 *She made some oblique remarks about his appearance.*
▸ indirect, roundabout

oblong *NOUN*
▸ rectangle
FOR OTHER SHAPES SEE **shape** *NOUN*

obscene *ADJECTIVE*
We were shocked by her obscene language.
▸ coarse, crude, disgusting, filthy, foul, improper, indecent, objectionable, offensive, pornographic, rude, shocking, smutty, vulgar
AN OPPOSITE IS decent

obscure *ADJECTIVE*
1 *An obscure figure could be seen in the distance.*
▸ blurred, dim, hidden, indistinct, misty, murky, shadowy, unclear, vague
AN OPPOSITE IS clear
2 *His joke seemed rather obscure.*
▸ confusing, incomprehensible, puzzling
AN OPPOSITE IS obvious
3 *Henry Kirke White is an obscure poet.*
▸ forgotten, minor, undistinguished, unheard of, unimportant, unknown
AN OPPOSITE IS famous

obscure *VERB*
Mist obscured the view.
▸ block out, conceal, cover, disguise, envelop, hide, mask, screen, shroud
AN OPPOSITE IS reveal

observant *ADJECTIVE*
If you're observant, you might see a kingfisher by the river.
▸ alert, attentive, perceptive, sharp-eyed, vigilant, watchful
AN OPPOSITE IS inattentive

observation *NOUN*
1 *They took him to hospital for observation.*
▸ scrutiny, study, watching
2 *She made observations about their behaviour.*
▸ comment, opinion, remark, statement

observe *VERB*
1 *Astronomers observed the eclipse last night.*
▸ look at, study, view, watch
2 *They observed a change in his behaviour.*
▸ detect, discern, note, notice, perceive, see, spot, witness
3 *It's important to observe the rules.*
▸ abide by, adhere to, follow, heed, keep to, obey, respect, submit to
4 *She observed that it was a nice day.*
▸ comment, declare, mention, remark, say

obsession *NOUN*
Football is his obsession.
▸ addiction, mania, passion

obsolete *ADJECTIVE*
Computers quickly become obsolete.
▸ antiquated, dated, discarded, disused, old-fashioned, out of date
AN OPPOSITE IS current *ADJECTIVE*

obstacle *NOUN*
1 *They drove around the obstacles in the road.*
▸ barricade, barrier, obstruction
2 *His age proved to be an obstacle.*
▸ catch, difficulty, hindrance, hurdle, problem, snag

obstinate *ADJECTIVE*
The obstinate donkey would not move.
▸ contrary, defiant, perverse, stubborn, uncooperative, unreasonable, wilful
AN OPPOSITE IS cooperative

obstruct *VERB*
1 *The path was obstructed.*
▸ block, make impassable
2 *The demonstrators obstructed the traffic for over an hour.*
▸ check, curb, halt, hamper, hinder, hold up, restrict, slow down, stop

obtain *VERB*
The police wanted to know where he had obtained the money.
▸ acquire, come by, find, get, get hold of, (*informal*) pick up
▹ To obtain something by paying for it is to buy or purchase it.

obtuse *ADJECTIVE*
He was too obtuse to understand her point.
▸ (*informal*) dense, dull, slow, stupid, (*informal*) thick, unintelligent

obvious *ADJECTIVE*
1 *It was silly to make so many obvious mistakes.*
▸ glaring, noticeable, pronounced
2 *The castle is an obvious landmark.*
▸ conspicuous, distinct, notable, prominent, visible
AN OPPOSITE IS inconspicuous
3 *She didn't say much, but what she was thinking was obvious.*
▸ clear, evident, plain, unconcealed, undisguised, unmistakable
AN OPPOSITE IS hidden

occasion *NOUN*
1 *They needed to wait for the right occasion to tell him.*
▸ chance, moment, opportunity, time
2 *The wedding was a happy occasion.*
▸ affair, celebration, ceremony, event, happening, incident, occurrence

occasional *ADJECTIVE*
The weather forecaster predicted occasional showers.
▸ infrequent, intermittent, irregular, odd, scattered, unpredictable
AN OPPOSITE IS frequent or regular

occupant *NOUN*
The present occupants of the house are moving out shortly.
▸ inhabitant, occupier, resident, tenant

occupation *NOUN*
1 *He's not happy with his present occupation.*
▸ business, employment, job, post, profession, trade, work
FOR VARIOUS OCCUPATIONS SEE **job**
2 *His favourite occupation is reading.*
▸ activity, hobby, pastime, pursuit

occupied *ADJECTIVE*
She's very occupied in her work.
▸ absorbed, busy, engaged, engrossed, involved
AN OPPOSITE IS idle

occupy *VERB*
1 *They occupy the house next door.*
▸ dwell in, inhabit, live in, reside in
2 *She got rid of the piano because it occupied too much space.*
▸ fill, take up, use up
3 *Troops occupied the town.*
▸ capture, conquer, invade, take over, take possession of

occur *VERB*
1 *She told us what had occurred.*
▸ arise, come about, develop, happen, take place
2 *The disease only occurs in certain parts of the world.*
▸ crop up, exist, turn up

occurrence *NOUN*
An eclipse of the sun is an unusual occurrence.
▸ event, happening, incident, occasion, phenomenon

ocean *NOUN*
THE GREAT OCEANS OF THE WORLD
Antarctic, Arctic, Atlantic, Indian, Pacific

odd *ADJECTIVE*
1 *Her behaviour seemed very odd.*
▸ abnormal, curious, eccentric, funny, peculiar, puzzling, queer, strange, unconventional, unusual, weird
AN OPPOSITE IS normal
2 *He could only find a couple of odd socks.*
▸ left over, single, spare
3 *He does odd jobs to earn money.*
▸ casual, irregular, occasional, various

oddments *PLURAL NOUN*
She put the oddments in a box.
▸ bits, bits and pieces, fragments, leftovers, odds and ends, offcuts, remnants, scraps

odour *NOUN*
There's a nasty odour coming from the fridge.
▹ A nice smell is a fragrance or perfume. A nasty smell is a reek, stench, or stink.

offence *NOUN*
He was punished for his offence.
▸ crime, fault, outrage, sin, wrongdoing
▹ In games, an offence is a foul or an infringement.
to give offence
SEE **offend**

offend *VERB*
1 *His remarks offended her.*
▸ anger, annoy, disgust, give offence to, hurt your feelings, insult, upset, vex
2 *You'll be punished if you offend again.*
▸ break the law, do wrong

offensive *ADJECTIVE*
1 *She was shocked by their offensive language.*
▸ abusive, disgusting, impolite, insulting, nasty, obscene, revolting, rude, sickening, unpleasant, vulgar
AN OPPOSITE IS pleasant
2 *The police arrested him for carrying an offensive weapon.*
▸ aggressive, dangerous, threatening, warlike

offer *VERB*
1 *A reward was offered for his capture.*
▸ make available, propose, put forward, suggest
2 *He offered to help with the work.*
▸ volunteer

offer *NOUN*
Their offer of help was gratefully received.
▸ proposal, suggestion

office *NOUN*
PEOPLE WHO WORK IN AN OFFICE
cashier, clerk, filing clerk, office boy or office girl, receptionist, secretary, shorthand typist, telephonist, typist, word processor operator
EQUIPMENT USED IN AN OFFICE
answering machine, calculator, computer, copier, desk, diary, dictating machine, duplicator, fax, files, filing cabinet, intercom, photocopier, stapler, stationery, telephone, typewriter, word processor

officer *NOUN*
FOR POLICE OFFICERS SEE **police**
FOR OFFICERS IN THE ARMED SERVICES SEE **rank**

official *ADJECTIVE*
It was an official announcement.
▶ approved, authentic, authorized, formal, genuine, legitimate, proper
AN OPPOSITE IS unofficial

official *NOUN*
We spoke to an official of the organization.
▶ officer, organizer, person in charge, representative
OFFICIALS IN A CLUB OR ORGANIZATION
chairman or chairperson or chairwoman, secretary, treasurer
OFFICIALS AT A SPORTING EVENT
assistant referee, linesman, marshal, referee, steward, touch judge, umpire

officious *ADJECTIVE*
He got annoyed with the officious car park attendant.
▶ (*informal*) bossy, interfering, zealous

often *ADVERB*
It often rains in April.
▶ again and again, constantly, frequently, many times, regularly, repeatedly, time after time

oil *VERB*
He oiled the hinge to stop it squeaking.
▶ grease, lubricate

oily *ADJECTIVE*
Fried food is too oily for me.
▶ fatty, greasy

ointment *NOUN*
The nurse gave her some ointment for the rash.
▶ cream, lotion

old *ADJECTIVE* This word is often overused. Here are some alternatives:
1 *She doesn't like growing old.*
▶ aged, decrepit, doddery, elderly, (*slang*) past it
AN OPPOSITE IS young
2 *The old church was being restored.*
▶ ancient, crumbling, decayed, decaying, ruined
▷ Something that you respect because it is old is **venerable**.
3 *I put on old clothes to do some gardening.*
▶ scruffy, shabby, worn, worn out
AN OPPOSITE IS new
4 *The car he used to drive was an old model.*
▶ antiquated, early, obsolete, old-fashioned, out of date, primitive
▷ Valuable old cars are **veteran** or **vintage** cars. Other things which are valuable because they are old are **antique**.
AN OPPOSITE IS up to date
5 *She wondered what life was like in the old days.*
▶ earlier, former, past, previous, remote
▷ Times before written records were kept are **prehistoric** times. The ancient Greeks and Romans lived in **classical** times. The Middle Ages are **medieval** times.
AN OPPOSITE IS modern

old-fashioned *ADJECTIVE*
He has some rather old-fashioned ideas.
▶ obsolete, out of date, traditional, unfashionable
AN OPPOSITE IS modern or stylish

omen *NOUN*
They hoped that the storm was not an omen of disaster.
▶ indication, sign, warning

ominous *ADJECTIVE*
The rumble of thunder was an ominous sign of a coming storm.
▶ forbidding, grim, menacing, sinister, threatening, unlucky

omission *NOUN*
There are some surprising omissions from the list.
▶ exclusion, gap, oversight

A B C D E F G H I J K L M N **O** P Q R S T U V W X Y Z

omit *VERB*
1 *His article was omitted from the magazine.*
▶ cut, eliminate, exclude, leave out, miss out, overlook, pass over, skip
2 *Don't omit to turn off the lights.*
▶ fail, forget, neglect

one-sided *ADJECTIVE*
The driver gave a very one-sided account of the accident.
▶ biased, prejudiced, unfair

onlooker *NOUN*
The onlookers did nothing to stop the fight.
▶ bystander, eyewitness, observer, spectator, witness

ooze *VERB*
Oil was oozing out of the damaged tank.
▶ dribble, leak, seep

opaque *ADJECTIVE*
The dirt had turned the window opaque.
▶ cloudy, dull, hazy, muddy, murky, obscure, unclear
AN OPPOSITE IS transparent

open *ADJECTIVE*
1 *The puppy escaped through the open door.*
▶ ajar, gaping, unfastened, unlocked, wide open
AN OPPOSITE IS closed
2 *There aren't many open spaces where children can play.*
▶ accessible, clear, empty, extensive, public, uncrowded, unrestricted
AN OPPOSITE IS enclosed
3 *He was open about what he had done wrong.*
▶ communicative, frank, honest, outspoken, sincere, straightforward
AN OPPOSITE IS deceitful
4 *The captain faced open rebellion from the crew.*
▶ obvious, plain, unconcealed, undisguised
AN OPPOSITE IS concealed
5 *It's an open question as to whether they'll win the next election.*
▶ arguable, debatable, unanswered, undecided, unfinished, unresolved

open *VERB*
1 *Please open the door.*
▶ unbolt, unfasten, unlock
▷ To open a locked door is to **unbolt**, **unfasten**, or **unlock** it. To open an umbrella is to **unfurl** it. To open a wine bottle is to **uncork** it. To open a map is to **unfold** or **unroll** it. To open a parcel is to **undo** or **unwrap** it.
2 *The jumble sale opens at 2 p.m.*
▶ begin, commence, (*informal*) get going, start
3 *A new rail service has just been opened.*
▶ initiate, launch, set up
AN OPPOSITE IS close

opening *NOUN*
1 *The animals got out through an opening in the fence.*
▶ breach, break, gap, hole, split
2 *We enjoyed the opening of the concert.*
▶ beginning, commencement, start
3 *I attended the opening of the new sports centre.*
▶ initiation, launch
4 *The job offers a good opening for a keen young person.*
▶ chance, opportunity

open-minded *ADJECTIVE*
She has an open-minded attitude to new ideas.
▶ fair, impartial, neutral, objective, unbiased, unprejudiced
AN OPPOSITE IS biased

operate *VERB*
1 *This watch operates even under water.*
▶ function, go, perform, work
2 *Do you know how to operate this machine?*
▶ deal with, drive, handle, manage, use, work
3 *The surgeon operated to remove her appendix.*
▶ carry out an operation, perform surgery

operation *NOUN*
1 *Her main concern was the safe operation of the machines.*
▶ functioning, performance, working
2 *He had an operation to remove his appendix.*
▶ surgery
3 *Tracking down those ruthless criminals was a dangerous operation.*
▶ action, activity, enterprise, exercise, manoeuvre, process, project, task

opinion *NOUN*
He was asked for his honest opinion.
▶ attitude, belief, comment, conclusion, feeling, idea, impression, judgement, notion, point of view, theory, thought, view

opponent *NOUN*
He fought fiercely against his opponent.
▸ adversary, challenger, enemy, foe, rival
▹ Your opponents in a game are the **opposition.**
AN OPPOSITE IS ally

opportunity *NOUN*
1 *There were few opportunities to relax.*
▸ chance, moment, occasion, time
2 *The job offers a good opportunity for a keen young person.*
▸ (*informal*) break, opening

oppose *VERB*
Many people opposed the building of the new road.
▸ argue against, attack, be against, be hostile towards, disapprove of, fight against, (*informal*) make a stand against, resist

opposite *ADJECTIVE*
1 *They have opposite views about politics.*
▸ conflicting, contradictory, contrary, contrasting, different, incompatible, opposed, opposing
AN OPPOSITE IS similar
2 *She lives on the opposite side of the road.*
▸ facing

opposite *NOUN*
She says one thing and does the opposite.
▸ contrary, converse, reverse

opposition *NOUN*
1 *She hadn't expected so much opposition to her idea.*
▸ disapproval, hostility, resistance, scepticism, unfriendliness
AN OPPOSITE IS support
2 *The opposition were stronger than they expected.*
▸ opponents, rivals

oppress *VERB*
1 *The people were oppressed by the military government.*
▸ abuse, crush, exploit, misuse, persecute
2 *The atmosphere in the room oppressed them.*
▸ concern, grieve, sadden, trouble, upset, weigh down, worry

oppressive *ADJECTIVE*
1 *The oppressive ruler made the people's lives miserable.*
▸ brutal, cruel, harsh, repressive, severe, tyrannical, unjust
2 *This weather feels very oppressive.*
▸ airless, close, heavy, hot, humid, muggy, stifling, stuffy

optical *ADJECTIVE*
VARIOUS OPTICAL INSTRUMENTS
bifocals, binoculars, field glasses, glasses, lens, magnifier, magnifying glass, microscope, opera glasses, periscope, spectacles, sunglasses, telescope

optimistic *ADJECTIVE*
She's optimistic about her chances of success.
▸ buoyant, cheerful, confident, expectant, hopeful, positive
AN OPPOSITE IS pessimistic

option *NOUN*
He had the option of staying or leaving.
▸ alternative, choice, possibility

optional *ADJECTIVE*
Everyone has to pay for the basic holiday, but the excursions are optional extras.
▸ possible, voluntary
AN OPPOSITE IS compulsory

oral *ADJECTIVE*
He gave an oral report of what happened.
▸ spoken, verbal
AN OPPOSITE IS written

orbit *VERB*
The earth orbits the sun in about 365 days.
▸ circle, travel round

ordeal *NOUN*
He went through a horrific ordeal.
▸ difficulty, experience, (*informal*) nightmare, suffering, test, torture

order *NOUN*
1 *The captain gave the order to abandon ship.*
▸ command, instruction
2 *She gave the newsagent an order for the new magazine.*
▸ application, demand, request, reservation
3 *The army restored order after the riot.*
▸ calm, control, discipline, good behaviour, law and order, obedience, organization, peace
4 *They put the library books in alphabetical order.*
▸ arrangement, sequence, series, succession
5 *She keeps her bike in good order.*
▸ condition, state

A B C D E F G H I J K L M N **O** P Q R S T U V W X Y Z

order *VERB*
1 *She ordered them to be quiet.*
▸ command, instruct, require, tell
2 *He ordered the new magazine.*
▸ apply for, book, request, reserve

orderly *ADJECTIVE*
1 *Her work was always very orderly.*
▸ careful, methodical, neat, organized, systematic, tidy, well arranged, well organized
AN OPPOSITE IS untidy
2 *The police expect orderly behaviour at the demonstration.*
▸ law-abiding, obedient, peaceful, restrained, well behaved, well disciplined
AN OPPOSITE IS disorderly

ordinary *ADJECTIVE*
1 *It was just an ordinary sort of day.*
▸ customary, everyday, familiar, habitual, normal, regular, routine, standard, typical, usual
2 *She's just an ordinary sort of person.*
▸ average, common, conventional, humble, modest, plain, simple, undistinguished, unexceptional, unexciting
3 *It was a very ordinary game.*
▸ indifferent, mediocre, unimpressive, uninteresting
AN OPPOSITE IS special or unusual

organic *ADJECTIVE*
Some farmers are going back to using organic fertilizers instead of chemical ones.
▸ biological, living, natural

organism *NOUN*
Evolution has produced millions of different organisms.
▸ creature, living thing

organization *NOUN*
1 *She works for a charitable organization.*
▸ institution, (*informal*) set-up
BUSINESS ORGANIZATIONS
business, company, corporation, firm
ORGANIZATIONS FOR LEISURE, SPORT, ETC.
association, club, league, society
POLITICAL ORGANIZATIONS
confederation, federation, party, union
2 *Who was responsible for the organization of the conference?*
▸ arrangement, coordination, organizing, planning, running

organize *VERB*
1 *It took her ages to organize the car-boot sale.*
▸ coordinate, make arrangements for, plan, run, see to, set up
2 *The librarian has to organize the books in the library.*
▸ arrange, classify, put in order, sort out, tidy up

organized *ADJECTIVE*
It was an organized fire drill.
▸ methodical, orderly, planned, systematic, well run
AN OPPOSITE IS chaotic

origin *NOUN*
1 *We know very little about the origin of life on earth.*
▸ beginning, birth, cause, creation, source, start
AN OPPOSITE IS end *NOUN*
2 *He became very rich, despite his humble origins.*
▸ ancestry, background, descent, family, parentage, pedigree, stock

original *ADJECTIVE*
1 *The settlers drove out the original inhabitants.*
▸ aboriginal, earliest, first, initial, native
2 *The story was very original.*
▸ creative, fresh, imaginative, inspired, inventive, new, novel, unconventional, unfamiliar, unusual
3 *Is that an original work of art or a copy?*
▸ authentic, genuine, real, unique

originate *VERB*
1 *Where did the idea originate?*
▸ begin, commence, crop up, emerge, start
2 *They originated a new style of dancing.*
▸ be the inventor of, conceive, create, design, give birth to, introduce, invent, launch

ornament *NOUN*
A few ornaments will make the place more attractive.
▸ adornment, decoration

ornamental *ADJECTIVE*
He bought an ornamental glass vase.
▸ attractive, decorative, pretty

orthodox *ADJECTIVE*
He disagreed with her orthodox views about religion.
▸ accepted, approved, conventional,

customary, established, normal, official, ordinary, regular, standard, traditional, usual, well established
AN OPPOSITE IS unconventional

outbreak *NOUN*
1 *Everyone feared an outbreak of disease.*
▸ epidemic, plague
2 *The armies prepared for the outbreak of war.*
▸ beginning, commencement, start

outburst *NOUN*
There was an outburst of laughter from the next room.
▸ eruption, explosion, storm

outcome *NOUN*
What was the outcome of the meeting?
▸ consequence, effect, result, upshot

outcry *NOUN*
There was an outcry over the closure of the hospital.
▸ fuss, protest, uproar

outdoor *ADJECTIVE*
The hotel had an outdoor swimming pool.
▸ open-air, out of doors, outside

outer *ADJECTIVE*
He was wearing a thick jumper and waterproof outer garments.
▸ exterior, external, outside
AN OPPOSITE IS inner

outfit *NOUN*
1 *She bought a new outfit for the wedding.*
▸ costume, suit
2 *The puncture repair outfit is in the boot.*
▸ equipment, gear, paraphernalia

outing *NOUN*
They've gone on their annual outing to London.
▸ excursion, expedition, jaunt, picnic, trip

outlaw *NOUN*
A band of outlaws held up the train.
▸ bandit, brigand, criminal, fugitive, outcast, robber

outlet *NOUN*
If you instal a fire, you must provide an outlet for the fumes.
▸ channel, mouth, opening, way out

outline *NOUN*
1 *She could see the outline of the house in the dim light.*
▸ form, profile, shadow, shape, silhouette
2 *He gave us a brief outline of his plan.*
▸ framework, précis, rough idea, summary

outline *VERB*
He outlined his plan.
▸ describe, summarize

outlook *NOUN*
1 *The house has a pleasant outlook over the valley.*
▸ prospect, scene, sight, view
2 *He has a rather gloomy outlook on life.*
▸ attitude, frame of mind, point of view, view
3 *The outlook for the weekend is bright and sunny.*
▸ expectations, forecast, prediction

outlying *ADJECTIVE*
Children from the outlying areas came to school by bus.
▸ distant, far, outer, remote

outrage *NOUN*
1 *There was public outrage at the government's decision.*
▸ anger, disgust, fury, horror, indignation, resentment, revulsion, sense of shock
2 *The area has been the scene of some of the worst terrorist outrages.*
▸ atrocity, crime, disgrace, scandal

outrageous *ADJECTIVE*
1 *His behaviour was outrageous.*
▸ atrocious, disgraceful, disgusting, offensive, scandalous, shocking
2 *They charge outrageous prices at that shop.*
▸ excessive, unreasonable
AN OPPOSITE IS acceptable or reasonable

outside *ADJECTIVE*
Paint for outside use.
▸ exterior, external, outer

outside *NOUN*
We looked at the outside of a house, but we couldn't get in.
▸ exterior, shell, surface
AN OPPOSITE IS inside

A B C D E F G H I J K L M N O P Q R S T U V W X Y Z

outsider *NOUN*
She's lived there for years, but local people still treat her as an outsider.
▸ alien, foreigner, immigrant, newcomer, stranger, visitor

outskirts *PLURAL NOUN*
We live on the outskirts of town.
▸ edge, fringe, outer areas
▹ The outskirts of a big town are the suburbs.
AN OPPOSITE IS centre

outspoken *ADJECTIVE*
He's always been an outspoken critic of the government.
▸ blunt, frank, honest, plain, straightforward
AN OPPOSITE IS tactful

outstanding *ADJECTIVE*
1 *She will be an outstanding tennis player in a few years.*
▸ celebrated, conspicuous, distinguished, eminent, excellent, exceptional, extraordinary, great, impressive, notable, prominent, remarkable, superlative, well known
AN OPPOSITE IS ordinary
2 *There are still some outstanding bills to pay.*
▸ overdue, owing, unpaid

outward *ADJECTIVE*
Outward appearances can be deceptive.
▸ exterior, external, outer, outside, superficial, surface, visible

outwit *VERB*
The fox succeeded in outwitting the hounds.
▸ baffle, cheat, deceive, fool, trick

oval *ADJECTIVE*
The cake was on an oval plate.
▸ egg-shaped, elliptical

oven *NOUN*
The meat was roasting in the oven.
▸ cooker, stove
▹ A special oven for firing pottery, etc., is a kiln.

overcast *ADJECTIVE*
It's a bit overcast — it might rain.
▸ black, cloudy, dark, dismal, dull, gloomy, grey, leaden, stormy, threatening

overcome *VERB*
1 *He's finally managed to overcome his fear of flying.*
▸ conquer, cope with, deal with, defeat, sort out
2 *She was overcome by the fumes.*
▸ get the better of, make helpless, overpower, overwhelm

overflow *VERB*
The river had overflowed its banks.
▸ flood, pour over, spill over

overgrown *ADJECTIVE*
The back garden was completely overgrown.
▸ tangled, untidy, unweeded, weedy, wild

overhang *VERB*
Part of the cliff overhangs the beach.
▸ jut over, project over, protrude over, stick out over

overhaul *VERB*
1 *The boiler was recently overhauled.*
▸ check over, examine, inspect, put right, repair, restore, service
2 *The express overhauled a goods train.*
▸ leave behind, overtake, pass

overhead *ADVERB*
A seagull flew overhead.
▸ above, high up, in the sky

overlook *VERB*
1 *He seems to have overlooked one important fact.*
▸ fail to see, miss
2 *She's always willing to overlook his faults.*
▸ disregard, excuse, forget about, ignore, pardon, pay no attention to, (*informal*) turn a blind eye to
3 *The chateau overlooked fields of corn and olive trees.*
▸ face, have a view of, look on to

overpower *VERB*
It took three police officers to overpower him.
▸ beat, conquer, defeat, get the better of, overcome, subdue

overpowering *ADJECTIVE*
I felt an overpowering need to sneeze.
▸ compelling, irresistible, overwhelming, powerful, strong, uncontrollable

overrun *VERB*
The barn was overrun with rats and mice.
▸ invade, take over

oversight *NOUN*
The mix-up was due to an oversight on the part of the travel agent.
▸ carelessness, an error, a mistake, an omission

overtake *VERB*
We overtook the car in front.
▸ leave behind, overhaul, pass

overthrow *VERB*
The rebels overthrew the President.
▸ beat, conquer, defeat, (*informal*) throw out, topple

overturn *VERB*
1 *The boat overturned.*
▸ capsize, tip over, turn over, turn turtle
2 *She leapt to her feet, overturning her chair.*
▸ knock over, spill, tip over, topple, upset

overwhelm *VERB*
1 *The troops were overwhelmed by superior enemy forces.*
▸ beat decisively, crush, defeat, overcome, overpower
2 *A tidal wave overwhelmed the village.*
▸ bury, devastate, engulf, flood, inundate, submerge, swallow up

overwhelming *ADJECTIVE*
He was elected by an overwhelming majority.
▸ crushing, decisive, devastating, great
▹ An overwhelming victory at an election is a **landslide**.

owe *VERB*
▹ If you owe money to someone, you are in **debt**.

owing *ADJECTIVE*
There is still £50 owing.
▸ due, outstanding, overdue, owed, unpaid
owing to *Owing to the rain, the match is cancelled.*
▸ as a result of, because of, on account of, thanks to

own *VERB*
It was the first car she'd owned.
▸ be the owner of, possess
to own up *No one owned up to breaking the window.*
▸ admit your guilt, confess

Pp

pace *NOUN*
1 *Move forward two paces.*
▸ step, stride
2 *The front runner set a fast pace.*
▸ rate, speed
▹ A formal word is **velocity**.

pacify *VERB*
She was furious at first, but he managed to pacify her eventually.
▸ appease, calm, humour, quieten, soothe
AN OPPOSITE IS anger or annoy

pack *NOUN*
1 *There were four candles in each pack.*
▸ bale, bundle, package, packet
2 *The hikers picked up their packs and trudged off.*
▸ haversack, knapsack, rucksack

pack *VERB*
1 *She packed her suitcase and called a taxi.*
▸ fill, load up
2 *I forgot to pack my hairdryer.*
▸ stow away, wrap up
3 *They packed as many passengers as possible onto the train.*
▸ cram, crowd, jam, squeeze, stuff, wedge

package *NOUN*
The postman delivered a package.
▸ bundle, packet, parcel

pad *NOUN*
1 *She put a pad of cotton wool over the wound.*
▸ wad
▹ A pad to make a chair or bed comfortable is a **cushion** or **pillow**. A pad to kneel on in church is a **hassock** or **kneeler**.
2 *There's a pad for messages next to the phone.*
▸ jotter, notebook, writing pad

pad *VERB*
The seats are padded with foam rubber.
▸ fill, pack, stuff
▹ To put covers and padding on furniture is to **upholster** it.

A B C D E F G H I J K L M N O P Q R S T U V W X Y Z

padding *NOUN*
The padding is coming out of this armchair.
▶ filling, stuffing
▷ The covers and padding on furniture is upholstery.

paddle *VERB*
1 *The children paddled at the water's edge.*
▶ dabble, splash about
▷ To walk through deep water is to wade.
2 *He paddled his canoe along the canal.*
▷ To move a boat along with two oars is to row it.

paddock *NOUN*
The horses were kept in a paddock behind the farm.
▶ enclosure
▷ Other grassy areas are field, meadow, or pasture.

page *NOUN*
1 *Several pages have been torn out of this book.*
▶ leaf, sheet
2 *He wrote two pages of notes.*
▶ side
3 (*old use*) *The king summoned his page.*
▶ attendant, boy, servant

pageant *NOUN*
A pageant was put on to mark the centenary of the event.
▶ display, entertainment, parade, procession, spectacle

pageantry *NOUN*
He was greeted with all the pageantry of an official state visit.
▶ ceremony, display, grandeur, magnificence, pomp, show, spectacle, splendour

pail *NOUN*
He used a pail of water to put out the fire.
▶ bucket
FOR OTHER CONTAINERS SEE **container**

pain *NOUN*
Her back has been causing her a lot of pain.
▶ anguish, suffering
▷ A dull pain is an ache or soreness. Severe pain is agony, torment, or torture. A slight pain is discomfort. A slight pain which doesn't last long is a twinge. A sudden pain is a pang or stab. Pain in your head is a headache. Pain in your teeth is toothache. The pains a woman feels when giving birth are contractions or labour pains. To cause pain or to feel pain is to hurt.

painful *ADJECTIVE*
1 *My shoulder's still really painful.*
▶ aching, agonizing, hurting, inflamed, raw, smarting, stinging, sore, tender, throbbing
2 *The conversation brought back many painful memories.*
▶ distressing, nasty, unpleasant, upsetting
AN OPPOSITE IS painless

painless *ADJECTIVE*
1 *The treatment is quite painless.*
▶ comfortable, pain free
2 *This is a quick and painless way to learn a foreign language.*
▶ easy, effortless, simple, trouble free
AN OPPOSITE IS painful

painstaking *ADJECTIVE*
The discovery is the result of ten years' painstaking research.
▶ careful, conscientious, methodical, meticulous, systematic, thorough
AN OPPOSITE IS careless

paint *NOUN*
KINDS OF PAINT
distemper, emulsion, enamel, lacquer, oil colour, oil paint, pastel, primer, stain, tempera, undercoat, varnish, water colour, whitewash
▷ A layer of paint is a coat of paint. Paint which stays shiny when it dries is gloss paint. Paint which goes dull when it dries is matt paint.

paint *VERB*
1 *The walls were painted yellow.*
▶ colour, decorate
2 *He painted the view from his bedroom window.*
▶ depict, portray, represent

painter *NOUN*
▷ A person who paints houses, etc., is a decorator. A person who paints pictures is an artist.

painting *NOUN*
SEE **picture** *NOUN*

pair *NOUN*
▷ A pair of people who go out together are a couple. Two people who sing or play music together are a duet. Two people who work together are partners or a partnership. Two babies born together are twins.

palace *NOUN*
The palace was open to the public at weekends.
▶ castle, mansion, stately home

pale *ADJECTIVE*
1 *His illness made him look pale.*
▶ pallid, pasty, unhealthy, white
▷ If you suffer from a poor condition of the blood which makes you pale, you are **anaemic**.
AN OPPOSITE IS ruddy
2 *I don't like pale colours.*
▶ bleached, dim, faded, faint, light
▷ Pale colours which you use deliberately to get a soft effect are **pastel** colours.
AN OPPOSITE IS bright

pamper *VERB*
He's been pampered by his parents ever since he was a baby.
▶ humour, indulge, spoil

pamphlet *NOUN*
We were given a pamphlet about road safety.
▶ booklet, brochure, leaflet

pan *NOUN*
FOR UTENSILS USED IN COOKING SEE **cook** *VERB*

pandemonium *NOUN*
Pandemonium broke out when the results were announced.
▶ bedlam, chaos, confusion, din, disorder, excitement, fuss, hullabaloo, racket, row, tumult, turbulence, turmoil, upheaval, uproar

pane *NOUN*
There was a small crack in the pane of glass.
▶ sheet of glass, window

panel *NOUN*
A panel of experts was consulted.
▶ group, team

panic *NOUN*
People fled the streets in panic.
▶ alarm, hysteria

panic *VERB*
If a fire starts, don't panic!
▶ become hysterical, (*informal*) lose your head, stampede

panicky *ADJECTIVE*
The animals became panicky during the thunderstorm.
▶ alarmed, frantic, frightened, hysterical, overexcited
AN OPPOSITE IS calm

panorama *NOUN*
A beautiful panorama of lakes and mountains spread out in front of them.
▶ landscape, perspective, prospect, scene, view

pant *VERB*
He was panting by the time he reached the top.
▶ breathe quickly, gasp, puff

pants *PLURAL NOUN*
FOR UNDERCLOTHES SEE **underclothes**

paper *NOUN*
1 *She sat at the desk with pen and paper ready.*
VARIOUS KINDS OF MATERIAL FOR WRITING OR DRAWING ON
card, cardboard, cartridge paper, manila, notepaper, postcard, stationery, tracing paper, writing paper
▷ A piece of paper is a **leaf** or a **sheet**.
EARLY MATERIALS FOR WRITING ON WERE
papyrus, parchment, vellum
OTHER KINDS OF PAPER
tissue paper, toilet paper, wallpaper, wrapping paper
2 *There were some important papers in his briefcase.*
PAPERS WHICH MAY BE IMPORTANT
accounts, certificates, deeds, documents, forms, licences, receipts, records
3 *The story made the front page of the local paper.*
▶ newspaper

parade *NOUN*
The crowd cheered as the parade passed along the street.
▶ display, procession, show
▷ A parade of people on horseback is a **cavalcade**. A parade of soldiers is a **march past**.

parade *VERB*
The demonstrators paraded through the city.
▶ assemble, file past, line up, make a procession, march past

A B C D E F G H I J K L M N O P Q R S T U V W X Y Z

paradoxical *ADJECTIVE*
It seems paradoxical to make weapons in order to keep peace.
▸ absurd, contradictory, illogical

parallel *NOUN*
There is a parallel between their situations.
▸ analogy, comparison, likeness, match, resemblance, similarity

paralyse *VERB*
The shock paralysed him.
▸ cripple, deaden, immobilize

paraphernalia *NOUN*
The hall was full of the builder's paraphernalia.
▸ baggage, belongings, equipment, gear, odds and ends, stuff, tackle, things

paraphrase *VERB*
He paraphrased the story to make it easier to understand.
▸ interpret, translate

parcel *NOUN*
The postman delivered a parcel.
▸ package, packet

parched *ADJECTIVE*
1 *Nothing was growing in the parched earth.*
▸ arid, baked, barren, dry, scorched, sterile, waterless
2 *I'm parched!*
▸ thirsty

pardon *VERB*
Hundreds of political prisoners were pardoned and released.
▸ excuse, forgive, free, let off, release, set free, spare
▹ To pardon someone who is condemned to death is to reprieve them.

pardon *NOUN*
She knew she had done wrong, but she hoped for pardon.
▸ forgiveness, mercy
▹ A pardon for someone who is condemned to death is a reprieve. A general pardon for a whole group of people is an amnesty.

pardonable *ADJECTIVE*
It was a pardonable mistake.
▸ excusable, forgivable, minor, negligible, understandable
AN OPPOSITE IS unforgivable

parent *NOUN*
FOR FAMILY RELATIONSHIPS SEE **family**

park *NOUN*
DIFFERENT KINDS OF PARK
amusement park, arboretum, botanical gardens, forest park, nature reserve, public gardens, recreation ground, safari park, theme park
▹ A park with fields and trees around a big house is an estate or parkland.

park *VERB*
He parked her car outside her house.
▸ leave, place, position, station

parliament *NOUN*
▹ The British parliament consists of the House of Commons and the House of Lords.
FOR RELATED WORDS SEE **government**

parody *NOUN*
The film was a parody of a horror story.
▹ An informal synonym is send-up. A piece of writing which uses humour to make us think about how silly someone or something is, is a satire. A description which exaggerates amusing things about a person is a caricature.

parson *NOUN*
SEE **clergyman**

part *NOUN*
1 *All the parts of the engine are now working properly.*
▸ bit, component, constituent
2 *I only saw the first part of the programme.*
▸ element, piece, portion, section
3 *Which part of this organization deals with complaints?*
▸ branch, department, division
4 *Granny lives in another part of the town.*
▸ area, district, neighbourhood, region, sector
5 *He's just right to act the part of Romeo.*
▸ character, role

part *VERB*
1 *It was the first time she'd been parted from her parents.*
▸ divide, remove, separate
AN OPPOSITE IS join
2 *They exchanged a final kiss before parting.*
▸ depart, go away, leave, say goodbye, split up
AN OPPOSITE IS meet

partial *ADJECTIVE*
The play was only a partial success.
▸ imperfect, incomplete, limited
AN OPPOSITE IS complete
to be partial to *He's partial to a hot drink at bedtime.*
▸ appreciate, be fond of, be keen on, enjoy, like

participate *VERB*
She participates actively in local politics.
▸ be involved, cooperate, help, join in, share, take part

particle *NOUN*
The camera lens was covered with particles of dust.
▸ bit, fragment, grain, piece, scrap, shred, sliver, speck
▹ In science, particles of matter include atoms, neutrons, and protons.

particular *ADJECTIVE*
1 *He usually agreed with her, but in this particular case he thought she was wrong.*
▸ distinct, individual, unique
2 *She took particular care not to damage the parcel.*
▸ exceptional, notable, outstanding, special, unusual
3 *The cat's very particular about his food.*
▸ choosy, finicky, fussy, hard to please

particulars *PLURAL NOUN*
The police officer took down all the particulars.
▸ circumstances, details, facts, information

parting *NOUN*
Parting from him was very difficult.
▸ departure, going away, leaving, saying goodbye, separation, splitting up
AN OPPOSITE IS meeting

partition *NOUN*
A partition separates the two classrooms.
▸ room divider, screen

partly *ADVERB*
It was partly my fault.
▸ in part, to some extent, up to a point
AN OPPOSITE IS entirely

partner *NOUN*
He's a good friend, as well as my business partner.
▸ ally, associate, colleague
▹ In marriage, your partner is your **spouse** or your **husband** or **wife**. An animal's partner is its **mate**.

party *NOUN*
1 *They had a party at the end of term.*
▸ celebration, festivity, function, (*informal*) get-together
VARIOUS KINDS OF PARTY
ball, banquet, barbecue, birthday party, ceilidh, Christmas party, dance, disco, feast, house-warming, picnic, reception, reunion, tea party, wedding
2 *A party of tourists was going round the museum.*
▸ band, crowd, group
3 *They support different political parties.*
▸ alliance, association, league

pass *VERB*
1 *We watched the procession pass.*
▸ go by, move past
2 *She tried to pass the car in front.*
▸ overhaul, overtake
3 *We passed over the bridge.*
▸ advance, go, proceed, progress
4 *Could you pass me the vegetables, please?*
▸ deliver, give, hand over, offer, present
5 *Do you think you will pass your music exam?*
▸ be successful in, get through, succeed in
6 *How did you pass the time on holiday?*
▸ occupy, spend, use
7 *The pain will soon pass.*
▸ disappear, fade, go away, vanish
8 *Parliament has passed a new law against computer hacking.*
▸ approve, confirm, decree, establish

pass *NOUN*
1 *He has a pass which allows him to fish in the lake.*
▸ licence, permit, ticket
2 *The horses filed through a pass between the hills.*
▸ canyon, gap, gorge, ravine, valley

passable *ADJECTIVE*
1 *She has a passable knowledge of German.*
▸ acceptable, adequate, fair, satisfactory, tolerable
AN OPPOSITE IS unacceptable

a b c d e f g h i j k l m n o **p** q r s t u v w x y z

A B C D E F G H I J K L M N O P Q R S T U V W X Y Z

2 *The flooded road is passable again.*
▸ clear, open, unblocked, usable
AN OPPOSITE IS impassable

passage *NOUN*
1 *They discovered a secret passage.*
▸ corridor, passageway, tunnel
2 *The police forced a passage through the crowd.*
▸ path, route, way
3 *A sea passage takes longer than going by air.*
▸ crossing, journey, voyage
4 *She asked them to choose a favourite passage from a book.*
▸ episode, excerpt, extract, piece, quotation, section
5 *He hadn't changed, despite the passage of time.*
▸ advance, passing, progress

passenger *NOUN*
The bus has seats for 55 passengers.
▸ traveller
▹ Passengers who travel regularly to work are **commuters**.

passer-by *NOUN*
The policeman asked if any passer-by had witnessed the accident.
▸ bystander, onlooker, witness

passion *NOUN*
1 *'Romeo and Juliet' is a story of youthful passion.*
▸ emotion, love
2 *She has a passion for adventure.*
▸ appetite, craving, desire, eagerness, enthusiasm, obsession, thirst, urge, zest

passionate *ADJECTIVE*
1 *It was a passionate speech.*
▸ emotional, intense, strong
AN OPPOSITE IS unemotional
2 *He is a passionate follower of football.*
▸ avid, enthusiastic, fervent, zealous
AN OPPOSITE IS apathetic

passive *ADJECTIVE*
Instead of fighting back, the demonstrators remained passive.
▸ docile, inactive, patient, resigned, submissive, unresisting
AN OPPOSITE IS active

past *NOUN*
In the past, things were different.
▸ days gone by, old days, olden days, past times
▹ The study of what happened in the past is **history**. The things and ideas that have come down to us from the past are our **heritage**.
AN OPPOSITE IS future

past *ADJECTIVE*
Things were very different in past centuries.
▸ earlier, former, old, previous
AN OPPOSITE IS future

pasta *NOUN*
SOME KINDS OF PASTA
cannelloni, lasagne, macaroni, noodles, ravioli, spaghetti, tagliatelle, vermicelli

paste *NOUN*
She used some paste to stick pictures into the album.
▸ adhesive, glue, gum

pastime *NOUN*
What's your favourite pastime?
▸ activity, amusement, diversion, entertainment, game, hobby, occupation, recreation, relaxation, sport
SEE ALSO **game**, **sport**

pasture *NOUN*
Cattle were grazing on the pasture.
▸ field, grassland, meadow

pasty *ADJECTIVE*
He has a pasty complexion.
▸ pallid, pale, unhealthy, white

pat *VERB*
He patted her on the head.
▸ tap, touch
▹ To hit someone hard with an open hand is to **slap** them. To stroke someone with an open hand is to **caress** them. To touch something gently with something soft is to **dab** it.

patch *VERB*
I need to patch my jeans.
▸ mend, repair
▹ Another way to mend holes in clothes is to **darn** them or **stitch** them up.

patchy *ADJECTIVE*
The weather forecast warned of patchy outbreaks of rain.
▸ inconsistent, irregular, uneven, unpredictable, varying
AN OPPOSITE IS uniform

path *NOUN*
VARIOUS KINDS OF PATH
bridle path or bridleway, cart track, footpath, footway, pathway, pavement or (*American*) sidewalk, track, trail, walk, walkway
▹ A path above a beach is an **esplanade** or **promenade**. A path along a canal is a **towpath**. A path between buildings is an **alley**.
SEE ALSO **road**

pathetic *ADJECTIVE*
1 *The refugees were a pathetic sight.*
▸ distressing, heartbreaking, moving, pitiful, sad, touching, tragic
2 *The goalkeeper made a pathetic attempt to stop the ball.*
▸ inadequate, incompetent, laughable, useless, weak

patience *NOUN*
She waited with great patience for an hour.
▸ calmness, endurance, perseverance, persistence, resignation, restraint, self-control, tolerance
AN OPPOSITE IS impatience

patient *ADJECTIVE*
1 *She was very patient with the children.*
▸ calm, docile, easygoing, even-tempered, mild, philosophical, quiet, resigned, serene, tolerant, uncomplaining
2 *After hours of patient effort, the job was finished.*
▸ determined, persevering, persistent, steady, unhurried, untiring
AN OPPOSITE IS impatient

patrol *VERB*
Police patrolled the area all night.
▸ guard, keep watch over, tour
VARIOUS PEOPLE WHO PATROL
guard, lookout, nightwatchman, policeman, policewoman, scout, security officer, sentinel, sentry, watchman

patron *NOUN*
The theatre asked local business people to be patrons.
▸ backer, benefactor, sponsor, subscriber, supporter

patter *VERB*
FOR VARIOUS SOUNDS SEE **sound**

pattern *NOUN*
1 *Do you like the pattern on this wallpaper?*
▸ decoration, design
2 *She used a pattern when she was making the skirt.*
▸ example, guide, model, specimen, standard

pause *NOUN*
There was a pause while they got their breath back.
▸ break, gap, halt, lull, rest, stop, wait
▹ A pause in the middle of a performance is an **interlude** or **interval**. A pause in the middle of a cinema film is an **intermission**. A pause caused by something unexpected is an **interruption** or **stoppage**.

pause *VERB*
1 *She paused uncertainly, not sure what she should do.*
▸ hang back, hesitate, wait
2 *They paused to let the others catch up.*
▸ break off, halt, rest, stop, take a break

pave *VERB*
MATERIALS USED TO PAVE PATHS, ETC.
asphalt, cobbles, concrete, crazy paving, flagstones, paving stones, setts, tiles

paw *NOUN*
The cat left prints of her paws in the wet concrete.
▸ foot
▹ A horse's foot is a **hoof**. A pig's feet are its **trotters**. A bird's feet are its **claws**.

pay *VERB*
1 *She paid a lot for her new car.*
▸ (*informal*) fork out, give, hand over, spend
2 *He always pays his debts.*
▸ clear, pay off, refund, repay, settle
3 *They paid for all the damage they caused.*
▸ compensate, pay back
4 *Do you think the new business is likely to pay?*
▸ be profitable
5 *I'll make you pay for this!*
▸ suffer

payment *NOUN*
PAYMENTS WHICH YOU MAKE TO OTHER PEOPLE
▷ The total of all the payments you make is your **expenditure**. Payment made by a man or woman to a divorced wife or husband is **alimony**. A payment to make up for some wrong that you have done is **compensation**. A voluntary payment to a charity is a **contribution** or **donation**. A first payment of part of the price of something is a **deposit**. The payment you make to travel on public transport is the **fare**. A payment you have to make as a punishment is a **fine**. A payment for an insurance policy is a **premium**. A payment made to free a hostage or prisoner is a **ransom**. A payment you make which shows that you appreciate something someone has done is a **reward**. A payment to join a club is a **subscription**. If you have to make an extra payment on top of the normal price, it is a **supplement** or **surcharge**. A payment to use a private road or bridge is a **toll**. A voluntary payment to a waiter, etc., is a **tip**.
PAYMENTS WHICH OTHER PEOPLE MAKE TO YOU
▷ Payments you get for work you have done are your **pay**, **salary**, or **wages**. A payment you get for doing a single job is a **fee**. Regular payments you get when you have retired from work are your **pension**. Payment that you receive regularly from parents is **pocket money**. A payment you get if you paid too much for something is a **refund**.

peace *NOUN*
1 *After the war there was a period of peace.*
▸ agreement, friendliness, harmony
2 *She enjoys the peace of the countryside.*
▸ calmness, peacefulness, quiet, serenity, silence, stillness, tranquillity

peaceful *ADJECTIVE*
They enjoyed a peaceful day fishing.
▸ calm, gentle, placid, pleasant, quiet, relaxing, restful, serene, soothing, still, tranquil, undisturbed, untroubled
AN OPPOSITE IS noisy or troubled

peak *NOUN*
1 *The peak of the mountain was covered in snow.*
▸ cap, summit, tip, top
2 *At the peak of the storm I thought the house would be blown away!*
▸ climax, crisis, culmination, height, highest point

peal *VERB*
The bells pealed to celebrate the wedding.
▸ chime, ring
▷ If a bell rings slowly at a funeral, etc., it **tolls**.

pebbles *NOUN*
▷ A quantity of pebbles on a beach is **shingle**. Round stones like large pebbles are **cobbles**.

peculiar *ADJECTIVE*
1 *What's that peculiar smell?*
▸ abnormal, curious, extraordinary, funny, out of the ordinary, queer, strange, unusual
AN OPPOSITE IS ordinary
2 *He seemed a bit peculiar.*
▸ eccentric, odd, suspicious, weird
3 *He recognized her peculiar way of writing.*
▸ characteristic, different, distinctive, identifiable, individual, particular, personal, special, unique

peculiarity *NOUN*
Did you notice any peculiarity which would help us identify the man?
▸ abnormality, characteristic, eccentricity, oddity

pedigree *NOUN*
They have a complete record of the dog's pedigree.
▸ ancestry, descent, family history

peel *NOUN*
Orange peel is used in marmalade.
▸ rind, skin

peep, **peer** *VERBS*
SEE **look** *VERB*

peer, **peeress** *NOUNS*
▸ aristocrat, noble, nobleman or noblewoman
FOR TITLES OF NOBLES SEE **title**

pelt *VERB*
They pelted each other with snowballs.
▸ attack, bombard, shower
SEE ALSO **throw**

pen *NOUN*
1 *My pen has run out of ink.*
▸ ballpoint, felt-tipped pen, fountain pen
2 *The dog drove the sheep into the pen.*
▸ enclosure, fold

penalize *VERB*
In football, you will be penalized if you handle the ball.
▸ punish

penalty *NOUN*
The maximum penalty for this crime is ten years in prison.
▸ punishment

penetrate *VERB*
1 *He stepped on a nail that penetrated his foot.*
▸ bore through, get through, make a hole in, pierce
▹ When something penetrates a tyre, it punctures it.
2 *The soldiers penetrated the enemy's defences.*
▸ enter, get past, infiltrate

penitent *ADJECTIVE*
He was penitent about his mistake.
▸ apologetic, ashamed, regretful, remorseful, repentant, sorry
AN OPPOSITE IS unrepentant

people *PLURAL NOUN*
1 *There are always a lot of people in town on Saturdays.*
▸ folk, men and women and children
▹ People as opposed to animals are humans or human beings or mankind.
2 *The people will decide who governs the country.*
▸ citizens, common people, population, the public, society
3 *It would be wonderful if the peoples of the world could live in peace.*
▸ nation, race

peppery *ADJECTIVE*
He's not keen on food with a peppery taste.
▸ hot, spicy

perceive *VERB*
1 *They perceived a shape on the horizon.*
▸ become aware of, catch sight of, make out, notice, observe, recognize, see, spot
2 *He began to perceive what she meant.*
▸ comprehend, grasp, realize, understand

perceptible *ADJECTIVE*
There was a perceptible note of anger in his voice.
▸ clear, definite, distinct, evident, noticeable, obvious, recognizable, unmistakable, visible
AN OPPOSITE IS imperceptible

perceptive *ADJECTIVE*
She's very perceptive about people.
▸ acute, alert, clever, observant, quick, sensitive, sharp, shrewd
AN OPPOSITE IS unobservant

perch *VERB*
He perched on top of the wall.
▸ balance, rest, settle, sit

percussion *NOUN*
FOR VARIOUS PERCUSSION INSTRUMENTS SEE **music**

perfect *ADJECTIVE*
1 *She has a perfect set of teeth.*
▸ complete, faultless, flawless, ideal, intact, undamaged, whole
▹ A perfect stamp or coin is in mint condition.
2 *This photocopier makes perfect copies every time.*
▸ accurate, correct, exact, faithful, precise
AN OPPOSITE IS imperfect
3 *He was a perfect stranger.*
▸ absolute, total, utter

perfect *VERB*
He spent years perfecting his technique.
▸ improve, polish up, refine

perforate *VERB*
She perforated the paper with a pin.
▸ bore through, pierce, prick, puncture

perform *VERB*
1 *He's too shy to perform on a stage.*
▸ act, appear, dance, play, sing
2 *They performed a play about Cinderella.*
▸ present, produce, put on, take part in
3 *Soldiers are expected to perform their duty.*
▸ carry out, do, execute, fulfil
▹ To perform a crime is to commit a crime.

performance *NOUN*
1 *He really enjoyed the performance he saw at the theatre.*
▸ presentation, production, show
FOR DIFFERENT KINDS OF PERFORMANCE SEE **entertainment**
2 *She congratulated them on their good performance.*
▸ achievement, attempt, behaviour, conduct, effort, endeavour, exertion, work

A B C D E F G H I J K L M N O **P** Q R S T U V W X Y Z

performer *NOUN*
SEE **entertainer**

perfume *NOUN*
The perfume of roses filled the room.
▸ fragrance, scent, smell

perhaps *ADVERB*
Perhaps the weather will be better tomorrow.
▸ maybe, possibly
AN OPPOSITE IS definitely

peril *NOUN*
They bravely faced the peril which lay ahead.
▸ danger, risks, threat
AN OPPOSITE IS safety

perilous *ADJECTIVE*
They made a perilous trek through the mountains.
▸ dangerous, hazardous, risky
AN OPPOSITE IS safe

perimeter *NOUN*
They put up a fence round the perimeter of the field.
▸ border, boundary, edge
▹ The distance round the edge of something is the circumference.

period *NOUN*
1 *After a long period of hard work they had a rest.*
▸ span, spell, stretch, time
2 *The book is about the Victorian period.*
▸ age, epoch, era

periodical *NOUN*
She bought a computing periodical to read on the train.
▸ journal, magazine

perish *VERB*
1 *Many birds perish in cold weather.*
▸ be killed, die, expire, pass away
2 *There was a leak where the rubber hose had perished.*
▸ crumble away, decay, decompose, disintegrate, go bad, rot

permanent *ADJECTIVE*
1 *She told him to do a permanent repair, not just to patch it up.*
▸ durable, lasting
2 *If you live in a city, traffic noise is a permanent problem.*
▸ chronic, constant, continual, endless, everlasting, incessant, never-ending, perennial, perpetual, persistent, unending
3 *Marriage is a permanent relationship.*
▸ lifelong, long-lasting, stable, steady
AN OPPOSITE IS temporary

permissible *ADJECTIVE*
It is not permissible to smoke in here.
▸ acceptable, allowed, lawful, legal, permitted, right
AN OPPOSITE IS forbidden

permission *NOUN*
They had the teacher's permission to leave.
▸ agreement, approval, consent, (*informal*) go-ahead

permissive
His parents have a permissive attitude — they let him do what he wants.
▸ easy-going, indulgent, lenient, tolerant
AN OPPOSITE IS intolerant

permit *VERB*
The council doesn't permit fishing in the lake.
▸ agree to, allow, approve of, authorize, consent to, give permission for, license, tolerate
▹ Another way to say 'Permit me to speak' is to say 'Let me speak'.

permit *NOUN*
You need a permit to fish in the river.
▸ licence, pass, ticket

perpendicular *ADJECTIVE*
The Leaning Tower of Pisa is not perpendicular.
▸ upright, vertical

perpetual *ADJECTIVE*
The perpetual roar of traffic is very annoying.
▸ ceaseless, chronic, constant, continual, continuous, endless, eternal, everlasting, incessant, never-ending, non-stop, perennial, permanent, persistent, unceasing, unending
AN OPPOSITE IS temporary

perplex *VERB*
The question perplexed him.
▸ baffle, bewilder, confuse, muddle, mystify, puzzle, worry

persecute *VERB*
People were persecuted for their religious beliefs.
▸ bully, discriminate against, harass, intimidate, oppress, terrorize, torment, torture

persevere *VERB*
She persevered despite all the difficulties.
▸ continue, go on, (*informal*) keep at it, keep going, persist, (*informal*) stick at it
AN OPPOSITE IS give up

persist *VERB*
1 *He persists in his beliefs, despite the evidence.*
▸ be obstinate, keep on, persevere
AN OPPOSITE IS stop
2 *How long will this snow persist?*
▸ last, linger, remain
AN OPPOSITE IS disappear

persistent *ADJECTIVE*
1 *There are persistent rumours that she is getting married.*
▸ constant, continual, endless, eternal, everlasting, incessant, never-ending, repeated, unceasing
2 *He had a persistent cold all winter.*
▸ ceaseless, chronic, permanent, recurrent, recurring
3 *That dog is very persistent — he won't go away.*
▸ determined, obstinate, patient, persevering, resolute, steadfast, stubborn, tireless

person *NOUN*
Who was that person I saw you with last night?
▸ character, human being, individual
▹ An adult person is a man or woman. A young person is a baby, infant, child, or adolescent.

personal *ADJECTIVE*
1 *They have personal business to discuss.*
▸ confidential, intimate, private, secret
2 *Don't make personal remarks!*
▸ critical, insulting, offensive, rude

personality *NOUN*
1 *She has an attractive personality.*
▸ character, disposition, make-up, nature
2 *A crowd gathered to watch the show business personalities arrive.*
▸ celebrity, famous person, idol, public figure, star

personnel *NOUN*
The company promised that all personnel would get a pay rise.
▸ employees, staff, workers

perspire *VERB*
He perspires a lot in hot weather.
▸ sweat

persuade *VERB*
I persuaded him to come with us.
▸ coax, convert, convince
▹ To persuade someone to do something is also to talk them into doing it.
AN OPPOSITE IS dissuade

persuasion *NOUN*
It took a lot of persuasion to make him change his mind.
▸ argument, coaxing, convincing, persuading, reasoning

persuasive *ADJECTIVE*
She used some very persuasive arguments.
▸ convincing, credible, effective, logical, reasonable, sound, strong, valid
AN OPPOSITE IS unconvincing

perverse *ADJECTIVE*
He was acting in a rather perverse way.
▸ contrary, illogical, obstinate, stubborn, tiresome, uncooperative, unhelpful, unreasonable
AN OPPOSITE IS reasonable

pervert *VERB*
The police claimed that he had tried to pervert the course of justice.
▸ interfere with, lead astray, undermine

perverted *ADJECTIVE*
His perverted behaviour got him into trouble with the police.
▸ abnormal, corrupt, evil, immoral, improper, obscene, twisted, unnatural, warped, wicked, wrong
AN OPPOSITE IS normal

A B C D E F G H I J K L M N O **P** Q R S T U V W X Y Z

pessimistic *ADJECTIVE*
They were pessimistic about their chances of winning.
► cynical, despairing, gloomy, hopeless, negative, without hope
AN OPPOSITE IS optimistic

pest *NOUN*
1 *He won't use chemicals to get rid of garden pests.*
▷ Pests in general are **vermin**. An informal word for insect pests is **bugs**. A pest which lives on or in another creature is a **parasite**.
2 *Don't be a pest!*
► annoyance, bother, nuisance

pester *VERB*
Please don't pester me while I'm busy!
► annoy, (*informal*) badger, bother, harass, nag, plague, provoke, trouble, try, worry

pet *NOUN*
CREATURES COMMONLY KEPT AS PETS INCLUDE
budgerigar, canary, cat, dog, ferret, fish, gerbil, goldfish, guinea pig, hamster, mouse, parrot, pigeon, rabbit, rat, tortoise

petrify *VERB*
He was so petrified that he couldn't move.
► frighten, horrify, scare, shock, terrify

petrol *NOUN*
▷ In America, petrol is **gas** or **gasoline**.

petty *ADJECTIVE*
There were a lot of annoying petty rules.
► insignificant, minor, small, trivial, unimportant
AN OPPOSITE IS important

pharmacy *NOUN*
He went to the pharmacy for his medicine.
► chemist's, dispensary

phase *NOUN*
Going to a new school is the start of a new phase in your life.
► period, stage, step, time

phenomenal *ADJECTIVE*
The winner of the quiz had a phenomenal memory.
► amazing, exceptional, extraordinary, (*informal*) fantastic, incredible, outstanding, remarkable, unbelievable, unusual, wonderful
AN OPPOSITE IS ordinary

phenomenon *NOUN*
1 *Snow is a common phenomenon in winter.*
► event, fact, happening, occurrence
2 *The six-year-old pianist was quite a phenomenon.*
► curiosity, marvel, wonder

philosophical *ADJECTIVE*
1 *They had a philosophical debate about the meaning of life.*
► abstract, academic, analytical, intellectual, learned, logical, rational, reasoned, theoretical
AN OPPOSITE IS practical
2 *He was quite philosophical about losing the race.*
► calm, patient, reasonable, resigned, sensible, stoical, unemotional
AN OPPOSITE IS emotional

philosophy *NOUN*
Her philosophy can be summed up in the phrase, 'Respect all living things'.
► beliefs, convictions, values, way of thinking

phobia *NOUN*
He has a phobia about spiders.
► anxiety, dislike, dread, fear, (*informal*) hang-up, hatred, horror
▷ A fear of open spaces is **agoraphobia**. A fear of spiders is **arachnophobia**. A fear of enclosed spaces is **claustrophobia**. A fear of strangers or foreigners is **xenophobia**.

phone *VERB*
He phoned her to tell her the news.
► call, dial, ring, telephone

photocopy *VERB*
She photocopied the article.
► copy, duplicate, print off, reproduce

photograph *NOUN*
Have the holiday photographs been developed yet?
► photo, shot, snap or snapshot
▷ The photographs you get when a film is processed are **prints**. A photograph on the original film from which you have to make a print is a **negative**. A photograph which is larger than a normal print is an **enlargement**. A photograph for projecting onto a screen is a **slide** or **transparency**.

photograph *VERB*
She photographed him in fancy dress.
▸ shoot, snap, take a picture of
PHOTOGRAPHIC EQUIPMENT INCLUDES
(*old use*) box camera, cine-camera, darkroom, enlarger, exposure meter or light meter, (*trademark*) Polaroid camera, SLR or single lens reflex camera, telephoto lens, tripod, zoom lens

phrase *NOUN*
'I don't believe it!' is a common phrase.
▸ expression, saying

phrase *VERB*
She tried to phrase it politely.
▸ express, put into words

physical *ADJECTIVE*
1 *There's a lot of physical contact in rugby.*
▸ bodily
▹ Physical punishment is corporal punishment.
2 *Ghosts have no physical presence.*
▸ actual, earthly, real, solid, substantial

pick *VERB*
1 *They picked partners for the game.*
▸ choose, decide on, opt for, select, settle on, single out
2 *They decided to pick a new captain.*
▸ elect, nominate, vote for
3 *She picked some flowers from the garden.*
▸ collect, cut, gather
4 *I picked an apple off the tree.*
▸ pluck, pull off, take

picture *NOUN*
There were some good pictures in the book.
▸ illustration, image, likeness, portrayal, representation
PICTURES PRODUCED BY VARIOUS METHODS
cartoon, collage, doodle, drawing, engraving, etching, identikit picture, mosaic, oil painting, photograph, print, sketch, slide, snap or snapshot, transfer, transparency, water colour
▹ A picture which represents a particular person is a portrait. A picture which gives a side view of someone is a profile. A picture which exaggerates some aspect of a person is a caricature. A picture which gives just the general shape of someone or something is an outline or silhouette. A picture drawn quickly without much thought is a doodle. A picture which represents a group of objects is a still life. A picture which represents a country scene is a landscape. A picture which does not represent any person, thing, or scene is an abstract.
▹ A picture painted on a wall is a fresco or a mural. A picture painted by a famous painter of the past is an old master. A copy of a painting is a reproduction. Pictures on a computer are graphics. Moving pictures are films.

picture *VERB*
1 *They were pictured against a background of flowers.*
▸ depict, illustrate, portray, represent, show
2 *Can you picture what the world will be like in 100 years?*
▸ imagine, visualize

picturesque *ADJECTIVE*
1 *They stayed in a picturesque thatched cottage.*
▸ attractive, charming, pretty, quaint
AN OPPOSITE IS ugly
2 *It was a picturesque account of life in the Middle Ages.*
▸ colourful, descriptive, expressive, graphic, imaginative, lively, poetic, vivid

piece *NOUN*
A SUBSTANTIAL PIECE OF SOMETHING
bar, block, chunk, hunk, length, lump, part, sample, section, segment, slab, stick
A PIECE BROKEN OR CUT OFF SOMETHING
bit, chip, crumb, fragment, morsel, particle, scrap, shred, slice
A PIECE OF SOMETHING TO EAT
bite, crumb, helping, morsel, portion, share
ONE OF THE PIECES THAT SOMETHING IS MADE OF
component, constituent, element, part, unit
▹ A piece of clothing is an article or item of clothing.
FOR WORDS FOR A PIECE OF MUSIC OR WRITING SEE **music, writing**

pier *NOUN*
1 *The passengers disembarked at the pier.*
▸ jetty, landing stage, quay, wharf
▹ A structure built out into the sea as a protection against the waves is a breakwater.
2 *The flood nearly swept away the piers supporting the bridge.*
▸ column, pile, pillar, support

pierce *VERB*
This new drill will pierce almost anything.
▶ bore through, drill through, enter, go through, make a hole in, penetrate
▷ To pierce a hole through paper is to **punch** a hole or **perforate** it. To pierce a hole in a tyre is to **puncture** it. To pierce someone with a spike is to **impale** or **spear** them.

piercing *ADJECTIVE*
He heard a piercing scream.
▶ deafening, high-pitched, loud, penetrating, sharp, shrill

pig *NOUN*
▷ An old word for pigs is **swine**. A wild pig is a **wild boar**. A male pig is a **boar** or **hog**. A female pig is a **sow**. A baby pig is a **piglet**. A family of piglets is a **litter**. The smallest piglet in a litter is the **runt**.

pile *NOUN*
1 *Where did this pile of rubbish come from?*
▶ accumulation, heap, mass, mound, quantity, stack
2 *The pier is built on piles driven into the mud.*
▶ column, pier, post, support

pile *VERB*
Pile everything in the corner and we'll sort it out later.
▶ accumulate, assemble, bring together, build up, collect, concentrate, gather, heap up, stack

pill *NOUN*
The doctor told her to swallow the pills with some water.
▶ capsule, pellet, tablet

pillar *NOUN*
The roof was supported by tall pillars.
▶ column, pier, pile, post, prop, support

pillow *NOUN*
▷ A long kind of pillow is a **bolster**. A kind of pillow for a chair or sofa is a **cushion**.

pilot *VERB*
She piloted the aircraft back to safety.
▶ fly, guide, lead, navigate, steer

pimple *NOUN*
He had a pimple on his nose.
▶ boil, spot, swelling
▷ A lot of pimples or spots on your skin is a **rash**.

pin *NOUN*
▷ A pretty pin you might wear on a dress is a **brooch**. A pin to fix something on a noticeboard is a **drawing pin**. A pin to fix a baby's nappy in place is a **safety pin**.

pinch *VERB*
1 *He pinched his fingers in the door.*
▶ crush, nip, squeeze
2 (*informal*) *Who pinched my pen?*
▶ (*informal*) lift, (*informal*) make off with, pilfer, steal, take, (*informal*) walk off with

pine *VERB*
The dog pined when its master died.
▶ mope, mourn, sicken, waste away
to pine for *She was pining for her mother.*
▶ crave, long for, want, yearn for

pioneer *NOUN*
1 *They learned about the pioneers who first settled in America.*
▶ colonist, discoverer, explorer, settler
2 *Alexander Bell was a pioneer in the history of telecommunications.*
▶ innovator, inventor, originator

pious *ADJECTIVE*
The pious pilgrims knelt down when they reached the sacred place.
▶ holy, religious, reverent, saintly

pip *NOUN*
▷ A pip in an apple, orange, etc., is a **seed**. The pips on dice are **spots**. The pips of a time signal are **bleeps**.

pipe *NOUN*
The water flows away along this pipe.
▶ tube
▷ A length of pipe is **piping** or **tubing**. The system of water pipes in a house is the **plumbing**. A pipe used for watering the garden is a **hose**. A pipe in the street which supplies water for fighting fires, etc., is a **hydrant**. A pipe which carries oil, etc., over long distances is a **pipeline**.

pipe *VERB*
1 *They pipe water from the Welsh hills to Birmingham.*
▸ convey, transmit
2 *She began to pipe a tune on her recorder.*
▸ blow, play, sound, whistle

pirate *NOUN*
In the old days ruthless pirates sailed the high seas.
▸ buccaneer, marauder

pistol *NOUN*
FOR VARIOUS GUNS SEE **weapon**

pit *NOUN*
1 *They dug a deep pit.*
▸ abyss, chasm, crater, depression, excavation, hole, hollow, mine, pothole, quarry
2 *At one time, a lot of coal was mined from the pits in this area.*
▸ coal mine, colliery

pitch *NOUN*
The groundsman worked hard to prepare the pitch for the game.
▸ ground, playing field

pitch *VERB*
1 *They pitched the rubbish into the skip.*
▸ (*slang*) bung, cast, (*informal*) chuck, fling, heave, hurl, lob, sling, throw, toss
2 *It was hard trying to pitch the tent in the rain!*
▸ erect, put up, set up
3 *He lost his balance and pitched into the water.*
▸ drop, fall heavily, plunge, topple
4 *The ship pitched about in the storm.*
▸ dip, lurch, rock, roll, toss

pitfall *NOUN*
They tried to avoid the obvious pitfalls.
▸ catch, danger, difficulty, hazard, snag, trap

pitiful *ADJECTIVE*
1 *We could hear pitiful cries for help.*
▸ distressing, miserable, moving, pathetic, sad, touching, wretched
2 *The goalkeeper made a pitiful attempt to stop the ball.*
▸ contemptible, hopeless, inadequate, incompetent, laughable, pathetic, ridiculous, useless

pitiless *ADJECTIVE*
They kept up a pitiless bombardment until the town was flattened.
▸ barbaric, bloodthirsty, brutal, callous, cruel, heartless, inhuman, merciless, relentless, remorseless, ruthless, sadistic, savage, vicious
AN OPPOSITE IS merciful

pity *NOUN*
The thugs showed no pity.
▸ compassion, feeling, humanity, kindness, mercy, regret, sympathy, tenderness, understanding
AN OPPOSITE IS cruelty

pity *VERB*
She pitied anyone who was out in the storm.
▸ feel for, feel pity for, sympathize with, weep for

pivot *NOUN*
▹ The point on which a lever turns is the **fulcrum**. The point on which a spinning object turns is its **axis**. The point on which a wheel turns is the **axle** or **hub**.

placard *NOUN*
They put up a placard announcing the sale.
▸ advertisement, bill, notice, poster, sign

place *NOUN*
1 *They couldn't find the place on the map.*
▸ location, point, position, situation, spot
▹ A place where there is a particular building or something interesting is a **site**.
2 *This would be a nice place for a holiday.*
▸ area, country, district, locality, neighbourhood, region, vicinity
3 *Save me a place on the bus.*
▸ seat

place *VERB*
1 *The council placed a recycling centre next to the car park.*
▸ locate, situate
2 *They placed guards at regular intervals along the route.*
▸ position, stand, station
3 *Place your things on the table.*
▸ arrange, deposit, dump, lay, leave, put down, rest, set down

A B C D E F G H I J K L M N O **P** Q R S T U V W X Y Z

placid *ADJECTIVE*
1 *He won't get upset — he's a very placid character.*
▶ cool, even-tempered, level-headed, mild, sensible, unexcitable
AN OPPOSITE IS excitable or quarrelsome
2 *They had a placid voyage.*
▶ calm, peaceful, quiet, restful, tranquil, unruffled, untroubled
AN OPPOSITE IS stormy

plague *NOUN*
1 *Doctors worked hard to prevent the plague from spreading.*
▶ epidemic, infection, outbreak
2 *There was a plague of wasps this summer.*
▶ invasion, swarm

plague *VERB*
1 *Ants have plagued us all summer.*
▶ afflict, be a nuisance to, torment
▷ To be plagued by insects or vermin is to be infested by them.
2 *She has been plagued by bad luck.*
▶ annoy, irritate, nag, pester, trouble, vex, worry

plain *ADJECTIVE*
1 *The room was very plain.*
▶ austere, homely, modest, simple, undecorated
AN OPPOSITE IS elaborate
2 *Some people say she looks plain compared with her sister.*
▶ ordinary, unattractive
AN OPPOSITE IS attractive
3 *It was quite plain what he meant.*
▶ clear, comprehensible, definite, distinct, evident, obvious, unambiguous, unmistakable
AN OPPOSITE IS unclear
4 *He told her in plain words what he thought.*
▶ blunt, direct, frank, honest, outspoken, sincere, straightforward

plain *NOUN*
▷ A grassy plain in a hot country is called savannah. The large plains of North America are the prairies. The large plains of Russia are the steppes.

plaintive *ADJECTIVE*
He played a plaintive tune on his saxophone.
▶ melancholy, mournful, sad, sorrowful, wistful
AN OPPOSITE IS cheerful

plan *NOUN*
1 *The captain explained her plan to the rest of the team.*
▶ aim, idea, intention, policy, project, proposal, scheme, strategy
▷ A plan to do something bad is a plot.
2 *They looked at the plans for the new sports centre.*
▶ blueprint, design, diagram, drawing
3 *He drew a plan of the village.*
▶ chart, map, sketch map

plan *VERB*
1 *They planned a money-raising campaign.*
▶ arrange, contrive, design, devise, formulate, map out, organize, outline, prepare, think out, work out
▷ To plan to do something bad is to plot.
2 *What do you plan to do next?*
▶ aim, intend, mean, propose

plane *NOUN*
SEE **aircraft**

planet *NOUN*
Is there life on other planets?
▶ world
PLANETS OF THE SOLAR SYSTEM
Earth, Jupiter, Mars, Mercury, Neptune, Pluto, Saturn, Uranus, Venus
▷ The path followed by a planet is its orbit. Minor planets orbiting the sun are asteroids. Something which orbits a planet is a satellite. The earth's large satellite is the moon.

plank *NOUN*
SEE **timber**

plant *NOUN*
SOME KINDS OF PLANT
algae, bulb, cactus, cereal, fern, flower, fungus, grass, herb, lichen, moss, shrub, tree, vegetable, waterplant
SEE ALSO **flower**, **fruit**, **tree**, **vegetable**
PARTS OF VARIOUS PLANTS
bloom, blossom, branch, bud, flower, fruit, leaf, petal, pod, root, shoot, stalk, stem, trunk, twig
THINGS THAT PLANTS GROW FROM
bulb, corm, cutting, seed, tuber
▷ Annual plants live for just one year. Biennial plants live for two years. Perennial plants continue to live year after year. A plant which is growing where you don't want it is a weed. A young plant is a seedling. A word for plants in general is vegetation. A formal scientific word for plants in general is flora. The scientific study of plants is botany.

plant *VERB*
They will plant the seeds in April.
▸ set out, sow
▹ To move a plant from where it was growing and plant it somewhere else is to transplant it.

plaster *NOUN*
The nurse put a plaster on the cut.
▸ dressing, sticking plaster

plate *NOUN*
1 *She piled their plates with food.*
FOR ITEMS OF CROCKERY SEE **crockery**
2 *The sides of the warship were protected by steel plates.*
▸ panel, sheet
3 *There were some attractive plates in the book.*
▸ illustration, photo, picture

platform *NOUN*
She stood on the platform to make the speech.
▸ stage

play *NOUN*
1 *There was a good play on TV last night.*
▸ comedy, drama, performance, production, tragedy
2 *It is important to balance work and play.*
▸ amusement, fun, games, playing, recreation, sport
FOR VARIOUS GAMES AND SPORTS SEE **game**, **sport**

play *VERB*
1 *The children went out to play.*
▸ amuse yourself, have fun, romp about
2 *Would you like to play with us?*
▸ join in, participate, take part
3 *I'll play you at snooker.*
▸ challenge, compete against, oppose
4 *She played the piano at the school concert.*
▸ perform on
5 *He often plays tapes in the car.*
▸ have on, listen to, put on
6 *She played Mary in the nativity play.*
▸ act, portray, represent, take the part of
to play about, **to play up** *She gets angry if anyone starts to play up while she's reading a story.*
▸ behave badly, fool around, make mischief, mess about, misbehave

player *NOUN*
1 *You need four players for this game.*
▸ competitor, contestant, participant
2 *How many players were there in the band?*
▸ instrumentalist, musician, performer
▹ Someone who plays music on their own is a soloist.
FOR VARIOUS PERFORMERS SEE **entertainer**, **music**

playful *ADJECTIVE*
They were in a playful mood.
▸ cheerful, frisky, frivolous, impish, jaunty, joking, lively, mischievous, skittish, sprightly
AN OPPOSITE IS serious

playing field *NOUN*
They couldn't play because the playing field was too wet.
▸ ground, pitch, recreation ground, sports ground

plea *NOUN*
The judge ignored the accused man's plea for mercy.
▸ appeal, entreaty, request

plead *VERB*
He pleaded to be let off.
▸ appeal, ask, beg, entreat, implore, request

pleasant *ADJECTIVE* This word is often overused. It can refer to anything which pleases you, and there are many possible synonyms. We just give some common ones here:
1 *He seems to be a pleasant person.*
▸ amiable, amicable, approachable, cheerful, decent, friendly, genial, good-natured, hospitable, kind, likeable, sympathetic
2 *We had a pleasant time.*
▸ agreeable, delightful, enjoyable, entertaining, excellent, pleasing, relaxing
3 *You get pleasant views from the upstairs windows.*
▸ attractive, beautiful, charming, lovely, pretty
4 *The weather is quite pleasant today.*
▸ bright, clear, fine, mild, sunny, warm
5 *They played pleasant music while they had their dinner.*
▸ gentle, peaceful, soothing
AN OPPOSITE IS unpleasant

please *VERB*
1 *He did it to please her.*
▸ amuse, entertain, give pleasure to, make happy, satisfy
2 *Do as you please.*
▸ want, wish

A B C D E F G H I J K L M N O **P** Q R S T U V W X Y Z

pleased *ADJECTIVE*
Why do you look so pleased today?
▸ contented, delighted, elated, glad, grateful, happy, satisfied, thankful, thrilled
AN OPPOSITE IS annoyed

pleasure *NOUN*
1 *She gets a lot of pleasure from her garden.*
▸ comfort, contentment, delight, enjoyment, gladness, happiness, joy, satisfaction
▹ Very great pleasure is **bliss** or **ecstasy**.
2 *He talked about the pleasures of living in the country.*
▸ amusement, diversion, entertainment, luxury, recreation

pleat *NOUN*
It takes ages to iron the pleats in the skirt.
▸ crease, fold, tuck

pledge *NOUN*
She gave a pledge that the work will be done on time.
▸ assurance, guarantee, oath, promise, vow, word

plentiful *ADJECTIVE*
They had a plentiful supply of food.
▸ abundant, ample, generous, inexhaustible, lavish, liberal, profuse
AN OPPOSITE IS scarce

plenty *NOUN*
Don't buy any milk — there's plenty in the fridge.
▸ an abundance, a lot, a profusion
▹ More than you know what to do with is a **glut** or **surplus**.
AN OPPOSITE IS scarcity
plenty of *They've got plenty of food.*
▸ abundant, ample, heaps of, (*informal*) loads of, a lot of, lots of, (*informal*) masses of, piles of

pliable *ADJECTIVE*
She showed him how to weave a basket out of pliable twigs.
▸ flexible, springy, supple
AN OPPOSITE IS rigid

plight *NOUN*
He was concerned about the plight of the homeless.
▸ difficulty, dilemma, problem

plod *VERB*
1 *We plodded through the mud.*
▸ tramp, trudge
2 *She plodded away at her work without much enthusiasm.*
▸ labour at, persevere with

plot *NOUN*
1 *Guy Fawkes was involved in a plot against the government.*
▸ conspiracy, scheme, secret plan
2 *It was hard to follow the plot of the film.*
▸ narrative, story, thread
3 *He bought a plot of ground to build a retirement home.*
▸ area, lot, patch, piece
▹ A plot of ground for growing flowers or vegetables is an **allotment** or **smallholding**. A large plot of land is a **tract** of land.

plot *VERB*
1 *They plotted to rob a bank.*
▸ conspire, intrigue, scheme
2 *They were plotting mischief.*
▸ (*informal*) cook up, hatch

plough *VERB*
After one crop is harvested, they plough the ground for the next one.
▸ cultivate, till, turn over

pluck *VERB*
1 *He had to pluck the chicken before cooking it.*
▸ remove the feathers from, strip
2 *They plucked the apples off the tree.*
▸ collect, gather, harvest, pick, pull off
3 *A seagull plucked her sandwich out of her hand.*
▸ grab, jerk, pull, seize, snatch, tug, yank
4 *He began to pluck the strings of his guitar.*
▹ To run your finger or plectrum across the strings of a guitar is to **strum**. To pluck the strings of a violin or cello is to play **pizzicato**.

plucky *ADJECTIVE*
SEE **brave**

plug *NOUN*
They put a plug in the hole.
▸ bung, cork, stopper

plug *VERB*
1 *She tried to plug a leak in the water tank.*
▸ block up, bung up, close, fill, seal, stop up
2 (*informal*) *They asked the local radio station to plug our concert.*
▸ advertise, mention frequently, promote, publicize, recommend

plump *ADJECTIVE*
He's getting a bit plump.
▶ chubby, dumpy, podgy, portly, round, squat, stout
AN OPPOSITE IS skinny

plunder *VERB*
Rioters plundered the shops.
▶ loot, pillage, raid, ransack, rob, steal from

plunge *VERB*
1 *She plunged into the water.*
▶ dive, drop, fall, jump, leap, pitch, swoop down, tumble
2 *I plunged my hand in the water.*
▶ dip, immerse, lower, sink, submerge
3 *He plunged his spear into the animal's side.*
▶ force, push, stab, thrust

plural *ADJECTIVE*
AN OPPOSITE IS singular

pneumatic *ADJECTIVE*
The tricycle has pneumatic tyres.
▶ air-filled, pumped up

poach *VERB*
Robin Hood used to poach deer in Sherwood Forest.
▶ hunt illegally, steal

podgy *ADJECTIVE*
She needs more exercise — she's getting podgy.
▶ chubby, dumpy, plump, portly, round, stout
AN OPPOSITE IS skinny

poem *NOUN*
▷ Poems are **poetry**, **rhymes**, or **verse**.
SOME KINDS OF POEM
ballad, cinquain, clerihew, concrete poem, elegy, free verse, haiku, limerick, narrative poem, nonsense verse, nursery rhyme, ode, sonnet, tanka
▷ A poem divided into groups of lines with a regular pattern of rhymes is in **stanzas**. A poem with pairs of lines that rhyme is in **couplets**. Poor verse with silly-sounding rhymes is **doggerel**. A short poem which is meant to be set to music is a **lyric**.

poetic *ADJECTIVE*
They used poetic language in their descriptions.
▶ emotional, (*uncomplimentary*) flowery, imaginative, lyrical, poetical

point *NOUN*
1 *She hurt herself on that sharp point.*
▶ prong, spike, tip
2 *Remember to put in the decimal point.*
▶ dot, full stop, mark, spot
3 *He marked on the map the exact point where the accident happened.*
▶ location, place, position, site, situation
4 *At that point the rain started to come down.*
▶ instant, moment, time
5 *She said that his last point was a good one.*
▶ detail, idea, thought
6 *Honesty is one of his good points.*
▶ characteristic, feature, peculiarity
7 *What is the point of that story?*
▶ aim, intention, meaning, purpose, use, usefulness

point *VERB*
1 *She pointed the way.*
▶ draw attention to, indicate, point out, show, signal
2 *Can you point me in the right direction for the station?*
▶ aim, direct, guide, lead, steer

pointless *ADJECTIVE*
It's pointless to argue with him — he's so stubborn.
▶ futile, useless, vain
AN OPPOSITE IS worthwhile

poise *NOUN*
She showed great poise on her first public appearance.
▶ calmness, coolness, dignity, self-confidence

poise *VERB*
He poised himself on a narrow ledge.
▶ balance, support, suspend

poison *NOUN*
▷ A poison to kill plants is **herbicide** or **weedkiller**. A poison to kill insects is **insecticide** or **pesticide**. The poison in a snake bite is **venom**. Food poisoning can be caused by bacteria such as **salmonella**.
SOME POISONOUS SUBSTANCES
arsenic, belladonna, cyanide, DDT, hemlock, paraquat, strychnine, warfarin
▷ A substance which can save you from the effects of a poison is an **antidote**.

A B C D E F G H I J K L M N O **P** Q R S T U V W X Y Z

poisonous *ADJECTIVE*
He became very ill after receiving a poisonous snake bite.
▸ deadly, lethal, toxic, venomous

poke *VERB*
He poked me in the back with a stick.
▸ dig, jab, prod, stab, thrust
to poke out *She saw the kitten's head poking out of the basket.*
▸ project, protrude, stick out

polar *ADJECTIVE*
The polar night lasts for months.
▸ antarctic or arctic

pole *NOUN*
Four poles marked the corners of the field.
▸ bar, post, rod, shaft, stick
▹ A pole that you use when walking or as a weapon is a **staff**. A pole for a flag to fly from is a **flagpole**. A pole to support sails on a boat, etc., is a **mast** or **spar**. A pole with a pointed end to stick in the ground is a **stake**. Poles which a circus entertainer walks on are **stilts**.

police officer *NOUN*
ORDINARY POLICE OFFICERS
(*informal*) bobby, constable, (*slang*) cop or copper, policeman or policewoman
POLICE OFFICERS HIGHER IN RANK THAN A CONSTABLE
chief constable, inspector, sergeant, superintendent
▹ Someone training for the police force is a **cadet**. Someone who investigates crimes is a **detective**.

policy *NOUN*
She explained the government's policy on education.
▸ approach, plan of action, strategy
▹ A document which officially explains someone's policy is a **manifesto**.

polish *VERB*
She was polishing the car.
▸ rub down, shine, wax
to polish something off *They polished off the rest of the work quickly.*
▸ complete, conclude, end, finish, round off

polish *NOUN*
He rubbed hard to get a good polish on the car.
▸ brightness, brilliance, glaze, gloss, lustre, sheen, shine, sparkle

polished *ADJECTIVE*
1 *She could see her face in the polished surface.*
▸ bright, glassy, gleaming, glossy, lustrous, shining, shiny
AN OPPOSITE IS dull
2 *They gave a polished performance.*
▸ elegant, faultless, perfect, stylish, well prepared
AN OPPOSITE IS rough

polite *ADJECTIVE*
He's always very polite to me.
▸ chivalrous, civil, civilized, considerate, correct, courteous, gallant, obliging, respectful, tactful, well mannered, well spoken
AN OPPOSITE IS rude

politics *NOUN*
THE MAIN POLITICAL PARTIES IN BRITAIN
Conservative or Tory, Labour, Liberal Democrat
WORDS TO DESCRIBE VARIOUS POLITICAL BELIEFS
anarchist, capitalist, communist, conservative, democratic, fascist, liberal, Marxist, moderate, monarchist, nationalist, radical, republican, socialist
WORDS TO DESCRIBE PEOPLE WITH EXTREME POLITICAL VIEWS
extremist, revolutionary
▹ A politician who wants to make important changes can be described as **radical**.
DIFFERENT POLITICAL SYSTEMS
anarchy, capitalism, communism, democracy, dictatorship, monarchy, republic

poll *NOUN*
The result of the poll has been declared.
▸ ballot, election, vote
▹ A vote on a particular question by all the people in a country is a **referendum**. An official survey to find out about the population is a **census**.

pollute *VERB*
The river has been polluted by chemicals.
▸ contaminate, infect, poison

pomp *NOUN*
The coronation was conducted with great pomp.
▸ ceremony, display, formality, grandeur, magnificence, pageantry, spectacle, splendour

pompous *ADJECTIVE*
He spoke in a rather pompous manner.
▸ arrogant, haughty, self-important, snobbish, (*informal*) stuck-up
AN OPPOSITE IS modest

pond *NOUN*
SEE **pool**

pool *NOUN*
There are fish in that pool.
▸ pond
▹ A larger area of water is a **lake**. A small shallow area of water is a **puddle**. A pool of water in the desert is an **oasis**. A pool specially made to swim in is a **swimming pool** or **swimming bath**.

poor *ADJECTIVE*
1 *You can't afford luxuries if you are poor.*
▸ badly off, deprived, hard up, needy, penniless, underprivileged
AN OPPOSITE IS rich
2 *Her work was very poor.*
▸ bad, (*informal*) hopeless, inadequate, incompetent, inefficient, inferior, mediocre, shoddy, unsatisfactory, useless, weak, worthless
AN OPPOSITE IS good or superior
3 *They pitied the poor animals standing in the rain.*
▸ forlorn, miserable, pathetic, sad, unfortunate, unhappy, unlucky, wretched
AN OPPOSITE IS lucky

poorly *ADJECTIVE*
He stayed at home because he felt poorly.
▸ ill, sick, unfit, unwell
AN OPPOSITE IS well

popular *ADJECTIVE*
Disney has made a lot of popular children's films.
▸ celebrated, favourite, loved, well-known, well-liked, well-loved
▹ Clothes which are popular are **fashionable** or **trendy**.
AN OPPOSITE IS unpopular

populated *ADJECTIVE*
They stayed in a village populated mainly by holidaymakers.
▸ inhabited, lived in, occupied

population *NOUN*
The whole population turned out to welcome the victorious football team.
▸ citizens, community, inhabitants, residents

porch *NOUN*
She waited in the porch until the rain eased off.
▸ doorway, entrance

pore *VERB*
to pore over *The engineers pored over the printout of the computer programme to find out what was wrong.*
▸ examine, inspect, look closely at, scrutinize, study

porous *ADJECTIVE*
Porous substances soak up liquid.
▸ absorbent, spongy

port *NOUN*
The ship entered the port.
▸ anchorage, dock, harbour, haven, seaport
▹ A harbour for yachts and pleasure boats is a **marina**.

portable *ADJECTIVE*
They took a portable TV on holiday.
▸ easy to carry, handy, light, lightweight
▹ A portable phone is a **mobile phone**. A portable computer is a **laptop**.

portion *NOUN*
He asked for a small portion of pie.
▸ bit, helping, part, piece, quantity, ration, serving, share, slice

portrait *NOUN*
There's a portrait of the queen on every stamp.
▸ image, likeness, picture, profile, representation

portray *VERB*
The film portrays what life was like 1000 years ago.
▸ depict, describe, illustrate, represent, show

pose *NOUN*
1 *He adopted a suitable pose so that she could take a photo.*
▸ attitude, position, posture
2 *Don't take his behaviour seriously — it's only a pose.*
▸ act, pretence

A B C D E F G H I J K L M N O **P** Q R S T U V W X Y Z

pose *VERB*
She posed in front of the camera.
▸ model, sit
to pose as someone *The burglar posed as a gas man.*
▸ impersonate, pretend to be

posh *ADJECTIVE*
1 (*informal*) *They stayed in a posh hotel.*
▸ elegant, fashionable, high-class, (*uncomplimentary*) snobbish
2 (*informal*) *He put on posh clothes for the visit.*
▸ decent, formal, smart

position *NOUN*
1 *Mark the position on the map.*
▸ location, place, point, site, spot, whereabouts
2 *He shifted his position to avoid getting cramp.*
▸ pose, posture
3 *Losing all her money put her in a difficult position.*
▸ circumstances, condition, situation, state
4 *A referee should adopt a neutral position.*
▸ attitude, opinion, outlook, view
5 *She has a responsible position in her firm.*
▸ appointment, function, job

positive *ADJECTIVE*
1 *He was positive that he was right.*
▸ certain, confident, convinced, definite, emphatic, sure
AN OPPOSITE IS uncertain
2 *The teacher gave her some positive advice.*
▸ beneficial, constructive, helpful, optimistic, useful, worthwhile
AN OPPOSITE IS negative

possess *VERB*
He doesn't possess a car.
▸ have, own

possessions *PLURAL NOUN*
Many of their possessions were taken in the burglary.
▸ belongings, goods, property

possibility *NOUN*
There's a possibility that it may rain later.
▸ chance, danger, likelihood, risk

possible *ADJECTIVE*
1 *Is it possible that life exists on other planets?*
▸ credible, likely, probable
2 *It wasn't possible to move the piano.*
▸ feasible, practicable, practical
AN OPPOSITE IS impossible

possibly *ADVERB*
Possibly they'll arrive next week.
▸ maybe, perhaps

post *NOUN*
1 *He put up some posts for a new fence.*
▹ A long round post is a **pole**. A post or pole which you use to support something is a **prop**. A post driven into the ground to make a foundation for a building, etc., is a **pile**. A post supporting a roof, etc., is a **column** or **pillar**. A post supporting a bridge is a **pier**. A post with a sharpened end to be driven into the ground is a **stake**. A short post in the road or on a traffic island is a **bollard**. The post which marks the finish of a race is the **winning post**.
2 *The post was delivered late.*
▸ cards, letters, mail, packets, parcels, postcards
3 *She has been appointed to a new post.*
▸ appointment, job, position, situation
▹ If you are looking for a post, you are looking for **employment** or **work**.

post *VERB*
1 *Did you post those letters?*
▸ despatch or dispatch, mail, send
2 *The captain posted the team for Saturday's game on the noticeboard.*
▸ advertise, display, pin up, put up, stick up

poster *NOUN*
They put up a poster to advertise sports day.
▸ advertisement, announcement, bill, notice, placard, sign

postpone *VERB*
As the weather was bad, they decided to postpone the game.
▸ defer, delay, put off
▹ To stop what you are doing for a time, intending to start again later, is to **adjourn** or **suspend** it.

posture *NOUN*
You can tell he's a soldier because of his upright posture.
▸ bearing

pot *NOUN*
VARIOUS POTS YOU MIGHT FIND IN A KITCHEN
basin, bowl, casserole, cauldron, crock, dish, jar, pan, saucepan, teapot, urn
SEE ALSO **container**

potent *ADJECTIVE*
1 *The chemicals had a potent smell.*
▸ overpowering, overwhelming, powerful, strong
▷ A potent drink is an alcoholic or intoxicating drink.
2 *It was a very potent argument.*
▸ effective, forceful, influential
AN OPPOSITE IS weak

potential *ADJECTIVE*
1 *He's a potential champion.*
▸ budding, future, likely, possible, probable, promising
2 *These floods are a potential disaster for the farmers.*
▸ looming, threatening

potion *NOUN*
She drank a magic potion.
▸ drug, medicine, mixture

pottery *NOUN*
▷ A formal word for the art of making pottery is ceramics.
KINDS OF POTTERY
bone china, china, earthenware, porcelain, stoneware, terracotta
▷ The kind of pottery we eat and drink from is crockery.
THINGS OFTEN MADE OF POTTERY INCLUDE
basin, bowl, cup, dish, flowerpot, jug, mug, plate, pot, saucer, teapot, tureen, vase

pouch *NOUN*
He kept his money in a leather pouch.
▸ bag, purse, sack

poultry *NOUN*
KINDS OF POULTRY
bantam, chicken, duck, fowl, goose, guinea fowl, hen, pullet, turkey
▷ A male chicken specially fattened for eating is a capon.

pounce *VERB*
to pounce on *The cat pounced on the mouse.*
▸ ambush, attack, jump on, leap on, seize, snatch, spring at, swoop down on

pound *VERB*
Huge waves pounded the stranded ship.
▸ batter, beat, hit, smash
▷ To pound something hard until it is powder is to crush, grind, or pulverize it. To pound something soft is to knead, mash, or pulp it.

pour *VERB*
1 *Water poured through the hole.*
▸ flow, gush, run, spill, spout, stream
2 *I poured the milk out of the bottle.*
▸ serve, tip

poverty *NOUN*
His poverty led him into crime.
▸ hardship, need, shortage, want
▷ If you owe people money, you are in debt. If you can't pay your debts, you are bankrupt.
AN OPPOSITE IS wealth

powder *NOUN*
The powder got up her nose and made her sneeze.
▸ dust, particles

powder *VERB*
After bathing the baby, she powdered his bottom.
▸ cover with powder, dust, sprinkle

powdered *ADJECTIVE*
She used powdered coffee to make her drink.
▸ crushed, granulated, ground, pulverized
▷ Powdered milk, etc., is dehydrated or dried milk.

powdery *ADJECTIVE*
The wind blew the powdery soil away.
▸ dry, dusty, fine, loose

power *NOUN*
1 *They were impressed by the power of the machine.*
▸ energy, force, might, strength
2 *He has the power to keep an audience interested.*
▸ ability, competence, skill, talent
3 *A policeman has the power to arrest someone.*
▸ authority, privilege, right
4 *The king had power over everyone.*
▸ command, control, dominance, domination, influence

powerful *ADJECTIVE*
1 *He is the most powerful person in the land.*
▸ dominant, forceful, important, influential
2 *The wrestler was a powerful man.*
▸ muscular, strong, tough, vigorous
3 *The enemy had a powerful army.*
▸ formidable, invincible, irresistible, mighty, potent
4 *He used some powerful arguments.*
▸ convincing, effective, impressive, persuasive
AN OPPOSITE IS powerless or weak

powerless *ADJECTIVE*
The town was powerless against the enemy's might.
▸ defenceless, feeble, helpless, ineffective, weak
AN OPPOSITE IS powerful

practicable *ADJECTIVE*
Is the plan practicable?
▸ achievable, attainable, feasible, possible, practical, realistic, workable
AN OPPOSITE IS impracticable

practical *ADJECTIVE*
1 *She is very practical — she does her own car repairs.*
▸ capable, competent, expert, proficient, skilled
2 *He has a set of practical tools to make the heavy jobs easier.*
▸ convenient, handy, usable, useful
3 *He's very practical in a crisis.*
▸ businesslike, efficient, helpful, realistic, sensible
AN OPPOSITE IS impractical
practical joke *The plastic spider in his lunch box was meant to be a practical joke.*
▸ hoax, prank, trick

practically *ADVERB*
Keep going — we're practically there!
▸ almost, as good as, just about, nearly, virtually

practice *NOUN*
1 *They need more practice if they want to win.*
▸ exercises, preparation, rehearsal, training
2 *What will the plan involve in practice?*
▸ action, operation, reality, use
3 *Smoking used to be a common practice.*
▸ custom, habit, routine, tradition

practise *VERB*
1 *The gymnastics coach keeps telling them to practise.*
▸ do exercises, rehearse, train
▹ To practise just before you take part in an event is to **warm up**.
2 *Practise what you preach.*
▸ apply, carry out, do, follow, perform, put into practice

praise *VERB*
1 *The critics praised their performance in the concert.*
▸ commend, compliment, congratulate, exalt, pay tribute to, rave about
▹ To show that you think something is very good you can **applaud**, **cheer**, or **clap**.
AN OPPOSITE IS criticize
2 *People go to church to praise God.*
▸ adore, glorify, honour, worship

praise *NOUN*
She received a lot of praise for her work.
▸ admiration, applause, approval, compliments, congratulations, thanks, tribute

prance *VERB*
They started prancing about in a silly way.
▸ caper, cavort, dance, frisk, frolic, gambol, jump, leap, play, romp, skip

prayer *NOUN*
▹ Your private prayers are your **devotions** or **meditation**. An **intercession** is a prayer to God on behalf of someone else. A **petition** or **supplication** is a prayer to God on your own behalf. An **invocation** is a prayer asking for God's help. A **doxology** is a prayer of praise to God. Prayer in which the congregation alternates with the priest or minister is a **litany**. A **collect** is a short prayer in the Church of England and the Roman Catholic Church. The prayer which Jesus taught his followers is the **Lord's Prayer**. The **Fatiha** is a section of the Koran used as a prayer by Muslims. The **Kaddish** is a daily prayer in praise of God in Jewish services.

preach *VERB*
1 *The vicar preached about the Good Samaritan.*
▸ give a sermon
2 *She's a fine one to preach about punctuality — she's always late!*
▸ give advice, lecture people, tell people what to do

preacher *NOUN*
▷ Someone who preaches about the Christian gospel is an **evangelist**.
▷ Someone who goes to another country to preach is a **missionary**.
SEE ALSO **clergyman**

precarious *ADJECTIVE*
1 *The climbers were in a precarious situation on a narrow ledge.*
▸ dangerous, insecure, perilous, risky
2 *Take care — that ladder looks precarious!*
▸ rickety, shaky, unsafe, unstable, unsteady, wobbly
AN OPPOSITE IS secure

precaution *NOUN*
She took the precaution of locking everything in the safe.
▸ defence, insurance, protection, safeguard, safety measure

precede *VERB*
1 *A police motorcyclist preceded the procession.*
▸ come before, go before, lead
2 *The minister preceded his talk with an announcement.*
▸ introduce, lead into, start
AN OPPOSITE IS follow

precious *ADJECTIVE*
1 *Your health is the most precious thing you have.*
▸ beneficial, important, invaluable, useful, valuable, worthwhile
AN OPPOSITE IS unimportant
2 *The crown glittered with precious gems.*
▸ costly, expensive, valuable
AN OPPOSITE IS worthless

precipice *NOUN*
The climber fell down a precipice.
▸ cliff, crag, drop

précis *NOUN*
He gave a précis of the talk they heard yesterday.
▸ outline, summary

precise *ADJECTIVE*
1 *They must have precise measurements before they lay the new carpet.*
▸ accurate, correct, exact, meticulous, right
AN OPPOSITE IS inaccurate
2 *He gave us precise instructions about how to get to his house.*
▸ careful, clear, definite, detailed, specific
AN OPPOSITE IS vague

predator *NOUN*
The heron is one of the frog's predators.
▸ hunter

predatory *ADJECTIVE*
Predatory magpies stole eggs from a blackbird's nest.
▸ greedy, hunting, marauding, pillaging, plundering, preying

predict *VERB*
You can't predict what may happen in the future.
▸ forecast, foresee, foretell, prophesy

predictable *ADJECTIVE*
It was predictable that it would rain.
▸ expected, foreseeable, likely, probable
AN OPPOSITE IS unpredictable

predominate *VERB*
Girls predominate in the rounders team.
▸ be in the majority, dominate

preface *NOUN*
If you read the preface you'll find out what the book is about.
▸ introduction, prologue

prefer *VERB*
Do you prefer tea or coffee?
▸ choose, fancy, favour, incline towards, like, plump for, want

preferable *ADJECTIVE*
preferable to *She finds country life preferable to living in the city.*
▸ better than, more attractive than, more desirable than, nicer than, preferred to

preference *NOUN*
1 *He has a preference for sweet things.*
▸ desire, fancy, liking, wish
2 *There's milk or cream — what's your preference?*
▸ choice, inclination, option, pick

prefix *NOUN*
AN OPPOSITE IS suffix

pregnant *ADJECTIVE*
She went regularly to the clinic for a check-up when she was pregnant.
▸ carrying a child, (*informal*) expecting
▹ A pregnant woman is an **expectant** mother.

prehistoric *ADJECTIVE*
SOME PREHISTORIC REMAINS YOU MIGHT VISIT
barrow or tumulus, cromlech or stone circle, dolmen, hill fort, menhir or standing stone
▹ The prehistoric period when the best tools and weapons were made of stone was the **Stone Age**. Formal names for the Old, Middle, and New Stone Ages are **Palaeolithic**, **Mesolithic**, and **Neolithic** periods. The period when the best tools and weapons were made of bronze was the **Bronze Age**. The period when the best tools and weapons were made of iron was the **Iron Age**. A person who studies prehistory by excavating and analysing remains is an **archaeologist**. A person who studies fossils and ancient forms of life is a **palaeontologist**.

prejudice *NOUN*
1 *The referee was accused of showing prejudice.*
▸ bias, favouritism, unfairness
AN OPPOSITE IS impartiality
2 *They campaigned against racial prejudice.*
▸ discrimination, intolerance, narrow-mindedness
▹ Prejudice against other races is **racism**. Prejudice against other nations is **xenophobia**. Prejudice against the other sex is **sexism**. Male prejudice against women is sometimes called **male chauvinism**. Prejudice against other people because of your religion, etc., is **bigotry**.
AN OPPOSITE IS tolerance

prejudiced *ADJECTIVE*
The players thought the referee was prejudiced.
▸ biased, intolerant, narrow-minded, one-sided, unfair
▹ To be prejudiced against other races is to be **racist**. To be prejudiced against other nations is to be **xenophobic**. To be prejudiced against the other sex is to be **sexist**. To be prejudiced against other people because of your religion, etc., is to be **bigoted**.
AN OPPOSITE IS impartial or tolerant

preliminary *ADJECTIVE*
1 *Preliminary results with the new medicine are encouraging.*
▸ early, experimental, first, initial, provisional, trial
2 *She made some preliminary remarks before starting the main part of her talk.*
▸ introductory, opening, preparatory
▹ The preliminary rounds of a competition are the **qualifying** rounds.

prelude *NOUN*
The first match was an exciting prelude to the season.
▸ beginning, introduction, opening, preparation, start
▹ The introduction to an opera, etc., is also called an **overture**. The introduction to a book is a **preface** or **prologue**.
AN OPPOSITE IS conclusion or epilogue

premises *PLURAL NOUN*
Keep out — these are private premises.
▸ buildings, property

preoccupied *ADJECTIVE*
preoccupied in something *She didn't see me because she was preoccupied in her work.*
▸ absorbed in, concentrating on, engrossed in, intent on, interested in, involved in, obsessed with

preparation *NOUN*
The concert involved a lot of preparation.
▸ getting ready, making arrangements, organization, rehearsal

prepare *VERB*
1 *There are things to prepare if you're going to have visitors.*
▸ arrange, get ready, make arrangements for, organize, plan, set up
2 *A teacher prepares pupils for exams.*
▸ educate, instruct, teach
▹ To prepare for a play is to **rehearse**. To prepare people to take part in a sport is to **coach** them. To prepare yourself to take part in a sport is to **train**. To prepare yourself for an exam is to **revise**.
to be prepared *He wanted a volunteer who was prepared to stay behind and wash up.*
▸ be able, be ready, be willing

prescribe *NOUN*
1 *The doctor prescribed some medicine.*
▸ advise, recommend, suggest
2 *The law prescribes heavy penalties for this offence.*
▸ assign, fix, lay down, specify

presence *NOUN*
Your presence is required.
▸ attendance

present *ADJECTIVE*
1 *Is everyone present?*
▸ at hand, here, in attendance
2 *Who are the present champions?*
▸ current, existing

present *NOUN*
Did you get any presents on your birthday?
▸ gift
▹ Money that you give to a waiter, etc., is a **gratuity** or **tip**. Money that you give to a charity, etc., is a **contribution** or **donation**.

present *VERB*
1 *The mayor presents the prizes on sports day.*
▸ award, hand over
2 *They presented a play about the history of the town.*
▸ act, perform, put on
3 *He presented the new designs for approval.*
▸ display, exhibit, show
4 *They were presented to the Prime Minister.*
▸ introduce, make known

preserve *VERB*
1 *It's more difficult to preserve food in hot weather.*
▸ keep, save, store
WORDS TO DESCRIBE PRESERVED FOODS
bottled, canned, chilled, cured, dehydrated, desiccated, dried, freeze-dried, frozen, pickled, refrigerated, salted, smoked, tinned
2 *It's important to preserve the countryside.*
▸ conserve, defend, guard, look after, maintain, protect, safeguard
AN OPPOSITE IS destroy

preside *VERB*
The chairman was unable to preside at the meeting.
▸ be in charge, take charge

president *NOUN*
FOR PEOPLE IN CHARGE OF VARIOUS THINGS SEE **chief** *NOUN*

press *VERB*
1 *Those things will fit in the case if you press them down.*
▸ compress, cram, crush, force, push, shove, squash, squeeze
2 *She pressed her jeans.*
▸ flatten, iron, smooth
3 *They pressed him to stay a bit longer.*
▸ beg, entreat, implore, persuade, put pressure on, urge

press *NOUN*
1 *She read about the accident in the press.*
▸ magazines, newspapers
2 *The press came to the opening of the new sports centre.*
▸ journalists, photographers, reporters

pressure *NOUN*
1 *The pressure of the huge crowd broke down the barrier.*
▸ force, heaviness, pushing, shoving, squeezing, weight
2 *They kept up the pressure but couldn't score a winning goal.*
▸ attack
3 *If you were prime minister, could you stand the pressure?*
▸ (*informal*) hassle, strain, stress, tension

pressurize *VERB*
They pressurized him to join the gang.
▸ force, persuade, put pressure on, urge

prestige *NOUN*
Their prestige suffered when they lost.
▸ credit, fame, glory, good name, honour, renown, reputation

presume *VERB*
1 *I presume you'd like something to eat.*
▸ assume, believe, guess, imagine, suppose, take it for granted, think
2 *He wouldn't presume to tell her what to do!*
▸ be bold enough, be presumptuous enough, dare, take the liberty (of), venture

A B C D E F G H I J K L M N O **P** Q R S T U V W X Y Z

presumptuous *ADJECTIVE*
It was presumptuous of him to take charge.
▸ arrogant, bold, cheeky, forward, impertinent, impudent, self-important

pretence *NOUN*
She didn't fool them — they saw through her pretence.
▸ act, acting, deceit, deception, disguise, insincerity, lying, make-believe, pose, posing, pretending, sham, show, trickery

pretend *VERB*
1 *Don't believe her — she's pretending.*
▸ act, bluff, deceive someone, fool, hoax, (*informal*) kid, lie, mislead someone, play a part, pose, put on an act
▹ To pretend that something happens is to **fake**, **imagine**, or **simulate** it.
2 *He pretended that he could play the piano.*
▸ allege, claim, declare, make out
to pretend to be someone or **something**
She was pretending to be a policewoman.
▸ disguise yourself as, imitate, impersonate, play the part of, pose as, profess to be, put on an act as

pretty *ADJECTIVE*
1 *They saw some pretty scenery in the hills.*
▸ attractive, beautiful, lovely, nice, picturesque, pleasing
2 *The girl was wearing a pretty little dress.*
▸ charming, (*informal*) cute, dainty
AN OPPOSITE IS ugly

pretty *ADVERB*
(*informal*) *That's pretty good!*
▸ fairly, moderately, quite, rather, somewhat
AN OPPOSITE IS very

prevail *VERB*
1 *In Britain, south-westerly winds prevail.*
▸ dominate, predominate
2 *I think the more experienced team will prevail.*
▸ be victorious, come out on top, succeed, triumph, win

prevailing, **prevalent** *ADJECTIVES*
What's the prevailing colour in this year's fashions?
▸ accepted, common, current, dominant, fashionable, general, influential, normal, ordinary, orthodox, popular, predominant, principal, usual, widespread
AN OPPOSITE IS unusual

prevent *VERB*
1 *The driver could do nothing to prevent the accident.*
▸ avert, avoid
2 *The police prevented an attempted bank raid.*
▸ block, foil, frustrate, intercept
3 *There's not much you can do to prevent colds.*
▸ stave off, take precautions against, ward off
4 *The scarecrow prevents the birds from eating the seed.*
▸ deter, discourage, frighten off, stop

previous *ADJECTIVE*
1 *She had enjoyed her previous visits to the museum.*
▸ earlier, former
2 *He had phoned the previous day.*
▸ preceding
AN OPPOSITE IS subsequent

prey *NOUN*
The lion killed its prey.
▸ quarry, victim

prey *VERB*
to prey on *Owls prey on small animals.*
▸ eat, feed on, hunt, kill

price *NOUN*
£30 is a reasonable price for a second-hand bike.
▸ amount, cost, expense, figure, payment, sum
▹ The price you pay for a journey on public transport is a **fare**. The price you pay to send a letter is the **postage**. The price you pay to use a private road, bridge, or tunnel is a **toll**. The prices you have to pay at a hotel, etc., are their **charges**, **rates**, or **terms**.

priceless *ADJECTIVE*
1 *The museum contained many priceless antiques.*
▸ costly, dear, expensive, precious, rare, valuable
2 (*informal*) *The joke she told was priceless.*
▸ amusing, comic, funny, hilarious, witty

prick *VERB*
He pricked the balloon with a pin.
▸ jab, perforate, pierce, puncture, stab

prickle *NOUN*
She fell into a bush full of prickles.
▸ barb, needle, spike, spine, thorn

prickly *ADJECTIVE*
The bush was a bit prickly.
▸ bristly, scratchy, sharp, spiky, spiny, thorny

pride *NOUN*
1 *She looked with pride at what she had achieved.*
▸ dignity, satisfaction, self-respect
2 (*uncomplimentary*) *Pride goes before a fall.*
▸ arrogance, conceit, pomposity, self-importance, self-righteousness, snobbery, vanity
AN OPPOSITE IS humility

priest *NOUN*
▹ A priest of an ancient Celtic religion in Britain and France was a **Druid**. A Buddhist priest is a **lama**.
SEE ALSO **clergyman**

priggish *ADJECTIVE*
They hated the priggish way he looked down on the rest of them.
▸ pious, pompous, prim, self-righteous, snobbish, (*informal*) stuck-up, superior
AN OPPOSITE IS humble

prim *ADJECTIVE*
She's too prim to enjoy rude jokes!
▸ narrow-minded, priggish, proper, puritanical
AN OPPOSITE IS broad-minded

primarily *ADVERB*
He likes all kinds of music but primarily he's interested in jazz.
▸ above all, basically, chiefly, especially, first of all, fundamentally, mainly, mostly, predominantly, principally

primary *ADJECTIVE*
Their primary aim was to win the game.
▸ basic, chief, dominant, first, foremost, fundamental, greatest, leading, main, major, most important, outstanding, prime, principal, supreme, top

prime *ADJECTIVE*
1 *Her prime concern was to protect her children.*
SEE **primary**
2 *The local shop only sells prime beef.*
▸ best, excellent, first-class, select, top

primitive *ADJECTIVE*
1 *Primitive humans were hunters rather than farmers.*
▸ ancient, early, prehistoric, primeval
AN OPPOSITE IS civilized
2 *These days steam engines seem very primitive.*
▸ backward, basic, crude, elementary, obsolete, simple, undeveloped
AN OPPOSITE IS advanced

principal *ADJECTIVE*
Their principal aim is to bring peace.
▸ basic, chief, dominant, first, foremost, fundamental, greatest, leading, main, major, most important, outstanding, primary, prime, supreme, top

principle *NOUN*
She taught him the principles of geometry.
▸ belief, rule, theory
principles *He seemed to have no principles when it came to making money.*
▸ morals, standards

print *VERB*
1,000 copies of the book were printed.
▸ issue, publish

print *NOUN*
1 *She found the tiny print difficult to read.*
▸ characters, lettering, letters, printing, type
2 *I followed the prints of his feet in the snow.*
▸ impression, mark
3 *It's a print, not an original painting.*
▸ copy, duplicate, photocopy, reproduction
▹ Something printed from information stored in a computer is a **printout** or **hard copy**.

priority *NOUN*
Traffic on the main road has priority.
▸ precedence, right of way

prise *VERB*
She tried to prise the lid off the box.
▸ force, lever, wrench

prison *NOUN*
He was sentenced to six months in prison.
▸ confinement, imprisonment
PLACES WHERE VARIOUS PEOPLE MAY BE DETAINED
(*old use*) Borstal, compound, concentration camp, detention centre, (*old use*) dungeon, gaol or jail, guardhouse, (*informal*) lock-up, open prison, (*American*) penitentiary, police cell, (*American*) reformatory
▹ People detained in their own home are **under house arrest**. People detained before their trial are **in custody** or **on remand**. Before the trial they may be detained in a **remand centre**.

a b c d e f g h i j k l m n o **p** q r s t u v w x y z

prisoner *NOUN*
The prisoner tried to escape from jail.
▸ captive, convict
▹ A person who is held prisoner until some demand is met is a **hostage**.

private *ADJECTIVE*
1 *Keep out — this is private property.*
▸ privately owned
2 *What I write in my diary is private.*
▸ confidential, intimate, personal, secret
▹ Secret official documents are **classified** or **restricted** documents.
3 *Can we go somewhere a little more private?*
▸ concealed, hidden, isolated, little known, quiet, secluded
AN OPPOSITE IS public

privilege *NOUN*
Club members enjoy special privileges.
▸ advantage, benefit, concession, right

privileged *ADJECTIVE*
Rich people are in a privileged position compared with poor people.
▸ advantageous, favoured, powerful, special, superior

prize *NOUN*
He held on to his lead and won the first prize.
▸ award, reward, trophy
▹ Money that you win as a prize or in gambling is your **winnings**. Prize money that keeps increasing until someone wins it is a **jackpot**.

prize *VERB*
The necklace was one that her mother had prized for years.
▸ appreciate, cherish, esteem, hold dear, like, rate, regard, revere, treasure, value
AN OPPOSITE IS dislike

probable *ADJECTIVE*
If you've got toothache, it's probable that you need a filling.
▸ expected, feasible, likely, predictable, presumed
AN OPPOSITE IS improbable

probe *NOUN*
They were conducting a probe into corruption within the company.
▸ examination, inquiry, investigation, study

probe *VERB*
1 *The doctor probed the wound.*
▸ poke, prod
2 *New equipment can probe the depths of the sea.*
▸ explore, penetrate, see into
3 *The programme probed corruption within the police force.*
▸ examine, inquire into, investigate, look into, scrutinize, study

problem *NOUN*
1 *Can you help me solve this problem?*
▸ dilemma, mystery, poser, puzzle, question
▹ A puzzling question which people ask as a joke is a **conundrum** or **riddle**.
2 *Not having any money is a big problem.*
▸ difficulty, (*informal*) headache, snag, trouble, worry

procedure *NOUN*
She explained the procedure for making pastry.
▸ course of action, method, plan of action, process, system, technique, way
▹ A procedure which you follow regularly is a **routine**. A procedure which you are planning is a **scheme** or **strategy**.

proceed *VERB*
Settle down, then we can proceed.
▸ carry on, continue, go ahead, go on, make progress, move forward, progress

proceedings *PLURAL NOUN*
1 *The proceedings were interrupted by a fire alarm.*
▸ events, (*informal*) goings-on, happenings, matters, things
2 *He threatened to start proceedings if she didn't pay her debts.*
▸ a lawsuit, legal action

proceeds *PLURAL NOUN*
They added up the proceeds from the sale.
▸ earnings, income, profit, revenue, takings

process *NOUN*
They have developed a new process for making steel rustproof.
▸ method, operation, procedure, system, technique

process *VERB*
They process crude oil before we use it as fuel.
▸ alter, change, convert, deal with, prepare, refine, transform, treat

procession *NOUN*
The procession made its way slowly down the hill.
▸ column, line, parade
▹ A procession of people on horses is a **cavalcade**. A procession of motor vehicles is a **motorcade**. A procession of people in costume is a **pageant**. A funeral procession is a **cortège**.

proclaim *VERB*
The judges proclaimed that the winner was disqualified.
▸ announce, declare, make known, pronounce

prod *VERB*
He prodded me in the back with a ruler.
▸ dig, jab, nudge, poke, push

produce *VERB*
1 *Some lorries produce a lot of fumes.*
▸ cause, create, generate, give rise to
2 *The tree produced a good crop of apples this year.*
▸ grow, yield
3 *The factory produces cars and vans.*
▸ construct, make, manufacture
4 *The referee's decision produced angry shouts from the crowd.*
▸ arouse, provoke, result in, stimulate
5 *As a journalist, she has to produce interesting articles every day.*
▸ compose, invent, think up
6 *She can produce evidence to prove she was right.*
▸ bring out, present, put forward, reveal, supply

produce *NOUN*
The shop sells home-grown produce.
▸ fruit and vegetables, greengrocery
▹ The produce of a farm is its **crops** or **harvest**.

product *NOUN*
1 *The company launched a new range of beauty products.*
▸ article, item, substance
2 *The problems with the car are the product of years of neglect.*
▸ consequence, outcome, result, upshot

production *NOUN*
1 *Production at the factory has increased this year.*
▸ output
2 *They went to see a new production at the Arts Theatre.*
▸ performance, play, show

productive *ADJECTIVE*
1 *The soil is rich and productive.*
▸ fertile, fruitful
2 *It wasn't a very productive meeting.*
▸ beneficial, constructive, effective, profitable, rewarding, useful, valuable, worthwhile
AN OPPOSITE IS unproductive

profession *NOUN*
Nursing is a worthwhile profession.
▸ business, career, employment, job, occupation, work

professional *ADJECTIVE*
1 *She sought the advice of professional builders.*
▸ competent, efficient, expert, qualified, responsible, skilled, trained
2 *It's a very professional piece of work.*
▸ competent, efficient, proficient, skilful
AN OPPOSITE IS incompetent
3 *His ambition is to be a professional footballer.*
▸ paid
AN OPPOSITE IS amateur

proficient *ADJECTIVE*
She's a very proficient typist.
▸ accomplished, capable, efficient, experienced, expert, skilful, skilled
AN OPPOSITE IS incompetent

profile *NOUN*
1 *I didn't see his face properly — I just saw his profile.*
▸ outline, side view, silhouette
2 *The local paper published a profile of each of the candidates.*
▸ account, biography, sketch

profit *NOUN*
1 *They sold the business and bought a yacht with the profit.*
▸ gain, surplus
▹ The extra money you get on your savings is **interest**.
2 *There's no profit in shouting at the referee from the bench.*
▸ advantage, benefit

A B C D E F G H I J K L M N O P Q R S T U V W X Y Z

profit *VERB*
1 *Did you profit from the sale?*
▸ gain, make money
2 *It won't profit anyone to get angry.*
▸ benefit, help

profitable *ADJECTIVE*
1 *Selling things at a car-boot sale can be profitable.*
▸ advantageous, beneficial, productive, rewarding, worthwhile
2 *The business has been very profitable in recent years.*
▸ commercial, moneymaking, paying, profit-making
AN OPPOSITE IS unprofitable

profound *ADJECTIVE*
1 *They expressed their profound sympathy.*
▸ deep, sincere
AN OPPOSITE IS insincere
2 *The book is full of original and profound insights.*
▸ intellectual, knowledgeable, learned, philosophical, serious, thoughtful
AN OPPOSITE IS superficial

profuse *ADJECTIVE*
He offered his profuse apologies for the mistake.
▸ abundant, ample, extravagant, lavish, plentiful
AN OPPOSITE IS meagre

programme *NOUN*
1 *We worked out a programme for sports day.*
▸ plan, schedule, timetable
▹ A list of things to be done at a meeting is an agenda.
2 *There was a really good programme on TV last night.*
▸ broadcast, performance, production, transmission

progress *NOUN*
1 *I traced their progress on the map.*
▸ advance, journey, movements, route, travels, way
2 *Progress in computer technology has been amazingly rapid.*
▸ development, evolution, growth, improvement
▹ An important piece of progress is a breakthrough.

progress *VERB*
1 *Work on the new building was progressing rapidly.*
▸ advance, continue, forge ahead, go on, make headway, make progress, move forward, proceed
2 *Technology is bound to progress even further.*
▸ develop, evolve, improve
AN OPPOSITE IS retreat

progression *NOUN*
He followed the progression of events with interest.
▸ advance, development, evolution, sequence, series, succession

progressive *ADJECTIVE*
1 *There's been a progressive improvement in their performance this season.*
▸ accelerating, continuous, escalating, growing, increasing, ongoing, steady
AN OPPOSITE IS erratic
2 *The new manager has progressive ideas.*
▸ advanced, forward-looking, go-ahead, up-to-date
AN OPPOSITE IS conservative

prohibit *VERB*
They decided to prohibit smoking on the buses.
▸ ban, forbid, make illegal, outlaw, rule out, stop, veto
AN OPPOSITE IS allow

project *NOUN*
1 *We did a history project on the Victorians.*
▸ activity, assignment, piece of research, task
2 *The council announced a project to build a bypass.*
▸ plan, proposal, scheme

project *VERB*
1 *A narrow ledge projects from the cliff.*
▸ bulge, extend, jut out, overhang, protrude, stand out, stick out
2 *The lighthouse projects a beam of light.*
▸ cast, shine, throw out

prolong *VERB*
They prolonged their visit by a few days.
▸ draw out, extend, increase, lengthen, make longer, stretch out
AN OPPOSITE IS shorten

prominent *ADJECTIVE*
1 *He has very prominent cheekbones.*
▸ bulging, jutting out, projecting, protruding, sticking out
2 *The windmill on the hill is a prominent landmark.*
▸ conspicuous, noticeable, obvious, recognizable
AN OPPOSITE IS inconspicuous
3 *She's a prominent member of the society.*
▸ celebrated, distinguished, eminent, famous, important, leading, major, notable, outstanding, renowned, well-known
AN OPPOSITE IS unknown

promise *NOUN*
1 *We had promises of help from many people.*
▸ assurance, guarantee, pledge, vow, word, word of honour
2 *That young actor shows promise.*
▸ potential, talent

promise *VERB*
1 *She promised to come.*
▸ agree, consent, undertake
2 *He promised that he would pay me back.*
▸ assure someone, give your word, guarantee, swear, take an oath, vow

promising *ADJECTIVE*
1 *The new goalkeeper made a promising first appearance on Saturday.*
▸ encouraging, hopeful
2 *He's a promising young actor.*
▸ budding, likely, talented, (*informal*) up-and-coming

promontory *NOUN*
They stood on the promontory, looking out to the sea.
▸ cape, headland, peninsula

promote *VERB*
1 *He was promoted to captain.*
▸ elevate, exalt, move up, raise, upgrade
2 *They gave away free samples to promote the new shampoo.*
▸ advertise, make known, market, (*informal*) plug, publicize, sell
3 *The conference aimed to promote trade between the two countries.*
▸ back, encourage, help, support

promoter *NOUN*
One of the festival's promoters withdrew their support.
▸ backer, sponsor

prompt *ADJECTIVE*
She received a prompt reply to her letter.
▸ immediate, instant, punctual, quick, rapid, swift, unhesitating
AN OPPOSITE IS delayed

prompt *VERB*
1 *The demonstration prompted the police to increase security in the town.*
▸ encourage, motivate, persuade, provoke, stimulate
2 *The speaker was hesitant and the chairman had to prompt her.*
▸ jog your memory, remind

prone *ADJECTIVE*
1 *The victim was lying prone on the floor.*
▸ face down, on the front
▹ To lie face upwards is to be supine.
2 *She's prone to exaggerate.*
▸ inclined, liable, likely

prong *NOUN*
Pierce the sausage with the prongs of a fork.
▸ point, spike

pronounce *VERB*
1 *Try to pronounce the words clearly.*
▸ articulate, say, sound, speak, utter
2 *The doctor pronounced her fully recovered.*
▸ announce, declare, judge, proclaim

pronounced *ADJECTIVE*
She walked with a pronounced limp.
▸ clear, conspicuous, definite, distinct, evident, marked, noticeable, obvious, perceptible, prominent, striking, unmistakable
AN OPPOSITE IS imperceptible

pronunciation *NOUN*
The announcer's pronunciation was not very clear.
▸ accent, articulation, intonation

proof *NOUN*
The police say they have proof of her guilt.
▸ confirmation, evidence

A B C D E F G H I J K L M N O **P** Q R S T U V W X Y Z

prop *NOUN*
The construction was supported by 300 steel props.
▸ strut, support
▹ A stick to prop yourself on when you hurt a leg is a **crutch**. Part of a building which props up a wall is a **buttress**.

prop *VERB*
He propped his bike against the kerb.
▸ lean, rest, stand
to prop something up *The roof will have to be propped up while the repairs are carried out.*
▸ hold up, reinforce, support

propaganda *NOUN*
The play is nothing but political propaganda.
▸ advertising, indoctrination, publicity

propel *VERB*
The boat is propelled by using a long paddle.
▸ drive forward, move forward, push forward

propeller *NOUN*
▹ The large horizontal propeller of a helicopter is a **rotor**. The underwater propeller of a ship is a **screw**.

proper *ADJECTIVE*
1 *They had not followed the proper procedures.*
▸ acceptable, correct, normal, right, suitable, usual
AN OPPOSITE IS wrong or incorrect
2 *He should get the proper punishment for the crime.*
▸ appropriate, deserved, fair, fitting, just, lawful, legal, suitable, valid
AN OPPOSITE IS inappropriate
3 *In those days, it wasn't thought proper for a woman to go on the stage.*
▸ decent, respectable, tasteful
AN OPPOSITE IS rude
4 (*informal*) *He's in a proper mess!*
▸ absolute, complete, great, perfect, thorough, total, utter

property *NOUN*
1 *He owns a great deal of property.*
▸ assets, belongings, goods, possessions
▹ Property in the form of money is a **fortune** or **riches** or **wealth**.
2 *Keep off! Private property!*
▸ buildings, estate, land, premises
3 *An unusual property of this gas is its smell.*
▸ characteristic, feature, peculiarity, quality

prophecy *NOUN*
Her prophecy came true.
▸ forecast, prediction

prophesy *VERB*
She prophesied that it would rain.
▸ forecast, foresee, foretell, predict

prophet, prophetess *NOUNS*
PEOPLE WHO ARE SUPPOSED TO BE ABLE TO FORETELL THE FUTURE
clairvoyant, forecaster, fortune-teller, mystic, oracle, seer, soothsayer

proportion *NOUN*
1 *A large proportion of the audience were delighted.*
▸ fraction, part, section, share
2 *What is the proportion of girls to boys in your class?*
▸ balance, ratio
proportions *The sports centre is a building of large proportions.*
▸ dimensions, measurements, size

proposal *NOUN*
The council discussed a proposal to build a supermarket.
▸ plan, project, recommendation, scheme, suggestion

propose *VERB*
1 *He proposed a change in the rules.*
▸ ask for, recommend, suggest
2 *He proposes to attend next month's meeting.*
▸ aim, intend, mean, plan
3 *She was proposed as a candidate in the local election.*
▸ nominate, put forward

proprietor *NOUN*
He is the proprietor of a local restaurant.
▸ (*informal*) boss, manager, owner

prosecute *VERB*
They prosecuted him for dangerous driving.
▸ accuse (of), bring to trial, charge (with), start legal proceedings against
▹ To take someone to court to try to get money from them is to **sue** them.

prospect *NOUN*
1 *There's a prospect of a change in the weather.*
▸ chance, expectation, hope, likelihood, possibility, probability, promise
2 *The hotel has a lovely prospect across the valley.*
▸ outlook, panorama, view

prospect *VERB*
The petrol company is prospecting for oil.
▸ explore, search, survey

prosper *VERB*
He expects his business to prosper this year.
▸ become prosperous, be successful, boom, do well, expand, flourish, grow, progress, succeed, thrive
AN OPPOSITE IS fail

prosperity *NOUN*
Tourism has brought prosperity to the region.
▸ affluence, (*informal*) boom, growth, plenty, success, wealth

prosperous *ADJECTIVE*
The north of the country is more prosperous than the south.
▸ affluent, rich, successful, wealthy, well off
AN OPPOSITE IS poor

protect *VERB*
1 *A sentry was posted outside to protect the palace.*
▸ defend, guard, keep safe, safeguard, secure
2 *I put up an umbrella to protect myself from the sun.*
▸ insulate, preserve, screen, shade, shield

protection *NOUN*
Use a sun cream that will give you adequate protection against harmful ultra-violet rays.
▸ cover, defence, insulation, shelter
PEOPLE WHO PROTECT YOU
defender, guard, protector
▹ A guard who protects a person's life is their bodyguard. An informal word for a bodyguard is minder. Someone who protects someone's interests is their benefactor or patron.

protest *NOUN*
1 *The scheme was dropped following protests from local residents.*
▸ complaint, objection
▹ A general protest is an outcry.
2 *There was a big protest in the square.*
▸ (*informal*) demo, demonstration, march, rally

protest *VERB*
1 *Local residents protested about the introduction of the scheme.*
▸ argue, complain, express disapproval, grouse, grumble, make a protest, object (to)
2 *A big crowd protested in the square.*
▸ demonstrate, (*informal*) hold a demo, march

protrude *VERB*
His stomach protrudes above his waistband.
▸ bulge, jut out, poke out, project, stand out, stick out, swell

proud *ADJECTIVE*
1 *Her father's really proud of her.*
▸ delighted (with), pleased (with)
AN OPPOSITE IS disgusted (with)
2 (*uncomplimentary*) *He's too proud to mix with the likes of us!*
▸ arrogant, (*informal*) cocky, conceited, grand, haughty, self-important, self-righteous, snobbish, (*informal*) stuck-up, superior, vain
AN OPPOSITE IS humble

prove *VERB*
The evidence will prove that he is innocent.
▸ confirm, demonstrate, establish, verify
AN OPPOSITE IS disprove

proverb *NOUN*
SEE **saying**

proverbial *ADJECTIVE*
'Many hands make light work' is a proverbial saying.
▸ conventional, famous, traditional, well-known

provide *VERB*
1 *We'll provide the food if you bring something to drink.*
▸ arrange for, contribute, donate, lay on
▹ To provide food and drink for people is to cater for them.
2 *The council provided money for new equipment.*
▸ allot, allow, (*informal*) fork out, give, grant
▹ To provide money which you promise to give back later is to lend or loan it.

A B C D E F G H I J K L M N O P Q R S T U V W X Y Z

3 *They provided us with the essential equipment.*
► equip, supply
to provide for 1 *He had provided for an emergency of this sort.*
► get ready for, prepare for, take precautions against
2 *Parents have to provide for their children.*
► care for, look after, support, take care of

provision *NOUN*
Many parents would welcome the provision of childcare facilities at work.
► providing, setting up, supply, supplying
provisions *We had enough provisions for two weeks.*
► food, groceries, rations, stores, supplies

provisional *ADJECTIVE*
The list of players is only provisional.
► preliminary, temporary
AN OPPOSITE IS permanent

provocation *NOUN*
The dog won't attack without some provocation.
► (*informal*) aggravation, challenge, inducement, taunting, teasing

provoke *VERB*
1 *I didn't do anything to provoke him.*
► (*informal*) aggravate, anger, annoy, exasperate, incense, infuriate, irritate, offend, taunt, tease, torment, vex, worry
AN OPPOSITE IS pacify
2 *His jokes provoked a lot of laughter.*
► arouse, bring about, cause, generate, give rise to, induce, produce, prompt, spark off, stimulate, stir up, whip up

prowl *VERB*
Guard dogs prowled about the grounds of the palace.
► creep, roam, slink, sneak, steal

prudent *ADJECTIVE*
It would be prudent to start saving some money.
► careful, cautious, sensible, shrewd, thoughtful, wise
AN OPPOSITE IS reckless or unwise

prune *VERB*
Mum prunes her roses every spring.
► cut back, trim

pry *VERB*
Don't pry — it's none of your business!
► be curious, be inquisitive, (*informal*) be nosy, interfere, (*informal*) nose about or around, snoop
to pry into something *Don't pry into my affairs!*
► inquire into, interfere in, investigate, meddle in, (*informal*) poke your nose into, spy on

pseudonym *NOUN*
George Orwell isn't his real name — it's a pseudonym.
► alias, assumed name, false name

psychic *ADJECTIVE*
She was said to have psychic powers.
► supernatural, telepathic

psychological *ADJECTIVE*
The doctor said the patient's problem was psychological.
► emotional, mental

pub *NOUN*
They went to the pub for a drink.
► (*old use*) inn, (*informal*) local, public house, (*old use*) tavern
▷ Other places where alcoholic drinks are served are a **bar** or **wine bar**.

puberty *NOUN*
You reach puberty in your teens.
► adolescence, sexual maturity

public *ADJECTIVE*
1 *There have been proposals to ban smoking in all public places.*
► accessible, communal, open, shared
AN OPPOSITE IS private
2 *It's public knowledge that he went to prison.*
► common, familiar, general, popular, unconcealed, universal, well-known
AN OPPOSITE IS secret

public *NOUN*
the public *The public has a right to know how government works.*
► citizens, the community, everyone, the nation, people in general, the population, society, the voters
in public *Should people be allowed to smoke in public?*
► anywhere, in the open, openly, publicly

publication *NOUN*
She's celebrating the publication of her first novel.
▸ issuing, printing, production
▹ Various publications are **books** and **magazines**.

publicity *NOUN*
1 *Did you see the publicity for the play?*
▸ advertisements, advertising, promotion
2 *Famous people don't always enjoy publicity.*
▸ being in the limelight, fame, notoriety

publicize *VERB*
They asked the local radio station to publicize the concert.
▸ advertise, announce, make known, market, (*informal*) plug, promote

publish *VERB*
1 *The magazine is published every week.*
▸ bring out, circulate, issue, print, produce, release
2 *When will they publish the results?*
▸ announce, communicate, declare, disclose, make known, make public, publicize, report, reveal
▹ To publish information which is supposed to be secret is to **leak** it. To publish information on radio or TV is to **broadcast** it.

pudding *NOUN*
Do you want any pudding?
▸ dessert, sweet
FOR VARIOUS FOODS SEE **food**

puff *NOUN*
1 *A puff of wind caught his hat.*
▸ breath, flurry, gust
2 *A puff of smoke rose from the chimney.*
▸ cloud, whiff

puff *VERB*
1 *The engine puffed black smoke into the blue sky.*
▸ belch, blow out, emit, send out
2 *By the end of the race I was puffing.*
▸ breathe heavily, gasp, pant, wheeze
3 *The sails puffed out as the wind rose.*
▸ become inflated, billow, swell

pull *VERB*
1 *He pulled the chair nearer the desk.*
▸ drag, draw, haul, lug, tow, trail
AN OPPOSITE IS push
2 *Be careful — you nearly pulled my arm off!*
▸ jerk, pluck, rip, tug, wrench
to pull out 1 *She pulled the cork out of the bottle.*
▸ extract, remove, take out
2 *He had to pull out of the race.*
▸ back out, retire, withdraw
to pull someone's leg *I hope you aren't pulling my leg!*
▸ make fun of you, play a trick on you, tease you
to pull through *It was a bad accident, but the doctors expect her to pull through.*
▸ get better, recover, revive, survive
to pull up *She pulled up at the traffic lights.*
▸ draw up, halt, put the brakes on, stop

pulp *VERB*
The strawberries were pulped and mixed with the ice cream.
▸ crush, liquidize, mash, squash

pulse *NOUN*
You can feel the pulse of blood in your veins.
▸ beat, drumming, throb

pump *VERB*
The fire brigade pumped water out of the cellar.
▸ drain, draw off, empty, raise
▹ To move liquid from a higher container to a lower one through a tube is to **siphon** it.

punch *VERB*
1 *He punched me on the nose!*
▸ jab, poke, prod, thump
SEE ALSO **hit** *VERB*
2 *I need to punch another hole in my belt.*
▸ bore, pierce

punctual *ADJECTIVE*
The bus was punctual today.
▸ in good time, on time, prompt
AN OPPOSITE IS late

punctuation *NOUN*
PUNCTUATION MARKS
apostrophe, brackets, colon, comma, dash, exclamation mark, full stop, hyphen, question mark, quotation marks or speech marks, semicolon, square brackets
OTHER MARKS YOU USE IN WRITING
accent, asterisk or star, bullet point, slash

puncture *NOUN*
1 *I had a puncture on the way home.*
▶ burst tyre, flat tyre
2 *I found the puncture in my tyre.*
▶ hole, leak, pinprick

puncture *VERB*
A nail punctured my tyre.
▶ deflate, let down, perforate, pierce

punish *VERB*
Those responsible for this crime will be severely punished.
▶ make an example of, penalize

punishment *NOUN*
Many people believe that the punishment should fit the crime.
▶ correction, penalty
▷ Making someone suffer because they have harmed you is **revenge**.
▷ Punishing someone by taking their life is **capital punishment** or **execution**.
FORMS OF CAPITAL PUNISHMENT
beheading or decapitation or the guillotine, burning, crucifixion, electrocution, firing squad or shooting, gassing, hanging, injection, poisoning, stoning
▷ Punishing someone by hurting them physically is **corporal punishment**.
FORMS OF CORPORAL PUNISHMENT
a beating, the birch, the cane, flogging, (*informal*) a hiding, a spanking, torture, whipping
OTHER FORMS OF PUNISHMENT
banishment or exile, (*old use*) Borstal, community service, confiscation of property, deportation, detention, a fine, a forfeit, gaol or jail, an imposition, imprisonment, probation
FORMS OF PUNISHMENT YOU MAY READ ABOUT IN HISTORY BOOKS
ducking-stool, keelhauling, the pillory, the stocks, the treadmill

puny *ADJECTIVE*
He's rather a puny child.
▶ delicate, feeble, frail, pathetic, weak, weedy
AN OPPOSITE IS strong

pupil *NOUN*
There are 33 pupils in our class.
▶ learner, scholar, schoolchild, student
▷ Someone who follows a great teacher is a **disciple**.

purchase *VERB*
He used the money to purchase a new bike.
▶ acquire, buy, get, obtain, pay for

purchase *NOUN*
1 *She opened her bag and examined her purchases.*
▶ acquisition
2 *The climbers had difficulty getting any purchase on the rock face.*
▶ grasp, hold, leverage

pure *ADJECTIVE*
1 *The bracelet is made of pure gold.*
▶ authentic, genuine, real
2 *He was talking pure nonsense.*
▶ absolute, complete, perfect, sheer, total, utter
3 *Their products are made from pure ingredients.*
▶ natural, wholesome
4 *They swam in the pure, clear water of the lake.*
▶ clean, fresh, unpolluted
▷ Water which is purified by boiling it and condensing the vapour is **distilled** water.
AN OPPOSITE IS impure

purge *VERB*
The boss took action to purge all dishonest employees.
▶ expel, get rid of, remove, root out

purify *VERB*
You can't drink this water unless you purify it.
▶ clean, make pure
▷ You destroy germs by **disinfecting** or **sterilizing** things. You take solid particles out of liquids by **filtering** them. To purify water by boiling it and condensing the vapour is to **distil** it. To purify crude oil is to **refine** it.

puritanical *ADJECTIVE*
He's rather puritanical about moral matters.
▶ austere, narrow-minded, prim, severe, strict
AN OPPOSITE IS broad-minded

purpose *NOUN*
1 *Have you got a particular purpose in mind?*
▶ aim, ambition, end, goal, hope, intention, objective, outcome, plan, result, target, wish
2 *What's the purpose of this gadget?*
▶ point, use, usefulness, value

purposeful *ADJECTIVE*
Her purposeful look showed she meant business.
▶ decisive, determined, positive
AN OPPOSITE IS aimless or hesitant

purposeless *ADJECTIVE*
He felt he was leading a purposeless existence.
▶ aimless, pointless, senseless, unnecessary, useless
AN OPPOSITE IS useful

purposely *ADVERB*
Was it an accident, or did he do it purposely?
▶ consciously, deliberately, intentionally, knowingly, on purpose
AN OPPOSITE IS accidentally

purse *NOUN*
She lost all her money when her purse was stolen.
▶ bag, handbag, pouch
▷ A container for paper money, credit cards, etc., is a **wallet**.

pursue *VERB*
1 *He ran off, pursued by two police officers.*
▶ chase, follow, go in pursuit of, hound, hunt, run after, tail, track down
2 *She pursued her acting career with great determination.*
▶ carry on, continue, keep up with, proceed with, work at

pursuit *NOUN*
1 *The pursuit of the fox lasted for hours.*
▶ chase, hunt, tracking down, trail
2 *They both enjoyed outdoor pursuits.*
▶ activity, hobby, interest, occupation, pastime, pleasure

push *VERB*
1 *They pushed us out of the way.*
▶ barge, drive, elbow, force, hustle, jostle, propel, shove, thrust
AN OPPOSITE IS pull
2 *He pushed his things into a bag.*
▶ compress, cram, crush, insert, pack, press, put, ram, squash, squeeze
3 *They pushed him to work even harder.*
▶ bully, (*informal*) lean on, persuade, pressurize, put pressure on, urge
4 *The firm is pushing its new product hard.*
▶ advertise, market, (*informal*) plug, promote, publicize

put *VERB* This word is often overused.
1 *The council plans to put a recycling centre next to the car park.*
▶ locate, situate
2 *Put the books on the shelf.*
▶ arrange, dump, leave, place, set down, stand
3 *Put your head on the cushion.*
▶ lay, lean, rest
4 *I'll put some pictures on the wall.*
▶ attach, fasten, fix, hang
5 *They put guards outside the bank.*
▶ position, stand, station
6 *She wanted to put her point of view.*
▶ express, say, state
to put something off *They had to put off their visit because of the fog.*
▶ defer, delay, postpone
to put something out *The firemen quickly put out the blaze.*
▶ extinguish, quench, smother
to put something up 1 *It doesn't take long to put up the tent.*
▶ construct, erect, set up
2 *I'm going to buy a new bike before they put up the price.*
▶ increase, raise
to put up with something *I don't know how you put up with that noise.*
▶ bear, endure, stand, tolerate

puzzle *NOUN*
Can you solve this puzzle for me?
▶ difficulty, dilemma, mystery, (*informal*) poser, problem, question

puzzle *VERB*
1 *I was very puzzled by her reply.*
▶ baffle, bewilder, confuse, fox, mystify, perplex
2 *We puzzled over the problem for hours.*
▶ brood, meditate, ponder, think, worry

puzzling *ADJECTIVE*
There were many puzzling aspects of the affair.
▶ baffling, bewildering, confusing, inexplicable, insoluble, mysterious, mystifying, perplexing
AN OPPOSITE IS straightforward

Qq

quadrangle *NOUN*
▷ The covered path round the inside of a courtyard next to a cathedral or monastery is the **cloisters**.

quail *VERB*
She quailed at the furious expression on his face.
▸ back away, falter, flinch, hesitate, quake, recoil, show fear, shrink back, tremble

quaint *ADJECTIVE*
They stayed in a quaint thatched cottage.
▸ antiquated, charming, curious, old-fashioned, picturesque

quake *VERB*
The whole building quaked when the bomb went off.
▸ quiver, rock, shake, sway, tremble, vibrate, wobble

qualification *NOUN*
He gave his approval to the scheme, but with several qualifications.
▸ condition, exception, reservation
qualifications *Have you got the qualifications to do the job properly?*
▸ ability, competence, experience, know-how, knowledge, skill, suitability, training

qualified *ADJECTIVE*
1 *This job needs a qualified electrician.*
▸ competent, experienced, professional, skilled, trained
AN OPPOSITE IS amateur
2 *He's not qualified for a lorry driver's job.*
▸ appropriate, eligible, suitable
3 *He received qualified praise for his efforts.*
▸ cautious, half-hearted, limited, modified

qualify *VERB*
1 *She doesn't qualify for unemployment benefit.*
▸ be eligible, be qualified, have the qualifications
2 *The first three runners will qualify to take part in the final.*
▸ get through, pass
3 *She felt the need to qualify her last statement.*
▸ limit, modify, restrict, soften, weaken

quality *NOUN*
1 *The butcher sells top quality meat.*
▸ class, grade, standard, value
2 *The most obvious quality of rubber is that it stretches.*
▸ characteristic, feature, peculiarity, property

quantity *NOUN*
1 *The council deals with a large quantity of rubbish every week.*
▸ amount, bulk, (*informal*) load, mass, volume, weight
2 *We had a large quantity of empty bottles to get rid of.*
▸ number
▷ When we add up numbers, we get a **sum** or **total**.
FOR WORDS WE USE WHEN MEASURING VARIOUS QUANTITIES SEE **measurement**

quarrel *NOUN*
We have quarrels, but really we are good friends.
▸ argument, clash, conflict, difference of opinion, disagreement, dispute, misunderstanding, row, squabble
▷ Continuous quarrelling is **strife**. A long-lasting quarrel is a **feud** or **vendetta**. A quarrel in which people become violent is a **brawl** or **fight**.

quarrel *VERB*
They quarrelled about money.
▸ argue, clash, differ, disagree, fall out, fight, row, squabble
to quarrel with something *I can't quarrel with your decision.*
▸ complain about, disagree with, object to, oppose, question, take exception to

quarrelsome *ADJECTIVE*
He's a very quarrelsome man.
▸ aggressive, bad-tempered, defiant, excitable, hostile, impatient, irritable, mutinous, quick-tempered, rebellious
AN OPPOSITE IS placid

quarry *NOUN*
1 *This quarry produces limestone for road building.*
▸ excavation
▷ A place with shafts and tunnels where minerals are dug out is a **mine** or **pit**.
2 *The lion stalked its quarry.*
▸ prey, victim

quarters *PLURAL NOUN*
The soldiers stayed in quarters in the town.
▸ accommodation, billets, housing, living quarters, lodgings

quaver *VERB*
His voice quavered.
▸ falter, quake, quiver, shake, tremble, waver

quay *NOUN*
The ship unloaded its cargo onto the quay.
▸ berth, dock, harbour, jetty, landing stage, pier, wharf

queasy *ADJECTIVE*
The sea was rough and I began to feel a bit queasy.
▸ ill, poorly, queer, sick, unwell

queer *ADJECTIVE*
1 *I heard a queer noise.*
▸ curious, eerie, funny, inexplicable, mysterious, puzzling, strange, uncanny, unusual, weird
2 *There's something queer going on.*
▸ abnormal, (*informal*) fishy, odd, peculiar, shady, suspicious
3 *He was feeling rather queer after eating so much chocolate.*
▸ poorly, queasy, sick, unwell
SEE ALSO **ill**
AN OPPOSITE IS normal

quench *VERB*
1 *The iced lemonade soon quenched her thirst.*
▸ cool, satisfy
2 *They dumped sand on the embers to quench the fire.*
▸ extinguish, put out, smother

query *NOUN, VERB*
SEE **question** *NOUN, VERB*

quest *NOUN*
The quest for a vaccine for the disease continues.
▸ hunt, search

question *NOUN*
1 *I'll try to answer your question.*
▸ demand, enquiry or inquiry, query
▹ A question which someone asks as a joke is a brain-teaser or conundrum or riddle. A series of questions asked as a game is a quiz. A set of questions which someone asks in order to get information is a questionnaire or survey.
2 *There's some question about his honesty.*
▸ argument, controversy, debate, dispute, doubt, problem, uncertainty

question *VERB*
1 *Four men were being questioned about the burglary.*
▸ ask, cross-examine, examine, grill, interrogate, interview, quiz
2 *He questioned the referee's decision.*
▸ argue over, challenge, dispute, object to, quarrel with, query

questionable *ADJECTIVE*
1 *It's questionable how necessary these changes are.*
▸ debatable, doubtful, uncertain, unclear
2 *The police said her evidence was questionable.*
▸ unconvincing, unreliable

questionnaire *NOUN*
They were asked to fill in a questionnaire.
▸ opinion poll, survey

queue *NOUN*
There was a queue of cars at the level crossing.
▸ column, file, line, row, string, tailback

queue *VERB*
Please queue at the door.
▸ form a queue, line up, wait in a queue

quick *ADJECTIVE*
1 *You'd better be quick — the bus leaves in 10 minutes.*
▸ fast, rapid, swift
2 *He made a quick exit.*
▸ hasty, headlong, hurried, (*informal*) nippy, speedy, sudden
3 *Do you mind if we have a quick rest?*
▸ brief, momentary, short
4 *I hope to get a quick reply.*
▸ early, immediate, instant, instantaneous, prompt, punctual, snappy, unhesitating
5 *She's very quick at mental arithmetic.*
▸ acute, alert, bright, clever, perceptive, sharp, smart
AN OPPOSITE IS leisurely or slow

quicken *VERB*
Their pace quickened.
▸ accelerate, become faster, hasten, hurry up, speed up

a b c d e f g h i j k l m n o p q r s t u v w x y z

A B C D E F G H I J K L M N O P Q R S T U V W X Y Z

quiet *ADJECTIVE*
1 *The deserted house was quiet.*
▸ noiseless, silent, soundless
AN OPPOSITE IS noisy
2 *They spoke in quiet whispers.*
▸ hushed, low, soft
▹ Something that is so quiet that you can't hear it is **inaudible**.
AN OPPOSITE IS loud
3 *She's a very quiet, modest person.*
▸ reserved, retiring, shy, thoughtful, uncommunicative
AN OPPOSITE IS talkative
4 *We were in a quiet mood.*
▸ calm, peaceful, placid, restful, serene, tranquil, untroubled
AN OPPOSITE IS excited
5 *We found a quiet place for a picnic.*
▸ isolated, lonely, private, secluded
AN OPPOSITE IS busy

quieten *VERB*
1 *Her mother was trying to quieten her.*
▸ calm, hush, pacify, soothe
2 *A silencer quietens the noise of the engine.*
▸ deaden, muffle, soften, suppress
▹ To use a special device to make a musical instrument quieter is to **mute** it.

quit *VERB*
1 *Police were called in when he refused to quit the building.*
▸ abandon, depart from, desert, forsake, go away from, leave
2 *When he became ill, he had to quit his job.*
▸ give up, resign from
3 (*informal*) *Quit pushing!*
▸ cease, leave off, stop

quite *ADVERB*
Take care how you use *quite*, as the two senses are almost opposites
1 *Yes, I have quite finished.*
▸ absolutely, altogether, completely, entirely, perfectly, totally, utterly, wholly
2 *They played quite well, but far from their best.*
▸ fairly, moderately, (*informal*) pretty, rather

quiver *VERB*
The jelly quivered when the table was banged.
▸ quake, quaver, shake, shiver, shudder, tremble, vibrate, wobble

quiz *VERB*
Four men have been quizzed about the crime.
▸ ask, cross-examine, examine, grill, interrogate, interview, question

quota *NOUN*
Make sure everyone gets their proper quota of food.
▸ allowance, helping, portion, ration, share

quotation *NOUN*
I copied a short quotation from the book.
▸ excerpt, extract, passage, piece
▹ A piece taken from a newspaper is a **cutting**. A piece taken from a film or TV programme is a **clip**.
quotation marks *In writing, you put quotation marks round the words someone has said.*
▸ inverted commas, speech marks

quote *VERB*
He quoted a passage from the Bible.
▸ repeat, speak

Rr

race *NOUN*
1 *They had a race to see who could get there first.*
▸ chase, competition, contest
VARIOUS KINDS OF COMPETITIVE RACING
cross-country, cycle racing, horse racing, hurdles, marathon, motor racing, regatta, relay race, road race, rowing, speedway racing, running races, sprinting, steeplechase, stock-car racing, swimming races
▹ A race to decide who will take part in the final is a **heat**.
VARIOUS PLACES WHERE RACES TAKE PLACE
circuit, dog track, racecourse, racetrack, stadium
▹ Once round a circuit or racetrack is a **lap**.
2 *We belong to different races but we are all humans.*
▸ ethnic group, nation, people
▹ A group of related families is a **clan**. A group of families living together ruled by a chief is a **tribe**.

race *VERB*
1 *They raced each other to the end of the road.*
▸ compete with, have a race with, try to beat
2 *She had to race home because she was late.*
▸ dash, fly, gallop, hurry, move fast, run, rush, sprint, tear, zoom

racism *NOUN*
Sadly, racism still exists in society.
▸ bias, chauvinism, discrimination, intolerance, prejudice, racial hatred, xenophobia

rack *NOUN*
He made a rack for his tools in the garage.
▸ frame, framework, shelf, stand

racket *NOUN*
1 *A racket is used to hit the ball in tennis.*
▷ In cricket and other games you hit the ball with a bat. In golf you hit the ball with a club.
2 *She complained about the racket from next door.*
▸ commotion, disturbance, hullabaloo, noise, pandemonium, row, tumult, uproar
3 (*slang*) *The police were investigating an insurance racket.*
▸ fraud, (*slang*) rip-off, swindle

radiant *ADJECTIVE*
Her radiant smile made everyone feel better.
▸ beautiful, bright, cheerful, happy, sunny, warm

radiate *VERB*
1 *This fire radiates a lot of heat.*
▸ emit, give off, send out
2 *The bus routes radiate from the centre of town.*
▸ spread out

radical *ADJECTIVE*
1 *We need a radical examination of what went wrong.*
▸ basic, drastic, fundamental, thorough
AN OPPOSITE IS superficial
2 *Some people were suspicious of the politician's radical views.*
▸ extreme, revolutionary
AN OPPOSITE IS moderate

radio *NOUN*
He turned on the radio.
▸ radio set, receiver, transistor, (*old use*) wireless
▷ Equipment which has a radio and also plays CDs and cassettes is a stereo or hi-fi. The radio receiver in hi-fi equipment is a tuner. A portable stereo is a personal stereo or (*trademark*) Walkman. Radio equipment which sends out programmes is a transmitter. Sending out radio programmes is broadcasting.

rag *NOUN*
She wiped the floor with a rag.
▸ cloth, scrap of cloth

rage *NOUN*
He was trembling with rage.
▸ anger, fury, indignation, (*old use*) wrath
▷ A child's rage is a tantrum or temper.

rage *VERB*
She raged about the delays.
▸ be angry, be fuming, flare up, lose your temper, seethe, storm

ragged *ADJECTIVE*
1 *Who was the man wearing ragged clothes?*
▸ frayed, old, patched, ripped, shabby, tattered, tatty, threadbare, torn, worn out
2 *A ragged line of refugees struggled along the road.*
▸ irregular, uneven

raid *NOUN*
The enemy raid caught them by surprise.
▸ assault, attack, blitz, invasion

raid *VERB*
1 *Police raided the house.*
▸ attack, descend on, invade, pounce on, rush, storm, swoop on
2 *They raided the larder when they were hungry.*
▸ loot, pillage, plunder, rob, steal from

raider *NOUN*
Raiders swooped down from the mountains.
▸ attacker, brigand, invader, looter, marauder, robber, thief
▷ Someone who raids ships at sea is a pirate. Someone who raids and steals cattle is a rustler.

rail *NOUN*
The fence was made of iron rails.
▸ bar, rod
▷ A fence made of rails is also called railings.

railway *NOUN*
▷ The rails which trains run on are the **line** or **permanent way** or **track**. The American term is **railroad**.
DIFFERENT KINDS OF RAILWAY
branch line, cable railway, funicular, light railway, main line, metro, mineral line, monorail, mountain railway, narrow gauge railway, rack-and-pinion railway, rapid transit system, sidings, standard gauge railway, tramway, the tube, underground railway
VARIOUS KINDS OF TRAIN
diesel, electric train, express, freight train or goods train, intercity, sleeper, steam train, stopping train, tram, underground train
▷ Vehicles which run on the railway are **locomotives** and **rolling stock**.
VARIOUS KINDS OF LOCOMOTIVE AND ROLLING STOCK
buffet car, cable car, carriage, coach, container wagon, dining car, engine, goods van, goods wagon, guard's van, locomotive, Pullman carriage, shunter, sleeping car, steam engine, tender, truck, wagon
THINGS YOU MIGHT SEE ALONG THE LINE
cutting, halt, level crossing, marshalling yard, points, signals, signal-box, sleepers, station, track, tunnel, viaduct
▷ The end of the line is the **terminus**.
THINGS YOU MIGHT SEE AT A STATION
booking office, buffers, buffet, information centre, left-luggage office, luggage trolley, platform, ticket office, timetable, waiting room
PEOPLE WHO WORK FOR THE RAILWAY INCLUDE
announcer, booking clerk, conductor, crossing keeper, driver, engineer, fireman, guard, platelayer, porter, signalman, station manager, stationmaster, steward

rain *NOUN, VERB*
VARIOUS KINDS OF RAIN
cloudburst, deluge, downpour, drizzle, rainstorm, shower, squall
VARIOUS WAYS IT CAN RAIN
drizzle, pelt, pour, (*informal*) rain cats and dogs, spit
▷ A formal word for rain, snow, etc., is **precipitation**. The rainy season in south and southeast Asia is the **monsoon**. When there is no rain for a long time you have a **drought**.
FOR OTHER WORDS TO DO WITH WEATHER SEE **weather**

raise *VERB*
The verb *to raise* can be used in many ways. We give some of the common ways you can use it here:
1 *Raise your hand if you need help.*
► hold up, lift, put up
2 *They raised a monument to the victims of the earthquake.*
► build, construct, erect, set up
3 *The box was too heavy for him to raise.*
► lift, pick up
▷ To raise a flag or sail is to **hoist** it. To raise a vehicle off the ground is to **jack it up**. To raise the barrel of a big gun is to **elevate** it. To raise prices is to **increase** them. To raise someone to a higher rank is to **promote** them.
4 *They aimed to raise £1000 for charity.*
► collect, get, make
5 *He raised some questions about the new policy.*
► bring up, introduce, mention, put forward, refer to, suggest
6 *The doctor didn't want to raise their hopes.*
► build up, encourage, stimulate
7 *The farmer raises prize cattle.*
► breed, rear
8 *She sold some of the tomato plants I had raised.*
► cultivate, grow, produce
9 *It's hard work trying to raise a family.*
► bring up, care for, educate, look after, nurture

rally *NOUN*
Some demonstrators held a rally in the town square.
► (*informal*) demo, demonstration, march, meeting, protest

ram *VERB*
The car rammed the one in front.
► bump, collide with, crash into, hit, smash into, strike

ramble *VERB*
1 *They rambled round the country park.*
► hike, meander, range, roam, rove, stroll, walk, wander
2 *He tends to ramble when he talks.*
► stray from the point, talk aimlessly

rambling *ADJECTIVE*
1 *They followed a rambling path.*
► indirect, meandering, roundabout, twisting, winding, zigzag
AN OPPOSITE IS **direct**

2 *She was bored by his rambling speech.*
▸ aimless, confused, wordy
AN OPPOSITE IS eloquent
3 *They stayed in a rambling old farmhouse.*
▸ sprawling, straggling
AN OPPOSITE IS compact

rampage *VERB*
Hooligans rampaged through the town.
▸ go berserk, go wild, race about, rush about

random *ADJECTIVE*
The inspectors looked at a random sample of their work.
▸ arbitrary, casual, chance, haphazard, unplanned
AN OPPOSITE IS deliberate

range *NOUN*
1 *There was a range of mountains to the south.*
▸ chain, line, row, series, string
2 *Supermarkets sell a wide range of goods.*
▸ selection, spectrum, variety
3 *The pianist said that playing jazz was outside his range.*
▸ limit, scope
4 *He can hit a target at a range of a hundred yards.*
▸ distance

range *VERB*
1 *Prices range from £10 to £15.*
▸ differ, extend, fluctuate, vary
2 *The flower pots were ranged in rows on the windowsill.*
▸ arrange, display, lay out, line up, set out
3 *Sheep range over the hills.*
▸ ramble, roam, rove, stray, wander

rank *NOUN*
1 *They lined up in a single rank.*
▸ column, file, line, row, series
2 *After he'd gained experience, he was promoted to a higher rank.*
▸ grade, level, position, status
RANKS IN THE AIR FORCE, IN DESCENDING ORDER OF SENIORITY
Marshal of the RAF, Air Chief Marshal, Air Marshal, Air Vice-Marshal, air commodore, group captain, wing commander, squadron leader, flight lieutenant, flying officer, pilot officer, warrant officer, flight sergeant, chief technician, sergeant, corporal, junior technician, senior aircraftman, leading aircraftman, aircraftman

RANKS IN THE ARMY, IN DESCENDING ORDER OF SENIORITY
Field Marshal, general, lieutenant general, major general, brigadier, colonel, lieutenant colonel, major, captain, lieutenant, second lieutenant or subaltern, warrant officer, staff sergeant, sergeant, corporal, lance corporal, private
RANKS IN THE NAVY, IN DESCENDING ORDER OF SENIORITY
Admiral of the Fleet, admiral, vice-admiral, rear admiral, commodore, captain, commander, lieutenant commander, lieutenant, sub-lieutenant, chief petty officer, petty officer, leading rating, able rating, ordinary rating

ransack *VERB*
1 *She ransacked the house looking for her purse.*
▸ comb, rummage through, scour, search, (*informal*) turn upside down
2 *Rioters ransacked the shops.*
▸ loot, pillage, plunder, wreck

rap *VERB*
He rapped on the door.
▸ knock, tap

rapid *ADJECTIVE*
They made rapid progress.
▸ brisk, fast, quick, speedy, swift
AN OPPOSITE IS slow

rare *ADJECTIVE*
1 *She died of a rare disease.*
▸ abnormal, curious, odd, peculiar, strange, uncommon, unusual
2 *A cuckoo is a rare sight in this area.*
▸ exceptional, infrequent, occasional, surprising
AN OPPOSITE IS common

rarely *ADVERB*
She rarely went out.
▸ infrequently, occasionally, seldom
AN OPPOSITE IS often

rash *ADJECTIVE*
He regretted his rash decision.
▸ careless, hasty, hurried, impulsive, incautious, reckless, risky, thoughtless
AN OPPOSITE IS careful

A B C D E F G H I J K L M N O P Q R S T U V W X Y Z

rash *NOUN*

1 *She had a rash on her skin.*
▸ spots
2 *There's been a rash of burglaries in the area.*
▸ outbreak

rate *NOUN*

1 *They set out at a fast rate.*
▸ pace, speed
▹ A formal word is **velocity**.
2 *What's the usual rate for washing a car?*
▸ amount, charge, cost, fee, figure, payment, price, wage

rate *VERB*

How do you rate their chance of winning?
▸ consider, estimate, evaluate, judge, regard

rather *ADVERB*

1 *She was rather ill.*
▸ fairly, moderately, (*informal*) pretty, quite, slightly, somewhat
2 *He said he'd rather not come.*
▸ preferably, sooner

ratio *NOUN*

The ratio of boys to girls is about 50–50.
▸ balance, fraction, proportion
▹ You can express a ratio as a **percentage**.

ration *NOUN*

They had their ration of sweets.
▸ allowance, helping, measure, portion, quota, share
rations *The expedition carried enough rations to last a month.*
▸ food, necessities, provisions, stores, supplies

ration *VERB*

In time of war the government may ration food supplies.
▸ allot, control, distribute fairly, limit, restrict, share equally

rational *ADJECTIVE*

1 *No rational person would do such a silly thing.*
▸ intelligent, normal, reasonable, sane, sensible, thoughtful, wise
2 *Don't get angry — et's have a rational discussion.*
▸ balanced, logical, lucid, reasoned, sound
AN OPPOSITE IS irrational

rationalize *VERB*

1 *The new manager tried to rationalize the company.*
▸ reorganize, sort out
2 *He couldn't rationalize his absurd fear of spiders.*
▸ be rational about, explain, justify, think through

rattle *NOUN VERB*

FOR VARIOUS WAYS TO MAKE SOUNDS SEE **sound** *VERB*

rave *VERB*

1 *He raved about the film he saw last week.*
▸ be enthusiastic, talk wildly
2 *The head raved angrily about our bad behaviour.*
▸ rage, roar, shout, storm, yell

ravenous *ADJECTIVE*

He felt ravenous and ate a huge dinner.
▸ famished, greedy, hungry, starved, starving

raw *ADJECTIVE*

1 *Raw vegetables are supposed to be good for you.*
▸ uncooked
AN OPPOSITE IS cooked
2 *The factory imports a lot of raw materials from abroad.*
▸ crude, natural, unprocessed, untreated
AN OPPOSITE IS manufactured or processed
3 *The raw beginners didn't know what to do.*
▸ ignorant, new, untrained
AN OPPOSITE IS experienced
4 *Her knee felt raw after she fell off her bike.*
▸ bloody, inflamed, painful, red, rough, sore, tender
5 *The raw wind made him shiver.*
▸ bitter, chilly, cold, unpleasant

ray *NOUN*

A ray of light shone between the curtains.
▸ beam, shaft, stream
▹ A strong narrow ray of light used in various technological devices is a **laser**.

razor *NOUN*

▹ A razor you throw away after using it is a **disposable razor**. An electric razor is also called a **shaver**.

reach *VERB*
1 *They hoped to reach Oxford by lunch time.*
▸ arrive at, get to, go as far as, make
2 *The appeal fund has reached its target.*
▸ achieve, attain
3 *He could just reach the handle.*
▸ get hold of, grasp, touch
to reach out *Reach out your hand.*
▸ extend, hold out, put out, raise, stick out, stretch out

reach *NOUN*
1 *The shelf was just within his reach.*
▸ grasp
2 *The shops are within easy reach.*
▸ distance, range

react *VERB*
How did she react when you asked for money?
▸ answer, behave, reply, respond

reaction *NOUN*
What was his reaction when you said it was too expensive?
▸ answer, reply, response
▷ Information about how people have reacted to something is **feedback**.

read *VERB*
He couldn't read her handwriting.
▸ decipher, make out, understand
▷ To read through something very quickly is to **skim through** it. To read here and there in a book is to **dip into** it. A device which enables a computer to read things is a **scanner** which **scans** pages.

readable *ADJECTIVE*
1 *It was a very readable book.*
▸ enjoyable, entertaining, interesting, well written
AN OPPOSITE IS boring
2 *Is his handwriting readable?*
▸ clear, decipherable, legible, plain, understandable
AN OPPOSITE IS illegible

readily *ADVERB*
1 *She readily agreed to help.*
▸ eagerly, gladly, happily, voluntarily, willingly
2 *The recipe uses ingredients which are readily available.*
▸ conveniently, easily, quickly

ready *ADJECTIVE*
1 *Dinner is ready.*
▸ available, done, obtainable, prepared, set out, waiting
AN OPPOSITE IS not ready
2 *He's always ready to help.*
▸ eager, glad, keen, pleased, willing
AN OPPOSITE IS reluctant
3 *She's always got a ready reply.*
▸ immediate, prompt, quick, sharp, smart
AN OPPOSITE IS slow
4 *This balloon is ready to burst at any moment!*
▸ liable, likely

real *ADJECTIVE*
1 *History is about real events.*
▸ actual, factual, true, verifiable
AN OPPOSITE IS fictitious or imaginary
2 *She likes stories about real life.*
▸ everyday, ordinary
AN OPPOSITE IS unreal
3 *There was real cream in the coffee.*
▸ authentic, genuine, natural, pure
AN OPPOSITE IS artificial
4 *You're a real friend!*
▸ dependable, reliable, sound, trustworthy
AN OPPOSITE IS untrustworthy
5 *She doesn't often show her real feelings.*
▸ honest, sincere, true
AN OPPOSITE IS insincere

realistic *ADJECTIVE*
1 *The film gives a realistic idea of what happened.*
▸ authentic, convincing, fair, faithful, genuine, lifelike, reasonable, recognizable, true to life, truthful
2 *Some people say it's not realistic to ban traffic from the city centre.*
▸ feasible, possible, practicable, practical, sensible, workable
AN OPPOSITE IS unrealistic

reality *NOUN*
Stop daydreaming and face reality.
▸ the facts, the real world, the truth

realize *VERB*
It took him a long time to realize what she meant.
▸ appreciate, become aware of, (*informal*) catch on to, comprehend, grasp, recognize, see, (*informal*) tumble to, (*informal*) twig, understand

A B C D E F G H I J K L M N O P Q R S T U V W X Y Z

really *ADVERB*
1 *Are you really going to Australia?*
▶ actually, certainly, definitely, genuinely, honestly, in fact, truly
2 *I saw a really good film last night.*
▶ exceptionally, extremely, unusually, very

realm *NOUN*
The king ruled the realm for fifty years.
▶ country, domain, empire, kingdom

reap *VERB*
1 *They used to reap corn with scythes.*
▶ cut, gather in, harvest, mow
2 *They hoped they would reap some benefit from all their efforts.*
▶ gain, get, obtain, receive, win

reappear *VERB*
The swallows reappeared after the winter.
▶ appear again, come back, return

rear *ADJECTIVE*
They found seats in the rear coach of the train.
▶ back, end, last
▷ The rear legs of an animal are its hind legs.
AN OPPOSITE IS front

rear *NOUN*
They walked through to the rear of the train.
▶ back, end, tail-end
▷ The rear of a ship is the stern.

rear *VERB*
1 *They have reared three children.*
▶ bring up, care for, feed, look after, nurture
2 *Farmers rear cattle.*
▶ breed, produce, raise
3 *The horse reared.*
▶ rise up
4 *The deer reared their heads when they caught his scent.*
▶ hold up, lift, raise

reason *NOUN*
1 *What was the reason for his behaviour?*
▶ cause, excuse, explanation, incentive, justification, motive
2 *Reason is what distinguishes us from other animals.*
▶ brains, intelligence, judgement, reasoning, understanding, wisdom
3 *She tried to make him see reason.*
▶ common sense, logic, sense

reason *VERB*
1 *He reasoned that if they started early they would reach their destination by noon.*
▶ calculate, conclude, deduce, draw the conclusion, infer, judge, work out
2 *She tried to reason with him, but he wouldn't change his mind.*
▶ argue, debate, use reason

reasonable *ADJECTIVE*
1 *He'll understand — he's a very reasonable person.*
▶ calm, intelligent, rational, realistic, sane, sensible, thoughtful, wise
AN OPPOSITE IS irrational
2 *Her argument seemed very reasonable.*
▶ believable, credible, justifiable, logical, sound
AN OPPOSITE IS illogical
3 *£10 is a reasonable price.*
▶ acceptable, average, fair, moderate, normal, proper, respectable
AN OPPOSITE IS excessive

reasonably *ADVERB*
1 *They all behaved reasonably.*
▶ intelligently, rationally, sanely, sensibly
2 *It is reasonably warm for the time of year.*
▶ fairly, moderately, (*informal*) pretty, quite, rather, tolerably

reasoning *NOUN*
She couldn't follow his reasoning.
▶ analysis, argument, case, deduction, line of thought, logic, reasons, thinking

reassure *VERB*
He reassured them and said everything would be all right.
▶ calm, comfort, encourage, give confidence to, support
AN OPPOSITE IS threaten

rebel *VERB*
The dictator feared that the people would rebel.
▶ revolt, rise up
▷ To rebel against the captain of a ship is to mutiny.
AN OPPOSITE IS obey

rebel *NOUN*
▷ A person who rebels violently against the government is a revolutionary. A person who thinks that all governments and laws are bad is an anarchist. A person who rebels against the captain of a ship is a mutineer.

rebellion *NOUN*
1 *As conditions got worse there were signs of rebellion among the men.*
▸ disobedience, rebelliousness, resistance
2 *The dictator sent soldiers to put down the rebellion.*
▸ revolt, revolution, uprising
▹ A rebellion on a ship is a mutiny.

rebellious *ADJECTIVE*
1 *Troops were sent to deal with the rebellious citizens.*
▸ disloyal, mutinous, revolutionary
2 *He was a very rebellious boy.*
▸ defiant, difficult, disobedient, quarrelsome, uncontrollable, unmanageable, unruly, wild
AN OPPOSITE IS obedient

rebound *VERB*
The ball rebounded off the wall.
▸ bounce back, spring back
▹ If a bullet rebounds off a wall, etc., it is said to ricochet.

rebuild *NOUN*
After the earthquake they started to rebuild the town.
▸ build again, renew, repair, restore

recall *VERB*
1 *The manufacturer recalled the faulty cars.*
▸ bring back, call back
2 *Try to recall what happened.*
▸ recollect, remember, think back to

recapture *VERB*
They spent ages trying to recapture my rabbit.
▸ get back, retrieve

recede *VERB*
When the rain stopped the flood receded.
▸ decline, ebb, go back, retreat, subside

receipt *NOUN*
Keep the receipt in case you need to take the goods back.
▸ account, bill, proof of purchase, ticket
receipts *He was pleased with the shop's receipts last month.*
▸ gains, income, profits, takings

receive *VERB*
1 *The captain went up to receive the winners' cup.*
▸ accept, be given, collect, take
AN OPPOSITE IS give or present
2 *He received some serious injuries.*
▸ experience, suffer, sustain, undergo
AN OPPOSITE IS inflict
3 *We went to the front door to receive our visitors.*
▸ greet, meet, welcome

recent *ADJECTIVE*
1 *He told her about the recent changes to the rules.*
▸ fresh, new
2 *She watches the news to keep up with recent events.*
▸ contemporary, current, up to date

reception *NOUN*
1 *They gave him a friendly reception.*
▸ greeting, welcome
2 *They enjoyed themselves at the wedding reception.*
▸ celebration, party
▹ More formal synonyms are function or gathering.

recess *NOUN*
1 *There was a statue in a recess in the wall.*
▸ alcove, bay, corner
2 *They had a recess for refreshments halfway through the meeting.*
▸ adjournment, break, interlude, intermission, interval, rest

recession *NOUN*
Many people lost their jobs in the recession.
▸ depression, slump

recipe *NOUN*
He was able to make a cake by following the recipe.
▸ directions, instructions, list of ingredients

recital *NOUN*
1 *He had to listen to a long recital of all her problems.*
▸ account, narration, repetition
2 *He gave a short recital of piano music.*
▸ concert, performance

recitation *NOUN*
She enjoyed his recitation of the poem.
▸ narration, performance, speaking, telling

recite *VERB*
She recited a poem she had written.
▸ deliver, narrate, perform

A B C D E F G H I J K L M N O P Q R S T U V W X Y Z

reckless *ADJECTIVE*
The police arrested him for reckless driving.
▸ careless, dangerous, hasty, impulsive, inattentive, incautious, irresponsible, negligent, rash, thoughtless, wild
AN OPPOSITE IS careful

reckon *VERB*
1 *I tried to reckon how much she owed me.*
▸ add up, assess, calculate, compute, count, estimate, figure out, total, work out
2 *I reckon it's going to rain.*
▸ believe, feel, guess, think

reclaim *VERB*
1 *They ought to reclaim all this derelict land.*
▸ make usable, restore, save
2 *They were able to reclaim their bus fares after the journey.*
▸ get back, put in a claim for, recover

recline *VERB*
He reclined lazily on the sofa.
▸ lean back, lie, loll, lounge, rest, sprawl, stretch out

recognizable *ADJECTIVE*
He is recognizable because he's much taller than the rest of us.
▸ distinctive, distinguishable, identifiable, unmistakable

recognize *VERB*
1 *If you saw him again, would you recognize him?*
▸ distinguish, identify, know, make out, notice, pick out, recall, recollect, remember, see, spot
2 *He should recognize that what he did was wrong.*
▸ accept, acknowledge, admit, be aware, confess, grant, realize, (*informal*) twig, understand

recoil *VERB*
She recoiled when she saw the blood.
▸ back away, draw back, falter, flinch, quail, shrink back, wince

recollect *VERB*
1 *She didn't recollect what happened.*
▸ have a memory of, recall, remember
2 *They sat for hours recollecting old times.*
▸ be nostalgic about, reminisce about, tell stories about, think back to
AN OPPOSITE IS forget

recollection *NOUN*
They exchanged recollections of last summer's holiday.
▸ memory, reminiscence

recommend *VERB*
1 *The doctor recommended a complete rest.*
▸ advise, advocate, counsel, prescribe, propose, suggest, urge
2 *The critics recommended the film.*
▸ approve of, commend, praise, speak well of

recommendation *NOUN*
1 *He acted on the doctor's recommendation.*
▸ advice, encouragement, suggestion
2 *It was her recommendation that got him the job.*
▸ approval, backing, praise, support

reconcile *VERB*
She managed to reconcile them after their quarrel.
▸ bring together, reunite
reconcile yourself to something *He could never reconcile himself to being dropped from the team.*
▸ accept, put up with, tolerate

record *NOUN*
1 *They spent the evening chatting and playing records.*
KINDS OF RECORD
album, compilation, EP or extended play, single
KINDS OF RECORDING
audiotape, cassette, CD-ROM, compact disc or CD, digital recording, long-playing record or LP, tape recording, video, video cassette, video disc, videotape
2 *He broke the world record for the high jump.*
▸ (*informal*) best, best performance
3 *She kept a record of what she did on holiday.*
▸ account, diary, file, journal, report
▹ The record of what happened at a meeting is the **minutes**. The record of a ship's voyage is the **log**. A record of people's names and information about them is a **register**. Records consisting of historical documents are **archives**.

record *VERB*
1 *She recorded the concert.*
▸ tape, video
2 *He recorded what he saw in a notebook.*
▸ enter, note, put down, set down, write down

record player *NOUN*
FOR EQUIPMENT FOR MAKING AND PLAYING RECORDINGS SEE **audio-visual**

recover *VERB*
1 *It took him a long time to recover after his illness.*
► come round, get better, heal, improve, mend, pull through, rally, revive
2 *They managed to recover the football they kicked over the fence.*
► find, get back, reclaim, retrieve, trace, track down

recovery *NOUN*
1 *His recovery from his illness took a long time.*
► convalescence, cure, healing, revival
2 *The police didn't offer much hope for the recovery of the stolen goods.*
► restoration, retrieval, salvaging

recreation *NOUN*
The people deserved some recreation after their hard work.
► amusement, diversion, enjoyment, entertainment, fun, leisure, play, pleasure, relaxation
▷ A particular activity you do as recreation is a **hobby** or **pastime**.

recruit *NOUN*
The new recruits were very inexperienced.
► beginner, learner, new member, novice
▷ A recruit learning a trade is an **apprentice** or **trainee**.

recruit *VERB*
The youth club needs to recruit new members.
► advertise for, bring in, enrol, take on
▷ To be recruited into the armed services is to **enlist** or **sign on**.

rectangle *NOUN*
► oblong

recur *VERB*
Go to the doctor if the symptoms recur.
► come again, happen again, persist, reappear, repeat itself, return

recycle *VERB*
We should recycle as much waste as we can.
► reclaim, recover, retrieve, reuse, salvage, use again

red *ADJECTIVE & NOUN*
WORDS TO DESCRIBE VARIOUS SHADES OF RED
blood-red, brick-red, cherry, crimson, flame-coloured, maroon, pink, rose, ruby, scarlet, vermilion, wine-coloured
▷ Something which is rather red is **reddish**.
WORDS TO DESCRIBE SOMEONE'S RED CHEEKS
blushing, flushed, glowing, rosy, ruddy
WORDS TO DESCRIBE REDDISH HAIR
auburn, carroty, ginger
WORDS TO DESCRIBE RED EYES
bloodshot, inflamed

redden *VERB*
His face reddened with embarrassment.
► become red, blush, colour, flush, glow

redeem *VERB*
He redeemed his watch from the pawnbroker's.
► buy back, reclaim, recover

reduce *VERB*
He reduced the time he spent reading so he had more time for football.
► cut, cut back, lessen, make less
▷ To reduce something by half is to **halve** it. To reduce the width of something is to **narrow** it. To reduce the length of something is to **shorten** or **trim** it. To reduce the height or level of something is to **bring it down** or **lower** it. To reduce speed is to **decelerate** or **slow down**. To reduce someone to a lower rank is to **demote** them. To reduce the strength of a liquid is to **dilute** it.
AN OPPOSITE IS increase

reduction *NOUN*
1 *The company announced a reduction in prices.*
► cut, decrease, drop
AN OPPOSITE IS increase
2 *With this voucher, you get a reduction of £5.*
► concession, discount, refund

redundant *ADJECTIVE*
The work was finished, so his offer of help was redundant.
► superfluous, unnecessary, unwanted
AN OPPOSITE IS essential

A B C D E F G H I J K L M N O P Q R S T U V W X Y Z

reel *NOUN*
She wound the tape onto the reel.
► spool

reel *VERB*
1 *The blow made his head reel.*
► spin, whirl
2 *He reeled along the road as if he was drunk.*
► lurch, roll, stagger, stumble, sway, totter, wobble

refer *VERB*
1 *She had to refer the decision to her boss.*
► hand over, pass on
2 *If they don't have what he wants, they'll refer him to another shop.*
► direct, recommend, send
to refer to **1** *Don't refer to this matter again.*
► allude to, bring up, comment on, draw attention to, make reference to, mention, speak of
2 *If he can't spell a word, he refers to his dictionary.*
► consult, go to, look up, turn to

referee *NOUN*
▷ A person who helps the referee in football is a linesman or touch judge or assistant referee. A person who makes sure players keep to the rules in some other games is an umpire. A person who acts as a judge in a competition is an adjudicator.

reference *NOUN*
1 *Don't make any reference to her dirty clothes.*
► comment (about), mention (of), remark (about)
2 *Which book does this reference come from?*
► example, illustration, quotation
3 *When you apply for a job you need a reference.*
► recommendation

refill *VERB*
She refilled her glass.
► top up
▷ To refill a fuel tank is to refuel.

refine *VERB*
1 *They have to refine crude oil before it can be used.*
► distil, process, purify
2 *She wrote a rough outline and then refined it.*
► amend, correct, improve, modify

refined *ADJECTIVE*
It was nice to meet someone who was so refined.
► civil, civilized, cultivated, cultured, polite, (*informal*) posh, sophisticated, well brought-up, well educated, well mannered, well spoken
AN OPPOSITE IS vulgar

reflect *VERB*
1 *Cat's-eyes reflect the light from a car's headlights.*
► send back, shine back, throw back
2 *Their success reflects their hard work.*
► demonstrate, exhibit, indicate, reveal, show
to reflect on *She had time to reflect on what had happened.*
► brood over, consider, contemplate, meditate on, ponder, think about

reflection *NOUN*
1 *He could see his reflection in the glass.*
► image, likeness
2 *Their success is a reflection of their hard work.*
► indication, outcome, result
3 *She needed some time for reflection.*
► contemplation, meditation, thinking

reflective *ADJECTIVE*
1 *You should wear reflective patches if you ride your bike at night.*
► reflecting, shiny
2 *You seem to be in a reflective mood.*
► serious, thoughtful

reflex *ADJECTIVE*
Blinking is usually a reflex action.
► automatic, instinctive, involuntary, spontaneous, unthinking
AN OPPOSITE IS conscious

reform *VERB*
She told him to reform his behaviour or be thrown out.
► amend, change, correct, improve, make better, modify

reform *NOUN*
The club introduced several reforms.
► amendment, change, improvement, modification

refrain *VERB*
to refrain from *Please refrain from smoking.*
► avoid, (*informal*) quit, stop

refresh *VERB*
1 *They refreshed themselves with a cup of tea.*
▶ cool, freshen, invigorate, restore, revive, stimulate
2 *Let me refresh your memory.*
▶ jog, prod, prompt

refreshments *PLURAL NOUN*
Refreshments were served during the interval.
▶ drinks, food, a snack

refrigerate *VERB*
Food keeps longer if it is refrigerated.
▶ chill, cool, freeze, keep cold

refuge *NOUN*
The climbers looked for refuge from the blizzard.
▶ cover, a haven, a hiding place, protection, safety, sanctuary, security, shelter

refugee *NOUN*
The refugees had no food or shelter.
▶ exile, outcast

refund *VERB*
She asked them to refund her money.
▶ give back, pay back, repay, return

refuse *VERB*
1 *He refused the invitation.*
▶ decline, reject, say no to, turn down
AN OPPOSITE IS accept
2 *They were refused help.*
▶ deny, deprive of, withhold
AN OPPOSITE IS allow

refuse *NOUN*
The refuse was taken to the tip.
▶ garbage, junk, litter, rubbish, scrap, trash, waste

regain *VERB*
1 *The troops regained possession of the town.*
▶ get back, recapture, win back
2 *They were glad to regain the safety of the harbour.*
▶ get back to, return to

regard *VERB*
1 *He regarded her as his best friend.*
▶ consider, judge, think of, value
2 *The cat regarded him curiously.*
▶ contemplate, eye, gaze at, look at, scrutinize, stare at, view, watch

regard *NOUN*
1 *She quailed under his stern regard.*
▶ gaze, look, scrutiny, stare
2 *Little regard was shown for their feelings.*
▶ attention, consideration, heed, notice, thought
3 *They have a great regard for her ability.*
▶ admiration, affection, esteem, respect

regarding *PREPOSITION*
He had received no answer regarding his request.
▶ about, concerning, connected with, involving, on the subject of, with reference to, with regard to

regardless *ADJECTIVE*
regardless of *He leapt into the water regardless of the danger.*
▶ careless about, heedless of, indifferent to, not caring about, unconcerned about

region *NOUN*
1 *The Antarctic is a cold region.*
▶ area, expanse, part of the world, place, territory, tract
2 *There are two local radio stations serving this region.*
▶ area, district, locality, neighbourhood, vicinity, zone

register *VERB*
1 *They registered as members of the club.*
▶ enlist, enrol, join, sign on
2 *The parents registered the birth of their child.*
▶ record, set down, write down
3 *The thermometer registered a very high temperature.*
▶ indicate, reveal, show

regret *NOUN*
1 *He felt no regret for his actions.*
▶ guilt, penitence, remorse, repentance, shame
2 *With great regret, I have to tell you that your friend is very ill.*
▶ grief, sadness, sorrow, sympathy

regret *VERB*
1 *She regrets losing her temper.*
▶ be sorry, feel regret, repent, reproach yourself
2 *Everyone regretted his death.*
▶ feel sad about, grieve, lament, mourn

A B C D E F G H I J K L M N O P Q R S T U V W X Y Z

regretful *ADJECTIVE*
1 *She gave him a regretful smile and said sorry.*
► apologetic, ashamed, conscience-stricken, penitent, remorseful, repentant, sad
AN OPPOSITE IS unrepentant
2 *He said a regretful goodbye to his friends.*
► melancholy, reluctant, sad, sorrowful, wistful
AN OPPOSITE IS happy

regrettable *ADJECTIVE*
It was a regrettable accident.
► deplorable, disgraceful, distressing, lamentable, shameful, shocking, undesirable, unfortunate, unlucky
AN OPPOSITE IS fortunate

regular *ADJECTIVE*
1 *You ought to have meals at regular times.*
► evenly spaced, fixed, predictable
▷ Words to describe various regular intervals are **daily**, **hourly**, **monthly**, **weekly**, **yearly**.
2 *She has beautiful regular teeth.*
► even, symmetrical
AN OPPOSITE IS uneven
3 *The drummer kept up a regular rhythm.*
► consistent, constant, measured, repeated, steady, uniform, unvarying
AN OPPOSITE IS erratic
4 *They went home by their regular route.*
► accustomed, customary, familiar, habitual, normal, ordinary, routine, usual
AN OPPOSITE IS unusual
5 *He filled out the form in the regular way.*
► common, conventional, correct, official, proper, standard, traditional
AN OPPOSITE IS unusual
6 *I'm a regular customer at the sweet shop.*
► dependable, faithful, frequent, reliable
AN OPPOSITE IS irregular or abnormal

regulate *VERB*
1 *Just turn the knob to regulate the temperature.*
► adjust, alter, change, get right, vary
2 *The council has a new scheme to regulate the traffic.*
► control, direct, govern, limit, manage, organize, restrict, supervise

regulation *NOUN*
The traffic regulations should be obeyed.
► law, requirement, restriction, rule
▷ A regulation which applies in a particular area is a **by-law**. A regulation imposed on you by someone of higher rank is a **decree** or **order**.

rehearsal *NOUN*
They had a rehearsal for the play.
► practice, preparation, (*informal*) try-out

rehearse *VERB*
They had to rehearse the scene all over again.
► go over, practise, try out

reign *VERB*
Which British monarch reigned the longest?
► be king or queen, be on the throne, govern, have power, rule

reinforce *VERB*
1 *He put up a concrete post to reinforce the fence.*
► prop up, strengthen, support
2 *They sent another hundred soldiers to reinforce the army.*
► add to, assist, back up, help

reinforcements *PLURAL NOUN*
The officer asked headquarters to send reinforcements.
► (*informal*) back-up, help, reserves, support

reject *VERB*
1 *She rejected his invitation.*
► decline, refuse, say no to, turn down, veto
2 *Shops reject poor quality goods.*
► discard, eliminate, get rid of, scrap, send back, throw away, throw out
AN OPPOSITE IS accept

rejoice *VERB*
They rejoiced when their team won the cup.
► be happy, celebrate, delight, exult
AN OPPOSITE IS grieve

relate *VERB*
1 *Doctors relate all these illnesses to poor diet.*
► associate, compare, connect, link
2 *The TV programme related to the music industry.*
► be relevant, concern, refer
3 *She related her story.*
► describe, narrate, report on, tell

relation *NOUN*
FOR YOUR VARIOUS RELATIONS SEE **family**

relationship *NOUN*
1 *Is there a relationship between wealth and happiness?*
▸ association, bond, connection, link
▹ The relationship between two numbers is a **ratio**.
2 *The twins have a close relationship.*
▸ attachment, friendship, understanding
3 *Are those two having a relationship?*
▸ love affair, romance

relative *NOUN*
FOR YOUR VARIOUS RELATIVES SEE **family**

relative *ADJECTIVE*
1 *The police gathered evidence relative to the crime.*
▸ allied, associated (with), connected (with), related, relevant
AN OPPOSITE IS irrelevant
2 *They live in relative comfort.*
▸ comparative

relax *VERB*
1 *They did some exercises to relax their cramped muscles.*
▸ ease, loosen
AN OPPOSITE IS tighten
2 *Don't relax your efforts!*
▸ lessen, reduce
AN OPPOSITE IS increase
3 *She likes to relax in front of the TV.*
▸ be relaxed, get comfortable, let up, rest, (*informal*) unwind

relaxation *NOUN*
People need some relaxation after work.
▸ informality, leisure, peace and quiet, recreation, relaxing, rest, tranquillity
AN OPPOSITE IS tension

relaxed *ADJECTIVE*
They enjoyed the relaxed atmosphere of the party.
▸ calm, carefree, casual, comfortable, contented, cosy, easygoing, friendly, good-humoured, happy, informal, leisurely, light-hearted, peaceful, restful, serene, tranquil, unhurried, untroubled
AN OPPOSITE IS tense

relay *VERB*
He relayed the information to the police.
▸ communicate, pass on, send out, spread, transmit

relay *NOUN*
1 *The rescuers worked in relays.*
▸ shift, turn
2 *There will be a live relay from the pop concert on TV.*
▸ broadcast, programme, transmission

release *VERB*
1 *The prisoners were released early.*
▸ allow out, discharge, free, let go, liberate, rescue, save, set free
▹ To release slaves is to **emancipate** them.
AN OPPOSITE IS imprison
2 *The dog was tied up — who released him?*
▸ let loose, set loose, unfasten, unleash, untie
3 *The group were about to release their new CD.*
▸ issue, make available, publish, send out

relegate *VERB*
At the end of the season the team was relegated to a lower division.
▸ demote, put down

relent *VERB*
She relented and let them off their punishment.
▸ be lenient, give in, show pity, soften, weaken, yield

relentless *ADJECTIVE*
1 *The guns continued a relentless bombardment.*
▸ cruel, fierce, merciless, pitiless, remorseless, ruthless, unfeeling
2 *They were sick of the relentless rain.*
▸ ceaseless, constant, continual, continuous, everlasting, incessant, never-ending, perpetual, persistent, unceasing

relevant *ADJECTIVE*
1 *The arguments she used weren't relevant to the case.*
▸ applicable, appropriate, connected, linked, related, significant, suitable
2 *Don't interrupt unless your comments are relevant.*
▸ to the point
AN OPPOSITE IS irrelevant

reliable *ADJECTIVE*
1 *She's a reliable friend.*
▸ constant, dependable, devoted, faithful, loyal, responsible, trustworthy
2 *I wish the weather was more reliable.*
▸ certain, consistent, predictable
3 *They have a reliable water supply.*
▸ regular, safe, sound, steady, sure
AN OPPOSITE IS unreliable

A B C D E F G H I J K L M N O P Q **R** S T U V W X Y Z

relic *NOUN*
The museum contains interesting relics from the past.
▸ reminder, souvenir, survival

relief *NOUN*
The pills gave some relief from the pain.
▸ comfort, ease, help, relaxation, release, rest

relieve *VERB*
The doctor said the pills would relieve the pain.
▸ calm, comfort, diminish, ease, help, lessen, lighten, make less, moderate, reduce, relax, soothe
AN OPPOSITE IS intensify

religion *NOUN*
People from all religions went to the service.
▸ belief, creed, cult, doctrine, faith, sect
SOME OF THE PRINCIPAL RELIGIONS OF THE WORLD
Buddhism, Christianity, Hinduism, Islam, Judaism, Shintoism, Sikhism, Taoism, Zen
▹ The study of religion is divinity or scripture or theology.

religious *ADJECTIVE*
1 *They went to a religious service.*
▸ divine, holy, sacred
2 *He's very religious.*
▸ pious, reverent, spiritual

reluctant *ADJECTIVE*
He was reluctant to help.
▸ grudging, half-hearted, hesitant, uncooperative, unenthusiastic, unhelpful, unwilling
AN OPPOSITE IS eager

rely *VERB*
You can rely on him.
▸ bank on, count on, depend on, have confidence in, trust

remain *VERB*
1 *Fog remained on the motorway all day.*
▸ continue, (*informal*) hang about, linger, stay
2 *Please remain as you are.*
▸ carry on, continue, keep on, stay, wait
3 *Little remained of the house after the fire.*
▸ be left, survive

remainder *NOUN*
Keep the remainder of the food for later.
▸ remains, remnants, rest, surplus

remains *PLURAL NOUN*
He cleared away the remains of the party.
▸ debris, fragments, odds and ends, remnants, scraps, traces
▹ The remains at the bottom of a cup are dregs. Remains of food after a meal are leftovers. The remains of a building or wall, etc., which has collapsed are rubble. Remains still standing after a building has collapsed are ruins. The remains of a crashed aircraft, ship, or vehicle are wreckage. The remains of a dead person are ashes or bones or the corpse. The remains of a dead animal are the carcass. Historic remains are relics or our heritage.

remark *VERB*
He remarked that it was a nice day.
▸ comment, declare, mention, note, observe, say, state

remark *NOUN*
They exchanged a few remarks about the weather.
▸ comment, mention, observation, statement, thought, word

remarkable *ADJECTIVE*
To win the competition three years running is a remarkable achievement.
▸ amazing, exceptional, extraordinary, important, impressive, interesting, notable, out of the ordinary, outstanding, phenomenal, special, strange, striking, surprising, tremendous, uncommon, unusual, wonderful
AN OPPOSITE IS ordinary

remedy *NOUN*
1 *There is no known remedy for his illness.*
▸ cure, medicine, relief, therapy, treatment
▹ A remedy to act against a poison is an antidote.
2 *It's a big problem, and I don't know the remedy.*
▸ answer, solution

remember *VERB*
1 *She didn't remember his name.*
▸ have a memory of, recall, recognize, recollect
2 *He was trying to remember his lines for the play.*
▸ get off by heart, keep in mind, learn, memorize
AN OPPOSITE IS forget
3 *She likes to remember the old days.*
▸ be nostalgic about, reminisce about, tell stories about, think back to

remind *VERB*
Remind me to buy some potatoes.
▶ jog your memory, prompt

reminder *NOUN*
1 *They sent him a reminder to pay the bill.*
▶ cue, hint, prompt
2 *He bought the picture as a reminder of his holidays.*
▶ relic, souvenir

reminisce *VERB*
to reminisce about *He likes to reminisce about his school days.*
▶ be nostalgic about, recall, remember, tell stories about, think back to

reminiscence *NOUN*
He told us his reminiscences of his childhood.
▶ memory, recollection

remnants *PLURAL NOUN*
They spent ages clearing up the remnants of the party.
▶ debris, fragments, odds and ends, remains, scraps, traces

remorse *NOUN*
He showed no remorse for what he'd done.
▶ grief, guilt, penitence, pricking of conscience, regret, repentance, sadness, shame, sorrow

remorseful *ADJECTIVE*
She seemed remorseful about her actions.
▶ apologetic, ashamed, conscience-stricken, penitent, regretful, repentant, sorry
AN OPPOSITE IS unrepentant

remorseless *ADJECTIVE*
They continued their remorseless bombardment of the town.
▶ constant, continual, continuous, cruel, fierce, incessant, merciless, never-ending, perpetual, persistent, pitiless, relentless, ruthless, unceasing, unfeeling

remote *ADJECTIVE*
1 *He liked to travel to remote parts of the world.*
▶ distant, faraway, inaccessible, isolated, lonely, out of reach, out of the way, unfrequented
AN OPPOSITE IS accessible
2 *The chances of him winning are remote.*
▶ improbable, negligible, poor, slender, slight, small, unlikely
AN OPPOSITE IS likely

removal *NOUN*
1 *The dentist said the removal of the tooth would be painless.*
▶ extraction, taking out
2 *The police were called to deal with the removal of the intruders.*
▶ dismissal, ejection, expulsion

remove *VERB*
1 *Please remove your rubbish.*
▶ clear away, take away
2 *The police removed the people who were causing trouble.*
▶ eject, expel, (*informal*) kick out, send away, throw out, turn out
▷ To remove people from a house where they are living is to **evict** them. To remove a monarch from the throne is to **depose** him or her.
3 *They removed the rude words from the film.*
▶ censor, cut out, delete, eliminate, erase, get rid of
4 *The men removed the furniture to her new house.*
▶ move, transfer, transport
5 *The dentist removed my bad tooth.*
▶ draw out, extract, pull out, take out, (*informal*) whip out
6 *She removed her coat.*
▶ dispense with, peel off, strip off, take off

render *VERB*
1 *The shock rendered her speechless.*
▶ leave, make
2 *She rendered him a great service.*
▶ give, provide

rendezvous *NOUN*
1 *They arranged a rendezvous for six o'clock.*
▶ appointment, engagement, meeting
▷ A rendezvous with your boyfriend or girlfriend is a **date**.
2 *Their usual rendezvous is by the swings in the park.*
▶ meeting place

renew *VERB*
VARIOUS WAYS TO RENEW THINGS
bring up to date, (*informal*) do up, mend, modernize, overhaul, recondition, redecorate, redesign, redo, refit, remake, renovate, repaint, repair, replace, replenish, restore, resume, resurrect, revitalize, revive, touch up, update

renown *NOUN*
He achieved great renown for his daring exploits.
▸ distinction, eminence, fame, glory, honour, prestige, prominence

renowned *ADJECTIVE*
The shop is renowned for its pork pies.
▸ celebrated, distinguished, famous, notable, outstanding, prominent, well known
AN OPPOSITE IS unknown

rent *VERB*
They rented a van to move their things.
▸ charter, hire
to rent something out *The garage down the road rents out various vehicles.*
▸ lease, let

repair *VERB*
1 *It took them a week to repair the damaged car.*
▸ fix, mend, overhaul, patch up, put right, service
2 *He tried to repair the hole in his jeans.*
▸ darn, patch, sew up

repay *VERB*
They repaid her expenses.
▸ pay back, refund
▹ To pay someone money for damage you have done is to compensate them.

repeat *VERB*
1 *She had to repeat her story all over again.*
▸ retell, say again
2 *He repeated everything she said.*
▸ echo, quote, tell
3 *They had to repeat the exercise.*
▸ do again, redo
4 *That shot was a fluke — he couldn't repeat it.*
▸ copy, duplicate, reproduce

repeat *NOUN*
Their new song is really just a repeat of their last one.
▸ copy, duplicate, replica, repetition

repeatedly *ADVERB*
He was warned repeatedly about his behaviour.
▸ again and again, constantly, continually, frequently, often, persistently, regularly, time after time

repel *VERB*
1 *The soldiers managed to repel the attack.*
▸ drive off, fend off, fight off, force away, hold off, push away, resist, ward off
2 *They were repelled by his bad language.*
▸ disgust, horrify, offend, revolt, sicken, (*slang*) turn you off

repellent *ADJECTIVE*
She found him quite repellent.
▸ disgusting, foul, hateful, hideous, horrible, loathsome, objectionable, offensive, repulsive, revolting, sickening, vile
AN OPPOSITE IS attractive

repent *VERB*
Do you truly repent your sins?
▸ be repentant about, regret, reproach yourself for

repentance *NOUN*
She showed genuine repentance for her sins.
▸ guilt, penitence, regret, remorse, sorrow

repentant *ADJECTIVE*
She was repentant when she saw what she'd done.
▸ apologetic, ashamed, conscience-stricken, penitent, regretful, remorseful, sorry
AN OPPOSITE IS unrepentant

repetitive *ADJECTIVE*
The work was very repetitive.
▸ boring, monotonous, tedious

replace *VERB*
1 *He replaced the books on the shelf.*
▸ put back, restore (to), return (to)
2 *Who will replace the captain when he leaves?*
▸ be a substitute for, come after, follow, succeed, take over from, take the place of
3 *They had to replace the tyres on the car.*
▸ change, renew

replacement *NOUN*
They had to find a replacement for the injured player.
▸ (*informal*) stand-in, substitute
▹ Someone who replaces an actor who is ill, etc., is an **understudy**.

replica *NOUN*
1 *The picture is a replica of a famous painting.*
▸ copy, duplicate, reproduction
▹ An exact copy of a document is a **facsimile**.
2 *They saw a replica of a space module.*
▸ model, reconstruction

reply *NOUN*
She didn't get a reply to her letter.
▸ acknowledgement, answer, reaction, response
▹ An angry reply is a **retort**.

reply *VERB*
to reply to *It took him a long time to reply to her letter.*
▸ acknowledge, answer, give a reply to, react to, respond to

report *VERB*
1 *The newspapers reported what happened.*
▸ announce, declare, describe, give an account of, proclaim, publish, record, state, tell
2 *He was told to report to reception when he arrived.*
▸ announce yourself, introduce yourself, make yourself known, present yourself
3 *She reported him to the police.*
▸ complain about, denounce, inform against, tell of

report *NOUN*
1 *There was a report in the paper about the crash.*
▸ account, article, description, news, record, story
2 *He was startled by the report of the gun.*
▸ bang, blast, crack, detonation, noise

reporter *NOUN*
A TV reporter interviewed them about the accident they witnessed.
▸ correspondent, journalist

represent *VERB*
1 *The picture represents a hunting scene.*
▸ act out, depict, describe, illustrate, picture, portray, show
▹ You can represent things by **drawing** or **painting** them.
2 *Santa Claus represents the spirit of Christmas.*
▸ stand for, symbolize
3 *He appointed a lawyer to represent him.*
▸ speak for

representation *NOUN*
There was a representation of Santa Claus at the side of the stage.
▸ image, likeness, model, picture, portrait, portrayal

repress *VERB*
1 *She always repressed her feelings.*
▸ bottle up, control, curb, restrain, stifle, suppress
AN OPPOSITE IS express
2 *The people were repressed by the government.*
▸ control, keep down, oppress

repressive *ADJECTIVE*
The people eventually rebelled against the repressive government.
▸ cruel, dictatorial, harsh, oppressive, severe, totalitarian, tyrannical, undemocratic
AN OPPOSITE IS liberal

reprieve *VERB*
The condemned man was reprieved only minutes before the execution.
▸ let off, pardon, set free, spare

reprimand *VERB*
He reprimanded them for their bad behaviour.
▸ condemn, criticize, reproach, scold, tell off, (*informal*) tick off
AN OPPOSITE IS praise

reprisal *NOUN*
She refused to name the criminals because she feared reprisals.
▸ revenge, vengeance

reproach *VERB*
She reproached him for letting her down.
▸ criticize, find fault with, reprimand, scold, show disapproval of, (*informal*) tell off, (*informal*) tick off
AN OPPOSITE IS praise

A B C D E F G H I J K L M N O P Q R S T U V W X Y Z

reproduce *VERB*
1 *The parrot can reproduce human voices.*
▸ imitate, mimic, simulate
2 *The photocopier will reproduce as many copies as you want.*
▸ copy, duplicate, photocopy, print, reprint
3 *Mice reproduce amazingly quickly.*
▸ breed, increase, multiply, produce offspring
▹ Fish reproduce by **spawning**. To reproduce plants is to **propagate** them. To reproduce exact copies of living things is to **clone** them.

reproduction *NOUN*
1 *Nature has devised many ways of reproduction.*
▹ The reproduction of animals is **breeding**. The reproduction of plants is **propagation**. The reproduction of exact copies of living things is **cloning**.
2 *Is that an original painting or a reproduction?*
▸ copy, duplicate, imitation, likeness, print, replica
▹ A reproduction of something which is intended to deceive people is a **fake** or **forgery**. An exact reproduction of a document is a **facsimile**.

reptile *NOUN*
SOME REPTILES
alligator, basilisk, chameleon, crocodile, lizard, salamander, snake, tortoise, turtle
FOR OTHER ANIMALS SEE **animal**

repulsive *ADJECTIVE*
They were put off by the animal's repulsive appearance.
▸ disgusting, foul, hateful, hideous, horrible, loathsome, objectionable, offensive, repellent, revolting, sickening, vile
AN OPPOSITE IS attractive

reputation *NOUN*
His reputation spread throughout the world.
▸ distinction, eminence, fame, name, prestige, renown

request *VERB*
They requested his help.
▸ appeal for, apply for, ask for, beg for, call for, entreat, implore, invite, pray for, seek

request *NOUN*
He wouldn't listen to their request for help.
▸ appeal, call, cry, demand, entreaty, plea
▹ A request for a job, etc., is an **application**. A request signed by a lot of people is a **petition**.

require *VERB*
1 *They require three runs to win.*
▸ be short of, lack, need, want
2 *The official required her to show her passport.*
▸ command, compel, direct, force, instruct, oblige, order, request

required *ADJECTIVE*
He didn't have the required documents.
▸ compulsory, essential, indispensable, necessary, needed, obligatory
AN OPPOSITE IS optional

rescue *VERB*
1 *The police rescued the hostages.*
▸ free, liberate, release, save, set free
▹ To rescue someone by paying money is to **ransom** them.
2 *The passengers had no time to rescue their belongings from the sinking ship.*
▸ recover, retrieve, salvage

research *NOUN*
Their research showed that many cars carry only one person.
▸ analysis, inquiry, investigation, probe, study

resemblance *NOUN*
It's easy to see the resemblance between the two sisters.
▸ closeness, likeness, similarity
AN OPPOSITE IS difference

resemble *VERB*
He resembled his father.
▸ be similar to, look like, (*informal*) take after

resent *VERB*
He resented her success.
▸ be angry about, begrudge, be resentful about, envy, grudge, object to, take exception to

resentful *ADJECTIVE*
She felt resentful about his interference.
▸ angry, annoyed, bitter, envious, grudging, indignant, jealous, offended, spiteful, upset, vexed

resentment *NOUN*
They felt a lot of resentment about the way they had been treated.
▸ anger, annoyance, bitterness, hatred, indignation, spite, unfriendliness, vexation

reservation *NOUN*
1 *They visited a wildlife reservation.*
▸ game park, reserve, safari park, sanctuary
2 *She had reservations about whether the plan would work.*
▸ doubt, hesitation
▹ If you have reservations about something, you are sceptical about it.

reserve *VERB*
1 *She decided to reserve some food for later.*
▸ hoard, hold back, keep, preserve, put aside, retain, save, set aside, stockpile, store up
2 *They had to reserve their seats on the train.*
▸ bag, book, order, pay for, secure

reserve *NOUN*
1 *The climbers kept a reserve of food in their base camp.*
▸ hoard, stock, stockpile, store, supply
▹ A reserve of money is a fund or savings.
2 *They put him down as a reserve for Saturday's game.*
▸ replacement, standby, substitute
▹ Someone who can take the place of an actor is an understudy. Someone who can take the place of a person in charge of something is a deputy. Soldiers brought in to help other soldiers are reinforcements.
3 *She saw many kinds of animal at the wildlife reserve.*
▸ game park, reservation, safari park, sanctuary

reserved *ADJECTIVE*
1 *These seats are reserved.*
▸ bagged, booked, ordered, paid for
2 *She is too reserved to speak up for herself.*
▸ bashful, coy, modest, quiet, retiring, secretive, self-conscious, shy, timid

reside *VERB*
to reside in *Most of the students reside in college.*
▸ dwell in, inhabit, live in, occupy

residence *NOUN*
The palace was the official residence of the head of state.
▸ (*old use*) abode, dwelling, home

resident *NOUN*
The local residents got together to set up a neighbourhood watch scheme.
▸ citizen, inhabitant
▹ A temporary resident in a hotel, apartment, etc., is a guest, lodger, occupant, tenant, or visitor.

resign *VERB*
to resign from something *She's just resigned from the committee.*
▸ give up, leave, pull out of, (*informal*) quit, withdraw from
▹ When a monarch resigns from the throne, he or she abdicates.
to resign yourself to something *When the bus broke down, I had to resign myself to being late.*
▸ accept, be patient about, put up with, tolerate

resist *VERB*
1 *They were too weak to resist an enemy attack.*
▸ defend yourself against, defy, oppose, stand up to, try to stop, withstand
2 *Sometimes it's hard to resist temptation.*
▸ avoid, deal with, fight
AN OPPOSITE IS surrender to

resistance *NOUN*
Their resistance crumbled when they ran out of ammunition.
▸ defence, fighting, opposition

resolute *ADJECTIVE*
Her voice sounded calm but resolute.
▸ bold, confident, courageous, decisive, determined, firm, strong-minded
▹ If you are resolute in a selfish or unhelpful way, you are obstinate or stubborn.
AN OPPOSITE IS hesitant

resolution *NOUN*
1 *They showed great resolution in the face of danger.*
▸ boldness, courage, firmness, perseverance, will-power
2 *We made a resolution to work harder.*
▸ commitment, decision, promise

A B C D E F G H I J K L M N O P Q **R** S T U V W X Y Z

resolve *VERB*
1 *We resolved to work harder.*
▸ agree, decide, determine, make a firm decision, promise, undertake
2 *They hoped the crisis could be resolved.*
▸ end, overcome, settle, sort out

resort *NOUN*
1 *We stayed in a resort on the coast.*
▸ holiday town
2 *As a last resort, we could always walk.*
▸ alternative, course of action, option

resort *VERB*
He didn't want to resort to violence.
▸ adopt, fall back on, make use of, rely on, start using, use

resound *VERB*
Our voices resounded in the cave.
▸ boom, echo

resources *PLURAL NOUN*
1 *We should all try to use natural resources wisely.*
▸ materials, raw materials, reserves
2 *He started a business with his own resources.*
▸ assets, capital, funds, money, riches, wealth

respect *NOUN*
1 *His colleagues had the deepest respect for him.*
▸ admiration, honour, love, regard, reverence
2 *Have some respect for other people's feelings.*
▸ concern, consideration, sympathy, thought
3 *In some respects, she's a better player than I am.*
▸ aspect, characteristic, detail, feature, particular, point, way

respect *VERB*
Everyone respects her for her courage.
▸ admire, esteem, honour, revere, think well of, value
AN OPPOSITE IS scorn

respectable *ADJECTIVE*
1 *He came from a very respectable family.*
▸ decent, honest, honourable, upright, worthy
2 *Could you change into something a bit more respectable?*
▸ clean, proper, suitable
3 *He earns a respectable income.*
▸ adequate, considerable, reasonable, satisfactory, sizeable, substantial, tolerable

respectful *ADJECTIVE*
1 *He gave us a respectful greeting.*
▸ civil, courteous, polite
AN OPPOSITE IS rude
2 *People expect respectful behaviour in a place of worship.*
▸ considerate, humble, proper, reverent
AN OPPOSITE IS disrespectful

respective *ADJECTIVE*
We all returned to our respective homes.
▸ individual, own, particular, personal, separate, specific

respond *VERB*
to respond to *He didn't respond to my question.*
▸ acknowledge, answer, react to, reply to

response *NOUN*
Did you get a response to your letter?
▸ acknowledgement, answer, reaction, reply
▹ An angry response is a retort. A response you may get to something you do for people is feedback.

responsible *ADJECTIVE*
1 *Parents are legally responsible for their children.*
▸ in charge
AN OPPOSITE IS not responsible
2 *He's a very responsible sort of person.*
▸ careful, conscientious, dependable, dutiful, honest, law-abiding, reliable, sensible, trustworthy
AN OPPOSITE IS irresponsible
3 *Looking after people's money is a responsible job.*
▸ important, serious
4 *I was responsible for the damage.*
▸ guilty (of), to blame

rest *NOUN*
1 *Let's have a rest.*
▸ break, breather, breathing-space, holiday, interlude, intermission, interval, lie-down, lull, nap, pause
2 *The doctor said the patient needed complete rest.*
▸ ease, idleness, leisure, quiet, relaxation, time off
3 *I made a rest for my telescope.*
▸ base, prop, stand, support
the rest *Take a few sweets now, but leave the rest for later.*
▸ the others, the remains, the remnants, the remainder, the surplus

rest *VERB*
1 *I think we should stop and rest for a while.*
▸ doze, have a rest, lie down, relax, sleep
2 *Rest the ladder against the wall.*
▸ lean, place, prop, stand, support

restaurant *NOUN*
VARIOUS PLACES WHERE YOU CAN BUY A MEAL AND EAT IT
buffet, burger bar, café, cafeteria, canteen, carvery, diner, dining room, grill, pizzeria, pub, snack bar, steakhouse
▹ A French-style restaurant is a bistro. A Greek-style restaurant is a taverna. An Italian-style restaurant is a trattoria.

restful *ADJECTIVE*
They spent a restful Sunday morning reading the papers.
▸ calm, comfortable, leisurely, peaceful, quiet, relaxing, soothing, tranquil, undisturbed, untroubled
AN OPPOSITE IS exhausting

restless *ADJECTIVE*
1 *The animals became restless during the storm.*
▸ agitated, anxious, edgy, excitable, fidgety, impatient, jumpy, nervous
AN OPPOSITE IS relaxed
2 *I'm tired — I had a restless night.*
▸ disturbed, interrupted, sleepless, troubled, uncomfortable, unsettled
AN OPPOSITE IS restful

restore *VERB*
1 *Please restore the book to its proper place on the shelf.*
▸ put back, replace, return
2 *My uncle loves to restore old cars.*
▸ clean up, (*informal*) fix, mend, rebuild, renew, repair, touch up
3 *The council is going to restore our local train service.*
▸ bring back
▹ To restore someone to health is to cure them.

restrain *VERB*
1 *Some members of the crowd had to be restrained by police.*
▸ control, keep back, keep under control, repress, restrict, subdue, tie up
THINGS USED TO RESTRAIN PEOPLE OR ANIMALS
bridle, chains, fetters, handcuffs, harness, irons, lead or leash, muzzle, reins, ropes
2 *She tried to restrain her anger.*
▸ control, curb, govern, stifle, suppress

restrict *VERB*
1 *The new law restricts the sale of fireworks.*
▸ control, limit, regulate
2 *The warders were ordered to restrict the prisoners to their cells.*
▸ confine, enclose (in), imprison (in), keep (in), restrain (in), shut (in)

restriction *NOUN*
1 *There are certain restrictions we must all obey.*
▸ check, control, curb, limitation, regulation, restraint, rule
2 *They imposed a speed restriction through the village.*
▸ ban, limit

result *NOUN*
1 *The water shortage is a result of the long drought.*
▸ consequence, effect, outcome, sequel (to), upshot
▹ The result of a game is the score. The result of a trial is the verdict.
2 *If you multiply 9 by 12, what is the result?*
▸ answer, product

result *VERB*
The road was closed to traffic, and chaos resulted.
▸ come about, develop, emerge, ensue, follow, happen, occur, take place, turn out
to result in *The accident resulted in the death of two pedestrians.*
▸ bring about, cause, develop into, give rise to, lead to, provoke

resume *VERB*
We'll resume work after lunch.
▸ begin again, carry on, continue, proceed with, recommence, restart, start again

resuscitate *VERB*
The doctors tried to resuscitate him.
▸ bring back to life, restore, revive

retain *VERB*
1 *Please retain your ticket.*
▸ (*informal*) hang on to, hold on to, keep, preserve, reserve, save
AN OPPOSITE IS surrender
2 *They built a dam to retain water.*
▸ hold back, keep in
AN OPPOSITE IS release

retire *VERB*
1 *He's hoping to retire next year.*
▸ finish working, give up work, leave your job, stop working
▹ To leave your job voluntarily is to **resign**.
2 *The attack failed and the soldiers had to retire.*
▸ give up, leave, quit, withdraw

retiring *ADJECTIVE*
As a child, he was very retiring.
▸ bashful, coy, quiet, reserved, shy, timid

retort *VERB*
'There's no need to be rude!' she retorted angrily.
▸ answer, react, reply, respond

retort *NOUN*
His sharp retort upset her.
▸ answer, reaction, reply, response

retrace *VERB*
to retrace your steps *The bridge had collapsed, so we had to retrace our steps.*
▸ go back, return

retreat *VERB*
1 *The army retreated.*
▸ back away, go away, leave, move back, retire, withdraw
▹ To retreat in a shameful way is to **run away**.
2 *The flood began to retreat when the rains stopped.*
▸ disappear, go down, recede, shrink
▹ When the tide retreats, it **ebbs**.

retrieve *VERB*
I was sent to retrieve the ball from next door's garden.
▸ fetch back, find, get back, recover, rescue, track down

return *VERB*
1 *I'll see you when you return.*
▸ come back, get back, reappear
2 *You'll have to return the way you came.*
▸ go back, retrace your steps
3 *Return the books to the shelf.*
▸ put back, replace, restore
4 *Faulty goods may be returned to the shop.*
▸ send back, take back
5 *Please return the money I lent you.*
▸ give back, refund, repay
6 *The illness may return.*
▸ happen again, recur

return *NOUN*
1 *We look forward to your return.*
▸ arrival, reappearance
2 *He's hoping for a good return from his investment.*
▸ gain, income, interest, profit

reveal *VERB*
1 *He decided to reveal the truth.*
▸ announce, communicate, confess, declare, disclose, make known, proclaim, publish, tell
▹ To reveal secret information in a sly way is to **leak** it.
2 *Next week the manufacturer will reveal a new design.*
▸ display, exhibit, show, unveil
3 *The nurse took off the bandage to reveal the wound.*
▸ expose, uncover
AN OPPOSITE IS **hide**

revenge *NOUN*
The assassination was an act of revenge.
▸ reprisal, vengeance
to take revenge on someone *He declared that he would take revenge on them all.*
▸ get even with, (*informal*) get your own back on, repay

revere *VERB*
He was greatly revered by his fellow poets.
▸ admire, adore, honour, idolize, respect, value, worship
AN OPPOSITE IS **despise**

reverence *NOUN*
He had a deep reverence for the traditions of the church.
▸ admiration, devotion, respect

reverent *ADJECTIVE*
The worshippers knelt in reverent silence.
▸ adoring, pious, respectful, solemn
AN OPPOSITE IS **irreverent**

reverse *NOUN*
He says one thing and does the reverse.
▸ contrary, converse, opposite

reverse *VERB*
1 *We decided to reverse the order in which we did things.*
▸ change, invert, turn round
2 *The driver tried to reverse into the parking space.*
▸ back, drive backwards, go backwards

review *NOUN*

1 *The council undertook a review of the town's traffic problems.*
▸ examination, inspection, study, survey
2 *We had to write reviews of our favourite books.*
▸ appraisal, criticism

review *VERB*

1 *The judge began to review the evidence.*
▸ appraise, assess, consider, evaluate, examine, go over, scrutinize, study, survey, weigh up
2 *He reviewed the play for the Sunday paper.*
▸ criticize, write a review of

revise *VERB*

1 *We revised the work we did last term.*
▸ go over, learn, review, study
2 *The new evidence forced me to revise my opinion.*
▸ alter, change, modify, reconsider, update
3 *The articles were revised before being published.*
▸ correct, edit, improve, rewrite

revive *VERB*

1 *Many songs from the seventies have been revived.*
▸ bring back
2 *He soon revived after the anaesthetic.*
▸ awaken, come back to life, come round, come to, rally, recover, wake
3 *A cold drink will revive you.*
▸ bring back to life, freshen up, invigorate, refresh, restore, wake up

revolt *VERB*

1 *The people revolted against the military dictatorship.*
▸ rebel, riot, rise up
▹ To revolt on a ship is to **mutiny**.
2 *Cruelty to animals revolted her.*
▸ appal, disgust, horrify, repel, sicken

revolting *ADJECTIVE*

What is that revolting smell?
▸ appalling, disgusting, foul, horrible, loathsome, nasty, offensive, repulsive, sickening, unpleasant
AN OPPOSITE IS attractive or pleasant

revolution *NOUN*

1 *The revolution brought in a new government.*
▸ civil war, rebellion, revolt, uprising
2 *Computers brought about a revolution in the way we do things.*
▸ change, transformation, (*informal*) U-turn
3 *One revolution of the earth takes 24 hours.*
▸ rotation, turn

revolutionary *ADJECTIVE*

He's full of revolutionary and exciting ideas.
▸ innovative, new, radical, (*informal*) unheard of
AN OPPOSITE IS conservative

revolutionize *VERB*

Computers have revolutionized the way people do business.
▸ change completely, transform

revolve *VERB*

The earth revolves once every 24 hours.
▸ rotate, turn
▹ To revolve quickly is to **spin** or **whirl**. To move round something is to **circle** or **orbit** it.

reward *NOUN*

▹ A reward for hard work is a **bonus** on top of your wages. A reward for bravery is a **decoration** or **medal**. A reward for winning something is an **award** or **prize**.
AN OPPOSITE IS punishment

reward *VERB*

She was generously rewarded for her work.
▸ compensate, repay
AN OPPOSITE IS punish

rewarding *ADJECTIVE*

They say that nursing is a rewarding job.
▸ pleasing, satisfying, worthwhile
AN OPPOSITE IS thankless

rhyme *NOUN*

She sang her sister little rhymes.
▸ poem, verse

rhythm *NOUN*

She could hear the rhythm of his heartbeat.
▸ beat, pulse
▹ The speed or type of rhythm of a piece of music is the **tempo**. The type of rhythm of a piece of poetry is its **metre**.

rhythmic *ADJECTIVE*
The rhythmic beat of the music makes you want to dance.
▸ rhythmical, regular, repeated, steady, throbbing

ribbon *NOUN*
She tied a red velvet ribbon in her hair.
▸ band, braid, strip

rich *ADJECTIVE*
1 *They must be rich to live in a huge house like that.*
▸ affluent, prosperous, wealthy, well-off
AN OPPOSITE IS poor
2 *The rooms were full of rich furnishings.*
▸ costly, elaborate, expensive, lavish, luxurious, splendid, valuable
3 *She wore a dress of a rich red colour.*
▸ deep, intense, strong, vivid
4 *This cake is a bit too rich for me.*
▸ creamy, fat, fattening, fatty

riches *PLURAL NOUN*
They acquired riches beyond their wildest dreams.
▸ affluence, fortune, prosperity, wealth

richly *ADVERB*
1 *The palace was richly furnished.*
▸ elaborately, expensively, lavishly, luxuriously
2 *They richly deserved their punishment.*
▸ absolutely, completely, thoroughly

rickety *ADJECTIVE*
Take care — that ladder looks rickety.
▸ decrepit, flimsy, shaky, unsteady, wobbly
AN OPPOSITE IS solid

ricochet *VERB*
The bullet ricocheted off the wall.
▸ bounce, rebound

rid *VERB*
The new vaccine may rid the world of this disease.
▸ clear, empty, free, purge
to get rid of **1** *I managed to get rid of him at last.*
▸ eject, evict, expel, remove, throw out
2 *He decided to get rid of his old car.*
▸ dispose of, dump, scrap, throw away

riddle *NOUN*
The police have not yet solved the riddle of her death.
▸ conundrum, mystery, problem, puzzle, question

ride *VERB*
Can you ride a horse?
▸ control, handle, manage, sit on

ride *NOUN*
He took us for a ride in his new car.
▸ drive, journey, outing, trip

ridicule *VERB*
Everyone ridiculed me because of my novel ideas.
▸ be sarcastic or satirical about, deride, jeer at, joke about, laugh at, make fun of, make jokes about, mock, scoff at, (*informal*) send up, sneer at, taunt, tease

ridiculous *ADJECTIVE*
1 *He looks ridiculous in that hat.*
▸ absurd, daft, funny, foolish, laughable, silly, stupid
2 *It was ridiculous to go out in that weather.*
▸ absurd, (*informal*) crazy, (*informal*) daft, foolish, ludicrous, senseless, silly, stupid, unreasonable
AN OPPOSITE IS sensible

right *ADJECTIVE*
1 *Most people write with their right hand.*
AN OPPOSITE IS left
▷ The right side of a ship when you face the bow is the **starboard** side.
2 *Put up your hand if you got the right answer.*
▸ correct, exact, true
3 *She was waiting for the right moment to tell him.*
▸ appropriate, fitting, proper, suitable
4 *It's not right to steal.*
▸ decent, fair, honest, honourable, just, lawful, legal, moral, upright, virtuous
5 *Have we come the right way?*
▸ best, convenient, normal, sensible, usual
AN OPPOSITE IS wrong

right *ADVERB*
1 *Turn right at the corner.*
AN OPPOSITE IS left
2 *Turn right round.*
▸ all the way, completely

3 *She stood right in the middle.*
▶ exactly, precisely
4 *Go right ahead.*
▶ directly, straight

right *NOUN*
1 *The post office is on the right along the High Street.*
AN OPPOSITE IS left
2 *People have the right to walk across the common.*
▶ freedom, liberty
3 *You don't have the right to tell me what to do.*
▶ authority, power

righteous *ADJECTIVE*
He was a devout and righteous man.
▶ blameless, good, guiltless, just, law-abiding, moral, pure, upright, virtuous
AN OPPOSITE IS sinful

rigid *ADJECTIVE*
1 *The tent was supported by a rigid framework.*
▶ firm, hard, solid, stiff
2 *The referee was rigid in applying the rules.*
▶ harsh, inflexible, stern, strict, uncompromising
AN OPPOSITE IS flexible

rim *NOUN*
She looked at him over the rim of her glass.
▶ brim, brink, edge, lip

ring *NOUN*
The wooden barrel had metal rings round it.
▶ band, circle, hoop

ring *VERB*
1 *The police ringed the whole area.*
▶ circle, encircle, enclose, surround
2 *The bell rang.*
▶ chime, clang, clink, jangle, peal, resound, tinkle, toll
3 *Ring me tomorrow evening.*
▶ call, phone, ring up, telephone

rinse *VERB*
Rinse the plates in clean water.
▶ clean, swill, wash
▷ To rinse out the lavatory is to flush it.

riot *NOUN*
The police moved in to stop the riot.
▶ commotion, disorder, disturbance, rioting, turmoil, uproar, violence
▷ Unruly behaviour by sailors on a ship is a mutiny.

riot *VERB*
The crowds were rioting in the streets.
▶ go wild, rampage, rebel, revolt, rise up, run wild

riotous *ADJECTIVE*
Their riotous behaviour led to their arrest.
▶ boisterous, disorderly, lawless, mutinous, noisy, rebellious, rowdy, unruly, violent, wild
AN OPPOSITE IS orderly

rip *VERB*
The barbed wire ripped my jeans.
▶ tear

ripe *ADJECTIVE*
Choose a nice ripe peach.
▶ mature, ready to eat

ripen *VERB*
The pears need to ripen.
▶ become riper, develop, mature

ripple *VERB*
The wind rippled the surface of the pond.
▶ disturb, make waves on, ruffle, stir

rise *VERB*
1 *The lark rose into the air.*
▶ ascend, climb, fly up, mount, soar
▷ When a plane rises into the air, it takes off. When a rocket rises into the air, it lifts off.
AN OPPOSITE IS descend
2 *A high cliff rose above us.*
▶ loom, stand out, stick up, tower
3 *They say that prices may rise soon.*
▶ go up, increase
AN OPPOSITE IS fall
4 *He rose and shook her hand.*
▶ get up, stand up
AN OPPOSITE IS sit
to rise up *The people rose up against the military dictatorship.*
▶ rebel, revolt, riot

A B C D E F G H I J K L M N O P Q R S T U V W X Y Z

rise *NOUN*
1 *The bad weather resulted in a rise in the price of vegetables.*
▶ increase, jump
AN OPPOSITE IS fall
2 *At the top of the rise they paused for a break.*
▶ ascent, bank, hill, incline, ramp, slope

risk *VERB*
He risked his life to save them.
▶ gamble, venture

risk *NOUN*
1 *All outdoor activities carry an element of risk.*
▶ danger, hazard, peril
2 *Starting a business involves risk.*
▶ a gamble, uncertainty
3 *The forecast says there's a risk of frost.*
▶ chance, likelihood, possibility

risky *ADJECTIVE*
Cycling on icy roads is risky.
▶ dangerous, hazardous, perilous, unsafe
AN OPPOSITE IS safe

ritual *NOUN*
Most religions have rituals, performed on special occasions.
▶ ceremony, rite, tradition

rival *NOUN*
He has no serious rival for the championship.
▶ adversary, competitor, contender, contestant, enemy, opponent

rival *VERB*
Few countries can rival Scotland for mountainous scenery.
▶ compete with, contend with

rivalry *NOUN*
There was fierce rivalry between the two teams.
▶ competition, competitiveness, opposition
AN OPPOSITE IS cooperation

river *NOUN*
▷ A small river is a stream or rivulet. A small river which flows into a larger river is a tributary. The place where a river begins is its source. The place where a river goes into the sea is its mouth. A wide river mouth is an estuary. The place where the mouth of a river splits into several channels before going into the sea is a delta. A river of ice is a glacier.

road *NOUN*
KINDS OF ROAD FOR TRAFFIC
bypass, dual carriageway, (*American*) freeway, highway, lane, main road, motorway, one-way street, ring road, trunk road
▷ A road on which a toll was collected at a toll gate in former times was a turnpike. A private road up to a house is a drive. A firm road across marshy land is a causeway.
KINDS OF ROAD IN TOWNS
alley, avenue, boulevard, crescent, cul-de-sac, side street, shopping street, street
THINGS WHICH MAY BE PART OF A ROAD SYSTEM
bridge, flyover or overpass, footbridge, ford, hairpin bend, junction, lay-by, level crossing, motorway interchange, pedestrian crossing, roundabout, service area or service station, signpost, slip road, traffic lights, underpass, viaduct
WAYS LIKE ROADS BUT NOT MADE FOR MOTOR VEHICLES
bridle path or bridleway, cart track, footpath, pedestrian precinct or pedestrianized street, track, trail, walkway
▷ A way along the side of a river or canal is a tow-path. A way for people to walk on along the sea front in a seaside town is an esplanade or promenade.
SURFACES USED TO MAKE ROADS AND PATHS
asphalt, cobbles, concrete, gravel, paving blocks or stones, sets or setts, (*trademark*) tarmac

roam *VERB*
1 *We roamed about town aimlessly.*
▶ meander, ramble, walk, wander
2 *Herds of wild deer roamed over the hills.*
▶ prowl, range, rove

roar *NOUN VERB*
FOR VARIOUS WAYS TO MAKE SOUNDS SEE **sound** *VERB*

rob *VERB*
Make sure no one robs you when you're taking money to the bank.
▶ mug, pick your pocket, steal from
SEE ALSO **steal, stealing**

robber *NOUN*
SEE **thief**

robbery *NOUN*
SEE **stealing**

robe *NOUN*
▷ A kind of robe you might wear in your bedroom is a **dressing gown** or **bathrobe**. Robes worn by a priest are **vestments**. The robe worn by a monk is a **habit**. A robe certain officials might wear at a ceremony is a **gown**. Robe is also a formal word for a woman's **dress**.

robust *ADJECTIVE*
1 *A mountaineer needs a robust constitution.*
▸ athletic, fit, hardy, healthy, muscular, powerful, strong, vigorous
AN OPPOSITE IS weak
2 *She wore a pair of robust leather shoes.*
▸ durable, hard-wearing, solid, sturdy, tough
AN OPPOSITE IS flimsy

rock *NOUN*
1 *We clambered over the rocks.*
▸ boulder, stone
2 *The rocks towered above them.*
▸ cliff, crag, precipice
▷ **Igneous** rocks have solidified from molten rock. **Metamorphic** rocks have been transformed by heat, or high pressure, or both. **Sedimentary** rocks were formed from layers of particles deposited by winds or water. Rock from which metal or other valuable minerals can be extracted is **ore**.
SOME KINDS OF ROCK
agglomerate, basalt, chalk, conglomerate, flint, granite, gypsum, lava, limestone, marble, quartz, sandstone, shale, slate, tufa

rock *VERB*
1 *I rocked the baby's cradle to and fro.*
▸ move gently, sway, swing
2 *The ship rocked in the storm.*
▸ lurch, pitch, reel, roll, shake, toss

rocky *ADJECTIVE*
1 *Nothing was growing in the rocky ground.*
▸ barren, pebbly, stony
2 *Take care — that chair's a bit rocky.*
▸ rickety, shaky, unsafe, unsteady, wobbly

rod *NOUN*
VARIOUS KINDS OF ROD
bar, baton, cane, curtain rail, fishing rod, pole, rail, shaft, spoke, staff, stick, strut, wand

rogue *NOUN*
Don't trust him — he's a rogue.
▸ cheat, (*slang*) conman, fraud, rascal, scoundrel, swindler, villain

roguish *ADJECTIVE*
He gave me a roguish smile.
▸ impish, mischievous, naughty, playful, wicked

role *NOUN*
1 *He plays the role of a journalist in his new film.*
▸ character, part
2 *Both sides have important roles to play in the discussions.*
▸ contribution, function, job, position, task

roll *VERB*
1 *The wheels began to roll.*
▸ move round, revolve, rotate, spin, turn, twirl, whirl
2 *I rolled up my beach-mat and carried it home.*
▸ coil, curl, twist, wind
▷ To roll up a sail on a yacht is to **furl** it.
3 *Roll out the pastry on a flat surface.*
▸ flatten, level out, smooth
4 *The ship rolled in the storm.*
▸ pitch, rock, sway, toss, wallow
5 *He rolled along the street as if he were drunk.*
▸ lumber, lurch, reel, stagger, totter

romance *NOUN*
1 *The moonlight gave the scene a touch of romance.*
▸ excitement, glamour
2 *She had a holiday romance during the summer.*
▸ affair, love affair, relationship

romantic *ADJECTIVE*
1 *Her boyfriend is very romantic.*
▸ emotional, sentimental, tender
2 *A holiday on a desert island sounds very romantic.*
▸ exotic, glamorous

romp *VERB*
The children romped around the playground.
▸ caper, dance about, frisk, frolic, leap about, play, prance, run about, skip about

A B C D E F G H I J K L M N O P Q R S T U V W X Y Z

roof *NOUN*
MATERIALS USED TO MAKE ROOFS
corrugated iron, roofing felt, slates, thatch, tiles
▷ A sloping roof is a **pitched roof**. The sloping beams in the framework of a roof are **rafters**. The overhanging edge of a roof is the **eaves**.

room *NOUN*
1 *How many rooms are there in your house?*
ROOMS YOU MIGHT FIND IN A HOUSE
bathroom, bedroom, conservatory, dining room, drawing room or living room or lounge or sitting room, hall, kitchen or kitchenette, landing, larder or pantry, lavatory or toilet or WC, nursery, parlour, scullery, spare room or guest room, study, utility room
ROOMS YOU MIGHT FIND IN A SCHOOL
assembly hall, classroom, cloakroom, corridor, laboratory, library, music room, office, staff room, storeroom, workshop
▷ A small room in a monastery or prison is a **cell**. An underground room is a **basement** or **cellar** or **vault**. The space in the roof of a house is the **attic** or **loft**. A room where an artist works is a **studio**. A room where you wait to see a dentist, etc., is a **waiting room**. A room in a boarding school where pupils sleep is a **dormitory**. A room in a hospital for patients is a **ward**.
2 *I need more room to spread my things out.*
► freedom, scope, space

roomy *ADJECTIVE*
It's a surprisingly roomy car.
► big, large, sizeable, spacious

root *NOUN*
We need to get to the root of the problem.
► basis, origin, source, starting point

rope *NOUN*
The sailors threw a rope to the men in the water.
► cable, cord, line
▷ The ropes that support a ship's mast and sails are the **rigging**. A rope for raising and lowering a sail is a **halyard**. A thick rope for mooring a ship is a **hawser**. A rope with a loop at one end used for catching cattle is a **lasso**.

rot *VERB*
The wooden fence had begun to rot.
► become rotten, crumble, decay, decompose, disintegrate
▷ If metal rots it is said to **corrode**. If rubber rots it is said to **perish**. If food rots it is said to **go bad** or **putrefy**.

rotate *VERB*
The globe rotates on its axis.
► pivot, revolve, spin, swivel, turn, twirl, twist, wheel, whirl

rotten *ADJECTIVE*
1 *The window frame is rotten.*
► crumbling, decayed, decaying, decomposed, disintegrating, unsound
▷ Rotten metal is **corroded** or **rusty** metal.
AN OPPOSITE IS sound
2 *The fridge smelled of rotten eggs.*
► bad, decomposing, foul, mouldy, perished, smelly
AN OPPOSITE IS fresh
3 (*informal*) *We had rotten weather.*
► (*informal*) abysmal, awful, bad, dreadful, nasty, poor, unpleasant
AN OPPOSITE IS good

rough *ADJECTIVE*
1 *A rough track led to the farm.*
► bumpy, craggy, irregular, jagged, rocky, rugged, stony, uneven
AN OPPOSITE IS even or smooth
2 *The sea was rough, and I was seasick.*
► choppy, heaving, stormy, tempestuous, turbulent
AN OPPOSITE IS calm
3 *The blanket felt rough against my skin.*
► bristly, coarse, harsh, scratchy
AN OPPOSITE IS soft
4 *He's been hanging around with some rough company.*
► badly behaved, boisterous, disorderly, noisy, riotous, rowdy, unruly, violent, wild
AN OPPOSITE IS well behaved
5 *At a rough guess there were a hundred people present.*
► approximate, imprecise, inexact, vague
AN OPPOSITE IS exact
6 *He carved a rough figure out of wood.*
► amateurish, careless, clumsy, crude, hasty, unskilful
AN OPPOSITE IS skilful

roughly *ADVERB*
There were roughly a hundred people present.
▸ about, approximately, around, close to, nearly

round *ADJECTIVE*
The plant has small round berries.
▸ rounded, spherical
▹ A flat round shape is **circular**.

round *NOUN*
We were knocked out in the first round of the competition.
▸ bout, contest, game, heat, stage

round *VERB*
The car rounded the corner at top speed.
▸ go round, travel round, turn
to round something off *They rounded the evening off with some songs.*
▸ bring to an end, complete, conclude, end, finish
to round up people or things *The captain rounded up his players.*
▸ assemble, bring together, collect, gather, muster, rally

roundabout *ADJECTIVE*
We went home by a roundabout route to avoid the traffic.
▸ devious, indirect, long, meandering, twisting, winding
AN OPPOSITE IS direct

rouse *VERB*
1 *She was roused by the sound of the telephone ringing.*
▸ arouse, awaken, call, wake up
2 *He was a quiet man, not easily roused to anger or jealousy.*
▸ agitate, excite, provoke, stimulate, stir up

rout *VERB*
We routed the opposition.
▸ conquer, crush, defeat, overwhelm, thrash

route *NOUN*
We drove home by the quickest route.
▸ course, direction, journey, path, road, way

routine *NOUN*
1 *His departure had upset her daily routine.*
▸ method, pattern, procedure, system, way
2 *The skaters performed a new routine.*
▸ act, performance, programme

row *NOUN*
1 *They arranged the chairs in a row.*(rhymes with go)
▸ column, line, sequence, series, string
▹ A row of people waiting for something is a **queue**. A row of people walking behind each other is a **file**. A row of soldiers standing side by side on parade is a **rank**. A row of police, etc., is a **cordon**.
2 *The class next door was making a terrible row.*(rhymes with cow)
▸ commotion, din, disturbance, hullabaloo, noise, racket, tumult, uproar
3 *They had a terrible row.*(rhymes with cow)
▸ argument, disagreement, dispute, fight, quarrel, squabble

rowdy *ADJECTIVE*
The crowd became rowdy.
▸ badly behaved, boisterous, disorderly, noisy, riotous, rough, unruly, violent, wild
AN OPPOSITE IS quiet

royalty *NOUN*
WORDS FOR MEMBERS OF A ROYAL FAMILY
Her or His Majesty, Her or His Royal Highness, king, monarch, prince, princess, queen, queen mother, sovereign
▹ The husband or wife of a royal person is a **consort**. A person who rules while a monarch is too young or too ill to rule is a **regent**.
SEE ALSO **ruler**

rub *VERB*
1 *She rubbed her stiff arms and legs.*
▸ knead, massage, stroke
2 *The heel of his shoe was rubbing his foot.*
▸ graze, scrape
3 *I rubbed the plate until it gleamed.*
▸ polish, scour, scrub, wipe
to rub something out *He rubbed out the pencil marks.*
▸ delete, erase, remove, wipe out

rubbish *NOUN*
1 *She took the rubbish out to the bin.*
▸ garbage, junk, litter, refuse, scrap, trash, waste
2 *Don't talk rubbish!*
▸ (*slang*) bilge, nonsense, (*informal*) rot, (*informal*) tripe

rubble *NOUN*
The building collapsed into a pile of rubble.
▸ broken bricks, debris, fragments, remains, wreckage

ruddy *ADJECTIVE*
He has a ruddy face because he spends so much time out of doors.
▸ fresh, glowing, healthy looking, red, sunburnt

rude *ADJECTIVE*
1 *That was a very rude remark.*
▸ abrupt, abusive, bad-mannered, blunt, cheeky, disrespectful, ill-mannered, impertinent, impolite, impudent, inconsiderate, insolent, insulting, saucy, tactless, uncivil, uncomplimentary, uncouth, unfriendly
▹ To be rude to someone is to **insult** them or **snub** them.
AN OPPOSITE IS **polite**
2 *He kept telling rather rude jokes.*
▸ coarse, crude, dirty, foul, improper, indecent, naughty, obscene, offensive, smutty, vulgar
▹ Words which are rude about sacred things are **blasphemous** or **irreverent**.
AN OPPOSITE IS **decent**

rudeness *NOUN*
I'm sick of her rudeness.
▸ abuse, bad manners, cheek, impertinence, impudence, insolence, insults, tactlessness, vulgarity
AN OPPOSITE IS **politeness**

ruffian *NOUN*
He was attacked by a gang of ruffians.
▸ bully, gangster, hooligan, lout, mugger, scoundrel, thug, villain

ruffle *VERB*
1 *A breeze ruffled the water.*
▸ agitate, disturb, ripple, stir
AN OPPOSITE IS **smooth**
2 *Some of the audience booed, and the speaker began to get ruffled.*
▸ annoy, fluster, irritate, (*informal*) rattle, unsettle, upset, worry
AN OPPOSITE IS **calm**

rug *NOUN*
▹ A rug to go on the floor is a **mat**. A rug to wrap yourself in is a **blanket**.

rugged *ADJECTIVE*
1 *He was tall and dark with rugged features.*
▸ irregular, rough, uneven
2 *It was difficult for boats to land on the rugged coast.*
▸ bumpy, craggy, jagged, rocky

ruin *VERB*
The storm had ruined the flowers in the garden.
▸ damage, demolish, destroy, devastate, flatten, shatter, spoil, wreck

ruin *NOUN*
1 *The ruin was covered in ivy.*
▸ ruined building
2 *The ruin of his business meant that he had to sell his house.*
▸ breakdown, collapse, failure
▹ Financial ruin is **bankruptcy**.
ruins *After the earthquake, people wandered hopelessly through the ruins.*
▸ debris, remains, rubble, wreckage

ruined *ADJECTIVE*
A notice near the ruined building told people to keep out.
▸ crumbling, derelict, uninhabitable, unsafe, wrecked

ruinous *ADJECTIVE*
Pollution is having a ruinous effect on the environment.
▸ calamitous, catastrophic, destructive, devastating, disastrous

rule *NOUN*
1 *Stick to the rules of the game.*
▸ law, principle, regulation
▹ A set of rules is a **code**.
2 *The country was formerly under French rule.*
▸ administration, authority, command, control, domination, government, management, power, reign

rule *VERB*
1 *The judge rules the courts.*
▶ administer, command, control, direct, dominate, govern, lead, manage, reign over, run
2 *Queen Victoria continued to rule for many years.*
▶ be ruler, reign
3 *The umpire ruled that the batsman was out.*
▶ decide, decree, determine, judge, pronounce

ruler *NOUN*
VARIOUS RULERS
caesar, dictator, emir, emperor, empress, governor, kaiser, king, lord, monarch, president, prince, princess, queen, rajah, regent, satrap, sovereign, sultan, tyrant, tzar, viceroy
SEE ALSO **chief** *NOUN*

rummage *VERB*
I rummaged through my bag looking for my purse.
▶ comb, hunt, scour, search

rumour *NOUN*
The rumour began with an anonymous telephone call to a newspaper.
▶ gossip, scandal

run *VERB* This word is often overused. Here are some alternatives:
1 *We ran as fast as our legs could carry us.*
▶ bolt, career, dash, hurry, race, rush, scamper, scurry, scuttle, speed, sprint, tear
▷ To run at a gentle pace is to jog. When a horse runs, it gallops or trots.
2 *Water ran down the wall.*
▶ dribble, flow, gush, leak, pour, spill, stream, trickle
3 *The bus doesn't run on Sundays.*
▶ go, operate, provide a service, travel
4 *The car runs well.*
▶ behave, function, operate, perform, work
5 *The government runs the country's affairs.*
▶ administer, conduct, control, direct, govern, look after, manage, rule, supervise
to run away *They ran away when they saw the policeman.*
▶ bolt, escape, flee, make off
to run into **1** *I didn't expect to run into you!*
▶ (*informal*) bump into, come across, encounter, meet
2 *A car ran into our bus.*
▶ collide with, hit

run *NOUN*
1 *We went for a run in the park.*
▷ A fast run is a **dash**, **gallop**, **race**, or **sprint**. A gentle run is a canter, jog, or trot.
2 *We went for a run in the car.*
▶ drive, journey, ride
3 *She's had a run of good luck recently.*
▶ sequence, series, stretch
4 *The animals lived in a run surrounded by wire netting.*
▶ compound, coop, enclosure, pen

runaway *NOUN*
▷ A person who has run away from the army is a deserter. A person who is running away from the law is a fugitive or outlaw.

runner *NOUN*
The runners were ready to start the race.
▶ athlete, competitor
▷ Someone who runs fast over short distances is a sprinter. Someone who runs to keep fit is a jogger.

runny *ADJECTIVE*
This gravy is too runny.
▶ fluid, liquid, thin, watery
AN OPPOSITE IS thick

rural *ADJECTIVE*
They live in a peaceful rural area.
▶ agricultural, pastoral, rustic

rush *VERB*
I rushed home with the good news.
▶ bolt, career, charge, dash, fly, gallop, hasten, hurry, race, run, scamper, scurry, scuttle, shoot, speed, sprint, tear, zoom
▷ When cattle rush along together they **stampede**.

rush *NOUN*
1 *We've got plenty of time, so what's the rush?*
▶ haste, hurry, urgency
2 *There was a sudden rush of water.*
▶ cataract, flood, gush

rust *VERB*
Iron rusts if you leave it exposed to the weather.
▶ become rusty, corrode, crumble away, oxidize, rot

rustic *ADJECTIVE*
The village had a rustic charm.
▶ agricultural, pastoral, rural

A B C D E F G H I J K L M N O P Q R S T U V W X Y Z

rusty *ADJECTIVE*
I found a rusty knife buried in the garden.
▸ corroded, oxidized, rotten

rut *NOUN*
The tractor left ruts along the track.
▸ channel, furrow, groove, indentation, pothole

ruthless *ADJECTIVE*
Many people were killed in the ruthless attack.
▸ barbaric, bloodthirsty, brutal, callous, cruel, ferocious, fierce, heartless, pitiless, sadistic, savage, vicious, violent
AN OPPOSITE IS merciful

Ss

sabotage *NOUN*
The sabotage was blamed on terrorists.
▸ damage, destruction, disruption, vandalism, wrecking

sabotage *VERB*
The machinery has been sabotaged.
▸ cripple, damage, destroy, put out of action, vandalize, wreck

sack *NOUN*
He bought a sack of potatoes.
▸ bag
SEE ALSO **container**
to get the sack (*informal*) *She got the sack because of her laziness.*
▸ be sacked, lose your job
to give someone the sack
SEE **sack** *VERB*

sack *VERB*
The boss threatened to sack him.
▸ dismiss, (*informal*) fire, (*informal*) give you the sack, make you redundant
▹ To lay off employees is to tell them there is no work for them at present.

sacred *ADJECTIVE*
The Koran is a sacred book.
▸ blessed, divine, holy, religious, revered

sacrifice *VERB*
1 *She sacrificed her weekend to finish the job.*
▸ give up, surrender
2 *They sacrificed animals to please the gods.*
▸ kill, offer up, slaughter

sad *ADJECTIVE* This word is often overused. Here are some alternatives:
1 *He was looking a bit sad.*
▸ broken-hearted, dejected, depressed, desolate, despairing, dismal, distressed, downcast, downhearted, forlorn, gloomy, glum, grave, heartbroken, in low spirits, (*informal*) low, miserable, regretful, sorrowful, sorry, tearful, troubled, unhappy, upset, wistful, woeful, wretched
▹ If you are sad because you are away from home, you are **homesick**.
AN OPPOSITE IS happy
2 *It was sad to see how badly the animals were treated.*
▸ depressing, distressing, heartbreaking, pathetic, pitiful, upsetting
AN OPPOSITE IS cheering
3 *They sang a sad song.*
▸ melancholy, mournful, moving, plaintive, touching, wistful
AN OPPOSITE IS cheerful
4 *She has had some sad news.*
▸ grim, painful, regrettable, serious, tragic, unfortunate, unpleasant
AN OPPOSITE IS pleasant

sadden *VERB*
The bad news saddened her.
▸ (*informal*) break your heart, depress, disappoint, distress, grieve, upset
AN OPPOSITE IS cheer up

sadistic *ADJECTIVE*
He takes a sadistic pleasure in hurting people.
▸ brutal, callous, cruel, heartless, inhuman
AN OPPOSITE IS kind

sadness *NOUN*
SEE **sorrow**

safe *ADJECTIVE*
1 *They got home safe in spite of the storm.*
▸ (*informal*) in one piece, intact, sound, undamaged, unharmed, unhurt, uninjured
AN OPPOSITE IS damaged or hurt
2 *They made their house safe from intruders.*
▸ defended, guarded, protected, secure
AN OPPOSITE IS vulnerable
3 *She's a safe driver.*
▸ cautious, dependable, reliable, trustworthy

4 *The dog's quite safe.*
▶ docile, friendly, gentle, harmless, tame
5 *This drinking water is safe.*
▶ drinkable, pure, uncontaminated
6 *You can eat the food — it's safe.*
▶ eatable, good, wholesome
▷ A safe car is **roadworthy**. A safe aircraft is **airworthy**. A safe ship is **seaworthy**.
AN OPPOSITE IS **dangerous**

safeguard *NOUN*
She made a copy of the computer disk as a safeguard.
▶ protection, security

safety *NOUN*
1 *You must wear a seat belt for your own safety.*
▶ protection, security
2 *The nurse assured him of the safety of the drug.*
▶ harmlessness, reliability

safety belt *NOUN*
It's against the law to drive without a safety belt on.
▶ safety harness, seat belt

sag *VERB*
The clothes line sagged in the middle.
▶ dip, droop, slump

sail *VERB*
1 *She sailed to France rather than going by air.*
▶ travel by ship
▷ To have a holiday sailing on a ship is to **cruise**.
2 *It needs a lot of experience to sail a boat.*
▶ navigate, pilot, steer

sailor *NOUN*
VARIOUS PEOPLE WHO WORK ON BOATS OR HELP TO SAIL THEM
able seaman, bargee, boatman, boatswain or bosun, captain, cox or coxswain, helmsman, mariner, mate, midshipman, navigator, pilot, rating, rower, seaman, yachtsman
▷ The team of sailors who sail a boat is the **crew**.
FOR RANKS IN THE NAVY SEE **rank**

saintly *ADJECTIVE*
He had such a saintly expression on his face.
▶ angelic, holy, innocent, pure, religious, virtuous
AN OPPOSITE IS **devilish**

sake *NOUN*
for my sake *He did it for my sake.*
▶ on my behalf, for my benefit, to help me

salad *NOUN*
VEGETABLES OFTEN EATEN IN SALADS
beetroot, carrot, celery, chicory, cress, cucumber, lettuce, mustard and cress, onion, peppers, potato, radish, spring onion, watercress
FOR OTHER VEGETABLES SEE **vegetable**

salary *NOUN*
He gets a salary of £15,000 a year.
▶ earnings, income, pay
▷ If your pay is calculated week by week, it is called **wages**.

sale *NOUN*
KINDS OF SALE
auction, bazaar, car-boot sale, closing-down sale, fair, jumble sale, market

salty *ADJECTIVE*
The water tasted salty.
▶ saline, salted
AN OPPOSITE IS **fresh**
▷ Salty water is **brine**. Water which is slightly salty is **brackish**. Food with a salty taste is said to have a **savoury** taste.

salvage *VERB*
They were able to salvage a few possessions from the wreck.
▶ reclaim, recover, rescue, retrieve, save

same *ADJECTIVE*
the same **1** *Each person will get the same amount.*
▶ equal, equivalent, identical
2 *Everyone in the choir wore the same clothes.*
▶ matching, similar, uniform
3 *She hadn't seen him since last year, but he looks the same.*
▶ unaltered, unchanged
▷ Lines which go in the same direction are **parallel**. Words which mean the same are **synonymous**.
AN OPPOSITE IS **different**

sample *NOUN*
He showed the visitor a sample of his work.
▶ example, illustration, instance, selection, specimen

A B C D E F G H I J K L M N O P Q R S T U V W X Y Z

sample *VERB*
She let him sample the home-made fudge.
▶ taste, test, try

sanctuary *NOUN*
The hunted fox found sanctuary in a wood.
▶ a haven, protection, refuge, safety, shelter

sand *NOUN*
He got some sand in his shoes.
▶ grit
sands *They played on the sands until the tide came in.*
▶ beach, shore
▷ Hills of sand along the coast are **dunes**.

sane *ADJECTIVE*
A sane person would not do something like that.
▶ rational, reasonable, sensible
AN OPPOSITE IS insane

sanitary *ADJECTIVE*
It's important to have sanitary conditions in a hospital.
▶ clean, disinfected, germ free, healthy, hygienic, pure, sterilized, uncontaminated, unpolluted
AN OPPOSITE IS insanitary

sanitation *NOUN*
Has the camp site got proper sanitation?
▶ drainage, drains, lavatories, sewage disposal, sewers

sarcasm *NOUN*
He found her constant sarcasm very irritating.
▶ derision, irony, mockery, ridicule, satire

sarcastic *ADJECTIVE*
She made some sarcastic remarks about politicians.
▶ ironical, mocking, satirical, sneering, taunting

satirical *ADJECTIVE*
There was a satirical article about him in the paper.
▶ ironic, irreverent, mocking, sarcastic
DEVICES USED IN SATIRE TO MAKE PEOPLE LAUGH
caricature, exaggeration, irony, mimicry, mockery, parody, ridicule

satisfaction *NOUN*
She gets a lot of satisfaction from her hobby.
▶ contentment, enjoyment, fulfilment, happiness, pleasure, pride, sense of achievement
AN OPPOSITE IS dissatisfaction

satisfactory *ADJECTIVE*
She said his work was not satisfactory.
▶ acceptable, adequate, all right, competent, good enough, passable, tolerable
AN OPPOSITE IS unsatisfactory

satisfy *VERB*
Nothing satisfies him — he's always complaining.
▶ make you happy, meet your needs, please
▷ To satisfy your thirst is to **quench** or **slake** it.
AN OPPOSITE IS frustrate

saturate *VERB*
Their clothes were saturated when they got caught in the storm.
▶ drench, soak
▷ If something is saturated, it is said to be **wringing wet**.

sauce *NOUN*
SOME KINDS OF SAUCE YOU EAT WITH VARIOUS FOODS
bread sauce, cheese sauce, cranberry sauce, curry sauce, custard, gravy, horseradish sauce, ketchup, mayonnaise, mint sauce, salad cream, sauce tartare

saucepan *NOUN*
FOR THINGS YOU COOK WITH SEE **cook** *VERB*

saucy *ADJECTIVE*
He was told off for making saucy remarks.
▶ cheeky, disrespectful, facetious, impertinent, impudent, insolent, rude
AN OPPOSITE IS respectful

saunter *VERB*
They sauntered through the park.
▶ amble, stroll, walk slowly
SEE ALSO **walk** *VERB*

savage *ADJECTIVE*
1 *The soldiers launched a savage attack against the enemy.*
▶ barbarous, bloodthirsty, brutal, cold-blooded, cruel, diabolical, merciless, murderous, pitiless, ruthless, sadistic, vicious, violent
AN OPPOSITE IS humane
2 *At one time Britain was the home of savage tribes.*
▶ barbaric, primitive, uncivilized
AN OPPOSITE IS civilized
3 *Savage beasts roam the plain in search of prey.*
▶ ferocious, fierce, untamed, wild
AN OPPOSITE IS domesticated

save *VERB*
1 *They tried to save their belongings from the fire.*
▶ recover, retrieve, salvage
2 *Most animals have an instinct to save their young from danger.*
▶ defend, guard, preserve, protect, shield
3 *She saved him from making a fool of himself.*
▶ deter, prevent, stop
4 *He saves £50 a month.*
▶ hoard, invest
5 *They saved some food for him.*
▶ hold on to, keep, reserve, set aside
6 *They discussed ways to save our natural resources.*
▶ be sparing with, conserve, economize on, use wisely

savings *PLURAL NOUN*
She kept her savings in the bank.
▶ investments, reserves, resources, riches, wealth

savoury *ADJECTIVE*
They had a savoury stew for dinner.
▶ appetizing, delicious, tasty
▷ Savoury food usually tastes salty.
AN OPPOSITE IS sweet

saw *NOUN*
SOME KINDS OF SAW
chainsaw, circular saw, cross-cut saw, fretsaw, hacksaw, jigsaw, ripsaw, tenon saw
FOR OTHER TOOLS SEE **tool**

say *VERB* This word is often overused. Here are some alternatives:
He sometimes finds it hard to say what he means.
▶ communicate, convey, express, put into words
VARIOUS WAYS WE SAY THINGS
announce, answer, ask, assert, comment, declare, exclaim, maintain, mention, query, recite, remark, repeat, reply, report, respond, retort, shout, state, suggest, utter, whisper
SEE ALSO **talk**

saying *NOUN*
'Many hands make light work' is a common saying.
▶ catchphrase, cliché, expression, motto, phrase, proverb, quotation, remark, slogan, statement

scales *PLURAL NOUN*
He weighed himself on the bathroom scales.
▶ balance, weighing machine

scamper *VERB*
The rabbits scampered away to safety.
▶ dash, hasten, hurry, run, rush, scuttle

scan *VERB*
1 *He scanned the horizon, hoping to see a ship.*
▶ examine, eye, gaze at, look at, scrutinize, search, study, survey, view, watch
2 *She scanned the newspaper looking for interesting news.*
▶ glance through, read quickly, skim

scandal *NOUN*
1 *The waste of food was a scandal.*
▶ disgrace, embarrassment, outrage, shame
2 *Newspapers shouldn't print scandal about people's private lives.*
▶ gossip, rumours

scandalous *ADJECTIVE*
It was a scandalous waste of money.
▶ disgraceful, outrageous, shameful, shocking, wicked

scanty *ADJECTIVE*
They had only a scanty supply of water.
▶ inadequate, insufficient, meagre, mean, (*informal*) measly, scarce, small, sparse
AN OPPOSITE IS plentiful

scar *NOUN*
The cut left a scar on his face.
▶ blemish, mark
▷ A scar which still has a clot of dried blood on it is a scab.

scar *VERB*
The injuries he received scarred him for life.
▶ deface, leave a scar on, mark

scarce *ADJECTIVE*
Fresh vegetables have been scarce during the drought.
▶ hard to find, in short supply, insufficient, lacking, scanty, sparse, (*informal*) thin on the ground, uncommon
AN OPPOSITE IS plentiful

scarcely *ADVERB*
She was so tired that she could scarcely walk.
▸ barely, hardly, only just

scarcity *NOUN*
SEE **shortage**

scare *NOUN*
The explosion gave them a nasty scare.
▸ alarm, fright, shock

scare *VERB*
The sudden noise scared us.
▸ alarm, frighten, petrify, shock, startle, terrify
AN OPPOSITE IS reassure

scatter *VERB*
1 *She scattered the seeds on the ground.*
▸ shower, sow, spread, sprinkle, strew, throw about
AN OPPOSITE IS collect
2 *The crowd scattered when the gun went off.*
▸ break up, disintegrate, disperse, split up
AN OPPOSITE IS gather

scene *NOUN*
1 *The police arrived quickly at the scene of the crime.*
▸ location, place, position, site, situation, spot
2 *They were rehearsing a scene from the play.*
▸ act, episode, part, section
3 *He gazed at the beautiful scene.*
▸ landscape, outlook, panorama, prospect, scenery, setting, sight, spectacle, view
4 *He created a scene because he didn't win the argument.*
▸ commotion, disturbance, fuss, quarrel, row

scenery *NOUN*
1 *They admired the scenery from the top of the hill.*
▸ landscape, outlook, panorama, prospect, scene, view
2 *He built the scenery for the play.*
▸ set

scent *NOUN*
1 *She loves the scent of roses.*
▸ fragrance, perfume
▹ A word often used for pleasant food smells is **aroma**. A word usually used for unpleasant smells is **odour**.
SEE ALSO **smell**
2 *He gave her a bottle of scent for her birthday.*
▸ perfume
3 *The dogs followed the scent of the fox.*
▸ trail

scented *ADJECTIVE*
He wrote the letter on scented notepaper.
▸ aromatic, fragrant, perfumed, sweet smelling
SEE ALSO **smell** *NOUN*

sceptical *ADJECTIVE*
She was a bit sceptical about the plan.
▸ cynical, disbelieving, distrustful, doubting, incredulous, suspicious, uncertain, unconvinced, unsure
AN OPPOSITE IS trustful

schedule *NOUN*
According to the schedule, it's his turn to wash up.
▸ list, plan, programme, timetable
▹ A schedule of topics to be discussed at a meeting is an **agenda**. A schedule of places to be visited on a journey is an itinerary.

scheme *NOUN*
1 *They worked out a scheme to raise some money.*
▸ method, plan, procedure, project, proposal, system
2 *The men involved in the dishonest scheme were arrested.*
▸ conspiracy, plot, (*informal*) racket

scheme *VERB*
They were scheming against her.
▸ conspire, intrigue, plan, plot

scholar *NOUN*
The professor is a real scholar.
▸ intellectual

scholarly *ADJECTIVE*
The professor is a very scholarly woman.
▸ academic, (*informal*) brainy, intellectual, studious

scholarship *NOUN*
1 *She got a scholarship to study at university.*
▸ award, grant
2 *The professor is a woman of great scholarship.*
▸ academic achievement, education, knowledge, learning, wisdom

school *NOUN*
VARIOUS KINDS OF SCHOOL
academy, boarding school, coeducational school, college, comprehensive school, grammar school, high school, infant school, junior school, kindergarten, nursery school, playgroup, preparatory or prep school, primary school, public school, secondary school
PARTS OF A SCHOOL
assembly hall, cafeteria or refectory, classroom, cloakroom, dormitory, foyer, gymnasium, hall, laboratory, library, office, playground, playing field, reception, staffroom, stockroom
PEOPLE WHO HELP RUN A SCHOOL
caretaker, groundsman, head teacher, librarian, monitor, prefect, principal, secretary, teacher, technician, tutor
▷ The people who are paid to help run a school or teach the children are the **staff**.

schoolchild *NOUN*
▸ pupil, scholar, schoolboy or schoolgirl, student

science *NOUN*
BRANCHES OF SCIENCE AND TECHNOLOGY INCLUDE
anatomy, anthropology, astronomy, biology, botany, chemistry, computer science, ecology, electronics, engineering, environmental science, food science, forensic science, genetics, geology, information technology, mechanics, medical science, meteorology, physics, psychology, telecommunications, veterinary science, zoology

scientific *ADJECTIVE*
They are very scientific in their approach.
▸ analytical, methodical, organized, systematic

scoff *VERB*
to scoff at *They scoffed at the idea.*
▸ deride, jeer at, laugh at, make fun of, mock, ridicule, sneer at

scold *VERB*
She scolded us for being late.
▸ criticize, find fault with, (*informal*) nag, reprimand, reproach, tell off, (*informal*) tick off

scoop *VERB*
Rabbits had scooped out holes in the turf.
▸ dig, excavate, gouge, hollow, scrape

scope *NOUN*
1 *They had plenty of scope to do what they wanted.*
▸ freedom, liberty, opportunity, room, space
2 *The coroner said the question of who was to blame was outside the scope of his inquiry.*
▸ capacity, competence, extent, limit, range

scorch *VERB*
The bonfire scorched the hedge.
▸ blacken, char, singe
SEE ALSO **burn**

score *NOUN*
She added up the score.
▸ marks, points, total
▷ The final score is the result.

score *VERB*
1 *How many did he score yesterday?*
▸ earn, gain, get, make
2 *The knife scored a line on the polished table.*
▸ cut, gouge, mark, scrape, scratch

scorn *NOUN*
She dismissed his suggestion with scorn.
▸ contempt, derision, disgust, dislike, disrespect, mockery, ridicule
AN OPPOSITE IS admiration

scorn *VERB*
They scorned his pathetic efforts.
▸ be scornful about, deride, despise, insult, jeer at, laugh at, look down on, make fun of, mock, ridicule, scoff at, sneer at
AN OPPOSITE IS admire

scoundrel *NOUN*
He'd like to catch the scoundrel who damaged his car!
▸ (*old use*) knave, rascal, rogue, ruffian, villain

scour *VERB*
1 *He scoured the pan till it was shiny.*
▸ clean, polish, rub, scrape, scrub
2 *She scoured the house looking for her purse.*
▸ comb, hunt through, ransack, rummage through, search

scout *NOUN*
They sent out scouts to find the enemy.
▸ lookout, spy

scowl *VERB*
He scowled when he saw her.
▸ frown, glower

scramble *VERB*
1 *He scrambled over the rocks to safety.*
▸ clamber, climb, crawl, move awkwardly
2 *The starving people scrambled to get at the food.*
▸ compete, fight, jostle, push, scuffle, struggle

scrap *NOUN*
1 *They fed the scraps of food to the birds.*
▸ bit, crumb, fragment, morsel, particle, piece, speck
2 *He took a pile of scrap to the tip.*
▸ junk, litter, odds and ends, refuse, rubbish, waste
▷ Scraps of cloth are **rags** or **shreds**.
3 (*informal*) *There was a scrap between the two gangs.*
▸ brawl, fight, scuffle, squabble

scrap *VERB*
1 *The car had to be scrapped after the accident.*
▸ discard, throw away, write off
2 *The plans for the new road have been scrapped.*
▸ abandon, abort, cancel, drop, give up
3 (*informal*) *They're always scrapping.*
▸ fight, quarrel, scuffle, squabble

scrape *VERB*
She scraped her knee when she fell over.
▸ graze, scratch
to scrape something clean *It took him ages to scrape the frying pan clean.*
▸ rub, scour, scrub

scrape *NOUN*
He's always getting into scrapes.
▸ (*informal*) jam, (*informal*) pickle
▷ Getting into scrapes is also getting into **mischief** or into **trouble**.

scrappy *ADJECTIVE*
She complained that my work was scrappy.
▸ careless, fragmentary, hurried, imperfect, incomplete, sketchy, slipshod, unfinished, unsatisfactory, untidy
AN OPPOSITE IS **perfect**

scratch *VERB*
1 *Someone scratched the side of the car.*
▸ gouge, graze, mark, score, scrape
2 *The cat tried to scratch her.*
▸ claw

scratch *NOUN*
Who made this scratch on the side of the car?
▸ gash, groove, line, mark, scrape

scrawl *VERB*
She scrawled his phone number on a scrap of paper.
▸ jot, scribble, write untidily

scream *NOUN VERB*
All these synonyms can be used both as nouns and verbs
▸ bawl, cry, howl, roar, screech, shout, shriek, squeal, wail, yell
FOR VARIOUS WAYS TO MAKE OTHER SOUNDS SEE **sound** *VERB*

screen *NOUN*
The room was divided into two by a screen.
▸ curtain, partition

screen *VERB*
1 *The farmer put up a fence to screen the manure heap.*
▸ camouflage, conceal, cover, disguise, hide, mask, veil
2 *A line of trees screened them from the sun.*
▸ protect, safeguard, shade, shelter, shield
3 *All employees are screened before being appointed.*
▸ examine, investigate, test

scribble *VERB*
He scribbled his phone number on a scrap of paper.
▸ jot, scrawl, write untidily
▷ To scribble a rough drawing or pattern, especially when you are bored, is to **doodle**.

script *NOUN*
▷ The script for a broadcast or a speech, etc., is the **text**. The script for a film is a **screenplay**. A handwritten or typed script is a **manuscript**.

scrounge *VERB* (*informal*)
He scrounged some money from friends.
▸ beg for, cadge

scrub *VERB*
She scrubbed the floor clean.
▸ brush, clean, rub, scour, wash

scruffy *ADJECTIVE*
Her clothes looked a bit scruffy.
▸ bedraggled, dirty, messy, ragged, shabby, slovenly, tatty, untidy
AN OPPOSITE IS smart

scrutinize *VERB*
He scrutinized the timetable to find the time of the next bus.
▸ examine, inspect, investigate, look at, search, study

scrutiny *NOUN*
His work was subjected to close scrutiny.
▸ examination, inspection, investigation, study

scuffle *NOUN*
Scuffles broke out between police and demonstrators.
▸ brawl, fight, (*informal*) scrap, (*informal*) squabble, struggle

sculpture *NOUN*
The ancient church was full of interesting sculptures.
▸ carving, figure, statue

scum *NOUN*
There was a nasty scum on the pond.
▸ dirt, film, foam, froth

sea *NOUN*
▹ The very large seas of the world are called **oceans**. An area of sea partly enclosed by land is a **bay** or **gulf**. A wide inlet of the sea is a **sound**. A wide inlet where a river joins the sea is an **estuary**, or in Scotland a **firth**. A narrow stretch of water linking two seas is a **strait**. The bottom of the sea is the **seabed**. The land near the sea is the **coast** or the **seashore**. Ships that travel long distances at sea are **ocean-going** or **seagoing** ships. People who work on ships at sea are **nautical** or **seafaring** people. Creatures that live in the sea are **marine** or **saltwater** creatures.
SEE ALSO **seaside**

seal *VERB*
▹ To seal an envelope is to **stick it down**. To seal a box or container is to **close**, **fasten**, **lock**, **secure**, or **shut** it. To seal a leak is to **plug** it or **stop** it.

seam *NOUN*
1 *The seam on his trousers split.*
▸ join
2 *Geologists discovered a seam of coal.*
▸ layer, stratum

search *VERB*
1 *He was searching for the book he had lost.*
▸ hunt, look, poke about, seek
▹ To search for gold or some other mineral is to **prospect**.
2 *The police searched the house but didn't find anything.*
▸ comb, explore, ransack, rummage through, scour
3 *Security staff searched all the passengers.*
▸ check, examine, (*informal*) frisk, inspect, scrutinize

search *NOUN*
After a quick search, she found her purse.
▸ check, hunt, look
▹ A long journey searching for something is a **quest**.

searching *ADJECTIVE*
The police asked some searching questions.
▸ deep, detailed, penetrating, probing, thorough
AN OPPOSITE IS superficial

seaside *NOUN*
▹ The land near the sea is the **coast**.
VARIOUS TYPES OF LAND ALONG THE COAST
cliffs, dunes, mudflats, rocks, sandy beach, shingle beach
▹ A town where you go to have fun by the sea is a **seaside resort**.
PLACES YOU OFTEN FIND IN A SEASIDE RESORT
amusement arcade, bed and breakfast place, bingo hall, café, guesthouse, hotel, nightclub, restaurant, shop, souvenir shop, theatre, tourist information office
▹ The area next to the sea where you play and sunbathe is the **beach** or **seashore**.
THINGS YOU MIGHT SEE ON OR NEAR THE BEACH
aquarium, beach huts, breakwater, cave, cliff, funfair, harbour, lifeboat station, lighthouse, marina, pier, promenade or esplanade, Punch and Judy, rock pool, rocks, seagulls and various sea birds
THINGS YOU MIGHT TAKE TO THE SEASIDE
bat and ball, beach ball, bucket and spade, deckchair or folding chair, fishing line or net, inflatable dinghy, snorkel, sunglasses, sunhat, sunshade, suntan cream or oil, swimming costume, towel, windbreak
THINGS YOU MIGHT DO AT THE SEASIDE
ball games, beachcombing, boat trip, building sandcastles, donkey ride, fishing, paddling, scuba diving, snorkelling, sunbathing, surfing, swimming, water-skiing, windsurfing

A B C D E F G H I J K L M N O P Q R S T U V W X Y Z

seaside *NOUN*
THINGS YOU MIGHT FIND LYING ON THE BEACH
driftwood, flotsam and jetsam, pebble, seashell, seaweed
WILDLIFE YOU MIGHT SEE ON OR NEAR THE BEACH
barnacle, cockle, cormorant, crab, cuttlefish, dolphin, fish, jellyfish, limpet, mussel, octopus, porpoise, sandhopper, sea anemone, seagull, seal, sea urchin, shrimp, squid, starfish, whelk
SEE ALSO **sea**

season *NOUN*
The hotels are full during the holiday season.
▸ period, time

seat *NOUN*
FURNITURE DESIGNED FOR PEOPLE TO SIT ON
armchair, bench, chair, chaise longue, couch, deckchair, dining chair, pew, pouffe, reclining chair, rocking chair, settee, settle, sofa, stool, throne, window seat
▹ A seat on a cycle or horse is a **saddle**. A seat for a passenger on a motor cycle is a **pillion**.

secluded *ADJECTIVE*
They found a secluded beach for their picnic.
▸ cut off, isolated, lonely, private, quiet, remote, sheltered, unfrequented
AN OPPOSITE IS crowded

second *ADJECTIVE*
She was given a second chance.
▸ additional, alternative, another, extra, further

second *NOUN*
1 *He was second in the race.*
▸ runner-up
2 *Between rounds the second gave the boxer some advice.*
▸ assistant, helper, supporter
3 *The pain only lasted a second.*
▸ flash, instant, (*informal*) jiffy, moment, (*informal*) tick

second *VERB*
1 *The boxer needed a reliable man to second him in his fight.*
▸ assist, encourage, help, side with
2 *She seconded the proposal.*
▸ back, support

secondary *ADJECTIVE*
When human lives are in danger, money is of secondary importance.
▸ inferior, lesser, lower, minor, subordinate

second-hand *ADJECTIVE*
She bought a second-hand car.
▸ used
AN OPPOSITE IS new

secret *ADJECTIVE*
1 *The spy was trying to get hold of secret information.*
▸ classified, (*informal*) hushed up, hush-hush
2 *The things he writes in his diary are secret.*
▸ confidential, intimate, personal, private
3 *They say there is a secret passageway into the castle.*
▸ concealed, disguised, hidden, underground
AN OPPOSITE IS well known

secretary *NOUN*
▹ A secretary who handles business for an important member of a firm is a **personal assistant**.
FOR OTHER PEOPLE WHO WORK IN OFFICES SEE **office**

secrete *VERB*
1 *He secreted his money in a drawer.*
▸ conceal, hide, put out of sight
2 *The pores of your body secrete sweat.*
▸ discharge, give out, let out, produce

secretive *ADJECTIVE*
Why is he so secretive about his private life?
▸ furtive, mysterious, quiet, reserved, uncommunicative
AN OPPOSITE IS communicative

section *NOUN*
If it is too long, divide it into sections.
▸ bit, division, fraction, fragment, part, portion, sector, segment
▹ A section of a book is a **chapter**. A section from a piece of classical music is a **movement**. A section taken from a book or from a long piece of music is a **passage**. A section of a journey is a **stage**. A section of business is a **branch** or **department**.

sector *NOUN*
Soldiers occupied one sector of the town.
▸ area, district, part, region, section, zone

secure *ADJECTIVE*
1 *The ladder was not very secure.*
▸ fast, firm, fixed, immovable, solid, steady
2 *She needs a secure job.*
▸ permanent, regular, steady
3 *Is the house secure against burglars?*
▸ defended, guarded, protected, safe
4 *They felt secure indoors.*
▸ snug, unharmed, unhurt
AN OPPOSITE IS insecure or unsafe

secure *VERB*
1 *The door wasn't properly secured.*
▸ fasten, lock, make safe
2 *He managed to secure two tickets for the concert.*
▸ buy, get hold of, order, reserve

security *NOUN*
You must wear a seat belt for your own security.
▸ protection, safety

sedate *ADJECTIVE*
The procession moved at a sedate pace.
▸ calm, cool, deliberate, dignified, grave, quiet, sensible, serene, serious, slow, sober, solemn, tranquil
AN OPPOSITE IS lively

sediment *NOUN*
They dredged a lot of sediment from the bottom of the canal.
▸ deposit, mud, sludge

see *VERB* This word is often overused. It can be used in many senses. These are some of the common ones and some useful alternatives:
1 *Did you see the film on TV last night?*
▸ look at, view, watch
2 *They saw a kingfisher.*
▸ catch sight of, distinguish, make out, note, notice, observe, perceive, recognize, sight, spot, spy
▹ To see something briefly is to **glimpse** it. To see an accident or some unusual event is to **witness** it.
3 *He asked her to see him in his office.*
▸ go to, report to, visit
4 *I didn't expect to see you here!*
▸ (*informal*) bump into, encounter, meet, run into
5 *She went to see her friend.*
▸ call on, drop in on, visit
6 *I see what you mean.*
▸ appreciate, comprehend, follow, grasp, realize, take in, understand
7 *She found it hard to see herself in the role.*
▸ imagine, picture, visualize
8 *Please see that the windows are shut.*
▸ ensure, make certain, make sure
9 *I'll see what I can do.*
▸ consider, investigate, reflect on, think about, weigh up
10 *He saw them to the door.*
▸ accompany, conduct, escort, guide, lead, take
to see to something *He said he would see to the dinner.*
▸ attend to, deal with, look after, make arrangements for, take care of

seed *NOUN*
▹ The seed in an orange, etc., is a **pip**. The seed in a plum, etc., is a **stone**.

seek *VERB*
1 *For many years he sought his long-lost brother.*
▸ hunt for, inquire after, look for, search for
2 *Most people seek happiness.*
▸ ask for, desire, pursue, strive after, want, wish for

seem *VERB*
1 *Everything seems to be all right.*
▸ appear, look
2 *She isn't the nice person she seems to be.*
▸ give the impression (of), pretend

seep *VERB*
Oil began to seep through the crack.
▸ dribble, drip, flow, leak, ooze, run, soak, trickle

seethe *VERB*
The water in the pan began to seethe.
▸ boil, bubble, foam, froth up
to be seething *She was seething when someone crashed into her car.*
▸ be angry, be agitated, be in a temper, rage, storm

segment *NOUN*
He ate a few segments of an orange.
▸ bit, division, fragment, part, portion, section, slice

segregate *VERB*
They segregated the visitors from the home supporters.
▸ cut off, isolate, keep apart, separate, set apart

seize *VERB*
1 *He stretched out to seize the rope.*
▸ catch, clutch, grab, grasp, grip, hold, pluck, snatch, take
2 *The police seized him in the act of committing the crime.*
▸ arrest, capture, detain, (*informal*) nab, take prisoner
▹ To seize someone's property as a punishment is to **confiscate** it. To seize someone's power or position is to **usurp** it. To seize an aircraft or vehicle during a journey is to **hijack** it.

seldom *ADVERB*
It seldom rains in the desert.
▸ infrequently, rarely
AN OPPOSITE IS often

select *VERB*
They had to select a new captain.
▸ appoint, choose, decide on, elect, nominate, opt for, pick, settle on, vote for

select *ADJECTIVE*
Only a select few were invited.
▸ carefully chosen, privileged, selected, special

selection *NOUN*
There's a wide selection to choose from.
▸ assortment, choice, range, variety

self-centred *ADJECTIVE*
She's very self-centred — she never thinks of other people.
▸ demanding, grasping, greedy, inconsiderate, selfish, thoughtless
AN OPPOSITE IS selfless

self-confident *ADJECTIVE*
He tried to look self-confident at the interview.
▸ assertive, bold, confident, cool, decisive, fearless, forceful, positive, sure of yourself
AN OPPOSITE IS insecure

self-conscious *ADJECTIVE*
She always feels self-conscious in front of an audience.
▸ awkward, bashful, coy, embarrassed, insecure, nervous, sheepish, shy, uncomfortable, unnatural
AN OPPOSITE IS confident

self-control *NOUN*
He showed a lot of self-control by not answering back.
▸ calmness, coolness, patience, restraint, will-power

self-evident *ADJECTIVE*
She had the stolen goods on her, so her guilt was self-evident.
▸ clear, evident, obvious, plain, unmistakable

self-important *ADJECTIVE*
He acted in a very self-important way.
▸ arrogant, haughty, pompous, snobbish, (*informal*) stuck-up
AN OPPOSITE IS modest

selfish *ADJECTIVE*
She's too selfish to even think of sharing her sweets.
▸ demanding, grasping, greedy, mean, miserly, self-centred, thoughtless
AN OPPOSITE IS selfless

selfless *ADJECTIVE*
He's so selfless — he'll do anything to help you.
▸ caring, considerate, generous, helpful, kind, thoughtful, unselfish
AN OPPOSITE IS selfish

self-respect *NOUN*
Losing his job made him lose a lot of self-respect.
▸ dignity, pride

self-righteous *ADJECTIVE*
He acted with self-righteous indignation.
▸ haughty, pious, pompous, priggish, proud, self-satisfied, superior
AN OPPOSITE IS humble

self-sufficient *ADJECTIVE*
The village used to be a self-sufficient community.
▸ independent, self-contained, self-supporting

sell *VERB*
The shop on the corner sells newspapers and sweets.
▸ deal in, offer for sale, retail, stock, trade in
▹ To sell things such as drugs illegally is to **traffic** in them.
VARIOUS WAYS TO BUY AND SELL THINGS
auction, barter, cash sale, hire purchase, on credit, part-exchange, trade-in
PEOPLE WHO SELL THINGS INCLUDE
dealer, (*old use*) hawker, market trader, merchant, pedlar, representative or (*informal*) rep, retailer, salesman or saleswoman, shopkeeper or storekeeper, stockist, street trader, supplier, trader, vendor, wholesaler
FOR PARTICULAR SHOPS SEE **shop**

send *VERB*
1 *She sent him a letter.*
▸ dispatch, post
2 *They plan to send a rocket to Mars.*
▸ direct, fire, launch, propel, shoot
to send something out *The chimney was sending out evil-smelling fumes.*
▸ belch, discharge, emit, give off, issue

senior *ADJECTIVE*
1 *She's the senior member of the team.*
▸ chief, oldest, principal
2 *He is a senior officer in the navy.*
▸ high-ranking, important
AN OPPOSITE IS junior

sensation *NOUN*
1 *She had a tingling sensation in her fingers.*
▸ feeling, sense
2 *The unexpected news caused a sensation.*
▸ excitement, thrill
▹ A sensation caused by something bad is an **outrage** or a **scandal**.

sensational *ADJECTIVE*
1 *The new roller coaster is a sensational experience!*
▸ exciting, hair-raising, spectacular, stimulating, stupendous, thrilling
2 *The newspaper contained a sensational account of a murder.*
▸ shocking, startling, violent
3 (*informal*) *Did you hear the sensational result of yesterday's match?*
▸ amazing, extraordinary, fantastic, remarkable, surprising, unexpected

sense *NOUN*
1 *A baby learns about the world through its senses.*
▹ Your five senses are **hearing**, **sight**, **smell**, **taste**, and **touch**.
2 *He has no sense of shame.*
▸ awareness, consciousness, feeling, perception
3 *If you had any sense you'd stay at home.*
▸ brains, cleverness, intelligence, judgement, wisdom
4 *The sense of the word is not clear.*
▸ gist, meaning, significance
to make sense *When she explained it, it began to make sense.*
▸ be intelligible, have a meaning, mean something
to make sense of something *She couldn't make sense of the message.*
▸ explain, follow, interpret, understand
out of your senses (*informal*) *You're out of your senses to go swimming in this weather!*
▸ crazy, daft, foolish, insane, mad, (*informal*) out of your mind, stupid

sense *VERB*
1 *He sensed that she didn't like him.*
▸ be aware, feel, guess, notice, perceive, realize, suspect
2 *The machine senses any change of temperature.*
▸ detect, respond to

senseless *ADJECTIVE*
1 *It was a senseless action.*
▸ crazy, daft, foolish, illogical, insane, irrational, mad, silly, stupid, unreasonable
AN OPPOSITE IS sensible
2 *The blow on the head left him senseless.*
▸ knocked out, unconscious
AN OPPOSITE IS conscious

sensible *ADJECTIVE*
1 *He made a sensible decision not to set sail until the weather improved.*
▸ careful, intelligent, logical, prudent, rational, reasonable, sane, sound, thoughtful, wise
AN OPPOSITE IS stupid
2 *Wear sensible shoes to go walking.*
▸ comfortable, practical
AN OPPOSITE IS impractical

A B C D E F G H I J K L M N O P Q R S T U V W X Y Z

sensitive *ADJECTIVE*
1 *She stays out of the sun because she has sensitive skin.*
▸ delicate, fine, soft, tender
2 *Take care what you say — he's very sensitive.*
▸ easily offended, quickly upset, touchy
3 *She's very sensitive towards other people.*
▸ considerate, sympathetic, tactful, thoughtful, understanding
AN OPPOSITE IS insensitive

sentence *VERB*
The judge sentenced the convicted man.
▸ condemn, pass judgement on, pronounce sentence on

sentiment *NOUN*
1 *What are your sentiments about experiments on animals?*
▸ attitude, belief, idea, judgement, opinion, thought, view
2 *There's no room for sentiment in this business.*
▸ emotion, feeling

sentimental *ADJECTIVE*
1 *He gets sentimental when he looks at old family photographs.*
▸ emotional, nostalgic, tearful
2 *She hates sentimental messages on birthday cards.*
▸ insincere, romantic, (*informal*) sloppy, (*informal*) soppy
AN OPPOSITE IS cynical

sentinel, sentry *NOUNS*
He gave the password to the sentry at the gate.
▸ guard, lookout, watchman

separate *ADJECTIVE*
1 *She keeps her books separate from his.*
▸ apart, distinct, independent, separated
2 *They slept in separate rooms.*
▸ detached, different
3 *The visiting supporters were kept separate from ours.*
▸ cut off, divided, fenced off, isolated, segregated
AN OPPOSITE IS combined

separate *VERB*
1 *The farmer wanted to separate the sheep from the lambs.*
▸ cut off, divide, fence off, isolate, keep apart, remove, segregate, set apart, take away
AN OPPOSITE IS combine or mix
▹ To separate something which is connected to something else is to **detach** or **disconnect** it. To separate things which are tangled together is to **disentangle** them.
2 *They walked along together until their paths separated.*
▸ branch, fork, split
AN OPPOSITE IS merge
3 *Her friend's parents have separated.*
▸ part company, split up
▹ To end a marriage legally is to **divorce**.

septic *ADJECTIVE*
The cut became septic.
▸ infected, inflamed, poisoned

sequel *NOUN*
1 *They looked forward to hearing the sequel to the story.*
▸ continuation
2 *The taxi broke down, and the sequel was that she missed her train.*
▸ consequence, outcome, result, upshot

sequence *NOUN*
1 *They learned about the sequence of events which led to the First World War.*
▸ chain, course, series, string, succession, train
2 *He arranged the cards in a logical sequence.*
▸ order, progression

serene *ADJECTIVE*
She had a serene smile on her face.
▸ calm, contented, peaceful, placid, quiet, tranquil, untroubled
AN OPPOSITE IS agitated

series *NOUN*
1 *We learned about the series of events that lead to the First World War.*
▸ chain, course, progression, sequence, set, succession, train
2 *The parade consisted of a series of floats depicting life in Victorian times.*
▸ line, procession, row, set, string
3 *Are you watching the new series on TV?*
▸ mini-series, serial
▹ A kind of TV drama series is a **soap** or **soap opera**. A kind of TV comedy series is a **sitcom** or **situation comedy**.

serious *ADJECTIVE*

1 *They had a serious debate about conservation.*
▸ deep, earnest, intellectual, profound, sincere
AN OPPOSITE IS frivolous
2 *It is a serious subject.*
▸ important, significant, weighty
AN OPPOSITE IS unimportant
3 *Her serious expression told them something was wrong.*
▸ grave, grim, solemn, stern, thoughtful, unsmiling
AN OPPOSITE IS cheerful
4 *There has been a serious accident on the motorway.*
▸ appalling, awful, dreadful, frightful, ghastly, hideous, horrible, nasty, shocking, terrible
AN OPPOSITE IS trivial
5 *His illness wasn't serious.*
▸ critical, dangerous, life-threatening, major, severe
AN OPPOSITE IS minor

servant *NOUN*

Many of the words given below are not often used. They apply to a past time when it was common for some people to be served by others
PEOPLE WHO WORK OR USED TO WORK IN SOMEONE ELSE'S HOUSE
butler, chambermaid, char or charwoman, chauffeur, cook, errand boy, footman, groom, home help, housekeeper, housemaid, kitchenmaid, maid, manservant, page, parlourmaid, retainer, valet
▹ A young person from another country who works for a time in someone's home is an au pair. The servant of an army officer is a batman.
PEOPLE WHO HELP US IN HOTELS, ETC.
attendant, barmaid or barman, doorman, steward or stewardess, waiter or waitress

serve *VERB*

1 *He wanted to serve the community.*
▸ aid, assist, help, work for
2 *How long did he serve in the army?*
▸ be employed, do your duty
3 *She serves in a shop at weekends.*
▸ be an assistant, sell things
4 *When everyone had sat down they served the first course.*
▸ dish up, distribute, give out, pass round
▹ To serve food at table is to wait.
5 *This room will serve as a study.*
▸ be suitable

service *NOUN*

1 *He was able to do her a small service.*
▸ favour, help, kindness
2 *Their marriage service was held in the local church.*
▸ ceremony
▹ A service in church is a meeting for worship.
3 *Mum says her car needs a service.*
▸ a check-over, maintenance, servicing
the services
SEE **armed services**

service *VERB*

The garage serviced her car.
▸ maintain, mend, overhaul, repair

session *NOUN*

1 *They have a training session on Thursday evenings.*
▸ period, time
2 *The Queen will open the next session of Parliament.*
▸ meeting, sitting

set *VERB*

The verb *to set* has many meanings. We give just some of the important ones here
1 *He set the vase on the sideboard.*
▸ place, position, put, stand
2 *She set the table.*
▸ arrange, lay, set out
3 *He set the clock to the correct time.*
▸ adjust, correct, put right, regulate
4 *The jelly will set quicker in the fridge.*
▸ become firm, harden, stiffen
5 *They decided to set the fence posts in concrete.*
▸ fasten, fix
6 *The teacher didn't set any homework.*
▸ prescribe, specify, suggest
7 *They set a date for the Christmas party.*
▸ allot, appoint, choose, decide, determine, establish, identify, name, settle
to set about something *He set about the job immediately.*
▸ begin, commence, start
to set someone free *The prisoners were set free.*
▸ free, let out, liberate, release, rescue

a b c d e f g h i j k l m n o p q r **s** t u v w x y z

A B C D E F G H I J K L M N O P Q R S T U V W X Y Z

to set off **1** *They set off on their journey.*
▸ depart, get going, leave, set out, start out
2 *They set off a bomb.*
▸ detonate, explode
to set something out *Her work is always very well set out.*
▸ display, exhibit, present
to set something up *She wanted to set up a playgroup.*
▸ bring into existence, create, found, initiate, introduce, launch

set *NOUN*
1 *He bought a set of spanners.*
▸ batch, collection
2 *She bought a new TV set.*
▸ apparatus, receiver
3 *They painted the set for the play.*
▸ scenery, setting

setting *NOUN*
The house stood in a rural setting.
▸ background, environment, location, place, position, site, surroundings

settle *VERB*
1 *They have settled what to do.*
▸ agree, choose, decide, determine
2 *They tried to settle their differences.*
▸ deal with, end, solve, sort out
3 *She settled in the chair.*
▸ make yourself comfortable, relax, rest, sit down
4 *They are planning to settle in Canada.*
▸ emigrate (to), go and live, make your home, move (to), set up home
5 *You can see lots of fish when the mud settles.*
▸ clear, sink to the bottom, subside
6 *She settled the bill.*
▸ pay

settlement *NOUN*
They established a settlement on the bank of the river.
▸ colony, community, encampment

settler *NOUN*
The early European settlers in America looked forward to beginning a new life.
▸ colonist, immigrant, newcomer, pioneer

sever *VERB*
The partners eventually decided to sever their relationship.
▸ break off, end, terminate
▹ To sever a branch of a tree is to **cut it off** or **remove** it. To sever a limb is to **amputate** it.

severe *ADJECTIVE*
1 *He was very severe with the children.*
▸ hard, harsh, stern, strict
AN OPPOSITE IS lenient
2 *The traffic warden gave him a severe look.*
▸ disapproving, grim, unkind, unsmiling, unsympathetic
AN OPPOSITE IS kind
3 *She had a severe bout of flu.*
▸ acute, bad, serious, troublesome
AN OPPOSITE IS mild
4 *The explorers experienced severe conditions.*
▸ dangerous, difficult, extreme, tough
▹ A severe frost is a **sharp** frost. Severe cold is **intense** cold. A severe storm is a **violent** storm.

sew *VERB*
He sewed up the tear in his jeans.
▸ darn, mend, repair, stitch, tack
▹ To sew pictures or designs is to do **embroidery** or **tapestry**.

sewers *PLURAL NOUN*
We expect modern cities to have efficient sewers.
▸ drainage, drains, sanitation

sex *NOUN*
What sex is the hamster?
▸ gender

sexist *ADJECTIVE*
She hates it when people make sexist remarks.
▸ male chauvinist, prejudiced

sexy *ADJECTIVE* (*informal*)
She looked very sexy.
▸ attractive, desirable, glamorous

shabby *ADJECTIVE*
1 *She'd like to throw away those shabby clothes and get new ones.*
▸ drab, dreary, faded, frayed, ragged, scruffy, tattered, tatty, threadbare, unattractive, worn, worn out
AN OPPOSITE IS smart
2 *That was a shabby trick!*
▸ dishonest, mean, nasty, shameful, unfair, unfriendly, unkind

shade *NOUN*
1 *They sat in the shade of a tree.*
▸ shadow
2 *She put up a shade to keep the sun off.*
▸ blind, canopy, parasol, screen
3 *They painted the room a pale shade of blue.*
▸ colour, hue, tinge, tint, tone

shade *VERB*
1 *She used her hand to shade her eyes from the sun.*
▸ hide, mask, protect, screen, shield
2 *He shaded the background of the picture with a pencil.*
▸ darken, fill in, make darker

shadow *NOUN*
Her face was deep in shadow.
▸ gloom, shade

shadow *VERB*
The detective was shadowing the suspect.
▸ follow, keep watch on, pursue, stalk, tail, track, trail

shadowy *ADJECTIVE*
1 *They walked along a shadowy path through the woods.*
▸ dark, dim, gloomy, shady, sunless
AN OPPOSITE IS bright
2 *She saw a shadowy figure in the mist.*
▸ faint, ghostly, hazy, indistinct, obscure, unclear, unrecognizable, vague
AN OPPOSITE IS clear

shady *ADJECTIVE*
1 *They found a shady spot under a tree.*
▸ cool, dark, shaded, shadowy, sheltered, sunless
AN OPPOSITE IS sunny
2 *He's involved in some shady business.*
▸ corrupt, (*informal*) crooked, dishonest, disreputable, doubtful, (*informal*) fishy, suspicious, untrustworthy
AN OPPOSITE IS honest

shaft *NOUN*
1 *The horse was harnessed between the shafts of the cart.*
▸ pole, rod
▹ An upright shaft is a column or pillar or post. A shaft that you shoot is an arrow. The shaft on a broom, etc., is the handle.
2 *He nearly fell into an old shaft.*
▸ hole, mine, pit
3 *A shaft of light shone through the window.*
▸ beam, ray

shaggy *ADJECTIVE*
You could hardly see his face behind his shaggy beard.
▸ bushy, hairy, rough, untidy, woolly

shake *VERB*
1 *An explosion made the ground shake.*
▸ quake, quiver, rattle, rock, shiver, shudder, sway, totter, vibrate, wobble
2 *She shook her umbrella.*
▸ brandish, flourish, twirl, wag, waggle, wave, wiggle
3 *They were shaken by the terrible news.*
▸ alarm, distress, disturb, frighten, shock, startle, surprise, upset
4 *He was so upset that his voice was shaking.*
▸ quaver, tremble

shaky *ADJECTIVE*
1 *Be careful — the table is rather shaky.*
▸ decrepit, flimsy, frail, insecure, precarious, rickety, unsteady, weak, wobbly
2 *He was so nervous that his hands were shaky.*
▸ quivering, shaking, trembling
3 *He spoke in a shaky voice.*
▸ faltering, nervous, quavering, tremulous
AN OPPOSITE IS steady

shallow *ADJECTIVE*
1 *They paddled about in the shallow water.*
Surprisingly, there are no convenient synonyms for this common sense of *shallow*
AN OPPOSITE IS deep
2 *She thought that the discussion was rather shallow.*
▸ foolish, frivolous, silly, superficial, trivial
AN OPPOSITE IS profound

sham *NOUN*
It was all a sham.
▸ deception, pretence

shambles *NOUN*
a shambles (*informal*) *It was so badly organized it turned into a shambles.*
▸ chaos, confusion, disorder, a mess, a muddle

shame *NOUN*
He was overcome with feelings of shame when he was caught stealing.
▸ disgrace, dishonour, embarrassment, guilt, humiliation

shameful *ADJECTIVE*
1 *Losing 10–0 was a shameful defeat.*
▸ embarrassing, humiliating
2 *They showed a shameful lack of concern.*
▸ contemptible, despicable, disgraceful, outrageous, scandalous, wicked
AN OPPOSITE IS honourable

A B C D E F G H I J K L M N O P Q R S T U V W X Y Z

shameless *ADJECTIVE*
1 *He's quite shameless about having cheated in the test.*
▸ brazen, unashamed, unrepentant
AN OPPOSITE IS ashamed
2 *Her shameless behaviour shocked everyone.*
▸ bold, improper, impudent, indecent, insolent, outrageous, rude
AN OPPOSITE IS modest

shape *NOUN*
The badge was in the shape of a star.
▸ form
▹ The shape of your body is your **figure**. A line showing the shape of a thing is the **outline**. A dark outline seen against a light background is a **silhouette**. A container for making things in a special shape is a **mould**.
FLAT SHAPES
circle, diamond, ellipse, heptagon, hexagon, oblong, octagon, oval, parallelogram, pentagon, polygon, quadrilateral, rectangle, rhombus, ring, semicircle, square, trapezium, triangle
THREE-DIMENSIONAL SHAPES
cone, cube, cylinder, hemisphere, polyhedron, prism, pyramid, sphere

shape *VERB*
The sculptor shaped the stone into a human figure.
▸ carve, cut, fashion, form, mould
▹ To shape something in a mould is to **cast** it.

share *NOUN*
Everyone got a share of the food.
▸ allowance, bit, (*informal*) cut, division, fraction, helping, part, piece, portion, quota, ration

share *VERB*
They shared the money equally.
▸ allot, deal out, distribute, divide, ration out, share out, split, subdivide

sharp *ADJECTIVE*
1 *The carving knife has a sharp edge.*
▸ keen, razor-sharp, sharpened
AN OPPOSITE IS blunt
2 *The barbed wire has sharp points all along it.*
▸ jagged, pointed, spiky
AN OPPOSITE IS smooth
3 *If you can see that, you must have sharp eyes!*
▸ alert, observant, perceptive, quick
AN OPPOSITE IS unobservant
4 *She's very sharp.*
▸ bright, clever, intelligent, quick-witted, shrewd, smart
AN OPPOSITE IS stupid
5 *We slowed down for a sharp bend in the road.*
▸ abrupt, sudden, unexpected
▹ A bend that doubles back on itself, such as you might find on a mountain road, is a **hairpin** bend.
AN OPPOSITE IS gradual
6 *The sharp frost killed mum's geraniums.*
▸ extreme, intense, serious, severe
AN OPPOSITE IS slight
7 *Focus the projector so that we get a sharp picture.*
▸ clear, distinct, focused, well defined
AN OPPOSITE IS blurred
8 *He felt a sharp pain in his side.*
▸ acute, stabbing, stinging
AN OPPOSITE IS dull
9 *This lemonade is a bit sharp.*
▸ acid, bitter, sour, tart
AN OPPOSITE IS sweet or tasteless

sharpen *VERB*
He sharpened the carving knife.
▸ grind, make sharp

shatter *VERB*
1 *The ball shattered a window.*
▸ break, destroy, smash, wreck
2 *The windscreen shattered when a stone hit it.*
▸ break, disintegrate, splinter
shattered *She was shattered by the bad news.*
▸ distressed, horrified, shaken, shocked, stunned, upset

sheaf *NOUN*
She had a sheaf of papers in her hand.
▸ bunch, bundle

sheath *NOUN*
He put his sword back in its sheath.
▸ casing, covering, scabbard, sleeve

shed *NOUN*
They kept their lawnmower in the garden shed.
▸ hut, outhouse, shack

shed *VERB*
A lorry shed its load on the motorway.
▸ drop, let fall, scatter, spill

sheen *NOUN*
He polished the car until it had a nice sheen.
▸ brightness, gleam, gloss, lustre, polish, shine

sheep *NOUN*
▷ A female sheep is a ewe. A young sheep is a lamb. A male sheep is a ram. Meat from sheep is mutton or lamb.

sheepish *ADJECTIVE*
When she caught him out, he gave her a sheepish look.
▸ ashamed, bashful, coy, embarrassed, self-conscious, shy, timid
AN OPPOSITE IS shameless

sheer *ADJECTIVE*
1 *The story he told was sheer nonsense.*
▸ absolute, complete, pure, total, utter
2 *Don't try to climb that sheer cliff.*
▸ perpendicular, vertical
3 *Her blouse was made of sheer silk.*
▸ fine, flimsy, see-through, thin, transparent

sheet *NOUN*
▷ A sheet of paper is a leaf or page. A sheet of glass is a pane or plate of glass. A sheet of ice is a covering or layer of ice. A sheet of water is an area or expanse of water.

shelf *NOUN*
She put the vase of flowers on the shelf.
▸ ledge

shell *NOUN*
A tortoise has a hard shell.
▸ case, casing, covering, exterior, outside

shell *VERB*
They shelled the town until it was in ruins.
▸ attack, bomb, bombard, fire at, shoot at

shellfish *NOUN*
SOME SPECIES OF SHELLFISH
barnacle, clam, cockle, conch, crab, crayfish, cuttlefish, limpet, lobster, mussel, oyster, prawn, scallop, shrimp, whelk, winkle
▷ Invertebrate creatures with a soft body and a shell are molluscs. Molluscs like oysters and mussels with two hinged shells are bivalves. Shellfish with legs like crabs, lobsters, and shrimps are crustaceans.

shelter *NOUN*
They reached shelter just before the storm broke.
▸ cover, protection, refuge, sanctuary, safety

shelter *VERB*
1 *The wall sheltered them from the wind.*
▸ defend, guard, protect, safeguard, screen, shield
2 *He sheltered from the rain under the trees.*
▸ hide, take refuge

shelve *VERB*
1 *The plans had to be shelved.*
▸ abandon, cancel, postpone, put off, reject
2 *The beach shelves steeply.*
▸ drop away, fall away, slope

shield *NOUN*
They erected a wind shield.
▸ barrier, defence, guard, protection, screen, shelter
▷ The part of a helmet that shields your face is the visor.

shield *VERB*
The bird tried to shield her chicks from danger.
▸ defend, guard, keep safe, protect, safeguard, shelter

shift *VERB*
1 *He asked his neighbour if she could shift her car.*
▸ move, remove
2 *He shoved the wardrobe but it wouldn't shift.*
▸ budge, change position, move

shine *VERB*
1 *A light shone in the window.*
▸ be visible, show up
DIFFERENT WAYS IN WHICH VARIOUS THINGS GIVE OUT OR REFLECT LIGHT
beam, blaze, burn, dazzle, flame, flash, flicker, glare, gleam, glimmer, glint, glisten, glitter, glow, radiate, shimmer, spark, sparkle, twinkle
▷ To shine in the dark is to be luminous or phosphorescent.
2 *He shines his shoes every morning.*
▸ clean, polish, rub
3 *She's good at all sports, but she shines at tennis.*
▸ do best, excel, stand out

shingle *NOUN*
The beach was shingle, not sand.
▸ gravel, pebbles, stones

A B C D E F G H I J K L M N O P Q R S T U V W X Y Z

shiny *ADJECTIVE*
She polished the silver until it was shiny.
▸ bright, dazzling, gleaming, glistening, glossy, lustrous, polished, reflective, shining, sleek
AN OPPOSITE IS dull
▹ Shiny paint is **gloss** paint. The opposite is matt paint.

ship *NOUN*
FOR VARIOUS SHIPS SEE **vessel**

ship *VERB*
The firm ships goods all over the world.
▸ convey, export, move, send, shift, take, transport

shirk *VERB*
He always shirks the unpleasant tasks.
▸ avoid, evade, get out of, ignore, neglect

shiver *VERB*
She began to shiver with cold.
▸ quake, quaver, quiver, shake, shudder, tremble

shock *NOUN*
1 *His sudden death was a great shock.*
▸ blow, surprise, (*informal*) upset
2 *People felt the shock of the explosion miles away.*
▸ bang, impact, jolt
3 *The driver involved in the accident was in a state of shock.*
▸ collapse, dismay, distress, fright
▹ A formal word for a state of shock is **trauma**.

shock *VERB*
1 *They were shocked by the news.*
▸ alarm, amaze, astonish, astound, dismay, distress, frighten, (*informal*) give you a turn, scare, shake, stagger, startle, stun, surprise, upset
▹ A formal synonym is **traumatize**.
2 *The bad language in the play shocked them.*
▸ appal, disgust, horrify, offend, outrage, repel, revolt

shoddy *ADJECTIVE*
1 *Their work was rather shoddy.*
▸ careless, messy, negligent, slipshod, sloppy, slovenly, untidy
AN OPPOSITE IS careful
2 *That shop sells shoddy goods.*
▸ cheap, inferior, poor quality, (*informal*) tacky, trashy, worthless
AN OPPOSITE IS superior

shoe *NOUN*
KINDS OF SHOE
ankle boot, boot, bootee, brogue, clog, court shoe, espadrille, flip-flop, galosh, gumboot, gymshoe, moccasin, mule, plimsoll, pump, sandal, slip-on, slipper, sneaker, trainer, wader, wellington

shoot *VERB*
1 *He prepared to shoot at the target.*
▸ aim, fire
2 *They were told to shoot the dangerous animal if necessary.*
▸ fire at, gun down, hit, open fire on, snipe at
3 *They watched the racing cars shoot past.*
▸ (*informal*) dash, hurtle, rush, speed, streak, (*informal*) zoom
4 *They are going to shoot a TV series in the town.*
▸ film, photograph

shoot *NOUN*
Young shoots grow in the spring.
▸ bud, new growth, sprout

shop *NOUN*
VARIOUS PLACES WHERE YOU CAN BUY THINGS
boutique, cash and carry, corner shop, department store, hypermarket, market, retailer's, shopping arcade, shopping centre, shopping mall, shopping precinct, supermarket, wholesaler's
PEOPLE INVOLVED IN SELLING THINGS TO US
dealer, market trader, merchant, retailer, salesman or saleswoman, shop assistant, shopkeeper, shop manager, stockist, storekeeper, supplier, trader, tradesman
SHOPS AND BUSINESSES DEALING IN DIFFERENT KINDS OF GOODS OR SERVICES
antique shop, baker, bank, barber, betting shop, bookmaker, bookshop, building society, butcher, chemist, clothes shop, confectioner, dairy, delicatessen, DIY or do-it-yourself shop, draper, electrician, estate agent, fish and chip shop, fishmonger, florist, furniture store, garden centre, greengrocer, grocer, haberdasher, hairdresser, hardware store, health-food shop, ironmonger, jeweller, launderette, newsagent, off-licence, pawnbroker, pharmacy, post office, shoemaker, stationer, tailor, tobacconist, toyshop, video shop, watchmaker

shop *VERB*
She was shopping for Christmas presents.
▶ buy things, go shopping

shopper *NOUN*
The market is crowded with shoppers on Saturdays.
▶ buyer, customer

shopping *NOUN*
He put the shopping in a carrier bag.
▶ goods, purchases

shore *NOUN*
They walked along the shore looking for seashells.
▶ beach, edge of the water, sands, seashore, seaside, shingle

short *ADJECTIVE* This word is often overused. Here are some alternatives:
1 *They live a short distance from the shops.*
There is no obvious synonym for *short* in this sense
AN OPPOSITE IS long
2 *It was a very short visit.*
▶ brief, fleeting, hasty, quick, temporary
AN OPPOSITE IS long
3 *He's very short.*
▶ dumpy, little, small, tiny
AN OPPOSITE IS tall
4 *During the drought water was in short supply.*
▶ inadequate, insufficient, limited, meagre, scanty, scarce
AN OPPOSITE IS plentiful
5 *He was short with her when she asked for a loan.*
▶ abrupt, bad-tempered, cross, grumpy, impolite, irritable, rude, sharp, unfriendly, unsympathetic
AN OPPOSITE IS friendly

shortage *NOUN*
The shortage of water is worrying.
▶ inadequacy, lack, scarcity
▷ A shortage of water is a **drought**. A shortage of food is a **famine**.

shortcoming *NOUN*
He has many shortcomings.
▶ defect, failing, fault, flaw, imperfection, weakness

shorten *VERB*
She had to shorten the speech because it was too long.
▶ abbreviate, compress, condense, curtail, cut down, prune, reduce, summarize, trim
AN OPPOSITE IS lengthen

shortly *ADVERB*
The post will arrive shortly.
▶ before long, presently, soon

shot *NOUN*
1 *They heard a shot.*
▶ bang, blast, crack
2 *He's a good shot!*
▷ A person who is good at shooting with a gun is a **marksman**.
3 *He had a shot at goal.*
▶ hit, kick, strike
4 *The photographer took some unusual shots.*
▶ photograph, picture, snap, snapshot
5 *She had a shot at solving the problem.*
▶ attempt, effort, go, try

shout *VERB*
You'll deafen me if you shout like that!
▶ bawl, bellow, call, cry out, exclaim, rant, roar, scream, screech, shriek, yell, yelp
AN OPPOSITE IS whisper

shove *VERB*
They shoved her out of the way.
▶ barge, drive, elbow, hustle, jostle, propel, push

shovel *VERB*
He shovelled the snow off the path.
▶ clear, dig, move, scoop, shift

show *VERB*
1 *He showed the garden to the visitors.*
▶ display, exhibit, present, reveal
2 *The photo shows them on holiday.*
▶ depict, illustrate, picture, portray, represent
3 *She showed them how to do it.*
▶ explain to, instruct, make clear to, teach, tell
4 *The evidence shows that he was right.*
▶ demonstrate, prove
5 *She showed him to the manager's office.*
▶ conduct, direct, guide
6 *The signpost shows the way.*
▶ indicate, point out
7 *His vest showed through his shirt.*
▶ appear, be seen, be visible
to show off *He's always showing off.*
▶ bluster, boast, brag, crow, gloat, swagger, (*informal*) swank

A B C D E F G H I J K L M N O P Q R S T U V W X Y Z

show *NOUN*
1 *They put up a show of his paintings.*
▸ display, exhibition, presentation
2 *There's a good show on at the theatre.*
▸ entertainment, performance, production
SEE ALSO **entertainment**

shower *NOUN*
FOR KINDS OF RAIN SEE **rain**

shower *VERB*
A passing bus showered mud over them.
▸ spatter, splash, spray, sprinkle

showy *ADJECTIVE*
She was wearing very showy jewellery.
▸ bright, conspicuous, flashy, gaudy, loud, striking
AN OPPOSITE IS plain

shred *NOUN*
The accused man said they didn't have a shred of evidence against him.
▸ bit, piece, scrap, trace
shreds *The barbed wire tore his shirt to shreds.*
▸ rags, ribbons, strips, tatters

shred *VERB*
She shredded the lettuce and put it in a salad bowl.
▸ cut into shreds, cut up, tear up
▷ To shred something hard like cheese is to grate it.

shrewd *ADJECTIVE*
He's too shrewd to be fooled like that.
▸ artful, bright, clever, crafty, cunning, ingenious, intelligent, quick-witted, sharp, smart, wily, wise
AN OPPOSITE IS stupid

shriek *NOUN, VERB*
All these synonyms can be used both as nouns and verbs
▸ bawl, cry, howl, scream, screech, shout, squeal, wail, yell
FOR VARIOUS WAYS TO MAKE SOUNDS SEE **sound** *VERB*

shrill *ADJECTIVE*
She heard the shrill sound of a whistle.
▸ high, high-pitched, penetrating, piercing, sharp
AN OPPOSITE IS gentle or low

shrink *VERB*
His clothes shrank in the wash.
▸ become smaller, contract
AN OPPOSITE IS expand
to shrink from *He shrinks from meeting strangers.*
▸ avoid, keep or stay away from

shrivel *VERB*
The plants shrivelled in the heat.
▸ become dehydrated, droop, dry out, dry up, shrink, wilt, wither, wrinkle

shroud *VERB*
The mountain was shrouded in mist.
▸ conceal, cover, envelop, hide, mask, screen, veil, wrap

shrub *NOUN*
She bought some shrubs at the garden centre.
▸ bush
SOME POPULAR GARDEN SHRUBS
azalea, berberis, broom, buddleia, camellia, daphne, forsythia, heather, hydrangea, jasmine, lavender, lilac, privet, rhododendron, rosemary, rue, viburnum

shudder *VERB*
He shuddered when he heard the gory details.
▸ quake, quiver, shake, shiver, tremble

shuffle *VERB*
1 *She shuffled upstairs in her slippers.*
FOR VARIOUS WAYS TO WALK SEE **walk** *VERB*
2 *Shuffle the cards before you deal them.*
▸ jumble, mix, mix up

shut *VERB*
Please shut the door.
▸ bolt, close, fasten, latch, lock, push to, seal, secure
▷ To shut a door with a bang is to slam it.
to shut down *The chip shop is going to shut down.*
▸ cease trading, close
to shut someone up *They shut him up in a dark room.*
▸ confine, detain, imprison
Shut up! ▸ Be quiet! Be silent! (*informal*) Hold your tongue! Hush! Keep quiet! (*informal*) Pipe down! Silence! Stop talking!

shy *ADJECTIVE*
He was too shy to say anything.
▸ bashful, cautious, coy, hesitant, inhibited, modest, nervous, reserved, self-conscious, timid, wary
AN OPPOSITE IS bold

sick *ADJECTIVE*
1 *She can't work because she's sick.*
▸ ailing, bedridden, diseased, ill, infirm, poorly, sickly, suffering, unhealthy, unwell
AN OPPOSITE IS healthy
2 *The sea was rough and he felt sick.*
▸ likely to vomit, queasy
to be sick *I think I'm going to be sick.*
▸ vomit
sick of **1** *They're sick of his rude behaviour.*
▸ annoyed by, disgusted by, upset by
2 *I'm sick of that tune.*
▸ bored with, (*informal*) fed up with, tired of

sicken *VERB*
She is sickened by cruelty to animals.
▸ appal, disgust, distress, offend, repel, revolt, shock, (*informal*) turn your stomach

sickly *ADJECTIVE*
He's a sickly child.
▸ ailing, delicate, frail, unhealthy, weak
AN OPPOSITE IS healthy

sickness *NOUN*
FOR VARIOUS ILLNESSES SEE **illness**

side *NOUN*
1 *Each side of the dice has a different number on it.*
▸ face, surface
2 *The path runs along the side of the field.*
▸ border, boundary, edge, fringe, limit, perimeter
▷ The side of a page is the margin. The side of a road is the verge.
3 *She could see both sides of the argument.*
▸ angle, aspect, point of view, view
4 *The football club has a strong side this year.*
▸ team

side *VERB*
to side with someone *She sided with him against the others.*
▸ agree with, back, give support to, stand up for, support

siege *NOUN*
The town held out against the siege for months.
▸ blockade

sieve *NOUN*
▷ A device for straining liquid from food is a colander or strainer. A device for sifting things in the garden is a riddle.

sift *VERB*
1 *He sifted the flour through a sieve.*
▸ filter, separate, strain
2 *They began to sift the evidence they had collected.*
▸ analyse, examine, review, scrutinize, select, sort out

sigh *NOUN VERB*
FOR VARIOUS WAYS TO MAKE SOUNDS SEE **sound** *VERB*

sight *NOUN*
1 *He has good sight.*
▸ eyesight, vision
2 *The woods in autumn are a lovely sight.*
▸ display, scene, show, spectacle
3 *They live within sight of the power station.*
▸ range, view
4 *She went to London to see the sights.*
▸ attraction, tourist attraction

sight *VERB*
The lookout sighted a ship on the horizon.
▸ distinguish, glimpse, make out, notice, observe, perceive, recognize, see, spot, spy

sightseer *NOUN*
London was full of sightseers.
▸ holidaymaker, tourist, visitor

sign *NOUN*
1 *A sign pointed to the exit.*
▸ notice, placard, poster, signpost
▷ The sign belonging to a particular business or organization is a logo. The sign on a particular brand of goods is a trademark.
2 *She gave no sign that she was angry.*
▸ clue, hint, indication, warning
3 *She gave them a sign to begin.*
▸ cue, gesture, reminder, signal

sign *VERB*
1 *She signed her name on the form.*
▸ inscribe, write
2 *He signed that he was turning left.*
▸ communicate, gesticulate, give or send a signal, indicate, signal
3 *The club signed a new player last week.*
▸ engage, enrol, recruit, take on

signal *NOUN*
She gave a clear signal.
▸ indication, sign, warning
SIGNALS USED IN VARIOUS SITUATIONS
alarm bell, beacon, bell, bugle call, burglar alarm, buzzer, flag, flare, gesture, gong, green light, hooter, indicator, lights, red light, rocket, semaphore signal, siren, smoke signal, traffic lights, warning light, whistle
SEE ALSO **gesture**

A B C D E F G H I J K L M N O P Q R S T U V W X Y Z

signal *VERB*
He signalled that he was ready.
▸ gesticulate, give a sign or signal, indicate

signature *NOUN*
The author wrote his signature in the book.
▸ autograph

significance *NOUN*
What's the significance of that remark?
▸ importance, meaning, message, point, relevance

significant *ADJECTIVE*
1 *They made a note of the significant facts.*
▸ important, meaningful, telling, valuable, vital
2 *He's made significant progress in maths.*
▸ considerable, noticeable, perceptible, striking
3 *He made a significant profit on the sale of his business.*
▸ biggish, largish, sizeable, substantial, worthwhile
AN OPPOSITE IS negligible

signify *VERB*
1 *A red light signifies danger.*
▸ be a sign of, denote, mean, represent, stand for, symbolize
2 *They signified their agreement by raising their hands.*
▸ communicate, convey, express, indicate, make known, signal

silence *NOUN*
There was silence while we sat the exam.
▸ calm, hush, peace, quiet, quietness, stillness
AN OPPOSITE IS noise

silence *VERB*
He tried to silence the noise of the engine.
▸ deaden, muffle, quieten, suppress
▹ To silence someone by putting something in or over their mouth is to **gag** them.
Silence! ▸ Be quiet! Be silent! (*informal*) Hold your tongue! Hush! Keep quiet! (*informal*) Pipe down! Shut up! Stop talking!

silent *ADJECTIVE*
1 *It was a silent night.*
▸ hushed, noiseless, quiet, soundless, still
▹ Something you can't hear is **inaudible**.
2 *He remained silent throughout the meeting.*
▸ dumb, mute, speechless, tongue-tied, uncommunicative
AN OPPOSITE IS talkative

silky *ADJECTIVE*
A cat has silky fur.
▸ fine, sleek, smooth, soft, velvety

silly *ADJECTIVE*
1 *It was silly of him to waste all his money.*
▸ brainless, crazy, foolish, idiotic, illogical, irrational, misguided, naïve, pointless, rash, reckless, senseless, stupid, thoughtless, unintelligent, unreasonable, unwise
AN OPPOSITE IS sensible
2 *She laughed at their silly games.*
▸ absurd, amusing, comic, frivolous, light-hearted, ludicrous, playful, ridiculous
AN OPPOSITE IS serious

similar *ADJECTIVE*
1 *Twin brothers are similar in appearance.*
▸ alike, identical, indistinguishable, matching, the same
2 *She tried to find a similar dress to the one she had lost.*
▸ comparable, matching
AN OPPOSITE IS different

similarity *NOUN*
It's easy to see the similarity between the twins.
▸ likeness, resemblance
AN OPPOSITE IS difference

simple *ADJECTIVE*
1 *Can you answer this simple question?*
▸ easy, elementary
AN OPPOSITE IS difficult
2 *This computer program is simple to use.*
▸ clear, foolproof, intelligible, lucid, straightforward, uncomplicated, understandable, user-friendly
AN OPPOSITE IS complicated
3 *She wore a simple dress.*
▸ austere, plain, undecorated
AN OPPOSITE IS elaborate
4 *He enjoys simple pleasures like walking and gardening.*
▸ homely, honest, humble, modest, ordinary, unsophisticated
AN OPPOSITE IS sophisticated
5 *He seems a bit simple.*
▸ brainless, foolish, idiotic, naïve, senseless, silly, stupid, unintelligent
AN OPPOSITE IS wise

simplify *VERB*
They simplified the rules so that they are easier to understand.
▶ clarify, make simpler
AN OPPOSITE IS elaborate

simulate *VERB*
The machine simulates space flight.
▶ counterfeit, imitate, reproduce

sin *NOUN*
The preacher said that everyone is guilty of sin.
▶ evil, immorality, sinfulness, vice, wickedness, wrongdoing

sin *VERB*
He said that he had sinned.
▶ do wrong, misbehave, offend

sincere *ADJECTIVE*
He sent her his sincere good wishes.
▶ frank, genuine, honest, open, real, straightforward, true, truthful
AN OPPOSITE IS insincere

sincerity *NOUN*
They doubted the sincerity of his welcome.
▶ frankness, genuineness, honesty, integrity, openness, straightforwardness, truthfulness

sinful *ADJECTIVE*
He asked forgiveness for his sinful behaviour.
▶ bad, corrupt, evil, guilty, immoral, perverted, unholy, unrighteous, villainous, wicked, wrong
AN OPPOSITE IS righteous

sing *VERB*
VARIOUS WAYS TO SING
chant, croon, descant, hum, trill, warble, yodel
DIFFERENT SINGING VOICES
alto, baritone, bass, contralto, soprano, tenor, treble
VARIOUS KINDS OF SINGER
choirboy or choirgirl, chorister, crooner, folk singer, (*old use*) minstrel, opera singer, pop singer, prima donna, vocalist
▷ A group of singers is a choir or chorus.
FOR KINDS OF MUSIC FOR SINGING SEE **song**

singe *VERB*
The hot iron singed his T-shirt.
▶ blacken, burn, char, scorch

single *ADJECTIVE*
1 *We saw a single house high on the moors.*
▶ isolated, solitary
▷ When only a single example of something exists, it is unique.
2 *She says she'll never marry: she wants to stay single.*
▶ unmarried
▷ An unmarried man is a bachelor. An unmarried woman is a spinster.

single *VERB*
to single someone out *He singled me out as the best player in the team.*
▶ choose, identify, pick out, select

single-handed *ADVERB*
You can't shift the piano single-handed.
▶ alone, independently, on your own, unaided, without help

singular *ADJECTIVE*
1 (*in grammar*) *You use the singular form of a word when you refer to only one person or thing.*
AN OPPOSITE IS plural
2 *It was a singular event.*
▶ abnormal, curious, extraordinary, odd, peculiar, remarkable, uncommon, unusual
AN OPPOSITE IS common

sinister *ADJECTIVE*
1 *He had a sinister smile on his face.*
▶ disturbing, evil, forbidding, frightening, menacing, threatening, upsetting, villainous
2 *There was something sinister about his behaviour.*
▶ bad, corrupt, criminal, dishonest, illegal, questionable, shady, suspicious

sink *VERB*
1 *The ship hit the rocks and sank.*
▶ become submerged, founder, go down
▷ To let water into a ship to sink it deliberately is to scuttle it.
2 *He fainted and sank to the ground.*
▶ drop, fall, slip down, subside
▷ When the sun sinks to the horizon it sets.

sit *VERB*
1 *Please sit on the bench.*
▶ be seated, perch, rest, seat yourself, settle down
▷ To sit on your heels is to squat. To sit to have your portrait painted is to pose.
2 *My cousin has to sit important exams this year.*
▶ (*informal*) go in for, take

A B C D E F G H I J K L M N O P Q R S T U V W X Y Z

site *NOUN*
This is the site for a new sports centre.
▸ location, place, plot, position, setting, situation

site *VERB*
They decided to site the shopping centre in the middle of the town.
▸ establish, locate, place, position, situate

sitting room *NOUN*
They were watching TV in the sitting room.
▸ drawing room, living room, lounge
FOR NAMES OF OTHER ROOMS SEE **room**

situated *ADJECTIVE*
The house is situated next to the park.
▸ located, positioned

situation *NOUN*
1 *The house is in a pleasant situation.*
▸ locality, location, place, position, setting, site, spot
2 *He was in an awkward situation.*
▸ circumstances, condition, plight
3 *She applied for a situation in the new firm.*
▸ appointment, employment, job, post

size *NOUN*
They were amazed by the sheer size of the building.
▸ dimensions, magnitude, proportions, scale
Size can be measured in many ways. Other synonyms we might use depend on how we would measure the thing we are talking about.
OTHER SYNONYMS MIGHT INCLUDE
amount, area, breadth, bulk, capacity, depth, extent, gauge, height, length, volume, width
FOR UNITS OF SIZE SEE **measurement**

sizeable *ADJECTIVE*
She gave them sizeable helpings of pudding.
▸ biggish, considerable, decent, generous, largish, significant, worthwhile
AN OPPOSITE IS small

skeleton *NOUN*
1 *They dug up a human skeleton.*
▸ bones
2 *So far they've only put up the skeleton of the building.*
▸ frame, framework, shell

sketch *NOUN*
1 *He drew a quick sketch of her.*
▸ drawing, outline, picture
▹ A sketch you do while you think of other things is a **doodle.**
2 *They performed a comic sketch.*
▸ scene, skit, turn

sketch *VERB*
He sketched the man the police were looking for.
▸ depict, draw, portray, represent

sketchy *ADJECTIVE*
She has a rather sketchy knowledge of the subject.
▸ fragmentary, imperfect, incomplete, rough, scrappy
AN OPPOSITE IS perfect

skid *VERB*
He skidded on the ice.
▸ go out of control, slide, slip

skilful *ADJECTIVE*
She's a skilful driver.
▸ able, accomplished, brilliant, capable, clever, deft, expert, gifted, talented
▹ If you are skilful at a lot of things, you are **versatile.** If you are skilful at deceiving people, you are **artful** or **crafty** or **cunning.**
AN OPPOSITE IS unskilful
SEE ALSO **skilled**

skill *NOUN*
1 *She showed great skill at the game.*
▸ ability, accomplishment, aptitude, capability, cleverness, competence, deftness, expertise, gift, ingenuity, proficiency, talent, versatility, workmanship
2 *He wanted to learn new skills.*
▸ art, craft, knack, technique

skilled *ADJECTIVE*
You need a skilled electrician to replace the wiring.
▸ competent, experienced, professional, proficient, qualified, trained
AN OPPOSITE IS amateur

skim *VERB*
1 *The stone skimmed across the surface of the pond.*
▸ glide, skid, slide, slip
2 *He skimmed through the book.*
▸ glance through, look through, scan, skip through

skin *NOUN*
People used to dress in animal skins.
▸ coat, fur, hide, pelt
▹ The type of skin you have on your face is your **complexion**. A scientific word for your skin is **epidermis**. Skin on fruit, vegetables, etc., is **peel** or **rind**. Skin that might form on top of a liquid, etc., is a **coating**, **film**, or **membrane**.

skinny *ADJECTIVE*
He's very skinny — he should eat more.
▸ bony, gaunt, lanky, spare, thin
AN OPPOSITE IS plump
SEE ALSO **thin**

skip *VERB*
1 *They skipped about the room.*
▸ bound, caper, dance, frisk, frolic, hop, jump, leap, prance, romp, spring
2 *He skipped the boring bits in the book.*
▸ ignore, leave out, miss out, pass over, skim through
3 *She was told off for skipping lessons.*
▸ be absent from, miss, play truant from

skirt *VERB*
The path skirts the playing field.
▸ circle, go round, pass round

skittish *ADJECTIVE*
They were in a skittish mood and couldn't get any work done.
▸ excitable, frisky, impish, lively, playful, sprightly
AN OPPOSITE IS sedate

sky *NOUN*
Clouds moved across the sky.
▸ air, heavens

slab *NOUN*
She took a slab of chocolate in case she got hungry.
▸ block, chunk, hunk, lump, piece

slack *ADJECTIVE*
1 *She had to tighten any guy-ropes that were slack.*
▸ limp, loose
AN OPPOSITE IS tight
2 *He's too slack in his approach to work.*
▸ casual, idle, lazy, negligent, relaxed, unbusinesslike
AN OPPOSITE IS businesslike
3 *Business has been slack this year.*
▸ quiet, slow
AN OPPOSITE IS busy

slacken *VERB*
1 *He slackened the ropes.*
▸ ease off, loosen, relax, release
AN OPPOSITE IS tighten
2 *The pace of the game slackened after half-time.*
▸ decrease, lessen, reduce, slow down
AN OPPOSITE IS increase

slam *VERB*
Don't slam the door!
▸ bang, shut loudly

slant *VERB*
1 *Her handwriting slants backwards.*
▸ be at an angle, incline, lean, slope, tilt
2 *He slanted the evidence in her favour.*
▸ distort, twist

slant *NOUN*
1 *The floor of the caravan was at a slant.*
▸ angle, gradient, incline, slope, tilt
▹ A slant on a damaged ship is a **list**. A slanting line joining opposite corners of a square, etc., is a **diagonal**. A surface slanting up to a higher level is a **ramp**.
2 *He didn't like the slant they gave to the news.*
▸ bias, distortion, emphasis, point of view

slap *VERB*
She was so angry she slapped him.
▸ smack, spank
FOR OTHER WAYS TO HIT THINGS SEE **hit** *VERB*

slash *VERB*
FOR VARIOUS WAYS TO CUT THINGS SEE **cut** *VERB*

slaughter *VERB*
They had to slaughter the cattle.
▸ kill, massacre, slay

slaughter *NOUN*
The battle ended in terrible slaughter.
▸ bloodshed, butchery, killing, massacre

slaughterhouse *NOUN*
▹ A formal word is **abattoir**.

slave *VERB*
They slaved all day to get the job done.
▸ exert yourself, labour, toil, work hard

slavery *NOUN*
Thousands of Africans were taken away into slavery.
▸ bondage, captivity
AN OPPOSITE IS freedom

A B C D E F G H I J K L M N O P Q R S T U V W X Y Z

slay VERB
(*old use*) *Many men were slain in the battle.*
▸ exterminate, kill, massacre, put to death, slaughter

sledge NOUN
The sledge sped down the snowy slope.
▸ sled, toboggan
▹ A large sledge pulled by horses is a **sleigh**. A sledge with steering and brakes used in winter sports is a **bobsleigh**.

sleek ADJECTIVE
The cat has a sleek coat.
▸ glossy, shiny, silky, smooth, soft, velvety
AN OPPOSITE IS coarse

sleep VERB
▹ To sleep peacefully is to **be asleep** or **slumber**. To sleep for a time during the day is to **snooze** or **take a nap**. To be half-asleep is to **doze** or **drowse**. To go to sleep is to **drop off** or **nod off**.
INFORMAL WORDS FOR A SHORT SLEEP
catnap, forty winks, kip, nap, shut-eye, snooze
▹ An afternoon sleep is a **siesta**. A deep sleep caused by an injury, etc., is a **coma**. The long sleep some animals have through the winter is **hibernation**.

sleepless ADJECTIVE
She had a sleepless night.
▸ restless, wide awake
▹ The formal name for sleeplessness is **insomnia**.

sleepy ADJECTIVE
He always feels sleepy after dinner.
▸ (*informal*) dopey, drowsy, heavy-eyed, lethargic, ready to sleep, tired, weary
AN OPPOSITE IS wide awake

slender ADJECTIVE
1 *She has a slender figure.*
▸ graceful, lean, slim, spare, trim
AN OPPOSITE IS fat
2 *The spider dangled on a slender thread.*
▸ delicate, fine, fragile, thin
AN OPPOSITE IS thick
3 *He's only got a slender chance of winning.*
▸ insignificant, negligible, poor, slight
AN OPPOSITE IS good
4 *He won by a slender margin.*
▸ narrow, small
AN OPPOSITE IS large

slice VERB
▹ To slice meat is to **carve** it.
SEE ALSO **cut** VERB

slick ADJECTIVE
The conjuror's slick movements deceived them all.
▸ artful, clever, cunning, deft, quick, smart
AN OPPOSITE IS clumsy

slide VERB
He began to slide down the icy slope.
▸ glide, skid, slip, slither
▹ To enjoy yourself sliding over ice or snow is to **skate** or **ski** or **toboggan**.

slight ADJECTIVE
1 *There is a slight problem with the system.*
▸ insignificant, minor, negligible, superficial, trifling, trivial, unimportant
AN OPPOSITE IS important
2 *In spite of his slight build he's a good runner.*
▸ delicate, fragile, frail, slender, slim, small, spare, thin, tiny
AN OPPOSITE IS stout

slightly ADVERB
She was slightly hurt in the accident.
▸ a little, hardly, only just, scarcely
AN OPPOSITE IS seriously

slim ADJECTIVE
1 *He stays slim by taking exercise.*
▸ graceful, lean, slender, spare, thin, trim
AN OPPOSITE IS fat
2 *Her chances of winning are slim.*
▸ insignificant, negligible, poor, slight
AN OPPOSITE IS good
3 *They won by a slim margin.*
▸ fine, narrow, small
AN OPPOSITE IS large

slim VERB
He's been trying to slim for years.
▸ become slimmer, diet, lose weight, reduce

slimy ADJECTIVE
She slipped in the slimy mud.
▸ mucky, slippery, squashy, sticky

sling *VERB*
He slung the rubbish into the skip.
▸ cast, (*informal*) chuck, fling, (*informal*) heave, hurl, lob, pitch, throw, toss

slink *VERB*
They tried to slink away without being seen.
▸ creep, move guiltily, slip, sneak, steal

slip *VERB*
1 *He slipped on the ice.*
▸ move out of control, skate, skid, slither
2 *The lifeboat slipped into the water.*
▸ glide, slide
3 *She slipped out of the room.*
▸ creep, edge, move quietly, slink, sneak, steal, tiptoe
to slip up *The burglar slipped up when he left his fingerprints on the window.*
▸ go wrong, make a mistake

slip *NOUN*
He made a silly slip.
▸ blunder, error, fault, lapse, mistake, oversight, (*informal*) slip-up
to give someone the slip *The robber gave them the slip.*
▸ escape, get away, run away

slippery *ADJECTIVE*
Take care — the floor is slippery.
▸ glassy, slithery, smooth
▹ A surface slippery with frost is **icy**. A surface slippery with grease is **greasy** or **oily**. To put oil on something to make it slippery is to **lubricate** it.

slipshod *ADJECTIVE*
His work was rather slipshod.
▸ careless, hasty, messy, shoddy, sloppy, slovenly, untidy
AN OPPOSITE IS careful

slit *NOUN*
He made slits in his jeans with a pair of scissors.
▸ cut, gash, hole, opening, split, tear

slit *VERB*
FOR VARIOUS WAYS TO CUT THINGS SEE **cut** *VERB*

slither *VERB*
The snake slithered away.
▸ glide, slide, slip

slog *VERB*
He slogged the ball over the boundary.
▸ (*informal*) bash, (*informal*) belt, clout, drive, hammer, hit, (*slang*) slosh, swipe, thump, (*informal*) wallop

slogan *NOUN*
They were trying to think up a new advertising slogan.
▸ catchphrase, motto, saying

slop *VERB*
He slopped tea into the saucer.
▸ slosh, spill, splash, upset

slope *VERB*
The beach slopes gently down to the sea.
▸ fall, rise, shelve

slope *NOUN*
1 *It was hard work pushing the cart up the slope.*
▸ bank, gradient, hill, incline, ramp, rise
▹ An upward slope is an **ascent**. A downward slope is a **descent**.
2 *There was a slope in the floor of the caravan.*
▸ slant, tilt

sloppy *ADJECTIVE*
1 *He stirred the sloppy mixture of flour, eggs, and milk.*
▸ liquid, messy, runny, watery, wet
2 *Her work was very sloppy.*
▸ careless, hasty, shoddy, slipshod, slovenly, untidy
3 (*informal*) *He hates sloppy love stories.*
▸ romantic, sentimental, (*informal*) soppy, weak

slosh *VERB*
1 *He sloshed water on to the dirty floor.*
▸ slop, spill, splash
2 (*slang*) *He sloshed the man on the chin.*
▸ (*informal*) bash, (*informal*) belt, clout, hit, thump, (*informal*) wallop

slot *NOUN*
1 *She put a coin into the slot.*
▸ chink, hole, opening, slit
2 *TV has a regular slot for local news.*
▸ place, space, time

slouch *VERB*
She told him to stop slouching.
▸ droop, lounge, shamble, slump, stoop

a b c d e f g h i j k l m n o p q r s t u v w x y z

A B C D E F G H I J K L M N O P Q R S T U V W X Y Z

slovenly *ADJECTIVE*
She told him off for his slovenly work.
▸ careless, hasty, messy, shoddy, sloppy, thoughtless, untidy
AN OPPOSITE IS careful

slow *ADJECTIVE*
1 *They made slow progress.*
▸ careful, cautious, deliberate, gradual, leisurely, plodding, tedious, unhurried
2 *She told them to hurry up — they were being too slow.*
▸ dawdling, idle, late, lazy, loitering, straggling
3 *He was slow to answer.*
▸ hesitant, reluctant
AN OPPOSITE IS quick

slow *VERB*
to slow down *Slow down — you're driving too fast.*
▸ brake, go slower, reduce speed
AN OPPOSITE IS accelerate

sludge *NOUN*
They cleared a lot of sludge out of the pond.
▸ muck, mud, ooze, slime

slump *VERB*
He slumped in his chair.
▸ collapse, flop, loll, sag, slouch

slump *NOUN*
There was a slump in trade after Christmas.
▸ collapse, decline, drop, fall
▹ A general slump in trade is a **depression** or **recession**.
AN OPPOSITE IS boom

sly *ADJECTIVE*
She thought he was a bit sly.
▸ artful, crafty, cunning, deceitful, devious, furtive, scheming, secretive, (*informal*) sneaky, stealthy, tricky, underhand, wily
AN OPPOSITE IS straightforward

smack *VERB*
His mother threatened to smack him.
▸ slap, spank
FOR WAYS OF HITTING SEE **hit** *VERB*

small *ADJECTIVE* This word is often overused. Here are some alternatives:
1 *The model village showed everything on a small scale.*
▸ compact, little, microscopic, miniature, minute, tiny
AN OPPOSITE IS big
2 *He complained that his helping of stew was rather small.*
▸ inadequate, insufficient, meagre, (*informal*) measly, scanty, stingy
AN OPPOSITE IS generous
3 *She had a small problem.*
▸ insignificant, minor, negligible, trifling, trivial, unimportant
AN OPPOSITE IS important

smart *ADJECTIVE*
1 *Everyone looked smart at the wedding.*
▸ chic, elegant, fashionable, neat, (*informal*) posh, spruce, stylish, tidy, trim, well-dressed
AN OPPOSITE IS scruffy
2 *It was smart of him to think of that.*
▸ acute, artful, bright, clever, crafty, ingenious, intelligent, shrewd
AN OPPOSITE IS stupid
3 *They set off at a smart pace.*
▸ brisk, fast, quick, rapid, speedy, swift
AN OPPOSITE IS slow

smart *VERB*
The cut will smart when she puts antiseptic on it.
▸ be painful, hurt, sting

smarten *VERB*
He smartened himself up before the visitors arrived.
▸ clean, tidy

smash *VERB*
1 *He dropped a plate and smashed it.*
▸ break, crush, squash
▹ When glass smashes it **shatters**. When wood smashes it **splinters**. To smash something completely is to **demolish** or **destroy** or **wreck** it.
2 *She thought the lorry was going to smash into them.*
▸ bang, bump, collide, crash, knock, ram, slam

smear *VERB*
The chef smeared butter over the cooking dish.
▸ dab, rub, smudge, spread, wipe

smear *NOUN*
There was a smear of paint on his face.
▸ mark, smudge, streak, trace

smell *NOUN*
PLEASANT SMELLS
aroma, fragrance, perfume, scent
▹ The smell of wine is its **bouquet**.
ADJECTIVES USED TO DESCRIBE THINGS WITH A PLEASANT SMELL
aromatic, fragrant, perfumed, savoury, scented, spicy, sweet, sweet-smelling
UNPLEASANT SMELLS
odour, (*informal*) pong, reek, stench, stink, whiff
ADJECTIVES USED TO DESCRIBE THINGS WITH AN UNPLEASANT SMELL
foul, musty, odorous, reeking, rotten, sharp, smelly, sour, stinking, (*informal*) whiffy

smell *VERB*
1 *She smelled the roses.*
▸ scent, sniff
2 *Those onions smell.*
▸ reek, stink

smelly *ADJECTIVE*
SEE **smell** *NOUN*
AN OPPOSITE IS fragrant or odourless

smile *VERB*
He smiled because he was pleased to see her.
▸ beam, grin
▹ To smile in a silly way is to **smirk**. To smile in an insulting way is to **sneer**.
All these words can be used both as nouns and as verbs.

smoke *NOUN*
The chimney sent out clouds of smoke.
▸ fumes, gases, steam, vapour
▹ The smoke given out by a car is **exhaust**. Poisonous fumes which hang in the air like fog are **smog**.

smoke *VERB*
1 *The bonfire was still smoking next morning.*
▸ smoulder
2 *He likes smoking cigars.*
▸ puff at
▹ To breath in tobacco smoke is to **inhale**.

smoky *ADJECTIVE*
The smoky air near the factory affected people's health.
▸ dirty, foggy, grimy, hazy, murky, sooty

smooth *ADJECTIVE*
1 *The road was smooth, with no bumps.*
▸ even, flat, level
AN OPPOSITE IS uneven
2 *They sailed across a smooth sea.*
▸ calm, glassy, peaceful, placid, quiet, unruffled
AN OPPOSITE IS rough
3 *The cat's fur was shiny and smooth.*
▸ silky, sleek, soft, velvety
AN OPPOSITE IS coarse
4 *The new trains give you a smooth ride.*
▸ comfortable, steady
AN OPPOSITE IS bumpy
5 *Whisk the ingredients to make a smooth mixture.*
▸ creamy, flowing, runny
AN OPPOSITE IS lumpy

smooth *VERB*
He smoothed down the wood with sandpaper.
▸ even out, flatten, level, level off
▹ To smooth metal you can **file** or **polish** it. To smooth wood you can **plane** or **sandpaper** it. To smooth cloth you can **iron** or **press** it.

smother *VERB*
1 *She was smothered with a pillow.*
▸ choke, stifle, suffocate
2 *The pudding was smothered with cream.*
▸ cover

smoulder *VERB*
A bonfire can smoulder for days.
▸ burn slowly, smoke

smudge *NOUN*
There was a smudge on the painting.
▸ blot, mark, smear, stain, streak
All these words can be used both as nouns and as verbs

snack *NOUN*
She eats a lot of snacks between meals.
▸ bite, (*informal*) nibble, refreshments
▹ A snack in the middle of the morning is sometimes called **elevenses**.

snag *NOUN*
An unexpected snag delayed the plan.
▸ complication, difficulty, hindrance, hitch, obstacle, problem

A B C D E F G H I J K L M N O P Q R S T U V W X Y Z

snake *NOUN*
▸ serpent
SOME KINDS OF SNAKE
adder, anaconda, boa constrictor, cobra, grass snake, mamba, puff adder, python, rattlesnake, sand snake, sea snake, sidewinder, tree snake, viper

snap *VERB*
1 *She heard a twig snap.*
▸ break, crack
2 *The dog is always snapping at people.*
▸ bite, nip
3 *She was in a bad mood and snapped at him.*
▸ speak angrily, speak irritably

snare *NOUN*
The rabbit was caught in a snare.
▸ booby trap, noose, trap

snare *VERB*
The poacher was trying to snare some game.
▸ catch, net, trap

snarl *VERB*
1 *The dog snarled at her.*
▸ bare the teeth, growl
2 *'Go away!' he snarled.*
FOR DIFFERENT WAYS TO SAY THINGS SEE **talk** *VERB*
snarled up *The motorway was completely snarled up.*
▸ at a standstill, blocked, congested, jammed, obstructed

snatch *VERB*
The thief snatched her bag and ran off.
▸ grab, grasp, pluck, seize, wrench away

sneak *VERB*
I managed to sneak in without anyone seeing.
▸ creep, move stealthily, slink, slip, steal, tiptoe
to sneak on someone (*informal*) *She sneaked on her sister.*
▸ inform against, report, (*informal*) split on, tell tales about

sneaky *ADJECTIVE*
(*informal*) *That was a really sneaky trick.*
▸ cheating, crafty, deceitful, devious, furtive, sly, underhand, untrustworthy
AN OPPOSITE IS honest

sneer *VERB*
to sneer at *They sneered at her ideas.*
▸ be scornful of, deride, jeer at, make fun of, mock, ridicule, scoff at

sniff *VERB*
FOR VARIOUS WAYS TO MAKE SOUNDS SEE **sound** *VERB*

snip *VERB*
She snipped off a lock of her hair.
▸ chop, clip, cut, trim

snippet *NOUN*
She could hear snippets of conversation from the next room.
▸ fragment, piece, scrap, snatch

snivel *VERB*
For goodness' sake, stop snivelling!
▸ cry, sniff, sob, weep, whimper, whine

snobbish *ADJECTIVE*
She's too snobbish to mix with us.
▸ arrogant, haughty, pompous, (*informal*) posh, (*informal*) stuck-up, superior
AN OPPOSITE IS humble

snoop *VERB*
She caught him snooping round her office.
▸ look furtively, poke, pry, rummage, spy

snooper *NOUN*
▹ A person who snoops is a busybody or a spy.

snore, snort *VERBS*
FOR VARIOUS WAYS WE MAKE SOUNDS SEE **sound** *VERB*

snout *NOUN*
The crocodile's snout was visible above the water.
▸ face, muzzle, nose

snub *VERB*
She deliberately ignored you in order to snub you.
▸ be rude or unfriendly to, humiliate, insult, offend, (*informal*) put you down

snug *ADJECTIVE*
I was tucked up snug in bed.
▸ comfortable, cosy, relaxed, safe, secure, warm
AN OPPOSITE IS uncomfortable

soak *VERB*
The rain had soaked his jacket and trousers.
▶ drench, saturate, wet thoroughly
▷ To put something into a liquid is to **immerse** or **submerge** it.
to soak up *A sponge soaks up water.*
▶ absorb, take in, take up

soaked, soaking *ADJECTIVES*
My jacket is soaked.
▶ drenched, dripping, saturated, soggy, sopping, waterlogged, wet through

soar *VERB*
1 *The bird spread its wings and soared into the air.*
▶ ascend, climb, fly, glide, rise
2 *The cost of living continued to soar.*
▶ go up, increase, rise, shoot up

sob *VERB*
She threw herself on the bed, sobbing loudly.
▶ cry, shed tears, weep

sober *ADJECTIVE*
1 *He drank a little wine, but he stayed sober.*
▷ A person who drinks very little alcohol is **abstemious** or **temperate**.
AN OPPOSITE IS drunk
2 *We'll discuss the problem when you are in a sober mood.*
▶ calm, composed, logical, lucid, rational, sensible, serious
AN OPPOSITE IS frivolous or irrational
3 *The funeral was a sober occasion.*
▶ dignified, grave, plain, sedate, solemn, sombre
AN OPPOSITE IS bright or showy

sociable *ADJECTIVE*
They are a pleasant, sociable couple.
▶ amiable, friendly, hospitable, neighbourly, welcoming
AN OPPOSITE IS unfriendly

social *ADJECTIVE*
1 *Elephants are social animals.*
▷ People and creatures who like to be in groups or communities are said to be **gregarious**.
AN OPPOSITE IS solitary
2 *They organized several social activities.*
▶ communal, community, group, public

society *NOUN*
1 *Britain is a multi-racial society.*
▶ civilization, community
2 *He's a member of a secret society.*
▶ association, club, group, organization
3 *She enjoyed the society of others.*
▶ companionship, company, fellowship, friendship

soft *ADJECTIVE*
1 *The baby can only eat soft food.*
▶ crumbly, pulpy, spongy, squashy
AN OPPOSITE IS hard
2 *The gloves are made of soft leather.*
▶ elastic, flexible, pliable, springy, supple
AN OPPOSITE IS rigid
3 *I sank into a soft chair.*
▶ comfortable, cosy, padded
AN OPPOSITE IS uncomfortable
4 *The cat's fur felt very soft.*
▶ downy, feathery, fleecy, furry, silky, sleek, smooth, velvety
AN OPPOSITE IS coarse
5 *A soft breeze stirred the leaves.*
▶ delicate, gentle, light, mild
AN OPPOSITE IS rough
6 *They spoke in soft whispers.*
▶ faint, muted, quiet
AN OPPOSITE IS loud
7 *Soft light created a romantic atmosphere.*
▶ diffused, dim, low, shaded, subdued
AN OPPOSITE IS bright or dazzling

soggy *ADJECTIVE*
1 *The ground was soggy after so much rain.*
▶ drenched, saturated, soaked, sopping, wet through
AN OPPOSITE IS dry
2 *The cake was rather soggy.*
▶ heavy, moist, stodgy
AN OPPOSITE IS light

soil *NOUN*
The plants grow best in well-drained soil.
▶ earth, ground, land
▷ Good fertile soil is **loam**. Decayed plant material which enriches the soil is **humus**. The fertile top layer of soil is **topsoil**. Soil under the topsoil is **subsoil**.

soil *VERB*
Their clothes were soiled with mud and grass stains.
▶ defile, dirty, make dirty

soldier *NOUN*

▷ A soldier in a regular army is a **serviceman** or **servicewoman**. Soldiers are also called **troops**. A person who is compelled to become a soldier is a **conscript**. A new soldier is a **recruit**. A young person training to be a soldier is a **cadet**. A soldier who makes a career in the army is a **regular** soldier. A soldier who makes money fighting for a foreign army is a **mercenary**. An old word for a soldier is **warrior**. Soldiers who use big guns are the **artillery**. Soldiers who fight on foot are the **infantry**.

VARIOUS KINDS OF SOLDIER
cavalryman, commando, guardsman, gunner, infantryman, marine, paratrooper, rifleman, sapper, sentry, trooper

POSITIONS SOLDIERS MAY HOLD IN THE ARMY
officer, non-commissioned officer or NCO, private

FOR RANKS IN THE ARMY SEE **rank**

sole *ADJECTIVE*

He is the sole survivor of the accident.
▸ lone, one, only, single, solitary, unique

solemn *ADJECTIVE*

1 *She sat down, a solemn expression on her face.*
▸ earnest, grave, serious, sober, sombre, thoughtful, unsmiling
AN OPPOSITE IS cheerful
2 *The coronation was a solemn occasion.*
▸ dignified, formal, grand, important, impressive, pompous, stately
AN OPPOSITE IS frivolous

solid *ADJECTIVE*

1 *A cricket ball is solid.*
There are no convenient synonyms for this sense of *solid*.
AN OPPOSITE IS hollow
2 *The water turned into solid ice.*
▸ dense, hard, rigid, unyielding
AN OPPOSITE IS soft
3 *The hut has a solid framework.*
▸ firm, robust, sound, stable, steady, strong, sturdy, tough
AN OPPOSITE IS weak
4 *He got solid support from his team-mates.*
▸ dependable, reliable, unanimous, undivided, united
AN OPPOSITE IS variable

solidify *VERB*

The lava from the volcano solidifies as it cools.
▸ become solid, harden, set, stiffen
AN OPPOSITE IS soften

solitary *ADJECTIVE*

1 *He was a solitary man and rarely spoke to others.*
▸ isolated, lonely, secluded, unsociable
▷ To be solitary is to be **alone**.
AN OPPOSITE IS sociable
2 *There was a solitary tree in the middle of the field.*
▸ one, only, single, sole

solitude *NOUN*

She enjoyed her few hours of solitude.
▸ isolation, loneliness, privacy, seclusion

solve *VERB*

He tried to solve the riddle his friend had set him.
▸ answer, decipher, explain, find the solution to, interpret, unravel, work out

sombre *ADJECTIVE*

1 *The room was decorated in sombre brown and grey.*
▸ cheerless, dark, depressing, dim, dingy, dismal, drab, dull
AN OPPOSITE IS bright
2 *He had a sombre expression.*
▸ gloomy, grave, melancholy, mournful, sad, serious, sober
AN OPPOSITE IS cheerful

song *NOUN*

VARIOUS KINDS OF MUSIC FOR SINGING
anthem, ballad, calypso, carol, chant, ditty, folk song, hymn, jingle, lament, love song, lullaby, nursery rhyme, pop song, psalm, shanty, spiritual

LONG COMPOSITIONS FOR SINGERS
anthem, cantata, chant, musical, opera, oratorio

▷ A song from a musical is a **number**. A song from an opera or oratorio is an **aria**. The words for a song are the **lyrics**.

FOR OTHER MUSICAL TERMS SEE **music**

soon *ADVERB*

I'll be ready soon.
▸ before long, in a short time, presently, quickly, shortly

soothe *VERB*
1 *The quiet music soothed her nerves.*
▸ calm, comfort, pacify, relax
2 *This cream will soothe the pain.*
▸ ease, lessen, relieve

soothing *ADJECTIVE*
They played soothing music.
▸ calming, gentle, peaceful, pleasant, relaxing, restful

sophisticated *ADJECTIVE*
1 *It's a play that will only appeal to a sophisticated audience.*
▸ adult, cultivated, cultured, grown-up, mature
AN OPPOSITE IS naïve
2 *They like going to sophisticated restaurants.*
▸ fashionable, (*informal*) posh, stylish
AN OPPOSITE IS unfashionable
3 *This is a sophisticated computer.*
▸ advanced, complex, complicated, elaborate
AN OPPOSITE IS primitive or simple

sorcerer, sorceress *NOUNS*
The sorcerer waved a magic wand.
▸ conjuror, magician, wizard

sore *ADJECTIVE*
1 *My feet are still sore from the walk.*
▸ aching, hurting, inflamed, painful, raw, red, sensitive, smarting, tender
2 (*informal*) *He's still sore because I forgot to phone him back.*
▸ angry, annoyed, bitter, resentful, upset

sore *NOUN*
I put ointment on the sore.
VARIOUS KINDS OF SORE PLACE
abscess, boil, carbuncle, graze, inflammation, laceration, pimple, rawness, scab, spot, ulcer, wound

sorrow *NOUN*
1 *It was a time of great sorrow.*
▸ anguish, dejection, depression, desolation, despair, distress, gloom, glumness, grief, heartache, heartbreak, melancholy, misery, sadness, tearfulness, unhappiness, woe, wretchedness
▹ Sorrow because of someone's death is **mourning**. Sorrow at being away from home is **homesickness**.
AN OPPOSITE IS happiness
2 *She expressed her sorrow for what she had done.*
▸ apologies, guilt, penitence, regret, remorse, repentance

sorrowful *ADJECTIVE*
Her face looked sorrowful.
▸ broken-hearted, dejected, distressed, grief-stricken, heartbroken, long-faced, melancholy, miserable, mournful, regretful, sad, sombre, sorry, tearful, unhappy, upset, woeful, wretched
AN OPPOSITE IS happy

sorry *ADJECTIVE*
1 *He's sorry for what he did.*
▸ apologetic, ashamed, penitent, regretful, remorseful, repentant
AN OPPOSITE IS unrepentant
2 *He felt sorry for her — she seemed so unhappy.*
▸ compassionate, pitying, sympathetic, understanding
AN OPPOSITE IS unsympathetic

sort *NOUN*
What sort of music do you like?
▸ category, class, description, form, kind, type, variety
▹ A particular sort of goods is a **brand** or **make**. A sort of animal is a **breed** or **species**.
sort of (*informal*) *'Do you see what I mean?' 'Sort of'.*
▸ a bit, a little, in a way, somewhat, to some extent

sort *VERB*
The books are sorted according to their subjects.
▸ arrange, catalogue, categorize, classify, divide, file, grade, group, organize
AN OPPOSITE IS mix
to sort something out 1 *Sort out the things you need.*
▸ choose, select, separate, set aside
2 *The problem has been sorted out.*
▸ attend to, clear up, cope with, deal with, solve

soul *NOUN*
Many people believe that a person's soul is immortal.
▸ spirit

sound *NOUN*
I heard the sound of people talking.
▸ noise
FOR OTHER WORDS, SEE THE NEXT ENTRY
SEE ALSO **noise**

sound *VERB*
1 *A loud buzzer sounded.*
▸ become audible, be heard, make a noise, resound
Many of these words can be used either as verbs or as nouns
VARIOUS WAYS PEOPLE MAKE SOUNDS
boo, clap, croak, cry, groan, hiccup, hum, jeer, lisp, moan, murmur, scream, shout, shriek, sigh, sing, sniff, snore, sob, splutter, wail, whimper, whisper, whistle, yell, yodel
SEE ALSO **talk**
WAYS VARIOUS ANIMALS MAKE SOUNDS
bark, bay, bellow, bleat, bray, buzz, croak, growl, grunt, hiss, howl, jabber, low, miaow, moo, neigh, purr, roar, snarl, snort, squeak, squeal, trumpet, whine, whinny, yap, yelp
WAYS VARIOUS BIRDS MAKE SOUNDS
cackle, caw, chirp, chirrup, cluck, coo, crow, honk, hoot, quack, screech, squawk, tweet, twitter, warble
WAYS VARIOUS THINGS MAKE SOUNDS
bang, blare, bleep, boom, chime, chink, clang, clank, clash, clatter, click, clink, crack, crackle, crash, creak, fizz, grate, gurgle, jangle, jingle, patter, peal, ping, plop, pop, rattle, ring, rumble, rustle, sizzle, slam, snap, swish, throb, thud, thunder, tick, ting, tinkle, twang, whir, whistle, whiz
2 *They sounded the depth of the river.*
▸ measure, plumb
to sound out *They did a survey to sound out public opinion.*
▸ examine, find out about, investigate, probe, test

sound *ADJECTIVE*
1 *The car engine seemed sound.*
▸ in good condition, undamaged, whole, working
AN OPPOSITE IS damaged
2 *They returned safe and sound.*
▸ fit, healthy, strong, well
AN OPPOSITE IS ill
3 *His ideas are sound.*
▸ convincing, logical, rational, reasonable, sensible, wise
AN OPPOSITE IS silly
4 *Savings certificates are usually a sound investment.*
▸ dependable, reliable, safe, secure, trustworthy
AN OPPOSITE IS unreliable

soup *NOUN*
SOME KINDS OF SOUP
broth, chowder, consommé, minestrone, mulligatawny, Scotch broth
There are many other kinds of soup. Often they are named after the main ingredient: *chicken soup, tomato soup*, etc
▷ The liquid in which you stew fish, meat, or vegetables is **stock**.

sour *ADJECTIVE*
1 *These apples are a bit sour.*
▸ acid, bitter, sharp, tart
AN OPPOSITE IS sweet
2 *She gave him a sour look.*
▸ cross, disagreeable, grumpy, ill-natured, irritable, unpleasant

source *NOUN*
The source of the river is in the hills.
▸ beginning, head, origin, start, starting point
▷ The source of a river or stream is usually a **spring**.

south *NOUN, ADJECTIVE, & ADVERB*
▷ The parts of a continent or country in the south are the **southern** parts. To travel towards the south is to travel **southward** or **southwards** or **in a southerly direction**. A wind from the south is a **southerly** wind. A person who lives in the south of Britain is a **southerner**.

souvenir *NOUN*
He brought home some souvenirs of his trip to Paris.
▸ reminder

sow *VERB*
▷ To sow seeds in the ground is to **plant** them. To sow an area of ground with seeds is to **seed** it.

space *NOUN*
1 *The six astronauts on board the shuttle will spend ten days in space.*
▷ Everything that exists in space is the **universe**. Distances in space stretch to **infinity**. Travel to other stars is **interstellar** travel. Travel to other planets is **interplanetary** travel. A traveller in space is an **astronaut**. A Russian traveller in space is a **cosmonaut**. In stories, an astronaut is often called a **spaceman** or **spacewoman**. In stories, beings from other planets are **alien** or **extraterrestrial** beings.

WORDS TO DO WITH TRAVEL IN SPACE
blast-off, booster rocket, capsule, countdown, docking bay, heat shield, life-support system, module, orbit, probe, re-entry, retrorocket, rocket, satellite, solar panel, spacecraft, spaceship, space shuttle, space station, spacesuit, spacewalk, splashdown, sputnik
FOR ASTRONOMICAL TERMS SEE **astronomy**

2 *There wasn't much space to move about.*
▸ freedom, room, scope
3 *He peered through the tiny space in the curtains.*
▸ blank, break, gap, hole, opening
▹ A space without any air in it is a vacuum. A space of time is an interval or period.

spacious *ADJECTIVE*
The living room is spacious and comfortably furnished.
▸ big, large, roomy, sizeable
AN OPPOSITE IS small

span *NOUN*
The arch had a span of 60 metres.
▸ breadth, distance, extent, length, width
▹ A span of time is a period or stretch.

span *VERB*
A narrow bridge spanned the river.
▸ arch over, cross, extend across, pass over, reach over, straddle, stretch over

spare *VERB*
1 *Can you spare any money for the homeless?*
▸ afford, do without, part with, provide, sacrifice
2 *She begged him to spare her.*
▸ be merciful to, forgive, free, (*informal*) let off, pardon, release, reprieve, save

spare *ADJECTIVE*
1 *The spare tyre is in the boot.*
▸ additional, extra, standby
2 *Have you any spare boxes I could have?*
▸ leftover, odd, remaining, surplus, unnecessary, unneeded, unused, unwanted
3 *He was tall and spare.*
▸ lean, slender, slim, thin, trim

sparing *ADJECTIVE*
He's sparing with his money.
▸ careful, economical, frugal, prudent, thrifty
INSULTING SYNONYMS ARE mean, miserly, stingy
AN OPPOSITE IS generous or wasteful

spark *NOUN*
There was a spark of light as he struck the match.
▸ flash, flicker, gleam, glint, sparkle

sparkle *VERB*
The diamond ring sparkled in the sunlight.
▸ flash, glint, glitter, spark, twinkle
FOR VARIOUS EFFECTS OF LIGHT SEE **light** *NOUN*

sparse *ADJECTIVE*
In the desert, vegetation is very sparse.
▸ inadequate, light, meagre, scanty, scarce, scattered, thin
AN OPPOSITE IS plentiful

spatter *VERB*
The bus spattered water over us.
▸ scatter, shower, slop, splash, spray, sprinkle

speak *VERB*
He was so shocked he couldn't speak.
▸ communicate, express yourself, say something, talk, utter your thoughts
SEE ALSO **talk**

speaker *NOUN*
▹ A person who gives a talk is a lecturer. A person who makes formal speeches is an orator. A person who speaks on behalf of an organization is a spokesperson.

spear *NOUN*
▹ A spear used in whaling is a harpoon. A spear thrown as a sport is a javelin. A spear carried by a knight fighting on horseback was a lance.

special *ADJECTIVE*
1 *They were keeping the champagne for a special occasion.*
▸ exceptional, extraordinary, important, memorable, momentous, notable, out-of-the-ordinary, significant, uncommon, unusual
AN OPPOSITE IS ordinary
2 *She had her own special way of doing things.*
▸ characteristic, different, distinctive, individual, recognizable, unique, unmistakable
3 *You need special tools for this job.*
▸ particular, proper, specialized, specific

specialist *NOUN*
She's a specialist in military history.
▸ authority, consultant, expert, professional
FOR SPECIALISTS WHO LOOK AFTER YOUR HEALTH SEE **medicine**

speciality *NOUN*
What's your speciality?
▸ expertise, special knowledge or skill, strength, strong point

specialize *VERB*
to specialize in **1** *She decided to specialize in chemistry.*
▸ be a specialist in, concentrate on
2 *The restaurant specializes in seafood.*
▸ be best at, have a reputation for

species *NOUN*
Many species of animals and birds are facing extinction.
▸ breed, class, kind, race, sort, type, variety

specific *ADJECTIVE*
1 *The instructions he gave were very specific.*
▸ detailed, exact, precise
AN OPPOSITE IS general
2 *There are several specific problems that need to be dealt with.*
▸ definite, particular, special, specified
AN OPPOSITE IS unspecified

specify *VERB*
He did not specify what action he would like them to take.
▸ be specific about, define, identify, name

specimen *NOUN*
The police asked for a specimen of his handwriting.
▸ example, illustration, instance, sample

speck *NOUN*
She brushed a speck of dust from her shoes.
▸ bit, dot, fleck, grain, mark, particle, spot, trace

speckled *ADJECTIVE*
A brown, speckled egg lay on the nest.
▸ dotted, flecked, mottled, spotted, spotty
▹ If you have a lot of brown spots on your skin you are **freckled**. Something with patches of colour is **dappled** or **patchy**.

spectacle *NOUN*
The military parade was a magnificent spectacle.
▸ display, exhibition, extravaganza, show

spectacles *PLURAL NOUN*
SEE **glass**

spectacular *ADJECTIVE*
1 *The flying display at the air show was really spectacular.*
▸ dramatic, exciting, impressive, magnificent, sensational, thrilling
2 *The flowers are spectacular at this time of year.*
▸ beautiful, breathtaking, colourful, eye-catching, showy, splendid

spectator *NOUN*
▹ The spectators at a show are the **audience**. The spectators at a football match are the **crowd**. A person watching TV is a **viewer**. If you see an accident or a crime you are an **eyewitness** or **witness**. If you just happen to see something going on you are a **bystander** or **onlooker**.

spectrum *NOUN*
The library caters for a wide spectrum of interests.
▸ range, variety

speech *NOUN*
1 *His speech was slurred and he looked tired.*
▸ articulation, elocution, pronunciation, speaking, talking
2 *She gave a speech lasting for more than an hour.*
▸ address, lecture, oration, presentation, talk
▹ A talk in church is a **sermon**. Speech between actors in a play is **dialogue**. A speech delivered by a single actor is a **monologue**.

speechless *ADJECTIVE*
She was speechless with surprise.
▸ dumb, mute, silent, tongue-tied
AN OPPOSITE IS communicative

speed *NOUN*
She worked with amazing speed.
▸ pace, quickness, rapidity, rate, swiftness
▹ A formal synonym is **velocity**. The speed of a piece of music is its **tempo**.

speed *VERB*
1 *They sped down the road.*
▸ career, dart, dash, (*informal*) fly, gallop, hasten, hurry, hurtle, move quickly, race, run, rush, shoot, sprint, streak, tear, (*informal*) zoom
2 *She was caught speeding on the motorway.*
▸ break the speed limit, go too fast
to speed up *The train began to speed up.*
▸ accelerate, go faster, increase speed, quicken, spurt ahead

speedy *ADJECTIVE*
They sent their best wishes for a speedy recovery.
▸ fast, immediate, prompt, quick, swift
AN OPPOSITE IS slow

spell *NOUN*
1 *After a brief spell in the navy, he decided to become a teacher.*
▸ period, session, stretch, time
2 *A magic spell put the princess to sleep for a thousand years.*
▸ charm, magic formula
▹ Making magic spells is sorcery or witchcraft or wizardry.

spend *VERB*
1 *I spent all my money.*
▸ exhaust, (*informal*) fork out, get through, (*informal*) lash out, pay out, use up
▹ To spend money unwisely is to fritter or squander it.
2 *She seems to spend all her time gossiping.*
▸ fill, occupy, pass
▹ To spend time doing something useless is to waste it.

sphere *NOUN*
1 *The earth has the shape of a sphere.*
▸ ball, globe
2 *He's an expert in his own sphere.*
▸ area, department, field, subject

spherical *ADJECTIVE*
The earth is spherical.
▸ ball-shaped, round

spice *NOUN*
SOME SPICES USED IN COOKING
allspice, aniseed, bayleaf, capsicum, cardamom, cayenne, chilli, cinnamon, cloves, coriander, cumin, curry powder, ginger, juniper, mace, nutmeg, paprika, pepper, pimento, saffron, sesame, turmeric

spike *NOUN*
The wall was topped with iron spikes.
▸ barb, nail, point, projection, prong

spill *VERB*
1 *You'll spill that tea if you're not careful.*
▸ overturn, tip over, upset
2 *Milk spilled onto the floor.*
▸ overflow, pour, run out, slop, slosh, splash
3 *The bag fell off the table, spilling its contents on to the floor.*
▸ drop, scatter, shed, tip

spin *VERB*
The rear wheels of the car spun round.
▸ revolve, rotate, twirl, whirl

spine *NOUN*
1 *Your spine runs down the middle of your back.*
▸ backbone, spinal column
▹ The bones in your spine are your vertebrae.
2 *A hedgehog has sharp spines.*
▸ bristle, needle, point, spike

spine-chilling *ADJECTIVE*
The ghost story was spine-chilling.
▸ creepy, exciting, frightening, (*informal*) scary

spirit *NOUN*
1 *Although he is dead, his spirit lives on.*
▸ soul
2 *The charm was meant to keep evil spirits away.*
VARIOUS SPIRITS YOU READ ABOUT IN STORIES
bogeyman, demon, devil, genie, ghost, ghoul, gremlin, hobgoblin, imp, incubus, nymph, phantom, poltergeist, spectre, sprite, sylph, wraith, zombie
3 *Everyone who knew her admired her spirit.*
▸ bravery, cheerfulness, confidence, courage, daring, determination, energy, enthusiasm, heroism, morale, optimism, pluck, valour
4 *It took a while to get into the spirit of the party.*
▸ atmosphere, feeling, mood

spiritual *ADJECTIVE*
The Dalai Lama is the spiritual leader of Tibet.
▸ holy, religious, sacred
AN OPPOSITE IS worldly

spite *NOUN*
She's only saying it out of spite.
▸ (*informal*) bitchiness, bitterness, hate, hostility, ill-feeling, malevolence, malice

spiteful *ADJECTIVE*
He made some really spiteful comments.
▸ (*informal*) bitchy, bitter, cruel, hostile, ill-natured, malevolent, malicious, nasty, unkind, venomous, vicious
AN OPPOSITE IS kind

splash *VERB*
1 *The bus splashed water over us.*
▸ shower, slop, slosh, spatter, spill, spray, sprinkle
2 *The children splashed about in the water.*
▸ bathe, dabble, paddle, wade

splendid *ADJECTIVE*
1 *The celebrations ended with a splendid banquet.*
▸ beautiful, brilliant, costly, dazzling, elegant, glorious, gorgeous, grand, great, imposing, impressive, lavish, luxurious, magnificent, majestic, marvellous, noble, (*informal*) posh, rich, stately, superb, wonderful
2 *That's a splendid idea!*
▸ admirable, excellent, first-class

splendour *NOUN*
They admired the splendour of the cathedral.
▸ brilliance, ceremony, colourfulness, display, glory, grandeur, magnificence, majesty, pageantry, pomp, show, spectacle

splinter *NOUN*
There were splinters of glass all over the floor.
▸ chip, flake, fragment, sliver

splinter *VERB*
The glass splintered into pieces.
▸ chip, crack, fracture, shatter, smash, split

split *VERB*
1 *He split the log in two.*
▸ chop, crack open, cut up, splinter
2 *He split his trousers climbing over the fence.*
▸ rip open, tear
3 *They split the profits.*
▸ distribute, share out
4 *The path splits here.*
▸ branch, fork, separate
to split up *The search party decided to split up.*
▸ break up, divide, go different ways, part, separate
▹ If a married couple splits up, they may divorce.

split *NOUN*
He had a split in the seat of his trousers.
▸ slash, slit, tear

spoil *VERB*
1 *Bad weather spoiled the holiday.*
▸ mar, mess up, ruin, wreck
There are many different ways you can spoil things. Here are just a few examples
▹ You can burn or overdo or undercook things you are cooking. You can blot or smudge your handwriting. You can crease or crumple a clean shirt. Vandals may deface or disfigure a public place. You can interrupt someone's enjoyment of something.
2 *The strawberries will spoil in this wet weather.*
▸ go bad, go off, perish, rot
AN OPPOSITE IS improve
3 *His parents have spoiled him since he was a baby.*
▸ indulge, make a fuss of, pamper

spoken *ADJECTIVE*
Her spoken French is excellent.
▸ oral
AN OPPOSITE IS written

sponge *VERB*
1 *The nurse gently sponged the wound.*
▸ clean, mop, wash, wipe
2 (*informal*) *He's been sponging off his friends for months.*
▸ cadge (from), (*informal*) scrounge (from)

spongy *ADJECTIVE*
The spongy material quickly soaked up the water.
▸ absorbent, porous, soft, springy

sponsor *NOUN*
The money for the pantomime came from local sponsors.
▸ backer, benefactor, patron, promoter

sponsor *VERB*
The event was sponsored by several local firms.
▸ back, be a sponsor of, finance, help, promote, subsidize, support

spontaneous *ADJECTIVE*
The audience broke into spontaneous applause.
▸ impromptu, impulsive, instinctive, involuntary, natural, unconscious, unplanned, unrehearsed, voluntary
▹ An action done without any conscious thought is a reflex action.

spoon *NOUN*
SEE **cutlery**

sport *NOUN*
I'm not very good at sport.
► exercise, games, pastime, play, recreation
OUTDOOR SPORTS INCLUDE
American football, archery, Association football or soccer, baseball, bowls, canoeing, climbing, cricket, croquet, cross-country running, diving, gliding, golf, hockey, horse racing, jogging, lacrosse, motor racing, mountaineering, netball, orienteering, polo, potholing, rock-climbing, roller skating, rounders, rowing, rugby, sailing or yachting, showjumping, skydiving, surfing or surfriding, swimming, tennis, volleyball, water polo, water-skiing, windsurfing
SEE ALSO **athletics**
INDOOR SPORTS INCLUDE
badminton, basketball, billiards, boxing, darts, gymnastics, martial arts, pool, snooker, squash, table tennis or (*informal*) ping-pong, trampolining, wrestling
WINTER SPORTS INCLUDE
bobsleigh, ice hockey, skating, skiing, tobogganing
BLOOD SPORTS INCLUDE
beagling, fishing, deer hunting, fox hunting, shooting

sporting *ADJECTIVE*
It was sporting of him to admit the ball was out.
► fair, generous, honourable

sportsman, sportswoman *NOUNS*
► contestant, participant, player

spot *NOUN*
1 *There were several spots of paint on the carpet.*
► blot, blotch, dot, fleck, mark, smudge, speck, stain
▷ Small brown spots on your skin are **freckles**. A small dark spot on your skin is a **mole**. A mark you have had on your skin since you were born is a **birthmark**. A small round swelling on your skin is a **pimple**. A lot of spots is a **rash**. A disease which gives you a lot of spots is **impetigo**.
2 *She felt a few spots of rain.*
► bead, blob, drop
3 *Here's a nice spot for a picnic.*
► locality, location, place, position, site, situation

spot *VERB*
1 *She spotted her friend in the crowd.*
► catch sight of, distinguish, make out, note, notice, observe, recognize, see, sight, spy
2 *The floor was spotted with paint.*
► blot, fleck, mark, mottle, spatter, speckle, stain

spotless *ADJECTIVE*
He polished his shoes until they were spotless.
► clean, shiny, unmarked
AN OPPOSITE IS dirty

spotty *ADJECTIVE*
She had a pale, spotty complexion.
► blotchy, pimply

spout *NOUN*
The teapot has a chipped spout.
► lip, nozzle, outlet
▷ A spout carved like an ugly face sticking out from a church roof is a **gargoyle**.

spout *VERB*
The volcano spouted ash and lava.
► erupt, flow, gush, pour, spurt, squirt, stream

sprawl *VERB*
1 *We sprawled on the lawn.*
► flop, lean back, lie, loll, lounge, recline, relax, slouch, slump, spread out, stretch out
2 *The housing estate had sprawled out into the countryside.*
► spread

spray *VERB*
A passing bus sprayed mud over us.
► scatter, shower, spatter, splash, sprinkle

spray *NOUN*
1 *The dog shook itself briskly, sending a spray of water over the floor.*
► fountain, mist, shower, splash, sprinkling
2 *She arranged a spray of freesias in a small glass vase.*
► arrangement, bouquet, bunch, posy

spread *VERB*
1 *I spread the map on the table.*
► arrange, display, lay out, open out, unfold
2 *Water leaked out and was spreading over the floor.*
► broaden, enlarge, expand, extend, get bigger or longer or wider, lengthen

A B C D E F G H I J K L M N O P Q R S T U V W X Y Z

3 *She's always spreading rumours about other people.*
▶ advertise, circulate, give out, make known, pass on, pass round, publicize, transmit
4 *She spread jam on a piece of toast.*
▶ smear
5 *He spread the seeds over the ground.*
▶ distribute, scatter

sprightly ADJECTIVE
She's quite sprightly for her age.
▶ active, agile, brisk, energetic, frisky, lively, nimble, quick
AN OPPOSITE IS inactive

spring VERB
He sprang over the gate.
▶ bound, hop, jump, leap, vault
▷ When a cat springs at a mouse, it **pounces**.
to spring up **1** *Fast food restaurants have sprung up all over the country.*
▶ appear, arise, develop, emerge
2 *Weeds spring up quickly in damp weather.*
▶ germinate, grow, shoot up, sprout

springy ADJECTIVE
The bed felt soft and springy.
▶ bouncy, elastic, flexible, pliable, stretchy
AN OPPOSITE IS rigid

sprinkle VERB
1 *He sprinkled vinegar on his chips.*
▶ drip, shower, spatter, splash, spray
2 *Sprinkle some cheese over the bread and grill for five minutes.*
▶ scatter

sprout VERB
The seeds will sprout if they are warm and damp.
▶ develop, emerge, germinate, grow, shoot up, spring up

spruce ADJECTIVE
He looked very spruce in a cream linen jacket.
▶ clean, elegant, neat, (*informal*) posh, smart, tidy, trim, well-dressed
AN OPPOSITE IS scruffy

spur VERB
The cheers of the crowd spurred them on to greater efforts.
▶ egg on, encourage, inspire, prompt, stimulate, urge

spurt VERB
1 *Water spurted from the hole.*
▶ erupt, flow, gush, shoot out, spout, spray, squirt
2 *She spurted ahead.*
▶ accelerate, go faster, increase speed, quicken, speed up

spy NOUN
He was accused of being a spy.
▶ agent, informer, secret agent

spy VERB
She spied a figure in the distance.
▶ catch sight of, distinguish, make out, notice, recognize, see, sight, spot
to spy on someone or **something** *She was sure her neighbours were spying on her.*
▶ keep an eye on, keep under surveillance, watch

squabble VERB
They were still squabbling about whose turn it was to wash up.
▶ argue, fall out, fight, quarrel

squalid ADJECTIVE
The refugees lived in squalid conditions.
▶ degrading, dingy, dirty, filthy, foul, mucky, nasty, unpleasant
AN OPPOSITE IS clean

squander VERB
He squandered his money on an expensive sports car.
▶ fritter, misuse, spend unwisely, waste
AN OPPOSITE IS save

square ADJECTIVE
All the tiles have square corners.
▶ right-angled
▷ A pattern of squares is a **chequered** pattern.

squarely ADVERB
The ball hit him squarely in the face.
▶ directly, exactly, head on, straight
AN OPPOSITE IS obliquely

squash VERB
1 *Don't put tomatoes at the bottom of the bag—they'll get squashed.*
▶ crush, flatten, smash
▷ To squash food, etc., deliberately is to **mash** or **pound** or **pulp** it.
2 *She squashed down her clothes and zipped up the suitcase.*
▶ compress, press
3 *Seven of us squashed into the car.*
▶ cram, crowd, pack, squeeze

squat *VERB*
She told us to squat on the ground.
▸ crouch, sit

squat *ADJECTIVE*
It's hard to look elegant if you have a squat figure like me.
▸ dumpy, plump, podgy, portly, stocky
AN OPPOSITE IS graceful

squawk, squeak, squeal *NOUNS & VERBS*
FOR VARIOUS WAYS TO MAKE SOUNDS SEE **sound** *VERB*

squeeze *VERB*
1 *She squeezed the water out of the sponge.*
▸ compress, press, wring
2 *Five of us squeezed into the back seat of the car.*
▸ cram, crowd, push, shove, squash, stuff, wedge
3 *He squeezed her affectionately.*
▸ clasp, embrace, hug
▹ To squeeze something between your thumb and finger is to pinch it.

squirm *VERB*
She managed to squirm out of his grasp.
▸ twist, wriggle, writhe

squirt *VERB*
He dropped the hosepipe, and water squirted all over him.
▸ gush, shoot, spout, spray, spurt

stab *VERB*
1 *He stabbed the sausage with his fork.*
▸ impale, jab, pierce, spear
2 *She stabbed a finger at him.*
▸ push, stick, thrust

stab *NOUN*
He felt a sudden stab of pain.
▸ pang, prick, sting

stabilize *VERB*
They had to move the cargo to stabilize the ship.
▸ balance, keep upright, make stable, steady
AN OPPOSITE IS upset

stable *ADJECTIVE*
1 *That ladder isn't very stable.*
▸ balanced, firm, fixed, solid, steady
AN OPPOSITE IS wobbly
2 *He's been in a stable relationship for years.*
▸ durable, established, lasting, permanent, secure, steady
AN OPPOSITE IS temporary

stack *NOUN*
There were stacks of books all over the floor.
▸ heap, mound, pile, quantity
▹ Another word for a stack of hay is a rick or hayrick.

stack *VERB*
Stack the books on the table.
▸ assemble, collect, gather, heap up, pile up

staff *NOUN*
There was a party at the hospital for all the staff.
▸ assistants, employees, personnel, team, workers, workforce
▹ The staff of a school are the teachers. The staff on a ship are the crew.

stage *NOUN*
1 *They went up on the stage to collect their prizes.*
▸ platform
2 *The final stage of the journey was made by coach.*
▸ leg, period, phase
3 *At this stage of his life, he had been very unhappy.*
▸ moment, point, step, time

stage *VERB*
1 *The show is being staged at the local theatre.*
▸ perform, present, produce, put on
2 *They decided to stage a protest.*
▸ arrange, organize

stagger *VERB*
1 *He staggered and fell.*
▸ falter, lurch, reel, stumble, sway, totter, walk unsteadily, waver, wobble
2 *Everyone was staggered at the jury's verdict.*
▸ amaze, astonish, astound, shake, shock, startle, stun, surprise

stagnant *ADJECTIVE*
The water was stagnant and smelt unpleasant.
▸ motionless, static, still
AN OPPOSITE IS flowing

stain *NOUN*
He had a large stain on his shirt.
▸ blemish, blot, blotch, fleck, mark, smudge, spot

A B C D E F G H I J K L M N O P Q R S T U V W X Y Z

stain *VERB*
1 *Her trousers were stained with mud.*
▸ blacken, dirty, make dirty, mark, soil, tarnish
2 *The wood can be stained a darker shade.*
▸ colour, dye, paint, tint, varnish

stair *NOUN*
She sat down on the bottom stair.
▸ step
▷ A set of stairs taking you from one floor to another is a flight of stairs, or a staircase or stairway. A moving staircase is an escalator.

stake *NOUN*
The sapling was supported by a stake.
▸ pile, pole, post, stave, stick

stale *ADJECTIVE*
The bread had gone stale.
▸ dry, hard, mouldy, old
AN OPPOSITE IS fresh

stalk *NOUN*
He was chewing a stalk of grass.
▸ shoot, stem, twig

stalk *VERB*
1 *The lion stalked its prey.*
▸ follow, hunt, pursue, shadow, tail, track, trail
2 *She turned and stalked out of the room.*
▸ stride, strut
FOR VARIOUS WAYS WE WALK SEE **walk** *VERB*

stall *VERB*
Don't stall — tell us where he's gone.
▸ delay, hang back, hesitate, hold things up, pause, put it off

stammer *VERB*
He went red and started stammering.
▸ falter, splutter, stumble, stutter

stamp *VERB*
1 *He stamped on the tent peg to get it in.*
▸ step, tread
2 *The librarian stamped his library book.*
▸ mark, print
▷ To stamp a postmark on a letter is to frank it. To stamp a mark on cattle with a hot iron is to brand them.

stampede *NOUN*
When the alarm went, there was a stampede towards the exit.
▸ charge, dash, rout, rush

stand *VERB*
1 *He was too weak to stand.*
▸ get to your feet, get up, rise
2 *They stood the ladder against the wall.*
▸ erect, put up, set up, situate, station
3 *The offer still stands.*
▸ be unchanged, continue, remain valid
4 *She couldn't stand the heat.*
▸ abide, bear, endure, put up with, suffer, tolerate
to stand for something 1 *She won't stand for any nonsense.*
▸ accept, allow, endure, permit, put up with, tolerate
2 *What do these initials stand for?*
▸ indicate, mean, represent, signify
to stand in for someone *She stood in for the regular teacher.*
▸ be a substitute for, deputize for, replace, take over from
to stand out *Her clothes made her stand out in a crowd.*
▸ be obvious, catch the eye, show, stick out
to stand up for someone *He always stands up for his friends.*
▸ defend, fight for, help, look after, protect, shield, side with, speak up for, (*informal*) stick up for, support

stand *NOUN*
▷ A three-legged stand for a camera, etc., is a tripod. A stand for a Bible or other large book is a lectern. A stand to put a statue on is a pedestal.

standard *NOUN*
1 *She praised the high standard of their work.*
▸ achievement, grade, level
2 *He considered the book good by any standard.*
▸ guidelines, ideal, measurement, model
3 *The soldiers carried their standard proudly.*
▸ colours, flag

standard *ADJECTIVE*
He did it according to the standard procedure.
▸ accepted, approved, basic, common, conventional, customary, established, familiar, habitual, normal, official, ordinary, orthodox, recognized, regular, routine, traditional, typical, usual
AN OPPOSITE IS abnormal

standby *NOUN*
They need a standby in case someone drops out.
▸ replacement, reserve, substitute

standstill *NOUN*
to come to a standstill *The traffic came to a standstill.*
▸ draw up, halt, pull up, stop

staple *ADJECTIVE*
Rice is the staple diet in many countries.
▸ chief, main, principal, standard

star *NOUN*
1 *Astronomers study the stars.*
FOR ASTRONOMICAL TERMS SEE **astronomy**
FOR SIGNS OF THE ZODIAC SEE **Zodiac**
▹ A mark in the shape of a star in a piece of writing is an **asterisk**.
2 *Many stars attended the premiere of the film.*
▸ celebrity, idol, personality

stare *VERB*
What are you staring at?
▸ contemplate, examine, gape at, gaze at, keep your eyes on, look at, peer at, scrutinize, study, watch
▹ To stare angrily at someone is to **glare** at them.

start *VERB*
1 *They were ready to start work.*
▸ begin, commence, (*informal*) get cracking on, get going on
AN OPPOSITE IS finish
2 *He plans to start a new business.*
▸ create, establish, found, initiate, institute, introduce, launch, open, originate, set up
AN OPPOSITE IS close
3 *She started when the gun went off.*
▸ flinch, jerk, jump, recoil, spring up, twitch, wince

start *NOUN*
1 *The start of something new is always exciting.*
▸ beginning, birth, commencement, creation, dawn, establishment, initiation, introduction, launch, opening
AN OPPOSITE IS finish
2 *His father gave him a start in business.*
▸ advantage, opportunity
3 *The explosion gave him a nasty start.*
▸ jolt, jump, shock, surprise

startle *VERB*
The sudden noise startled them.
▸ agitate, alarm, frighten, make you jump, make you start, scare, shock, surprise, take you by surprise, upset

starvation *NOUN*
The refugees were dying of starvation.
▸ famine, hunger, malnutrition

starve *VERB*
Many animals will starve if the drought continues.
▸ die of starvation, go hungry, go without, perish
▹ To choose to go without food is to **fast**. If prisoners protest by starving themselves, they are **on hunger strike**.

starving *ADJECTIVE* (*informal*)
What's for dinner? I'm starving!
▸ famished, hungry, (*informal*) peckish, ravenous

state *NOUN*
1 *The building was in a bad state.*
▸ condition, shape
▹ The state of a person or animal is their **fitness** or **health**.
2 *He was in a terrible state!*
▸ (*informal*) flap, panic, plight, situation
3 *The queen is the head of state.*
▸ country, nation
SEE ALSO **country**

state *VERB*
The prime minister stated that the election would be held in May.
▸ announce, communicate, declare, proclaim, pronounce, put into words, report, say

stately *ADJECTIVE*
They admired the stately way she walked into the room.
▸ dignified, elegant, formal, grand, imposing, impressive, majestic, noble, solemn, splendid
AN OPPOSITE IS informal

statement *NOUN*
The minister made a statement about the new policy.
▸ announcement, bulletin, communication, declaration, explanation, message, notice, proclamation, pronouncement

A B C D E F G H I J K L M N O P Q R S T U V W X Y Z

station *NOUN*
1 *The train stopped at the station.*
▷ The station at the end of a line is the **terminus**. A small platform without any station buildings is a **halt**.
FOR OTHER WORDS TO DO WITH RAILWAYS SEE ALSO **railway**
2 *They were taken to the police station.*
▶ depot, headquarters
3 *She enjoyed listening to the local radio station.*
▶ channel

station *VERB*
They stationed a lookout on the roof.
▶ locate, place, position, put, situate, stand

stationary *ADJECTIVE*
The car was stationary at the traffic lights.
▶ at a standstill, at rest, halted, immobile, motionless, parked, standing, static, still, unmoving
AN OPPOSITE IS moving

stationery *NOUN*
KINDS OF STATIONERY
cards, computer paper, copier paper, envelopes, exercise books, jotters, postcards, writing paper

statistics *PLURAL NOUN*
The newspaper reported the latest crime statistics.
▶ data, figures, numbers

statue *NOUN*
There a statue of Lord Nelson in Trafalgar Square.
▶ carving, figure, sculpture

status *NOUN*
They discussed the changing status of women in society.
▶ grade, importance, level, position, prestige, rank

staunch *ADJECTIVE*
He's a staunch supporter of the team.
▶ constant, dependable, faithful, firm, loyal, reliable, sound, strong
AN OPPOSITE IS unreliable

stave *VERB*
to stave something off *They did all they could to stave off disaster.*
▶ avert, avoid, fend off, prevent, ward off

stay *VERB*
1 *She stayed late at the office.*
▶ continue, hang about, remain, wait
AN OPPOSITE IS depart
2 *He planned to stay in the town for the rest of his life.*
▶ carry on, live, reside, settle, stop
3 *They are going to stay in a hotel.*
▶ be accommodated, board, lodge

stay *NOUN*
She came for a short stay.
▶ holiday, stop, visit

steady *ADJECTIVE*
1 *Is the ladder steady?*
▶ balanced, fast, firm, safe, secure, settled, solid, stable
AN OPPOSITE IS wobbly
2 *They need a steady supply of water.*
▶ ceaseless, continuous, dependable, non-stop, reliable, uninterrupted
AN OPPOSITE IS unreliable
3 *They kept up a steady pace.*
▶ constant, even, regular, rhythmic, unchanging, unvarying
AN OPPOSITE IS irregular

steady *VERB*
She tried to steady the boat.
▶ balance, stabilize

steal *VERB*
1 *He stole some money from her.*
▶ rob, take
INFORMAL OR SLANG SYNONYMS
knock off, lift, make off with, nick, pinch, swipe, whip
SEE ALSO **stealing**
2 *She stole quietly upstairs.*
▶ creep, move stealthily, slink, slip, sneak, tiptoe

stealing *NOUN*
The police accused him of stealing.
▶ robbery, theft
VARIOUS KINDS OF STEALING
▷ Stealing from someone's home is **burglary** or **housebreaking**. Stealing from someone in the street is **mugging** or **picking someone's pocket**. Stealing from a shop is **shoplifting**. Stealing from homes or shops during a riot is **looting**. Stealing small things is **pilfering**. Stealing fruit from people's gardens is **scrumping**. Stealing fish or game on someone else's land is **poaching**. Stealing from ships at sea is **piracy**. Stealing from the funds of a business is **embezzlement**.

stealthy *ADJECTIVE*
Why did you sneak out in that stealthy manner?
▸ cautious, furtive, inconspicuous, quiet, secret, secretive, sly, (*informal*) sneaky, underhand
AN OPPOSITE IS conspicuous

steam *NOUN*
She couldn't see through the steam.
▸ haze, mist, smoke, vapour
▹ Steam on a cold window is **condensation**.

steamy *ADJECTIVE*
1 *The bathroom gets steamy when he has a hot shower.*
▸ close, damp, humid, moist, muggy
2 *She wiped the steamy mirror.*
▸ cloudy, hazy, misty

steep *ADJECTIVE*
Climbing up the steep slope exhausted them.
▸ abrupt, sharp, sudden, uphill
▹ Something such as a cliff which goes straight up is **sheer** or **vertical**.
AN OPPOSITE IS gradual

steer *VERB*
He steered the car into the garage.
▸ direct, guide
▹ To steer a car is to **drive** it. To steer a boat is to **navigate** or **pilot** it.

stem *NOUN*
The gardener pulled out the dead stems.
▸ branch, shoot, stalk, twig
▹ The main stem of a tree is its **trunk**.

step *NOUN*
1 *The baby took her first steps yesterday.*
▸ footstep, pace, stride
2 *She stood on the bottom step.*
▸ doorstep, stair
▹ A set of steps going from one floor of a building to another is a **staircase**. A folding set of steps is a **stepladder**. The steps of a ladder are the **rungs**.
3 *Just take it one step at a time.*
▸ action, phase, stage

step *VERB*
Don't step in the mud!
▸ put your foot, stamp, trample, tread, walk
to step something up *They stepped up the pressure.*
▸ boost, increase, intensify, strengthen

sterile *ADJECTIVE*
1 *Very little grows in the sterile soil of the desert.*
▸ arid, barren, dry, infertile, lifeless
AN OPPOSITE IS fertile
2 *The nurse put a sterile bandage on the wound.*
▸ antiseptic, clean, disinfected, germ-free, hygienic, sterilized
AN OPPOSITE IS infected

sterilize *VERB*
1 *He sterilized the equipment before conducting the experiment.*
▸ clean, decontaminate, disinfect, make sterile
▹ Milk is partially sterilized by **pasteurizing** it.
AN OPPOSITE IS infect
2 *The vet is going to sterilize the cat.*
▸ neuter
▹ To sterilize a male horse is to **geld** it. To sterilize a female animal is to **spay** it.

stern *ADJECTIVE*
He gave them a stern look.
▸ disapproving, grim, hard, harsh, severe, strict, unsmiling
AN OPPOSITE IS lenient

stew *VERB*
FOR VARIOUS WAYS TO COOK FOOD SEE **cook** *VERB*

steward, stewardess *NOUNS*
▹ A steward on a ship, etc., is an **attendant** or a **waiter** or **waitress**. A steward at a football ground, etc., is an **official**.

stick *NOUN*
They collected sticks to make a fire.
▸ branch, stalk, twig
KINDS OF STICK MADE FOR VARIOUS PURPOSES
bar, bat, baton, cane, club, hockey stick, pole, rod, staff, stilt, walking stick, wand

stick *VERB*
1 *He stuck his fork into the potato.*
▸ dig, jab, poke, prod, stab, thrust
▹ To stick something into a tyre, etc., is to **puncture** it.
2 *She tried to stick the pieces of the broken vase together.*
▸ cement, fasten, glue, join
▹ To stick pieces of metal together using heat is to **fuse** or **weld** them.
3 *The stamp wouldn't stick to the envelope.*
▸ adhere, cling

4 *The door was always sticking.*
▸ become jammed, become wedged
5 *He can't stick people who are always complaining.*
▸ abide, bear, endure, put up with, stand, tolerate
to stick out *The shelf sticks out too far.*
▸ jut, overhang, poke out, project, protrude
to stick up for (*informal*) *She stuck up for him when he was in trouble.*
▸ defend, fight for, help, look after, protect, shield, side with, speak up for, stand up for, support

sticky *ADJECTIVE*
1 *She secured the parcel with sticky tape.*
▸ adhesive, glued, gummed
AN OPPOSITE IS non-adhesive
▹ Paint that is still wet is said to be tacky.
2 *They didn't like the hot sticky weather.*
▸ clammy, damp, humid, moist, muggy, steamy, sweaty
AN OPPOSITE IS dry
3 (*informal*) *The criminal came to a sticky end.*
▸ dreadful, grisly, gruesome, horrible, nasty, unpleasant

stiff *ADJECTIVE*
1 *Stir the flour and water to a stiff paste.*
▸ firm, hard, solid
AN OPPOSITE IS soft
2 *He mounted the picture on stiff card.*
▸ inflexible, rigid, thick
AN OPPOSITE IS pliable
3 *Her muscles were stiff after the long walk.*
▸ aching, painful, taut, tight
AN OPPOSITE IS supple
4 *It was a stiff exam.*
▸ difficult, hard, severe, tough
AN OPPOSITE IS easy
5 *His stiff manner made him hard to talk to.*
▸ awkward, cold, formal, tense, unfriendly, unnatural, wooden
AN OPPOSITE IS relaxed
6 *The judge imposed a stiff penalty.*
▸ harsh, severe, strict
AN OPPOSITE IS lenient
7 *A stiff wind was blowing.*
▸ brisk, fresh, strong
AN OPPOSITE IS gentle

stifle *VERB*
1 *He was almost stifled by the fumes.*
▸ choke, suffocate
▹ To kill someone by stopping their breathing is to strangle or throttle them.
2 *She stifled a yawn.*
▸ check, cover up, curb, hold back, repress, restrain, suppress

still *ADJECTIVE*
1 *He sat still and said nothing.*
▸ motionless, unmoving
2 *It was a beautiful still evening.*
▸ calm, hushed, noiseless, peaceful, placid, quiet, restful, serene, silent, tranquil, untroubled, windless

still *VERB*
She tried to still her fears.
▸ calm, lull, quieten, settle, soothe
AN OPPOSITE IS agitate

stimulate *VERB*
1 *His experiences stimulated him to write a book on the subject.*
▸ encourage, inspire, spur
2 *The exhibition stimulated her interest in painting.*
▸ arouse, excite, provoke, rouse, stir up, whip up
AN OPPOSITE IS discourage

stimulus *NOUN*
The prize acted as a stimulus to the competitors.
▸ encouragement, incentive, inducement, inspiration

sting *VERB*
1 *He was stung by a bee.*
▸ bite, nip
2 *The smoke made her eyes sting.*
▸ hurt, smart, tingle

stingy *ADJECTIVE*
He's too stingy to give money to charity.
▸ mean, (*informal*) mingy, miserly, selfish, tight, uncharitable, ungenerous
AN OPPOSITE IS generous

stink *NOUN*
The stink from the rubbish tip was overpowering.
▸ odour, smell, stench
SEE ALSO **smell** *NOUN*

stink *VERB*
The room stank of rotting food.
▸ reek, smell

stir *VERB*
1 *Pour in the cream and stir the mixture well.*
► agitate, beat, blend, mix, whisk
2 *He stirred in his sleep.*
► begin to move, change position, move, shift, toss, turn
to stir something up *She's always stirring up trouble.*
► arouse, cause, encourage, excite, provoke, set off, stimulate, whip up

stir *NOUN*
The news caused quite a stir.
► commotion, excitement, fuss, hullabaloo

stock *NOUN*
1 *Stocks of food were running low.*
► hoard, reserve, stockpile, store, supply
2 *The shopkeeper arranged his new stock.*
► goods, merchandise, wares
3 *The farmer took some of his stock to market.*
► animals, beasts, cattle, flocks, herds, livestock
4 *The duke is descended from royal stock.*
► ancestors, ancestry, family, line

stock *VERB*
Most supermarkets now stock organic fruit and vegetables.
► deal in, handle, keep in stock, sell, trade in

stocky *ADJECTIVE*
He had a strong stocky body.
► compact, dumpy, solid, squat, sturdy
AN OPPOSITE IS thin

stodgy *ADJECTIVE*
1 *The food was extremely stodgy.*
► filling, heavy, indigestible, solid, starchy
AN OPPOSITE IS light
2 *He thought the book was a bit stodgy.*
► boring, dull, slow, tedious, unexciting, uninteresting
AN OPPOSITE IS lively

stoke *VERB*
She stoked the fire to warm up the room.
► keep burning, put fuel on, tend

stomach *NOUN*
▷ The part of the body that contains the stomach is the abdomen.
INFORMAL OR SLANG SYNONYMS ARE belly, guts, insides, paunch, tummy

stomach *VERB* (*informal*)
I can't stomach any more of his rudeness!
► bear, put up with, take, tolerate

stone *NOUN*
STONES USED BY BUILDERS
block, flagstone, sett, slab, slate
▷ A large lump of stone is a rock. A large rounded stone is a boulder. Small rounded stones are pebbles. Small pieces of broken stone are chippings. A mixture of sand and small stones is gravel. Pebbles on the beach are shingle. Round stones used to pave a path, etc., are cobbles.
SEE ALSO **rock** *NOUN*
STONES USED TO MAKE JEWELLERY, ETC.
gem, jewel, semi-precious stone
SEE ALSO **jewellery**

stony *ADJECTIVE*
1 *The waves broke over the stony beach.*
► pebbly, rocky, rough, shingly
AN OPPOSITE IS sandy
2 *He gave me a stony look and said nothing.*
► cold, expressionless, hard, hostile, indifferent, uncaring, unemotional, unfriendly
AN OPPOSITE IS friendly

stoop *VERB*
The doorway was so low that he had to stoop to go in.
► bend, bow, duck, hunch your shoulders, lean forward

stop *VERB*
1 *Stop what you are doing.*
► break off, cease, conclude, end, finish, (*informal*) knock off, leave off, quit, suspend, terminate
AN OPPOSITE IS start
2 *The manager stopped the thief before he could escape.*
► arrest, capture, catch, detain, grab, hold, seize
3 *You can't stop me from going.*
► prevent
4 *How do you stop this machine?*
► immobilize, turn off
5 *Wait for the bus to stop.*
► come to rest, draw up, halt, pull up
6 *He tried to stop the leak in the pipe.*
► block up, bung up, close, plug, seal
7 *They planned to stop in London for a few days.*
► spend some time, stay

A B C D E F G H I J K L M N O P Q R S T U V W X Y Z

stop *NOUN*
1 *Everything suddenly came to a stop.*
▸ conclusion, end, finish, halt, standstill
2 *They drove down through France, with a short stop in Paris.*
▸ break, interval, pause
3 *This is my stop.*
▸ destination, station

store *VERB*
Squirrels need to store food for the winter.
▸ hoard, put away, reserve, save, set aside, stock up, stow away

store *NOUN*
1 *The building is now used as a grain store.*
VARIOUS PLACES WHERE PEOPLE STORE THINGS
armoury, arsenal, barn, cache, cellar, cold storage, depot, granary, larder, pantry, repository, safe, silo, stockroom, storage, storehouse, storeroom, strongroom, treasury, vault, warehouse
2 *He kept a large store of wine in the cellar.*
▸ accumulation, hoard, quantity, reserve, stock, stockpile, supply
3 *He's the manager of the local grocery store.*
▸ SEE **shop** *NOUN*

storey *NOUN*
The new building has six storeys.
▸ floor, level

storm *NOUN*
1 *Crops were damaged in the heavy storms.*
▸ tempest
VARIOUS KINDS OF STORM
blizzard, cyclone, deluge, dust-storm, gale, hurricane, rainstorm, sandstorm, squall, thunderstorm, tornado, typhoon, whirlwind
▹ The effect of a storm when you are in an aircraft is **turbulence**. An old word for storm is **tempest**.
2 *Plans to close the library caused a storm of protest.*
▸ eruption, outburst, tumult

storm *VERB*
The soldiers stormed the castle.
▸ charge at, rush at

stormy *ADJECTIVE*
1 *It was a dark, stormy night.*
▸ blustery, choppy, gusty, raging, rough, squally, tempestuous, wild, windy
AN OPPOSITE IS calm
2 *Several arguments broke out at the stormy meeting.*
▸ angry, bad-tempered, disorderly, ill-tempered, quarrelsome, turbulent
AN OPPOSITE IS orderly

story *NOUN*
1 *Tell me a story.*
▸ tale, (*informal*) yarn
VARIOUS KINDS OF STORY
crime story, detective story, fable, fairy tale, fantasy, folk tale, legend, mystery, myth, novel, parable, romance, saga, science fiction or SF, thriller
▹ Invented stories are all kinds of **fiction**.
2 *The book tells the story of her childhood in New York.*
▸ account, history, narrative
▹ A story of a person's life is a **biography**. The story of your life told by yourself is your **autobiography**.
3 *It was the front-page story in all the papers.*
▸ article, feature, news item, report
4 (*informal*) *She's been telling stories again.*
▸ fib, lie

stout *ADJECTIVE*
1 *He was a stout man with grey hair.*
▸ chubby, dumpy, fat, heavy, overweight, plump, portly, stocky, well-built
AN OPPOSITE IS thin
2 *They wore stout walking boots.*
▸ robust, sound, strong, sturdy, substantial, thick, tough
AN OPPOSITE IS weak
3 *They put up a stout resistance.*
▸ bold, brave, courageous, determined, fearless, gallant, heroic, intrepid, plucky, resolute, valiant
AN OPPOSITE IS cowardly

stove *NOUN*
▹ A stove used for heating is a **boiler** or **furnace**. A stove used for cooking is a **cooker** or an **oven**. An old-fashioned cooking stove is a **range**.

stow *VERB*
1 *He stowed the luggage in the boot.*
▸ pack, pile, load
2 *They stowed the books in the attic.*
▸ put away, store

straggle *VERB*
1 *Brambles straggled across the path.*
▸ grow untidily, spread out, trail
2 *The children straggled behind her.*
▸ dawdle, fall behind, lag, loiter, ramble about, stray, wander

straight *ADJECTIVE*
1 *They walked in a straight line.*
▸ direct, unswerving
AN OPPOSITE IS crooked
2 *It took a long time to get the room straight.*
▸ neat, orderly, tidy
AN OPPOSITE IS untidy
3 *She found it difficult to get a straight answer from him.*
▸ blunt, frank, honest, outspoken, plain, sincere, straightforward
AN OPPOSITE IS dishonest

straightforward *ADJECTIVE*
He's a very straightforward man.
▸ blunt, direct, frank, genuine, honest, open, plain, simple, sincere, straight, truthful, uncomplicated
AN OPPOSITE IS devious

strain *VERB*
1 *The dog was straining at its lead, eager to be off.*
▸ haul, pull, stretch, tug
2 *People were straining to see what was going on.*
▸ attempt, endeavour, exert yourself, make an effort, struggle, try
3 *Take it easy and don't strain yourself.*
▸ exhaust, tire out, weaken, wear out, weary

strain *NOUN*
The strain of his job was too much for him.
▸ anxiety, difficulty, hardship, pressure, stress, tension, worry

strand *NOUN*
The strands of the rope began to come apart.
▸ fibre, filament, thread

stranded *ADJECTIVE*
1 *A ship was stranded on the beach.*
▸ aground, (*informal*) high and dry, stuck
2 *He was stranded in London without any money.*
▸ abandoned, alone, deserted, helpless, in difficulties, lost, marooned, without help

strange *ADJECTIVE*
1 *A strange thing happened this morning.*
▸ abnormal, curious, exceptional, extraordinary, funny, odd, out of the ordinary, queer, remarkable, singular, surprising, uncommon, unexpected, unnatural, unusual
▷ If something is like nothing else, it is unique.
2 *He's a very strange man.*
▸ eccentric, peculiar, unconventional, weird, zany
3 *I heard strange noises in the night.*
▸ baffling, bewildering, eerie, inexplicable, mysterious, mystifying, perplexing, puzzling, sinister, uncanny
AN OPPOSITE IS familiar or ordinary

stranger *NOUN*
Please help me find the way — I'm a stranger here.
▸ alien, foreigner, guest, newcomer, outsider, visitor

strangle *VERB*
The victim had been strangled.
▸ throttle

strap *NOUN*
He fastened a leather strap around his case.
▸ band, belt

strategy *NOUN*
The government are developing a new strategy for dealing with unemployment.
▸ approach, method, plan, policy, procedure, programme, scheme, tactics

stratum *NOUN*
You can see different strata of rock in the cliff.
▸ layer, seam, thickness, vein

stray *VERB*
Tourists sometimes stray into dangerous areas.
▸ get lost, go astray, meander, ramble, range, roam, rove, straggle, wander

streak *NOUN*
1 *He had a streak of red paint on his face.*
▸ band, line, smear, stain, strip, stripe
2 *There's a streak of selfishness in her character.*
▸ element, trace

streak *VERB*
1 *Rain had begun to streak the window panes.*
► smear, smudge, stain
2 *Cars streaked past.*
► dash, flash, fly, hurtle, move at speed, rush, speed, tear, zoom

streaky *ADJECTIVE*
The kitchen wallpaper was old and streaky with grease.
► smeary, smudged, streaked

stream *NOUN*
1 *A stream flowed down the valley.*
► brook, small river
▷ In northern England, a stream is a **beck**. In Scotland, a stream is a **burn**.
2 *The dinghy was carried along with the stream.*
► current, flow, tide
3 *A stream of water poured through the hole.*
► cataract, flood, gush, jet, rush, torrent
4 *There was a steady stream of visitors.*
► line, series, string, succession

stream *VERB*
Water streamed through the hole.
► flood, flow, gush, issue, pour, run, spill, spout, spurt, squirt

streamlined *ADJECTIVE*
The new trains are streamlined.
▷ A formal word is **aerodynamic**.
AN OPPOSITE IS air resistant

street *NOUN*
SEE **road**

strength *NOUN*
1 *Despite being a small woman she still had great strength.*
► fitness, might, muscle, power, sturdiness, toughness
2 *Patience is her greatest strength.*
► advantage, asset, virtue
AN OPPOSITE IS weakness

strengthen *VERB*
1 *Regular exercise strengthens the muscles.*
► build up, harden, make stronger, toughen
2 *They need to strengthen their defence.*
► back up, bolster, fortify, prop up, reinforce
AN OPPOSITE IS weaken

strenuous *ADJECTIVE*
1 *They made strenuous efforts to improve security after the break-in.*
► determined, energetic, resolute, strong, tireless, vigorous
AN OPPOSITE IS feeble
2 *He was advised to avoid strenuous exercise.*
► demanding, difficult, exhausting, hard, laborious, tiring, tough, uphill
AN OPPOSITE IS easy

stress *NOUN*
1 *High winds put great stress on the structure of the building.*
► force, pressure
2 *Stress made him ill.*
► anxiety, strain, tension, worry
3 *He puts great stress on the need for discipline.*
► emphasis, importance

stress *VERB*
She stressed the importance of a healthy diet.
► draw attention to, emphasize, show clearly, underline

stretch *VERB*
1 *She stretched the piece of elastic until it snapped.*
► draw out, elongate, expand, extend, lengthen, pull out
2 *She stretched her arms wide.*
► extend, open out, spread out
3 *The road stretched into the distance.*
► continue, disappear, go on and on

stretch *NOUN*
1 *He had a 2-year stretch in the army.*
► period, spell, time
2 *There are often accidents on this stretch of road.*
► length, piece, section
3 *It's a beautiful stretch of countryside.*
► area, expanse, tract

strict *ADJECTIVE*
1 *The club has strict rules about smoking.*
► (*informal*) hard and fast, inflexible, rigid
AN OPPOSITE IS flexible
2 *His father was very strict.*
► firm, harsh, severe, stern
AN OPPOSITE IS lenient
3 *He used the word in its strict scientific sense.*
► correct, exact, precise
AN OPPOSITE IS approximate

stride *NOUN*
He took two strides forward.
► pace, step

strife *NOUN*
There has been a great deal of strife within the company.
► arguments, conflict, disagreements, fighting, friction, hostility, quarrelling

strike *VERB*
1 *She fell, and struck her head on the floor.*
▸ bang, bump, crack, hit, knock, (*informal*) wallop, whack
SEE ALSO **hit** *VERB*
2 *The enemy struck for the second time in a week.*
▸ attack
3 *The clock struck one.*
▸ chime, ring
4 *Workers threatened to strike over the proposed job losses.*
▸ stop work, take industrial action, withdraw labour

strike *NOUN*
During the strike, no buses were running.
▸ industrial action, stoppage, withdrawal of labour

striking *ADJECTIVE*
Her most striking feature was her long, curly red hair.
▸ conspicuous, distinctive, effective, interesting, noticeable, obvious, outstanding, prominent, remarkable
AN OPPOSITE IS inconspicuous

string *NOUN*
1 *She tied some string round the box.*
▸ cord, line, rope, twine
FOR MUSICAL INSTRUMENTS WITH STRINGS SEE **music**
2 *The incident was the latest in a string of burglaries.*
▸ chain, sequence, series, succession

string *VERB*
She strung the beads together.
▸ connect, join, link, thread

stringy *ADJECTIVE*
This meat is very stringy.
▸ chewy, fibrous, tough
AN OPPOSITE IS tender

strip *VERB*
1 *He stripped the paper off the present.*
▸ peel, remove
AN OPPOSITE IS cover or wrap
2 *He stripped and got into the bath.*
▸ get undressed, undress
AN OPPOSITE IS dress

strip *NOUN*
A strip of carpet covered the hall floor.
▸ band, bit, piece, ribbon

stripe *NOUN*
The tablecloth was white with blue stripes.
▸ band, bar, line, strip

strive *VERB*
They were striving to finish the decorations in time for the party.
▸ aim, attempt, make an effort, try hard

stroke *NOUN*
1 *He split the log with a single stroke.*
▸ action, blow, effort, hit, movement
2 *She added a few quick pencil strokes to her drawing.*
▸ line, mark

stroke *VERB*
She was curled up on the sofa, stroking the cat.
▸ caress, pat, rub, touch

stroll *VERB*
They strolled quietly home.
▸ amble, saunter, walk slowly
SEE ALSO **walk**

strong *ADJECTIVE* This word is often overused. Here are some alternatives:
1 *He became very strong after taking up weightlifting.*
▸ (*informal*) beefy, brawny, burly, fit, hefty, mighty, muscular, powerful, robust, sturdy, tough, well-built, wiry
2 *The chair wasn't strong enough and broke when he sat on it.*
▸ durable, hard-wearing, stout, substantial
3 *He made a strong effort to improve.*
▸ determined, forceful, resolute, vigorous
4 *The lights were too strong.*
▸ bright, brilliant, clear, dazzling, glaring
5 *The cheese had a strong taste.*
▸ definite, highly-flavoured, hot, obvious, overpowering, pronounced, spicy, unmistakable
6 *The drink was too strong for her.*
▸ alcoholic, intoxicating
7 *The police have strong evidence that she's guilty.*
▸ convincing, persuasive, solid, sound, valid
8 *He's a strong supporter of the team.*
▸ avid, enthusiastic, fervent, genuine, keen, passionate, zealous
AN OPPOSITE IS weak or feeble or flimsy

stronghold *NOUN*
They besieged the enemy stronghold for months.
▸ castle, fort, fortress, garrison

A B C D E F G H I J K L M N O P Q R **S** T U V W X Y Z

structure *NOUN*
1 *The cathedral is a magnificent structure.*
▸ building, construction, framework
FOR VARIOUS KINDS OF STRUCTURE SEE **building**
2 *She explained the structure of the poem.*
▸ arrangement, composition, design, organization, plan, shape

struggle *VERB*
1 *He was struggling to get free.*
▸ endeavour, fight, make an effort, strain, strive, try hard, tussle, wrestle, wriggle about, writhe about
2 *She had to struggle through deep mud.*
▸ flounder, stagger, stumble, wallow

struggle *NOUN*
After a long struggle she got what she wanted.
▸ battle, contest, fight, match, (*informal*) scrap, tussle

stubborn *ADJECTIVE*
He's too stubborn to give in now.
▸ defiant, difficult, disobedient, inflexible, obstinate, pig-headed, uncooperative, wilful
AN OPPOSITE IS docile

stuck-up *ADJECTIVE* (*informal*)
Nobody likes her — she's so stuck-up.
▸ arrogant, (*informal*) cocky, conceited, haughty, pompous, (*informal*) posh, proud, self-important, snobbish, superior
AN OPPOSITE IS humble

student *NOUN*
▹ A student at school is a pupil. A old word for a pupil is scholar. A student at university is an undergraduate.

studious *ADJECTIVE*
She's a quiet, studious girl.
▸ academic, (*informal*) brainy, clever, intellectual, scholarly, thoughtful

study *VERB*
1 *He went to university to study medicine.*
▸ learn about, research into
2 *They studied the evidence carefully.*
▸ analyse, consider, contemplate, enquire into, examine, investigate, look closely at, read carefully, scrutinize, survey, think about
3 *She has to study for her exams.*
▸ cram, revise, (*informal*) swot

stuff *NOUN*
1 *What's this stuff in the saucepan?*
▸ matter, substance
2 *That's his stuff on the table.*
▸ articles, belongings, gear, possessions, things

stuff *VERB*
1 *She managed to stuff everything in the suitcase.*
▸ compress, cram, force, jam, pack, push, ram, shove, squeeze, stow
2 *The cushions are stuffed with foam rubber.*
▸ fill, pad

stuffy *ADJECTIVE*
1 *Open a window — it's stuffy in here.*
▸ airless, close, (*informal*) fuggy, humid, muggy, musty, stale, unventilated
AN OPPOSITE IS airy
2 *She found the lecture a bit stuffy.*
▸ boring, dreary, dull, formal, humourless, pompous, stodgy
AN OPPOSITE IS informal or lively

stumble *VERB*
1 *He stumbled on a tree root.*
▸ flounder, lurch, stagger, totter, trip
2 *She stumbled over her words.*
▸ falter, hesitate, stammer, stutter
to stumble across something *He stumbled across some old photos.*
▸ come across, dig up, discover, encounter, find, unearth

stump *VERB*
They were all stumped by the problem.
▸ baffle, bewilder, defeat, fox, mystify, outwit, perplex, puzzle

stun *VERB*
1 *The blow stunned him.*
▸ daze, knock out, knock senseless, make unconscious
2 *She was stunned by the news.*
▸ amaze, astonish, astound, bewilder, confuse, shake, shock, stagger, surprise

stunt *NOUN*
We watched the daredevils performing their stunts.
▸ exploit, feat, trick

stupendous *ADJECTIVE*
Everyone congratulated her on her stupendous achievement.
▸ amazing, colossal, enormous, exceptional, extraordinary, huge, incredible, marvellous, miraculous, notable, phenomenal, remarkable, sensational, singular, special, staggering, tremendous, unbelievable, wonderful
AN OPPOSITE IS ordinary

stupid *ADJECTIVE*
1 *He's such a stupid man.*
All these words can be insulting, and some can be more insulting than others. Many are informal. Therefore you need to think carefully how you use them.
▸ brainless, dense, dim, dopey, dull, dumb, feeble-minded, foolish, half-witted, idiotic, ignorant, mindless, moronic, naïve, silly, simple, slow, thick, unintelligent, unwise
2 *It was a stupid thing to do.*
▸ absurd, crazy, daft, irrational, laughable, ludicrous, (*informal*) mad, pointless, rash, reckless, ridiculous, senseless, thoughtless
AN OPPOSITE IS intelligent

sturdy *ADJECTIVE*
1 *She is short and sturdy.*
▸ athletic, brawny, burly, healthy, hefty, husky, muscular, powerful, robust, stocky, strong, vigorous, well-built
AN OPPOSITE IS weak
2 *She bought some sturdy walking boots.*
▸ durable, solid, sound, substantial, tough, well made
AN OPPOSITE IS flimsy

stutter *VERB*
She tends to stutter when she's nervous.
▸ stammer, stumble

style *NOUN*
1 *He doesn't like the new styles of clothes.*
▸ design, fashion, pattern
2 *The book is written in an informal style.*
▸ manner, tone, way, wording
3 *He dresses with great style.*
▸ elegance, sophistication, stylishness, taste

stylish *ADJECTIVE*
She always wears stylish clothes.
▸ chic, elegant, fashionable, modern, smart, sophisticated, (*informal*) trendy, up to date
AN OPPOSITE IS old-fashioned

subdue *VERB*
1 *The army managed to subdue the rebels.*
▸ beat, conquer, control, crush, defeat, overcome, overpower, vanquish
2 *He tried to subdue his anger.*
▸ check, curb, hold back, quieten, repress, restrain, suppress

subdued *ADJECTIVE*
They were all in a subdued mood.
▸ depressed, grave, quiet, serious, silent, sober, solemn, thoughtful
AN OPPOSITE IS excited

subject *NOUN*
1 *She had strong views on the subject.*
▸ issue, matter, point, question, theme, topic
2 *Maths is his favourite subject.*
SUBJECTS WHICH STUDENTS STUDY
agriculture, anatomy, anthropology, archaeology, architecture, art, astronomy, biology, botany, business studies, chemistry, classics, domestic science, drama, economics, electronics, engineering, English, environmental science, foreign languages, geography, geology, history, ICT, law, mathematics, medicine, music, pharmacy, philosophy, physics, politics, psychology, religious studies, science, scripture, sociology, sport, surveying, technology, theology, zoology
3 *They are British subjects.*
▸ citizen, passport-holder

subject *VERB*
They subjected him to a string of questions.
▸ expose, submit

subjective *ADJECTIVE*
1 *Our reactions to music are bound to be subjective.*
▸ emotional, in the mind, instinctive, intuitive
2 *It was a very subjective account of what had happened.*
▸ biased, prejudiced
AN OPPOSITE IS objective

submerge *VERB*
1 *He watched the submarine submerge.*
▸ dive, go under
2 *They feared that the flood would submerge the village.*
▸ cover, drown, engulf, immerse, inundate, overwhelm, swallow up, swamp

A B C D E F G H I J K L M N O P Q R S T U V W X Y Z

submission *NOUN*
1 *They starved the town into submission.*
▸ giving in, surrender
2 *The judge accepted counsel's submission.*
▸ claim, idea, presentation, proposal, suggestion

submissive *ADJECTIVE*
He's too submissive — he needs to stand up for himself.
▸ docile, gentle, humble, meek, obedient, passive, tame, uncomplaining
AN OPPOSITE IS assertive

submit *VERB*
1 *They finally submitted to the enemy.*
▸ give in, surrender, yield
2 *He submitted the plans to the council for approval.*
▸ give in, hand in, present

subordinate *ADJECTIVE*
1 *An officer can give orders to soldiers of subordinate rank.*
▸ inferior, junior, lesser, lower
AN OPPOSITE IS higher or superior
2 *The other issues are subordinate to that one.*
▸ minor, secondary, subsidiary
AN OPPOSITE IS major

subscribe *VERB*
to subscribe to *She subscribes to several good causes.*
▸ contribute to, donate to, give to, pay a subscription to, support

subscriber *NOUN*
The book club sent a letter to all its subscribers.
▸ patron, regular customer, supporter

subscription *NOUN*
He couldn't afford the club subscription.
▸ contribution, fee, regular payment

subside *VERB*
1 *The wall cracked when the house subsided.*
▸ settle, sink
2 *When the rain stopped the flood began to subside.*
▸ decline, ebb, fall, go down, recede, shrink
3 *The pain eventually subsided.*
▸ decrease, diminish, dwindle, lessen, moderate, wear off

subsidize *VERB*
The project was subsidized by the government.
▸ back, finance, sponsor, support

subsidy *NOUN*
Public transport gets a subsidy from taxes.
▸ backing, financial help or support, a grant

substance *NOUN*
1 *The scientists couldn't identify the substance.*
▸ material, matter, stuff
2 *What was the substance of the book?*
▸ essence, gist, subject matter, theme

substantial *ADJECTIVE*
1 *He gave them a substantial amount of money.*
▸ big, considerable, generous, large, significant, sizeable, worthwhile
AN OPPOSITE IS small
2 *He built a substantial fence to keep the cattle out.*
▸ durable, hefty, solid, sound, strong, sturdy, well made
AN OPPOSITE IS flimsy

substitute *VERB*
1 *In most recipes you can substitute margarine for butter.*
▸ exchange, (*informal*) swap
Other ways you can express the example sentence are: *Margarine can take the place of butter*, or *You can replace butter with margarine*
2 *He substituted for the injured goalkeeper.*
▸ deputize, stand in, take the place (of)

substitute *NOUN*
They had to bring on a substitute during the match.
▸ deputy, replacement, reserve, standby
▹ A substitute for a regular teacher is a supply teacher. A substitute for a sick actor is an understudy. A substitute for a thing that isn't available is an alternative.

subtle *ADJECTIVE*
1 *There was a subtle smell of perfume in the room.*
▸ delicate, faint, mild, slight
2 *His jokes are too subtle for them.*
▸ ingenious, sophisticated
3 *He gave her a subtle hint.*
▸ gentle, indirect, tactful
AN OPPOSITE IS obvious

subtract *VERB*
Subtract 5 from 20 and you have 15 left.
▸ deduct, remove, take away
AN OPPOSITE IS add

suburbs *PLURAL NOUN*
They lived in the suburbs of the city.
▸ fringes, outer areas, outlying areas, outskirts
▹ The suburbs of large towns are also known as suburbia.

succeed *VERB*
1 *You have to work hard if you want to succeed.*
▸ be successful, do well, flourish, (*informal*) make it, prosper, thrive
2 *She hoped the plan would succeed.*
▸ be effective, (*informal*) catch on, produce results, work
AN OPPOSITE IS fail
3 *Elizabeth II succeeded George VI.*
▸ come after, follow, replace, take over from

success *NOUN*
1 *She talked about her success as an actress.*
▸ achievement, attainment, fame
2 *They congratulated the team on their success.*
▸ triumph, victory, win
3 *The group's recent CD was a success.*
▸ hit, (*informal*) winner
4 *The success of the plan depends on their cooperation.*
▸ completion, effectiveness, successful outcome
AN OPPOSITE IS failure

successful *ADJECTIVE*
1 *She runs a successful business.*
▸ booming, flourishing, profitable, prosperous, rewarding, thriving
2 *His final attempt to fix it was successful.*
▸ effective
3 *The supporters cheered the successful team.*
▸ triumphant, victorious, winning
AN OPPOSITE IS unsuccessful

succession *NOUN*
They suffered a succession of disasters.
▸ run, sequence, series, string

successive *ADJECTIVE*
It rained on seven successive days.
▸ consecutive, in succession, uninterrupted
You can also say: *It rained on several days in succession.*

suck *VERB*
to suck something up *A sponge will suck up water.*
▸ absorb, draw up, soak up

sudden *ADJECTIVE*
1 *He made a sudden decision.*
▸ hasty, hurried, impulsive, quick, rash
2 *The bus came to a sudden halt.*
▸ abrupt, swift
3 *A sudden bang made her jump.*
▸ sharp, startling, unexpected
AN OPPOSITE IS expected

suffer *VERB*
1 *He suffers terribly with his back.*
▸ feel pain, hurt
2 *He will suffer for his crime.*
▸ be punished, pay
3 *She had to suffer the disgrace of coming last.*
▸ bear, cope with, endure, experience, feel, go through, put up with, stand, tolerate, undergo

suffering *NOUN*
The refugees experienced terrible suffering.
▸ deprivation, hardship, illness, misery, pain, torture
SEE ALSO **pain**

sufficient *ADJECTIVE*
They had sufficient money to live on.
▸ adequate, enough, satisfactory
AN OPPOSITE IS insufficient

suffix *NOUN*
AN OPPOSITE IS prefix

suffocate *VERB*
He was suffocated by the fumes.
▸ choke, stifle
▹ To stop someone's breathing by squeezing their throat is to strangle or throttle them. To stop someone's breathing by covering their nose and mouth is to smother them.

sugar *NOUN*
VARIOUS FORMS OF SUGAR
brown sugar, cane sugar, caster sugar, demerara, glucose, granulated sugar, icing sugar, lump sugar, molasses, sucrose, syrup, treacle
▹ Things you eat which are made mainly of sugar are sweets.

A B C D E F G H I J K L M N O P Q R S T U V W X Y Z

suggest *VERB*
1 *She suggested going to the zoo.*
▸ advise, advocate, propose, recommend
2 *Her yawn suggests that she's bored.*
▸ hint, imply, indicate, mean, signal

suggestion *NOUN*
They didn't like his suggestion.
▸ advice, offer, plan, proposal, recommendation

suit *VERB*
1 *The ten o'clock train would suit them very well.*
▸ be acceptable or convenient to, fit in with, satisfy
AN OPPOSITE IS displease
2 *Her new haircut didn't suit her.*
▸ be appropriate to, become, look good on

suitable *ADJECTIVE*
1 *They wore clothes suitable for cold weather.*
▸ acceptable, appropriate, apt, fit, well chosen
2 *Is this a suitable time to have a chat?*
▸ convenient, proper, satisfactory
AN OPPOSITE IS unsuitable

sulk *VERB*
He sulked for days when he was dropped from the team.
▸ be resentful or sullen, brood, mope

sullen *ADJECTIVE*
1 *She became sullen when she lost.*
▸ bad-tempered, brooding, cross, gloomy, moody, morose, resentful, silent, sour, sulky
AN OPPOSITE IS cheerful
2 *The sullen sky promised rain.*
▸ cloudy, dark, dismal, dull, grey, overcast, sombre
AN OPPOSITE IS bright

sum *NOUN*
1 *The sum of 2 and 2 is 4.*
▸ result, total
2 *He lost a large sum of money.*
▸ amount, quantity
sums *She doesn't like doing sums.*
▸ adding up, arithmetic, (*informal*) maths, mathematical problems
FOR OTHER MATHEMATICAL TERMS SEE **mathematics**

sum *VERB*
to sum up SEE **summarize**

summarize *VERB*
1 *The judge began to summarize the evidence.*
▸ make a summary of, outline, (*informal*) recap, sum up
2 *He had to summarize his story because of the lack of time.*
▸ abbreviate, condense, reduce, shorten
AN OPPOSITE IS elaborate

summary *NOUN*
She wrote a short summary of her story.
▸ condensation, outline, précis

summit *NOUN*
The summit of the mountain was covered in snow.
▸ cap, peak, tip, top
AN OPPOSITE IS base

summon *VERB*
The head will summon you when she's ready to see you.
▸ call, command you to come, order you to come, send for
▹ To ask someone politely to come is to invite them.

sun *NOUN*
They went out into the garden to sit in the sun.
▸ sunlight, sunshine

sunbathe *VERB*
She spent the whole holiday sunbathing on the beach.
▸ bask in the sun, get a tan, sun yourself

sunburned, sunburnt *ADJECTIVE*
▹ If you are often in the sun you become **bronzed** or **tanned** or **weather-beaten**. If your skin is damaged by the sun you may be **blistered** or **peeling**.

sunlight *NOUN*
Most plants can only grow in sunlight.
▸ daylight, sun, sunshine
▹ Rays of light from the sun are **sunbeams**.

sunny *ADJECTIVE*
1 *It was a lovely sunny day.*
▸ clear, cloudless, fine
AN OPPOSITE IS cloudy
2 *She worked in a nice sunny office.*
▸ bright, cheerful, sunlit
AN OPPOSITE IS gloomy

sunrise *NOUN*
He always woke up at sunrise.
▸ dawn, daybreak

sunset *NOUN*
They finished work at sunset.
▸ dusk, evening, nightfall, twilight

sunshade *NOUN*
She sat under a sunshade.
▸ canopy, parasol

superb *ADJECTIVE*
It was a superb goal.
▸ excellent, exceptional, impressive, magnificent, marvellous, outstanding, remarkable, splendid, wonderful
INFORMAL SYNONYMS
brilliant, fabulous, fantastic, great, smashing, super

superficial *ADJECTIVE*
1 *It's only a superficial wound.*
▸ on the surface, shallow, slight, unimportant
AN OPPOSITE IS deep
2 *He gave the car a superficial examination.*
▸ careless, casual, hasty, hurried, quick
AN OPPOSITE IS thorough
3 *Her arguments seemed superficial.*
▸ frivolous, simple, trivial, unconvincing, unsophisticated
AN OPPOSITE IS profound

superfluous *ADJECTIVE*
They put the superfluous cups back in the box.
▸ excess, redundant, spare, surplus, unnecessary, unwanted, waste
AN OPPOSITE IS necessary

superintend *VERB*
SEE **supervise**

superior *ADJECTIVE*
1 *In the army, a major is superior in rank to a lieutenant.*
▸ greater, higher, more important, senior
2 *You have to pay more to get superior quality.*
▸ better, first-class, first-rate, select, top
3 *They didn't like her superior attitude.*
▸ arrogant, haughty, self-important, smug, snobbish, stuck-up
AN OPPOSITE IS inferior

supernatural *ADJECTIVE*
She claimed to have supernatural powers.
▸ inexplicable, magical, miraculous, mysterious, spiritual, unearthly, unnatural
AN OPPOSITE IS natural

superstition *NOUN*
It's a superstition that 13 is an unlucky number.
▸ myth

supervise *VERB*
He supervised the men unloading the lorry.
▸ be in charge of, control, direct, lead, look after, manage, organize, preside over, run, superintend, watch over
▹ To supervise candidates in an exam is to invigilate.

supervision *NOUN*
They worked under the supervision of the manager.
▸ administration, control, management

supervisor *NOUN*
Her supervisor told her off for being late.
▸ administrator, controller, director, inspector, manager, organizer
▹ The person who supervises you in an exam is the invigilator.

supple *ADJECTIVE*
The shoes are made of nice supple leather.
▸ flexible, pliable, soft
AN OPPOSITE IS brittle or rigid

supplementary *ADJECTIVE*
You have to pay a supplementary fare to travel first class.
▸ additional, extra

supplier *NOUN*
The store ordered more goods from the suppliers.
▸ dealer, retailer, seller, shopkeeper, wholesaler

supply *VERB*
The supermarket supplies everything you need.
▸ give, provide, sell

supply *NOUN*
They have a good supply of food.
▸ quantity, reserve, stock, store
supplies *He bought supplies for the camping trip.*
▸ equipment, food, necessities, provisions

A B C D E F G H I J K L M N O P Q R S T U V W X Y Z

support *NOUN*
1 *She thanked them for their support.*
▸ aid, assistance, backing, cooperation, encouragement, friendship, help, interest, loyalty
2 *The support of a local business enabled them to buy sports equipment.*
▸ contributions, donations, sponsorship
3 *The supports prevented the wall from collapsing.*
▸ prop
▹ A support for a shelf is a bracket. A support built against a wall is a buttress. A support for someone with an injured leg is a crutch. A support for a roof is a pillar. A support for a broken arm is a sling. A bar of wood or metal supporting a framework is a strut. A support put under a board to make a table is a trestle.

support *VERB*
1 *The rope couldn't support his weight.*
▸ bear, carry, hold up
2 *The beams support the roof.*
▸ prop up, reinforce, strengthen
3 *They supported him when he was in trouble.*
▸ aid, assist, back, comfort, defend, encourage, give support to, rally round, reassure, side with, speak up for, stand by, stand up for
4 *They agreed to support her proposal.*
▸ advocate, agree with, argue for, promote, uphold
5 *She had to work to support her family.*
▸ bring up, feed, keep, maintain, provide for
6 *He supports OXFAM.*
▸ contribute to, donate to, give to
7 *He supports Nottingham Forest.*
▸ be a supporter of, follow

supporter *NOUN*
1 *The supporters cheered their team.*
▸ fan, follower
2 *The government's supporters welcomed the new law.*
▸ ally, backer, collaborator, helper
▹ The supporter of the main speaker in a debate is the seconder. A supporter of someone in a fight is their second.

suppose *VERB*
1 *I suppose you want to borrow some money.*
▸ assume, believe, expect, guess, infer, presume, think
2 *Just suppose you had lots of money!*
▸ fancy, imagine, pretend
to be supposed to do something *She's supposed to get up at 7.30.*
▸ be due to, be expected to, be meant to, have a duty to, need to, ought to

supposition *NOUN*
That's only a supposition — we don't know if its really true.
▸ assumption, guess, hypothesis, opinion, suggestion, theory

suppress *VERB*
1 *He managed to suppress his anger.*
▸ bottle up, conceal, cover up, hide, repress, smother
▹ To suppress ideas for political or moral reasons is to censor them.
2 *The army suppressed the rebellion.*
▸ crush, overcome, put an end to, put down, stamp out, stop, subdue

supremacy *NOUN*
The country has achieved military supremacy.
▸ dominance, lead, predominance

supreme *ADJECTIVE*
Her supreme achievement was winning a gold medal.
▸ best, greatest, highest, outstanding, top

sure *ADJECTIVE*
1 *I'm sure that I'm right.*
▸ certain, confident, convinced, definite, positive
2 *He's sure to come.*
▸ bound, certain
3 *A high temperature is a sure sign of illness.*
▸ clear, guaranteed, true, undeniable
4 *He's a sure friend.*
▸ dependable, faithful, firm, loyal, reliable, trustworthy
AN OPPOSITE IS uncertain

surface *NOUN*
1 *Much of the surface of the earth is covered with sea.*
▸ exterior, outside
▹ The surface of something may be covered with a crust or shell or skin. A thin surface of expensive wood on furniture is a veneer.
AN OPPOSITE IS centre
2 *A dice has dots on each surface.*
▸ face, side
AN OPPOSITE IS inside
3 *Oil floated on the surface of the water.*
▸ top
AN OPPOSITE IS bottom

surface *VERB*
1 *They surfaced the road with asphalt.*
▸ coat, cover
▹ To surface cheap wood with a thin layer of expensive wood is to **veneer** it.
2 *The submarine surfaced.*
▸ appear, come up, emerge, (*informal*) pop up, rise to the surface

surge *VERB*
1 *Water surged around them.*
▸ billow, heave, make waves, rise, roll, swirl
2 *The crowd surged forward.*
▸ push, rush, sweep

surgery *NOUN*
1 *She went to see the doctor at the surgery.*
▸ clinic, health centre, medical centre
2 *She had surgery in the local hospital.*
▸ an operation

surpass *VERB*
It will be hard to surpass their score.
▸ beat, do better than, exceed, outdo

surplus *NOUN*
Eat what you want and put the surplus in the fridge.
▸ excess, extra, (*informal*) leftovers, remainder

surprise *NOUN*
She looked up in surprise when he walked in.
▸ alarm, amazement, astonishment, dismay, incredulity, shock, wonder

surprise *VERB*
1 *They were surprised by the news.*
▸ alarm, amaze, astonish, astound, shock, stagger, startle, stun, take aback, take by surprise
2 *She surprised the burglars as they went through her cupboards.*
▸ catch, catch red-handed, come upon, detect, discover

surprised *ADJECTIVE*
He gave her a surprised look when she told him.
▸ alarmed, amazed, astonished, astounded, dismayed, dumbfounded, (*informal*) flabbergasted, shocked, speechless, startled, stunned, taken aback

surprising *ADJECTIVE*
It was a surprising decision.
▸ amazing, astonishing, astounding, extraordinary, incredible, shocking, staggering, startling, sudden, unexpected, unplanned, unpredictable
AN OPPOSITE IS **predictable**

surrender *VERB*
1 *The soldiers refused to surrender.*
▸ admit defeat, give in, submit, yield
2 *She surrendered her ticket to the driver.*
▸ give, hand over

surround *VERB*
1 *The courtyard was surrounded by buildings.*
▸ enclose, fence in, wall in
2 *The police surrounded the suspects.*
▸ besiege, encircle, hem in

surroundings *PLURAL NOUN*
They lived in very pleasant surroundings.
▸ conditions, environment, location, setting

survey *NOUN*
1 *They did a survey of local leisure facilities.*
▸ investigation, study
▹ A survey to count the number of people, cars, etc., is a **census**.
2 *The builders did a survey of the house.*
▸ examination, inspection

survey *VERB*
1 *From the hill you can survey the whole valley.*
▸ examine, inspect, look over, scrutinize, study, view
2 *They surveyed the damage done by the storm.*
▸ appraise, assess, evaluate, investigate, weigh up
3 *The contractors surveyed the building plot.*
▸ map out, measure, plan out

survive *VERB*
1 *You can't survive without water.*
▸ carry on, continue, keep going, last, live, remain alive, stay alive
AN OPPOSITE IS **die**
2 *She survived her husband by twenty years.*
▸ outlast
3 *Will the birds survive this cold weather?*
▸ come through, endure, live through, weather, withstand

suspect *VERB*
1 *They suspected his motives.*
▸ doubt, have suspicions about, mistrust
2 *I suspect that it will rain.*
▸ expect, guess, imagine, sense, think it likely

A B C D E F G H I J K L M N O P Q R S T U V W X Y Z

suspend *VERB*
1 *The chairman suspended the meeting.*
▸ adjourn, break off, interrupt
2 *The head threatened to suspend the troublemakers from school.*
▸ bar, dismiss, exclude, expel
3 *They suspended the rope from a branch.*
▸ dangle, hang, swing

suspense *NOUN*
He could hardly bear the suspense of waiting to know what had happened.
▸ anxiety, drama, excitement, expectation, tension, uncertainty, waiting

suspicion *NOUN*
He had a suspicion that she was lying.
▸ feeling, hunch, impression, inkling, intuition, uncertain feeling

suspicious *ADJECTIVE*
1 *There was something about his story which made her suspicious.*
▸ cautious, distrustful, doubtful, incredulous, sceptical, unconvinced, uneasy, wary
AN OPPOSITE IS trusting
2 *What do you make of her suspicious behaviour?*
▸ (*informal*) fishy, peculiar, questionable, shady

sustain *VERB*
1 *Is there enough food to sustain the animals through the winter?*
▸ keep alive, keep going, preserve
2 *The runners couldn't sustain the high speed.*
▸ keep up, maintain
3 *Will the branch sustain his weight?*
▸ bear, carry, stand, support

swallow *VERB*
Chew your food properly before swallowing it.
▸ consume
▹ To swallow food is to eat. To swallow liquid is to drink.
to swallow something up *They were swallowed up in the fog.*
▸ cover, envelop, hide

swamp *VERB*
A huge wave swamped the ship.
▸ engulf, flood, inundate, overwhelm, sink, submerge, swallow up

swamp *NOUN*
He began to sink into the swamp.
▸ bog, fen, marsh, mud, quicksands

swampy *ADJECTIVE*
She warned them not to go near the swampy ground.
▸ boggy, marshy, muddy, soft, soggy, unstable, waterlogged, wet
AN OPPOSITE IS firm

swan *NOUN*
▹ A male swan is a **cob**. A young swan is a **cygnet**.

swap or **swop** *VERB* (*informal*)
She swapped the computer game for a CD.
▸ change, exchange, substitute

swarm *VERB*
The crowd swarmed around him.
▸ crowd, flock
swarming with *The garden is swarming with ants.*
▸ alive with, full of, infested with, overrun by, teeming with

sway *VERB*
The trees swayed in the breeze.
▸ bend, lean from side to side, rock, swing, wave

swear *VERB*
1 *Do you swear to tell the truth?*
▸ give your word, pledge, promise, take an oath, vow
2 *She swore when she hit her finger.*
▸ blaspheme, curse, use swear words

swear word *NOUN*
He was told off for using swear words.
▸ curse, oath, obscenity
▹ Using swear words is **bad language**. Using religious words when you swear is **blasphemy**.

sweat *VERB*
He sweats a lot in hot weather.
▸ perspire

sweaty *ADJECTIVE*
Her hands were sweaty.
▸ clammy, damp, moist, perspiring, sticky, sweating

sweep *VERB*
1 *She swept the floor.*
▶ brush, clean, dust
2 *The bus swept past.*
▶ shoot, speed, zoom
to sweep something away **1** *He tried to sweep away the rubbish.*
▶ clear away, get rid of, remove
2 *The flood swept away several houses.*
▶ destroy, flatten, level

sweet *ADJECTIVE*
1 *The pudding was too sweet for him.*
▶ sickly, sugary, sweetened, syrupy
AN OPPOSITE IS acid or bitter or savoury
2 *The sweet smell of roses filled the room.*
▶ fragrant
AN OPPOSITE IS foul
3 *I heard the sweet sound of a harp.*
▶ melodious, pleasant, soothing, tuneful
AN OPPOSITE IS ugly
4 *What a sweet little cottage!*
▶ attractive, charming, dear, lovely, pretty, quaint
AN OPPOSITE IS unattractive

sweet *NOUN*
1 *Would you like a sweet?*
▷ An American word is candy. A formal word for sweets is confectionery.
VARIOUS KINDS OF SWEET
acid drop, barley sugar, boiled sweet, bull's-eye, butterscotch, candyfloss, caramel, chewing gum, chocolate, fruit pastille, fudge, humbug, liquorice, lollipop, marshmallow, marzipan, mint or peppermint, nougat, rock, toffee, Turkish delight
2 *They had apple crumble for sweet.*
▶ dessert, pudding

swell *VERB*
The balloon swelled as it filled with hot air.
▶ become bigger, billow, blow up, bulge, enlarge, expand, grow, inflate, puff up, rise
AN OPPOSITE IS shrink

swelling *NOUN*
He had a painful swelling on his foot.
▶ blister, bulge, bump, growth, inflammation, lump
▷ A **tumour** is a serious swelling on the body.

swelter *VERB*
They sweltered in the heat.
▶ become hot, perspire, sweat

swerve *VERB*
The car swerved to avoid a hedgehog.
▶ change direction, dodge, swing, turn aside, veer

swift *ADJECTIVE*
1 *He set off at a swift pace.*
▶ brisk, fast, nimble, (*informal*) nippy, quick, rapid, speedy
2 *She didn't expect such a swift reaction.*
▶ hasty, hurried, immediate, instantaneous, prompt, snappy, sudden, unhesitating
AN OPPOSITE IS slow

swill *VERB*
He swilled the front steps with soapy water.
▶ clean, rinse, sponge down, wash
▷ To swill out the lavatory is to flush it.

swim *VERB*
She loves to swim in the sea.
▶ bathe, go swimming, take a dip
VARIOUS SWIMMING STROKES
backstroke, breaststroke, butterfly, crawl
PLACES WHERE YOU CAN SWIM
baths, leisure pool, lido, swimming bath or swimming pool
CLOTHING YOU WEAR TO SWIM IN
bathing costume, bathing suit, bikini, swimming costume, swimsuit, swimwear, trunks

swindle *VERB*
She was arrested for trying to swindle an insurance company.
▶ cheat, (*slang*) con, deceive, (*informal*) diddle, double-cross, fool, hoax, (*slang*) rip off, trick

swindle *NOUN*
They were victims of a swindle.
▶ deception, fraud, (*informal*) racket, (*slang*) rip-off, trick

swing *VERB*
1 *The bucket swung from the end of a rope.*
▶ dangle, flap, hang, sway, wave about
2 *He swung the car round to avoid the bus.*
▶ swerve, turn, twist

A B C D E F G H I J K L M N O P Q R S T U V W X Y Z

swing *NOUN*
There was a swing in public opinion before the election.
▸ change, movement, shift, variation

swirl *VERB*
The water swirls as it goes down the plughole.
▸ churn, spin, twirl, whirl

switch *VERB*
1 *He switched off the light.*
▸ turn
2 *She switched her attention to more important matters.*
▸ change, shift
3 *They switched places.*
▸ exchange, (*informal*) swap

swivel *VERB*
He swivelled in his chair.
▸ pivot, revolve, rotate, spin, turn, twirl

swoop *VERB*
The owl swooped and caught the mouse.
▸ descend, dive, drop, fall, fly down, pounce
to swoop on *The police swooped on the criminals' hideout.*
▸ attack, descend on, invade, pounce on, raid, rush, storm

swop *VERB*
SEE **swap**

sword *NOUN*
FOR VARIOUS WEAPONS SEE **weapon**

syllabus *NOUN*
The teacher explained what was on the syllabus for next term.
▸ course, curriculum, programme of study

symbol *NOUN*
The dove is a symbol of peace.
▸ emblem, image, sign
▹ The symbols we use in writing are **characters** or **letters**. The symbols used in ancient Egyptian writing were **hieroglyphics**. The symbol of a school, sports club, etc., is their **badge**. The symbol of a firm or organization is their **logo**. A religious symbol is an **icon**.

symbolize *VERB*
The dove symbolizes peace.
▸ be a sign of, indicate, mean, represent, signify, stand for, suggest

symmetrical *ADJECTIVE*
The garden was designed in a symmetrical shape.
▸ balanced
AN OPPOSITE IS asymmetrical

sympathetic *ADJECTIVE*
1 *She was sympathetic when my dog died.*
▸ caring, comforting, compassionate, concerned, kind, merciful, pitying, tender, understanding
2 *He took a sympathetic interest in what they were doing.*
▸ benevolent, friendly, interested, open-minded, positive
AN OPPOSITE IS unsympathetic

sympathize *VERB*
to sympathize with *He sympathized with the people who had lost their homes.*
▸ be sorry for, feel for, identify with, pity, show sympathy for, understand

sympathy *NOUN*
She showed no sympathy for him.
▸ compassion, consideration, feeling, kindness, mercy, pity, tenderness, understanding

symptom *NOUN*
A rash is one symptom of measles.
▸ indication, sign, warning

synonym *NOUN*
AN OPPOSITE IS antonym

synthetic *ADJECTIVE*
Nylon is a synthetic material.
▸ artificial, man-made, manufactured, unnatural
AN OPPOSITE IS natural

system *NOUN*
1 *Large towns need an efficient railway system.*
▸ network, organization, (*informal*) set-up
2 *She couldn't see any system in his work.*
▸ arrangement, logic, order, structure
3 *They've introduced a new system for teaching people languages.*
▸ method, plan, procedure, process, routine, scheme, technique

systematic *ADJECTIVE*
He worked in a very systematic way.
▸ businesslike, logical, methodical, orderly, organized, scientific
AN OPPOSITE IS unsystematic

Tt

table *NOUN*
KINDS OF TABLE
coffee table, dining table, gate-leg table, kitchen table, trestle table
SPECIAL TABLES FOR PLAYING GAMES ON
billiard table, card table, snooker table, table tennis table
FOR OTHER ITEMS OF FURNITURE SEE **furniture**

tablet *NOUN*
1 *The doctor prescribed some tablets.*
▸ capsule, pellet, pill
2 *She bought a tablet of scented soap.*
▸ bar, block, chunk, piece

tack *VERB*
1 *She tacked down the carpet.*
▸ nail, pin
2 *She tacked up the hem of her skirt.*
▸ sew, stitch

tackle *VERB*
1 *They left him to tackle the washing-up.*
▸ attempt, attend to, cope with, deal with, do, face, grapple with, handle, manage, set about
2 *Another player tackled him and got the ball.*
▸ attack, challenge, intercept

tackle *NOUN*
1 *He kept his fishing tackle in a special case.*
▸ apparatus, equipment, gear, kit, paraphernalia
2 *The referee said it was a fair tackle.*
▸ block, challenge, interception

tact *NOUN*
He showed tact in discussing the problem.
▸ consideration, diplomacy, tactfulness, thoughtfulness, understanding
AN OPPOSITE IS tactlessness

tactful *ADJECTIVE*
She gave him some tactful advice.
▸ considerate, diplomatic, discreet, judicious, polite, thoughtful
AN OPPOSITE IS tactless

tactics *PLURAL NOUN*
They discussed their tactics for the next game.
▸ approach, course of action, plan, policy, procedure, scheme, strategy

tactless *ADJECTIVE*
She made a tactless remark about his illness.
▸ impolite, inappropriate, inconsiderate, insensitive, rude, thoughtless, undiplomatic, unkind, untimely
AN OPPOSITE IS tactful

tag *NOUN*
The price is marked on the tag.
▸ label, sticker, ticket

tag *VERB*
Every item is tagged with a price label.
▸ identify, label, mark
to tag along with someone *She tagged along with them when they left.*
▸ accompany, follow, go with, join
to tag something on *He tagged on a PS at the end of his letter.*
▸ add, attach, tack on

tail *NOUN*
He joined the tail of the queue.
▸ back, end, rear

tail *VERB*
The police tailed the car for miles.
▸ follow, go after, pursue, track
to tail off *The number of tourists tails off in October.*
▸ decline, decrease, diminish, dwindle, flag, lessen, reduce, subside, wane

take *VERB* This word is often overused. Here are some alternatives:
The verb *to take* has many meanings. We give the commoner ones here
1 *He took her hand.*
▸ clutch, get hold of, grab, grasp, hold, seize, snatch
2 *The soldiers took many prisoners.*
▸ capture, catch, detain, secure, trap
3 *Someone took his pen.*
▸ move, pick up, remove, steal
4 *The caravan can take six people.*
▸ accommodate, contain, have room for, hold
5 *He wanted to take her to the party.*
▸ accompany, conduct, escort, lead
6 *The bus will take you into the city.*
▸ bring, carry, convey, drive, transport
7 *They took a taxi to the station.*
▸ catch, engage, hire, travel by
8 *Do you take sugar?*
▸ have, make use of, use
9 *She can't take rich food.*
▸ abide, bear, endure, put up with, stand, (*informal*) stomach

10 *He finds it hard to take criticism.*
► accept, experience, receive, suffer, tolerate, undergo
11 *It'll take two people to lift that table.*
► need, require
12 *He took their names and addresses.*
► make a note of, record, write down
13 *She took a new name.*
► adopt, choose, select
14 *He takes them for history.*
► look after, organize, supervise, teach
15 *Take 2 from 8 and you get 6.*
► deduct, subtract, take away
to take someone in *They were taken in by his lies.*
► cheat, deceive, delude, fool, mislead, trick
to take off *The plane took off on time.*
► depart, leave the ground, lift off
to take something off *Take off your coat.*
► peel off, remove, strip off
to take part in something *Would you like to take part in a quiz?*
► be involved in, join, share in, participate in
to take place *When did the accident take place?*
► come about, happen, occur
to take something up *He's taken up a new hobby.*
► begin, commence, embark on, start

takings *PLURAL NOUN*
The takings in the shop were better last week.
► earnings, income, proceeds, profits, revenue

tale *NOUN*
She told a tale of adventure.
► account, narrative, report, story, (*informal*) yarn
FOR VARIOUS KINDS OF STORY SEE **story**

talent *NOUN*
She is a musician of great talent.
► ability, aptitude, expertise, skill
▷ Unusually great talent is **genius**.

talented *ADJECTIVE*
He's a very talented painter.
► able, accomplished, brilliant, capable, clever, expert, gifted, skilled
▷ If you are talented in many different ways, you are **versatile**.

talk *VERB*
He learned to talk at a very early age.
► communicate, express yourself, pronounce words, say things, speak, use language
DIFFERENT THINGS WE MAY DO WHEN WE TALK
address people, advise people, answer questions, argue, ask for something, beg for something, complain, confer, converse, declare our intentions, deliver a speech, discuss problems, explain things, express opinions, give information or orders, have a conversation, negotiate, object to something, plead for something, pray, preach, read aloud, recite a poem, tell each other things
DIFFERENT WAYS TO TALK OR SAY THINGS
babble, bawl, bellow, blurt out, burble, call out, chat, chatter, croak, cry, drawl, drone, exclaim, gabble, gossip, grunt, howl, intone, jabber, lisp, moan, mumble, murmur, mutter, prattle, rant, rave, roar, scream, screech, shout, shriek, slur, snap, snarl, splutter, squeal, stammer, stutter, wail, whimper, whine, whinge, whisper, yell

talk *NOUN*
1 *She had a long talk with him.*
► chat, conversation, discussion, gossip
▷ The talk in a novel or play is the **dialogue**.
2 *He gave a talk on his visit to China.*
► address, lecture, presentation, speech
▷ A talk in church is a **sermon**.

talkative *ADJECTIVE*
She's a very talkative child.
► chatty, communicative, eloquent, fluent, vocal, wordy
▷ A talkative person is a **chatterbox** or a **gossip**.

tall *ADJECTIVE*
1 *She is tall for her age.*
► big
AN OPPOSITE IS short
2 *The city is full of tall buildings.*
► giant, high, lofty, towering
▷ Buildings with many floors are **high-rise** or **multi-storey** buildings.
AN OPPOSITE IS low

tally *VERB*
to tally with *Her story didn't tally with her sister's.*
► agree with, correspond with, match

tame *ADJECTIVE*
1 *The animals are quite tame.*
▸ docile, domesticated, gentle, manageable, obedient, safe, submissive
AN OPPOSITE IS wild
2 *The film seemed very tame.*
▸ boring, dull, feeble, tedious, unadventurous, unexciting, uninteresting
AN OPPOSITE IS exciting

tame *VERB*
They were trying to tame a wild horse.
▸ control, subdue, train

tamper *VERB*
to tamper with something *Someone has been tampering with the lock.*
▸ fiddle about with, interfere with, meddle with, tinker with

tan *VERB*
She tans quickly in the sun.
▸ get a tan, go brown
▹ If your skin goes red in the sun, you get sunburn.

tang *NOUN*
The drink has a tang of lemon.
▸ sharp flavour or smell, sharpness

tangle *VERB*
1 *He tangled all the ropes together.*
▸ confuse, muddle, twist
▹ Tangled hair is dishevelled or matted hair.
2 *A fish tangled itself in the net.*
▸ catch, entangle, trap

tangle *NOUN*
She sorted out a tangle of wires.
▸ confusion, jumble, knot, muddle

tank *NOUN*
▹ A water tank is a cistern. A tank to keep fish in is an aquarium.
FOR OTHER CONTAINERS SEE **container**

tantalize *VERB*
They were tantalized by the smell of food.
▸ taunt, tease, tempt, torment

tantrum *NOUN*
He had a tantrum when he didn't get his own way.
▸ fit of anger, fit of temper, rage

tap *VERB*
Someone tapped on the door.
▸ knock, rap, strike

tape *NOUN*
1 *The parcel was tied with tape.*
▸ braid, ribbon
2 *She bought a tape of her favourite pop group.*
▸ tape recording
▹ A tape for listening to is an audiotape. A tape for watching on TV is a videotape. You usually buy tapes in a cassette.

tape *VERB*
He taped the film so he could watch it later.
▸ record, video

target *NOUN*
1 *Their target was to raise £100.*
▸ aim, ambition, goal, hope, intention, objective, purpose
2 *She was the target of his insults.*
▸ object, victim

tarnish *VERB*
1 *Most metals tarnish in the open air.*
▸ corrode, discolour
▹ When iron corrodes it rusts.
2 *The scandal tarnished his reputation.*
▸ blot, mar, spoil, stain

tart *ADJECTIVE*
Lemons have a tart taste.
▸ acid, sharp, sour
AN OPPOSITE IS sweet

task *NOUN*
1 *He was given a number of tasks to do.*
▸ chore, errand, job, work
2 *The soldiers' task was to capture the hill.*
▸ assignment, duty, mission, operation, undertaking

taste *VERB*
She tasted the soup to see if it needed some more salt.
▸ sample, try
WORDS TO DESCRIBE HOW THINGS TASTE
acid, bitter, creamy, fresh, fruity, hot, juicy, meaty, mellow, mild, peppery, rancid, refreshing, salty, savoury, sharp, sour, spicy, stale, strong, sugary, sweet, syrupy, tangy, tart, tasteless, tasty, watery

A B C D E F G H I J K L M N O P Q R S T U V W X Y Z

taste *NOUN*
1 *I love the taste of strawberries.*
▸ flavour
2 *He gave her a taste of the cheese.*
▸ bit, bite, morsel, mouthful, nibble, piece, sample
3 *Her taste in clothes is a bit odd.*
▸ choice, discrimination, judgement, preference

tasteful *ADJECTIVE*
He usually wears tasteful colours.
▸ artistic, attractive, elegant, fashionable, in good taste, smart, stylish
AN OPPOSITE IS tasteless

tasteless *ADJECTIVE*
1 *The decorations seemed rather tasteless.*
▸ crude, gaudy, showy, ugly, unattractive, unfashionable
2 *He keeps making tasteless jokes.*
▸ improper, in bad taste, unpleasant, vulgar
AN OPPOSITE IS tasteful

tasty *ADJECTIVE*
That pie was very tasty.
▸ appetizing, delicious

tattered *ADJECTIVE*
Why does she wear tattered clothes?
▸ frayed, ragged, ripped, tatty, torn, worn out
AN OPPOSITE IS smart

tatters *PLURAL NOUN*
His jeans were in tatters.
▸ rags, ribbons, shreds

tatty *ADJECTIVE*
He was wearing tatty old clothes.
▸ frayed, old, patched, ragged, ripped, scruffy, shabby, tattered, torn, threadbare, untidy, worn out
AN OPPOSITE IS smart

taunt *VERB*
They taunted the losers.
▸ barrack, insult, jeer at, laugh at, make fun of, mock, ridicule, sneer at
AN OPPOSITE IS flatter or praise

taut *ADJECTIVE*
Make sure the rope is taut.
▸ stretched, tense, tight
AN OPPOSITE IS slack

tax *NOUN*
SOME TAXES PEOPLE HAVE TO PAY
airport tax, council tax or (*old use*) rates, customs duty, death duty, income tax, road tax, (*old use*) tithes, VAT or value-added tax

teach *VERB*
If you want to learn about computers, you need an expert to teach you.
▸ educate, inform, instruct
▹ To teach people to play a sport is to **coach** or **train** them. To teach one person at a time or a small group is to **tutor** them. To teach a large group of people is to **lecture** to them. To try to fill people's minds with your ideas is to **brainwash** or **indoctrinate** them.

teacher *NOUN*
VARIOUS PEOPLE WHO MIGHT TEACH US
coach, counsellor, (*old use*) governess, guru, headteacher or principal, instructor, lecturer, preacher, professor, schoolteacher or schoolmaster or schoolmistress, trainer, tutor

team *NOUN*
He was left out of the team.
▸ side
FOR VARIOUS KINDS OF GROUP SEE **group**

tear *VERB*
1 *The barbed wire tore his clothes.*
▸ gash, rip, shred, slit, split
2 *He tore home to watch TV.*
▸ career, dash, hurry, race, run, rush, zoom

tear *NOUN*
There was a tear in his shirt.
▸ cut, gap, gash, hole, opening, rip, slit, split

tearful *ADJECTIVE*
She was tearful when they said goodbye.
▸ crying, emotional, sad, sobbing, weeping

tease *VERB*
They teased him about his new haircut.
▸ annoy, bait, irritate, laugh at, make fun of, mock, pester, provoke, ridicule, tantalize, taunt, torment, vex, worry

technical *ADJECTIVE*
You need someone with technical knowledge to mend this equipment.
▸ expert, professional, scientific, specialized, technological

technique *NOUN*
1 *The musician's technique was flawless.*
▸ art, craft, expertise, know-how, skill
2 *They use modern techniques.*
▸ method, procedure, way

technological *ADJECTIVE*
Modern aircraft are full of technological equipment.
▸ advanced, automated, computerized, electronic, scientific

tedious *ADJECTIVE*
It was a tedious journey.
▸ boring, dreary, dull, long, monotonous, slow, tiresome, tiring, unexciting, uninteresting
AN OPPOSITE IS exciting

tedium *NOUN*
She complained about the tedium of the meeting.
▸ boredom, dullness, monotony, slowness, tediousness
AN OPPOSITE IS excitement

teem *VERB*
to teem with *The pond teemed with tadpoles.*
▸ abound in, (*informal*) be crawling with, be full of, be infested by, be overrun by, swarm with

teenager *NOUN*
The film was designed to appeal to teenagers.
▸ adolescent, youngster
▹ A word for a teenage boy is youth.

telephone *VERB*
He telephoned her to say he couldn't come.
▸ call, dial, phone, ring

televise *VERB*
The match is being televised.
▸ broadcast, relay, send out, transmit

television *NOUN*
She bought a new television.
▸ receiver, set, (*informal*) telly, (*short form*) TV
▹ The part of a computer system with a screen is the monitor.
VARIOUS TYPES OF TELEVISION PROGRAMME
cartoon, chat show, comedy, documentary, drama or play, film or movie, interview, mini series, news, panel game, quiz, serial, series, (*informal*) sitcom or situation comedy, (*informal*) soap or soap opera
▹ TV programmes recorded on tape are videos.
SEE ALSO **entertainment**

tell *VERB*
The verb *to tell* can be used in many ways. We give some of the more important ways here
1 *Tell us what you can see.*
▸ describe, explain, reveal, say
2 *Tell me when you are ready.*
▸ announce, communicate, inform
3 *He told them what they ought to do.*
▸ advise, recommend, suggest
4 *Tell them to stop.*
▸ command, direct, instruct, order
5 *She told them a story.*
▸ narrate, relate
6 *He told her she could trust him.*
▸ assure, promise
7 *She couldn't tell who it was in the dark.*
▸ discover, identify, make out, perceive, recognize, see
8 *Can you tell one from the other?*
▸ distinguish, separate
to tell someone off *She told them off for being late.*
▸ reprimand, reproach, scold, (*informal*) tick off
to tell tales about someone *She didn't like him because he was always telling tales.*
▸ betray, inform against, report, (*informal*) sneak on

telling *ADJECTIVE*
She made a telling contribution to the discussion.
▸ effective, important, impressive, meaningful, significant, striking
AN OPPOSITE IS unimportant

temper *NOUN*
1 *He couldn't put up with her bad temper.*
▸ humour, mood, state of mind
2 *He flew into a temper.*
▸ fit of anger, fury, rage, tantrum
to keep your temper *Try to keep your temper.*
▸ calm down, control yourself, stay calm, stay cool
to lose your temper *She lost her temper with him.*
▸ become angry, flare up, get annoyed, rage

tempestuous *ADJECTIVE*
It was a tempestuous night.
▸ rough, stormy, turbulent, violent, wild, windy
AN OPPOSITE IS calm

A B C D E F G H I J K L M N O P Q R S **T** U V W X Y Z

temple *NOUN*
FOR PLACES OF WORSHIP SEE **worship** *VERB*

temporary *ADJECTIVE*
It's just a temporary arrangement until they can find something better.
▸ makeshift, provisional
AN OPPOSITE IS permanent

tempt *VERB*
Can I tempt you to have more pudding?
▸ coax, persuade
▹ To tempt someone by offering them money is to **bribe** them. Something used to tempt an animal into a trap is **bait** or a **decoy**.

tempting *ADJECTIVE*
The shop has some tempting special offers.
▸ appealing, attractive, desirable, irresistible

tend *VERB*
1 *The shepherd was tending the sheep.*
▸ keep, mind, protect, watch over
2 *He spends a lot of time tending his garden.*
▸ cultivate, manage
3 *Nurses tend the sick.*
▸ attend to, care for, look after, nurse, treat
to tend to do something *She tends to eat too much.*
▸ be inclined to, be liable to, have a tendency to

tendency *NOUN*
He has a tendency to be lazy.
▸ bias, inclination

tender *ADJECTIVE*
1 *Frost may damage tender plants.*
▸ delicate, soft
AN OPPOSITE IS hardy or strong
▹ The opposite of tender meat is **tough** meat.
2 *The bruise is still tender.*
▸ aching, painful, sensitive, sore
AN OPPOSITE IS numb
3 *She gave him a tender smile.*
▸ affectionate, caring, compassionate, fond, gentle, kind, loving, merciful, soft-hearted, sympathetic
AN OPPOSITE IS cruel

tense *ADJECTIVE*
1 *He tried to relax his tense muscles.*
▸ strained, stretched, taut, tight
2 *Everyone was tense as they waited for the game to start.*
▸ anxious, apprehensive, edgy, excited, fidgety, jumpy, nervous, touchy, (*informal*) uptight, worried
3 *It was a tense moment.*
▸ exciting, nerve-racking, stressful, worrying
AN OPPOSITE IS relaxed

tension *NOUN*
1 *He checked the tension on the guy ropes.*
▸ strain, tautness, tightness
2 *They felt the tension as the spacecraft lifted off.*
▸ anxiety, excitement, nervousness, stress, suspense, worry

tent *NOUN*
KINDS OF TENT
bell tent, big top, frame tent, marquee, ridge tent, tepee, trailer tent, wigwam

tepid *ADJECTIVE*
By the time he got into the bath, the water was tepid.
▸ lukewarm, slightly warm

term *NOUN*
1 *He was sentenced to a term in prison.*
▸ period, spell, stretch, time
2 *He didn't understand the technical terms.*
▸ expression, phrase, saying, word
terms *The others wouldn't agree to the terms.*
▸ conditions

terminal *NOUN*
She spends all day working at a terminal.
▸ computer screen, VDU or visual display unit
▹ A desk with a terminal where you work on a computer is a **workstation**.

terminate *VERB*
The company terminated his contract.
▸ end, finish, put an end to, stop

terminus *NOUN*
They stayed on the bus until it reached the terminus.
▸ destination, terminal

terrible *ADJECTIVE*
They saw a terrible accident.
▸ appalling, awful, distressing, dreadful, (*informal*) fearful, frightful, ghastly, horrible, horrific, horrifying, revolting, shocking
The adjective *terrible* is most commonly used informally to mean *very bad*. See **bad** for the many other synonyms you could use

terrific *ADJECTIVE* (*informal*)
1 *The fish he caught was a terrific size.*
▸ Big, colossal, enormous, giant, gigantic, great, huge, immense, impressive, large, massive, mighty, monstrous, monumental, stupendous, tremendous, vast
2 *She's a terrific tennis player.*
▸ excellent, exceptional, first-class, good, marvellous, outstanding, phenomenal, remarkable, sensational, superb, supreme, unequalled, wonderful
INFORMAL SYNONYMS ARE
brilliant, fabulous, fantastic, great, incredible, smashing
The adjective *terrific* is used informally to describe anything which is extreme in some way, and synonyms you might use depend on what you are talking about. Here are some examples of words you could use as synonyms in particular senses:
▹ A terrific noise is a **loud** or **deafening** noise. A terrific storm is a **violent** storm. Terrific food is **delicious** food. A terrific speed is a very fast speed.

terrify *VERB*
The dog was terrified by thunder.
▸ alarm, dismay, frighten, horrify, make afraid, petrify, scare

territory *NOUN*
They entered the enemy's territory.
▸ area, country, district, land, region, sector, zone
▹ A territory which is part of a country is a **province**.

terror *NOUN*
They were filled with terror when the volcano erupted.
▸ alarm, dread, fear, fright, horror, panic

terrorist *NOUN*
▹ A terrorist may be a **gunman** or a **bomber**. A terrorist who kills someone is an **assassin**. A terrorist who takes over an aircraft or vehicle is a **hijacker**.

terrorize *VERB*
The local people were terrorized by a gang.
▸ bully, frighten, intimidate, menace, persecute, scare, terrify, threaten

test *NOUN*
She did very well in the test.
▸ appraisal, assessment, evaluation, examination
▹ A set of questions you answer for fun is a **quiz**. A test for a job as an actor or singer is an **audition**. A test to find the truth about something is an **experiment** or **trial**.

test *VERB*
1 *They were tested on all that they had learned.*
▸ examine, question
2 *They test a new medicine before they let people use it.*
▸ appraise, assess, check, evaluate, experiment with, investigate, try out

testify *VERB*
He testified that he had seen the robbery take place.
▸ declare, give evidence, state on oath, swear

testimonial *NOUN*
Her boss gave her a testimonial when she applied for a new job.
▸ commendation, recommendation, reference

tether *VERB*
He tethered the goat to a post.
▸ chain up, fasten, secure, tie up

text *NOUN*
1 *She studied the text of the document.*
▸ contents, wording, words
2 *He quoted a text from the Bible.*
▸ extract, passage, sentence, verse

textiles *PLURAL NOUN*
FOR VARIOUS KINDS OF TEXTILES SEE **cloth**

texture *NOUN*
Silk has a smooth texture.
▸ feel, quality, touch

thankful *ADJECTIVE*
He was thankful for her help.
▸ appreciative, grateful, happy, pleased, relieved
AN OPPOSITE IS ungrateful

thanks *PLURAL NOUN*
She sent him a card to show her thanks.
▸ appreciation, gratefulness, gratitude

A B C D E F G H I J K L M N O P Q R S T U V W X Y Z

thaw *VERB*

1 *The snow began to thaw when the sun came out.*

▸ melt

2 *Leave frozen food to thaw before cooking it.*

▸ defrost, soften, unfreeze

AN OPPOSITE IS freeze

theatre *NOUN*

PARTS OF A THEATRE

auditorium, balcony, bar, boxes, box office, circle, dress circle, dressing rooms, foyer, gallery, orchestra pit, stage, stalls

PEOPLE WHO PERFORM OR WORK IN A THEATRE

actor, actress, ballerina, dancer, director, dresser, make-up artist, musician, producer, prompter, scene shifter, stage manager, understudy, usher or usherette

VARIOUS THINGS YOU MIGHT GO TO SEE AT A THEATRE

ballet, comedy, drama, farce, mime, music hall, opera, operetta, pantomime, play

FOR OTHER ENTERTAINMENTS SEE **entertainment**

theft *NOUN*

He was found guilty of theft.

▸ robbery, stealing

FOR VARIOUS KINDS OF THEFT SEE **stealing**

theme *NOUN*

1 *What was the theme of the lecture?*

▸ argument, idea, subject, topic

2 *The band played themes from well-known films.*

▸ air, melody, tune

theoretical *ADJECTIVE*

The book is too theoretical.

▸ abstract, hypothetical

theory *NOUN*

1 *He has a theory about what happened.*

▸ belief, explanation, hypothesis, idea, notion, suggestion, view

2 *She began to study musical theory.*

▸ laws, principles, rules

therapy *NOUN*

He needs therapy after his accident.

▸ treatment

SOME KINDS OF THERAPY

acupuncture, aromatherapy, chemotherapy, homeopathy, hydrotherapy, hypnotherapy, occupational therapy, osteopathy, physiotherapy, psychotherapy, radiotherapy

FOR OTHER KINDS OF MEDICAL TREATMENT SEE **medicine**

thick *ADJECTIVE*

The shed was made from thick planks of wood.

▸ chunky, stout, substantial

The adjective *thick* is used in many other ways, and synonyms you might use often depend on what you are talking about. We give some common examples here:

▹ A thick line is a **broad** or **wide** line. A thick book is a **bulky** or **chunky** book. Thick snow is **deep** snow. Thick cloth is **heavy** cloth. Thick rope is **stout** or **substantial** rope. Thick fog is **dense** fog. Thick mud is **sticky** or **stiff** mud.

AN OPPOSITE IS thin

▹ Thick is also an informal word for **stupid**.

thief *NOUN*

The police managed to catch the thief.

▸ robber

▹ Someone who steals from people's homes is a **burglar** or **housebreaker**. Someone who steals from people in the street is a **mugger** or **pickpocket**. Someone who steals from shops is a **shoplifter**. Someone who steals by cheating people is a **con man** or **swindler**. A person who steals fish or game on someone else's land is a **poacher**. Someone who steals from homes or shops during a riot is a **looter**. Someone who used to steal from travellers was a **highwayman**. Sailors who steal from other ships at sea are **pirates**.

thin *ADJECTIVE* This word is often overused. Here are some alternatives:

The refugees were dreadfully thin.

▸ bony, gaunt, lean, skinny, spare, underweight

▹ Someone who is thin and tall is **lanky**. Someone who is thin but strong is **wiry**. Someone who is thin but attractive is **slim** or **slender**.

The adjective *thin* is used in many other ways, and synonyms you might use often depend on what you are talking about. We give some common examples here

▹ A thin line is a **fine** or **narrow** line. A thin book is a **slim** book. A thin covering of snow is a **light** covering. Thin cloth is **delicate** or **flimsy** cloth. Thin fog is **slight** or **wispy** fog. Thin gravy is **runny** or **watery** gravy.

AN OPPOSITE IS fat or thick

thin *VERB*
He thinned the paint.
► dilute, water down, weaken
to thin out *The crowd thinned out later in the day.*
► become less dense, diminish, disperse

thing *NOUN*
The word *thing* can be used instead of almost any other noun, apart from nouns which refer to people. The list of synonyms, therefore, could be virtually endless. We give just some of the more general synonyms here:
WORDS FOR A THING YOU CAN TOUCH AND HOLD
article, device, implement, item, object
WORDS FOR A THING THAT HAPPENS
affair, event, happening, incident, occurrence, phenomenon
WORDS FOR A THING YOU TALK OR THINK ABOUT
concept, detail, fact, factor, idea, point, statement, thought
WORDS FOR A THING YOU HAVE TO DO
act, action, job, task
things *Put your things on the table.*
► baggage, belongings, equipment, gear, luggage, possessions, stuff

think *VERB*
1 *Think before you do anything rash.*
► consider, deliberate, reason, reflect, use your intelligence, work things out
▷ To think hard about something is to **concentrate** on it or **contemplate** it. To think quietly and deeply about something is to **meditate**. To keep thinking anxiously about something is to **brood** on it.
2 *Do you think this is a good idea?*
► accept, admit, be convinced, believe, conclude, judge
3 *What do you think this is worth?*
► assume, estimate, feel, guess, imagine, presume, reckon, suppose
to think something out *She thought out a solution to the problem.*
► analyse, calculate, puzzle out, work out
to think something up *They thought up a plan.*
► conceive, create, design, devise, invent, make up

thirsty *ADJECTIVE*
She was thirsty after her long walk.
► parched
▷ If someone is ill through lack of fluids, they are **dehydrated**.

thorn *NOUN*
Don't scratch yourself on the thorns.
► needle, prickle, spike, spine

thorny *ADJECTIVE*
1 *He fell into a thorny gorse bush.*
► bristly, prickly, scratchy, sharp, spiky, spiny
2 *They discussed the thorny problem for hours.*
► baffling, complex, complicated, difficult, formidable, hard, involved, perplexing, ticklish, tricky

thorough *ADJECTIVE*
1 *The mechanic made a thorough examination of the car.*
► attentive, careful, comprehensive, conscientious, full, methodical, meticulous, observant, orderly, organized, painstaking, systematic, thoughtful
AN OPPOSITE IS superficial
2 *He's made a thorough mess of it!*
► absolute, complete, downright, perfect, total, utter

thought *NOUN*
1 *She gave a lot of thought to the problem.*
► attention, consideration, deliberation, study
2 *He spent much time in thought.*
► brooding, contemplation, meditation, reflection, thinking
3 *He explained his thoughts about the issue.*
► belief, conclusion, idea, notion, opinion

thoughtful *ADJECTIVE*
1 *She had a thoughtful expression on her face.*
► absorbed, attentive, brooding, reflective, serious, solemn, studious, wary
AN OPPOSITE IS carefree
2 *It was a thoughtful piece of work.*
► careful, conscientious, methodical, meticulous, systematic, thorough
AN OPPOSITE IS careless
3 *It was very thoughtful of her to visit him in hospital.*
► caring, considerate, friendly, good-natured, helpful, kind, unselfish
AN OPPOSITE IS thoughtless

thoughtless *ADJECTIVE*
He acted in a thoughtless way.
► careless, forgetful, inconsiderate, irresponsible, negligent, rash, reckless, selfish, uncaring, unthinking
AN OPPOSITE IS thoughtful

thrash *VERB*
1 *She hated seeing him thrash that donkey.*
▸ hit, thump, (*informal*) wallop, whack, whip
2 *We thrashed them 6–0.*
▸ beat, defeat, win against

thread *NOUN*
There was a loose thread hanging from her dress.
▸ fibre, strand
SOME KINDS OF THREAD
cotton, nylon, silk, string, twine, wool, yarn

threadbare *ADJECTIVE*
The beggar wore threadbare clothes.
▸ frayed, old, shabby, tattered, tatty, worn, worn out

threat *NOUN*
1 *The terrorists issued a threat against his life.*
▸ warning
2 *They lived under constant threat of famine.*
▸ danger, menace, risk

threaten *VERB*
1 *A gang of hooligans threatened them.*
▸ intimidate, make threats against, menace, terrorize
2 *The forecast threatened rain.*
▸ warn of
3 *The species is threatened with extinction.*
▸ endanger, put at risk

three *NOUN*
▹ A group of three musicians is a **trio**. Three babies born at the same time are **triplets**. A shape with three sides is a **triangle**. To multiply a number by three is to **triple** it.

thrifty *ADJECTIVE*
She's very thrifty and manages to save a lot of money.
▸ careful, economical, frugal, prudent, sparing
AN OPPOSITE IS extravagant

thrill *NOUN*
He loves the thrill of rock climbing.
▸ adventure, (*slang*) buzz, excitement, (*informal*) kick, sensation, tingle

thrill *VERB*
The music thrilled them.
▸ delight, electrify, excite, rouse, stimulate, stir
AN OPPOSITE IS bore

thriller *NOUN*
She was reading an exciting thriller.
▸ crime story, detective story, murder story, mystery story

thrive *VERB*
Tomato plants thrive in the greenhouse.
▸ do well, flourish, grow, prosper, succeed

thriving *ADJECTIVE*
He runs a thriving business.
▸ booming, expanding, healthy, profitable, prosperous, successful
AN OPPOSITE IS unsuccessful

throb *NOUN*
He felt the throb of the ship's engine.
▸ beat, pulse, rhythm, vibration

throb *VERB*
She could feel the blood throbbing through her veins.
▸ beat, pound

throng *NOUN*
There were throngs of people on the street.
▸ crowd, horde, swarm
SEE ALSO **group**

throttle *VERB*
The mugger tried to throttle him.
▸ choke, strangle, suffocate

throw *VERB*
1 *I threw a stone into the pool.*
▸ (*slang*) bung, cast, (*informal*) chuck, fling, pitch, sling, toss
▹ To deliver the ball in cricket is to **bowl**. To throw the shot in athletics is to **put** the shot. To throw something high in the air is to **lob** it. To throw something heavy is to **heave** it. To throw something with great force is to **hurl** it. If someone throws a lot of things at you, they **pelt** you.
2 *The horse threw its rider.*
▸ dislodge, shake off, throw off
to throw away *She threw away her old clothes.*
▸ discard, dispose of, (*informal*) dump, get rid of, scrap

thrust *VERB*
1 *He thrust his hands into his pockets.*
▸ force, push, shove
2 *They saw the murderer thrust with a dagger.*
▸ jab, lunge, poke, prod, stab

thump *VERB*
Someone thumped him and left him with a black eye.
▸ (*informal*) bash, hit, punch, slog, (*informal*) slosh, wallop
SEE ALSO **hit** *VERB*

thunder *NOUN VERB*
They could hear the thunder.
▹ You can also speak of a clap, crack, peal, or roll of thunder.

thunderous *ADJECTIVE*
The audience greeted the actors with thunderous applause.
▸ deafening, loud, noisy, resounding
AN OPPOSITE IS quiet

tick *VERB*
A clock was ticking in the background.
FOR VARIOUS WAYS TO MAKE SOUNDS SEE **sound** *VERB*
to tick someone off (*informal*) *She ticked him off for talking in class.*
▸ reprimand, reproach, scold, tell off

ticket *NOUN*
1 *They got free tickets for the concert.*
▸ coupon, pass, permit, token, voucher
2 *What does it say on the price ticket?*
▸ label, tab, tag

tickle *VERB*
1 *She giggled when he tickled her feet.*
FOR VARIOUS WAYS TO TOUCH SOMEONE SEE **touch** *VERB*
2 *This idea will tickle you.*
▸ amuse, cheer you up, make you laugh, please

ticklish *ADJECTIVE*
1 *He's very ticklish.*
▸ sensitive
2 *It was a ticklish problem.*
▸ awkward, complex, complicated, difficult, hard, involved, perplexing, thorny, tricky

tide *NOUN*
The moon determines the sea's tides.
▸ current, movement, rise and fall
▹ When the tide is coming in it is flowing. When the tide is going out it is ebbing. Tides when there is the biggest difference between high and low water are spring tides. Tides when there is the least difference between high and low water are neap tides.

tidy *ADJECTIVE*
He always kept his room tidy.
▸ neat, orderly, smart, spruce, straight, trim, uncluttered
AN OPPOSITE IS untidy

tie *VERB*
1 *She tied the rope around the tree.*
▸ bind, fasten, hitch, knot, loop, secure
AN OPPOSITE IS untie
▹ To tie up a boat is to moor it. To tie up an animal is to tether it.
2 *The two teams tied.*
▸ be equal, be level, draw, score the same

tight *ADJECTIVE*
1 *The lid was too tight for him to unscrew.*
▸ close, firm, secure, snug
▹ If it is so tight that air cannot get through, it is airtight. If it is so tight that water cannot get through, it is watertight.
AN OPPOSITE IS loose
2 *They squeezed into the tight space.*
▸ cramped, crowded, packed, small
AN OPPOSITE IS spacious
3 *The ropes were too tight.*
▸ rigid, stretched, taut, tense
AN OPPOSITE IS slack
4 *She's tight with her money.*
▸ mean, (*informal*) mingy, miserly, stingy
AN OPPOSITE IS extravagant or generous

tighten *VERB*
1 *She tightened her grip on his hand.*
▸ hold tighter, squeeze
2 *You need to tighten the guy ropes.*
▸ make taut, pull tighter, stretch
3 *He tried to tighten the screw.*
▸ make tighter, screw up
AN OPPOSITE IS loosen

till *VERB*
Farmers use tractors to till the land.
▸ cultivate, dig, plough, prepare

tilt *VERB*
The caravan tilted to one side.
▸ incline, keel over, lean, slant, slope, tip
▹ When a ship tilts to one side, it lists.

timber *NOUN*
He bought some timber to build a shed.
▸ wood
VARIOUS FORMS OF TIMBER
beams, boards or boarding, deal, hardwood, laths, logs, lumber, planks or planking, posts, softwood, stakes, tree trunks
MANUFACTURED KINDS OF BOARD
blockboard, chipboard, hardboard, plywood

time *NOUN*
1 *Is this a convenient time to phone?*
▸ moment, occasion, opportunity
2 *Spring is her favourite time of the year.*
▸ phase, season
3 *He spent a time in prison.*
▸ session, spell, stretch, term, while
4 *Shakespeare lived in the time of Elizabeth I.*
▸ age, days, epoch, era, period
5 *Please try to keep time with the music.*
▸ beat, rhythm, tempo
in good time , on time *Please try to be on time.*
▸ prompt, punctual
UNITS WE USE TO MEASURE TIME
second, minute, hour, day, week, fortnight, month, year, decade, century, millennium, eternity
DEVICES FOR MEASURING TIME
calendar, chronometer, clock, digital clock, digital watch, hourglass, stopwatch, sundial, timer, watch, wristwatch

timetable *NOUN*
They worked out a timetable for sports day.
▸ programme, rota, schedule

timid *ADJECTIVE*
She was too timid to say anything.
▸ afraid, anxious, apprehensive, bashful, cowardly, coy, fearful, nervous, sheepish, shy, unadventurous
AN OPPOSITE IS brave or confident

tin *NOUN*
He opened a tin of beans.
▸ can
FOR OTHER CONTAINERS SEE **container**

tingle *VERB*
Her fingers were tingling with the cold.
▸ itch, prickle, sting, tickle

tingle *NOUN*
1 *She felt a tingle in her foot.*
▸ itch, itching, pins and needles, prickling, stinging, tickle, tickling
2 *He felt a tingle of excitement.*
▸ quiver, sensation, shiver, thrill

tinker *VERB*
He tinkered with the TV, trying to get it to work.
▸ fiddle, interfere, meddle, mess about, play about, tamper

tinny *ADJECTIVE*
The car seemed rather tinny.
▸ cheap, inferior, poor quality, trashy

tint *NOUN*
The paint she chose had a nice blue tint.
▸ colour, hue, shade, tone
FOR NAMES OF COLOURS SEE **colour**

tiny *ADJECTIVE*
You can hardly see it — it's so tiny.
▸ little, microscopic, midget, miniature, minute
AN OPPOSITE IS big

tip *NOUN*
1 *The tip of his nose felt cold.*
▸ end, point, sharp end
▹ The tip of an ink pen is a **nib**.
2 *The tip of the mountain was covered in snow.*
▸ cap, head, peak, summit, top, (*formal*) vertex
3 *He gave them some useful tips on first aid.*
▸ clue, hint, piece of advice, suggestion, warning
4 *They took a load of rubbish to the tip.*
▸ dump, recycling centre, rubbish heap

tip *VERB*
1 *She tipped the waiter.*
▸ give a tip to, reward
2 *The caravan tipped to one side.*
▸ incline, keel over, lean, slant, slope, tilt
▹ When a ship tips slightly to one side, it lists. When a ship tips right over, it **capsizes**.
3 *He tipped his stuff on to the table.*
▸ dump, empty, turn out, unload
to tip over *He tipped the milk bottle over.*
▸ knock over, overturn, topple, upset

tiptoe *VERB*
FOR VARIOUS WAYS WE WALK SEE **walk** *VERB*

tire *VERB*
The long game tired them.
▸ exhaust, wear out
AN OPPOSITE IS refresh or rest

tired *ADJECTIVE*
Have a lie down if you're tired.
▸ (*informal*) all in, drowsy, exhausted, fatigued, flagging, listless, sleepy, weary, worn out
to be tired of something *I'm tired of watching TV.*
▸ bored with, (*informal*) fed up with, sick of
▹ If you are not interested in anything, you are **apathetic**.

tireless *ADJECTIVE*
She's a tireless worker.
▸ determined, energetic, persistent, unflagging, untiring
AN OPPOSITE IS lazy

tiresome *ADJECTIVE*
The children were being rather tiresome.
▸ (*informal*) aggravating, annoying, exasperating, irritating, troublesome, trying, unwelcome, vexing
AN OPPOSITE IS welcome

tiring *ADJECTIVE*
Digging the garden is tiring work.
▸ demanding, difficult, exhausting, fatiguing, hard, laborious, tough
AN OPPOSITE IS refreshing

title *NOUN*
She couldn't think of a title for the story.
▸ heading, name
▹ The title above a newspaper story is a **headline**. A title or brief description next to a picture is a **caption**.
▹ A person's title shows their **position**, **rank**, or **status** in society.
TITLES USED BEFORE THE NAMES OF MOST ORDINARY PEOPLE
Miss, Mr, Mrs, Ms
The full forms of these words no longer exist, although you can use *mister* informally for *Mr*, and *missis* or *missus* informally for *Mrs*.
OTHER TITLES USED BEFORE A PERSON'S NAME
Doctor or (*short form*) Dr, Professor, Reverend or (*short form*) Rev
TITLES OF NOBLES OR KNIGHTS
Baron, Baroness, Count, Countess, Dame, Duchess, Duke, Earl, Lady, Lord, Marchioness, Marquis, Sir, Viscount, Viscountess
TITLES YOU MIGHT USE WHEN SPEAKING TO PEOPLE
madam, my lady, my lord, sir, sire, your grace, your honour, your majesty
A person's rank in the armed services may also be used as a title before their name. SEE **rank**

toast *VERB*
1 *He toasted the stale bread.*
▸ brown, grill
2 *They toasted the bride and groom.*
▸ drink a toast to, drink the health of, raise your glass to

together *ADVERB*
1 *They walked to school together.*
▸ hand in hand, shoulder to shoulder, side by side
2 *The men all shouted together.*
▸ all at once, at the same time, in chorus, in unison, simultaneously
AN OPPOSITE IS independently or separately

toil *VERB*
He's been toiling all day.
▸ exert yourself, labour, slave, struggle, work hard

toilet *NOUN*
Can you tell me where the toilet is?
▸ cloakroom, conveniences, lavatory, WC

token *NOUN*
1 *You can exchange this token for a free drink.*
▸ counter, coupon, voucher
2 *They gave her the flowers as a token of their affection.*
▸ evidence, expression, indication, reminder, sign, signal, symbol

tolerable *ADJECTIVE*
1 *The heat was tolerable.*
▸ acceptable, bearable, endurable
2 *The food was tolerable.*
▸ adequate, all right, fair, mediocre, (*informal*) OK, passable, satisfactory
AN OPPOSITE IS intolerable

tolerant *ADJECTIVE*
She's very tolerant towards other people.
▸ broad-minded, easygoing, forgiving,

A B C D E F G H I J K L M N O P Q R S T U V W X Y Z

generous, indulgent, lenient, liberal, open-minded, permissive, sympathetic, understanding, unprejudiced, willing to forgive
AN OPPOSITE IS intolerant

tolerate *VERB*
1 *He won't tolerate bad language.*
▸ accept, forgive, make allowances for, permit, put up with
2 *She can't tolerate pain.*
▸ abide, bear, endure, (*informal*) stand, stick, (*informal*) stomach, suffer

tomb *NOUN*
PLACES WHERE DEAD PEOPLE ARE BURIED
catacomb, crypt, grave, mausoleum, sarcophagus, sepulchre, vault
THINGS WHICH MARK PLACES WHERE PEOPLE ARE BURIED
gravestone, headstone, memorial, monument, plaque, tombstone

tone *NOUN*
1 *There was an angry tone to her voice.*
▸ inflection, intonation, manner, note, quality, sound
2 *The house was painted in subtle tones.*
▸ colour, hue, shade, tint
3 *Eerie music created the right tone for the film.*
▸ atmosphere, effect, feeling, mood, spirit

tone *VERB*
to tone something down *He asked them to tone down the noise.*
▸ lessen, quieten, reduce, soften, turn down
to tone in with *The new curtains tone in with the background.*
▸ blend with, fit in with, match, merge into

tongue-tied *ADJECTIVE*
He gets tongue-tied when he's embarrassed.
▸ dumb, mute, silent, speechless

tool *NOUN*
He keeps his tools in the garage.
▸ apparatus, appliance, device, gadget, implement, instrument, utensil
TOOLS YOU MIGHT USE DOING WOODWORK
auger, awl, brace and bit, bradawl, chisel, clamp, drill, gimlet, hammer, jigsaw, mallet, pincers, plane, power drill, rasp, router, sander, saw, set square, spokeshave, T-square, vice
SEE ALSO **saw**
TOOLS YOU MIGHT USE IN THE HOME
brush, cooking utensil, needle, penknife, scales, scissors, tape measure, tweezers
FOR VARIOUS COOKING UTENSILS SEE **cook** *VERB*
TOOLS YOU MIGHT USE IF YOU HAVE A COAL FIRE
bellows, poker, tongs
TOOLS YOU MIGHT USE IN GARDENING, ETC.
axe, chain saw, chopper, crowbar, dibber, fork, grass rake, hoe, ladder, lawnmower, mattock, pick, pickaxe, pitchfork, rake, roller, scythe, secateurs, shears, shovel, sickle, sledgehammer, spade, strimmer, trowel
TOOLS YOU MIGHT USE ON A BIKE OR CAR, ETC.
Allen key, box spanner, file, jack, lever, pliers, pump, ring spanner, screwdriver, wrench

tooth *NOUN*
VARIOUS TEETH IN A PERSON'S MOUTH
canine tooth, eyetooth, incisor, molar, wisdom tooth
▹ A dog's or wolf's canine tooth is a **fang**. A long tooth that sticks out of an animal's mouth is a **tusk**.
FALSE TEETH
bridge or bridgework, dentures, plate
SOME PROBLEMS PEOPLE HAVE WITH THEIR TEETH
caries, cavity, decay, plaque, toothache
SEE ALSO **dentist**

top *NOUN*
1 *They climbed to the top of the hill.*
▸ crest, crown, head, peak, summit, tip, (*formal*) vertex
AN OPPOSITE IS bottom
2 *The table top was covered with newspapers.*
▸ surface
3 *He couldn't get the top off the jar.*
▸ cap, cover, covering, lid

top *ADJECTIVE*
1 *She got top marks in the exam.*
▸ best, highest, most, winning
2 *They set off at top speed.*
▸ greatest, high, maximum
AN OPPOSITE IS low
3 *She's the top executive in her firm.*
▸ most important, senior, supreme
AN OPPOSITE IS junior

top *VERB*
1 *She topped the cake with chopped nuts.*
▸ cover, decorate, finish off
2 *Their new record topped the charts.*
▸ be at the top of, dominate

topic *NOUN*
They discussed several topics.
▸ issue, matter, question, subject, talking-point

topical *ADJECTIVE*
He asked what the topical issues were.
▸ current, up to date

topple *VERB*
1 *He toppled off the wall.*
▸ fall, tumble
2 *The gale toppled their TV aerial.*
▸ knock down, overturn, tip over, upset
3 *They managed to topple the prime minister.*
▸ get rid of, overthrow, remove

torment *VERB*
1 *Toothache tormented her.*
▸ afflict, hurt, inflict pain on, torture
2 *He told them to stop tormenting the other children.*
▸ annoy, bother, bully, distress, harass, pester, tease, vex, worry
▹ To torment people continually is to plague or victimize them. To torment people because of their beliefs is to persecute them.

torment *NOUN*
She was in great torment.
▸ affliction, agony, anguish, distress, misery, pain, persecution, plague, purgatory, scourge, suffering, torture

torrent *NOUN*
A torrent of water flowed down the hill.
▸ cascade, flood, gush, rush, stream

torrential *ADJECTIVE*
They got caught in a torrential rainstorm.
▸ heavy, soaking, violent
▹ Torrential rain is sometimes called a cloudburst or deluge or downpour.

torture *NOUN*
1 *He died under torture.*
▸ cruel treatment, persecution
2 *She was suffering the torture of a bad toothache.*
▸ affliction, agony, anguish, pain, suffering, torment

torture *VERB*
They tortured prisoners who refused to cooperate.
▸ be cruel to, cause pain to, hurt, inflict pain on, persecute, torment

toss *VERB*
1 *He tossed a coin into the wishing-well.*
▸ cast, (*informal*) chuck, fling, lob, pitch, sling, throw
2 *They tossed a coin to see who would go first.*
▸ flick, flip, spin
to toss about 1 *The little boat tossed about on the waves.*
▸ bob up and down, lurch, pitch, rock, roll
2 *She tossed about in the uncomfortable bed.*
▸ move restlessly, twist and turn, writhe

total *NOUN*
Add the figures and tell me the total.
▸ amount, answer, sum

total *ADJECTIVE*
1 *The bill shows the total amount due.*
▸ complete, entire, full, whole
2 *The party was a total disaster.*
▸ absolute, downright, perfect, sheer, thorough, utter

total *VERB*
1 *He totalled the figures.*
▸ add up, calculate, count, find the total of, reckon up, work out
2 *The collection totalled £37.*
▸ add up to, amount to, come to, make, reach

totter *VERB*
The child tottered across the floor.
▸ reel, stagger, stumble, wobble
FOR VARIOUS WAYS TO WALK SEE **walk** *VERB*

touch *VERB*
1 *He doesn't like people touching him.*
▸ caress, feel, finger, fondle, handle, nuzzle, pat, paw, pet, rub, stroke, tickle
2 *The car just touched the gatepost.*
▸ brush, contact, graze, hit, knock
3 *Their speed touched 100 m.p.h.*
▸ reach, rise to
4 *She was touched by the sad music.*
▸ affect, move, stir
to touch down *They expect the plane to touch down on time.*
▸ arrive, get in, land
to touch something up *She touched up the paintwork on her car.*
▸ improve, repair

A B C D E F G H I J K L M N O P Q R S T U V W X Y Z

touch *NOUN*
1 *I felt a touch on my arm.*
► caress, contact, pat, stroke, tap
2 *Working with animals requires a special touch.*
► ability, knack, manner, sensitivity, skill, technique, understanding, way
3 *There's a touch of frost in the air.*
► hint, suggestion, trace

touchy *ADJECTIVE*
Be careful what you say because he's very touchy.
► easily offended, irritable, quick-tempered

tough *ADJECTIVE*
1 *You'll need tough shoes for the climb.*
► durable, hard-wearing, robust, stout, strong, sturdy, substantial, well made
AN OPPOSITE IS flimsy
2 *The meat was very tough.*
► chewy, gristly, leathery, rubbery
AN OPPOSITE IS tender
3 *They played against tough opposition.*
► determined, powerful, resistant, resolute, ruthless, stiff, strong, stubborn
AN OPPOSITE IS weak
4 *The police deal with some tough criminals.*
► brutal, disorderly, rough, unruly, violent
AN OPPOSITE IS feeble
5 *It was a tough climb.*
► demanding, exhausting, gruelling, laborious, strenuous, tiring
AN OPPOSITE IS gentle
6 *The problem was too tough for him.*
► baffling, difficult, hard, knotty, puzzling, thorny
AN OPPOSITE IS easy

toughen *VERB*
Joining the army will toughen him up.
► harden, make tougher, strengthen

tour *NOUN*
They went on a sightseeing tour.
► drive, excursion, expedition, jaunt, journey, outing, ride, trip

tourist *NOUN*
The cathedral was full of tourists.
► holidaymaker, sightseer, traveller, visitor

tournament *NOUN*
He reached the semi-final of the tennis tournament.
► championship, competition, contest, series

tow *VERB*
They towed the car to the garage.
► drag, draw, haul, pull, tug along

tower *NOUN*
VARIOUS KINDS OF TOWER
belfry, castle, fort, fortress, keep, minaret, silo, skyscraper, steeple, turret
▷ The pointed structure on a church tower is a **spire**.

tower *VERB*
to tower above something *The castle towers above the village.*
► dominate, loom over, rise above, stand above, stick up above

town *NOUN*
▷ A town with its own local council is a **borough**. An important town, often with a cathedral, is a **city**. Several towns that merge into each other are a **conurbation**.
PLACES OR THINGS YOU MAY FIND IN TOWNS
bank, bus station, café, car park, cinema, college, concert hall, council offices, factory, filling station, flats, garage, hotel, housing estate, industrial estate, leisure centre, library, market, market place, museum, office block, park, police station, post office, pub, railway station, recreation ground, residential area, restaurant, roads, school, shopping centre, shops, snack bar, sports centre, square, suburb, supermarket, theatre, university, warehouse

toxic *ADJECTIVE*
The toxic fumes made him ill.
► dangerous, deadly, harmful, poisonous
AN OPPOSITE IS harmless

toy *NOUN*
SOME TOYS CHILDREN PLAY WITH
ball, balloon, board game, building bricks, card game, computer game, construction kit, doll, doll's house, frisbee, hoop, kaleidoscope, kite, marbles, puppet, puzzle, rattle, rocking horse, rollerblades, roller skates, skateboard, skipping rope, teddy bear, top, tricycle, water pistol, yo-yo
The names of some toys are simply names of real things with the word *toy* or *model* before them. For example, *toy car*, *toy theatre*, *model aeroplane*, etc. Many toys have names which are trademarks, which we don't give here

trace *NOUN*
1 *He left no trace of his presence.*
▸ clue, evidence, hint, indication, mark, sign, track, trail
▹ A trace left by an animal might be its footprint or scent or spoor.
2 *They found traces of poison in the food.*
▸ tiny amount

trace *VERB*
1 *She was trying to trace her lost relatives.*
▸ seek out, track down
2 *They managed to trace the cause of the fire.*
▸ discover, find

track *NOUN*
1 *He walked along a track past the farm.*
▸ bridle path or bridleway, cart track, footpath, path, way
2 *They followed the fox's tracks for miles.*
▸ footmark or footprint, scent, trail
3 *They laid the track for a tram system.*
▸ line, rails
4 *They ran round the track.*
▸ circuit, course, racetrack

track *VERB*
The hunters were tracking a fox.
▸ chase, follow, hound, hunt, pursue, stalk, tail, trail
to track someone or **something down** *They tracked down the owner of the car.*
▸ discover, find, trace

tract *NOUN*
They had to cross a tract of desert.
▸ area, expanse, stretch

trade *NOUN*
1 *The shopkeeper says that trade is good at present.*
▸ business, buying and selling, commerce, dealing, the market, trading
2 *He wanted to learn a trade.*
▸ craft, occupation, profession
FOR VARIOUS KINDS OF EMPLOYMENT SEE **job**

trade *VERB*
to trade in something *The company trades in second-hand computers.*
▸ buy and sell, deal in, do business in, retail, sell
FOR VARIOUS PEOPLE WHO SELL THINGS SEE **sell**
▹ To trade in something illegally is to traffic in it.
to trade something in *She wants to trade her old car in.*
▸ exchange, offer in part exchange, (*informal*) swap

tradition *NOUN*
It's a tradition to sing 'Auld Lang Syne' on New Year's Eve.
▸ convention, custom, fashion, habit, routine

traditional *ADJECTIVE*
They wore traditional costumes.
▸ conventional, customary, familiar, habitual, historic, normal, regular, typical, usual

traffic *NOUN*
FOR VARIOUS KINDS OF VEHICLE SEE **vehicle**

traffic *VERB*
He was accused of trafficking in drugs.
▸ trade illegally

tragedy *NOUN*
1 *'Romeo and Juliet' is a tragedy.*
AN OPPOSITE IS comedy
2 *His death was a tragedy.*
▸ calamity, catastrophe, disaster, misfortune

tragic *ADJECTIVE*
1 *He died in a tragic accident.*
▸ awful, calamitous, catastrophic, disastrous, distressing, dreadful, fatal, terrible, unfortunate, unlucky
2 *She had a tragic expression on her face.*
▸ distressed, hurt, mournful, pathetic, pitiful, sad, sorrowful, woeful, wretched
AN OPPOSITE IS comic or happy

trail *NOUN*
1 *They walked along a trail through the woods.*
▸ path, pathway, route, track
2 *The hounds followed the fox's trail.*
▸ footprints, scent, signs, spoor, traces
▹ The trail left in the water by a ship is its wake.

trail *VERB*
1 *The hounds trailed the fox for miles.*
▸ chase, follow, hunt, pursue, shadow, stalk, tail, track
2 *He trailed a cart behind him.*
▸ drag, draw, haul, pull, tow
3 *They told him to stop trailing behind.*
▸ dawdle, hang about, lag, loiter, straggle

train *NOUN*
1 *They went to London by train.*
FOR WORDS CONNECTED WITH TRAVEL BY TRAIN SEE **railway**
2 *It was a strange train of events.*
▸ chain, sequence, series, string, succession

A B C D E F G H I J K L M N O P Q R S T U V W X Y Z

train *VERB*
1 *He trains the football team every Saturday.*
▸ coach, instruct, prepare, teach
2 *She needs to train harder.*
▸ do exercises, exercise, get fit, practise, prepare yourself
3 *He trained his rifle on the target.*
▸ aim (at), line up, point (at)

trainer *NOUN*
1 *Their trainer makes them work hard.*
▸ coach, instructor, teacher
2 *Where are my trainers?*
FOR THINGS YOU WEAR ON YOUR FEET SEE **shoe**

traitor *NOUN*
The traitor betrayed his country.
▸ collaborator, defector, deserter, double-crosser, spy, turncoat

tramp *VERB*
They tramped across the hills.
▸ hike, march, plod, stride, trek, trudge
FOR VARIOUS WAYS WE WALK SEE **walk** *VERB*

trample *VERB*
Don't trample the flowers!
▸ crush, flatten, squash, stamp on, tread on, walk over

trance *NOUN*
He was lost in a trance.
▸ daydream, daze, dream
▹ One way to be in a trance is to be **hypnotized**. Unconsciousness caused by an illness or accident is a **coma**.

tranquil *ADJECTIVE*
They led a tranquil life in the country.
▸ calm, peaceful, placid, quiet, restful, serene, still, undisturbed
AN OPPOSITE IS exciting or stormy

transact *VERB*
He has some business to transact.
▸ attend to, carry out, deal with, do, execute, perform, undertake

transfer *VERB*
1 *They transferred some of the books to another classroom.*
▸ carry, convey, move, remove, take
2 *He transferred all the money to her.*
▸ give, hand over

transform *VERB*
He transformed the attic into a bedroom.
▸ adapt, alter, change, convert, modify, turn

transformation *NOUN*
They were amazed by the transformation in her appearance.
▸ alteration, change, difference, improvement

transition *NOUN*
The transition from child to adult is a gradual process.
▸ alteration, change, change-over, evolution, movement, progression, shift, transformation

translate *VERB*
She translated the Russian visitors remarks into English.
▸ interpret

translator *NOUN*
▹ A person who translates a foreign language is an **interpreter**. An expert in languages is a **linguist**.

transmission *NOUN*
▹ A transmission on radio or TV is a **broadcast**.

transmit *VERB*
1 *The ship's radio began to transmit a distress signal.*
▸ broadcast, emit, relay, send out
2 *He transmitted the information through the computer network.*
▸ communicate, convey, dispatch, pass on, send
AN OPPOSITE IS receive

transparent *ADJECTIVE*
The box had a transparent lid.
▸ clear, (*informal*) see-through
▹ Something which is not fully transparent, but allows light to shine through, is **translucent**.

transplant *VERB*
She transplanted the seedlings into the flower bed.
▸ move, shift, transfer

transport *VERB*
They have to transport goods from the factory to the shops.
▸ bring, carry, convey, fetch, haul, move, shift, ship, take, transfer
METHODS OF TRANSPORT
TRANSPORT BY AIR
airship, helicopter, plane
SEE ALSO **aircraft**

TRANSPORT BY ROAD
bus, car, coach, cycle, horse, lorry, minibus, taxi, tram, van
SEE ALSO **vehicle**
TRANSPORT BY RAIL
Metro, monorail, train, tram
SEE ALSO **railway**
TRANSPORT BY WATER
barge, boat, ferry, ship
SEE ALSO **vessel**
FOR VARIOUS WAYS TO TRAVEL SEE **travel**

trap *NOUN*
The animal was caught in a trap.
▸ booby trap, net, noose, snare
▹ Something used to tempt something into a trap is **bait** or a **decoy**.

trap *VERB*
They tried to trap the mouse.
▸ capture, catch, corner, snare

trash *NOUN*
1 *He put the trash into the bin.*
▸ garbage, junk, litter, refuse, rubbish, waste
2 *Don't listen to that trash!*
▸ nonsense

travel *VERB*
She likes to travel at a leisurely speed.
▸ go, journey, move along, proceed, progress
VARIOUS WAYS TO TRAVEL
commute, cruise, cycle, drive, fly, go by rail, hike, hitch-hike, motor, pedal, ramble, ride, roam, row, sail, tour, trek, voyage, walk, wander
▹ When birds travel from one country to another they **migrate**. When people travel to another country to live there they **emigrate**.
FOR VARIOUS METHODS OF TRANSPORTSEE ALSO **transport**
PEOPLE WHO TRAVEL AS A WAY OF LIFE
gypsy, itinerant or tramp, nomad, traveller
PEOPLE WHO TRAVEL FOR VARIOUS REASONS
astronaut or cosmonaut, commuter, cyclist, driver or motorist, explorer, flyer or aviator, hitch-hiker, holidaymaker, motorcyclist, passenger, pedestrian, rambler or walker, sailor, tourist
▹ A person who travels to a religious place is a **pilgrim**. A person who travels illegally on a ship or plane is a **stowaway**. A person who likes travelling round the world is a **globetrotter**.

treacherous *ADJECTIVE*
1 *A treacherous member of the team revealed our plan to the other side.*
▸ cheating, deceitful, disloyal, double-crossing, faithless, false, (*informal*) sneaky, unfaithful, untrustworthy
AN OPPOSITE IS loyal
▹ A treacherous person is a **traitor**.
2 *The roads are often treacherous in winter.*
▸ dangerous, hazardous, perilous, risky, unpredictable, unreliable, unsafe
AN OPPOSITE IS safe

treachery *NOUN*
They were appalled by his treachery.
▸ betrayal, disloyalty, treason, untrustworthiness
AN OPPOSITE IS loyalty

tread *VERB*
Please tread carefully.
▸ put your foot down, step, walk
to tread on *He asked them not to tread on the flowers.*
▸ crush, flatten, squash, stamp on, step on, trample, walk on

treason *NOUN*
He was executed for treason.
▸ betrayal (of), disloyalty (to), rebellion, treachery
AN OPPOSITE IS loyalty

treasure *NOUN*
The treasure was buried somewhere on the island.
▸ fortune, hoard, riches, wealth
▹ Treasure which someone has found hidden is **treasure trove**.
TREASURE MIGHT CONSIST OF
bullion, coins, gems or precious stones, gold or other precious metals, jewellery, valuables

treasure *VERB*
He treasures the letter she sent him.
▸ cherish, prize, value

treat *VERB*
1 *She always treated him kindly.*
▸ behave towards, deal with
2 *The doctor treated her for flu.*
▸ give treatment to, prescribe medicine for
▹ To treat a wound is to **dress** it. To treat an illness or wound successfully is to **cure** or **heal** it.
3 *He didn't have any money so she treated him.*
▸ give you a treat, pay for

a b c d e f g h i j k l m n o p q r s t u v w x y z

treat *NOUN*
They took him to the zoo as a birthday treat.
▸ special event, surprise

treatment *NOUN*
1 *She was angry at the poor treatment of the animals.*
▸ attention, care
2 *His rough treatment of the equipment led to some breakages.*
▸ handling, management, use
3 *He went to the hospital for treatment.*
▸ cure, nursing, remedy, therapy
▹ Treatment you give someone before a medical person arrives is **first aid**.
FOR KINDS OF MEDICAL TREATMENT SEE **medicine, therapy**

treaty *NOUN*
The two sides signed a peace treaty.
▸ agreement, armistice, ceasefire, truce

tree *NOUN*
▹ Trees which lose their leaves in winter are **deciduous**. Trees which have leaves all year round are **evergreen**. Trees which grow cones are **conifers**. A young tree is a **sapling**. Small, low trees are **bushes** or **shrubs**. Miniature trees grown in small containers are **bonsai** trees.
SOME VARIETIES OF TREE
ash, bay, beech, birch, cedar, chestnut, cypress, elder, elm, eucalyptus, fir, hawthorn, hazel, holly, horse chestnut, larch, lime, maple, oak, olive, palm, pine, plane, poplar, rowan, spruce, sweet chestnut, sycamore, tamarisk, willow, yew
FOR NAMES OF FRUIT TREES SEE **fruit**

tremble *VERB*
She was trembling with cold.
▸ quake, quiver, shake, shiver, shudder

tremendous *ADJECTIVE*
1 *They heard a tremendous bang.*
▸ awful, big, enormous, fearful, frightful, great, huge, massive, mighty, (*informal*) terrific
2 *Winning first prize was a tremendous achievement.*
▸ excellent, exceptional, impressive, magnificent, marvellous, outstanding, remarkable, superb, wonderful

tremor *NOUN*
A tremor in her voice showed she was nervous.
▸ hesitation, quavering, quivering, shaking, trembling, vibration, wobble

trend *NOUN*
1 *The general trend is for prices to go up.*
▸ bias, direction, movement, shift, tendency
2 *What's the latest trend in clothes?*
▸ craze, fad, fashion, style

trendy *ADJECTIVE* (*informal*)
His clothes weren't very trendy.
▸ contemporary, fashionable, modern, stylish, up to date
AN OPPOSITE IS old-fashioned

trial *NOUN*
1 *Scientists conducted trials on the new drug.*
▸ experiment, test
2 *The judge predicted that the trial would last a long time.*
▸ case, hearing
▹ A military trial is a **court martial**.

triangular *ADJECTIVE*
▹ A triangular shape is **three-cornered** or **three-sided**.

tribe *NOUN*
▹ A group of people who are closely related is a **family**. A group of related Scottish families is a **clan**. A succession of people from the same powerful family is a **dynasty**.

tribute *NOUN*
They heard a moving tribute to the dead woman's courage.
▸ appreciation, commendation, compliment
▹ If you pay tribute to someone, you **praise** them.

trick *NOUN*
1 *She played a trick on him.*
▸ joke, practical joke, prank
▹ Tricks which are supposed to look like magic are **conjuring tricks**.
2 *The so-called special offer was just a trick.*
▸ cheat, (*informal*) con, deception, fraud, hoax, pretence, swindle
3 *He learnt the tricks of the trade.*
▸ art, dodge, knack, secret, skill, technique

trick *VERB*
He tricked them into buying worthless rubbish.
▸ cheat, (*slang*) con, deceive, (*slang*) diddle, fool, hoax, swindle

trickle *VERB*
Water trickled from the tap.
▸ dribble, drip, flow slowly, leak, ooze, seep
AN OPPOSITE IS gush

tricky *ADJECTIVE*
1 *It was a very tricky job.*
▸ awkward, complicated, difficult, intricate, involved, ticklish
AN OPPOSITE IS straightforward
2 *He's a tricky person to deal with.*
▸ crafty, cunning, deceitful, dishonest, sly, (*informal*) sneaky, untrustworthy, wily
AN OPPOSITE IS trustworthy

trifle *VERB*
She told him not to trifle with her.
▸ behave frivolously, fool about, play about

trifling *ADJECTIVE*
It was a trifling sum of money.
▸ insignificant, minor, negligible, paltry, petty, small, tiny, trivial, unimportant
AN OPPOSITE IS important or large

trigger *VERB*
to trigger something off *The burnt toast triggered off the smoke alarm.*
▸ activate, set off, start, switch on

trim *ADJECTIVE*
He keeps his garden trim.
▸ neat, orderly, smart, spruce, tidy, well kept
AN OPPOSITE IS untidy

trim *VERB*
1 *He asked the hairdresser just to trim his hair.*
▸ clip, cut, shorten
2 *She trimmed her blouse with lace.*
▸ adorn, decorate

trip *NOUN*
They went on a trip to the seaside.
▸ day out, excursion, expedition, jaunt, journey, outing, visit

trip *VERB*
1 *He tripped on the loose carpet.*
▸ catch your foot, fall, stagger, stumble, tumble
2 *She was tripping happily along.*
▸ run, skip

triumph *NOUN*
1 *They celebrated their great triumph over their opponents.*
▸ conquest, success, victory, win
2 *They returned in triumph.*
▸ celebration

triumphant *ADJECTIVE*
1 *They cheered the triumphant team.*
▸ conquering, successful, victorious, winning
AN OPPOSITE IS unsuccessful
2 *He could hear their triumphant laughter.*
▸ elated, exultant, gleeful, joyful, jubilant

trivial *ADJECTIVE*
Don't bother him with trivial details.
▸ frivolous, insignificant, little, minor, negligible, paltry, petty, silly, slight, small, superficial, trifling, unimportant, worthless
AN OPPOSITE IS important

troop *NOUN*
A troop of soldiers marched past.
▸ company, force, group, platoon, squad

troop *VERB*
They trooped along the road.
▸ march, parade, proceed, walk
▷ To walk one behind the other is to file along.

troops *PLURAL NOUN*
SEE **armed services**

trophy *NOUN*
She won a trophy in swimming.
▸ award, cup, medal, prize

trouble *NOUN*
1 *He's had a lot of trouble recently.*
▸ affliction, anxiety, burden, difficulty, distress, grief, hardship, illness, inconvenience, misery, misfortune, pain, problem, sadness, sorrow, suffering, unhappiness, vexation, worry
2 *The police dealt with trouble in the crowd.*
▸ bother, commotion, disorder, disturbance, fighting, fuss, misbehaviour, quarrelling, turmoil, unrest, violence
to take trouble *He took trouble to get it right.*
▸ take care, labour, make an effort, struggle, take pains, work hard

A B C D E F G H I J K L M N O P Q R S **T** U V W X Y Z

trouble *VERB*

1 *Something is troubling her.*
▸ afflict, concern, distress, grieve, hurt, pain, torment, upset, vex
2 *He asked them not to trouble him just now.*
▸ annoy, bother, disturb, interfere with, interrupt, pester, worry
▷ To trouble people in an unfriendly way is to **molest** or **threaten** them. To trouble people over a long period is to **plague** them.
3 *Nobody troubled to tidy up the room.*
▸ bother, take care, make an effort, take pains, take trouble, work hard

troublesome *ADJECTIVE*

1 *He found the heat troublesome.*
▸ annoying, distressing, inconvenient, irritating, tiresome, trying, upsetting, vexing, worrying
2 *She told off the troublesome children.*
▸ badly behaved, disobedient, disorderly, naughty, rowdy, unruly
AN OPPOSITE IS helpful

trousers *PLURAL NOUN*
GARMENTS WITH LEGS
breeches, corduroys, (*informal*) drainpipes, dungarees, (*informal*) flares, jeans, jodhpurs, overalls, (*American*) pants, shorts, ski pants, slacks, tights, (*Scottish*) trews, trunks
FOR OTHER GARMENTS SEE **clothes**

truant *NOUN*

to play truant
▷ If you play truant from school you are **absent without permission**. To run away from the army is to **desert**.

truce *NOUN*

The two sides agreed on a truce.
▸ armistice, ceasefire, end to hostilities, peace

true *ADJECTIVE*

1 *His story sounded true.*
▸ accurate, authentic, correct, exact, factual, genuine, real, right, undeniable
AN OPPOSITE IS untrue or fictional
2 *The police asked him if he was the true owner of the car.*
▸ authorized, legal, legitimate, official, proper, rightful
AN OPPOSITE IS false or illegal
3 *She's a true friend.*
▸ constant, dependable, devoted, faithful, honest, loyal, reliable, sincere, steady, trustworthy, trusty
AN OPPOSITE IS unreliable

truncheon *NOUN*

FOR VARIOUS WEAPONS SEE **weapon**

trundle *VERB*

A wagon trundled up the road.
▸ lumber, lurch, move heavily

trunk *NOUN*

▷ The trunk of a tree is its main **stem**. A formal word for an elephant's trunk is **proboscis**. A trunk to keep things in is a **box** or **chest**. Another word for a person's trunk is **torso**.

trust *VERB*

1 *They trusted him to do what he had promised.*
▸ bank on, believe in, be sure of, count on, depend on, have confidence in, have faith in, rely on
2 *I trust you are well.*
▸ hope

trust *NOUN*

1 *He has trust in her ability.*
▸ belief, confidence, faith
2 *She's in a position of trust.*
▸ responsibility

trustful *ADJECTIVE*

He's too trustful of other people.
▸ trusting, unquestioning, unsuspecting, unwary
▷ If you are trustful but easily deceived, you are **gullible** or **naïve**.
AN OPPOSITE IS suspicious

trustworthy *ADJECTIVE*

She's a trustworthy friend.
▸ dependable, honest, loyal, reliable, responsible, sensible, trusty, truthful, upright
AN OPPOSITE IS deceitful or untrustworthy

truth *NOUN*

1 *The police doubted the truth of her story.*
▸ accuracy, authenticity, correctness, genuineness, reliability, truthfulness, validity
AN OPPOSITE IS inaccuracy or falseness
2 *He wasn't telling the truth.*
▸ facts
AN OPPOSITE IS lies

truthful *ADJECTIVE*

1 *She's a truthful person.*
▸ frank, honest, reliable, sincere, straight, straightforward, trustworthy
2 *He gave a truthful answer.*
▸ accurate, correct, credible, proper, right, true, valid
AN OPPOSITE IS dishonest

try *VERB*
1 *He always tries to do his best.*
▸ aim, attempt, endeavour, make an effort, strive, struggle
2 *She tried her new computer.*
▸ evaluate, examine, experiment with, test, try out
3 *He tries them with his constant chatter.*
▸ annoy, bother, exasperate, irritate, provoke, trouble, upset, vex, worry

try *NOUN*
1 *He may not succeed, but it's worth a try!*
▸ attempt, effort, go, shot
2 *He had a try of her new pen.*
▸ experiment, test, trial

tub *NOUN*
FOR VARIOUS CONTAINERS SEE **container**

tube *NOUN*
▹ A flexible tube is a **hose**. A rigid tube is a **pipe**. A very narrow tube like a hair is a **capillary** tube. A large tube carrying water or sewage underground is the **main**. A tube which liquid pours out of is a **spout**.

tuck *VERB*
He tucked the flap inside the envelope.
▸ hide, insert, push, stuff

tuft *NOUN*
He had a tuft of hair sticking up.
▸ bunch, clump

tug *VERB*
1 *They tugged the rope.*
▸ jerk, pluck, twitch, wrench, yank
2 *He tugged the cart up the hill.*
▸ drag, draw, haul, heave, lug, pull, tow

tumble *VERB*
He tumbled into the water.
▸ collapse, drop, fall, flop, pitch, stumble, topple, trip up

tumult *NOUN*
He had to shout to be heard above the tumult.
▸ bedlam, chaos, commotion, confusion, disorder, noise, pandemonium, racket, turmoil, upheaval, uproar

tumultuous *ADJECTIVE*
Tumultuous applause greeted her winning shot.
▸ boisterous, excited, noisy, wild
AN OPPOSITE IS gentle or restrained

tune *NOUN*
They sang her favourite tune.
▸ air, melody, song, theme

tune *VERB*
He was trying to tune the TV.
▸ adjust, regulate

tuneful *ADJECTIVE*
It was a nice, tuneful song.
▸ catchy, melodious, pleasant, singable
AN OPPOSITE IS tuneless

tunnel *NOUN*
▹ A tunnel dug by rabbits is a **burrow**. A system of burrows is a **warren**. A tunnel in a mine is a **gallery**. A tunnel beneath a road is a **subway** or **underpass**.

tunnel *VERB*
A rabbit tunnelled under the fence.
▸ burrow, dig a tunnel, excavate a tunnel

turbulent *ADJECTIVE*
1 *The turbulent sea made him feel sick.*
▸ agitated, boisterous, heaving, rough, stormy, tempestuous, violent, wild, windy
AN OPPOSITE IS calm
▹ If the sea is turbulent with small waves it is said to be **choppy**. A turbulent journey by air is said to be **bumpy**.
2 *The police were trying to control the turbulent crowd.*
▸ badly-behaved, disorderly, excited, restless, riotous, rowdy, unruly
AN OPPOSITE IS well-behaved

turmoil *NOUN*
The whole place was in turmoil.
▸ bedlam, chaos, commotion, confusion, disorder, disturbance, ferment, pandemonium, tumult, upheaval, uproar
AN OPPOSITE IS calmness or order

turn *VERB*
1 *A wheel turns on its axle.*
▸ pivot, revolve, roll, rotate, spin, swivel, twirl, twist, whirl
2 *He signalled before he turned.*
▸ change direction, corner
▹ To turn unexpectedly is to **swerve** or **veer**

A B C D E F G H I J K L M N O P Q R S T U V W X Y Z

off course. If you turn to go back in the direction you came from, you **do a U-turn**. If marching soldiers change direction, they **wheel**.
3 *She turned quite pale.*
▸ become, go
4 *They turned the basement into a games room.*
▸ adapt, alter, change, convert, make, modify, transform
to turn something down *He turned the invitation down.*
▸ decline, refuse, reject
to turn into *The tadpoles will turn into frogs.*
▸ become, be transformed into, change into, develop into
to turn something on or **off** *He turned on the TV.*
▸ switch on or off
to turn out *Everything turned out well in the end.*
▸ happen, result
to turn over *The boat turned over.*
▸ capsize, flip over, keel over, overturn, turn upside down
to turn up *A friend turned up unexpectedly.*
▸ appear, arrive, come, drop in, visit

turn *NOUN*

1 *She gave the handle a turn.*
▸ spin, twirl, twist, whirl
▹ A single turn of wheel, etc., is a **revolution**. The process of turning is **rotation**.
2 *The house is just past the next turn in the road.*
▸ angle, bend, corner, curve, junction
▹ A sharp turn in a mountain road is a **hairpin bend**.
3 *It was his turn to bat.*
▸ chance, duty, go, job, opportunity, task
4 *He did a comic turn in the concert.*
▸ item, performance, scene, sketch, skit
5 (*informal*) *He had a nasty turn.*
▸ attack, bout, fit
6 (*informal*) *Seeing that accident gave her quite a turn.*
▸ fright, shock, surprise

tussle *NOUN*

The argument led to a bit of a tussle.
▸ contest, fight, (*informal*) scrap, scuffle, struggle

twiddle *VERB*

He was twiddling a knob on the radio.
▸ fiddle with, fidget with, turn, twirl, twist

twig *NOUN*

They gathered twigs to make a fire.
▸ branch, shoot, stalk, stem, stick

twin *NOUN*

This statue is a twin of one they saw in the antique shop.
▸ clone, double, duplicate, lookalike, match, one of a pair

twinkle *VERB*

The stars twinkled in the sky.
▸ glint, glitter, shine, sparkle

twirl *VERB*

1 *The dancers twirled faster and faster.*
▸ revolve, rotate, spin, turn, whirl
2 *He twirled his umbrella.*
▸ twiddle, twist

twist *VERB*

1 *She twisted the rope round a post.*
▸ coil, curl, loop
2 *Twist the handle to open the door.*
▸ revolve, rotate, turn
3 *The road twists through the hills.*
▸ curve, weave, wind, zigzag
4 *The snake twisted and turned.*
▸ wriggle, writhe
5 *He tried to twist the lid off the jar.*
▸ unscrew, wrench
6 *Heat can twist metal out of shape.*
▸ bend, buckle, crumple, distort, warp

SHAPES THINGS MAKE IF YOU TWIST THEM
coil, corkscrew, curl, kink, knot, loop, screw, spiral, tangle, zigzag

twitch *VERB*

The dog twitched in his sleep.
▸ fidget, jerk, jump, start, tremble

two *NOUN*

▹ Two musicians playing or singing together is a **duet**. Two people or things who belong together are a **couple** or a **pair**. To multiply a number by two is to **double** it.

type *NOUN*
1 *She doesn't like that type of film.*
▸ category, class, description, kind, sort, variety
2 *The book was printed in large type.*
▸ characters, lettering, letters, print

typical *ADJECTIVE*
He described a typical day at work.
▸ average, conventional, normal, ordinary, predictable, standard, unsurprising, usual
AN OPPOSITE IS unusual

tyrannical *ADJECTIVE*
The tyrannical government was finally overthrown.
▸ cruel, dictatorial, hard, harsh, merciless, oppressive, ruthless, severe, unjust, unkind
AN OPPOSITE IS liberal

tyrant *NOUN*
The people rejoiced when the tyrant died.
▸ dictator, oppressor
FOR OTHER KINDS OF RULER SEE **ruler**

Uu

ugly *ADJECTIVE*
1 *The room was filled with ugly furniture.*
▸ horrid, nasty, plain, tasteless, unattractive, unpleasant
AN OPPOSITE IS beautiful
2 *It was a fat, ugly dog.*
▸ grotesque, hideous, repulsive, revolting, unattractive
AN OPPOSITE IS beautiful
3 *The crowd was in an ugly mood.*
▸ angry, dangerous, hostile, menacing, ominous, sinister, threatening, unfriendly
AN OPPOSITE IS friendly

ultimate *ADJECTIVE*
Their ultimate aim was to force him to resign.
▸ eventual

umpire *NOUN*
OTHER OFFICIALS WHO MAKE SURE PLAYERS KEEP TO THE RULES
adjudicator, assistant referee, linesman, referee, touch judge

un- *PREFIX*
There are so many words beginning with the prefix *un-* that we can give synonyms for only a few of the more interesting ones. For some other words beginning with *un-*, we suggest another entry which you can look up to find synonyms.
If you want synonyms for words which we do not include, look up the root word — that is, the word to which *un-* has been added. There you will often find words to which you can add the prefix *un-* or the word *not*. For example, if you look up *able*, you can work out that you could use *not allowed*, *unwilling*, etc. as synonyms for *unable*.

unaided *ADJECTIVE*
She can no longer walk unaided.
▸ on your own, single-handed, without help

unanimous *ADJECTIVE*
It was a unanimous decision.
▸ collective, joint, united
▹ A decision where most but not all people agree is a majority decision.

unattractive *ADJECTIVE*
SEE **ugly**

unavoidable *ADJECTIVE*
The accident was unavoidable.
▸ bound to happen, certain, destined, inevitable, sure to happen

unaware *ADJECTIVE*
SEE **ignorant**

unbearable *ADJECTIVE*
The toothache was unbearable.
▸ impossible to bear, intolerable, unacceptable, unendurable

unbelievable *ADJECTIVE*
1 *Her excuse was unbelievable.*
▸ far-fetched, improbable, incredible, unconvincing, unlikely
2 *He scored an unbelievable goal.*
▸ amazing, astonishing, extraordinary, (*informal*) fantastic, phenomenal, remarkable

uncalled for *ADJECTIVE*
SEE **unnecessary**

uncanny *ADJECTIVE*
SEE **eerie**

A B C D E F G H I J K L M N O P Q R S T U V W X Y Z

uncertain *ADJECTIVE*
1 *I was uncertain what to do next.*
▸ doubtful, in two minds, unconvinced, unsure, wavering
2 *They are facing an uncertain future.*
▸ indefinite, undecided, unknown, unreliable
3 *The weather will be uncertain.*
▸ changeable, erratic, inconsistent, unpredictable, unreliable, variable
AN OPPOSITE IS certain

unclean *ADJECTIVE*
SEE **dirty**

unclear *ADJECTIVE*
SEE **uncertain**

uncomfortable *ADJECTIVE*
1 *The seats were extremely uncomfortable.*
▸ cramped, hard, lumpy
2 *She complained that her shoes were uncomfortable.*
▸ restrictive, stiff, tight, tight-fitting
3 *He spent an uncomfortable night, tossing and turning in the strange bed.*
▸ disagreeable, restless, troubled, uneasy
AN OPPOSITE IS comfortable

uncommon *ADJECTIVE*
SEE **unusual**

uncomplimentary *ADJECTIVE*
SEE **rude**

unconscious *ADJECTIVE*
1 *He's been unconscious for two days.*
▹ If you are unconscious because of a hit on the head, you are **knocked out**. If you are unconscious for an operation, you are **anaesthetized**. If you are unconscious because of an accident or illness, you are in **a coma**.
2 *She's unconscious of the effect she has on other people.*
▸ ignorant, unaware
3 *They laughed at her unconscious slip of the tongue.*
▸ accidental, unintended, unintentional
AN OPPOSITE IS conscious

uncontrollable *ADJECTIVE*
SEE **unruly**

uncooperative *ADJECTIVE*
SEE **unhelpful**

uncover *VERB*
1 *She uncovered the surprise gift her sister had bought for her.*
▸ disclose, expose, reveal, show, unveil, unwrap
▹ To uncover your body is to **bare** yourself, or **strip** or **undress**.
2 *Archaeologists have uncovered the ruins of a Roman fort.*
▸ come across, dig up, discover, expose, locate, unearth
AN OPPOSITE IS cover

undecided *ADJECTIVE*
SEE **uncertain**

undeniable *ADJECTIVE*
SEE **true**

underclothes *PLURAL NOUN*
▸ underclothing, undergarments, underwear, (*informal*) undies
▹ Women's underclothes are **lingerie**.
VARIOUS UNDERGARMENTS
bra or brassière, briefs, corset, drawers, garter, girdle, knickers, panties, pants, pantyhose, petticoat, slip, suspenders, tights, trunks, underpants, underskirt, vest
FOR OTHER GARMENTS SEE **clothes**

undergo *VERB*
She underwent a three-hour operation.
▸ be subjected to, endure, experience, go through, put up with, suffer

undergrowth *NOUN*
They cleared a path through the undergrowth.
▸ bushes, ground cover, plants, vegetation

underhand *ADJECTIVE*
He had been involved in underhand financial deals.
▸ deceitful, devious, furtive, secret, secretive, sly, (*informal*) sneaky, unfair

underline *VERB*
The accident underlines the need to take care.
▸ draw attention to, emphasize, give emphasis to, show clearly, stress

undermine *VERB*
Her criticism undermined his confidence.
▸ destroy, lessen, reduce, ruin, weaken
AN OPPOSITE IS support

underprivileged ADJECTIVE
He works for underprivileged children.
▸ badly off, deprived, needy, poor

understand VERB
1 *Do you understand what I mean?*
▸ appreciate, comprehend, fathom, follow, grasp, interpret, make sense of, realize, recognize, see, take in, (*informal*) twig, work out
2 *Can you understand this writing?*
▸ decipher, make out, read
▹ To understand something in code is to **decode** it.
3 *She understands animals.*
▸ know, show understanding of, sympathize with
4 *I understand you've been ill?*
▸ believe, hear

understanding NOUN
1 *The tutor was amazed by his young pupil's understanding.*
▸ cleverness, insight, intellect, intelligence, judgement, perceptiveness, sense, wisdom
2 *He has only a limited understanding of the problem.*
▸ appreciation, awareness, comprehension, grasp, knowledge
3 *The two sides reached an understanding.*
▸ accord, agreement, arrangement, bargain, contract, deal, settlement, treaty
4 *There was a great deal of understanding between them.*
▸ friendship, harmony, sympathy, tolerance

understanding ADJECTIVE
She's an understanding person.
▸ broad-minded, caring, friendly, helpful, kind, open-minded, sympathetic, tolerant, unprejudiced

undertake VERB
He undertook to deliver the letter right away.
▸ agree, commit yourself, consent, guarantee, promise

undertaking NOUN
Organizing the festival has been a difficult undertaking.
▸ enterprise, job, mission, operation, project, task, venture

underwear NOUN
SEE **underclothes**

undisguised ADJECTIVE
SEE **obvious**

undo VERB
1 *Undo the ropes.*
WORDS MEANING TO UNDO THINGS THAT ARE JOINED TOGETHER
detach, disconnect, loosen, part, separate, unclip, uncouple, unfasten, unhook, unravel, untether, untie
2 *She undid the parcel carefully.*
WORDS MEANING TO UNDO THINGS THAT ARE CLOSED OR SEALED OR WRAPPED UP
open, unbutton, unclasp, unfold, unlock, unpin, unroll, unscrew, unseal, unstick, unwind, unwrap, unzip
3 *It was too late to undo the damage.*
▸ cancel out, reverse, wipe out

undoubtedly ADVERB
She is undoubtedly our best player.
▸ certainly, definitely, doubtless, of course, surely

undress VERB
She undressed quickly and got into bed.
▸ get undressed, strip, take off your clothes
AN OPPOSITE IS dress

unearth VERB
1 *The dog unearthed an old bone.*
▸ dig up, uncover
2 *She unearthed some old diaries in the attic.*
▸ come across, discover, find, stumble upon, track down

unearthly ADJECTIVE
They heard an unearthly cry.
▸ eerie, frightening, ghostly, (*informal*) scary, sinister, (*informal*) spooky, strange, supernatural, uncanny, unnatural, weird

uneasy ADJECTIVE
1 *She had an uneasy feeling that something was wrong.*
▸ anxious, apprehensive, edgy, fearful, insecure, nervous, tense, troubled, uncertain, upsetting, worried
AN OPPOSITE IS confident
2 *She passed an uneasy night.*
▸ disturbed, restless, uncomfortable, unsettled
AN OPPOSITE IS comfortable

A B C D E F G H I J K L M N O P Q R S T U V W X Y Z

unemployed *ADJECTIVE*
Since the factory closed, many people have been unemployed.
► jobless, (*informal*) on the dole, out of work
▷ To be unemployed because there is not enough work for you to do is to be redundant.
AN OPPOSITE IS employed or working

uneven *ADJECTIVE*
1 *The ground was very uneven in places.*
► broken, bumpy, jagged, rough, rutted
AN OPPOSITE IS smooth
2 *Their performance has been uneven this season.*
► erratic, fluctuating, inconsistent, irregular, unpredictable, variable, varying
AN OPPOSITE IS consistent
3 *It was a very uneven contest.*
► ill-matched, one-sided, unbalanced, unequal, unfair
AN OPPOSITE IS balanced

unexpected *ADJECTIVE*
Her reaction was totally unexpected.
► sudden, surprising, unforeseen, unpredictable
AN OPPOSITE IS expected

unfair *ADJECTIVE*
SEE **unjust**

unfaithful *ADJECTIVE*
SEE **disloyal**

unfamiliar *ADJECTIVE*
SEE **strange**

unfashionable *ADJECTIVE*
SEE **old-fashioned**

unfasten *VERB*
SEE **undo**

unfavourable *ADJECTIVE*
1 *The new television series received unfavourable reviews.*
► attacking, critical, disapproving, hostile, negative, uncomplimentary, unfriendly, unkind, unsympathetic
2 *Unfavourable weather conditions prevented the journey.*
► adverse, bad, unhelpful
AN OPPOSITE IS favourable

unfinished *ADJECTIVE*
Her last novel was unfinished.
► incomplete, uncompleted
AN OPPOSITE IS complete

unfit *ADJECTIVE*
1 *He never gets any exercise and is really unfit.*
► out of condition, unhealthy
AN OPPOSITE IS fit
2 *She is unfit for the job.*
► unsatisfactory, unsuitable, useless

unforgettable *ADJECTIVE*
It was an unforgettable occasion.
► impressive, memorable, notable, outstanding, remarkable
AN OPPOSITE IS ordinary

unforgivable *ADJECTIVE*
Losing your temper with him was unforgivable.
► shameful, unjustifiable, unpardonable
AN OPPOSITE IS excusable

unfortunate *ADJECTIVE*
1 *It was an unfortunate mistake.*
► calamitous, dreadful, unlucky
AN OPPOSITE IS fortunate or lucky
2 *He was unfortunate enough to lose his job.*
► luckless, unlucky, unsuccessful
AN OPPOSITE IS fortunate or lucky
3 *His unfortunate remark silenced the whole room.*
► inappropriate, regrettable, tactless, unsuitable, untimely

unfriendly *ADJECTIVE*
He was abrupt and unfriendly.
► cold, cool, disagreeable, distant, hostile, impolite, inhospitable, uncivil, unhelpful, unkind, unsociable, unsympathetic, unwelcoming
AN OPPOSITE IS friendly

ungrateful *ADJECTIVE*
Don't be so ungrateful.
► unappreciative, unthankful
AN OPPOSITE IS grateful

unhappy *ADJECTIVE*
You look unhappy today — what's the matter?
► brokenhearted, dejected, depressed, desolate, despairing, dismal, distressed, (*informal*) down, downcast, downhearted, forlorn, gloomy, glum, grave, heartbroken, in low spirits, miserable, regretful, sad, sorrowful, sorry, tearful, troubled, upset, wistful, woeful, wretched
AN OPPOSITE IS happy

unhealthy *ADJECTIVE*
1 *He looked extremely unhealthy.*
▸ ailing, delicate, diseased, feeble, frail, ill, infirm, poorly, sick, sickly, suffering, (*informal*) under the weather, unwell, weak
2 *They were living in damp and unhealthy conditions.*
▸ dirty, harmful, insanitary, polluted, unclean, unhygienic, unwholesome
AN OPPOSITE IS healthy

unheard-of *ADJECTIVE*
SEE **exceptional**

unhelpful *ADJECTIVE*
The shop assistant was unhelpful.
▸ inconsiderate, reluctant to help, slow, uncooperative, unfriendly, unwilling to help
AN OPPOSITE IS helpful

unidentified *ADJECTIVE*
An unidentified benefactor gave the school a computer.
▸ anonymous, nameless, unknown, unnamed, unrecognized, unspecified
AN OPPOSITE IS named

uniform *ADJECTIVE*
The planks should be of uniform width.
▸ consistent, identical, regular, the same, similar, unvarying
AN OPPOSITE IS different or inconsistent

unify *VERB*
His main aim was to unify the different groups within the organization.
▸ amalgamate, bring together, combine, integrate, join, merge, unite
AN OPPOSITE IS separate

unimportant *ADJECTIVE*
Don't worry about unimportant details.
▸ insignificant, irrelevant, minor, negligible, petty, secondary, slight, small, trifling, trivial, uninteresting, worthless
AN OPPOSITE IS important

uninhabited *ADJECTIVE*
SEE **unoccupied**

unintelligent *ADJECTIVE*
SEE **stupid**

unintelligible *ADJECTIVE*
SEE **incomprehensible**

unintentional *ADJECTIVE*
If he upset you, I'm sure it was unintentional.
▸ accidental, unconscious, unintended, unplanned
AN OPPOSITE IS deliberate

uninterested *ADJECTIVE*
SEE **apathetic**

uninteresting *ADJECTIVE*
SEE **boring**

union *NOUN*
▹ A union of two organizations or parties is an **amalgamation** or **merger**. A union of two groups is their **integration**. A union of two countries is their **unification**. A union of two substances is a **compound** or **fusion** or **synthesis**. A union of two people is a **marriage** or **partnership**.

unique *ADJECTIVE*
Strictly, *unique* means *being the only one of its kind*. However, it is often used informally to mean *very unusual*.
1 *Your fingerprints are unique.*
▸ different, distinctive, individual, peculiar to you, special
2 (*informal*) *She is a woman of unique talent and determination.*
SEE **unusual**

unit *NOUN*
You can build up the units into a complex system.
▸ bit, component, element, module, part, piece, section, segment
FOR UNITS OF MEASUREMENT SEE **measurement** *NOUN*

unite *VERB*
1 *The store manager decided to unite the two departments.*
▸ amalgamate, bring together, combine, integrate, join, link, merge, unify
AN OPPOSITE IS separate
2 *The two groups united to demand changes in the law.*
▸ become allies, collaborate, cooperate, go into partnership, join forces
AN OPPOSITE IS compete
▹ To unite to do something bad is to **conspire**.

A B C D E F G H I J K L M N O P Q R S T U V W X Y Z

universal *ADJECTIVE*
It's an issue of universal interest.
▸ general, global, international, worldwide

unjust *ADJECTIVE*
The referee's decision was unjust.
▸ biased, prejudiced, unfair, unjustifiable, unjustified, unlawful, unreasonable, wrong
AN OPPOSITE IS just

unkind *ADJECTIVE*
That was an unkind thing to do!
▸ callous, hard-hearted, harsh, heartless, impolite, inconsiderate, inhumane, malicious, mean, nasty, ruthless, selfish, spiteful, tactless, thoughtless, uncaring, unfriendly, unpleasant, unsympathetic, vicious
People can be unkind in many ways, and there are many other words you can use in addition to those listed here. For example, SEE **angry**, **cruel**, **rude**, **unjust**, etc.
AN OPPOSITE IS kind

unknown *ADJECTIVE*
1 *The man was unknown to her.*
▸ unidentified, unrecognized
AN OPPOSITE IS known
2 *The author of the story is unknown.*
▸ anonymous, nameless, unnamed, unspecified
AN OPPOSITE IS named
3 *The explorers entered unknown territory.*
▸ alien, foreign, strange, undiscovered, unexplored, unfamiliar
AN OPPOSITE IS familiar
4 *The part was played by an unknown actor.*
▸ little-known, obscure, undistinguished, unheard of
AN OPPOSITE IS famous

unlike *ADJECTIVE*
Surprisingly, the twins are unlike each other.
▸ different from, distinct from, distinguishable from
AN OPPOSITE IS similar

unlikely *ADJECTIVE*
It seemed an unlikely explanation of the events.
▸ far-fetched, improbable, incredible, suspicious, unbelievable, unconvincing
AN OPPOSITE IS likely

unload *VERB*
1 *The driver unloaded the boxes from the back of the van.*
▸ drop off, (*informal*) dump, take off
2 *We unloaded the van.*
▸ clear, empty
AN OPPOSITE IS load

unlucky *ADJECTIVE*
1 *It was an unlucky accident.*
▸ unfortunate
2 *They were unlucky not to win.*
▸ luckless, unfortunate
AN OPPOSITE IS lucky

unmarried *ADJECTIVE*
▹ If you are unmarried, you are **single**. If your marriage has been legally ended, you are **divorced**. An unmarried man is a **bachelor**. An unmarried woman is a **spinster**. A man whose wife is dead is a **widower**. A woman whose husband is dead is a widow.

unmistakable *ADJECTIVE*
SEE **obvious**

unnatural *ADJECTIVE*
1 *It's unnatural for the weather to be so warm in March.*
▸ abnormal, extraordinary, odd, queer, strange, unusual
2 *They thought the acting in the film was unnatural.*
▸ insincere, self-conscious, stiff, theatrical, unrealistic, unspontaneous
3 *Her hair was an unnatural orange colour.*
▸ artificial, manufactured, simulated, synthetic
AN OPPOSITE IS natural

unnecessary *ADJECTIVE*
All this food is unnecessary.
▸ excessive, extra, non-essential, redundant, superfluous, surplus, uncalled for, unneeded, unwanted, useless
AN OPPOSITE IS necessary

unoccupied *ADJECTIVE*
1 *Since the fire, the flats have been unoccupied.*
▸ abandoned, deserted, empty, uninhabited, unused, vacant
AN OPPOSITE IS occupied
2 *The bathroom is unoccupied.*
▸ available, vacant
AN OPPOSITE IS engaged

unofficial *ADJECTIVE*
The police gave him an unofficial warning.
▸ informal
AN OPPOSITE IS official

unplanned *ADJECTIVE*
SEE **spontaneous**

unpleasant *ADJECTIVE* This word is often overused. Here are some alternatives:
1 *He's a thoroughly unpleasant man.*
▸ bad-tempered, disagreeable, malicious, nasty, spiteful, unfriendly, unkind
2 *Her visit to the dentist had been an unpleasant experience.*
▸ awful, disagreeable, nasty, uncomfortable
3 *The smell from the drain was very unpleasant.*
▸ dirty, disgusting, filthy, foul, horrible, horrid, objectionable, repulsive, revolting
AN OPPOSITE IS pleasant

unpopular *ADJECTIVE*
He was unpopular at work.
▸ despised, disliked, hated, unloved
AN OPPOSITE IS popular

unreal *ADJECTIVE*
It seemed as unreal as a dream.
▸ fanciful, fictional, imaginary, unrecognizable
AN OPPOSITE IS real

unrealistic *ADJECTIVE*
1 *The film gives an unrealistic picture of everyday life.*
▸ false, unconvincing, unlifelike, unnatural, unrecognizable
2 *His ideas were unrealistic.*
▸ impracticable, impractical, too ambitious, unworkable
AN OPPOSITE IS realistic

unreasonable *ADJECTIVE*
It's unreasonable to expect him to pay.
▸ absurd, crazy, illogical, irrational, nonsensical, senseless, silly, unfair, unjustifiable
AN OPPOSITE IS reasonable

unreliable *ADJECTIVE*
1 *The prosecution claimed the evidence was unreliable.*
▸ inaccurate, misleading, unsound
2 *He's lazy and unreliable.*
▸ changeable, inconsistent, irresponsible, unpredictable, untrustworthy
AN OPPOSITE IS reliable

unrest *NOUN*
The delay caused unrest in the crowd.
▸ commotion, discontent, disorder, disturbance, rioting, trouble

unruly *ADJECTIVE*
The police found it hard to control the unruly mob.
▸ badly behaved, disobedient, disorderly, naughty, rebellious, troublesome, uncontrollable, unmanageable
AN OPPOSITE IS well behaved

unsafe *ADJECTIVE*
SEE **dangerous**

unsatisfactory *ADJECTIVE*
Her work was unsatisfactory.
▸ disappointing, inadequate, incompetent, inefficient, insufficient, poor, unacceptable
AN OPPOSITE IS satisfactory

unseemly *ADJECTIVE*
It's unseemly to tell rude jokes in church.
▸ improper, inappropriate, offensive, out of place, unsuitable, untimely
AN OPPOSITE IS suitable

unseen *ADJECTIVE*
SEE **invisible**

unselfish *ADJECTIVE*
She's loyal and unselfish.
▸ caring, charitable, considerate, generous, humane, humanitarian, kind, selfless, thoughtful
AN OPPOSITE IS selfish

unsound *ADJECTIVE*
SEE **unreliable, weak**

unstable *ADJECTIVE*
SEE **unsteady**

unsteady *ADJECTIVE*
1 *The table was a bit unsteady.*
▸ insecure, precarious, rickety, shaky, unbalanced, unsafe, unstable, wobbly
2 *The unsteady candlelight flickered.*
▸ changeable, erratic, inconstant, intermittent, irregular, quavering, quivering, trembling, variable, wavering
AN OPPOSITE IS steady

unsuccessful *ADJECTIVE*
He made several unsuccessful attempts to see her.
▸ fruitless, futile, ineffective, ineffectual, unlucky, unproductive, unsatisfactory, useless, vain

A B C D E F G H I J K L M N O P Q R S T U V W X Y Z

unsuitable *ADJECTIVE*
The remarks she made were unsuitable at a funeral.
► inappropriate, incongruous, out of place, unsatisfactory, unseemly, untimely, wrong
AN OPPOSITE IS suitable

unsure *ADJECTIVE*
SEE **uncertain**

unsympathetic *ADJECTIVE*
She complained to the authorities but they were unsympathetic.
► indifferent, uncaring, unhelpful, uninterested, unmoved
AN OPPOSITE IS sympathetic

untidy *ADJECTIVE*
1 *The room wasn't dirty, but it was dreadfully untidy.*
► chaotic, cluttered, disorderly, (*informal*) higgledy-piggledy, jumbled, littered, messy, (*informal*) topsy-turvy, (*informal*) upside down
2 *His work was untidy and full of mistakes.*
► careless, confused, disorganized, haphazard, muddled, slapdash, (*informal*) sloppy
3 *He looked very untidy.*
► rumpled, scruffy, slovenly
4 *She smoothed her untidy hair.*
► dishevelled, tangled, uncombed, ungroomed
AN OPPOSITE IS tidy

untie *VERB*
She quickly untied the knots.
► free, loosen, undo, unfasten
▷ To untie a boat is to **cast off**. To untie an animal is to **release** or **untether** it.

untimely *ADJECTIVE*
SEE **unsuitable**

untrue *ADJECTIVE*
SEE **false**

untrustworthy, **untruthful** *ADJECTIVES*
SEE **dishonest**

unused *ADJECTIVE*
Any unused goods may be returned or exchanged.
► new, unopened
▷ An unused recording tape is a **blank** tape. Unused paper is **clean** paper. Unused clothes are **unworn**. Unused coins are in **mint condition**.
AN OPPOSITE IS used

unusual *ADJECTIVE*
1 *The weather was unusual for the time of year.*
► abnormal, exceptional, extraordinary, irregular, odd, out of the ordinary, peculiar, remarkable, singular, strange, surprising, unconventional, unexpected, unheard-of, (*informal*) unique, unnatural, untypical
AN OPPOSITE IS ordinary
2 *She has a very unusual name.*
► rare, uncommon, unfamiliar
AN OPPOSITE IS common

unwanted *ADJECTIVE*
SEE **unnecessary**

unwelcome *ADJECTIVE*
He had attracted a lot of unwelcome attention.
► disagreeable, objectionable, unacceptable, undesirable, unwanted
AN OPPOSITE IS welcome

unwell *ADJECTIVE*
SEE **ill**

unwilling *ADJECTIVE*
SEE **reluctant**

unwise *ADJECTIVE*
SEE **silly**

update *VERB*
The files are updated every week.
► amend, bring up to date, correct, revise

upgrade *VERB*
They plan to upgrade their computer.
► enhance, expand, improve, make better

upheaval *NOUN*
Moving to a new house causes such an upheaval.
► commotion, disturbance, fuss, turmoil, upset

uphill *ADJECTIVE*
1 *The last part of the road is uphill all the way.*
► ascending, rising, steep, upward
2 *It was an uphill struggle, but eventually she achieved her objectives.*
► arduous, difficult, exhausting, gruelling, hard, laborious, never-ending, stiff, strenuous, taxing, tough

upkeep *NOUN*
The upkeep of a car can be expensive.
► care, maintenance, running

upper *ADJECTIVE*
My bedroom is on the upper floor.
▸ higher, upstairs

upright *ADJECTIVE*
1 *The builder made sure the scaffolding poles were upright.*
▸ erect, perpendicular, standing straight up, vertical
AN OPPOSITE IS horizontal
2 *He's an upright member of society.*
▸ conscientious, fair, good, honest, honourable, just, moral, righteous, trustworthy, virtuous
AN OPPOSITE IS corrupt

uproar *NOUN*
The meeting ended in uproar.
▸ bedlam, chaos, commotion, confusion, din, disorder, disturbance, hullabaloo, noise, pandemonium, riot, row, turmoil

upset *VERB*
1 *The accusation upset her.*
▸ dismay, displease, distress, disturb, grieve, irritate, offend, ruffle
2 *Bad weather upset the train timetable.*
▸ affect, disrupt, interfere with, interrupt, spoil
3 *She upset the bottle of milk.*
▸ knock over, spill, tip over, topple
4 *A large wave upset the boat.*
▸ capsize, overturn

upset *NOUN*
1 *He's got a stomach upset.*
▸ ailment, (*informal*) bug, illness, infection
2 *They caused a major upset by winning 7--0.*
▸ shock, surprise

upside-down *ADJECTIVE*
1 *I can't read it if it's upside-down.*
▸ inverted, wrong way up
2 (*informal*) *They'd left the room upside-down as usual.*
▸ chaotic, cluttered, disorderly, (*informal*) higgledy-piggledy, jumbled, littered, messy, (*informal*) topsy-turvy, untidy

uptight *ADJECTIVE* (*informal*)
She's really uptight about the interview.
▸ anxious, apprehensive, edgy, fearful, jumpy, on edge, tense, upset, worried
AN OPPOSITE IS relaxed

up to date *ADJECTIVE*
You write it as *up-to-date* if it goes immediately before a noun.
1 *The spacecraft uses up-to-date technology.*
▸ advanced, current, the latest, modern, new, present-day, recent
AN OPPOSITE IS out of date or or out-of-date
2 *Her clothes are always up to date.*
▸ contemporary, fashionable, stylish, (*informal*) trendy
AN OPPOSITE IS old-fashioned

upward *ADJECTIVE*
He started on the steep, upward climb.
▸ ascending, rising, uphill

urban *ADJECTIVE*
Most of the population live in urban areas.
▸ built-up, densely populated

urge *VERB*
He urged her to reconsider her decision.
▸ advise, appeal to, beg, counsel, entreat, implore, plead with, press
▹ To urge someone to do something is also to advocate or recommend it.
to urge someone on *The fans urged their team on.*
▸ egg on, encourage, spur on
AN OPPOSITE IS discourage

urge *NOUN*
I had an urge to buy sweets.
▸ desire, eagerness, impulse, itch, longing, wish, yearning, (*informal*) yen

urgent *ADJECTIVE*
1 *He had urgent business in Paris.*
▸ essential, important, necessary, pressing, top priority, unavoidable
AN OPPOSITE IS unimportant
2 *If it's an urgent problem, deal with it immediately.*
▸ acute, immediate, severe
3 *She spoke in an urgent whisper.*
▸ anxious, earnest, insistent

usable *ADJECTIVE*
1 *The lift is not usable today.*
▸ fit for use, functional, functioning, operating, working
AN OPPOSITE IS unusable
2 *This ticket is usable only on certain trains.*
▸ acceptable, valid
AN OPPOSITE IS invalid

A B C D E F G H I J K L M N O P Q R S T U V W X Y Z

use *VERB* This word is often overused. Here are some alternatives:
1 *She used a calculator to add the figures up.*
▸ employ, make use of, utilize
▹ To use your knowledge is to **apply** it. To use your muscles is to **exercise** them. To use a musical instrument is to **play** it. To use an axe, sword, etc., is to **wield** it. To use people or things selfishly is to **exploit** them.
2 *Show me how to use this machine.*
▸ deal with, handle, manage, operate, work
3 *You've used all the hot water.*
▸ consume, exhaust, spend, use up

use *NOUN*
1 *Are these things any use to you?*
▸ advantage, profit, value
2 *This tool has many uses.*
▸ point, purpose

useful *ADJECTIVE*
1 *A microwave is useful for preparing meals quickly.*
▸ convenient, effective, efficient, handy, practical
2 *He gave me some useful advice.*
▸ beneficial, constructive, good, helpful, invaluable, positive, profitable, valuable, worthwhile
3 *He's a very useful player.*
▸ able, capable, competent, gifted, proficient, skilful, successful, talented
AN OPPOSITE IS useless

useless *ADJECTIVE*
1 *This old vacuum cleaner is useless.*
▸ broken down, (*slang*) duff, ineffective, inefficient, impractical, unusable
2 *Her advice was completely useless.*
▸ fruitless, futile, pointless, unhelpful, unprofitable, worthless
3 *He's useless at football.*
▸ incapable, incompetent, ineffectual, unskilful, unsuccessful
AN OPPOSITE IS useful

user-friendly *ADJECTIVE*
Computers should be as user-friendly as possible.
▸ easy to use, straightforward, uncomplicated, understandable

usual *ADJECTIVE*
1 *I'll meet you at the usual place.*
▸ accustomed, customary, familiar, habitual, normal, regular, standard
2 *It's usual to tip the waiter or waitress if the service has been good.*
▸ accepted, common, conventional, traditional
AN OPPOSITE IS unusual

utensil *NOUN*
The shelves were loaded with cooking utensils.
▸ appliance, device, gadget, implement, instrument, machine, tool
FOR VARIOUS TOOLS SEE **tool**

utilize *VERB*
SEE **use**

utter *ADJECTIVE*
He stared at her in utter amazement.
▸ absolute, complete, extreme, perfect, total

utter *VERB*
He didn't dare to utter his thoughts.
▸ communicate, express, pronounce, put into words, say, speak
SEE ALSO **talk** *VERB*

vacancy *NOUN*
They have vacancies for secretaries with word processing experience.
▸ job, opening, position, post, situation

vacant *ADJECTIVE*
1 *The house over the road is still vacant.*
▸ deserted, uninhabited, unoccupied
AN OPPOSITE IS occupied
2 *He gave her a vacant stare.*
▸ absent-minded, blank, expressionless, inattentive, mindless, vague
AN OPPOSITE IS alert

vacate *VERB*
Guests must vacate their rooms by midday.
▸ evacuate, leave, quit, withdraw from

vacation *NOUN*
(*mainly American use*) *She spent her vacation in Europe.*
▸ holiday, leave, time off

vaccinate *VERB*
The children were vaccinated against measles.
▸ immunize, inoculate

vacuum *NOUN*
▹ A trade name used as a synonym for a vacuum cleaner is Hoover. A trade name used as a synonym for a vacuum flask is Thermos.

vague *ADJECTIVE*
1 *His description was rather vague.*
▸ ambiguous, broad, general, generalized, indefinite, uncertain, unclear, woolly
AN OPPOSITE IS exact
2 *A vague shape could be seen through the mist.*
▸ blurred, dim, hazy, indistinct, shadowy, unrecognizable
AN OPPOSITE IS definite
3 *She's always been a bit vague.*
▸ absent-minded, careless, forgetful, inattentive
AN OPPOSITE IS attentive

vain *ADJECTIVE*
1 *He's vain about his appearance.*
▸ arrogant, boastful, (*informal*) cocky, conceited, haughty, proud, self-satisfied, (*informal*) stuck-up
AN OPPOSITE IS modest
2 *She made a vain attempt to tidy the room.*
▸ fruitless, futile, ineffective, pointless, unsuccessful, useless, worthless
AN OPPOSITE IS successful

valiant *ADJECTIVE*
He made a valiant attempt to break the world record.
▸ bold, brave, courageous, daring, fearless, gallant, heroic, plucky
AN OPPOSITE IS cowardly or feeble

valid *ADJECTIVE*
1 *The ticket is valid for three months.*
▸ approved, authentic, authorized, current, legal, official, permitted, proper, suitable, usable
2 *He made several valid points.*
▸ acceptable, convincing, genuine, legitimate, reasonable, sound
AN OPPOSITE IS invalid

valley *NOUN*
VARIOUS KINDS OF VALLEY
canyon, chasm, dale, defile, dell, glen, gorge, gulch, gully, hollow, pass, ravine, vale

valour *NOUN*
He was decorated for valour in battle.
▸ bravery, courage, daring, gallantry, heroism, pluck
AN OPPOSITE IS cowardice

valuable *ADJECTIVE*
1 *Apparently the painting is very valuable.*
▸ costly, dear, expensive, precious, priceless
2 *He gave her some valuable advice.*
▸ beneficial, constructive, good, helpful, invaluable, positive, useful, valued, worthwhile
AN OPPOSITE IS worthless
Notice that *invaluable* is not the opposite of *valuable*

value *NOUN*
1 *The alterations greatly increased the value of the house.*
▸ cost, price, worth
2 *He stressed the value of taking regular exercise.*
▸ advantage, benefit, importance, merit, significance, use, usefulness

value *VERB*
1 *He had always valued her advice.*
▸ appreciate, esteem, have a high opinion of, prize, respect, treasure
2 *A surveyor was sent to value the house.*
▸ assess, estimate the value of, evaluate, price

van *NOUN*
FOR VARIOUS VEHICLES SEE **vehicle**

vandal *NOUN*
The windows of the shop were smashed by vandals.
▸ delinquent, hooligan, lout, ruffian, troublemaker

vanish *VERB*
By the time she came back he had vanished.
▸ disappear, go away, melt away
AN OPPOSITE IS appear

A B C D E F G H I J K L M N O P Q R S T U V W X Y Z

vanity *NOUN*
He spoke without a trace of vanity.
▶ arrogance, (*informal*) cockiness, conceit, pride, self-esteem, self-importance

vanquish *VERB*
He successfully vanquished his opponent.
▶ beat, conquer, crush, defeat, overcome, overwhelm, (*informal*) thrash

vaporize *VERB*
Water vaporizes when it boils.
▶ dry up, evaporate, turn to vapour
AN OPPOSITE IS condense

vapour *NOUN*
Smelly vapour hung in the air.
▶ fumes, gas, smoke, steam
▷ Vapour hanging in the air is **haze**, **fog**, **mist**, or **smog**.

variable *ADJECTIVE*
The temperature is variable at this time of year.
▶ changeable, erratic, fluctuating, inconsistent, uncertain, unpredictable, unreliable, unstable, unsteady, (*informal*) up-and-down, varying, wavering
▷ If your loyalty to friends is variable, you are **fickle**.
AN OPPOSITE IS constant

variation *NOUN*
There are wide regional variations in house prices.
▶ alteration, change, difference, fluctuation, shift

variety *NOUN*
1 *The centre offers a variety of leisure activities.*
▶ array, assortment, miscellany, mixture
2 *The supermarket has over thirty varieties of pasta.*
▶ brand, kind, make, sort, type
▷ A variety of animal is a **breed** or **species**.
3 *Her job lacked variety.*
▶ change, difference, diversity, variation

various *ADJECTIVE*
The shirts are available in various colours.
▶ assorted, contrasting, different, differing, diverse, miscellaneous, mixed, several, varying

vary *VERB*
1 *The price of fruit and vegetables varies with the seasons.*
▶ alter, change, differ, fluctuate, go up and down
2 *He tried to vary his diet.*
▶ adjust, alter, change, modify

vast *ADJECTIVE*
1 *The miser accumulated a vast fortune.*
▶ enormous, great, huge, immense, large, massive
2 *A vast expanse of water stretched ahead of them.*
▶ big, broad, extensive, wide
AN OPPOSITE IS small

vault *VERB*
to vault over something *He vaulted over the fence.*
▶ bound over, clear, hurdle, jump over, leap over, spring over

vault *NOUN*
The gold was stored in the vaults of the bank.
▶ strongroom, treasury
▷ An underground part of a house is a **cellar**. An underground part of a church is a **crypt** or **undercroft**.

veer *VERB*
The car veered across the road.
▶ change direction, dodge, swerve, turn

vegetable *NOUN*
GREEN VEGETABLES
broccoli, Brussels sprout, cabbage, cauliflower, Chinese cabbage, kale, spinach
ROOT VEGETABLES
beetroot, carrot, parsnip, swede, turnip
▷ **Sugar beet** is a root vegetable used to make sugar. A **mangel** or **mangel-wurzel** is a root vegetable used for cattle.
LEGUMES OR PULSES
beans, chickpeas, dhal, lentils, mangetout or sugar pea, peas
FOR VARIOUS BEANS SEE **bean**
OTHER VEGETABLES
artichoke, asparagus, aubergine, celeriac, celery, courgette, garlic, leek, marrow, mushroom, okra, onion, pepper, potato, pumpkin, shallot, sweet corn, sweet potato, water chestnut, yam
FOR VEGETABLES EATEN IN SALADS SEE **salad**

vegetarian *NOUN*
▷ A person who doesn't eat any products that come from animals is a **vegan**. An animal that feeds only on plants is a **herbivore**. The opposite — a person or animal that eats flesh — is a **carnivore**.

vegetation *NOUN*
The gardens were filled with lush vegetation.
▸ foliage, greenery, growing things, growth, plants, undergrowth, weeds

vehicle *NOUN*
VEHICLES WHICH CARRY PEOPLE
ambulance, bus, cab, camper, car or motor car, caravan, (*old use*) charabanc, coach, double-decker, go-kart, jeep, minibus, minicab, (*old use*) omnibus, police car, rickshaw, single-decker, taxi, tram, trolleybus
SEE ALSO **car**, **cycle**
VEHICLES USED TO TRANSPORT THINGS
articulated lorry, breakdown vehicle, dump truck, HGV or heavy goods vehicle, horsebox, juggernaut, lorry, milk float, pantechnicon or removal van, pick-up truck, tanker, traction engine, tractor, trailer, transporter, truck, van
OTHER MECHANICAL VEHICLES
bulldozer, dustcart, fire engine, hearse, roadroller or (*old use*) steamroller, snowplough, tank
OLD HORSE-DRAWN VEHICLES
carriage, cart, chariot, coach, gig, hackney carriage, omnibus, phaeton, stagecoach, trap, wagon

veil *VERB*
Her face was veiled with a silk scarf.
▸ conceal, cover, hide, mask, shroud

vein *NOUN*
▷ A tube in the body that carries blood away from the heart is an **artery**. Veins and arteries are **blood vessels**. Delicate hairlike blood vessels are **capillaries**.

velocity *NOUN*
The rocket has to reach a great velocity before it can leave the earth's atmosphere.
▸ rate, speed, swiftness

venerable *ADJECTIVE*
The Bank of England is a venerable institution.
▸ aged, ancient, dignified, old, respected, revered, worthy of respect

vengeance *NOUN*
His cruel heart was set on vengeance.
▸ reprisal, revenge

venomous *ADJECTIVE*
The adder is Britain's only venomous snake.
▸ poisonous

vent *NOUN*
A vent in the roof lets the smoke out.
▸ gap, hole, opening, outlet, slit
to give vent to *She gave vent to her anger.*
▸ express, let go, release

ventilate *VERB*
Ventilate the greenhouse properly.
▸ air, freshen, let fresh air in

venture *NOUN*
He became involved in one business venture after another.
▸ enterprise, project, undertaking

venture *VERB*
They ventured out into the snow.
▸ dare to go, have an expedition, risk going

verdict *NOUN*
What was the jury's verdict?
▸ conclusion, decision, judgement, opinion

verge *NOUN*
Don't park on the verge of the road.
▸ edge, margin, side
▷ A stone or concrete edging beside a road is a **kerb**. The flat strip of tarmac or concrete beside a motorway is the **hard shoulder**.

verify *VERB*
Several witnesses verified his statement.
▸ (*informal*) check out, confirm, prove, show the truth of, support

vermin *NOUN*
The barn was infested with vermin.
▸ pests
▷ Vermin such as fleas that live on other animals are **parasites**.

versatile *ADJECTIVE*
He's one of the game's most versatile players.
▸ adaptable, all-round, gifted, talented

verse *NOUN*
1 *Most of the play is written in verse.*
▸ lines, rhyme
▹ The rhythm of a line of verse is its metre. Something written in verse is poetry or a poem.
SEE ALSO **poem**
2 *She'd managed to learn the first two verses of the poem by heart.*
▸ stanza

version *NOUN*
1 *The two newspapers gave different versions of the accident.*
▸ account, description, report, story
2 *It's an English version of a French play.*
▸ adaptation, interpretation, paraphrase
▹ A version of something which was originally in another language is a translation.
3 *They brought out a new version of the car last summer.*
▸ design, form, model, variation

vertical *ADJECTIVE*
The fence posts must be vertical.
▸ erect, perpendicular, upright
▹ A vertical drop is a sheer drop.
AN OPPOSITE IS horizontal

very *ADVERB* This word is often overused.
Her work is always very good.
▸ enormously, especially, exceedingly, extremely, highly, intensely, (*informal*) jolly, outstandingly, particularly, really, remarkably, (*informal*) terribly, (*informal*) terrifically, truly, uncommonly, unusually
AN OPPOSITE IS slightly

vessel *NOUN*
1 *Their fishing vessel collided with a tanker in rough seas.*
▸ boat, craft, ship
VESSELS USED TO TRANSPORT PEOPLE OR GOODS
barge, coaster, collier, cruise liner, dhow, ferry, freighter, gondola, hovercraft, hydrofoil, junk, lighter, liner, merchant ship, narrow boat, oil tanker, steamship, supertanker, tanker, tramp steamer
OTHER WORKING VESSELS
dredger, ice-breaker, lifeboat, lightship, trawler, tug, whaler
MILITARY VESSELS
aircraft carrier, battleship, corvette, cruiser, destroyer, frigate, gunboat, landing craft, minesweeper, submarine, torpedo boat, troop ship, warship
VESSELS USED MAINLY FOR LEISURE
cabin cruiser, canoe, catamaran, dinghy, houseboat, launch, motor boat, powerboat, punt, raft, rowing boat, sailing boat, speed boat, yacht
SOME VESSELS USED IN FORMER TIMES
brigantine, clipper, coracle, cutter, dugout, galleon, galley, man-of-war, packet boat, paddle steamer, schooner, trireme, windjammer
WORDS FOR PARTS OF A VESSEL
boom, bow, bowsprit, bridge, bulwark, cabin, conning tower, crow's nest, deck, engine room, fo'c'sle or forecastle, funnel, galley, helm, hull, keel, mast, poop, porthole, propeller, prow, quarterdeck, rigging, rudder, sail, stern, tiller**2** *Archaeologists discovered gold and silver vessels at the site.*
FOR VARIOUS CONTAINERS SEE **container**
blood vessels
▹ Blood vessels are your arteries, capillaries, and veins.

veteran *NOUN*
He is a veteran of the Second World War.
▸ old soldier, survivor

veto *NOUN*
They couldn't have a party because of the head's veto.
▸ ban, prohibition, refusal, rejection
AN OPPOSITE IS approval

veto *VERB*
The boss vetoed the proposed holiday.
▸ ban, forbid, prohibit, refuse, reject, rule out, say no to, turn down
AN OPPOSITE IS approve

vex *VERB*
It vexed her that he had forgotten her birthday.
▸ anger, annoy, exasperate, irritate, make you cross, upset, worry

vibrate *VERB*
You can feel the engine vibrate.
▸ quake, quiver, rattle, shake, shudder, throb, tremble

vibration *NOUN*
The vibrations from the earthquake could be felt for miles around.
▸ pulse, quivering, rattling, shaking, shuddering, throbbing, trembling, tremor

vicar *NOUN*
SEE **clergyman**

vice *NOUN*
1 *The police wage war on crime and vice.*
▸ corruption, evil, immorality, sin, wickedness, wrongdoing
2 *Vanity is not one of his vices.*
▸ bad habit, blemish, defect, failing, fault, imperfection, shortcoming, weakness
AN OPPOSITE IS virtue

vicinity *NOUN*
The car was found in the vicinity of the station.
▸ district, locality, neighbourhood, surrounding area

vicious *ADJECTIVE*
1 *He suffered a vicious attack.*
▸ atrocious, barbaric, barbarous, beastly, bloodthirsty, brutal, callous, cruel, diabolical, fiendish, inhuman, merciless, murderous, pitiless, ruthless, sadistic, savage, violent
2 *He's not a vicious person.*
▸ evil, heartless, immoral, malicious, perverted, spiteful, villainous, wicked
3 *Take care — that dog's vicious.*
▸ aggressive, bad-tempered, dangerous, ferocious, fierce
4 *A vicious wind was blowing.*
▸ nasty, severe, sharp, unpleasant
AN OPPOSITE IS gentle

victim *NOUN*
1 *Ambulances took the victims to hospital.*
▸ casualty
▹ Victims of an accident are also the injured or the wounded. A person who dies in an accident is a fatality.
2 *The hawk seized its victim.*
▸ prey
▹ People who are attacked and killed because of their beliefs are martyrs.

victimize *VERB*
He was victimized at school because he hated sport.
▸ bully, intimidate, oppress, persecute, pick on, terrorize, torment, treat unfairly
▹ To victimize people who work for you is to exploit them. To victimize people because of their race, religion, etc., is to discriminate against them.

victor *NOUN*
After the match, the victors returned in triumph.
▸ champion, conqueror, winner

victorious *ADJECTIVE*
A trophy was presented to the victorious team.
▸ conquering, leading, successful, top, top-scoring, triumphant, unbeaten, undefeated, winning
AN OPPOSITE IS defeated

victory *NOUN*
The streets were full of people celebrating the team's victory in the world cup.
▸ success, triumph, win
AN OPPOSITE IS defeat

view *NOUN*
1 *There's a good view from the top of the hill.*
▸ outlook, panorama, prospect, scene, scenery
2 *He has strong views about politics.*
▸ attitude, belief, conviction, idea, notion, opinion, thought
in view of something *In view of his recent conduct, the club has decided to suspend him.*
▸ as a result of, because of, considering, taking account of

view *VERB*
1 *Thousand of tourists come to view the cathedral each year.*
▸ contemplate, examine, eye, gaze at, inspect, look at, observe, see, stare at, survey
2 *She viewed the prospect of an interview with dread.*
▸ consider, regard, think of

viewer *NOUN*
▹ People who view a performance are the audience or spectators. People who view something as they happen to pass by are bystanders or onlookers or witnesses.

vigilant *ADJECTIVE*
He warned the public to be vigilant and report anything suspicious.
▸ alert, attentive, careful, observant, on the lookout, on your guard, wary, watchful
AN OPPOSITE IS negligent

A B C D E F G H I J K L M N O P Q R S T U V W X Y Z

vigorous *ADJECTIVE*
1 *Vigorous exercise does you good.*
▸ active, brisk, energetic, enthusiastic, lively, strenuous
2 *I gave the door a vigorous push.*
▸ forceful, mighty, powerful
3 *He was a vigorous man in the prime of life.*
▸ healthy, strong
AN OPPOSITE IS feeble

vigour *NOUN*
1 *He tackled the job with vigour.*
▸ energy, enthusiasm, keenness, liveliness, spirit, vitality, zeal, zest
2 *I banged on the door with vigour.*
▸ force, might, power, strength

vile *ADJECTIVE*
1 *What a vile smell!*
▸ disgusting, filthy, foul, horrible, loathsome, nasty, offensive, repellent, repulsive, revolting, sickening, unpleasant
AN OPPOSITE IS pleasant
2 *Murder is a vile crime.*
▸ contemptible, dreadful, evil, ugly, vicious, wicked

villain *NOUN*
The police have caught the villains who broke into the shop.
▸ criminal, delinquent, offender, rogue, wretch, wrongdoer
SEE ALSO **criminal** *NOUN*
▹ An informal word for the villain in a story is baddy.
AN OPPOSITE IS hero

villainous *ADJECTIVE*
People were appalled by his villainous behaviour.
▸ corrupt, cruel, diabolical, dreadful, evil, immoral, perverted, sinful, terrible, vicious, vile, wicked
AN OPPOSITE IS virtuous

violate *VERB*
1 *He was penalized for violating the rules.*
▸ break, disobey, ignore
2 *It's rude to violate someone's privacy.*
▸ abuse, interfere with, invade, show disrespect for

violation *NOUN*
He's guilty of a violation of the rules.
▸ breach, breaking, offence (against)
▹ A violation of the rules of a game is a foul or an infringement.

violence *NOUN*
1 *The violence of the attack horrified us.*
▸ barbarity, brutality, cruelty, ferocity, fierceness, fury, savagery, viciousness
AN OPPOSITE IS gentleness
2 *The violence of the storm uprooted trees.*
▸ destructiveness, intensity, power, rage, severity, strength
AN OPPOSITE IS feebleness
3 *The terrorists are prepared to use violence to achieve their objectives.*
▸ fighting, force, might, war
AN OPPOSITE IS non-violence or pacifism

violent *ADJECTIVE*
1 *There were violent clashes between demonstrators and police.*
▸ brutal, cruel, ferocious, fierce, frenzied, furious, savage, vicious, wild
AN OPPOSITE IS gentle
2 *The bridge was washed away in a violent storm.*
▸ destructive, devastating, forceful, intense, powerful, raging, rough, serious, severe, strong, tempestuous, (*informal*) terrific, turbulent, wild
AN OPPOSITE IS feeble

virtual *ADJECTIVE*
virtual reality Virtual reality is an imitation or simulation of the real world.

virtually *ADVERB*
I've virtually finished.
▸ almost, as good as, in effect, more or less, nearly, practically

virtue *NOUN*
1 *She has the virtue of a saint!*
▸ decency, goodness, honesty, honour, integrity, morality, nobility, righteousness, sincerity, uprightness, worthiness
2 *Our car's main virtue is that it's cheap to run.*
▸ advantage, asset, good point, merit, strength
AN OPPOSITE IS vice

virtuous *ADJECTIVE*
She's always led a virtuous life.
▸ good, honest, honourable, innocent, just, law-abiding, moral, praiseworthy, pure, righteous, trustworthy, upright, worthy
AN OPPOSITE IS wicked

visible *ADJECTIVE*
The spire of the church is visible from miles away.
▸ apparent, clear, conspicuous, distinct, evident, noticeable, obvious, perceptible, plain, recognizable, unconcealed
AN OPPOSITE IS invisible

vision *NOUN*
1 *He had perfect vision.*
▸ eyesight, sight
2 *He claimed he saw his future in a vision.*
▸ dream, hallucination
▹ Something travellers in the desert think they see is a **mirage**.
3 *He is a man of great political vision.*
▸ foresight, imagination, insight, understanding

visit *VERB*
She's visiting friends in London.
▸ call on, come to see, drop in on, go to see, pay a call on, stay with

visit *NOUN*
1 *My grandmother came for a visit.*
▸ call, stay
2 *We went to London for a visit.*
▸ day out, excursion, outing, trip

visitor *NOUN*
1 *They've got some visitors from Ireland staying with them.*
▸ caller, guest
2 *Rome welcomes millions of visitors every year.*
▸ holidaymaker, sightseer, tourist, traveller

visual aids *PLURAL NOUN*
FOR AUDIO-VISUAL EQUIPMENT USED IN SCHOOLS SEE **audio-visual**

visualize *VERB*
I can't visualize you with long hair.
▸ conceive, imagine, picture

vital *ADJECTIVE*
This leaflet contains vital information for travellers.
▸ crucial, essential, imperative, important, indispensable, necessary, relevant
AN OPPOSITE IS unimportant

vitality *NOUN*
Although she's quite old, she's still full of vitality.
▸ animation, energy, exuberance, life, liveliness, spirit, sprightliness, vigour, zest

vivid *ADJECTIVE*
1 *She loved to dress in vivid colours.*
▸ bright, brilliant, colourful, dazzling, (*uncomplimentary*) gaudy, glowing, intense, showy, striking, strong
2 *He gave a vivid description of the scene.*
▸ clear, graphic, imaginative, lifelike, lively, memorable, powerful, realistic
AN OPPOSITE IS dull

vocal *ADJECTIVE*
Usually she's quiet, but today she's quite vocal.
▸ chatty, communicative, outspoken, talkative
AN OPPOSITE IS uncommunicative

vocalist *NOUN*
FOR OTHER KINDS OF SINGER SEE **sing**

voice *NOUN*
I recognized her voice.
▸ accent, speaking, speech, tone

voice *VERB*
He voiced several objections to the plan.
▸ communicate, express, give vent to, put into words, speak

volcano *NOUN*
▹ Lava, ash, etc., pouring from a volcano is an **eruption**.

volley *NOUN*
A volley of shots rang out.
▸ barrage, bombardment

volume *NOUN*
1 *What is the volume of the container?*
▸ capacity, dimensions, size
2 *The firm couldn't deal with the volume of orders it received.*
▸ amount, bulk, mass, quantity
3 *He turned down the volume.*
▸ loudness
4 *She published two volumes of poetry.*
▸ book

voluntary *ADJECTIVE*
She does voluntary work for a charity.
▸ optional, unpaid
AN OPPOSITE IS compulsory

A B C D E F G H I J K L M N O P Q R S T U V W X Y Z

volunteer *VERB*
She volunteered to wash up.
▸ be willing, offer, put yourself forward

vomit *VERB*
The smell made him want to vomit.
▸ be sick, bring up your food

vote *VERB*
Everyone has a right to vote in the election.
▸ cast your vote
to vote for someone or **something** *Who did you vote for?*
▸ choose, elect, nominate, opt for, pick, select, settle on

vote *NOUN*
The results of the vote were printed in the newspaper.
▸ ballot, election, poll, referendum, show of hands

voucher *NOUN*
Exchange this voucher for a free drink.
▸ coupon, ticket, token

vow *NOUN*
She made a vow never to tell anyone what she'd heard.
▸ pledge, promise

vow *VERB*
He vowed that one day he would return.
▸ give an assurance, give your word, guarantee, pledge, promise, swear, take an oath

voyage *NOUN*
▹ A holiday voyage is a **cruise**. A voyage across a channel or sea is a **crossing**. A long voyage is a **sea passage**. A short voyage in a yacht is a **sail**.
FOR OTHER WAYS TO TRAVEL SEE **travel**

vulgar *ADJECTIVE*
1 *The jokes were rather vulgar.*
▸ coarse, foul, impolite, improper, indecent, obscene, offensive, rude, smutty
AN OPPOSITE IS polite
2 *Those gaudy colours look vulgar.*
▸ common, crude, in bad taste, tasteless, unsophisticated
AN OPPOSITE IS tasteful

vulnerable *ADJECTIVE*
1 *The soldiers were in a vulnerable position.*
▸ at risk, defenceless, exposed, open, unguarded, unprotected, weak
AN OPPOSITE IS safe
2 *He's a kind and vulnerable man.*
▸ easily hurt, sensitive, thin-skinned
AN OPPOSITE IS insensitive or robust

Ww

wad *NOUN*
He took a wad of banknotes from his pocket.
▸ bundle, mass, pad, roll

wag *VERB*
The dog wagged its tail.
▸ move to and fro, shake, waggle, wave, wiggle

wage *NOUN*
Her weekly wage is £350.
▸ earnings, income, pay, pay packet
▹ A fixed regular amount an employer agrees to pay you is a **salary**.

wage *VERB*
The government waged a war against crime.
▸ carry on, conduct, fight

wager *NOUN*
He had a wager that she would win.
▸ bet

wail *VERB*
Upstairs, the baby began to wail.
▸ cry, howl, moan, shriek

wait *VERB*
Wait here until I get back.
▸ (*informal*) hang about or around, (*informal*) hold on, linger, pause, remain where you are, stay, stop
to wait on someone *The owner of the restaurant waits on his customers from time to time.*
▸ serve

wait *NOUN*
There was a long wait before the bus came.
▸ delay, hold-up, interval, pause

wake, waken *VERBS*

1 *I usually wake at about 8.*
▸ become conscious, (*informal*) come to life, get up, rise, stir, wake up
2 *She woke me at 7.*
▸ arouse, awaken, call, disturb, rouse

walk *VERB* This word is often overused.
VARIOUS WAYS PEOPLE OR ANIMALS WALK
amble, crawl, creep, dodder, hike, hobble, limp, lope, lurch, march, mince, pace, pad, paddle, parade, plod, prowl, ramble, saunter, scuttle, shamble, shuffle, slink, stagger, stalk, steal, step, (*informal*) stomp, stride, stroll, strut, stumble, swagger, tiptoe, (*informal*) toddle, totter, traipse, tramp, trek, troop, trot, trudge, waddle, wade

walk *NOUN*

1 *We went for a walk in the country.*
▸ hike, ramble, saunter, stroll, tramp, trek, trudge
2 *There are some lovely walks in the surrounding countryside.*
▸ path, route

walker *NOUN*

▹ When you walk along the street, you are a **pedestrian**. If you go for long walks, you are a **hiker** or **rambler**.

wall *NOUN*
VARIOUS KINDS OF WALL
barricade, barrier, dam, dike, dividing wall, embankment, fence, fortification, hedge, obstacle, paling, palisade, parapet, partition, rampart, screen, sea wall, stockade

wallow *VERB*

1 *Hippos like to wallow in mud.*
▸ flounder, lie, roll about, wade
2 *She was wallowing in a hot bath.*
▸ indulge yourself, take delight

wander *VERB*

1 *The sheep wandered about the hills.*
▸ go aimlessly, meander, ramble, range, roam, rove, stray, travel, walk
2 *They'd wandered off the path.*
▸ stray, swerve, turn, veer

wane *VERB*

1 *At sunset, the light began to wane.*
▸ become dimmer, disappear, fade, fail
AN OPPOSITE IS brighten
2 *Her enthusiasm waned after a while.*
▸ decline, decrease, diminish, dwindle, lessen, subside, weaken
AN OPPOSITE IS strengthen

want *VERB*

1 *You can't always have what you want.*
▸ crave, desire, fancy, hanker after, (*informal*) have a yen for, hunger after, itch to have, long for, pine for, (*informal*) set your heart on, wish for, yearn for
▹ If we want something, we can say that we **would like** it, or we **wish** it would happen.
2 *My hair wants cutting.*
▸ need, require

want *NOUN*

1 *The hotel staff saw to all their wants.*
▸ demand, desire, need, requirement, wish
2 *The plants died from want of water.*
▸ absence, lack, need, scarcity, shortage

war *NOUN*
The incident led to war between the two countries.
▸ conflict, fighting, hostilities, military action, strife, warfare
▹ A war fought in the Middle Ages for religious reasons was a **crusade**.
VARIOUS THINGS THAT HAPPEN IN WAR
ambush, assault, attack or counter-attack, battle, blitz, blockade, bombardment, campaign, espionage, guerrilla warfare, invasion, manoeuvres, negotiations, operation, resistance, retreat, siege, skirmish, surrender, withdrawal
SEE ALSO **fight** *NOUN*

ward *VERB*

to ward off someone or **something** **1** *He turned to ward off his attackers.*
▸ beat off, fend off, keep away, push away
2 *The ritual was intended to ward off evil spirits.*
▸ avert, block, check, deflect, repel, stave off, turn aside

warder *NOUN*
He was handcuffed to a warder and taken to prison.
▸ gaoler or jailer, guard, keeper, prison officer

warehouse *NOUN*
The goods were stored in a warehouse.
► depot, store, storehouse

wares *PLURAL NOUN*
The market traders displayed their wares.
► commodities, goods, merchandise, produce, stock

warlike *ADJECTIVE*
The Picts were a notoriously warlike people.
► aggressive, fierce, hostile, militant, quarrelsome, violent
AN OPPOSITE IS peaceful

warm *ADJECTIVE*
1 *It was a warm September evening.*
► pleasantly hot
▷ Weather which is unpleasantly warm is close or sultry. Water or food which is only just warm is lukewarm or tepid.
AN OPPOSITE IS cold
2 *She changed into her warm clothes.*
► cosy, thick, woolly
▷ Underwear specially made to keep you warm is thermal underwear.
AN OPPOSITE IS thin
3 *They gave us a warm welcome.*
► affectionate, enthusiastic, friendly, genial, kind, loving, sympathetic, warm-hearted
AN OPPOSITE IS unfriendly

warm *VERB*
She sat by the fire, warming her hands and feet.
► heat, make warmer, raise the temperature (of), thaw, thaw out
AN OPPOSITE IS chill

warn *VERB*
He warned her not to walk home alone.
► advise, alert, caution, remind
▷ To warn people of a disaster is to raise the alarm.

warning *NOUN*
1 *There was no warning of the danger ahead.*
► advance notice, indication, sign, signal
FOR VARIOUS SIGNALS SEE **signal** *NOUN*
2 *The police let him off with a warning.*
► caution, reprimand, (*informal*) ticking off

warp *VERB*
The girders warped in the heat.
► become deformed, bend, buckle, curl, curve, distort, twist

warrant *VERB*
The allegations are serious enough to warrant investigation.
► deserve, justify, merit

warrior *NOUN*
SEE **fighter**

wary *ADJECTIVE*
I had a wary look round before I went in.
► apprehensive, attentive, careful, cautious, distrustful, suspicious, vigilant, watchful
AN OPPOSITE IS reckless

wash *VERB*
1 *If it's dirty, you'd better wash it.*
► clean
▷ To wash something with a cloth, etc., is to mop, sponge, or wipe it. To wash something with a brush is to scrub it. To wash something in clean water is to rinse, sluice, or swill it. To wash your hair is to shampoo it. To wash yourself all over is to bath or shower. To wash and iron clothes is to launder them.
2 *Waves washed over the beach.*
► flow, splash

waste *VERB*
Don't waste money on things you don't really need.
► fritter away, misuse, squander, throw away
AN OPPOSITE IS save
to waste away *She was visibly wasting away.*
► become thinner, lose weight

waste *ADJECTIVE*
1 *Ensure that waste materials are carefully disposed of.*
► discarded, left over, spare, superfluous, unnecessary, unwanted
2 *There was a patch of waste ground behind the factory.*
► derelict, empty, overgrown, uncultivated, undeveloped, unused, wild

waste *NOUN*
1 *The organization was keen to avoid any waste of resources.*
► unnecessary use, wastage
2 *A lot of household waste can be recycled.*
► garbage, junk, litter, refuse, rubbish, trash
▷ Waste food is leftovers. Waste timber is offcuts. Waste fabrics are remnants. Waste metal is scrap. Waste from our bodies is sewage.

wasteful *ADJECTIVE*
It's wasteful to cook more food than is necessary.
▸ extravagant, needless, prodigal, reckless, thriftless, uneconomical
AN OPPOSITE IS economical

watch *VERB*
1 *She sat and watched the children playing in the garden.*
▸ contemplate, gaze at, look at, see, stare at, view
2 *Watch how I do it.*
▸ attend to, concentrate on, heed, keep your eyes on, note, observe, pay attention to, take notice of
3 *Could you watch my bag for a few minutes?*
▸ care for, defend, guard, keep an eye on, keep watch over, look after, mind, protect, safeguard, shield, supervise, tend
to watch out *Watch out — there's a car coming!*
▸ be careful, beware, pay attention, take care, take heed

watch *NOUN*
INSTRUMENTS USED TO MEASURE TIME
chronometer, clock, digital watch, hourglass, stopwatch, sundial, timepiece, timer, wristwatch

watchful *ADJECTIVE*
She kept a watchful eye on the time.
▸ alert, attentive, observant, perceptive, sharp-eyed, vigilant

watchman *NOUN*
He found a job as a watchman in a local factory.
▸ caretaker, guard, lookout, nightwatchman, security guard

water *NOUN*
VARIOUS KINDS OF WATER
bathwater, bottled water, brine, distilled water, drinking water, rainwater, seawater, spa water, spring water, tap water
VARIOUS STRETCHES OF WATER
brook, canal, lake, lido, (*Scottish*) loch, ocean, pond, pool, reservoir, river, sea, stream

water *VERB*
She went out to water the plants.
▸ dampen, drench, irrigate, moisten, soak, sprinkle, wet
to water something down *The milk had been watered down.*
▸ dilute, thin, weaken

waterlogged *ADJECTIVE*
The match had to be abandoned because the pitch was waterlogged.
▸ full of water, saturated, soaked

waterproof *ADJECTIVE*
These shoes aren't waterproof.
▸ showerproof, water-resistant, weatherproof
▹ Joints or containers that do not let water through are **watertight**.

watery *ADJECTIVE*
1 *The soup was watery and tasteless.*
▸ diluted, runny, thin, watered down
2 *The smoky air made her eyes watery.*
▸ damp, moist, tear filled, tearful, wet

wave *VERB*
1 *The flags waved in the breeze.*
▸ flap, flutter, move to and fro, sway, swing
2 *Demonstrators waved banners and placards as they marched through the town.*
▸ brandish, flourish, shake, twirl, wag, waggle, wiggle

wave *NOUN*
1 *I watched the waves break on the shore.*
▸ billow, breaker, roller
▹ A very small wave is a **ripple**. A huge wave caused by an earthquake, etc., is a **tidal wave**. A number of white waves following each other is **surf**. The top of a wave is the **crest** or **ridge**.
2 *A wave of anger spread through the crowd.*
▸ outbreak, surge
3 *With a wave of his hand he walked off.*
▸ flourish, gesture, shake

waveband *NOUN*
The radio isn't tuned to the right waveband.
▸ channel, station, wavelength

waver *VERB*
1 *She wavered, uncertain whether to accept his offer or not.*
▸ be uncertain, dither, falter, hesitate, pause, think twice
2 *The candle flame wavered in the draught.*
▸ flicker, shake, sway, tremble

wavy *ADJECTIVE*
The paper was decorated with wavy gold lines.
▸ curling, curly, curving, rippling, winding, zigzag
AN OPPOSITE IS straight

way *NOUN*
1 *He walked along the covered way between the two buildings.*
▸ path, road, street
2 *Show me the way to your house.*
▸ direction, route
3 *Is it a long way from here?*
▸ distance, journey
4 *I'll show you the way to make a pancake.*
▸ knack, method, procedure, process, system, technique
5 *She behaved in a mature way.*
▸ fashion, manner, style
6 *They are very alike in some ways.*
▸ aspect, detail, feature, particular, respect
7 *Things are in a bad way.*
▸ condition, state

weak *ADJECTIVE*
1 *The bridge was too weak to carry heavy traffic.*
▸ decrepit, flimsy, fragile, rickety, shaky, unsafe, unsound, unsteady
2 *He was too weak to walk very far.*
▸ delicate, exhausted, feeble, frail, helpless, infirm, sickly
3 *Weak leadership was blamed for the current crisis.*
▸ ineffective, ineffectual, powerless, useless
4 *The soldiers were in a weak position.*
▸ defenceless, exposed, unguarded, unprotected, vulnerable
5 *The play was quite entertaining but the plot was a bit weak.*
▸ feeble, lame, unconvincing, unsatisfactory
6 *She gave me a cup of weak tea.*
▸ diluted, tasteless, thin, watery
AN OPPOSITE IS strong

weaken *VERB*
1 *Hunger weakened their resistance.*
▸ diminish, lessen, lower, make weaker, reduce, sap, undermine
2 *Our resolve weakened.*
▸ become weaker, decline, decrease, dwindle, ebb away, fade, flag, give way, wane
AN OPPOSITE IS strengthen

weakness *NOUN*
1 *Engineers discovered a structural weakness in the aircraft.*
▸ defect, fault, flaw, imperfection, mistake, shortcoming
2 *Most people saw her sensitivity as a sign of weakness.*
▸ fragility, inadequacy, incompetence, ineffectiveness, uselessness
AN OPPOSITE IS strength

wealth *NOUN*
No one knew how she had acquired her wealth.
▸ affluence, assets, capital, fortune, money, opulence, possessions, property, prosperity, riches
AN OPPOSITE IS poverty
a wealth of *There's a wealth of information in this book.*
▸ an abundance of, (*informal*) heaps of, lots of, much, plenty of, a profusion of

wealthy *ADJECTIVE*
He must be wealthy to live in a house like that.
▸ affluent, opulent, prosperous, rich, well-off, well-to-do
AN OPPOSITE IS poor

weapon *NOUN*
VARIOUS KINDS OF GUN
airgun, automatic pistol or rifle, bazooka, (*old use*) blunderbuss, Bren gun, cannon, Gatling gun, handgun, howitzer, machine-gun, mortar, (*old use*) musket, pistol, revolver, rifle, shotgun, Sten gun, sub-machine gun, tommy-gun, water-cannon
▹ Heavy guns are artillery. A set of heavy guns on a warship, etc., is a battery. Hand-held guns are firearms or small arms.
VARIOUS MODERN BOMBS AND MISSILES
atom bomb, ballistic missile, depth charge, grenade, H-bomb, incendiary bomb, landmine, mine, napalm bomb, nuclear weapons, rocket, time bomb, torpedo, warhead
OTHER MODERN WEAPONS
biological weapons, chemical weapons, CS gas, flame-thrower, tear gas
OLD WEAPONS OR WEAPONS WHICH DO NOT USE MODERN TECHNOLOGY
baton, battering ram, battleaxe, bayonet, blowpipe, boomerang, bow and arrow, broadsword, catapult, club, cosh, crossbow, cudgel, cutlass, dagger, dart, harpoon, javelin, lance, longbow, machete, pike, pole-axe, quarterstaff, rapier, sabre, scimitar, sling, spear, staff, sword, tomahawk, trident, truncheon
▹ Weapons in general are armaments, munitions, or weaponry. A collection or store of weapons is an armoury or arsenal or magazine.

wear *VERB*
1 *She was wearing a short, black dress.*
▸ be dressed in, clothe yourself in, dress in, have on
2 *The carpets were starting to wear.*
▸ fray, wear away, wear out
3 *The boots haven't worn well.*
▸ endure, last, survive
to wear off *The pain soon wore off.*
▸ die down, disappear, ease, fade, lessen, moderate, subside, weaken

weary *ADJECTIVE*
She looked pale and weary.
▸ (*informal*) all in, exhausted, fatigued, flagging, sleepy, tired, worn out

weather *NOUN*
▹ The prevalent weather conditions in a particular area is the **climate**. The study of weather is **meteorology**.
VARIOUS ASPECTS OF WEATHER WHICH PEOPLE NOTICE
blizzard, breeze, cloud, cyclone, deluge, dew, downpour, drizzle, drought, fog, frost, gale, hail, haze, heatwave, high or low temperatures, hoar frost, hurricane, ice, lightning, mist, rain, rainbow, shower, sleet, slush, snow, snowstorm, squall, storm, sunshine, tempest, thaw, thunder, tornado, typhoon, whirlwind, wind
WORDS USED TO DESCRIBE DIFFERENT KINDS OF WEATHER
autumnal, blustery, breezy, bright, chilly, clear, close, cloudless, cloudy, cold, drizzly, dry, dull, fair, fine, foggy, freezing, frosty, grey, hazy, hot, humid, icy, inclement, misty, overcast, pouring, rainy, rough, showery, slushy, snowy, springlike, squally, stormy, sultry, summery, sunless, sunny, sweltering, thundery, torrential, turbulent, wet, wild, windy, wintry

weather *VERB*
The ship weathered the storm.
▸ come through, endure, live through, survive, withstand

weave *VERB*
He managed to weave his way through the crowd.
▸ twist and turn, wind, wriggle, zigzag

web *NOUN*
The map was a web of criss-cross lines.
▸ mesh, net, network

wedding *NOUN*
She was a bridesmaid at her cousin's wedding.
▸ marriage
PEOPLE INVOLVED IN A WEDDING
best man, bride, bridegroom, bridesmaid, groom, maid or matron of honour, page, registrar, usher, wedding guests
OTHER WORDS TO DO WITH WEDDINGS
bouquet, ceremony, church service, confetti, honeymoon, reception or wedding breakfast, registry office, signing the register, trousseau, vows, wedding bells, wedding dress, wedding march, wedding ring

wedge *VERB*
Wedge the door open.
▸ jam, stick

weedy *ADJECTIVE*
1 *A weedy path led to the front door.*
▸ overgrown, untidy, unweeded, wild
2 (*insulting*) *A weedy little man opened the front door.*
▸ feeble, puny, thin

weep *VERB*
She buried her face in her hands and began to weep.
▸ cry, shed tears, sob
▹ To weep or cry in an annoying way is to **snivel** or **whimper**.

weigh *VERB*
to weigh someone down **1** *Her troubles weighed her down.*
▸ afflict, depress, sadden, worry
2 *She was weighed down with shopping.*
▸ load
to weigh something up *They weighed up the evidence.*
▸ assess, consider, evaluate, examine, give thought to, meditate on, ponder, study, think about

weight *NOUN*
Take care when lifting heavy weights.
▸ burden, load, mass
FOR UNITS OF WEIGHT SEE **measurement**

weighty *ADJECTIVE*
1 *He lifted a weighty volume off the shelf.*
▸ heavy, massive, ponderous
AN OPPOSITE IS light
2 *They had weighty matters to discuss.*
▸ important, major, pressing, serious, urgent
AN OPPOSITE IS unimportant

A B C D E F G H I J K L M N O P Q R S T U V W X Y Z

weird *ADJECTIVE*
1 *Weird shrieks were heard in the darkness.*
▸ creepy, eerie, ghostly, mysterious, (*informal*) scary, (*informal*) spooky, supernatural, uncanny, unearthly, unnatural
AN OPPOSITE IS natural
2 *Some of her clothes were a bit weird.*
▸ curious, extraordinary, (*informal*) funny, grotesque, odd, peculiar, queer, quirky, strange, unconventional, unusual
AN OPPOSITE IS ordinary

welcome *NOUN*
She gave us a friendly welcome.
▸ greeting, reception

welcome *ADJECTIVE*
1 *A cup of tea would be very welcome.*
▸ acceptable, agreeable, pleasant, pleasing
AN OPPOSITE IS unacceptable
2 *You're welcome to use my bike.*
▸ allowed, free, permitted
AN OPPOSITE IS forbidden

welcome *VERB*
1 *She welcomed us at the door.*
▸ greet, receive, say hello to
2 *The company welcomes customers' comments.*
▸ accept, appreciate, approve of, like, want

weld *VERB*
Panels of steel are welded together to form the body of the car.
▸ fix, fuse, join, solder

welfare *NOUN*
Her only concern was the welfare of her children.
▸ happiness, health, interests, well-being

well *NOUN*
PLACES WHERE YOU GET WATER OR OIL OUT OF THE GROUND
artesian well, borehole, geyser, gusher, oasis, oil well, shaft, spring, waterhole, wishing-well

well *ADVERB*
1 *The whole team played well.*
▸ admirably, effectively, efficiently, expertly, marvellously, satisfactorily, skilfully, successfully, wonderfully
AN OPPOSITE IS badly
2 *It was a difficult job but they paid him well.*
▸ fairly, generously, properly, reasonably, suitably
3 *I know her well.*
▸ closely, intimately, personally

well *ADJECTIVE*
You look well.
▸ fit, healthy, hearty, in good health, lively, robust, sound, strong, thriving, vigorous
AN OPPOSITE IS ill

well-known *ADJECTIVE*
A well-known television personality opened the new shop.
▸ celebrated, distinguished, eminent, famous, notable, outstanding, prominent, renowned
AN OPPOSITE IS unknown

well-mannered *ADJECTIVE*
They were well-mannered and eager to please.
▸ civil, considerate, courteous, polite, respectful, tactful
AN OPPOSITE IS rude

west *NOUN, ADJECTIVE, ADVERB*
▹ The parts of a continent or country in the west are the **western** parts. People from countries west of the oriental countries — especially from Europe and N. America — are called **westerners**. To travel towards the west is to travel **westward** or **westwards**. A wind from the west is a **westerly** wind.

wet *ADJECTIVE*
1 *She took off her wet clothes and had a hot bath.*
▸ clammy, damp, drenched, dripping, moist, soaked, sopping, wringing wet
2 *The field's wet, so we can't play.*
▸ dewy, muddy, saturated, soaking, soggy, submerged, waterlogged, watery
3 *Take care — the paint is still wet.*
▸ runny, sticky, tacky
4 *It was a miserable, wet day.*
▸ drizzly, misty, pouring, rainy, showery
AN OPPOSITE IS dry

wet *VERB*
Wet the clay before you start to mould it.
▸ dampen, moisten, soak, water
AN OPPOSITE IS dry

wheel *NOUN*
▹ A small wheel under a piece of furniture is a **caster**. A set of wheels under one end of a railway carriage is a **bogie**. The centre of a wheel is the **hub**. The outer edge of a wheel is the **rim**.

wheel *VERB*
1 *Gulls wheeled overhead.*
► circle, move in circles
2 *The column of soldiers wheeled to the right.*
► change direction, swerve, swing round, turn, veer

wheeze *VERB*
He was coughing and wheezing all night.
► breathe noisily, cough, gasp, pant, puff

whiff *NOUN*
As she walked by, he caught a whiff of her perfume.
► hint, puff, smell

while *NOUN*
I waited for a while.
► period, spell, time

whimper, whine *VERBS*
The dog whimpered in the corner of the room.
► cry, moan

whip *VERB*
1 *They whipped the horse with a leather belt.*
► beat, cane, flog, hit, lash, thrash
VARIOUS INSTRUMENTS USED FOR WHIPPING
birch, cane, cat, cat-o'-nine-tails, crop, horsewhip, lash, riding crop, scourge, switch, whip
2 *Whip the cream until it is thick.*
► beat, stir vigorously, whisk

whirl *VERB*
The snowflakes whirled in the icy wind.
► circle, reel, revolve, rotate, spin, turn, twirl, twist

whisk *VERB*
Whisk the egg yolks together in a bowl.
► beat, mix, stir, whip

whiskers *PLURAL NOUN*
He had long whiskers on his face.
► bristles, hairs, a moustache

whisper *VERB*
What are you two whispering about?
► murmur, speak softly

whistle *VERB*
FOR VARIOUS WAYS TO MAKE SOUNDS SEE **sound** *VERB*

white *ADJECTIVE & NOUN*
SHADES OF WHITE
cream, ivory, off-white, platinum, silvery, snow-white, whitish
▷ When coloured things become whiter they become bleached or faded or pale.

whole *ADJECTIVE*
1 *She told us the whole story.*
► complete, entire, full, total, unabbreviated
AN OPPOSITE IS incomplete
2 *Much of the building was damaged, but the front wall remained whole.*
► in one piece, intact, perfect, sound, unbroken, undamaged, unharmed
AN OPPOSITE IS broken or in pieces

wholesale *ADJECTIVE*
The storm caused wholesale destruction.
► complete, comprehensive, extensive, general, total, universal, widespread
▷ Something which affects the whole world is global or worldwide.

wholesome *ADJECTIVE*
The food was plentiful and wholesome.
► good, healthy, nourishing, nutritious
AN OPPOSITE IS unhealthy

wicked *ADJECTIVE*
1 *He is a wicked, cruel man.*
► corrupt, evil, immoral, perverted, sinful, vicious, villainous
▷ People who are not seriously wicked are mischievous or naughty.
2 *It was a wicked attack on a defenceless woman.*
► bad, cruel, diabolical, dreadful, fiendish, foul, malevolent, malicious, scandalous, shameful, spiteful, terrible, vile, wrong
AN OPPOSITE IS virtuous

wide *ADJECTIVE*
1 *The cottage was not far from the wide sandy beach.*
► broad, expansive, extensive, large
AN OPPOSITE IS narrow
2 *She has a wide knowledge of classical music.*
► comprehensive, encyclopedic, vast, wide-ranging
AN OPPOSITE IS limited

widely ADVERB
The story of Cinderella is widely known.
▸ commonly, everywhere, far and wide

widespread ADJECTIVE
After the drought famine was widespread.
▸ common, extensive, general, prevalent, universal
▹ Something which spreads over the whole world is **global** or **worldwide**.
AN OPPOSITE IS uncommon

width NOUN
The room is about eight feet in width.
▸ breadth
▹ The distance across a circle is its **diameter**.

wield VERB
The lumberjack was wielding his axe.
▸ brandish, flourish, hold, use

wild ADJECTIVE
1 *She didn't like seeing wild animals in captivity.*
▸ undomesticated, untamed
AN OPPOSITE IS tame
2 *The hedgerow was full of wild flowers.*
▸ natural, uncultivated
AN OPPOSITE IS cultivated
3 *It's a wild, mountainous region.*
▸ deserted, desolate, rough, rugged, uncultivated, waste
AN OPPOSITE IS cultivated
VARIOUS AREAS OF WILD COUNTRY
(*informal*) barren wastes, the bush, desert, heath, jungle, marsh, moorland, wasteland, wilderness, (*informal*) the wilds
4 *The crowd were wild with excitement.*
▸ aggressive, boisterous, disorderly, excited, hysterical, noisy, out of control, rash, reckless, riotous, rowdy, uncontrollable, uncontrolled, unruly, violent
AN OPPOSITE IS gentle or restrained
5 *Outside, a wild wind was blowing.*
▸ blustery, stormy, tempestuous, turbulent, windy
AN OPPOSITE IS calm

wilful ADJECTIVE
1 *He's a very wilful child.*
▸ determined, obstinate, stubborn
2 *She told him off for wilful disobedience.*
▸ conscious, deliberate, intentional, planned

will NOUN
He seemed to have lost the will to win.
▸ aim, desire, determination, intention, purpose, resolution, will-power, wish

willing ADJECTIVE
1 *I'm willing to help.*
▸ eager, happy, pleased, prepared, ready
2 *The task will be a lot easier if you can find a couple of willing helpers.*
▸ cooperative, enthusiastic, helpful, obliging
AN OPPOSITE IS unwilling

wilt VERB
The plants wilted in the heat.
▸ become limp, droop, fade, flop, shrivel, wither
AN OPPOSITE IS flourish

wily ADJECTIVE
He was constantly outwitted by his wily opponents.
▸ artful, clever, crafty, cunning, deceitful, devious, furtive, scheming, sly, (*informal*) sneaky, tricky

win VERB
1 *Who do you think will win?*
▸ be successful or victorious, come first, prevail, succeed, triumph
▹ To win against someone is also to **beat**, **conquer**, **defeat** or **overcome** them.
AN OPPOSITE IS lose
2 *She won first prize in the poetry competition.*
▸ gain, get, obtain, (*informal*) pick up, receive, secure

wind NOUN
▹ A gentle wind is a **breath**, **breeze**, or **draught**. A violent wind is a **cyclone**, **gale**, **hurricane**, or **tornado**. A sudden unexpected wind is a **blast**, **gust**, **puff**, or **squall**.
wind instruments
FOR MUSICAL INSTRUMENTS PLAYED BY BLOWING SEE **music**

wind VERB
1 *He wound the line on to a reel.*
▸ coil, curl, curve, loop, roll, turn
2 *The road winds up the hill.*
▸ bend, curve, meander, ramble, twist and turn, zigzag

window *NOUN*
KINDS OF WINDOW
casement, dormer, double-glazed window, fanlight, French window, pane, sash window, shop window, skylight, stained-glass window, windscreen

windy *ADJECTIVE*
1 *It was a cold, windy day.*
▸ blustery, breezy, gusty, squally, stormy
AN OPPOSITE IS calm
2 *This spot is too windy for a picnic.*
▸ bare, bleak, exposed
AN OPPOSITE IS sheltered

wine *NOUN*
FOR VARIOUS DRINKS SEE **drink**

wink *VERB*
1 *He winked at me.*
▹ To shut and open both eyes quickly is to **blink**.
2 *The lights winked on and off.*
▸ flash, flicker, sparkle, twinkle

winner *NOUN*
The winner was presented with a silver trophy.
▸ champion, conqueror, medallist, victor
AN OPPOSITE IS loser

winning *ADJECTIVE*
The winning team went up to receive their medals.
▸ champion, conquering, first, leading, successful, top, triumphant, unbeaten, undefeated, victorious
AN OPPOSITE IS losing

wintry *ADJECTIVE*
It was a grey, wintry day.
▸ arctic, bitter, cold, freezing, frosty, icy, snowy

wipe *VERB*
I wiped the table with a cloth.
▸ dry, dust, mop, polish, rub
to wipe something out *Whole villages were wiped out by the plague in the Middle Ages.*
▸ annihilate, destroy, exterminate, get rid of, kill

wire *NOUN*
▹ A wire to carry electric current is **cable** or **flex** or **a lead**. The system of electric wires in a building is the **wiring**.

wiry *ADJECTIVE*
His body was wiry and athletic.
▸ lean, strong, thin, tough
AN OPPOSITE IS flabby

wisdom *NOUN*
She's a woman of great wisdom.
▸ cleverness, common sense, good sense, insight, intelligence, judgement, prudence, reason, sense, understanding

wise *ADJECTIVE*
1 *He's a very wise man.*
▸ clever, intelligent, knowledgeable, perceptive, prudent, rational, reasonable, sensible, shrewd, thoughtful, well-informed
2 *I think you made a wise decision.*
▸ appropriate, fair, just, proper, right, sound
AN OPPOSITE IS foolish

wish *NOUN*
Her dearest wish was to have a family of her own one day.
▸ ambition, craving, desire, fancy, hope, longing, request, urge, want, yearning, (*informal*) yen

wish *VERB*
I wish they'd be quiet.
▹ If we wish something would happen, we can say that we **would like** it, or we **want** it to happen.
to wish for *It's no use wishing for things you can't have.*
▸ crave, desire, fancy, hanker after, long for, want, yearn for

wisp *NOUN*
She brushed a wisp of hair away from her eyes.
▸ shred, strand

wispy *ADJECTIVE*
The moon was partly hidden behind some wispy clouds.
▸ feathery, fluffy, light, soft, woolly

wistful *ADJECTIVE*
Her voice trailed off and she looked wistful.
▸ nostalgic, sad

wit *NOUN*

1 *He didn't have the wit to realize what she meant.*

▸ brains, cleverness, intelligence, quickness, sharpness, understanding

2 *His sharp wit had them all laughing.*

▸ comedy, humour, jokes, puns

3 *He was a great wit and an entertaining storyteller.*

▸ comedian, comic, joker

witchcraft *NOUN*

She didn't believe in the power of witchcraft.

▸ black magic, charms, sorcery, spells, wizardry

withdraw *VERB*

1 *The general withdrew his troops.*

▸ call back, pull out, recall

AN OPPOSITE IS send in

2 *She withdrew her offer.*

▸ cancel, take back

AN OPPOSITE IS make or present

3 *The attackers withdrew.*

▸ back away, draw back, fall back, leave, move back, retire, retreat, run away

AN OPPOSITE IS advance

4 *Some competitors withdrew at the last minute.*

▸ back out, drop out, pull out

AN OPPOSITE IS enter

wither *VERB*

The flowers had withered and died.

▸ become dry or limp, droop, dry up, flag, flop, shrink, shrivel, waste away, wilt

AN OPPOSITE IS flourish

withhold *VERB*

He was accused of withholding information from the police.

▸ hold back, keep back, refuse

AN OPPOSITE IS grant

withstand *VERB*

These desert plants are able to withstand extremes of temperature.

▸ bear, cope with, endure, hold out against, resist, stand up to, survive, tolerate, weather

witness *NOUN*

A witness said that the car was going too fast.

▸ bystander, eyewitness, looker-on, observer, onlooker, spectator

witty *ADJECTIVE*

He made several witty remarks about the situation.

▸ amusing, clever, comic, funny, humorous, quick-witted

AN OPPOSITE IS dull

wizard *NOUN*

1 *Suddenly everyone froze, as if a wizard had cast a spell over them.*

▸ magician, sorcerer

2 *He's a wizard with computers.*

▸ clever person, expert, specialist

wobble *VERB*

1 *The cyclist wobbled all over the road.*

▸ move unsteadily, sway, totter, waver

2 *The pile of bricks wobbled and fell over.*

▸ quake, quiver, rock, shake, tremble

wobbly *ADJECTIVE*

1 *She's still a bit wobbly on her legs after her illness.*

▸ insecure, shaky, unsafe, unsteady

2 *This table is a bit wobbly.*

▸ loose, rickety, unstable

AN OPPOSITE IS steady

woeful *ADJECTIVE*

He had such a woeful look on his face.

▸ dejected, gloomy, melancholy, miserable, mournful, sad, sorrowful, sorry, unhappy, wretched

AN OPPOSITE IS cheerful

woman *NOUN*

▹ A polite word for a woman is **lady**. A married woman is a **wife**. A woman who has children is a **mother**. A woman who stays at home to look after the house is a **housewife**. An unmarried woman is a **spinster**. A woman whose husband has died is a **widow**. A woman on her wedding day is a **bride**. A woman who is engaged to be married is a **fiancée**. A woman who is going out with a man is his **girlfriend**. A man who plays the part of a woman in a pantomime is the **dame**. Words for a young woman are **girl**, **lass**. Old words for a young woman are **maid**, **maiden**.

wonder *NOUN*

1 *The sight of the Taj Mahal filled them with wonder.*

▸ admiration, amazement, astonishment, awe, reverence, surprise

2 *It's a wonder that she recovered.*

▸ marvel, miracle

wonder *VERB*
I wonder why she left in such a hurry.
▸ ask yourself, be curious about, ponder, question yourself, think
to wonder at *People wondered at his bravery.*
▸ admire, be amazed or astonished by, marvel at

wonderful *ADJECTIVE*
1 *It's wonderful what doctors can do these days.*
▸ amazing, astonishing, astounding, extraordinary, incredible, marvellous, miraculous, phenomenal, remarkable, surprising, unexpected
2 *It was a wonderful party.*
▸ excellent, exceptional, magnificent, splendid, superb
▸ (*informal synonyms*) brilliant, fabulous, fantastic, great, terrific, tremendous
AN OPPOSITE IS ordinary

wood *NOUN*
1 *The garden shed was made of wood.*
▸ timber
VARIOUS FORMS OF TIMBER
beams, boards or boarding, deal, hardwood, laths, logs, lumber, planks or planking, posts, softwood, stakes, tree trunks
KINDS OF WOOD OFTEN USED TO MAKE THINGS
balsa, beech, cedar, chestnut, ebony, elm, mahogany, oak, pine, rosewood, sandalwood, teak, walnut
MANUFACTURED KINDS OF WOOD
blockboard, chipboard, hardboard, plywood
2 *We walked through the wood.*
▸ trees, woodland, woods
▹ Planting an area with trees is afforestation.

wooded *ADJECTIVE*
Many birds prefer to live in wooded areas.
▸ tree-covered, woody
DIFFERENT KINDS OF WOODED AREA
coppice, copse, covert, forest, grove, jungle, orchard, plantation, spinney, thicket, wood

wooden *ADJECTIVE*
1 *They sat down on a wooden bench.*
▸ timber, wood
2 *The acting was a bit wooden.*
▸ awkward, emotionless, expressionless, lifeless, stiff, unemotional, unnatural

woodwind *NOUN*
FOR MUSICAL INSTRUMENTS SEE **music**

woodwork *NOUN*
He went to evening classes to learn how to do woodwork.
▸ carpentry, joinery

woolly *ADJECTIVE*
1 *She wore a thick woolly jumper.*
▸ wool, woollen
2 *The animal had a woolly coat.*
▸ cuddly, downy, fleecy, furry, fuzzy, hairy, soft
3 *His ideas were rather woolly.*
▸ confused, hazy, indefinite, uncertain, unclear, unfocused, vague

word *NOUN*
1 *What's the Spanish word for 'table'?*
▸ expression, term
▹ All the words we know are our vocabulary.
IN DICTIONARIES, WORDS ARE CLASSIFIED ACCORDING TO THE JOB THEY DO
adjective, adverb, conjunction, exclamation or interjection, noun, preposition, pronoun, verb
▹ A word or part of a word that has one separate sound when you say it is a syllable. Syllables that you add to the beginning of a word to change its meaning are prefixes. Syllables that you add to the end of a word to change its meaning or function are suffixes. The main part of a word to which endings like -ing or -ed can be added is the stem.
2 *You gave me your word.*
▸ assurance, guarantee, pledge, promise, vow
3 *There has been no word from him for several weeks.*
▸ information, message, news

word *VERB*
She spent ages thinking how to word the letter.
▸ express, phrase, put into words

wording *NOUN*
The wording of the question was not precise.
▸ choice of words, language, phrasing, style

work *NOUN*
1 *Digging the garden involves a lot of hard work.*
▸ effort, exertion, labour, toil
2 *He set the class some work.*
▸ an assignment, a chore, homework, housework, a job, a project, a task, an undertaking

A B C D E F G H I J K L M N O P Q R S T U V **W** X Y Z

3 *What kind of work does he do?*
▸ business, employment, job, occupation, profession, trade, vocation
FOR VARIOUS KINDS OF WORK SEE **job**

work *VERB*
1 *He'd been working in the garden all morning.*
▸ be busy, exert yourself, make efforts, slave, toil
2 *She works in the local department store.*
▸ be employed, earn your living, go to work, have a job
3 *My watch isn't working.*
▸ be effective, function, go, operate
4 *This video recorder is easy to work.*
▸ deal with, manage, operate, run, use
to work something out *I can't work this problem out.*
▸ answer, calculate, explain, find the solution to, solve

workable *ADJECTIVE*
Her plan isn't workable.
▸ feasible, possible, practicable, practical, realistic
AN OPPOSITE IS impracticable

worker *NOUN*
Local government workers went on strike.
▸ employee
▹ All the workers in a business or factory are the staff or workforce.
PEOPLE WHO DO VARIOUS TYPES OF WORK
businessman or businesswoman, craftsman, executive, labourer, manager, operative, operator, servant, skilled worker, tradesman, unskilled worker, workman
FOR WORKERS DOING SPECIFIC JOBS SEE **job**

workmanship *NOUN*
The car is a wonderful example of British workmanship.
▸ art, competence, craft, craftsmanship, expertise, handicraft, handiwork, skill, technique

world *NOUN*
1 *Scotland is a very beautiful part of the world.*
▸ earth, globe
2 *Scientists are still not certain if there's life on other worlds.*
▸ planet

worldly *ADJECTIVE*
He had no interest in worldly success or power.
▸ earthly, materialistic, mundane, physical
AN OPPOSITE IS spiritual

worm *VERB*
He wormed through the undergrowth.
▸ crawl, creep, slither, squirm, wriggle, writhe

worried *ADJECTIVE*
He had a worried expression.
▸ agitated, anxious, apprehensive, bewildered, bothered, concerned, distressed, disturbed, edgy, fearful, nervous, perplexed, puzzled, tense, troubled, uneasy, unhappy, upset
AN OPPOSITE IS relaxed

worry *VERB*
1 *There's no need to worry.*
▸ be anxious or worried, brood, fret
2 *It worried her that he hadn't replied to her letter.*
▸ bewilder, disturb, mystify, perplex, puzzle, trouble, upset
3 *Don't worry her now — she's busy.*
▸ annoy, (*informal*) badger, bother, harass, irritate, nag, pester, tease, torment, vex

worry *NOUN*
1 *He's been a constant source of worry to her.*
▸ anxiety, distress, fear, tension, uneasiness, vexation
2 *She has a lot of financial worries at the moment.*
▸ burden, care, concern, problem, trouble

worsen *VERB*
1 *Complaining may only worsen the situation.*
▸ aggravate, make worse
2 *The patient's condition worsened during the night.*
▸ become worse, degenerate, deteriorate, get worse
AN OPPOSITE IS improve

worship *VERB*
1 *People go to church to worship God.*
▸ glorify, praise, pray to
VARIOUS PLACES WHERE PEOPLE WORSHIP
abbey, basilica, cathedral, chapel, church, meeting house, minster, mosque, oratory, pagoda, sanctuary, synagogue, tabernacle, temple
2 *She adores her sons and they worship her.*
▸ adore, be devoted to, idolize, look up to, love, revere

worship *NOUN*
The priests led the congregation.
▶ adoration, devotion, glorification, praise, prayer
▷ Your worship of God or gods is your faith or **religion**. The worship of idols is **idolatry**.

worth *NOUN*
This artist's paintings are of lasting worth.
▶ importance, merit, quality, significance, value
to be worth something *How much is the ring worth?*
▶ be priced at, cost, have a value of

worthless *ADJECTIVE*
It's nothing but a worthless piece of junk.
▶ (*informal*) trashy, unusable, useless, valueless
AN OPPOSITE IS valuable

worthwhile *ADJECTIVE*
It might be worthwhile to get a second opinion.
▶ beneficial, helpful, important, profitable, useful, valuable
AN OPPOSITE IS useless

worthy *ADJECTIVE*
They gave the money to a worthy cause.
▶ admirable, commendable, deserving, good, honest, praiseworthy, respectable, worthwhile
AN OPPOSITE IS unworthy

wound *NOUN*
Soldiers returned from the war with dreadful wounds.
▶ injury
KINDS OF WOUND
amputation, bite, bruise, burn, cut, fracture, gash, graze, laceration, scab, scald, scar, scratch, sore, sprain, sting, strain

wound *VERB*
Seven people were seriously wounded in the attack.
▶ harm, hurt, injure
WAYS PEOPLE, THINGS, OR ANIMALS CAN WOUND YOU
bite, blow up, bruise, burn, claw, crush, cut, fracture bones, gash, gore, graze, hit, impale, knife, lacerate, maim, mangle, maul, mutilate, scald, scratch, shoot, sprain, stab, sting, strain, torture

wrap *VERB*
1 *She wrapped the presents in shiny gold paper.*
▶ bind up, cover, pack
▷ To wrap water pipes, etc., is to **insulate** or **lag** them.
2 *The mountain was wrapped in mist.*
▶ cloak, conceal, envelop, hide, shroud, surround

wreathe *VERB*
The altar was wreathed in flowers.
▶ adorn, decorate, encircle, festoon, surround

wreck *VERB*
1 *His car was wrecked in the accident.*
▶ break up, crumple, crush, demolish, destroy, shatter, smash, write off
2 *The injury wrecked his chances of a professional football career.*
▶ ruin, spoil

wreckage *NOUN*
Investigators sifted through the wreckage of the aircraft.
▶ bits, debris, fragments, pieces, remains
▷ The wreckage of a building is **rubble** or **ruins**.

wrench *VERB*
He wrenched the door open.
▶ force, jerk, prise, pull, strain, tug, twist, (*informal*) yank

wrestle *VERB*
1 *He wrestled with the intruders.*
▶ grapple, struggle, tussle
SEE ALSO **fight** *VERB*
2 *I wrestled with my maths for hours.*
▶ try to solve, worry over

wretched *ADJECTIVE*
1 *She lay in bed with a migraine feeling absolutely wretched.*
▶ dejected, depressed, miserable, pitiful, unfortunate, unhappy, woeful
2 *The wretched car won't start!*
▶ annoying, exasperating, maddening, tiresome, useless

wriggle *VERB*
The snake wriggled away.
▶ squirm, twist, worm, writhe, zigzag

wring *VERB*
1 *He wrung the water out of his shirt.*
▸ press, squeeze, twist
2 *He wrung her hand enthusiastically.*
▸ clasp, grip, shake, wrench
wringing wet *My towel is wringing wet.*
▸ drenched, dripping, saturated, soaked, sopping

wrinkle *NOUN*
His face was covered in wrinkles.
▸ crease, crinkle, fold, furrow, line, ridge
▹ A small hollow on someone's skin is a **dimple**.

wrinkle *VERB*
Someone will trip over if you wrinkle the rug.
▸ crease, crinkle, crumple, fold, make wrinkles in, pucker up
AN OPPOSITE IS smooth

write *VERB*
1 *I'll write a shopping list.*
▸ compile, compose, draw up, jot down, note, print, scrawl, scribble, set down, take down
▹ To write letters to people is to **correspond** with them. To write a rough version of a story, etc., is to **draft** it. To write on a document or surface is to **inscribe** it.
2 *She decided at an early age that she wanted to write for a living.*
▸ be an author
THINGS YOU WRITE WITH
ballpoint, biro, chalk, crayon, felt tip, fountain pen, ink pen, pencil, typewriter, word processor
THINGS YOU WRITE ON
blackboard or chalkboard, card, exercise book, form, jotter, notepaper, pad, paper, parchment, postcard, stationery, whiteboard, writing paper

writer *NOUN*
▹ A person who writes books is an **author**, **biographer**, or **novelist**. A person who writes plays, films, etc., is a **dramatist**, **playwright**, or **scriptwriter**. A person who writes for newspapers is a **correspondent**, **journalist**, or **reporter**. A person who writes poetry is a **poet**. A person who writes music is a **composer**.

writhe *VERB*
He was writhing in agony.
▸ squirm, thrash about, twist, wriggle

writing *NOUN*
1 *Can you read his writing?*
▸ handwriting
▹ Untidy writing is **scrawl** or **scribble**. Neat writing is **copperplate**. The art of beautiful handwriting is **calligraphy**.
2 *The writing on the stone was very faint.*
▸ inscription
3 (*often plural*) *He introduced her to the writings of Charles Dickens.*
▸ literature, works
KINDS OF LITERATURE
autobiography, biography, children's story, comedy, crime or detective story, diary, drama or play, essay, fable, fairy story or fairy tale, fantasy, fiction, film or TV script, folk tale, history, journalism, legend, letters or correspondence, lyrics, myth, newspaper article, non-fiction, novel, parody, philosophy, poetry or verse, prose, romance, satire, science fiction or SF, thriller, tragedy, travel writing

wrong *ADJECTIVE*
1 *It is wrong to steal.*
▸ corrupt, criminal, (*informal*) crooked, deceitful, dishonest, evil, illegal, immoral, irresponsible, naughty, sinful, unfair, unjust, unlawful, wicked
2 *His calculations were wrong.*
▸ inaccurate, incorrect, mistaken, unacceptable
3 *Did I say the wrong thing?*
▸ improper, inappropriate, unconventional, unsuitable
4 *There's something wrong with the car.*
▸ defective, faulty, not working, out of order
AN OPPOSITE IS right

wrong *NOUN*
to do wrong *He has done wrong and must be punished.*
▸ behave badly, be naughty, break the law, misbehave, offend, sin

wrong *VERB*
He felt that he'd been wronged.
▸ harm, hurt, treat unfairly

wry *ADJECTIVE*
1 *He gave me a wry smile.*
▸ crooked, distorted, twisted
2 *She has a wry sense of humour.*
▸ dry, ironic, mocking, sarcastic

X-ray *NOUN*
▷ Taking X-ray pictures is radiography. Medical treatment using X-rays is radiotherapy.

yacht *NOUN*
FOR VARIOUS KINDS OF BOAT SEE **vessel**

yard *NOUN*
WORDS FOR PIECES OF GROUND BESIDE OR SURROUNDED BY BUILDINGS
cloister, court, courtyard, enclosure, farmyard, garden, parking space, patio, precinct, quadrangle or (*informal*) quad

yearly *ADJECTIVE*
The car is due for its yearly service.
► annual

yearn *VERB*
to yearn for something *She yearned for some peace and quiet!*
► (*informal*) be dying for, desire, long for, pine for, want, wish for

yell *VERB*
I yelled to attract her attention.
► bawl, bellow, call out, cry out, shout

yellow *ADJECTIVE & NOUN*
VARIOUS SHADES OF YELLOW
amber, chrome yellow, cream, gold, golden, lemon, tawny

yield *VERB*
1 *The government refused to yield to the hijackers' demands.*
► admit defeat, give in, submit, surrender
2 *Drivers must yield to vehicles on the main road.*
► give way
3 *The apple trees yielded a good crop of fruit.*
► bear, grow, produce, supply
4 *This savings account yields a high interest.*
► earn, pay out, provide

yield *NOUN*
1 *They got a good yield from the orchard this year.*
► crop, harvest, produce
2 *Investors get an annual yield of 10%.*
► earnings, income, interest, profit

young *ADJECTIVE*
1 *A lot of young people went to the concert.*
► juvenile, youngish, youthful
2 (*sometimes insulting*) *She's rather young for her age.*
► babyish, childish, immature, infantile
YOUNG PEOPLE
adolescent, baby, boy, child, girl, infant, juvenile, (*informal*) kid, lad, lass, teenager, toddler, youngster, youth
YOUNG ANIMALS
▷ A young animal is a baby. A young cow: calf, heifer. A young horse: colt, foal. A young fox, wolf, etc.: cub. A young deer: fawn. A young goat: kid. A young cat: kitten. A young sheep: lamb. A young hare: leveret. A young pig: piglet. A young dog: pup or puppy.
YOUNG BIRDS
▷ A young bird is a chick, fledgling, or nestling. A young swan: cygnet. A young duck: duckling. A young goose: gosling. A young farmyard hen: pullet.
YOUNG FISH
▷ Young fish are fry. A young eel: elver. A young salmon: grilse.
YOUNG PLANTS
▷ A young plant is a cutting or seedling. A young tree: sapling.

young *PLURAL NOUN*
The female bird feeds its young until they are able to leave the nest.
► children, family, offspring, young ones
▷ A family of young birds is a brood. A family of young cats, dogs, etc., is a litter.

youth *NOUN*
1 *In her youth, she had been a keen tennis player.*
► adolescence, childhood, teens
2 *The fight had been started by a group of youths.*
When you use it like this, the noun *youth* usually refers to boys rather than girls
► adolescent, juvenile, (*informal*) kid, (*informal*) lad, teenager, young man, youngster

A B C D E F G H I J K L M N O P Q R S T U V W X Y Z

youthful *ADJECTIVE*
1 *It's a popular radio station with a big, youthful audience.*
▶ juvenile, young, youngish
2 *She has a very youthful appearance.*
▶ fresh, lively, sprightly, vigorous, young-looking

Zz

zany *ADJECTIVE*
The audience laughed at his zany humour.
▶ absurd, crazy, daft, eccentric, funny, ludicrous, ridiculous, silly

zealous *ADJECTIVE*
The council was extremely zealous in enforcing the new regulations.
▶ conscientious, eager, enthusiastic, fervent, keen
AN OPPOSITE IS apathetic

zero *NOUN*
Four minus four makes zero.
▶ nothing, nought
▷ A score of zero in football is **nil**, in cricket it is a **duck**, in tennis it is **love**.

zest *NOUN*
She has a great zest for life.
▶ eagerness, enjoyment, enthusiasm

zigzag *VERB*
The road zigzags up the hill.
▶ bend, meander, twist, wind
▷ When a sailing boat zigzags to make use of the wind, it **tacks**.

zodiac *NOUN*
THE SIGNS OF THE ZODIAC
Aquarius [*THE WATER-CARRIER*], Aries [*THE RAM*], Cancer [*THE CRAB*], Capricorn [*THE GOAT*], Gemini [*THE TWINS*], Leo [*THE LION*], Libra [*THE SCALES*], Pisces [*THE FISH*], Sagittarius [*THE ARCHER*], Scorpio [*THE SCORPION*], Taurus [*THE BULL*], Virgo [*THE VIRGIN*]

zone *NOUN*
No one may enter the forbidden zone.
▶ area, district, locality, neighbourhood, region, sector, territory, vicinity

zoo *NOUN*
Which is your favourite animal in the zoo?
▶ menagerie, safari park, zoological gardens
FOR ANIMALS YOU MIGHT SEE IN A ZOO SEE **animal**

zoom *VERB*
(*informal*) *Cars zoomed along the motorway.*
▶ dash, hurry, hurtle, race, rush, speed, tear, (*informal*) whizz, (*informal*) zip

Supplement

Help with punctuation

These are the punctuation marks that will make your writing easier to understand:

apostrophe	’	Use an apostrophe to show that a letter has been left out of a word for example, *don’t*, or to show belonging, for example, *the cat’s tail*.
brackets	( )	You use brackets around things that are interesting but not necessary, for example, *the cat’s tail (which was black and very long)* was caught in the door.
colon	:	You use a colon when you have a list of things coming after a heading.You also use a colon in a sentence when you have examples to list, for example, *I got a lot of birthday presents: a camera, a chess set, a skateboard, a jacket and an ink pen*. A colon is also used when you have two sentences and the second sentence explains what is meant in the first, for example, *the cat is in trouble again: it is stuck in the tree*.
comma	,	You use a comma to show a small break in a sentence.
dash	–	Dashes are useful to show an interruption or bigger break in a sentence.
exclamation mark	!	An exclamation mark shows surprise or urgency.
full stop	.	A full stop is used at the end of a sentence.
hyphen	-	A hyphen joins words or parts of words together, for example, *hard-boiled*.
question mark	?	A question mark shows a question is being asked.
semi-colon	;	You use a semi-colon to show more of a break than a comma.
speech marks	‘ ’	You use these to around the words that a person speaks, for example, ‘*You are in the team,*’ *said Miss Johnson*.

Word classes (parts of speech)

There are eight word classes, or parts of speech:

Adjective	An **adjective** is a word which describes a noun and tells you what something is like, for example how big it is, how old it is, what colour it is, what it looks like and feels like. In the phrase, *a big, colourful rainbow, big* and *colourful* are adjectives. Many adjectives can be used to compare things - they have two forms: **comparative** and **superlative**. You use the comparative form such as *bigger* or *smaller* and superlative form such as *biggest* or *smallest* to compare different things. The comparative and superlative form is often made by adding *-er* and *-est* to the adjective. This does not work for some adjectives such as *dangerous*. To create the comparative form you would need to use *more colourful* or *most colourful*.
Adverb	An **adverb** is a word which tells you how, when, or where something happens. Some adverbs tell you how someone does something, for example *quickly, slowly, carefully* and *lazily*.
Conjunction	A **conjunction** is a word which joins words or ideas. *And* or *but* are conjunctions.
Interjection or exclamation	Words like *Hello!* or *Well!* are **exclamations**.
Noun	A **noun** is the name of a person, thing or idea. *House* and *gift* are nouns. **Proper nouns** are the names of particular places, persons or things. Nouns can be **countable**, for example, *girl* and *car*. You can say *three girls* and *four cars*. They can also be **uncountable**, for example, *grass* or *butter*. You cannot say *two grasses* or *three butters*. **Abstract nouns** are those things that you can't see or touch such as *air*, *happiness* or *luck.* **Collective nouns** are words for groups or sets of things e.g. a *herd* of cattle, a *flock* of sheep.

	Plural nouns are nouns that do not have a singular form e.g. *trousers.*
Preposition	**Prepositions** are words that give information on the position of things e.g. *on, under, behind, at*. In the phrases, *across the drive*, or *under the car*, *across* and *under* are prepositions.
Pronoun	A **pronoun** is a word which you use instead of a noun. For example, instead of saying *The dog ran away*, you can say *It ran away*, and instead of saying *I like my teacher*, you san say *I like her.*
	Personal pronouns are *you, me, I, he, him, she, her, it*. The plurals of these personal pronouns are *you, we, us, you, they, them.*
	Possessive pronouns show who something belongs to e.g. *my, your, his, her, its, our, their* and *mine, yours, hers, ours, theirs*. Other pronouns such as *who, what, some, which* and *whose* are for asking questions.
Verb	A **verb** is a doing word which shows what someone does or what happens. In the sentence *Jo ran home,* and *the rain stopped*, *ran* and *stopped* are verbs.

Using prefixes

prefix	meaning	examples
aero-	to do with air or aircraft	*aerobatics*
anti-	against or opposite	*antifreeze*. If the word you are adding *anti-* to begins with a vowel, you use a hyphen, e.g. *anti-aircraft*
audio-	to do with sound or hearing	*audio-visual*
auto-	self	*autobiography, automatic*
bi-	two	*bicycle, bilateral*
bio-	life	*biology, biography*
co-	together with someone else	*co-pilot, co-author, cooperate, coordinate*
counter-	opposite	*counterproductive, counter-claim, counterbalance*
cross-	across	*crossroads, crosswinds, cross-curricular*
de-	to take something away	*debug, de-ice, defrost*
dis-	opposite	*dislike, disagree, disobey*
e-	electronic	*email, e-shopping*
ex-	in the past	*ex-policeman, ex-president*
geo-	earth	*geography, geology*
in- (also im-)	opposite, not	*incorrect, insane, impossible, impolite*
micro-	small	*microchip, micro-organism*
mid-	in the middle	*midday, midnight, midsummer*
mini-	very small	*minibus, miniskirt*
mis-	badly or wrongly	*misbehave, misspell*
multi-	many	*multicoloured, multicultural*
non-	not	*non-existent, non-fiction, non-stop*
over-	too much	*overactive, oversleep*
photo-	light	*photocopy, photograph*
pre-	before	*prefabricated*, *pre-school*

re-	again	*rebuild, re-cover, re-enter, reheat*
semi-	half	*semicircle, semi-final, semi-detached*
sub-	under	*submarine, subway*
super-	bigger or very good	*super-hero, superhuman, supermodel*
un-	opposite, not	*unable, uncomfortable, unhappy*

Using suffixes

for making nouns

-hood	*child-childhood, father-fatherhood*
-ity	*stupid-stupidity, pure-purity*
-ness	*happy-happiness, kind-kindness*
-ment	*enjoy-enjoyment, move-movement*
-ship	*friend-friendship, champion-championship*
-sion	*divide-division, persuade-persuasion*
-tion	*subtract-subtraction, react-reaction*

for making adjectives

-able	*enjoy-enjoyable, forgive-forgivable*
-ful	*hope-hopeful, colour-colourful*
-ible	*eat-edible, reverse-reversible*
-ic	*allergy-allergic, science-scientific*
-ish	*child-childish*
-ive	*explode-explosive*
-less	*fear-fearless, hope-hopeless*
-like	*life-lifelike*
-y	*anger-angry, hair-hairy*

for making nouns that mean a person who does something

-er, -or	*act-actor, paint-painter*
-ist	*science-scientist, art-artist*

for making feminine nouns

-ess *actor-actress, lion-lioness*

for making adverbs

-ly *careful-carefully, quick-quickly*

for making verbs

-ate *active-activate, pollen-pollinate*

-en *damp-dampen, short-shorten*

-ify *solid-solidify, liquid-liquify*

-ize, -ise *apology-apologize, fossil-fossilize*

Notes

Notes

Notes

Notes

Notes

Notes

Notes

Notes

Notes

Notes

Notes

Notes

Notes

Notes

Notes

Notes

Notes

Notes

OXFORD
Dictionaries and Thesauruses for home and school

Oxford Very First Dictionary

Oxford First Dictionary
Oxford First Thesaurus

Oxford Junior Illustrated Dictionary
Oxford Junior Illustrated Thesaurus

Oxford Junior Dictionary
Oxford Junior Thesaurus

Oxford Primary Dictionary
Oxford Primary Thesaurus

Oxford Children's Dictionary
Oxford Children's Thesaurus

Oxford Concise School Dictionary
Oxford Concise School Thesaurus

Oxford School Dictionary
Oxford School Thesaurus

Oxford Pocket School Dictionary
Oxford Pocket School Thesaurus

Oxford Mini School Dictionary
Oxford Mini School Thesaurus

Oxford Student's Dictionary

Large print

Oxford Young Readers' Dictionary
Oxford Young Readers' Spelling Dictionary